Sentencing Policies and Practices in Western Countries: Comparative and Cross-National Perspectives

Sentencing Policies and Practices in Western Countries: Comparative and Cross-National Perspectives

Edited by Michael Tonry

Crime and Justice
A Review of Research
Edited by Michael Tonry

VOLUME 45

The University of Chicago Press, Chicago and London

The University of Chicago Press, Chicago 60637
The University of Chicago Press, Ltd., London

© 2016 by The University of Chicago
All rights reserved.
Printed in the United States of America

ISSN: 0192-3234

ISBN: 978-0-226-33757-9

LCN: 80-642217

Library of Congress Cataloging-in-Publication Data

Sentencing policies and practices in Western countries : comparative and cross-national perspectives / edited by Michael Tonry—(Crime and justice : a review of research; volume 45)
Chicago ; London : University of Chicago Press, 2016.
LCCN 2016031726 | ISBN 9780226440774 (cloth)
LCSH: Sentences (Criminal procedure)—Western countries. | Western countries.
LCC K5121 .S47 2016 | DDC 345/.0772091821—dc23 LC

2014036003

The paper used in this publication meets the minimum requirements of American National Standard for Information Sciences—Permanence of Paper for Printed Library Materials, ANSI Z39.48-1984. ♾

Contents

Preface

Nothing that can reasonably be described as a comparative literature on sentencing existed before the 1990s. Occasional articles and books discussed individual countries, but no one made it their business to look systematically and repeatedly across national boundaries to see what was happening elsewhere. Some systems no doubt were more just, effective, or efficient than others, but no one could have said which or why or in what ways.

Fundamental recent changes in American sentencing systems and punishment policies catalyzed development of a comparative literature. Policy makers, public officials, and scholars in many countries observed what was happening and wondered and worried whether America's present might be their future. The collapse of indeterminate sentencing, decline in confidence in rehabilitative programs, and increased support for punitive ways of thinking in the United States reverberated in the English-speaking countries and to a lesser extent in Western Europe. Most developed countries did not make major changes, but all considered them. More ominously, American imprisonment rates tripled between 1973 and 1990, reaching a then unprecedented 500 per 100,000 population. For countries in which rates seldom exceeded 100, that was worrisome.

Figuring out why what happened in the United States happened, whether other countries were at risk of it happening to them, and, more generally, how sentencing systems work and when and why they change, seemed important. Rod Morgan and Chris Clarkson organized a meeting at the University of Bristol in 1993 to discuss papers commissioned on national systems. The resulting book, *The Politics of Sentencing Reform* (1995), was the first in a series that document the evolution of sentencing policies and practices over four decades. The second, *Sentencing and Sanctions in Western Counties* (2001), edited by Richard S. Frase and me, emerged from a 1998 meeting in Minneapolis sponsored by the University of Minnesota Law School and the Max Planck Institute for

Comparative and International Criminal Law in Freiburg. The third, *Crime, Punishment, and Politics in Comparative Perspective* (2007), based on papers prepared for a 2005 Minneapolis conference, appeared as volume 36 of *Crime and Justice*. This book is based on papers prepared for a 2014 meeting in Bologna, Italy. Funding was provided by the Robina Foundation through grants to the University of Minnesota Law School.

The four volumes provide sentencing policy histories for a number of English-speaking and European countries. Each essay provides a snapshot of systems, sanctions, and punishment patterns, and charts recent changes. Some important things were learned. Late twentieth century American developments proved not to be harbingers of major changes elsewhere. Crime rates rose rapidly and steeply in all Western countries between the 1960s and 1990s, but only the United States responded with vastly harsher laws and severer punishments. Only in America did sentencing policy become a galvanizing political issue. We now understand why that happened, and why it did not happen elsewhere. Policies and practices changed in many places, but usually only slightly and in small steps. In no other country did imprisonment rates skyrocket or punishments become unprecedentedly severe.

There are major differences between national sentencing systems. In most countries, save for new community sanctions, new diversion programs, and diverse restorative justice and mediation initiatives, systems in 2015 looked little different than they had in 1975. Sentencing remained a solemn proceeding governed by established norms and practices. Professional prosecutors and judges remained resolutely determined not to let politics, media attention, or public opinion influence their decisions.

This volume followed the process typical of *Crime and Justice* thematic volumes. A small planning meeting was convened to decide whether a sufficiently ample literature had accumulated since publication of the 2007 volume to justify pulling it together and if so to decide what to commission and from whom. A conference attended by the writers and other subject-matter experts was convened to discuss and illuminate the drafts. The drafts were later distributed to paid referees for critical reactions. All were substantially rewritten.

The meeting in Bologna could not have succeeded had Rossella Selmini not pointed us to hotels, conference sites, and restaurants. Logistics were handled by Jo Hendricks and Alessandro Corda. In addition to the writers, the meeting was attended by Michele Caianiello (University of Bologna), Nora Demleitner (Washington and Lee University), Oren Gazal-Ayal (University of Haifa), Rhys Hester (University of Minnesota), Miklos Levay (Eötvös Loránd University), Grazia Mannozzi (University of Insubria), Ian O'Donnell (University College Dublin), Michael O'Hear (Marquette University), Ryan Scott (University of Indiana), Rossella Selmini (University of Minnesota), Cassia Spohn (Arizona State University), and Dirk van Zyl Smit (University of Nottingham).

Writers exhibited remarkable patience and good will. Meeting participants did their reading ahead of time and offered useful advice and criticism. Referees prepared reports substantially more detailed and reflective than is common. Rossella, Alessandro, and Jo provided indispensable help behind the scenes. I am enormously grateful to them all but especially to Su Smallen, who oversaw production of the book. She did her usual painstaking work and made this book better than it otherwise could have been.

Michael Tonry
Bagnaia, Isola D'Elba, June 2016

Michael Tonry

Differences in National Sentencing Systems and the Differences They Make

There are enormous variations in the quality of justice accorded people convicted of crimes in different countries. It is not simply that punishments are more severe, or different, in some places than in others. They are, but the differences are more fundamental than that. They involve basic human rights; procedural fairness; and commitment to the ideas that only the morally guilty should be convicted, that those convicted should be treated consistently and evenhandedly, and that no one should be punished more severely than he or she deserves.

Convicted offenders in different countries receive more or less severe, or different, punishments generally or for specific offenses, but that is a predictable result of diverse cultural traditions and norms. Practitioners and policy makers in Scandinavian and German-speaking countries have less of a taste for harsh punishments, for example, than do those in first-language English-speaking countries. No one is surprised that prison sentences are shorter in Finland or Germany than in England and the United States. Few short prison sentences are imposed in Germany because they are believed to accomplish nothing useful and to do unnecessary harm to people convicted of crimes; many are imposed in the Netherlands and Scandinavia because they are thought to be useful in reinforcing basic

Grateful thanks to Andrew Ashworth, Alessandro Corda, Anthony N. Doob, Richard S. Frase, Allan Manson, and Julian V. Roberts for comments on a draft of this essay.

1

social norms.[1] Swedes and Americans have more moralistic attitudes toward drug use and trafficking than do the Portuguese, the Spanish, or the Swiss; it is not surprising that punishments for drug possession and sale are harsher in the former countries than in the latter. If differences of these sorts were all that distinguished sentencing in different countries, this essay could be the length of an op-ed.

The organizational charts of Western countries' criminal justice systems look much the same: requirements of fair notice, legal assistance, and proof beyond a reasonable doubt; professional police; autonomous public prosecutors; independent judges; and mostly state-run institutional and community corrections systems. Processes and normative frameworks for handling criminal cases and sentencing convicted offenders, however, vary enormously and produce widely divergent results. Behind institutional similarities lurk basic differences that make stark injustices more and less likely.

Later in this essay, I discuss explanations that have been offered to explain those basic differences. In the end it comes down to this: in almost all developed countries except the United States, parts at least of eastern Europe, and, to a lesser extent, England and Wales, Australia, and New Zealand, convictions and punishments of individuals are regarded as matters solely of substantive justice. They must be handled dispassionately, rationally, and evenhandedly without regard to public emotion, media preoccupations, or politicians' interests or preferences. Elected politicians enact laws establishing statutory frameworks, but decisions in individual cases must be made by neutral, nonpartisan professionals. In the United States, England and Wales, and at least parts of eastern Europe, by contrast, sentencing is seen by many as quintessentially political, a subject concerning which elected officials including judges and prosecutors are, appropriately, democratically accountable. Prosecutors and judges may, within limits, take account of public opinion and politicians' preferences. If legislatures wish to enact laws requiring unjustly severe or disproportionate punishments, so be it. Practitioners generally feel obliged to enforce them even if they result in unjustly severe punishments of in-

---

[1] Sentencing conventions and practices systematically differ between countries in other ways also, including relative presences in prison populations of pretrial detainees and convicted offenders, the balance between short and long sentences, and rates of prison admissions compared with stock imprisonment population rates (Young and Brown 1993; Kommer 1994, 2004; Tonry 2007).

dividuals. Such enactments may or may not be good-faith expressions of public preferences, but in theory, they are justifiable because they are the handiwork of elected officials. After all, if a majority of voters disapprove, they can throw the rascals out in the next elections.

The first section of this essay sets out eight propositions about core features of national sentencing systems. A clear pattern stands out. Systems in English-speaking countries tend to be more severe and less focused on fairness, proportionality, and human dignity than those in western Europe. The second section proposes a model for encapsulating the differences.

I. Differences in National Sentencing Systems

Prosecutors and judges in developed countries other than the United States are expected to be apolitical, impartial, unemotional, and as concerned to exonerate the innocent as to convict the guilty. Except in a few Swiss cantons where some judges and prosecutors are chosen in nonpartisan local elections, prosecutors and judges in developed countries other than the United States are career civil servants or are appointed for life or for lengthy terms through nonpartisan processes. Prosecutors in continental Europe are formally part of the judiciary or are subject to judicial behavioral standards and ethical norms. In the United States, most chief prosecutors and a large majority of judges are elected or appointed by elected officials. No one is surprised that political considerations, personal ambitions, public emotions and attitudes, and media attention influence decisions in individual cases. Substantial empirical evidence shows that prosecutorial and judicial decisions often become more severe when reelection campaigns loom (e.g., Huber and Gordon 2004; Gordon and Huber 2007; Bandyopadhyay and McCannon 2014). In other English-speaking countries, prosecutors are expected to be impartial and apolitical. Chief prosecutors are neither elected nor appointed through partisan political processes; line prosecutors are career civil servants (Tonry 2012).

Prosecutors dominate sentencing in the United States but have little or no role in sentencing in most developed countries. In many countries, except for diversion programs that result in financial or community penalties, sentencing is a function solely of judges.[2] In continental Europe, prosecutors

---

[2] In the Netherlands, Belgium, and Germany, charges are suspended and usually later dismissed; admissions of guilt are not required (van de Bunt and van Gelder 2012; Scheirs,

seldom propose specific sentences. Prosecutors in common law countries other than the United States act as adversaries in relation to guilt, but generally not at the sentencing stage. In Australia, prosecutors are forbidden to make sentence recommendations. In Canada they now do, generally in joint submissions from the prosecutor and defense counsel, but as recently as the 1970s, they could not. In England, where until recently it was widely believed recommendations impinged on judicial authority, prosecutors may provide information but seldom argue for specific sentences. Irish prosecutors in recent years have resisted judicial pressures to propose recommended sentences for individual cases (O'Malley 2011).

In the United States, more than 95 percent of convictions result from guilty pleas, mostly negotiated. Often they specify the sentence to be imposed or involve charges and charge dismissals that tie judges' hands. Federal Court of Appeals Judge Gerald Lynch observed, "The prosecutor, rather than a judge or jury, is the central adjudicator of facts (as well as replacing the judge as arbiter of most legal issues and of the appropriate sentence to be imposed).... Potential defenses are presented by the defendant and his counsel not in a court, but to a prosecutor.... Mitigating information, similarly, is argued not to the judge, but to the prosecutor, who decides what sentence the defendant should be given in exchange for his plea" (2003, pp. 1403–4). Lynch was describing federal prosecutors, but his words also describe prosecutorial power in state courts.

Judicial fact finding for adjudication and sentencing is an indispensable part of the processing of criminal cases in most developed countries, but not in English-speaking common law countries. In most continental European countries, cases not disposed of informally come before the court in a single proceeding for adjudication and sentencing. Dossiers prepared by prosecutors or specialist investigating judges are typically available that set out material facts and circumstances. Even an admission of guilt generally does not eliminate the need for a hearing. Fact-finding by judges is required. Defendants in common law countries who do not plead guilty are effectively penalized. This is sometimes referred to as the "trial tax."

Beyens, and Snacken 2016; Weigend 2016). In Scandinavia and elsewhere in Europe, "penal orders" involving similar penalties require admissions (Lappi-Seppälä 2016). Suspects are free to reject proposed informal dispositions without penalty. There is no American or English-style "trial tax" in any of these systems.

Negotiated pleas in the United States typically result in an agreement about the sentence to be imposed or in dismissal of charges. In other English-speaking countries, sentences following guilty pleas are expected to be reduced by the judge. In England, a system of declining discounts provides for 33, 20, or 10 percent or other sentence reductions depending on when the defendant pled guilty. Judges, of course, may reject guilty pleas, but seldom do. They are expected to satisfy themselves that the defendant is guilty of the offense charged. In the United States, judges ask the defendant to acknowledge facts implied by the conviction offense and that his or her guilty plea is voluntary, but that is all, and often it is pro forma.[3] Judges in other English countries are generally less pro forma. However, simply requesting defendants to confirm their guilt is less rigorous than fact-finding by continental European judges.

Rules, standards, and guidelines for sentencing decisions vary enormously, from general and permissive to detailed prescription. Australian appellate courts zealously safeguard judges' discretion in individual cases to engage in "intuitive syntheses" of what public safety and justice require. Austrian judges, at least through the 1990s, engaged in equivalent "existential conversations" with themselves about sentences to be imposed. Canadian laws establish a set of sentencing principles that, because they encompass the full range of retributive and instrumental purposes, do not significantly constrain judges' discretion (except when a handful of modest mandatory minimum sentence laws apply). Judges in most European systems possess broad discretion, unconstrained by detailed guidelines or rules. At the other extreme, until the US Supreme Court in *US v. Booker*, 543 US 220 (2005), struck them down, "mandatory" federal guidelines prescribed detailed standards based almost exclusively on offense characteristics and criminal histories. In between are a wide array

---

[3] Rather than clutter the text with citations at the end of each sentence, references for major points in this and the next few paragraphs are given in footnotes. Concerning the United States, Lynch (2003), Bogira (2005), and Stuntz (2011) provide the fullest law-in-action accounts of plea negotiation and case processing. On other English-speaking countries: on Canada, Manson et al. (2008) and Doob and Webster (2016); on England and Wales, Ashworth (2001, 2015) and Roberts and Ashworth (2016); on Australia, Freiberg (2001, 2014, 2016). On western Europe: on Belgium, Scheirs, Beyens, and Snacken (2016); on France, Roché (2007) and Hodgson and Soubise (2016); on Germany, Weigend (2001, 2016); on Italy, Caianiello (2012) and Corda (2016); on the Netherlands, Tak (2001) and van de Bunt and van Gelder (2012); on Scandinavia, Hinkkanen and Lappi-Seppälä (2011), Asp (2012), and Lappi-Seppälä (2016); on Poland, Krajewski (2012, 2016); on Hungary, Levay (2012).

of diverse rules and standards, ranging from statutory principles in Scandinavia through weak sentencing guidelines in England and Wales and some American states and stronger "presumptive" guidelines in a few. In the Netherlands, prosecutors make recommendations in every case on the basis of quantitative sentence recommendation guidelines, but sentences are not negotiated. It is commonly said that judges take account of the recommendations though generally impose somewhat less severe sentences than are proposed.[4]

Politicians in some countries attempt to influence decisions in individual cases, but in most that is verboten. English and American politicians often comment on and disparage sentences judges impose in politically salient or notorious cases and make clear how they want some kinds of crimes to be punished. Dutch, Scandinavian, and Japanese prosecutors in theory are subject to oversight by government ministers, but that power is never exercised. It would be seen as scandalous if it were. In Sweden and other Scandinavian countries, as a safeguard against political or other unwarranted attempts to influence decisions, line prosecutors have complete autonomy in handling individual cases. Political influence in individual cases has been a chronic problem in postcommunist Poland. The Director of Public Prosecutions in England and Wales, a political appointee, sets detailed priorities for line prosecutors (e.g., Burney and Rose 2002), as do the US Department of Justice, politically appointed US attorneys, and elected chief prosecutors in the United States.[5]

Normative ideas governing sentencing vary widely between countries. Inevitably some mixture of retributive and consequentialist ideas influences sentencing decisions, but the balances among them vary widely between legal systems. Retributive ideas about proportionality and consistency are paramount in Scandinavian countries, although this is not understood to require that punishments be severe. Community punishments are the norm. Imprisonment is seldom imposed, sentences of weeks and months are common, and sentences longer than a year or two are rare. Punishments must be proportionate because that is just, and because doing anything else would undermine basic social norms. Primary institutions such as families, schools, churches, and local communities

---

[4] The sources listed in n. 2 apply here. Discussion of the Austrian judges' metaphysical conversations can be found in Tonry (1995).

[5] The sources in n. 2 apply here, plus Johnson (2012) and Krajewski (2012, 2016).

are understood to do the heavy lifting in socializing people into good values, and it would be seen as perverse for courts to undermine their efforts (Lappi-Seppälä 2011).

In English-speaking countries, retributive values are intermingled with instrumental goals of deterrence, incapacitation, and rehabilitation, and expressive aspirations to placate public opinion and maintain public confidence. Judges typically have broad discretion. Appellate sentence review systems are usually weak and deferential to sentencing judges. Proportionality and consistency are commonly said to be important, but this is often lip service. Unwarranted disparities in sentencing are common.

In southern and some other European countries, notably Belgium, France, and Italy, sentencing is highly individualized and resocialization of offenders is a major goal. Judges take retributive ideas into account in setting sentences but are not subject to significant constraints on their discretion. However, in all three countries specialized judges oversee implementation of sentences and have discretion to change the sentence initially imposed, usually for reasons the judge believes are associated with greater likelihood of the offender's successful reintegration into community living (Corda 2016; Hodgson and Soubise 2016; Scheirs, Beyens, and Snacken 2016).

Community sanctions have proliferated in most countries in recent decades but are used very differently. Many widely used community dispositions, including community service, victim-offender mediation, electronic monitoring, and intensive forms of supervision, were pioneered in the United States. Although most were initially conceived as alternatives to imprisonment, they were seldom used in that way in the United States and commonly became more focused on surveillance and crime prevention than on reintegration of offenders. "Net widening" was the most common finding of evaluations. Revocations and imprisonments for breaches of conditions became common (Morris and Tonry 1990). By contrast, in many continental European countries, newly developed community dispositions, especially mediation, community service, and electronic monitoring, are successfully used as pretrial diversion programs, prison alternatives, or early release mechanisms and focus on service provision (Tonry 1998, 1999).[6]

---

[6] Details for individual countries are provided in the essays contained in vol. 45 of *Crime and Justice: A Review of Research*.

Most Western countries have neither adopted "expressive" sentencing policies meant to convey political messages to the general public nor enacted new legislation, such as three-strikes, life without parole, truth in sentencing, or mandatory minimum sentence laws, meant to require judges to impose unprecedentedly severe punishments. Policies and laws meant primarily to be expressive have rarely been adopted except in the English-speaking countries (Garland 2001). Laws meant to mandate unprecedentedly severe punishments have been enacted only in the United States. Other English-speaking countries have enacted small numbers of mandatory minimum sentence laws, though never requiring sentences measured in decades or lifetimes as in the United States (Ashworth 2001; Pratt and Clark 2005; Tonry 2009, 2016; Doob and Webster 2016; Freiberg 2016). One notable, American-style exception is England and Wales's 2003 law authorizing indeterminate sentences for large numbers of offenders believed by judges to be especially dangerous (Jacobson and Hough 2010; Roberts and Ashworth 2016).

The reasons why such developments are distinctly Anglo-Saxon and predominantly American are clear. The jurisprudence of sentencing in northern Europe is based on ideas about proportionality and consistency, and there is widespread skepticism about the deterrent effectiveness of sanctions in individual cases. In southern Europe and the German-speaking countries, the jurisprudence of sentencing includes retributive ideas about proportionality but also incorporates strong support for ideas about the importance of facilitating reintegration of offenders into their communities. Both of these approaches are incompatible with laws mandating lengthy terms of imprisonment irrespective of offenders' circumstances or crimes' distinctive features. The jurisprudence of sentencing in the English-speaking countries is much more focused on crime prevention and denunciation of wrongdoing; just treatment of offenders and avoidance of unwarranted disparities are less important. Differences between the United States and other English-speaking countries derive from the much greater politicization of crime policy in recent decades in the United States, aggravated by the election and partisan political designation of judges and prosecutors (Tonry 2004).

II. A Typology of National Sentencing Systems

These differences among national sentencing systems importantly influence what happens in individual cases. They can be collapsed into two polar models. The Substantive Justice Model characterizes most of western Europe. The focus is on fair and respectful treatment of individual offenders. Respect for human dignity is often described as the fundamental value at stake (Whitman 2004). The overriding goal is to assure that cases are handled on their merits and that what happens to individuals is a product of impartial consideration of the seriousness of crimes and of defendants' blameworthiness and personal circumstances. There is no room for influence by public emotions or attitudes, preferences of politicians or government officials, or ambitions and personal interests of judges or prosecutors. Taking account of any of those considerations would widely be seen as wrong, unethical, and unjust.

The Democratic Accountability Model is fundamentally different. Public attitudes and emotions are considered to be germane to what happens in individual cases and classes of cases. Elected officials believe themselves entitled to make their voices heard and their wishes known. Legislators feel entitled to prescribe sentences in individual cases by means of mandatory minimum sentence and similar laws. Differences in outcomes of individual cases are influenced by the idiosyncrasies of prosecutors and judges, public opinion and the media, personal interests of officials, and inflexibility of sentencing laws. This is not necessarily celebrated but is seen as inevitable. Fair, consistent, evenhanded, and respectful treatment of individual offenders is seldom a high priority.

Ideas about democratic accountability underlie a series of US Supreme Court decisions over the past 30 years that make disproportionately severe punishments lawful and almost irremediable. *Rummel v. Estelle*, 445 U. S. 263, 274 (1980), upheld a sentence of life in prison for a defendant convicted of a $120.75 theft. The court observed that the Eighth Amendment's proportionality principle "would ... come into play in the extreme example ... if a legislature made overtime parking a felony punishable by life imprisonment." In *Hutto v. Davis*, 454 U. S. 370, 374 (1982), the defendant received two consecutive 20-year prison terms for possession of 9 ounces of marijuana. The court affirmed those sentences, explaining that "*Rummel* stands for the proposition that federal courts should be reluctant to review legislatively mandated terms of imprisonment, and that successful challenges to the proportionality of particular sentences should be exceedingly rare." In *Ewing v. California*, 538 U.S. 11 (2003), involving a 25-years-to-life sentence for stealing three golf clubs, the court observed that granting Ewing's appeal "would fail to accord proper deference to the policy judgments that find expression in the legislature's choice of sanctions" (p. 29). The bottom line is that if legislatures choose to enact laws that require unjustly severe punishments, the courts will almost never intervene. The United States is the extreme case, but similar albeit milder laws are enacted and enforced in other English-speaking countries.

Models are heuristic devices. Life is more complicated. Even so, the polar models capture real differences. Political agendas and theater, public and media reactions, and politicians' self-interest are major parts of the sentencing policy stories of the United States, England, and at least parts of eastern Europe, less often in other English-speaking countries, and only rarely in western Europe.

The substantive justice and democratic accountability models capture important differences between systems more fully than do Herbert Packer's Crime Control and Due Process models (1964). They distinguish between ways of thinking that differ over emphases to be given to crime prevention and procedural fairness, but neither implies support for unjustly severe and disproportionate punishments. Packer after all wrote during the indeterminate sentencing period when few mandatory minimum sentence laws existed and parole boards decided when prisoners were released.

Likewise, the classic distinction between the civil law inquisitorial criminal law systems of continental Europe and the common law adversarial systems of the English-speaking countries has no implications concerning the acceptability of laws that require unjust punishments. That is a structural distinction describing differences between legal systems in how disputed factual claims are to be disentangled (Damaška 1974).

James Q. Whitman's (2016) depiction of an American system predicated on a presumption of innocence and European systems based on a presumption of mercy comes closer. The attentions of American lawyers and processes, he argues, center on avoidance of the wrongful conviction of innocent people but focus much less on what happens to individuals after they are convicted. Before conviction, constitutional criminal procedures, evidentiary rules, and standards of proof exist to protect the innocent. After conviction, sentencing processes are informal, the law of evidence does not apply, there are no or low standards of proof, and until the advent of sentencing guidelines and mandatory sentencing laws, there were no standards or rules governing judges' sentencing decisions (Frankel 1973; Tonry 2016).

European systems, by contrast, Whitman suggests, avoid convicting innocent people but also give heavy weight to acknowledgment of human difference and avoidance of imposition of unnecessary suffering on people convicted of crimes. Reasonable people might disagree whether "presumption of mercy" is an optimal way to describe the effort to avoid imposition of gratuitous suffering, but the core idea is a familiar one. More than 200 years ago, Jeremy Bentham ([1789] 1970) used the term "frugality" to describe it; imposition of unnecessary punishment, he said, was "evil." Norval Morris (1974) used the term "parsimony." The drafters of the Model Sentencing Act used the phrase "the least restrictive alternative" (Advisory Council of Judges 1963).

Whitman's distinction is accurate enough in describing differences between American and continental European criminal law systems, but in two respects it fails. First, it applies as accurately to differences that existed in the 1960s, when indeterminate sentencing systems were ubiquitous in the United States, as to differences in the twenty-first century. Thus, unless relatively greater American concerns to prevent wrongful convictions entail utter indifference to the interests of people convicted of crimes, it does not help us understand why American sentencing laws changed radically in the 1980s and 1990s and sentencing laws in continental Europe did not.

Second, Whitman's distinction does not adequately explain contemporary differences in sentencing jurisprudence between the United States and other English-speaking countries. Whitman's seminal book *Harsh Justice* (2003) attributed fundamental differences between punishment practices in English-speaking and European countries to historically different eighteenth-century criminal justice system responses to Enlightenment ideas about equality. Before that, privileged offenders everywhere were often treated much more humanely and respectfully than the poor. Challenged to reconcile those differences with equality values, Europeans "leveled up" to treat all offenders decently and the English leveled down. Penal values of all the English-speaking countries in that analysis flow from historical English decisions about equality. Recent penal policies in the United States and other English-speaking countries, however, are not the same. They are as different, Franklin E. Zimring famously said in an oral presentation, as a haircut and a beheading.

Why countries have particular sentencing policies, values, and institutions is a subject for another day. So is the larger, broader question of why in the United States radical ideas about democratic accountability trumped long-standing values of mercy, parsimony, frugality, and the desirability of always using the least restrictive alternative in punishing people convicted of crimes. From perspectives of human rights, human dignity, and equality, continental western European systems despite their diversity are considerably more admirable than those in the English-speaking countries and especially the United States. That may not always be so. American systems were not always more punitive and less humane than those elsewhere, but they are today. It is difficult to imagine how they will become much better any time soon.

REFERENCES

Advisory Council of Judges, National Council on Crime and Delinquency. 1963. *Model Sentencing Act*. Hackensack, NJ: National Council on Crime and Delinquency.

Ashworth, Andrew. 2001. "The Decline of English Sentencing and Other Stories." In *Sentencing and Sanctions in Western Countries*, edited by Michael Tonry and Richard S. Frase. New York: Oxford University Press.

———. 2015. *Sentencing and Criminal Justice*. 6th ed. Cambridge: Cambridge University Press.

Asp, Petter. 2012. "The Prosecutor in Swedish Law." In *Prosecutors and Politics: A Comparative Perspective*, edited by Michael Tonry. Vol. 41 of *Crime and Justice: A Review of Research*, edited by Michael Tonry. Chicago: University of Chicago Press.

Bandyopadhyay, Siddhartha, and Bryan C. McCannon. 2014. "The Effect of the Election of Prosecutors on Criminal Trials." *Public Choice* 16(1):141–56.

Bentham, Jeremy. 1970. "The Utilitarian Theory of Punishment." In *An Introduction to Principles of Morals and Legislation*, edited by Jeremy Bentham, J. H. Burns, and H. L. A. Hart. London: Athlone. (Orig. published 1789.)

Bogira, Steve. 2005. *Courtroom 302—a Year Behind the Scenes in an American Criminal Courthouse*. New York: Knopf.

Burney, Elizabeth, and Gerry Rose. 2002. "Racist Offences—How Is the Law Working? Implementation of the Legislation on Racially Aggravated Offences in the *Crime and Disorder Act 1998*." Research Study no. 244. London: Home Office.

Caianiello, Michele. 2012. "The Italian Public Prosecutor: An Inquisitorial Figure in Adversarial Proceedings?" In *The Prosecutor in Transnational Perspective*, edited by Erik Luna and Marianne Wade. New York: Oxford University Press.

Corda, Alessandro. 2016. "Sentencing and Penal Policies in Italy, 1985–2015: The Tale of a Troubled Country." In *Sentencing Policies and Practices in Western Countries: Comparative and Cross-National Perspectives*, edited by Michael

Tonry. Vol. 45 of *Crime and Justice: A Review of Research*, edited by Michael Tonry. Chicago: University of Chicago Press.

Damaška, Mirjan. 1974. "Structures of Authority and Comparative Criminal Procedure." *Yale Law Journal* 84:480–543.

Doob, Anthony N., and Cheryl Marie Webster. 2016. "Weathering the Storm? Testing Long-Standing Canadian Sentencing Policy in the Twenty-First Century." In *Sentencing Policies and Practices in Western Countries: Comparative and Cross-National Perspectives*, edited by Michael Tonry. Vol. 45 of *Crime and Justice: A Review of Research*, edited by Michael Tonry. Chicago: University of Chicago Press.

Frankel, Marvin. 1973. *Criminal Sentences: Law without Order*. New York: Hill & Wang.

Freiberg, Arie. 2001. "Three Strikes and You're Out—It's Not Cricket: Colonization and Resistance in Australian Sentencing." In *Sentencing and Sanctions in Western Countries*, edited by Michael Tonry and Richard S. Frase. New York: Oxford University Press.

———. 2014. *Fox and Freiberg's Sentencing: State and Federal Law in Victoria*. 3rd ed. Melbourne: Thomson Reuters.

———. 2016. "The Road Well Traveled in Australia: Ignoring the Past, Condemning the Future." In *Sentencing Policies and Practices in Western Countries: Comparative and Cross-National Perspectives*, edited by Michael Tonry. Vol. 45 of *Crime and Justice: A Review of Research*, edited by Michael Tonry. Chicago: University of Chicago Press.

Garland, David. 2001. *The Culture of Control*. Oxford: Oxford University Press.

Gordon, Sanford C., and Gregory A. Huber. 2007. "The Effect of Electoral Competitiveness on Incumbent Behavior." *Quarterly Journal of Political Science* 2:107–38.

Hinkkanen, Ville, and Tapio Lappi-Seppälä. 2011. "Sentencing Theory, Policy, and Research in the Nordic Countries." In *Crime and Justice in Scandinavia*, edited by Michael Tonry and Tapio Lappi-Seppälä. Vol. 40 of *Crime and Justice: A Review of Research*, edited by Michael Tonry. Chicago: University of Chicago Press.

Hodgson, Jacqueline, and Laurène Soubise. 2016. "Understanding the Sentencing Process in France." In *Sentencing Policies and Practices in Western Countries: Comparative and Cross-National Perspectives*, edited by Michael Tonry. Vol. 45 of *Crime and Justice: A Review of Research*, edited by Michael Tonry. Chicago: University of Chicago Press.

Huber, Gregory A., and Sanford C. Gordon. 2004. "Accountability and Coercion: Is Justice Blind When It Runs for Office?" *American Journal of Political Science* 48:247–63.

Jacobson, J., and M. Hough. 2010. *Unjust Deserts: Imprisonment for Public Protection*. London: Prison Reform Trust.

Johnson, David. 2012. "Japan's Prosecution System." In *Prosecutors and Politics: A Comparative Perspective*, edited by Michael Tonry. Vol. 41 of *Crime and Justice: A Review of Research*, edited by Michael Tonry. Chicago: University of Chicago Press.

Kommer, Max. 1994. "Punitiveness in Europe: A Comparison." *European Journal of Criminal Policy and Research* 2(1):29–43.

———. 2004. "Punitiveness in Europe Revisited." *Criminology in Europe* 3(1):1, 8–12.

Krajewski, Krzysztof. 2012. "Prosecution and Prosecutors in Poland: In Quest of Independence." In *Prosecutors and Politics: A Comparative Perspective*, edited by Michael Tonry. Vol. 41 of *Crime and Justice: A Review of Research*, edited by Michael Tonry. Chicago: University of Chicago Press.

———. 2016. "Sentencing in Poland: Failed Attempts to Reduce Punitiveness." In *Sentencing Policies and Practices in Western Countries: Comparative and Cross-National Perspectives*, edited by Michael Tonry. Vol. 45 of *Crime and Justice: A Review of Research*, edited by Michael Tonry. Chicago: University of Chicago Press.

Lappi-Seppälä, Tapio. 2011. "Sentencing and Punishment in Finland: The Decline of the Repressive Ideal." In *Why Punish? How Much?* edited by Michael Tonry. New York: Oxford University Press.

———. 2016. "Nordic Sentencing." In *Sentencing Policies and Practices in Western Countries: Comparative and Cross-National Perspectives*, edited by Michael Tonry. Vol. 45 of *Crime and Justice: A Review of Research*, edited by Michael Tonry. Chicago: University of Chicago Press.

Levay, Miklos. 2012. "Penal Policy, Crime, and Political Change [in Hungary]." In *Crime and Transition in Central and Eastern Europe*, edited by A. Šelih and A. Završnik. New York: Springer Science and Business.

Lynch, Gerard E. 2003. "Screening versus Plea Bargaining: Exactly What Are We Trading Off?" *Stanford Law Review* 55:1399–1408.

Manson, Allan, P. Healy, J. V. Roberts, and D. Ives, eds. 2008. *The Law of Sentencing and Penal Policy in Canada*. 2nd ed. Toronto: Emond Montgomery.

Morris, Norval. 1974. *The Future of Imprisonment*. Chicago: University of Chicago Press.

Morris, Norval, and Michael Tonry. 1990. *Between Prison and Probation: Intermediate Punishments in a Rational Sentencing System*. New York: Oxford University Press.

O'Malley, Thomas. 2011. *Sentencing: Towards a Coherent System*. Dublin: Thomson Reuters.

Packer, Herbert L. 1964. "Two Models of the Criminal Process." *University of Pennsylvania Law Review* 113:1–68.

Pratt, John, and Marie Clark. 2005. "Penal Populism in New Zealand." *Punishment and Society* 7(3):303–22.

Roberts, Julian V., and Andrew Ashworth. 2016. "The Evolution of Sentencing Policy and Practice in England and Wales, 2003–2015." In *Sentencing Policies and Practices in Western Countries: Comparative and Cross-National Perspectives*, edited by Michael Tonry. Vol. 45 of *Crime and Justice: A Review of Research*, edited by Michael Tonry. Chicago: University of Chicago Press.

Roché, Sebastian. 2007. "Criminal Justice Policy in France: Illusions of Severity." In *Crime, Punishment, and Politics in Comparative Perspective*, edited by Michael Tonry. Vol. 36 of *Crime and Justice: A Review of Research*, edited by Michael Tonry. Chicago: University of Chicago Press.

Scheirs, Veerle, Kristel Beyens, and Sonja Snacken. 2016. "Belgian Sentencing as a Bifurcated Practice?" In *Sentencing Policies and Practices in Western Countries: Comparative and Cross-National Perspectives*, edited by Michael Tonry. Vol. 45 of *Crime and Justice: A Review of Research*, edited by Michael Tonry. Chicago: University of Chicago Press.

Stuntz, William J. 2011. *The Collapse of American Criminal Justice*. Cambridge, MA: Harvard University Press.

Tak, Peter J. 2001. "Sentencing and Punishment in the Netherlands." In *Sentencing and Sanctions in Western Countries*, edited by Michael Tonry and Richard S. Frase. New York: Oxford University Press.

Tonry, Michael. 1995. "Sentencing Reform across National Boundaries." In *The Politics of Sentencing Reform*, edited by Chris Clarkson and Rod Morgan. Oxford: Oxford University Press.

———. 1998. "Transfer of Criminal Justice Policies across National Boundaries." In *Internationale Perspektiven in Kriminologie und Strafrecht*, edited by Hans-Jörg Albrecht. Berlin: Duncker & Humblot.

———. 1999. "Parochialism in American Sentencing Policy." *Crime and Delinquency* 45(January):48–65.

———. 2004. *Thinking about Crime: Sense and Sensibility in American Penal Culture*. New York: Oxford University Press.

———. 2007. "Determinants of Penal Policies." In *Crime, Punishment, and Politics in Comparative Perspective*, edited by Michael Tonry. Vol. 35 of *Crime and Justice: A Review of Research*, edited by Michael Tonry. Chicago: University of Chicago Press.

———. 2009. "The Mostly Unintended Effects of Mandatory Penalties: Two Centuries of Consistent Findings." In *Crime and Justice: A Review of Research*, vol. 38, edited by Michael Tonry. Chicago: University of Chicago Press.

———. 2012. "Prosecutors and Politics in Comparative Perspective." In *Prosecutors and Politics: A Comparative Perspective*, edited by Michael Tonry. Vol. 41 of *Crime and Justice: A Review of Research*, edited by Michael Tonry. Chicago: University of Chicago Press.

———. 2016. "Equality and Human Dignity: The Missing Ingredients in American Sentencing." In *Sentencing Policies and Practices in Western Countries: Comparative and Cross-National Perspectives*, edited by Michael Tonry. Vol. 45 of *Crime and Justice: A Review of Research*, edited by Michael Tonry. Chicago: University of Chicago Press.

van de Bunt, Henk, and Jean-Louis van Gelder. 2012. "The Dutch Prosecution Service." In *Prosecutors and Politics: A Comparative Perspective*, edited by Michael Tonry. Vol. 41 of *Crime and Justice: A Review of Research*, edited by Michael Tonry. Chicago: University of Chicago Press.

Weigend, Thomas. 2001. "Sentencing and Punishment in Germany." In *Sentencing and Sanctions in Western Countries*, edited by Michael Tonry and Richard S. Frase. New York: Oxford University Press.

———. 2016. "No News Is Good News: Criminal Sentencing in Germany since 2000." In *Sentencing Policies and Practices in Western Countries: Comparative and Cross-National Perspectives*, edited by Michael Tonry. Vol. 45 of *Crime and Justice: A Review of Research*, edited by Michael Tonry. Chicago: University of Chicago Press.

Whitman, James Q. 2003. *Harsh Justice*. New York: Oxford University Press.

———. 2004. "The Two Western Cultures of Privacy: Dignity versus Liberty." *Yale Law Journal* 113:1151–1221.

———. 2016. "Presumption of Innocence or Presumption of Mercy? Weighing Two Western Modes of Justice." *Texas Law Review* 94:933–93.

Young, Warren, and Mark Brown. 1993. "Cross National Comparisons of Imprisonment." In *Crime and Justice: A Review of Research*, vol. 17, edited by Michael Tonry. Chicago: University of Chicago Press.

Tapio Lappi-Seppälä

Nordic Sentencing

ABSTRACT

Broad harmony and much commonality characterize the basic principles and core priorities of the sentencing systems of the four larger Nordic countries, notwithstanding rich diversity in details. Since 1960, there have been three distinctive phases in criminal justice policy and associated law reforms. A liberal period of "human and rational penal policy" from the late 1960s to early 1990s reformulated principles of penological thinking and resulted, among other things, in a radical reduction in the use of imprisonment in Finland. A second phase beginning in the mid-1990s, the "punitive turn—Nordic style," with Sweden playing the central role, included a gradual politicization of criminal justice policy and intensification in penal control especially in relation to drugs, violence, and sexual offenses. Political and police trends in the 2000s have been somewhat contradictory but include success in controlling the use of imprisonment and expanding the use of community penalties. Imprisonment rates rose slightly in the late 1990s but since 2005 have been either stable or declining. There is rich diversity in details among the Nordic countries but also broad harmony in basic principles and priorities.

The Nordic countries of Denmark, Finland, Norway, and Sweden share a long common history, sometimes, as now, as separate countries, other times as parts of single countries. Repeated wars occurred among Denmark, Norway, and Sweden between the fourteenth and nineteenth centuries, with countries controlling one another in different periods, including one when all three were joined by the 1397 Treaty of Kalmar under Danish domination. Sweden broke away in 1523, but Norway remained united with Denmark until 1814 and after that was coupled with

Electronically published July 8, 2016

Tapio Sappi-Seppälä is professor of criminal law and criminology at the University of Helsinki.

17

Sweden (as a "personal union") until 1905. From 1323 until 1809, Finland was a fully integrated part of Sweden but then became an autonomous grand duchy within the Russian Empire. During political unrest in Russia, Finland declared independence in 1917 but in the following decades followed a different path from its Nordic neighbors. A bloody civil war in 1918 created long-lasting internal conflicts and divisions and was followed by two wars with the Soviet Union (1939–40 and 1941–44) and one against Germany (1944–45). Ten percent of the population lost their homes.

This common history and its brutal interruptions are reflected in criminal justice statistics. Today the Nordic countries share a common imprisonment profile and their crime trends walk hand in hand (von Hofer, Lappi-Seppälä, and Westfelt 2012). This was much the same 100 years ago, but in between, developments in Finland differed radically from those elsewhere (von Hofer and Lappi-Seppälä 2014). Figure 1 displays trends in imprisonment rates since the early nineteenth century to 2012 in Norway, Sweden, and Finland.

Through the end of the nineteenth century, imprisonment rates in Norway, Sweden, and Finland moved in parallel; this has continued to the present in Norway and Sweden, with rates generally fluctuating between 50 and 75 per 100,000 population. In the twentieth century, however, Finland followed another course, with rates doubling and at times tripling from the 1900 level. These peaks were reactions to successive socioeconomic and political crises and steep crime waves associated

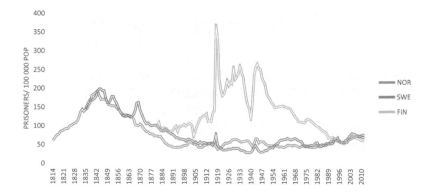

Fig. 1.—Nordic imprisonment rates, 1814–2013. Source: Christie (1968); Aho and Karsikas (1980); von Hofer, Lappi-Seppälä, and Westfelt (2012).

with them, sometimes accompanied by crises of political legitimacy. The crime waves often provoked intensified use of imprisonment (the principal punitive measure in use in the 1930s and 1940s). Serious prison overcrowding resulted, which resulted in ad hoc "back-door" initiatives and amnesties, which in turn produced steep short-term population declines.

Social and political conditions in Finland started to normalize and the economy grew stronger in the 1950s. In the 1960s and 1970s, Finland began more closely to resemble its neighbors, to participate in joint Nordic policy initiatives, and to join the Nordic approach to social welfare policy. Criminal justice policies also changed, which is visible in declining imprisonment rates beginning in the 1960s and reaching parity with the other countries in the 1990s.

This account of one country illustrates several stories. One is about overriding Scandinavian unity, interrupted in Finland by outside factors, but resumed once conditions normalized. Another is about the turbulent 1920s–40s, when Finland was shaken by succeeding crises, with deep consequences for crime and crime control. The third story is about Finland's reform of its criminal justice, which eventually closely resembled those of its Nordic neighbors.[1] The fourth is about current "Nordic unity" in criminal justice policy with internationally low and stable incarceration rates during periods when other countries experienced tightening of penal control and expansion of their prison systems. This essay is mainly about that fourth, latest, story, but it needs some background on the changes that brought penal policies in these countries back together.

---

[1] These changes are discussed at length elsewhere (Lappi-Seppälä 2001, 2007, 2011). On the effects of the war years on crime, see Takala and Tham (1987). About the effects of political crises on the criminal justice system, see Hannula (2004). For long-term historical accounts, see Pratt and Eriksson (2013) and von Hofer and Lappi-Seppälä (2014); for shorter-term analysis, see Träskman (2015). While Finland was part of Russia, its imprisonment rates were on the same level as in the other Nordic countries. Penal reforms at that time were progressive, including the abolition of the death penalty in 1826, law enforcement legislation based on progressive and rehabilitative principles in 1866, and a massive modern prison building program in the 1880s inspired by reform movements in England, Germany, Austria, and the other Nordic countries. Prison population peaks after 1918 and in the early 1930s occurred under the "white power" (the winners in the 1918 civil war against the reds) and later in connection with wars against the Soviet Union. The assertion that Finland's high imprisonment rates in the first half of the century demonstrated "Russian influence" (as suggested by Christie [1997]) fits poorly with historical facts (see Laine 2015).

I start in Section I with the general trends in penal policy since the late 1960s that shaped sentencing policies and principles of the following decades. Section II discusses the general structure of the sentencing systems, the systems of sanctions, and sentencing principles. Section III outlines the development and profiles of sentencing practices. It gives a concise statistical overview of major trends but also provides more detailed information on sentencing patterns for selected individual offenses. Discussion and conclusions follow in Section IV.

I. Penal Policy Trends, 1960s through the 2010s
There has been more continuity than change in fundamental Nordic approaches to crime and criminals since the 1960s with the exception of Finland's sustained effort over three decades to reach the Nordic level of imprisonment. Even so, three periods of changing emphases are discernible.

A. Humane and Rational Criminal Justice Policy
All Nordic countries experienced a period of penal liberalization during the 1970s. Its roots were in research-based liberal criticism of criminal justice practices and compulsory treatment programs in the 1960s. The first targets were treatment and forced labor for alcoholics and mental patients. From there, mistrust of coerced care and institutional treatment expanded to encompass child welfare and the prison system (Galtung 1959; Christie 1960; Goffman 1961; Aubert and Mathiesen 1962; Eriksson 1967; Siren 1967).

The criticism was fueled by empirical research that emphasized the ineffectiveness of custodial treatment. Reoffending seemed either to be unaffected by the type of intervention or even to make it more likely after imprisonment (Börjeson 1966; Uusitalo 1968; Bondeson 1977). All Nordic countries were affected by these findings, but most radically in Finland, where reform ambitions were boosted by data showing that Finnish imprisonment rates were three times higher than elsewhere in Scandinavia (Christie 1968). These observations quickly became parts of arguments in the public debate for decarceration. This strategic aim was supported by intensified Nordic cooperation. The 1962 Helsinki Treaty urged harmonization of Scandinavian criminal justice systems. For the Finns, that meant harmonization downward.[2]

---

[2] On the "Golden Age of Nordic Cooperation," see Lahti (2000) and Träskman (2013).

The discussions took somewhat divergent courses between countries, as penal and social welfare practices varied. In Finland, the critique of compulsory care merged with a reform program directed against an outdated and overly severe criminal code and the excessive use of custodial sentences generally (Anttila 1967). Still, the basic demands of the 1960s reform program in the Nordic countries can be summarized as follows:

- No hypocrisy: punishments should not be imposed under the false label of treatment.
- Separation of care and control: Supportive and rehabilitative activities should be the responsibility of the institutions best suited to that purpose—the general social welfare agencies. Coercion was to be left solely to the criminal justice system.
- Deinstitutionalization: The use of custodial sanctions and treatment methods should be reduced to a minimum. This applied to alcohol treatment, mental health services, and child welfare, as well as to imprisonment.

The first initiatives to realize these aims were undertaken in the 1960s in relation to social welfare, mental health care, and child protection, with criminal justice reforms following in the 1970s. The reforms carried out mainly in the 1960 and 1970s fully realized the principles that became characterized in Finland as "humane and rational criminal policy" (Lahti 2000).

Principles for penal reform in each country were formulated in four important documents published in 1976–78. The Finnish Criminal Law Committee report in 1976 (Committee Report 72:1976) was the most encompassing, covering both principles for criminalization and sanctions reforms. The Swedish report "New Penal System" (1977) mainly discussed the principles of the sanctions reform, which were further elaborated in much more detail in a 1986 report (SOU 1986:13–15). The Danish reform plan "Alternatives to Deprivation of Liberty 1977" and the Norwegian Ministry of Justice report "On Crime Policy" (1978) concentrated mainly on identifying new penalties to be used to reduce the prison population. All stressed, with differing emphases, the need to reduce the severity of sanctions (especially for property offenses), to replace short prison sentences with new community alternatives, to restrict the use of indeterminate sentences, and to develop a sentencing system that respected principles of proportionality and humanity. The ensuing law reforms followed the same path.

1. *Sanctions: Against Indeterminacy and Inflexibility.* In the 1970s and 1980s all Nordic countries restricted or abolished the use of indeterminate sanctions. The use of preventive detention was severely reduced in Finland in 1971 and in Denmark in 1973 and was abolished altogether in Sweden in 1981. Youth prisons, which included the possibility of extended confinement, were closed in law or in practice (Lappi-Seppälä 2011, pp. 220–21). Prison regimes in all the Nordic countries were relaxed by expanding the use of furloughs, open prisons, and routine early release programs.

Finland enacted three parole reforms between 1966 and 1989 to reduce sentence lengths, all with substantial effect on imprisonment rates. Sweden made one major downward change in the early 1980s by adopting a policy of automatic release after service of half the sentence (however, this was rescinded in 1993). In Denmark the minimum time for parole was reduced from 4 to 2 months in 1982. The adoption of fixed (semiautomatic) release was partly motivated by concern about legal safeguards, as the wide discretion given to prison administration to set release dates was seen as a threat to legal security and as a source for unequal and socially discriminatory release decisions. Denmark and Sweden, which had provided treatment programs in special institutions, abolished these programs or restricted their use. Investments in rehabilitative work remained quite modest throughout the 1980s. However, during the 1990s and 2000s, various treatment orders were introduced into the sanction systems in Denmark and Norway, either as conditions for conditional sentences or in combination with other sanctions. Sweden incorporated alcohol and substance abuse treatment back into the system in 1989 under the name "contract care."

2. *Specific Offenses: Decriminalization and Depenalization.* Public drunkenness was decriminalized in the Nordic countries in the 1960s and 1970s. This led to dramatic falls in the numbers of fine defaulters, especially in Finland. The next new initiatives with comparable effect on the overall use of imprisonment involved property offenses and drunk driving.

The number of property offenses increased quickly in and after the 1960s as a result of changes in opportunity structures: there were many more small valuable things to steal. Strict sentencing policies and inflexible recidivism rules led to disproportionately long sentences for persistent petty property offenders. As a result, penalty scales for theft were reduced in Finland in 1972 and again in 1991. Denmark did the same in 1973 and 1982. Recidivism rules were amended in Finland (1976), in Denmark (1973), and in Sweden in two phases (1976 and 1989). In addition, new restrictions on the use of preventive detention targeted habitual property offenders. Sweden relaxed penalties for theft by expanding the scope for nonprosecution. This general depenalization of theft had a substantial effect on use of imprisonment. In the mid-1970s the Finnish courts imposed 2,500 prison years for theft (the number sentenced to prison times the average sentence), in the early 1990s about 1,000, and in 2010 only 250.

3. *Drunken Driving.* Scandinavian countries' penal systems have paid more attention to drinking and driving than have most other countries. In the 1960s drunk drivers were the largest single group in Finnish prisons. Moralistic attitudes, and difficulties dealing with alcohol in the same rational way that other harmful behaviors are dealt with, for decades have kept drunk driving among the key problems of Scandinavian criminal justice policy (Hauge 1978).

Sentence levels for drunken driving were reduced in Finland in 1977, but only after long and bitter battles among researchers, conservative judges, and health care and alcohol treatment professionals. A new law on drunken driving replaced former unconditional prison sentences with a combination of conditional imprisonment and day fines. At the same time, criminalization expanded when a fixed limit of 0.05 percent was adopted. Denmark in 1981 and Norway in 1988 also relaxed drunken driving sanctions, but with less dramatic results. In Norway the normal penalty of 21 days for minor forms of drunk driving was replaced in 1988 with fines and conditional sentences (but drivers exceeding the limit of 0.1 percent blood alcohol content still had to go to prison). Even though the use of imprisonment was successfully reduced, moralistic tendencies did not disappear.

Restrictions in the use of prison sentences were followed by expansions of penal control of drunken driving by lowering blood alcohol limits from 0.5 to 0.2 first in Sweden in 1990 and then in Norway in 2000. Finland increased penal control by decreasing the limit for aggravated drunk driving from 1.5 to 1.2 in 1994 and in 2003 by adopting a Swedish-style zero limit for drugs in traffic. Overall, Nordic drunk driving policies can be seen as a mixture of efforts to rationalize the sentencing system by developing alternatives for custodial sanctions, coexisting with often moralistic views about the way people should organize their lives in relation to alcohol. Many reforms can be read mainly as symbolic statements underlining the message that "alcohol and traffic do not belong together," but too often without practical relevance for traffic safety.

4. *Alternatives to Imprisonment.* The traditional alternatives, fines and conditional imprisonment (suspended sentences), proved to be effective means to reduce use of imprisonment, especially in Finland. Fines were made heavier in Finland in the late 1970s in order to offer a more credible alternative to short prison sentences. The use of conditional imprisonment was expanded by relaxing prerequisites for its use. The annual number of conditional sentences rose from 4,000 in 1960 to 18,000 in 1990.

Testing of new alternatives took off in the early 1980s. Denmark began experimenting with community service in 1982. Norway followed in 1984. However, community service was not introduced on a wide scale in Nordic sanctions systems until the 1990s. Finland started with community service later than the other countries, but with better initial success. After a short experimental period in 1993–95, it was made permanent in 1995. The annual number of community service orders quickly reached the level of 3,500–4,000, replacing 35 percent of unconditional prison sentences of less than 8 months.

Other Nordic countries expanded use of community service in the early 2000s, using different approaches. Sweden created a combination of community service and suspended sentence in 2000, increasing the number of annual orders from 2,000 to 4,000. Denmark at the same time authorized use of community service for drunken driving (which was previously forbidden). Over 2 years this increased the number of orders from 1,000 to 4,000. Norway, in turn, increased the credibility of community service by changing its title to community punishment, including other elements in the sentence, and expanding its scope to include drunken driving. This resulted in an increase from 500 to 2,500 cases annually. Iceland began experimenting with community service in 1995 and made it permanent in 1998 (Olafsdottir and Bragadottir 2006). In contrast to the other Nordic countries, the decision about use of community service is made by the prison administration, not the courts.

Technically, community service appears in different forms. Finland and Norway treat it as an independent sanction. In Denmark and Sweden, it is attached either to conditional imprisonment or to a probation order. Iceland treats community service as a form of enforcement of a prison sentence. The maximum number of hours of work varies between 200 in Finland and 420 in Norway. Countries also differ in how strictly community service is defined as an alternative to imprisonment. Finland has followed the strictest policy, by requiring a two-step procedure. First, the court must make its sentencing decision according to normal principles and criteria without considering the possibility of community service. Second, if the result of this deliberation is unconditional imprisonment (and certain requirements are fulfilled), the court may transform the sentence into community service. Because of this, community service replaced prison sentences in Finland without notable net widening. That is also true in Iceland, where the prison authorities make the decision. In Denmark and Sweden, by contrast, community service has effectively replaced some of what would otherwise be prison sentences, but it has also to some extent replaced conditional sentences. In Norway replacement ratios look somewhat less favorable (Lappi-Seppälä 2012).

Figure 2 summarizes the main law reforms affecting specific offenses and the system of sanctions from the 1960s to the 1990s. The reforms are classified in terms of their "punitive direction" either as mitigating punishment, especially prison use (reforms restricting the scope or intensity of penal control) or aggravating (reforms expanding or intensifying penal control). Full lists of law reforms in the four countries are shown in appendix table A1.[3]

Practically all sanction reforms from the 1960s to the 1980s were designed to reduce the use of imprisonment or to mitigate the detrimental effects of incarceration. Most of the reforms at that time dealing with specific offenses shared these same aims (with the exception of drugs; see below). This is illustrated in figure 2.

Concrete results can be seen in Nordic imprisonment rates from 1960 to 1990 (see fig. 3). There was a steep decline in the Finnish imprisonment rate from around 160 per 100,000 population to 60. The Swedish imprisonment rates decreased in the short term from 70 per 100,000 in the mid-1960s to 50 in the mid-1970s.

B. The Punitive Turn, Nordic Style

After the 1980s things started to change. The sanction reforms still aimed at reduction in the use of imprisonment, but other legislation was revised with different motives. From the 1990s onward, most changes

---

[3] The appendix also provides a rough assessment of the effects of the various reforms on the use of imprisonment (marked as one to three pluses or minuses). This calculation is based less on statistics than on sporadic observations (and subjective judgment). The lists are not exhaustive. Only major reforms, and only those dealing with offenses and sanctions, are included. For a fuller list for Sweden, see von Hofer and Tham (2013), and for an earlier version of all the lists, see Lappi-Seppälä (2007).

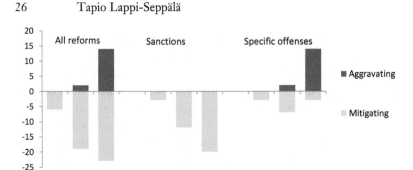

Fig. 2.—Prison use mitigating and aggravating law reforms, 1960s–80s. Source: Author's analyses.

dealing with specific offenses have increased punishment severity or expanded criminalization. The 1991 theft reform in Finland was the last that decreased penalties for common offenses (and it was enacted in 1988). For drug offenses, changes occurred long before that. Figure 4 shows law reforms from 1990 to early 2010, on the same basis as figure 2.

1. *Drugs: Between Moral Panics and Harm Reduction.* Sweden and Norway adopted strict policies for drug offenses in the 1960s. In 1968, Sweden increased the maximum penalty for trafficking from 6 months to 4 years. Maximum penalties were raised in 1969 from 4 to 6 years and in 1972 from 6 to 10 years. During the 1980s the focus shifted from man-

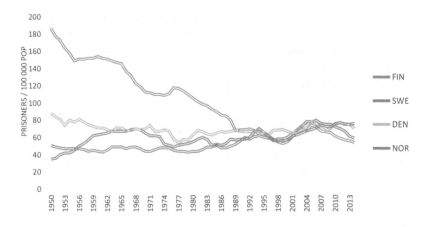

Fig. 3.—Imprisonment rates per 100,000 population, 1950–2013. Source: von Hofer, Lappi-Seppälä, and Westfelt (2012); Kristoffersen (2016).

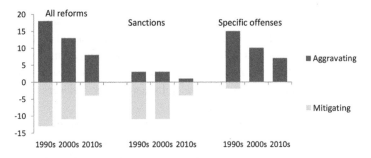

FIG. 4.—Mitigating and aggravating law reforms, 1990s–2010s. Source: Author's analyses.

ufacturers and dealers to consumers; the concept of "drug-free Sweden" emerged. The list of changes is long: Nonprosecution for drug crimes was restricted in 1980; penalties were increased in 1981; compulsory treatment for adults was enacted in 1982 and was expanded to juveniles in 1989; the scope of criminalization increased in 1983 and 1988; and penalties were further increased in 1985, 1988, and 1993 (Tham 2003, 2005). In 1981, Norway placed serious drug offenses in the same category as first-degree murder (with a maximum of 21 years' imprisonment). Iceland increased drug penalties in 2001.

Denmark and Finland have been more restrained. Denmark long showed very little interest in punishing drug consumption. However, during the 1990s, Denmark started to tighten its drug control. In 1996, penalties for repeat drug dealing were tripled. In 2004 the maximum sentence for drug offenses was lifted from 10 to 16 years, and penalties for consumption, possession, and dealing were increased.

The vision of a drug-free society was explicitly abandoned in Finland during the 1990s. Drug programs were based in principle on the notion of harm reduction. But despite these differences in policy principles, sanctioning practices in Finland closely resemble those elsewhere in Scandinavia, falling somewhere between the Swedish and Danish. In general, Finland imposes more fines for minor infractions compared with the other Nordic countries, and drug offenses are no exception.

2. *Violence.* All countries have increased punishments for violence against women. Initiatives concerning domestic violence occurred in Sweden during the early 1980s. In 1981 domestic violence was prioritized for public prosecution. Penalties were increased in 1984 and 1993. In 1998 a new gender-specific violence crime—the "breach of women's

peace"—was introduced. Similar developments spread quickly. Norway increased penalties for domestic violence in 1988 and again in 2006. In 1994, Finland defined assaults in public places as offenses under public prosecution. In 2004 nonprosecution of domestic violence was restricted, and in 2010 domestic violence and assaults against persons were excluded from the category of minor assault.

Penalties have also been raised for most forms of serious and gang-related violence. In 2010 Sweden increased penalties for serious violent offenses (see Prop. 2009–10:147, Skärpta Straff för Allvarliga Våldsbrott M.M, Regeringens Proposition). The law encouraged the courts to impose harsher punishments and to increase the weight accorded recidivism in sentencing. It introduced new and more severe penalty scales for a large number of violent offenses. The aim was generally to increase the "penal value" (seriousness) of violent offenses. In order generally to do that, a statement was added to general sentencing provisions: "When considering the penal value of the offense, special attention should be placed on whether the offense has included a serious infringement of someone's life, health, or security." Pre-enactment legislative reports indicated that penalties should be increased by 20–30 percent. In order to widen the breadth of applicable penalty scales, in both directions, the thresholds for taking account of mitigating and aggravating were lowered. The proposal was heavily criticized by experts, but without notable effect (see du Rées and Sarnecki 2013; Estrada and Tham 2013, 2015). Published court statistics after implementation indicated only modest changes in sentencing practice. This led the minister of justice in 2013 to appoint another inquiry to examine other possibilities for raising penalty levels. A spring 2014 plan published by the chief prosecutor proposed to lift minimum penalties for several violent offenses, including aggravated assault, robbery, and manslaughter (SOU 2014, p. 18).[4]

---

[4] These conclusions may have been premature. Postreform sentencing statistics hardly serve as a full evaluation of impact. A recently published follow-up, based on both quantitative and qualitative methods with three different types of data, indicates that penalties for aggravated assault increased by 20–30 percent, which matches the intention. Penalties for murder increased by 4 years, which may be a consequence of increasing the maximum prison term from 14 to 18 years (Brå 2014, p. 51). The 2010 changes were fundamentally political. They were unaffected by principled arguments from criminologists concerning the declining trend of serious violence while the proposal was drafted and presented. Nor did convincing evidence from a carefully designed public sense-of-justice study, which showed that the Swedish public did not demand harsher sentences for violent offenders, make a difference (Jerre and Tham 2010).

Denmark increased penalties for violent offenses in 1988. Penalties for repeat violence were lifted in 1994, for serious violence in 1997, and for gang violence in 2002. In 2014, new laws targeted organized violent crime—especially motorcycle gangs—with stiffer penalties. They authorized a doubling of sentences and tighter early release conditions for offenders who satisfied defined criteria of organized crime.

A Norwegian sexual offense package included increased maximum penalties for several violent offenses. In Finland the minimum penalty for aggravated assault was increased from 6 to 12 months in 2001. This resulted in a substantial increase in imposed prison years (71 percent from 1998 to 2004; Lappi-Seppälä 2008, p. 343). Unrelated to legislative changes, the use of life imprisonment, which is possible in Finland only for murder, increased. The average daily number of prisoners serving a life sentence increased from 30 in the early 1990s to 200 in the 2010s.

3. *Sexual Offenses.* Penalties for sexual offenses were made stiffer throughout the 1990s and 2000s. In Sweden, penalties for rape increased, the legal definition of rape was expanded, and sexual molestation of children was defined as "child rape" (Tham, Rönneling, and Rytterbro 2011). There was an immediate effect on the numbers of recorded and reported offenses and on conviction and incarceration rates. In 2001 Denmark increased penalties for rape by 1 year. This was heavily influenced by reported gang rapes involving immigrant offenders and by a media-based campaign claiming that Denmark had the shortest prison sentences in Scandinavia (Träskman and Kyvsgaard 2002). In 2010, Norway increased penalties for sexual offenses by 30–100 percent. The minimum penalty for rape was lifted from 2 to 3 years (and for homicide from 6 to 8 years). In Finland, penalties for rape were increased by 6 months in 1999. In 2010 penalties for sexual crimes against children were increased, in 2011 the definition of rape was expanded, and in 2012 the ministry of justice published a plan that anticipates further increases in rape penalties.

4. *Prostitution and Pornography.* Sweden enacted stricter laws against child pornography and the use of prostitution services (criminalization in 1999; expanded in 2005). In the other Nordic countries, similar changes have been motivated either by international obligations or by purportedly positive experiences in Sweden. In Finland penalties for human trafficking, procuring, and child pornography were increased in 2004 primarily to meet EU commitments. In 2006 prohibition of purchasing prostitution services, heavily influenced by the Swedish example, entered

into force. However, the scope of criminalization was restricted only to cases in connection with human trafficking or organized procurement. There have been very few convictions. The minister of justice recently announced that the government will draft a new bill, more closely following the "Swedish model." The government of Norway decided in 2004 not to follow the Swedish example, but changed course in 2007 by introducing criminalization that came into force in 2009. Iceland did the same in 2009. There is little doubt that Nordic law reforms in violent crimes, sexual offenses, prostitution, and pornography have been inspired by Swedish models, which in turn have been heavily influenced by the strong Swedish feminist and women's rights movements (Tham, Rönneling, and Rytterbro 2011; for Iceland, see Olafsdottir and Bragadottir [2006]).

5. *Penal Rhetoric of the 1990s.* Restrictive Nordic drug policies have long been regarded as an anomaly, a deviation from otherwise rational, knowledge-based, and less moralistic penal policies (Träskman 2004). The long list of sentencing law changes for violent and sexual offenses represents another deviation. They have very little to do with evidence-based crime prevention, but much more with openly punitive demands for harsher sentences. Does this mean that the fundamentals of Nordic criminal policy have changed in a way that justifies talk of an "Anglo-style" new punitive turn?

Something certainly changed, if criminal justice policy discussions of the 1970s are compared with those of the 1990s. While in the 1970s the Swedish minister of justice forecast that Sweden would reduce the number of prisoners from 3,000 to 500 in the near future, a conservative successor in 1993 published a booklet entitled *To Restore a Degenerated Criminal Policy*, which defined crime as a "threat to democracy," condemned the criminal justice policies of the 1980s, adopted openly tougher sentences, and endorsed more repressive crime control policies. For the first time in Swedish history, penal policy became an issue in a national election. The subsequent change in government in 1994 had little effect on policy, as the new social democratic minister of justice declared that there was no difference in practice between the crime policy of the Social Democrats and that of the other parties (Victor 1995; Tham 2001; von Hofer and Tham 2013).

Something similar took place in Denmark in the early 2000s. After a change of government in 2001, the new conservative minister of justice launched a series of policy changes that increased penalties for violence,

sexual offenses, and drugs, but also for property offenses. While defer-
ence to research-based expertise had been a distinctive mark of Nordic
political culture, experts seem to have lost much of their authority. This
was openly stated by a former Danish prime minister, who declared that
the politicians do not need any "arbiters of taste" to tell them what to do
about crime (Balvig 2004).

Similar statements were made by a Finnish minister of justice in
1998: "The criminal policy of the 1970s has come to its end." A newly
appointed prosecutor general sought increased penalties, especially for
sexual and violent offenses. The media, and some law professors, joined
the criticism, asserting that criminal justice policy discussions of the previous decade were dominated by a "Criminal Political Mafia" that had
"lost its touch on social reality" and is "unfamiliar with the new forms
of organized transnational crime" (Lappi-Seppälä 2008, p. 353).

This all reflected a changed and more punitive attitude especially toward sexual and violent offenses. It resulted in a substantial number of
law reforms, with a notable effect on increasing imprisonment rates.
But whether it justifies talk of an overall "US-style" punitive turn is less
clear. At least in Finland, general policy plans published by the ministry
of justice in 1999 and 2006 were committed to traditional liberal aims
and principles and an ambition to "control" incarceration rates. The
prison population fell from almost 4,000 in 2006 to 3,200 in 2010 and
3,100 in 2014. Much the same happened in Sweden. New punitive elements have entered in the penal landscape, but there were also counter-
acting forces.

C. Mixed Trends in the New Millennium

So far I have analyzed penal reforms from the perspective of punitiveness and whether they intensify or relax the scope of penal control.
That ignores changes in sanctions law and policy that tell a different
story. Changes targeting offenses are more directly politically motivated and provide simple ways to make political statements. Sanctions
reforms are often needed, however, to balance pressures created by
offense-focused changes, for example, by opening the prison's back door
or providing alternatives to imprisonment (Lappi-Seppälä 2007, pp. 258–
59). In the 2000s, this division of labor continued. All specific offense
reforms continued the line of penal expansion, in the form of new criminalization or increased sentence severity. Sanctions changes, however,
ameliorate them. Some policy changes are hard to fit into a simple clas-

sification based on punitiveness, as criminal justice policy does not concern only the severity of sanctions.

1. *Prison Reform.* All Nordic countries undertook major reforms of prison law in the 2000s, and prison regimes have undergone other changes. As Danish commentators note, several changes involve tougher actions and increased control (Balvig 2004; Greve 2007). Safe custody, risk management, and expansion of security have reached the Swedish prisons (Bruhn, Lindberg, and Nylander 2012). Several Nordic prisons have been altered to incorporate electrified fences, airport-like security checks, and specialized security wings. Some changes are attributable to the need to control narcotic substances in prisons, but others such as security units are established for offenders deemed particularly high-risk (such as motorcycle gangs; for a critical overview, see Ugelvik and Dullum [2012]).

However, it would be unfair to characterize twenty-first-century Nordic prison reforms in terms only of increased control and security. They are also influenced by the international human rights movement, new constitutionalism, and protection of prisoners' fundamental rights (albeit with national differences; see Greve 2007). For example, the 2006 Prison Act in Finland aims to bring prison law into line with requirements of the new constitution, to define the obligations of prison authorities in more detail, and to increase legal safeguards and transparency in prison administration. It also aims to reorganize imprisonment into a more structured and planned process and to increase investments in rehabilitative programs and treatment (and thereby also to reduce recidivism; Lappi-Seppälä 2009).

2. *Youth Justice.* Similar ambiguity applies to youth justice. From the 1990s onward, inspired by a reborn belief in penal rehabilitation, there has been increased interest in development of specific youth sanctions (Lappi-Seppälä 2011). These developments are differently motivated in different countries. In some instances the goal is more intensive and effective interventions, as with the semi-institutional "Danish juvenile punishment" in 2001 (Storgaard 2009). Sometimes as with Swedish "closed youth care" in the early 2000s, the aim was to replace imprisonment with other institutional arrangements, and sometimes as with "youth punishment" in Finland in 1994 to build a new step in the penal ladder in order to avoid use of imprisonment for juveniles.

The Nordic countries have been successful in their efforts to limit the use of penal custody for juveniles. Nordic child welfare, and to a large extent Nordic youth justice, are predominantly guided by the principle of the best interest of the child, not by punitive motives. Nonetheless, expansion of placements in child welfare institutions in Finland, and creation of hybrid institutions between prison and child welfare in Denmark (Storgaard 2009), may still raise serious concerns. Recent Danish changes in age limits tell their own story. In 2010 the Danish government reduced the age of criminal responsibility from 15 to 14, as a part of a political agreement with a radical right-wing party. The next year the new government changed the age limit back to 15 years! This may be one of the quickest European legislative turnovers on fundamentals of criminal liability.

3. *Fine Default.* Reforms with default penalties for unpaid fines provide another example of continuing efforts to restrict the use of imprisonment. Sweden ceased to convert fines to imprisonment in 1983. Denmark did the same in 2006. Finland excluded all prosecutors' fines from the default process in 2006, reducing the daily population of fine defaulters by two-thirds. Norway has introduced community alternatives as default penalties. Similar plans were proposed in Finland in 2013.

4. *Electronic Monitoring.* Electronic monitoring (EM) falls into the same category. EM was introduced in Sweden in mid-1990 as a form of enforcement of prison sentences up to 3 (now 6) months. A back-door version was adopted in 2001 as a part of early release programs for prisoners serving sentences of at least 18 months. In 2010 a total of 3,673 offenders entered into EM (with a daily average of 532).

Denmark started use of EM as a front-door option in 2005. All prisoners under age 25 with a sentence of not more than 6 months may apply to serve it in EM. In 2010, 1,898 offenders entered EM (with a daily average of 188 offenders at any one time). Norway started experimenting with EM in September 2008, in both front- and back-door versions, as part of the government's plan to get rid of waiting lists for prison admission. In Norway the correctional services can decide that prison sentences up to 4 months will be served at home. They can also decide that inmates serving longer sentences will have EM during the last 4 months before parole release. In 2010, 1,001 offenders entered into EM (with a daily average of 87).

Finland introduced a back-door version of EM after an experimental phase in 2006 in connection with a new form of early release (at most 6 months before normal conditional release). In late 2015, there were just over 100 prisoners in EM. The front-door version was adopted in

2011 as part of a new supervision order. It is reserved for offenders who do not pass the suitability test for community service, provided that it is "deemed to be justified in order to uphold and promote the offender's social skills." Besides EM supervision, the sanction requires work, education, or participation in rehabilitation programs.

Notwithstanding the criticism that EM expands penal control to civil society, it has several benefits over an unconditional prison term (provided that it is really used to replace prison sentences). In terms of daily prison populations, EM plays a substantial role so far only in Sweden, corresponding to just under 10 percent of the prison population. However, in terms of flow, the number of offenders entering EM corresponds to more than one-third of annual prison admissions. The stability or slight decline in the number of annual entries into penal institutions seems to be partly attributable to introduction of EM in Denmark and Norway. The Swedish imprisonment rates would also look different without EM (for details, see Lappi-Seppälä [2012, p. 99] and Kristoffersen [2016, pp. 15–19]).

5. *Mediation.* Informal restorative justice schemes began in the Nordic countries in the early 1980s. The first experiments were heavily influenced by the abolitionist writings in the 1970s of Thomas Mathiesen and Nils Christie in Norway and Louk Hulsman in the Netherlands. Informality, voluntariness, and community involvement were crucial from the beginning. Mediation started first in Norway in 1981 as an independent criminal sanction and was acknowledged as such in the code of criminal proceedings. Finland started experiments in 1983. The practice spread quickly, reaching 5,000 referrals by the early 1990s. Denmark and Sweden experimented with it during the 1990s on a smaller scale. During the 2000s, mediation was established in law in Finland in 2006, Denmark in 2010, and Sweden in 2002. Norway had done so in 1991.[5]

Today all Nordic countries have national legislation on mediation, and the system is well established. Participation is always voluntary for all parties. In Norway, mediation is an independent sanction and automatically replaces other criminal sanctions. Elsewhere, mediation has a more informal role. Criminal codes generally acknowledge mediation as one possible justification for prosecutors to waive charges or for judges

---

[5] On mediation in the Nordic countries, see Holmboe (2002), Wahlin (2005), and Lappi-Seppälä (2015a).

to waive or mitigate sentences, except in Denmark, where mediation cannot replace prosecution (Lappi-Seppälä and Storgaard 2015).

In statistical terms, mediation is most common in Finland, with over 12,000 cases per year. Norway closely follows. However, the diversionary role of mediation is most prominent in Norway. This has been reinforced by incorporating mediation as an element in new juvenile punishments—to be used instead of short prison sentences.[6]

II. Sentencing Law and Sanctions Systems

Standards governing Nordic sentencing are set out in legislation. Application of criminal law is guided by strict interpretation of the legality principle, confirmed in constitutions or criminal codes (or both as in Finland). Statutory regulation covers the process, the contents, and the application of specific sanctions and sentencing discretion. The term "sentencing" can refer to one of these areas or all of them. I take a broad view here.

A. The Process

The court system consists of local courts, regional appellate courts, and supreme courts. Courts enjoy constitutionally granted independence (as does the prosecution service). Civil servants and criminal justice officials (judges, prosecutors, police) are permanent nonpartisan career officials. The process may be characterized as inquisitorial with accusatorial elements or as accusatorial with inquisitorial elements. There has been a shift in recent decades from a judge-centered inquisitorial process toward an adversarial, prosecutor-centered process. The prosecutor has been given more responsibilities in moving cases through the process, more power to decide which should be handled by the court, and more independent powers to decide on the final disposition. However, the process still involves important inquisitorial elements, including the "incumbent pre-investigation," principles of legality and objectivity in prosecution, free assessment of the evidence, and a critical view toward plea bargaining and crown witnesses.

1. *Pre-investigations and Prosecution.* The principle of objectivity governs investigations and prosecutions in all countries. In the investigation,

---

[6] See Prop. 135 (2010–11), Endringer I Straffeloven, Straffeprosessloven, Straffegjennomföringsloven, Konflikrådsloven M.FL. Barn och Straff Det Kongelige Justis-og Politidepartement.

the police must take into account facts and evidence both against and in favor of the accused. The prosecutor, in turn, must act in an impartial and unprejudiced manner and is obliged to establish all facts of the case including those in favor of the accused. This applies also to cases involving confessions.

   a. Nonprosecution.   Not all reported offenses lead to investigations. "Complainant offenses," defamation and breach of domestic peace, can be investigated by the police only if the injured party notifies the police or a prosecutor that he or she wants punishment for the offender. If these demands are withdrawn during the investigation, the police will desist.

   In all countries, the prosecutor has the powers to close investigations in minor offenses for reasons of procedural expediency. Formal requirements vary. Thus, in Sweden, discontinuation is possible with the consent of the injured party, if the expected outcome would be nonprosecution or at most 3 months' imprisonment, provided that prosecution is not required on the basis of the general interest of the society. In Finland this option is reserved only for cases that would result in waiver of prosecution and if dropping the investigations would not breach any important private or public interest.

   The Nordic countries fall into two groups concerning prosecutors' discretionary powers. Finland and Sweden follow the principle of legality. The prosecutor is obliged to pursue charges if there is probable cause. In Denmark and Norway, prosecution is governed by the opportunity principle. This grants the prosecutor wider discretion. However, in practice, the differences are almost nonexistent, as the strict requirements of the legality principle are softened by extensive rules of nonprosecution in both Finland and Sweden.[7] The grounds for nonprosecution are defined in the law in detail. In both countries, they give the prosecutor fairly wide discretion in four types of cases:[8] minor offenses, young offenders, and cases in which the offender is suspected for several offenses (concurrence). The fourth case deals with extraordinary reasons of equity

---

   [7] Similar provisions can be found in Norway and Denmark but defined in broader terms. On prosecutors in Sweden, see Asp (2012); on Finland, see Lappi-Seppälä (2004).

   [8] For reasons of conceptual clarity it is necessary to make a clear distinction between two types of nonprosecution: decisions based on procedural circumstances such as lack of evidence and statutes of limitations where there are legal obstacles to prosecution ("procedural" nonprosecution) and when there is enough evidence to support prosecution, but the prosecutor chooses to drop the charge for other reasons, often related to the petty nature of the offense or the young age of the offender ("diversionary" nonprosecution). The text discusses the latter version.

and criminal political expediency. For example, in Finland, the prosecutor may drop charges "when trial and punishment are deemed unreasonable or pointless considering the reconciliation between the offender and the complainant or other action taken by the offender to prevent or remove the effects of his offense, his personal circumstances, other consequences of the offense to him, actions by the social security and health authorities, or other circumstances" (Lappi-Seppälä 2004, pp. 164–65).

Nonprosecution occurs in conditional and unconditional forms. In conditional forms, it is attached with conditions that must be met lest the case be taken into court. This makes the decision look more like a suspended sentence. This form of nonprosecution is in use in Norway. Denmark uses both conditional and unconditional nonprosecution. In Sweden and Finland all nonprosecution decisions are unconditional.

The scope of nonprosecution has varied over time. Finland followed very strict and legalistic policies until the early 1990s but then loosened the conditions. Sweden followed a very generous policy until the late 1990s but has since tightened conditions.

b. Prosecutors' Sanctioning Powers. All countries provide the prosecutor the right to impose penalties in summary processes. This has been gradually extended, and the prosecutor has received more independent power to act. Thus, in Finland, summary fines were confirmed by a judge at the request of the prosecutor until 1994. Since then the prosecutor decides on the request of police. The right to impose summary sanctions includes also forfeiture and revocation of driving licenses.[9]

In practice, prosecutorial fines (penalty orders, summary fines) occupy a central position as the standard sanction for minor offenses. This includes midrank traffic offenses (trivial ones are handled by the police and more serious ones by the courts) and petty property offenses. For example, in Finland, the police impose around 200,000 fixed ticket fines and prosecutors issue around 200,000 penalty orders (summary day fines). Around 60,000 offenders are sentenced by the courts, of whom 35,000 receive day fines, 16,000 receive suspended sentences, 5,000 receive unconditional prison sentences, and 3,000 receive community service orders. Police and prosecutors play the central roles in imposition of criminal sanctions in numbers. Any decisions that concern loss of liberty, however, must be made by the criminal court.

---

[9] The police have been given authority to impose small fixed monetary penalties in all countries mostly for traffic offenses.

c. The Role of the Victim.   The position of the Nordic victim has traditionally been strong (Joutsen 1987). The victim has a secondary right of prosecution should the prosecutor decide not to bring charges. More importantly, several arrangements serve the victim's compensatory and restorative interests. These include full application of the adhesion process. Civil law claims are almost always investigated and tried in the same proceeding as the offense. No separate process is needed (Lappi-Seppälä 1996). In addition, the public prosecutor has an obligation to pursue civil claims at the victim's request, if this is possible without major inconvenience and if the claim is not obviously ill founded. Unlike many other countries, Nordic countries do not use or admit victim impact statements. Victim's interests are implicated in issues relating to restitution, compensation, and support, but not the imposition of punishment.

2. *Cooperation and Sentence Negotiations.*   All Nordic criminal justice systems allow limited mitigation based on cooperation during the proceedings (but only concerning the defendant's case, not those of other defendants) and the offender's postact behavior and contributions in clearing up the offense. None of the countries allow full-blown plea bargaining, but negotiations between the parties have increased effect on sentencing discretions.

a. Confession and Clearing Up the Offense.   In Norway and Denmark, confessed cases may be dealt with under a simplified process with just one trained judge for offenses with a maximum authorized penalty of 10 years or less. Confession and helping clear up one's own offense may lead to different sorts of mitigation. All countries have provisions on this in their general sentencing rules. Mitigation is justified more openly on the basis of simplifying the process. In Sweden mitigation is based on the moral value of remorse. However, a recent proposal (SOU 2012, p. 231) would allow mitigation on more pragmatic grounds.

For all cases and in all countries this is confined to one's own offense. All countries have rejected mitigation as rewards for information concerning offenses committed by others (concerning Sweden, see SOU [2005, p. 73]).

b. Sentence Bargaining in Finland.   Finland took a further step toward adversarial processes in 2015 by introducing a limited form of plea bargaining. This was grounded in resource-based arguments. The European Court of Human Rights several times has criticized Finland about overly long criminal proceedings, especially for economic crimes. Plea bargaining was introduced—as an alternative measure—to speed up the pretrial phase and court proceedings and to allocate scarce criminal justice resources more effectively.

This option is restricted and its use is tightly defined. The prosecutor holds the key position. The prosecutor may act on his or her own initiative or at the injured party's initiative by drafting a proposition for sentencing. The offender agrees to plead guilty and the prosecutor agrees to propose sentencing from the mitigated penal scale. The prosecutor may also decide not to prosecute one or several suspected crimes. The law also provides opportunity to limit the scope of pre-investigations if the offender is suspected of several offenses. This decision is made by the prosecutor.

There are three sets of requirements. The maximum authorized penalty may not exceed 6 years. This rules out crimes such as homicide, aggravated assaults, and aggravated drug offenses. Offenses directed against the personal integrity of the victims are excluded (covering almost all sexual offenses and most violent crime). The victim must agree with use of this procedure. These restrictions will effectively confine plea bargaining mostly to economic, tax, and property offenses (as was intended).

Court proceedings after plea bargaining (the so-called confession process) are less complicated than are normal court proceedings. The parties have the opportunity to state their views of the agreement and to make closing statements. The process should save both time and money. Perhaps the most substantial savings will result from the absence of sentence reviews in the appellate court.

The effects of plea bargaining on sentencing are defined in the criminal code. The court must impose a mitigated sentence, provided that the plea has been voluntary and guilt is beyond a reasonable doubt. If so, the maximum penalty applicable will be reduced by one-third, and the courts are not bound by minimum penalties. To ensure the contemplated implementation of these provisions, the courts should state what the penalty would have been without a successful guilty plea.[10]

3. *Criminal Court Process.* Today, the inquisitorial features have disappeared from the criminal procedure, especially in dealing with serious crimes. The prosecutor is responsible to prove the defendant's guilt beyond a reasonable doubt.

---

[10] The government must monitor implementation and report to the Parliament in 2017. Early experience indicates restricted implementation (after the first 9 months about 20 cases, with sentence reductions of about one-third).

a. The Prosecutor's Changing Role.   The court remains passive through the proceedings, although the judge may clarify ambiguities and "fill in gaps" in the trial material by asking the parties questions. The court may not summon a witness on its own initiative for a complainant offense, and very rarely does that in other cases.

The court is tied to the charge. Section 3 of the Finnish Criminal Procedure Act states, "The court may pass a sentence only for the act for which a punishment has been requested or for which the court may pass a sentence on its own initiative. The court is not bound by the heading or the reference to the applicable provisions in the charge." This provision has been given a restrictive interpretation. The court may not base a decision against the defendant on facts not presented by the prosecutor. However, the court is not tied to the prosecutor's interpretation of the law. For instance, the court may decide differently from the prosecutor concerning whether the act proved was theft or robbery.

Nordic prosecutors have traditionally remained silent concerning the type and amount of punishment. This, too, has slowly been changing. Prosecutors have been encouraged to express their concrete views and proposals on sentencing issues, but in fairly broad terms by indicating mainly the type of sanction (e.g., fines or imprisonment, conditional or unconditional sentence, imprisonment or community service). Only in serious cases in which the only appropriate sanction is unconditional imprisonment may the prosecutor suggest the length of the sentence. However, the court is not bound by the prosecutor's proposal. The judge may order a sentence more severe than the prosecutor proposed (on Sweden, see Lappi-Seppälä [2004]; SOU [2013, p. 17]).

b. The Composition of the Courts.   The composition of the district court varies with the offense in question. Minor offenses punishable by fines or short prison terms are usually handled in simplified processes by one legally trained judge. In more serious cases, the number of legally trained judges increases, and they are complemented by lay members. These compositions vary between countries. Fines, in the majority of all dispositions, are usually imposed by one trained judge. In Denmark, midrank offenses are handled by one trained judge and two laymen. Offenses punishable by at least 4 years' imprisonment are dealt with by three trained judges and six laymen. In Norway, simple cases are dealt with by one legally trained judge, including when there is a guilty plea (and the maximum penalty is 10 years or less). Other cases are dealt with by one trained judge and two laymen. In Sweden, offenses that lead to sanctions more severe than fines are handled by one trained judge and three laymen. In Finland, a single-judge process is possible in cases in which the maximum punishment is at most 18 months, but the judge at most can impose a fine. The normal composition of a district court is one legally trained judge and three lay judges. In the most serious cases, this is enlarged by a second judge and a fourth lay member.

   c. Appeal.   Appeal rights and procedures have changed. Formerly unrestricted rights of appeal for all parties have gradually been restricted. Finland was the last country to do so in 2011. All parties including the victim have independent rights of appeal, but these rights have been restricted in minor offenses. In most countries, the defendant's unrestricted right pertains only to cases for which the sentence is more severe than a fine. In Finland, unrestricted appeal is available only in cases leading to 4-month or longer prison terms. For lesser offenses the defendant may petition to appeal for reasons related to uniform application of the law or for other specific reasons. Procedures and appellate court compositions vary between countries depending on the seriousness of the case. Recent changes have moved the proceedings toward oral hearings. The procedure follows the same basic principles as in local trial courts.

   The appeal may pertain to all or part of the grounds of the decision or the sentence. Appellate courts review the lower court ruling on factual and legal grounds (including guilt and punishment). In all countries appeals to the highest court require that the court grant leave to appeal.

B. The System of Sanctions

Nordic sanction alternatives can be scaled in severity from least to most intrusive. The scale consists of formal warnings in the form of nonprosecution, summary fines, court-imposed day fines, community sanctions, and imprisonment.

   1. *Fines.*   Fines are the most commonly used penalties in all Nordic countries. Denmark, Finland, and Sweden adopted day fine systems in the 1920s and 1930s. They aim to ensure comparable severity for offenders of different incomes and wealth. The number of day fines is based on the seriousness of the offense, and the amount of a single day fine depends on the financial situation of the offender.[11]

---

[11] The technical counting rules differ between countries, but the end result is about the same. The amount of a Swedish day fine is slightly lower than in Finland, but the number of day fines is a little higher. Sweden, unlike Finland and Denmark, established a general maximum for one day fine (1,000 Swedish crowns).

A fine may be imposed in an ordinary trial or, for petty offenses, by the prosecutor or the police using summary proceedings. Some summary fines are imposed both as day fines and as fixed fines. Police authority is usually limited to traffic offenses. A majority of prosecutors' fines are also imposed for traffic offenses. However, a substantial number of minor criminal offenses can be sanctioned by prosecutorial fines. The vast majority of fines are ordered in a summary process.[12]

2. *Community Alternatives.* Community sanctions are the middle range between fines and imprisonment. There are national differences in details, but the basic patterns are broadly similar (for an overview, see Kyvsgaard [2001]). Conditional imprisonment and suspended sentences form the backbone. However, the list of community sanctions has increased, especially since the 1990s. Today community sanctions encompass four to five basic options: conditional or suspended sentence, possibly combined with other sanctions; probation or supervision as an independent or a complementary sanction; community service as an independent or a complementary sanction; and treatment orders—usually as a complementary sanction. Electronic monitoring may be classified as a form of supervision order or as a way of serving a prison sentence.

a. Conditional and Suspended Sentences. The lower end of community punishments consists of suspended sentences or conditional imprisonment, with or without stipulated time. In Finland and Denmark, the court imposes the sentence but postpones enforcement. In Sweden, the court postpones the pronouncement of the sentence for a probation period. In Norway, both options are in use; postponement of enforcement (conditional imprisonment or sentence) is more common. In Finland, sentences of imprisonment up to 2 years may be imposed conditionally. Norway and Denmark have no formal limits, but conditional sentences lasting more than 2 years are rare.

Conditional imprisonment can be combined with supervision, fines, community service, or in Denmark and Norway with prison. A person sentenced to conditional imprisonment may be ordered to serve the prison sentence if a new offense is committed during the suspension period, usually 1–2 years. Thresholds for revocation vary. In Finland, revocation is possible only if the court imposes a sentence of imprisonment

---

[12] For more details on the use of fines, see Lappi-Seppälä (2011, pp. 229–30).

for the new offense. A behavioral infraction alone is not enough to trigger enforcement of a conditional prison sentence.

b. Community Service.   Community service appears in different forms. Finland and Norway treat it as an independent sanction (in 2001, Norway renamed community service as community punishment). In Denmark and Sweden, community service is attached either to conditional imprisonment or to a probation order. In Finland, conditional prison sentences over 1 year may be combined with a 20–60-hour community service order. In Denmark, community service may be combined with fines and unconditional imprisonment and may be amplified with additional conditions concerning residence, school attendance, or work. Norway allows conditions concerning the offender's dwelling, work, and treatment. The maximum number of hours varies between 200 (Finland) and 420 (Norway).

c. Probation and Supervision Orders.   Sweden has a separate probation sanction. "Protective supervision" is for 3 years, of which the sentenced person is supervised for the first year. Probation may be used alone (simple probation) or with other attached penalties. Swedish probation is a kind of "frame" penalty. Fines or a short prison sentence of 14 days to 3 months may be attached. It can also be combined with a treatment order and community service.

Introduction of electronic monitoring has lifted the profile of supervision as a community sanction. In Sweden, Denmark, and Norway, EM is a way to serve a prison sentence. After the judge orders a prison sentence, the offender may apply to serve it at home under EM. The decision is made by enforcement agencies. In Finland, EM is part of a new supervision order imposed by the court. It is designed for offenders who would not qualify for community service and are at risk of being sentenced to prison. Both arrangements are meant to replace short prison sentences.

d. Treatment Orders.   The roles of treatment orders are strongest in Sweden and Denmark. Swedish *contract treatment* is intended primarily for long-term substance abusers when there is a link between the abuse and crime. Contract treatment can be used as a normal condition of probation or as the reason not to impose a prison sentence. A contract is made between the court and the offender on institutional care in a home or an open clinic. If the person misbehaves, the sentence can be converted into a prison sentence. Treatment lasts 6–24 months. Part occurs in an institution. In contract treatment, treatment is always voluntary (but choices are limited: go to prison or not).

In Denmark, treatment orders are used both with conditional imprisonment and as a form of prison enforcement. In connection with a conditional sentence, persons suffering from substance abuse or a mental disturbance may be required to participate in treatment for alcohol or drug abuse or outpatient psychiatric treatment. Persons sentenced to prison for 60 days or less can apply for suspension of the sentence if in obvious need of alcohol abuse treatment.

3. *Imprisonment.* All Nordic countries have abolished the death penalty. The most severe sentence that may be imposed for a single offense in Denmark, Finland, and Sweden is "life," which in practice means a prison term of 15–18 years. Norway has abolished the life sentence and replaced it with a 21-year maximum term. The maximum term of imprisonment for a single offense not eligible for a life sentence is 16 years in Denmark, 12 years in Finland, and 10 years in Sweden (but 18 for murder). For multiple offenses, and in Denmark and Sweden in case of recidivism, these limits may be exceeded. These are nominal sentence lengths, which are substantially diminished by remission allowances and parole release.

Prison sentences are served in open or closed institutions. Open institutions hold between 20 percent (Sweden) and 40 percent (Denmark) of prisoners, including before trial. Open institutions are prisons without walls: prisoners must stay in the prison area, but neither guards nor fences keep them there. Closed prisons are small. The largest house 200 to over 300 prisoners; the norm is 50–100.

Extensive, and in some countries nearly automatic, early release on parole, combined with restrained revocation procedures, are distinguishing Nordic features. In Finland, adult prisoners are released on parole after serving half or two-thirds of their sentences and juveniles after serving either a third or half. In Denmark and Norway, release occurs after two-thirds of the sentence has been served or in exceptional cases (often first offenders or juveniles) after half. Sweden follows a standard rule of two-thirds. The minimum time to be served before early release is 14 days in Finland, 1 month in Sweden, and 2 months in Denmark and Norway. Probation periods are imposed individually in Denmark and Norway, or determined by the remaining sentence in Finland and Sweden, with the usual maximum being 3 years. Revocations generally occur only following commission of a new offense during the parole period.

Mere breach of conditions may justify only a short period of revocation (14 days in Finland), which is used very rarely, if at all.[13] Automatic early release means that most prisoners (practically all in Finland) are released on parole.[14]

4. *Sanctions for Young Offenders.* Youth justice takes a distinctive form in the Nordic countries. During the early years of the twentieth century, the Nordic countries developed systems of child protection legislation that authorized municipal authorities to intervene in children's behavior. This model differs in important respects from continental European and Anglo-Saxon youth justice systems characterized by special courts and codes for young offenders. Offenders under age 15 are dealt with only by the child welfare authorities. Offenders aged 15–17 fall under the jurisdiction of both the child welfare and criminal justice systems. Young adults aged 18–20 are dealt with by the criminal justice authorities (and to some extent the child welfare system by providing aftercare).[15]

All Nordic countries restrict the use of imprisonment for young offenders. Offenders aged 15–17 can be imprisoned only for exceptional reasons. The numbers of children under 18 held in penal institutions in recent years in each country have varied in absolute numbers between zero and 10.

Child welfare authorities have the main responsibility for dealing with young offenders, but all the Nordic countries have developed community sanctions for juveniles. These include "juvenile punishment orders" in Finland, the "youth contract" in Denmark, and "youth care" and "youth service" in Sweden. Norwegian "community punishment" contains many of the same elements as the other countries' youth sanctions. However, it is not designed as a penalty only for young offenders. The systems differ in precisely how specific sanctions are implemented. The Swedish and Danish systems are more differentiated than in Finland and Norway.

---

[13] Parole and early release in Finland are discussed in detail in Lappi-Seppälä (2010).

[14] The only restriction may follow from the minimum times before parole release eligibility. This may have notable relevance in countries that use short prison sentences, such as Denmark and Norway. In 2009, 8,020 prisoners were released in Denmark. Of these, 60 percent (4,845) were released after serving a full sentence. Of the remaining 3,173, 86 percent (2,819) were released after serving two-thirds. In Finland, except for the 30–40 prisoners serving a full sentence (and those sentenced to 14 days), all are released on parole.

[15] Nordic youth justice is discussed in detail in Lappi-Seppälä (2011, 2015c); see also Janson (2004) and Kyvsgaard (2004).

5. *Sanctions for Serious and Repeat Violent Offenders.* Offenders who have committed the most serious offenses or present the most compelling risks to public security are potentially subject to three special dispositions: life imprisonment, preventive detention based on perceived risk of future offending, and placement of violent offenders into involuntary institutional mental health care.[16]

Life imprisonment plays a different role in each country. Norway abolished life sentences in 1981 as a reaction to indeterminate sanctions in general. Denmark, Finland, and Sweden retain life imprisonment but use it on different scales. However, the normative structure is basically the same. A life sentence can be imposed only for the most serious cases of intentional lethal violence (and high treason and some crimes against humanity). In practice, life imprisonment is relevant only to homicide and murder cases, and all prisoners serving life sentences are released on parole. There is no "life without parole," although there is no absolute fixed maximum time to be served under a life sentence. Release processes were changed during the 2000s to remove clemency and pardoning powers from the government and vest release authority in the judiciary. Life sentences have recently become longer. Before the 2000s, time before release on parole was around 11 years in Finland. This increased to 13–14 years in the 2000s and to 15 in the 2010s. In some isolated cases, prisoners may serve even longer periods, but hardly ever over 20 years. Corresponding figures from Sweden would indicate an even stronger increase and longer prison terms.

In Finland, the release decision is made by the Helsinki Court of Appeal on the basis of the prisoner's application.[17] For adult prisoners, release may occur at the earliest after 12 years (for juveniles under 21 at the time of the offense, after 10 years). If the application is rejected, the matter can be reconsidered after 1 year. The prisoner may appeal to the supreme court under the general rules. All prisoners released from life imprisonment are on probation for 3 years. Parole can be canceled because of a new offense. The prison term to be revoked in this case would be 3 years at most (or shorter, depending on the nature of the new offense).

---

[16] For more detail, see Johnsen (2011, 2013), Johnsen and Engbo (2015), and Lappi-Seppälä (2015*b*).

[17] However, the possibility of a pardon remains (e.g., when the personal circumstances or health conditions of the prisoner have radically changed during the sentence).

Release from life sentences in Sweden takes place through a conversion process in which life sentences are commuted to fixed prison terms. Once the sentence has been commuted, release takes place under normal parole and early release rules, granting release after two-thirds. The decision is made by the Örebro district court on application of the prisoner and can occur after the prisoner has served at least 10 years. An important additional restriction is that the commuted sentence may not be shorter than the maximum prison term provided by the law. When the release rules were amended in Sweden in 2006, the maximum term was 10 years. However, it has subsequently been raised to 18 years. The conversion rule was not meant to change existing pardoning practice under which the converted sentence length (not the minimum term) would vary between 18 and 25 years (and release would occur after 12–16.3 years).

Danish rules provide two regular forms of release. After serving 12 years, and under favorable conditions, the prisoner may be released on the basis of an administrative decision. Should that not happen, applications may be made to the court after serving 14 years. In Denmark the duration of life imprisonment for prisoners released in 2006–12 was 14.5 years.

The roles of indeterminate security measures vary. Finland and Sweden have abolished preventive detention. Denmark and Norway have retained it under the label *"forvaring."* This option is applicable in Norway "when a sentence for a specific term is deemed to be insufficient to protect society." The conditions relate to the nature and seriousness of new offenses, past criminal history, and assessments of future offending risk. For the most serious offenses, *forvaring* is possible after first convictions and with lower reoffending risks compared with less serious offenses. The law sets initial durational limits, usually not to exceed 15 years and never to exceed 21 years (the 21-year upper limit was used in 2012, when Anders Breivik was sentenced to preventive detention after being convicted for 77 murders and terrorism). However, this term may be extended on application of the prosecutor for up to 5 years at a time. A minimum period not exceeding 10 years must also be specified.

Prisoners in *forvaring* are released on probation for a period of 1–5 years. On average, release seldom occurs until nearly 2 years (mean: 1 year, 9 months) have passed beyond the minimum specified in the court ruling. The Danish *forvaring* is classified as a "measure," not a punishment. It may be imposed on both criminally responsible and nonresponsible offenders. Preconditions distinguish between violent and sexual offenses (with somewhat lower thresholds). In both cases, the criteria fall into three parts: related to the seriousness of the offense, the risk of reoffending, and the requirement of necessity. In contrast to Norway, there is no specific minimum or maximum time. However, the prosecutor is obliged to ensure that the confinement does not last longer than needed. To ensure this, there are specific rules and procedures. Release and termination of confinement are decided by the court. The offender or the placement unit may request the prosecutor to take the case before the court. If the court decides to continue confinement, a new request may be made after 6 months. Once confinement has lasted 3 years, the placement unit is obliged to take the matter to the prosecutor once a year. Once released, prisoners are usually placed on probation. In contrast to Norway, no formal probation period is fixed. The final termination of *forvaring* takes place by court decision and usually occurs after a year of problem-free probation. However, probation periods may also last much longer, even indeterminately. Lengths of Danish *forvaring* terms seem to be increasing (and to exceed Norwegian ones). In the early 1990s, the mean term before release on probation was 7.3 years; in 2006–11, it was 14.3 years (Johnsen and Engbo 2015).

Finland abolished preventive detention in 2006. However, a compensating scheme was introduced that authorizes the courts to order serious violent offenders to serve their sentences in full. This option is reserved for the same category of high-risk violent recidivists as were affected by preventive detention. The aim was neither to expand nor to restrict the use of long-term confinement for this offender group. Use of the new option occurs in two stages. First, at the request of the prosecutor the district court orders that a person serve the sentence in full, following criteria set out in the law. Second, the Helsinki Court of Appeal needs to confirm the order to serve the sentence in full once the regular release time for parole is approaching. In all cases, the prisoner must be released on supervised probationary liberty 3 months before the prison term is fully served. The rationale for this is that releasing high-risk prisoners into society without any form of supervision or support is impractical, inhumane, and unwise. Prisoners serving their sentences in full may be released only after a risk assessment. Nineteen prisoners were released from serving their sentences in full between 2006 and 2011. In half these cases, the prisoner had served at least 8 years. On December 16, 2011, 34 of 3,246 prisoners were serving sentences in full. The typical offense is repeated homicide.

Most serious cases of violent crime raise mental health and criminal responsibility issues. Systems vary in handling this. Swedish law does not recognize the concept of criminal responsibility. Mentally ill people are held criminally responsible but may not be sentenced to imprisonment. Instead, there are specific treatment orders for this group, which are classified as criminal sanctions. In Denmark and Norway, care orders for mentally disturbed persons are defined in the criminal code, although they are classified as "specific measures," not as punishments. In all three countries, care orders are imposed by the courts; implementation criteria are set out in the criminal code. The Finnish system makes a clear separation between criminal law and mental health. Criminal law as such does not allow compulsory treatment. All care orders are issued by medical authorities, and regulation is provided in the Mental Health Act. Finland and Sweden represent opposite ends of a continuum, with Denmark and Norway falling in between (concerning Danish and Norwegian psychiatric care orders, see Kamber [2013]).

C. Sentencing Guidance

Efforts to guide sentencing discretion are fairly new. Continental legal doctrine at the beginning of the twentieth century treated sentencing not as an application of law but as an art, based on intuition rather than on rules and rational argument. Reasons for decisions were rarely expected. During the latter half of the century, the dogma of "free and unfettered discretion" was gradually overcome by judicialization of sentencing discretion in many countries (Lappi-Seppälä 1987, pp. 15–17). In the English-speaking countries, this shift toward stronger legal (or political) guidance took the form of numerical sentencing guidelines and mandatory minimum sentence laws from the 1970s onward. Continental and Nordic solutions followed civil law traditions, including the primacy of written law and the traditional division of powers between legislatures and courts. European codes increasingly included chapters on sentencing, also beginning in the 1970s. In Finland this took place in 1976 and in Sweden in 1988. Denmark (2004) and Norway (2005) followed suit.

1. *Regulating Sentencing Decisions.* Standards governing Nordic sentencing are set out in legislation. This guidance is expressed in penalty scales, classification of offenses, and statutory sentencing criteria. Sentenc-

ing councils and commissions, advisory boards, and guidelines, familiar in English-speaking countries, do not exist.[18] There are other sources of law. Supreme court decisions play an important role. In Norway, a country with less detailed statutory sentencing provisions, the supreme court has provided precedents that guide sentencing practices, especially for high-volume offenses. From a theoretical point of view, Nordic supreme court decisions are not legally binding in the sense that they are in common law countries, even though they are often called "precedents." The rulings have guiding force, but the force is based on the persuasiveness of the reasons given. But even though the Nordic supreme courts do not create law (at least criminal law), they elaborate it (Tolonen 2003, p. 125). This role has increased in recent decades in Finland and Sweden, partly in response to the enactment of sentencing rules. After the Finnish sentencing reform of 1976, the supreme court began to create reasoned precedents on sentencing. These decisions had a strong modeling effect for lower courts. As a result, each court ruling has a separate section for reasons related to both the type and severity of chosen sanctions. Legislative background works also are seen as a source of law. The Nordic legal tradition characterizes them as "allowed" or "weakly binding." The form and status of these documents vary between countries, but courts in all pay respect to statements in legislative documents.

Existing practice, as shown and described in statistical and legal analyses, has a peculiar role. It has been known for long to be perhaps the most influential "source" of sentencing decisions ("ask older colleagues"), although it has no clear normative status. However, uniformity and consistency in sentencing practice have long been central values and leading principles (Hinkkanen and Lappi-Seppälä 2011, pp. 356–57). Courts cannot simply dismiss existing practice in similar or comparable cases. In Finland this has been formulated into a heuristic decision-making model called "the notion of normal punishments." The relative influence of court practice has been strengthened by effective dissemination via electronic databases, handbooks, and systematic commentaries.

Various kinds of "soft law" instruments have been developed. In some cases the judiciary has developed informal guidelines for certain types of offenses. Prosecutors' practices may be guided by detailed instructions,

---

[18] See, in more detail, Lappi-Seppälä (1987, 2001) and Hinkkanen and Lappi-Seppälä (2011).

especially for common offenses. The normative status of these lower-level sources of sentencing guidance is unclear. Written law is the only authoritative source. In most cases these supplementary sources, including statistical analyses, are tools that provide concrete starting points. But as they may help in making the right decision, they have substantial practical relevance.

2. *The General Structure of Sentencing Law.* Nordic criminal codes define offenses and indicate punishment severity by providing a minimum and maximum for each. Most offenses in Finland and Sweden are graded into two or three subcategories according to their internal seriousness (typically petty, standard, aggravated), each with a specific minimum and maximum penalty (the Danish and Norwegian codes provide only a few minimums).

The resulting penalty ranges resemble statutory determinate sentencing and some systems of presumptive and voluntary sentencing guidelines in the United States (Tonry 2013). The ranges, however, are broad. Upper limits are binding and with minor exceptions may not be exceeded. Minimums, however, differ from those known in common law countries as mandatory minimums. They are fairly low (a few months for many aggravated offenses) and seldom compel courts to impose more severe penalties than they otherwise would. Moreover, the minimums are only presumptive.

In practice, imposed penalties tend to be closer to the minimum, usually in the lower quarter or third of the authorized range. From time to time this has been interpreted as a sign of unfounded leniency on the assumption that the average penalty should fall in the middle of the range (thus for a range of 1–10 years, around 5 years). The preparatory works for the latest Finnish sentencing reform point out that this is a misconception. Penalties cluster close to the minimum because there are always many more minor crimes than serious ones. The statistical distribution of crime severity does not follow the bell curve. There are fewer brutal murders than normal manslaughters and fewer aggravated assaults than normal assaults. This "tendency toward the minimum" was observable empirically from the initial adoption of the range system in the nineteenth century (Annerstedt 1869; Exner 1931). It flows from the nature of things, not from the soft-heartedness of judges.

Sentencing involves two main decisions: the type of sanction and its severity. These decisions partly overlap and are regulated by largely the same criteria and principles, but not entirely. The question of severity is very much the question of proportionality. To the extent that different kinds of penalties represent sanctions of different degrees of severity (say fines compared with imprisonment), the choice of sanction is also a decision about proportionality. However, there are also qualitative differences between sanctions, and other values besides proportionality are involved. To take these into account, the codes separately regulate both decisions related to the severity and decisions related to the choice of sanction. Arguments and principles concerning offense seriousness and sanction severity are general in nature, but decisions about the choice of sanction and the roles of other possible aims and values vary, depending on the characteristics of the sanction system. For that reason, I mostly discuss issues related to proportionality (about the choice of sanctions in Finland and Sweden, see Hinkkanen and Lappi-Seppälä [2011, pp. 368–73]).

3. *Sentencing Principles and Criteria.* Humane neoclassicism, the Nordic sentencing theory formulated in the 1970s and 1980s, stresses principles of proportionality, predictability, and equality. They are most clearly expressed in the opening paragraphs of the Finnish and Swedish sentencing chapters. Section 6.4 of the Finnish Penal Code, for example, states, "The sentence shall be determined so that it is in just proportion to the harmfulness and dangerousness of the offense, the motives for the act, and the other culpability of the offender manifested in the offense." The Swedish and Danish codes have similar language.

The principle of proportionality has its roots in the concept of the rule of law (*Rechtstaat*), legal safeguards, and the guarantees to citizens against misuse, arbitrariness, and excessive use of force. It is more important to prevent overly harsh and unjustified penalties than to prevent overly lenient ones. The main function of the proportionality principle is, thus, to impose upper limits that the punishment may never exceed. This asymmetry can be demonstrated in several ways. Courts have a general right to go below prescribed minimums whenever exceptional reasons justify it. The grading of offenses reflects this same idea. Lists of aggravating criteria are exhaustive. Lists of mitigating criteria are always open-ended. The phrasing of mitigating criteria usually leaves greater scope for judicial discretion than does the phrasing of aggravated criteria.

Attention must also be paid to uniformity or consistency in sentencing. The first appearance of this expectation was in the Finnish Penal Code in 1976. Similar requirements were included in the Swedish law in 1988 and in Denmark in 2004. These laws point out the importance of the principle of equality and the need to avoid unwarranted disparities in sentencing.

The principle of proportionality demands that there should be "just" or "fair" proportion between the seriousness of the offense and the severity of the punishment. Further criteria for assessing seriousness are given in the law. The criteria refer to both the extent of consequences (harm) and the (moral) blameworthiness of the offender (culpability).

Concerning the consequences of the act, attention must be paid not only to harms that resulted but also to harms that could have been anticipated (the principle of endangerment). The "principle of subjective coverage" limits harms to be taken into account only to those the actor foresaw (intentional crimes) or should have foreseen (crimes of negligence). Culpability, in turn, relates to the actor's mental state at the time of the offense. The wording of the Finnish law (culpability "manifested in the offense") stresses "act orientation." Evaluation of the actor's blameworthiness must be limited to the offense and may not encompass the offender's personality or the moral merits of his or her way of life. Intent and purpose reflect greater culpability than does mere foresight of consequences. Likewise, the degree of planning and premeditation, the firmness of the criminal decision, and the offender's decisiveness modulate the degree of culpability (Lappi-Seppälä 2001, pp. 125–26).

The amount of blame and punishment must be graded according to the actor's ability to conform to the law. Important statutory sentencing criteria describe situations in which the actors' ability to comply with the law is influenced by external or internal impulses or forces. Motives matter. Unlawful acts committed for respectable and altruistic motives or with the intention to benefit other members of society incur lesser punishments.

Prior convictions also matter, even though the reasons for regarding recidivism as an aggravating factor in punishment of subsequent offenses are not altogether clear. Nordic countries have rejected mechanical recidivism rules that link the number of prior convictions to specific time limits or compel courts to increase penalties by a certain percentage. Most codes attempted in the 1970s and 1980s to reduce the influence of recidivism on sentencing. This was a main aim of the 1976 Finnish sentencing reform. Aggravation of punishment because of previous convictions was allowed only when recidivism implied increased culpability. Previous criminality may increase the penalty only "if the relation between the offenses on the basis of their similarity or for another reason shows that the offender is apparently heedless of the prohibitions and commands of the law." Casual or occasional repetition should, thus, not increase punishments. This has a social dimension as well: Culpability is assessed on the basis of the offender's ability to conform to the law. This may well be diminished with socially marginalized property offenders for whom crime has become a lifestyle, largely because of external conditions.

There are signs that recidivism is coming to occupy a more central role in sentencing. Denmark removed recidivism altogether as an aggravating criterion from the Danish criminal code in 1973. However, the Parliament changed course in 1994, increasing penalties for recidivists, especially for repeat violent offenses. In the 2004 sentencing reform, recidivism was reintroduced as a general sentencing criterion. The Swedish Parliament also restricted the role of previous convictions by specifying in 1988 that recidivism, as a rule, should be taken into account mainly in making the choice between sanctions, but not in deciding the severity of the sanctions chosen (Hinkkanen and Lappi-Seppälä 2011). However, as a part of the new punitive approach in Sweden, this was partly rescinded in 2009 by statutory changes that increased sanctions for violent offenses (Bäcklund 2015).

4. *Other Principles and Values in Sentencing.* Along with proportionality, consistency, and predictability, other aims and values need to be acknowledged. Two major ones need to be addressed.

Since the enactment of sentencing codes, there has been agreement that the requirements of strict proportionality sometimes need to be softened on the basis of pragmatic considerations and values such as humaneness, equity, and mercy. These considerations are noted in the sentencing codes, which provide long lists of exceptional circumstances related to postact behavior, personal conditions, and cumulation of sanctions that justify downward deviations from the "normal punishments" (Hinkkanen and Lappi-Seppälä 2011, pp. 361–63). It is a matter of dispute whether and to what extent these factors lie outside the principle of proportionality (or "penal value"). Much depends on how strict an interpretation is given to this principle (von Hirsch and Ashworth 2005).

Another set of relevant factors relates to prevention and the expected effects of criminal sanctions. The sentencing reforms of the 1970s and 1980s moved away from prognostic sentencing: sentencing became backward-looking and guided by values of proportionality and predictability. However, after a period of strong neoclassicism in the 1980s, support for rehabilitative aims reemerged. This first took the form of new community sanctions, which introduced concepts such as consent, suitability, and promotion of social adjustment as legitimate sentencing considerations. This tendency continued in the 2000s. This is especially true concerning youth justice; an increasing number of juvenile sanctions lie at the border between child welfare and criminal justice, with clear emphases on individual prevention and rehabilitation (Lappi-Seppälä 2011).

Law reforms carried out since the 1960s severely restricted the use of indeterminate sanctions, especially in Sweden and Finland. While both Denmark and Norway still retain the possibility of indeterminate confinement for risk-based arguments, their application is narrowly restricted. There are no code provisions that would justify imposition of sanctions for reasons related to deterrence or the need to provide exemplary sentences. Such decisions would violate the requirements of both proportionality and equality (Hinkkanen and Lappi-Seppälä 2011, pp. 374–75).

III. Sentencing Practice
In this section, I provide an overview of sentencing trends and present practices, beginning with a snapshot of the distribution in percentages of all dispositions of different punishments. Since percentage shares may sometimes be misleading, I also show the use of different alternatives relative to population. I then describe trends from 1960 to 2014 using the same indicators and provide more detailed information on sentencing practice for different offense groups.

A. Overview
The use of different sentencing options in 2013–14 is displayed in table 1. Sanctions are divided into fines, conditional or suspended sentences, community service, and immediate imprisonment. Only court fines are included (summary fines imposed by prosecutors or the police are omitted).

Fines are the most common sanction (50–67 percent of cases, except in Norway). The proportion of sentences of immediate imprisonment is usually below 20 percent, Finland being lowest (9 percent of all imposed sanctions). The average length of prison terms ranges from 5.7 (Norway) to 12.4 months (Finland). Similar, albeit smaller, differences

TABLE 1
Sanction Patterns, Nordic Countries, Rates per 100,000 Population and Percentages, 2013–14

	Rate			
	Finland	Sweden	Denmark	Norway
A. Court dispositions (2013/14):				
Prison	93 (9.3%)	113 (18.6%)	169 (14.6%)	229 (53.1%)
Community service	35 (3.6)	52 (8.5)	56 (4.8)	48 (11.1)
Conditional/probation/other community	249 (25.1)	140 (23.0)	156 (13.4)	119 (27.8)
Fines in court	616 (62.0)	303 (49.8)	779 (67.2)	33 (7.8)
All	994 (100.0)	608 (100.0)	1,160 (100.0)	428 (100.0)
B. Imposed prison term (months)	12.4 (2014)	8.8 (2014)	6.3 (2014)	5.7 (2013)
C. Imposed prison years (2014)	5,219 (2014)	7,989 (2014)	4,997 (2014)	5,546 (2013)
Per 100,000 population	96	83	89	109
D. Prison statistics (2014):				
Prison term (months, mean)	10.3	7.7	8.9	7.0
Admissions per 100,000	63	92	94	131
Prisoners per 100,000	54	59	70	76

SOURCE.—Rows A–C are compiled from national statistics by the author; row D is from Kristoffersen (2016).

NOTE.—Percentages are in parentheses. Imprisonment figures for Denmark and Norway also include combinations of imprisonment and other sanctions.

can be detected in times served (from 7.0 to 10.3 months). These differences partly compensate for each other, so the annual number of prison sentences relative to population varies between 83 (Sweden) and 109 (Norway). Despite these differences, the total number of imposed prison years relative to population remains similar, from 83 per 100,000 in Sweden to 109 in Norway.

Enforcement statistics reveal substantial differences in admission rates. The Norwegian prisons receive more than twice as many admissions (131 per 100,000) as the Finnish (63). However, because of differences in sentence lengths, the difference between the annual average number of prisoners is much smaller (Finland 54, Norway 76).[19]

B. Sentencing Trends, 1960–2014

In this subsection, I examine the use of different sentencing alternatives in court practice from 1960 to 2014. The focus is on court-ordered sanctions and only on offenses resulting in penalties heavier than fines.[20]

1. *Custody and Community Alternatives.* Figures 5 and 6 show long-term sentencing patterns for immediate prison sentences, conditional or suspended prison sentences, and community service. Statistics on use of fines are hard to compare, because the handling of summary offenses varies substantially. Lines between summary and court processes also are drawn differently and under constant change, which hampers trend analyses. Community sanctions are divided into two groups. The term "conditional sentence" refers to conditional imprisonment and suspended sentences, probation in Sweden, and all noncustodial juvenile penalties. "CSO" covers both community service and community punishment (in Norway).

The dominant feature in Finland is the steep increase in the use of community sanctions from 1960 to 1990 (from 83 per 100,000 to 350). The number of prison sentences increased, but this took place only in

---

[19] Figures for Denmark may vary in international comparisons depending on whether placements in other treatment institutions (for mental health or substance abuse related) are included.

[20] Minor offenses punishable by fines dominate the statistics. They also predominate in court caseloads. Consequently, the growth of mass infractions related to changing opportunity and target structures (and resulting changes in the overall mix of offenses) easily conceals changes in sentence severity in the middle ranks of more serious offenses.

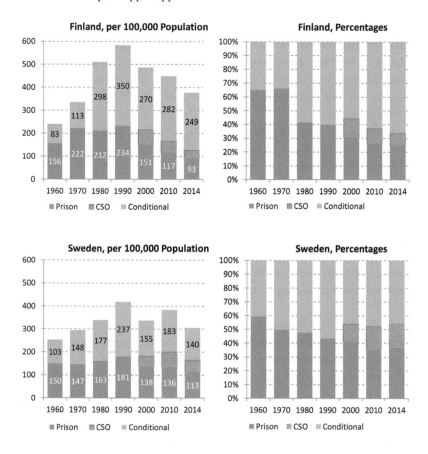

Fig. 5.—Court-imposed sanctions (other than fines), 1960–2010, Finland and Sweden, all offenses, all age groups. Source: National statistics, compiled by the author.

1960–70 (156 per 100,000 to 222). From 1970 to 1990, the imprisonment number remained stable and declined after that almost by 50 percent (from 233 to 124). Percentage changes reveal two major shifts. From 1970 to 1980, prison sentences were replaced by conditional sentences. From 1990 to 2010, this trend continued. The overall result is that the balance between unconditional and conditional imprisonment has changed dramatically. Sixty-five percent of "prison sentences" in the 1970s were unconditional. In the 2010s, only 26 percent were. Except for fines, still the most prevalent dispositions (see table 1 above), conditional prison sen-

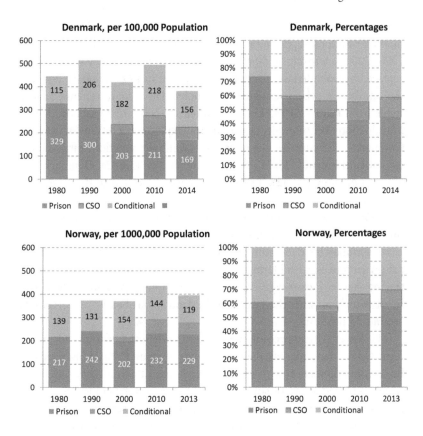

Fig. 6.—Court-imposed sanctions (other than fines), 1980–2010, Denmark and Norway, all offenses, all age groups. Source: National statistics, compiled by the author.

tences are now the norm.[21] The Swedish sanction profile resembles the Finnish one but with smaller changes. The introduction of community service mainly replaced other community sanctions and, to a lesser extent, imprisonment. However, Swedish sentencing statistics count electronic monitoring as imprisonment, which would reduce the real number of prison sentences.

[21] Table 1 also includes court fines; figs. 5 and 6 show only community sanctions and unconditional imprisonment. However, table 1 does not include summary fines, which are the vast majority of all sanctions imposed in the Nordic countries. For more detailed comparisons, see Lappi-Seppälä (2015c, table 2.8).

Data for Norway and Denmark are for 1980–2013. In Denmark the number of imposed prison sentences fell from 300 per 100,000 to 200 in 1990–2000 as a result of short-term prison sentences. They were largely replaced by extended use of community service in 1990–2000. In Norway the number of prison sentences and their relative share remained fairly stable from 1980 to 2013. The same applies to community sanctions. The introduction of community service mainly replaced conditional sentences. Comparing all countries, the prison to community sanctions ratio is most favorable in Finland (25/75), followed by Sweden (38/62), Denmark (45/55), and Norway (58/42). These differences are related to the lengths of prison sentences.

2. *Prison Sentences, 1960–2014.* Figure 7 provides a more detailed picture of prison sentences imposed during 1960–2010. The upper-left panel summarizes data from previous figures, showing the evolution of prison sentences, with Denmark having the largest decrease and Norway staying stable. Percentage changes (upper-right panel) show decreases in all countries, with the largest in Finland (from below 70 percent to around 25 percent).

The lower panels provide new data. The lengths of imposed prison term (lower left) increased in all countries from 1990. This needs to be seen in connection with the increase in use of community sanctions, which replaced short prison sentences. Thus fewer people are sent to prison but for offenses that are, on average, more serious. The lower-right panel shows the effects of changes in imposed prison years (as a function of numbers and lengths of prison terms). The overall trend is stable, despite steep short-term increases and decreases in individual countries. The final result is that, measured by imposed prison years relative to population, all Nordic countries were at the level of 100–120 in 2010. In 2014 the differences became somewhat bigger, with Norway highest at around 105 years and Denmark and Sweden, after a steep drop, the lowest between 80 and 90.[22]

3. *Life Imprisonment and Preventive Detention.* Figure 8 shows the use of the most severe sanctions, life imprisonment and preventive detention. It displays the numbers of court-imposed life sentences from 1980 to 2013 and the numbers of prisoners serving a life sentence from 1990 to 2013.

---

[22] Some prison years are commuted to electronic monitoring during the enforcement phase.

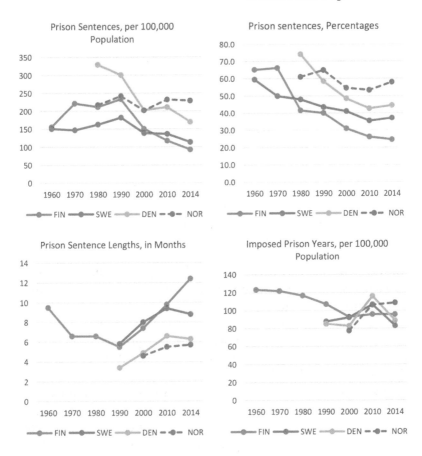

Fig. 7.—Court-imposed prison sentences, 1960–2014. Data show ratios of imprisonment and community alternatives (in percent), lengths of prison term, number of prison sentences per 100,000 population, and the total numbers of imposed prison years per 100,000 population for all offenses. Source: Compiled from national statistics by the author.

Life imprisonment plays a very small role in Denmark (left). In the 1980s, the Finnish courts imposed three to four life sentences per year. In the 1990s, the number increased to eight to nine and after that rose to nearly 20. This increase is not related to specific law reforms, but to changes in psychiatric practice and more restrictive application of the concept of diminished responsibility. In Finland, life imprisonment is mandatory for murder. However, those with diminished responsibility typically receive 12 years. In the 1980s, this was still the case for two of every three convicted murderers. During the 1990s, the scope of dimin-

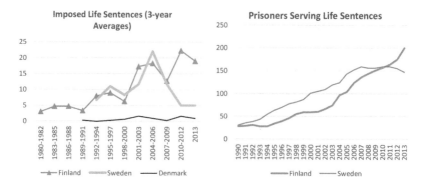

Fig. 8.—Imposed life sentences and absolute numbers of prisoners serving life sentences. Source: Compiled from national statistics.

ished responsibility was narrowed in psychiatric practice, and the fraction of offenders in murder cases classified as partially responsible fell from 64 to 10 percent. As a result, fixed prison sentences were replaced by life sentences, the norm for murder (90–95 percent of cases).

The reasons behind the Swedish changes are equally complex but different. The increase from six to seven in the early 1990s to over 20 in the mid-2000s parallels the generally tightening attitude toward violent offenses in Sweden. An unexpected drop to five cases per year from 2006 to 2010 does not. In 2008, a supreme court ruling reserved life imprisonment for only the most serious cases of lethal violence. Since 2006 life sentences can be commuted into fixed prison terms, which may have provoked some courts to impose determinate prison sentences. However, the most important explanation is probably that in 2009 the maximum prison term for murder was lifted from 10 years to 18. The goal was to increase penalties for serious forms of violent crime. However, concerning life sentences, the outcome may have been the reverse. The courts seem to have replaced previous life sentences with determinate sentences of 10 or more years. This result was clearly not what the government intended. The Swedish Ministry of Justice has since had another law enacted, effective July 1, 2014, that obliges the courts to use the life sentence as a presumptive penalty for serious cases of intentional lethal violence (see Lappi-Seppälä 2015b).

These changes have cumulative effects in enforcement statistics. In Finland, the number of prisoners serving a life sentence has grown from 30 in 1990 to 200 in 2013, which represents 6–7 percent of the prison population. The number of life prisoners in Swedish prisons increased from 30 in 1990 to 159 in 2007 (2.5 percent of the prison population). However, since then the figures have stabilized and slightly declined. This is mainly due to the declining number of life sentences imposed but also is partly a result of the conversion processes.[23] The Danish prison statistics do not report the exact number of prisoners serving a life sentence separately. However, the proportion varied between 0.8 and 1.1 percent of all prisoners in 2008–13, which gives an overall number of around 20.[24]

Figures on the use of preventive detention in Denmark and Norway are displayed in table 2. In 2002–13, the Norwegian courts imposed, on average, 14 *forvaring* orders. There is no clear trend; the last 2 years remain below the average. *Forvaring* are used less often in Denmark and average about four cases per year. Again no clear trend is visible, but during the 2000s there were, on average, five orders. The most common crime in both countries is rape (half of *forvaring* offenses). In Norway, homicide comes next (24 percent), followed by other violent crime (15 percent). In Denmark the figures are 12 percent for homicide and 25 for other types of violence (Johnsen and Engbo 2015, p. 180). The highest number of imposed orders is visible for detainees, who in Norway number 74 and in Denmark 32 for the whole period. The Danish figures show a clear and consistent increase (as a result of increased lengths of *forvaring*) from 25 to 45, while the Norwegian figures are fairly stable.

C. Sentencing in Selected Offense Groups

Table 3 compares sentencing patterns for homicide, assault, theft, robbery, rape, drunk driving, and drugs. Criminal codes grade each of these offenses into several (usually three) grades of seriousness, each with a differentiated penalty scale. Sentencing is expected to fall within these ranges unless there are valid reasons to go below the minimum.

---

[23] Since 2006, some life sentences have been commuted to determinate prison sentences, which disappear from the life imprisonment statistics. In March 2014 there were 15 prisoners serving a sentence that had been commuted to life; see Prop. 2013/14:194, Skärpt Straff för Mord, Regeringens Proposition (p. 11).

[24] See Kriminalforsorgen (2013, table 3.8). The most recent data give the figure of 18 prisoners. Norwegian prison statistics do not report the number of prisoners serving the maximum sentence of 21 years. A personal communication from the Norwegian prison administration indicates that the number varies around 15.

TABLE 2

Preventive Detention in Norway and Denmark, 2002–13

	2002	2003	2004	2005	2006	2007	2008	2009	2010	2011	2012	2013	Mean
Court decisions:													
Norway	4	23	12	17	17	14	12	13	10	22	13	10	13.9
Denmark	4	1	5	4	0	3	2	5	5	6	5	4	3.7
Prisoners in preventive detention:													
Norway	58	669	72	76	75	78	76	72	71	79	84	85	74.6
Denmark	24	23	26	28	28	31	33	33	36	39	43	45	32.4

SOURCE.—Compiled from national statistics.

TABLE 3
Punishment Ranges

	Finland	Sweden	Norway	Denmark
Lethal violence:				
Homicide	8–12 years	6–10 years	8–15 (21 years)[a]	5 years to life
Murder	Life	10 years to 18 to life		
Mitigating circumstances	4–10 years			
Assault:				
Assault	Fines to 2 years	Maximum 2 years	Fines to 1 year	Fines to 3 years
Aggravated assault	1–10 years	1–6 years	Maximum 6–10 years[b]	Maximum 6 years (10 years)[c]
Petty assault	Fines	Fines to 6 months		
Robbery:				
Robbery	4 months–6 years	1–6 years	Maximum 6 years	Maximum 6 years
Aggravated robbery	2–10 years	4–10 years	Maximum 15 years (21 years)[d]	Maximum 10 years
Sexual offenses:				
Rape	1–6 years	2–6 years	Maximum 10 years	Maximum 8 years
Aggravated rape	2–10 years	4–10 years	Maximum 21 years	Maximum 12 years
Forced intercourse	Maximum 3 years	Maximum 2–4 years	Maximum 6 years	Maximum 4 years 10 months
Theft:				
Theft	Fines to 1 year 6 months	Maximum 2 years	Fines to 2 years	Maximum 1 year 6 months
Aggravated theft	4 months–4 years	6 months–6 years	Fines to 6 years	
Petty theft	Fines	Fines to 6 months		
Drugs:				
Drug offenses	Fines to 2 years	Fines to 3 years	Fines to 2 years	Fines to 2 years; maximum 10 years
Aggravated drug offenses	1–10 years	2–10 years	Maximum 10 years (21 years)[e]	Maximum 16 years
Petty drug offenses	Fines to 6 months	Fines to 6 months	Fines to 6 months	

[a] For Norway, aggravated scale maximum is 21 years for serious cases.

[b] For Norway, maximum is 6–10 years depending on the seriousness of injury and other circumstances defined in the law.

[c] For Denmark, maximum is 10 years under especially serious circumstances.

[d] For Norway, maximum is 21 years when resulting in death or serious injury.

[e] For Norway, maximum is 21 years under especially serious circumstances.

The table reveals structural differences. Finland and Sweden provide narrower scales with minimum penalties, while Denmark and Norway usually prescribe only the applicable maximum. Norway has differentiated the maximums according to the consequences of the act. Comparisons between the Finnish and Swedish ranges reveal no marked differences.

Table 4 shows sentencing practices. To simplify the presentation, results are given for aggregate offense categories. Court-ordered sentences are grouped into three categories: Prison includes immediate custodial sanctions and all combinations of prison with community sentences, "youth sanctions" in Denmark and "closed youth care" in Sweden. Community sanctions cover conditional and suspended sentences, community service, probation in Sweden, and specific noncustodial juvenile

TABLE 4

Sanction Practices, Selected Offenses, 2012–13

	Convicted per 100,000 (1)	Prison per 100,000 (2)	Mean Prison in Months (3)	Prison Percentage (4)	Prison Percentage, No Fines (5)	Prison Years per 100,000 (6)
Assault:						
Denmark	73	33	5.6	45.1	52.8	15.3
Finland	187	16	11.6	8.8	25.0	15.9
Sweden	77	17	8.5	21.8	25.9	11.3
Rape:						
Denmark	1	.8	25.2	78.9	93.8	1.7
Finland	3.1	1.1	32.1	42.9	42.9	3.6
Sweden	1.9	1.6	26.6	88.0	88.0	3.5
Theft:						
Denmark	316	38	4.9	12.1	59.0	15.4
Finland	115	15	7.5	12.9	42.8	9.3
Sweden	185	24	4.6	12.8	33.8	8.6
Robbery:						
Denmark	13	10	19.5	76.9	85.7	15.8
Finland	8	4	19.2	53.4	53.6	7.0
Sweden	9	6	19.9	65.3	65.4	7.0
Drunk driving:						
Denmark	164	16	1.7	9.7	33.6	2.3
Finland	299	22	3.4	7.2	12.4	6.1
Sweden	67	22	1.5	32.0	49.3	2.3
Drugs:						
Denmark	270	27	14.9	10.0	66.8	33.5
Finland	73	11	22.3	14.9	40.6	20.3
Sweden	177	16	14.6	9.0	48.4	17.7

punishments (mainly in Sweden) and their combinations. Only fines imposed by courts count as sole sanctions. Data are given for the number of court-imposed sanctions and prison sentences per 100,000 population (cols. 1 and 2), mean lengths of prison terms (col. 3), the percentage of prison sentences among all court-imposed sanctions (col. 4) and as a share of the sum of prison sentences, and community sanctions (col. 5). Column 6 provides information on the total number of imposed prison years relative to population.

1. *Assault.* The assault conviction rate is twice as high in Finland as in the other Nordic countries. The difference is not related to the prevalence of crime, but to more effective and legalistic case processing. Despite this difference, Denmark imposes twice as many prison sentences for assault as Finland (or Sweden). But prison terms are twice as long in Finland. The end result is that the total volumes of prison years are similar in Denmark and Finland but lower in Sweden.

2. *Rape.* The conviction rate is, again, highest in Finland. However, only half of convicted offenders receive a custodial sentence. In imprisonment rates for rape relative to population, Finland (1.1 per 100,000) lies between Denmark (0.8) and Sweden (1.6). The length of prison terms is longest in Finland (32 months) compared to Sweden (27) and Denmark (25), partly reflecting that the threshold for imprisonment in Finland is higher. The total number of imposed prison years is about the same in Finland and Sweden but twice as high as in Denmark.

3. *Robbery and Theft.* Robbery seems to be a special problem in Denmark. Both the conviction and imprisonment rates are double those in Finland and Sweden. The proportion of prison sentences is fairly high, and the total number of imposed prison years is double those in Finland and Sweden. Much the same pattern applies to theft offenses. The number and proportion of prison sentences are much higher in Denmark, sentences are longer, and the overall number of imposed prison years is double those in Finland and Sweden.

4. *Drunk Driving.* Drunk driving is a special problem in Finland. Finland has a much higher conviction rate compared with the other countries.[25] However, the number of imposed prison sentences is on the same

[25] This applies also to recorded crime. However, drunken driving as measured by routine tests seems to be on the same level of around 0.2–0.3 percent of all drivers (or even lower in Finland; see *Rikollisuustilanne* 2014, p. 162). This suggests that Finnish police and courts give more attention to drunk driving than occurs in other Nordic countries.

level in all three countries. Prison terms, however, are more than twice as long in Finland, and nearly three times as many prison years are imposed relative to population.

5. *Drug Offenses.* Drugs are a major issue in all Nordic countries. The total numbers of convictions vary depending on how minor offenses (mainly use) are handled. Denmark imposes at least twice as many prison sentences as Finland and Sweden. The number of prison sentences is lowest in Finland, but terms are much longer. Because of the large number of processed cases, the proportion of prison sentences attributable to drugs is high in Denmark. The number of prison years is double that in Sweden (and also much higher than in Finland).

6. *Lethal Violence.* The last comparison concerns homicide and murder. The offense is defined and classified differently in each country. Finland has three grades of seriousness, Sweden and Norway have two, and Denmark has just one. The sanction structures also vary. Norway does not have life imprisonment, but the three other countries do. Penalties for homicide may also be affected by the use of preventive detention and compulsory psychiatric care orders. Finland and Sweden do not use preventive or secure detention. Denmark and Norway do. Sweden defines compulsory mental care as a criminal sanction; in the other countries care orders fall outside the criminal justice system. An additional difficulty is that Swedish sentencing statistics do not separate attempts from completed offenses, which makes a big difference. With all these caveats in mind, table 5 presents the data.

Finland imposes an average sentence of 14 years (when life is valued at 25 years) for completed offenses; 10 percent of offenders are under mental health care. For Norway and Denmark the corresponding figure is 12 years; 20–25 percent of offenders are placed in care. Counted in this manner, sentencing practice is slightly stricter in Finland than in Denmark and Norway. However, the 2-year difference may be diminished by more generous early release rules in Finland. Sweden imposes, on average, 11-year prison terms for homicide and murder, including attempts; 10 percent are in compulsory care. The corresponding average prison term for attempts and completed offenses in Finland is 7.8 years. Given the number of convictions, the proportion of attempts is probably higher in Finland.

Despite differences in institutional arrangements, lethal violence seems to be punished similarly in all Nordic countries. Prison terms for completed offenses are 12–14 years. Differences occur mainly in the use of

TABLE 5
Penalties for Homicide

Completed	Finland (2009–14)	Denmark (2007–14)	Norway (2002–13)	Sweden (2014)
Mean (years):				
Including life	14.0	12.0	12.3	
Including attempts	7.8			11.0
Care order	10%	25%	20%–30%	
Including attempts				10%
Life imprisonment	25%–30%	2%–3%		5%–7%
Imposed prison years	1,000	300	220	
Including attempts				1,300
Imposed prison years per 100,000 population	18.5	5.3	4.4	
Including attempts	26.0			13.5
Convictions per year	170–175			130
Completed	70–75	25	20–25	
Attempts	100	20	10–15	
Victims, lethal violence, per 100,000 population (health data, last 5-year average)	1.87	.79	.96	.79

SOURCE.—Compiled from national statistics.

psychiatric care instead of the criminal justice system. Whether there are differences in treatment periods cannot be answered on the basis of available data.

The remaining major difference is the three to four times higher number of imposed prison years in Finland relative to population compared with Norway and Denmark (and at least twice as high as in Sweden). This is directly linked to the higher Finnish murder rate and the higher resulting number of convictions, which will keep homicide and life imprisonment high on the Finnish criminal justice policy agenda.

IV. Conclusion and Discussion
The Nordic countries have been successful in limiting use of penal custody and humanizing the criminal justice system. Tools include curbs in the use of indeterminate sanctions, extension of open prisons, expansion in use of conditional and early release programs, depenalization of property offenses, and reduction in use of imprisonment for fine defaulters in

Sweden and Denmark. Use of community sanctions as substitutes for imprisonment has continued successfully in the 2000s. Some new community sanctions such as electronic monitoring and youth punishment in Denmark are quite demanding, but they provide a more constructive and less destructive alternative than imprisonment. Nordic countries continue to have among the lowest incarceration rates in Europe (Lappi-Seppälä 2012). All countries experienced short-term increases around 2000, but since 2005, rates have been stable in Norway and Denmark and declining in Finland and Sweden.[26]

Imprisonment rates alone are an insufficient comparative measure of penal policy or sentencing trends. That imprisonment rates have been stable, or declining, is a sign of success in one field—conversion of prison sentences into community sanctions. However, there have been marked recent increases in penalties for sexual and violent offenses, and earlier for drug offenses. Concerning criminal justice policy more generally, when compared with the 1970s and 1980s, crime policy has become more aggressive, more politicized, and more responsive to the views and voices of the media. The role of penal expertise has diminished, being partly replaced by grassroots knowledge, influential interest groups, and politicians. Crime victims have come to occupy a central position in Danish and Swedish policy debates, with deep ramifications in political discourse, public perceptions, and penal practices (Demker and Duus-Otterström 2009; Tham, Rönneling, and Rytterbro 2011). There are signs that elected politicians are showing interest in achieving greater control over courts' sentencing practices.[27]

These are changes that may prove influential in the longer term. Tendencies are evident of use of criminal justice policy as a tool to promote ends other than traditional crime prevention, such as penalty increases aiming to reinforce national identity as a "drug-free zone" or to emphasize the importance of gender dimensions of all legal regulation (Tham,

[26] Recent data from Denmark also report declining numbers of prisoners (Träskman 2015, p. 170). Changes in Finland, Sweden, and Denmark are partly attributable to declining crime and partly to expanded use of electronic monitoring and supervision orders.

[27] There are also observable tensions between courts and elected politicians (e.g., the minister of justice). During recent years the Swedish supreme court has lowered sentences for drug offenses several times, which led the ministry to appoint a commission to clarify "the unclear legal situation." Something similar happened with violent offenses when sentencing changes did not meet the minister's expectations (Estrada and Tham 2013; Träskman 2013, pp. 346–49).

Rönneling, and Rytterbro 2011; Träskman 2013, pp. 351–52). However, there is also a shift away from pragmatic and rational policy making toward resort to public opinion as a justification for setting statutory sentencing levels. The "general sense of justice" has become the standard rationale for penalty increases for sexual and violent offenses. This has happened repeatedly in Sweden (Andersson 2002; von Hofer and Tham 2013), but not only there. The program for 2015–19 of the current conservative Finnish government states that punishments should "correspond to the general sense of justice." This short statement could be no more than a concession by the other parties to the demands of the right-wing True Finns Party, whose demands on other more important questions were neglected by the coalition government. However, other institutional arrangements may increase the influence of popular beliefs and direct democracy. In 2010, the Green Party achieved its goal of including a citizens' initiative provision in the Finnish Constitution. It obliges the Parliament to consider any proposal supported by 50,000 signatures. In the age of the Internet, Facebook, and popular bloggers, this is not hard to achieve. So far, proposals to increase penalties have been submitted concerning drunk driving and sexual abuse of children. The Parliament is not bound to act on these proposals, but they will likely be endorsed in one way or another. Few politicians want to oppose the "will of the people" (even the will of only 50,000 people).

Green proponents of direct democracy and right-wing populists seem to have common cause in support for policies that risk replacement of rational and humane criminal justice policies with obeisance to calls for popular punishments. Pragmatic consequentialist approaches calling for careful assessments of evidence and experience traditionally provided barriers against the unfounded overuse of the criminal law (Törnudd 1996). For example, it was possible to provide research-based evidence showing that, from a pragmatic crime prevention perspective, society would be wiser to invest scarce resources in social and situational prevention programs than in imprisonment. If that consequentialist approach to the use of criminal law failed, we should be ready to reevaluate whether the use of penal power can be defended. Justifications for policy derived from the general sense of justice may put an end to this approach. This happened when the Swedish government increased penalties for lethal violence during a time when crime was in steep decline by noting that the changes probably would have no effect on crime rates, but that was irrelevant as they were required by the general sense of justice (von Hofer and Tham 2013, p. 49).

There may be ways to weaken and refine the popular punishment argument (Ryberg and Roberts 2015). The gap between public demands and actual practices may grow smaller, or diminish, when respondents are given enough information about criminal cases in the context of deliberative polling.[28] It may even be possible to show that the public sense of justice does not want the public sense of justice to be followed. People may think it more important that judges work as impartial, objective professionals and follow their own professional principles and judgments, regardless of public opinion (e.g., in the Netherlands: Elffers and de Keijser 2008). However, even after all these and other caveats, there is a moral problem. Is it "right and just" to let the majority of the people decide how to treat the unpopular minorities, including lawbreakers? From the point of view of constitutional democracy and human rights, the answer must be no.[29] It would be advisable and useful to conduct careful and sophisticated public opinion surveys (as has been done by Balvig et al. [2015]), but this is not to accept that what we find should be assumed to be indicative of authoritative moral norms.

APPENDIX

TABLE A1

Nordic Law Reforms and Major Policy Proposal from the Late 1960s to the Present

Direction and Impact	Reform	Main Area	
		Sanctions	Offenses
	Finland		
– –	1966 Parole reform: minimum time from 6 to 4 months	x	
– –	1967 Amnesty (independence 60 years)	x	
– –	1969 Decriminalization of public drunkenness		x

[28] The Finnish Ministry of Justice's reaction was not to prepare legislation for tougher sentences, but to commission an independent study on the general sense of justice.

[29] For a fuller discussion, see Snacken (2012).

TABLE A1 (*Continued*)

Direction and Impact	Reform	Main Area	
		Sanctions	Offenses
	Finland		
−	1969 Day fine reform: the number of day fines reduced	x	
−	1969 Assault reform: less emphasis on unintended harm		x
− −	1972 Reduced penalties for theft		x
− −	1973 Restricting the use of preventive detention	x	
−	1973 Discount rules for remand	x	
−	1976 Reform of the prison law: minimum time for parole 4 months to >3 months	x	
−	1977 Conditional sentence expanded	x	
−	1977 Sentencing reform; the impact of recidivism reduced	x	
−	1977 Day fine reform: heavier fines to replace imprisonment	x	
− −	1977 DWI reform: fines and condition sentence instead of prison		x
−	1989 Fine default exchange rate reduced	x	
− −	1989 Minimum for parole 3 months to >14 days	x	
−	1989 The use of prison for juveniles restricted	x	
−	1989 The length of pretrial detention reduced	x	
−	1991 Reduced penalties for theft		x
−	1991 Expanding the scope of nonprosecution	x	
− −	1992 Introduction of CSO	x	
+	1994 Aggravated DWI 1.5 to >1.2‰		x
−	1994 Experiment on (nonresidential) juvenile penalty	x	
+	1995 Domestic violence under public prosecution		x
+ +	1999 Increasing penalties for assault		x
+	2000 Increasing penalties for rape		x
+	2001 More fines for drug users		x
+	2003 Zero limits for drugs in traffic		x
−	2000/4 Combination sentence (conditional + CSO)	x	
−	2006 New prison law, parole expanded	x	
− −	2006 Fine default abolished for prosecutors fines	x	
+	2006 Criminalization of purchasing prostitution services		x
+	2010 Increasing penalties for domestic violence		x
+	2010 Increasing penalties for sexual abuse of children		x
+ +	2011 Increasing penalties for rape		x
+	2013 Stalking criminalized		x
+	2014 Increasing penalties for rape		x

Direction and Impact	Reform	Main Area	
		Sanctions	Offenses
	Sweden		
−	1970 Decriminalizing moral offenses (including abortion)		x
−	1973 Discount rules for time served in remand	x	
−	1974 Revocation of parole restricted	x	
−	1976 Aggravated penalty scales for recidivism abolished	x	
−	1976 Breaking and entering defined as ordinary theft (and not aggravated theft)		x
	1977 Plan: new sanction system based on proportionality	x	
−	1977 Decriminalization of public drunkenness		x
+	1978 Stiffer penalties for child pornography		x
−	1979 Experiment on contractual treatment	x	
+	1980 Stiffer penalties for child pornography		x
−	1980 Extending probation as an alternative to imprisonment	x	
−	1980 Restrictions on the use of imprisonment for juveniles under 21	x	
−	1981 Preventive detention abolished	x	
−	1982 Minimum time before parole 3 months to >2 months, revocation of parole	x	
+	1981 Domestic violence under public prosecution		x
− −	1983 Release on parole after half	x	
− −	1983 Fine default abolished	x	
+	1984 Stiffer penalties for sex crimes and broader definition of rape		x
+	1985 Stiffer penalties for drug offenses		x
+	1985 Stiffer penalties for video violence		x
	1986 Plan: prison committee (SOU 1988:13–15): overall reduction of penalty levels	x	
+	1988 Nonprosecution for juveniles restricted	x	
−	1988 Contractual treatment stabilized	x	
−	1989 Sentencing reform (neoclassicism)	x	
−	1990 Experiment on community service	x	
−	1990 Drunk driving limit from 0.5 to 0.2‰; restrictions for imprisonment		x
+	1993 Stiffer penalties for several violence and sexual offenses		x
+	1993 Stiffer penalties for drug offenses, doping criminalization		x
+ +	1993 Abolishing halftime release in parole	x	
+	1994 Aggravated drunk driving 1.2 to >1.0‰, increased maximum penalty		x

TABLE A1 (*Continued*)

Direction and Impact	Reform	Main Area	
		Sanctions	Offenses
	Sweden		
−	1994 Experiment with electronic monitoring	x	
+	1998 Criminalization of the possession of child pornography		x
+	1998 Criminalization of the use of prostitution services		x
+	1999 New (residential) juvenile penalty	x	
− −	1999 Electronic monitoring for enforcement of maximum 3-month prison sentences	x	
− −	1999 Community service, extension and stabilization	x	
−	2001 Experiment on electronic monitoring in parole phase	x	
− −	2005 Electronic monitoring expanded to 6 months; parole experiment stabilized	x	
−/+	2007 New youth sanctions (restricting use of fines, expanded social work interventions)	x	
+	2010 Stalking criminalized		x
+ + +	2010 Increasing penalties for serious violence		x
+ +	2010 Increasing role of recidivism in sentencing		x
+ +	2014 More life sentences for murder		x
	Denmark		
−	1969 Guidelines not to prosecute for personal consumption of drugs in minor cases		x
−	1973 Abolishment of indeterminate penalties and specific institutions	x	
− − −	1973 Decreasing penalties for traditional property offenses		x
−	1977 Plan: alternatives to imprisonment (bet 806)	x	
+	1981 Increasing penalties for rape		x
− −	1981 Replacing short-term prison sentences by fines in less serious forms of DWI		x
− −	1982 Decreasing penalties for theft		x
− −	1982 Minimum time for parole dropped from 4 months to 2 months	x	
−	1982 Experiment of community service	x	
+ +	1989 Increasing penalties for lenient cases of assault		x
+	1989 Increasing penalties for child pornography		x
−	1990 Treatment in rehabilitation center instead of prison for drunk drivers	x	
+	1992 Experiment on juvenile contract	x	
+	1992 Increasing penalties for involuntary manslaughter (from 4 months to 4 years)		x

TABLE A1 (*Continued*)

Direction and Impact	Reform	Main Area	
		Sanctions	Offenses
	Denmark		
++	1994 Stiffer sentences for violent recidivists and violence against specific groups (i.e., taxi drivers)		x
−	1995 Drug treatment as a condition for suspended sentence to replace prison	x	
++	1992 Increasing penalties for drug dealing		x
−	1997 Treatment for sex offenders as a condition for suspended sentence to replace prison	x	
−	1997 Expanding CS as a combination order with fine or conditional sentence	x	
+++	1997 Stiffer sentences for aggravated assault		x
?	1998 Youth contract made permanent	x	
−	2000 Expanding the use of community service to drunk driving	x	
− − −	2000 Conditional sentence + treatment instead of prison for drunk drivers	x	
−+	2000 Abolishment of short-term prison sentence	x	
+	2001 Introduction of new (institutional) juvenile sanction	x	
++	2002 Stiffer penalties for rape, intercourse with children, and violent offenses		x
+	2002 Increasing penalties for car theft		x
++	2004 Stiffer sentences for serious recidivists	x	
+	2004 Increasing maximum sentence for drugs offenses from 10 to 16 years		x
+	2004 Increased penalties for carrying a knife in public		x
− −	2005 Experiment with electronic monitoring	x	
− −	2007 Restricting (abolishing) the use of default imprisonment for fines	x	
−	2010 Expanding the use of community service	x	
+++	2014 Stiffer sentences for organized crime (motorcycle gangs)		x
+	2014 Increased penalties for carrying a knife in public		x
−	2015 Expanding the the use of community service	x	
	Norway		
−	1970 Decriminalization of public drunkenness		x
+	1972 Stiffer penalties for drug offenses (maximum 6 to >10 years)		x
−	1977 Plan: Stortingsmelding (nr. 104 1977–78)	x	
+	1981 Stiffer penalties for drug offenses (maximum 10 to >15 years)		x

TABLE A1 (*Continued*)

Direction and Impact	Reform	Main Area Sanctions	Offenses
	Norway		
−	1981 Abandonment of life sentence to >21 years	x	
+	1981 Stiffer penalties for drug offenses (maximum 15 years to > 21 years)		x
+	1982 Video violence criminalization		x
−	1984 Experiment on CSO	x	
−	1985 Age of criminal responsibility 14 years to >15 years	x	
−	1988 CSO stabilized	x	
+	1988 Domestic violence under public prosecution		x
+	1988 Stiffer penalties for sex crimes against children		x
+	1988 Stiffer penalties for causing death in traffic		x
−	1988 Reduced penalties for DWI		x
−	1989 CSO extended	x	
+	1990 Stiffer penalties for tax evasion		x
−	1992 Stiffer penalties for tax evasion		x
+	1992 Doping criminalized		x
+	2000 DWI limit from 0.5 to 0.2‰		x
+	2000 Stiffer penalties for sexual offenses; broader rape definition		x
+	2001 CSO replaced by community punishment; extension	x	
− +	2001 New prison law	x	
−	2006 Drug program to replace prison sentences (for DWI)	x	
−	2008 Electronic monitoring to replace prison sentences (? front/back)		
+++	2010 Increasing penalties for rape and sexual offenses		x
− −	2012 New juvenile sanction replacing custody (community mediation)	x	
− −	2014 Default imprisonment replaced by "fine service"	x	

REFERENCES

Aho, Timo, and Vuokko Karsikas. 1980. *Vankien Taustaan ja Vankilukuun Liittyviä Tilastoja, 1881–1978*. Vankeinhoidon historiaprojektin julkaisu 3/1980. Helsinki: Oikeusministeriön vankeinhoito-osasto.
"Alternatives to Deprivation of Liberty" [Alternativ til Frihedstraf et Debatoplaeg]. 1977. Betaenking Kobenhavn. 806.

Andersson, Robert. 2002. "Kriminalpolitikens Väsen." Stockholm: Avhandlingsserie Kriminologiska Institutionen, Stockholms Universitet.

Annerstedt, Ludvig. 1869. *Om Straffmätning*. Uppsala: Universitets Årskrift.

Anttila, Inkeri. 1967. "Konservativ och Radikal Kriminalpolitik I Norden." *Nordisk Tidsskrift for Kriminalvidenskab* (3):237–51.

Asp, Petter. 2012. "Prosecutor in Swedish Law." In *Prosecutors and Politics: A Comparative Perspective*, edited by Michael Tonry. Vol. 41 of *Crime and Justice: A Review of Research*, edited by Michael Tonry. Chicago: University of Chicago Press.

Aubert, Vilhelm, and Thomas Mathiesen. 1962. "Förbrytelse og Sykdom." *Tidsskrift for Samfunnsforskning* 3:169–92.

Bäcklund, A. 2015. "En Kriminalpolitisk Nödvändighet? Om Tidigare Brottslighet och dess Betydelse vid Straffmätning." *Svensk Juristtidning* (5-6): 397–408.

Balvig, Flemming. 2004. "When Law and Order Returned to Denmark." *Journal of Scandinavian Studies in Criminology* 5:167–87.

Balvig, Flemming, Helgi Gunnlaugsson, Kristina Jerre, Henrik Tham, and Aarne Kinnunen. 2015. "The Public Sense of Justice in Scandinavia: A Study of Attitudes towards Punishments." *European Journal of Criminology* 12(3): 342–61.

Bondeson, Ulla. 1977. *Kriminalvård i Frihet*. Stockholm: Liber.

Börjeson, Bengt. 1966. *Om Påföljders Verkningar*. Uppsala: Almqvist & Wiksell.

Brå. 2014. *Skärpta Straff för Allvarliga Våldsbrott: Utvärdering av 2010 års Straffmätningsreform*. Stockholm: Brottsförebyggande rådet.

Bruhn, Anders, Odd Lindberg, and Per Åke Nylander. 2012. "A Harsher Prison Climate and a Cultural Heritage Working against It: Subcultural Divisions among Swedish Prison Officers." In *Penal Exceptionalism? Nordic Prison Policy and Practice*, edited by T. Ugelvik and J. Dullum. London: Routledge.

Christie, Nils. 1960. *Tvangsarbeid og Alkoholbruk*. Oslo: Universitetsforlaget.

————. 1968. "Changes in Penal Values." In *Scandinavian Studies in Criminology 2*. Oslo: Universitetsforlaget.

————. 1997. "Straffens Geografi." *Nordisk Tidsskrift for Kriminalvidenskab* (2): 89–102.

Demker, Marie, and Goran Duus-Otterström. 2009. "Realigning Criminal Policy: Offender and Victim in the Swedish Party System over Time." *International Review of Sociology* 19(2):273–96.

du Rées, H., and J. Sarnecki. 2013. "Skärpta Straff fel Metod att Minska Brottsligheten." *DN Debatt* (April 8). http://www.dn.se/debatt/skarpta-straff-fel-metod-att-minska-brottsligheten/.

Elffers, Henk, and Jan W. de Keijser. 2008. "Different Perspectives, Different Gaps: Does the General Public Demand a More Responsive Judge?" In *Fear of Crime: Punitivity, New Developments in Theory and Research*, edited by Helmut Kury. Frankfurt: University Press Bochum Brockmeyer.

Eriksson, Lars D., ed. 1967. *Pakkoauttajat*. Helsinki: Tammi.

Estrada, Felipe, and Henrik Tham. 2013. "Debattörerna: Varför vill du Sätta fler I Fängelse, Ask?" *DN Debatt* (March 18).

————. 2015. "Kriminalpolitiska Utspel Saknar Stöd I Forskningen." *DN Debatt* (August 30). http://www.dn.se/debatt/kriminalpolitiska-utspel-saknar-stod-i -forskningen/

Exner, Franz. 1931. *Studien Über Strafzumessungs-praxis der Deutschen Gerichte.* Kriminalistische Abhandlungen, Heft 16. Leipzig: Wiegandt.

Galtung, Johan. 1959. *Fengelssamfunnet.* Oslo: Universitetsforlaget.

Goffman, Erving. 1961. *Asylums: Essays on the Social Situation of Mental Patients and Other Inmates.* New York: Anchor.

Greve, Vagn. 2007. "Trends in Prison Law." In *Festschrift in Honour of Raimo Lahti*, edited by Kimmo Nuotio. Publications of the Faculty of Law. Helsinki: University of Helsinki.

Hannula, Illari. 2004. *Rikosoikeudellinen Järjestelmä Kriisissä: The Criminal Justice System in a Time of Crisis.* Vammala: Suomalainen Lakimiesyhdistys.

Hauge, Red. 1978. "Drinking and Driving in Scandinavia." In *Scandinavian Studies in Criminology 6*, edited by Red Hauge. Norwich, UK: Universitetsforlaget.

Hinkkanen, Ville, and Tapio Lappi-Seppälä. 2011. "Sentencing Theory, Policy, and Research in the Nordic Countries." In *Crime and Justice in Scandinavia*, edited by Michael Tonry and Tapio Lappi-Seppälä. Vol. 40 of *Crime and Justice: A Review of Research*, edited by Michael Tonry. Chicago: University of Chicago Press.

Holmboe, Morten. 2002. *Konfliktrådsloven: Kommentarutgave.* 4th ed. Oslo: Universitetsforlaget.

Janson, Carl-Gunnar. 2004. "Youth Justice in Sweden." In *Youth Crime and Youth Justice: Comparative and Cross-National Perspectives*, edited by Michael Tonry and Anthony N. Doob. Vol. 31 of *Crime and Justice: A Review of Research*, edited by Michael Tonry. Chicago: University of Chicago Press.

Jerre, K., and Henrik Tham. 2010. "Svenskarnas syn på Straff Rapport 2010:1." Stockholm: Stockholms Universitet, Kriminologiska Institutionen.

Johnsen, Berit. 2011. "Forvaring: Fra Saerreaksjon og 'Straff; till Lovens Strengeste Straff: Ett Skritt Frem Eller ett Tilbake?" *Nordisk Tidskrift for Kriminalvidenska* (1):2–16.

————. 2013. "Elleve år med Forvaring: Löslatelser–Praksis og Rettpraksis–og Tilbakefall." *Lov og Rett* (6):385–405.

Johnsen, Berit, and H. Engbo. 2015. "Forvaring I Norge, Danmark, og Grönland: Noen Likheter og Ulikheter." *Nordisk Tidskrift for Kriminalvidenskab* (2):175–94.

Joutsen, Matti. 1987. *The Role of the Victim in the European Criminal Justice Systems.* HEUNI Publications. Helsinki: European Institute for Crime Prevention and Control (for the United Nations).

Kamber, S. 2013. "Psykisk Syge Lovovertraedere I Komparativt Lys." *Nordisk Tidskrift for Kriminalvidenskab* (3):358–68.

Kriminalforsorgen. 2013. Statistikberetning 2013. http://www.http://kriminal forsorgen.dk/%C3%85rlige-statistikberetninger-1365.aspx.

Kristoffersen, R. 2016. *Correctional Statistic of Denmark, Finland, Iceland, Norway and Sweden, 2010–2014.* Oslo: Correctional Service of Norway Staff Academy.

Kyvsgaard, Britta. 2001. "Harmoni Eller Disharmoni Mellem de Nordiske Lande." *Nordisk Tidskrift for Kriminalvidenskab* (2):89–93.

———. 2004. "Youth Justice in Denmark." In *Youth Crime and Youth Justice: Comparative and Cross-National Perspectives,* edited by Michael Tonry and Anthony N. Doob. Vol. 31 of *Crime and Justice: A Review of Research,* edited by Michael Tonry. Chicago: University of Chicago Press.

Lahti, Raimo. 2000. "Towards a Rational and Humane Criminal Policy: Trends in Scandinavian Penal Thinking." *Journal of Scandinavian Studies and Crime Prevention* 2000(1):141–55.

Laine, M. 2015. "Rysssland och Finlands Kriminalpolitik." *Nordisk Tidskrift for Kriminalvidenskab* (1):79–84.

Lappi-Seppälä, Tapio. 1987. *Rangaistuksen määräämisestä I. Teoria ja yleinen osa.* Vammalan kirjapaino: Vammala.

———. 1996. "Reparation in Criminal Law: Finnish National Report." In *Wiedergutmachung im Strafrecht,* edited by Eser Albin and Susanne Walther. Saarbrücken: Max Planck Institut.

———. 2001. "Sentencing and Punishment in Finland: The Decline of the Repressive Ideal." In *Punishment and Penal Systems in Western Countries,* edited by Michael Tonry and Richard Frase. New York: Oxford University Press.

———. 2004. "The Finnish Prosecution Service." In *Tasks and Powers of the Prosecution Services in the EU Member States,* edited by Peter Tak. Nijemegen, Neth.: Wolf Legal.

———. 2007. "Penal Policy in Scandinavia." In *Crime, Punishment, and Politics in a Comparative Perspective,* edited by Michael Tonry. Vol. 36 of *Crime and Justice: A Review of Research,* edited by Michael Tonry. Chicago: University of Chicago Press.

———. 2008. "Politics or Policy: Fluctuations in the Finnish Penal Policy." In *Ikke Kun Straf: Festskrift til Vagn Greve.* Copenhagen: Juris- og Ökonomiforbundets Forlag.

———. 2009. "Imprisonment and Penal Policy in Finland." In *Scandinavian Studies in Law,* edited by Peter Wahlgren. Stockholm: Stockholm University of Law Faculty.

———. 2010. "Parole and Early Release in Finland." In *Release from Prisons: European Policy and Practice,* edited by Nicola Padfield, Dirk Zyl van Smit, and Frieder Dünkel. New York: Willan.

———. 2011. "Nordic Youth Justice: Juvenile Sanctions in Four Nordic Countries." In *Crime and Punishment in Scandinavia,* edited by Michael Tonry and Tapio Lappi-Seppälä. Vol. 40 of *Crime and Justice: A Review of Research,* edited by Michael Tonry. Chicago: University of Chicago Press.

———. 2012. "Penal Policies in the Nordic Countries 1960–2010." *Journal of Scandinavian Studies in Criminology and Crime Prevention* 13(suppl. 1):85–111.

———. 2015a. "Mediation in Finland: National Report." In *Restorative Justice and Mediation in Penal Matters,* edited by Frieder Dünkel, Joanna Grzywa-Holten, and Philip Horshfeld. Mönchengladbach: Forum Verlag Godesberg.

———. 2015b. "Preventive Detention and Life Imprisonment in Four Nordic Countries." In *Kriminalistiske Pejlinger: Festskrift til Flemming Balvig,* edited by Britta Kyvsgaard, Jørn Vestergaard, Lars Holmberg, and Thomas Elholm. Copenhagen: Jurist-og Økonomforbundets Forlag.

———. 2015c. "Youth Justice without a Juvenile Court: A Note on Scandinavian Exceptionalism. " In *Juvenile Justice in Global Perspective*, edited by Franklin E. Zimring, Maximo Langer, and David S. Tanenhaus. New York: New York University Press.

Lappi-Seppälä, Tapio, and A. Storgaard. 2015. "Nordic Mediation: Comparing Denmark and Finland." *Neue Kriminalpolitik* 2015(2):137–47.

Nytt Straffsystem. 1977. "New Penal System: Brottsfölrebygganbde Rådet." Rapport 7. Stockholm: Brå.

Olafsdottir, Hildigunnur, and Ragnheidur Bragadottir. 2006. "Crime and Criminal Policy in Iceland: Criminology on the Margins of Europe." *European Journal of Criminology* 3(2):221–53.

"Om kriminalpolitiken" [On crime policy]. 1978. St. meld. no. 104. Oslo: Justis-og politidepartamentet.

Pratt, John, and Anna Eriksson. 2013. *Contrasts in Punishment: An Explanation of Anglophone Excess and Nordic Exceptionalism.* London: Routledge.

Rikollisuustilanne. 2014. *Kriminologian ja Oikeuspolitiikan Instituutti. Katsauksia 4/2015.* Helsinki.

Ryberg, Jesper, and Julian V. Roberts. 2015. *Popular Punishment: On the Normative Significance of Public Opinion.* Oxford: Oxford University Press.

Siren, P. 1967. "Ei Kotia, Ei Koulua." *Pakkoauttajat* 78–107. Helsinki: Kustannusosakeyhtiö Tammi.

Snacken, Sonja. 2012. "Conclusion: Why and How to Resist Punitiveness in Europe." In *Resisting Punitiveness in Europe: Welfare, Human Rights, and Democracy*, edited by Sonja Snacken and Els Dumortier. London: Routledge.

SOU (Statens Offentliga Utredningar). 1986. *Påföljd för Brott Huvudbetänkande av Fängelsestraffkommittén.* 1986:13–15. Stockholm: Justitiedepartement.

———. 2005. *Ett Effektivare Brottmålsförfarande Några Ytterligare Åtgärder.* 2005:117. Anmärkning: Slutbetänkande; Stockholm: Justitiedepartement.

———. 2012. *Nya Påföljder.* Del 1–4. 2012:34. Stockholm: Justitiedepartement.

———. 2013. *Brottmålsprocessen.* Del 1–2. 2013:17. Stockholm: Justitiedepartement.

———. 2014. *Straffskalorna för Allvarliga Våldsbrott. Betänkande av Utredningen om Skärpta Straff för Allvarliga Våldsbrott.* 2014:18. Stockholm: Justitiedepartement.

Storgaard, Anette. 2009. "The Youth Sanction: A Punishment in Disguise." In *Scandinavian Studies in Law*, vol. 54, edited by Peter Wahlgren. Stockholm: Stockholm Institute for Scandinavian Law.

Takala, Hannu, and Tham Henrik. 1987. *Krig og Moral: Kriminalitet og Kontroll I Norden Under Andre Verdenskrig.* Oslo: Universitetsforlaget Oslo Bergen Tromsa.

Tham, Henrik. 2001. "Law and Order as a Leftist Project?" *Punishment and Society: The International Journal of Penology* 3(3):409–26.

———. 2003. "Forskare om Narkotikapolitiken." Rapport 2003:1. Stockholm: Department of Criminology, Stockholm University.

———. 2005. "Swedish Drug Policy and the Vision of the Good Society." *Journal of Scandinavian Studies in Criminology and Crime Prevention* 6:57–73.

Tham, Henrik, Anita Rönneling, and Lise-Lotte Rytterbro. 2011. "The Emergence of the Crime Victim: Sweden in a Scandinavian Context." In *Crime and Justice in Scandinavia*, edited by Michael Tonry and Tapio Lappi-Seppälä. Vol. 40 of *Crime and Justice: A Review of Research*, edited by Michael Tonry. Chicago: University of Chicago Press.

Tolonen, Hannu. 2003. *Oikeuslähdeoppi*. Helsinki: WSOY.

Tonry, Michael. 2013. "Sentencing in America, 1975–2025." In *Crime and Justice in America, 1975–2025*, edited by Michael Tonry. Vol. 41 of *Crime and Justice: A Review of Research*, edited by Michael Tonry. Chicago: University of Chicago Press.

Törnudd, P. 1996. *Facts, Values, and Visions: Essays in Criminology and Crime Policy*. Publication no. 138, edited by Inkeri Anttila, Kauko Aromaa, Risto Jaakkola, Tapio Lappi-Seppälä, and Hannu Takala. Helsinki: National Research Institute of Legal Policy.

Träskman, Per Ole. 2004. "Drug Control and Drug Offences in the Nordic Countries: A Criminal Political Failure Too Often Interpreted as a Success." *Journal of Scandinavian Studies in Criminology and Crime Prevention* 5:236–56.

———. 2013. "'The Golden Age of Nordic Cooperation.' Har de Nordiska Kronjuvelerna Kommit på Museum? Den Nordiska Brottskontrollen: Nutid, Dåtid och Framtid." *Nordisk Tidskrift for Kriminalvidenskap* 2013(3):333–55.

———. 2015. "Brottslight of Brottskontroll I Finland och de Andra Nordiska Länderna: Banbrytare eller Eftersläntare?" *Nordisk Tidskrift for Kriminalvidenskap* 2015(2):149–75.

Träskman, Per Ole, and Britta Kyvsgaard. 2002. "Vem eller vad Styr Straffrättspolitiken." In *Flores Juris et Legum Festskrift till Nils Jareborg*, edited by P. Asp, C. E. Herlitz, and L. Holmqvist. Uppsala: Iustus Förlag.

Ugelvik, Thomas, and Jane Dullum. 2012. *Penal Exceptionalism? Nordic Prison Policy and Practice*. London: Routledge.

Uusitalo, P. 1967. *Vankila ja Työsiirtola Rangaistuksena*. Helsinki: Kirjapaino.

Victor, D. 1995. "Politics and the Penal System: A Drama in Progress." In *Beware of Punishment: On the Utility and Futility of Criminal Law*, edited by Annika Snare. Vol. 14 of *Scandinavian Studies in Criminology*, edited by Annika Snare. Oslo: Pax Forlag.

von Hirsch, Andrew, and Andrew Ashworth. 2005. *Proportionate Sentencing: Exploring the Principles*. New York: Oxford University Press.

von Hofer, Hanns, and Tapio Lappi-Seppälä. 2014. "The Development of Crime in Light of Finnish and Swedish Criminal Justice Statistics: 1750–2010." *European Journal of Criminology* 2014(2):169–94.

von Hofer, Hanns, Tapio Lappi-Seppälä, and Lars Westfelt. 2012. *Nordic Criminal Statistics, 1950–2010: Summary of a Report*. 8th ed. Stockholm: Kriminologiska Institutionen, Stockholms Universitet.

von Hofer, Hanns, and Henrik Tham. 2013. "Punishment in Sweden." In *Punishment in Europe: A Critical Anatomy of Penal Systems*, edited by Ruggiero Vincenzo and Ryan Mick. Palgrave Studies in Prisons and Penology Series. Basingstoke, UK: Palgrave Macmillan.

Wahlin, L. 2005. *Medling vid Brott I Sverige Under 2000-talet*. Rapport 2005:14. Stockholm: Brottsförebyggande Rådet.

Thomas Weigend

No News Is Good News: Criminal Sentencing in Germany since 2000

ABSTRACT

Sentencing practice in Germany has long been stable, reflecting slightly falling crime rates. Public prosecutors dismiss the majority of cases that the police file with them as "cleared." In a significant percentage of provable cases, prosecutors demand a penance payment of suspects in exchange for dismissal; many others are dismissed without any consequence for the suspect. Criminal courts dispose of more than half of cases in a written procedure, routinely accepting the sentence proposals of prosecutors. A growing number of trials result in "bargained" sentences, that is, sentences agreed on among the judge and the parties. Sentence severity in Germany is generally low. Life sentences are exceptional, and release on parole is available. Overall, only 5 percent of convicted offenders must serve a prison sentence. Another 12 percent receive a suspended prison sentence, and the rest are fined. German society at present does not appear to regard crime and criminal justice as pressing problems. Operating in the shadow of the public interest, agents of criminal justice can pursue a fairly liberal and rational course.

As readers of older science fiction know, it is fun to look back at the prophesies of 100 years ago and smile at odd things writers imagined for the distant future (typical predictions included colonies of humans on Mars and the replacement of meals by pills; fortunately none of this has yet come true). The exercise can be a bit less uplifting when looking

Electronically published June 22, 2016
  Thomas Weigend is professor of criminal law and criminal procedure at the University of Cologne, Germany.

at one's own prophesies, especially when they are just 15 years old. But if the purpose of this essay is to assess recent developments in criminal sanctioning, one cannot avoid taking a position in the past and looking from that viewpoint to the present. Before I revisit the predictions I made in 2001 (see Weigend 2001), I present a brief sketch of the status quo of German sentencing. I then compare it with the situation at the turn of the twenty-first century and speculate on the reasons for changes—or their absence. The greatest surprise is the stability of the German criminal justice system over the last two decades. Dramatic developments all over the world seem to have left Germany's crime scene largely untouched. Facing a decrease rather than an increase in recorded crime, the justice system has stuck to its policy of relative leniency, dismissing the great majority of cases at the prosecutorial level and sending to prison only a small fraction of convicted offenders.

I. Sentencing in Germany

The main actors are the legislature, the public prosecutor, and the criminal court. The legislature defines minimum and maximum sentences for each offense, often providing for extensions in especially serious and less serious cases of crimes. Typically, the Penal Code leaves the courts great leeway in sentencing. For example, the minimum punishment for forgery is a fine of €5; the maximum for aggravated cases is 10 years' imprisonment. Some serious crimes carry mandatory prison sentences. This applies, for example, to manslaughter, mayhem, robbery, and rape. Sentencing judges have no discretion to impose a sentence less than the statutory minimum. Prison sentences of 2 years or less, however, may be suspended if it is expected that the offender will not commit further crimes if left at large. Murder (intentional killing with aggravating circumstances) carries a mandatory life sentence. Yet, even those convicted of murder may be released on parole after having served a minimum of 15 years in prison.

The public prosecutor is responsible for investigating cases and for submitting them to the court. When the prosecutor files an indictment, he or she selects an offense definition for the defendant's alleged conduct; but the trial court is not bound by that choice and, after proper warning given to the defendant (§ 265 Code of Criminal Procedure), may enter a conviction for a crime other than the one named in the indictment as long as the court's decision is based on the incident described in the indictment. The prosecutor therefore cannot make certain that the defendant, if convicted, will receive a sentence within a certain range. For example, if the prosecutor charges the defendant with simple theft (§ 242 Penal Code), which carries a statutory maximum sentence of 5 years' imprisonment, the court may also convict the defendant of robbery (maximum sentence 15 years) if it finds on the basis of the evidence presented at the trial that the defendant stole the object by using threats or violence. Although the prosecutor cannot directly influence the sentence through the charging decision, in less serious cases, he or she may decline to prosecute even if there is sufficient evidence to convict. The only exceptions are cases of felonies with a 1-year statutory minimum sentence; in these cases, the prosecutor, at least theoretically, is obliged to file charges if there is sufficient evidence.[1]

In nonfelony cases, the prosecutor may also settle cases by compromise: he or she may offer the suspect nonprosecution in exchange for a payment to the state or to a charitable organization, or in exchange for some other positive activity such as reconciliation with the victim (§ 153a Code of Criminal Procedure). If the suspect agrees and makes the required payment, the presumption of innocence remains intact and further prosecution for a nonfelony is precluded. This option was originally intended as a prosecutorial sentencing tool for everyday offenses of lesser seriousness; but since most business crimes (e.g., fraud, abuse of trust, tax offenses) are technically not felonies, "penance" payments—which have no statutory maximum—have sometimes been set at millions of euros. In August 2014, Formula 1 boss Bernie Ecclestone paid $100 million in exchange for dropping of corruption charges by the public prosecutor in Munich (Kudlich 2015). Although such payments are not technically criminal fines, because the suspect is never convicted of any crime, they are imposed as an official reaction to the allegation that the suspect has committed a criminal offense and are thus the functional equivalent of a fine without trial. In more serious cases, the deal needs to be approved by a judge (§ 153 sec. 1), but approval is almost never withheld.[2]

---

[1] See § 170 sec. 1 of the Code of Criminal Procedure in connection with § 12 Penal Code (defining "felony"). In practice, prosecutors may sometimes "overlook" aggravating factors that turn a less serious crime into a felony.

[2] For studies on the practice of conditional dismissals, see Rieß (1983) and Meinberg (1985).

Another tool of prosecutorial sentencing is the penal order (§§ 407–412). Formally, a penal order is a written judgment issued by the court. But in practice, the prosecutor drafts the judgment for the judge to sign without trial and without negotiation. By issuing a penal order, the judge may impose a fine, suspend the defendant's driver's license, and impose a suspended prison sentence of not more than 1 year; in the latter case, the defendant must be assisted by a lawyer (§ 407 sec. 2). If the judge, who receives the file of the prosecutor's pretrial investigation along with the draft penal order, does not agree with the proposed verdict or sentence, he or she may reject it and set the case for trial. The defendant's consent is not needed for the initiation of the penal order process; within 2 weeks, the defendant can file an appeal against the penal order, and the case is then set for trial. In that case, the sentence imposed by the penal order loses effect.[3] A penal order may also be issued when the defendant fails to appear for trial. In that case, the prosecutor may orally apply for a penal order based on the indictment, and the judge may sign it on the spot (§ 408a). Defendants who wish to submit their cases to trial must take the initiative by filing appeals. A penal order that is not appealed has the legal force of a trial judgment (§ 410 sec. 3).

Since 2009, the German Code of Criminal Procedure has provided for the option of a negotiated judgment (Weigend 2008; Turner and Weigend 2014).[4] The judge initiates that proceeding by proposing, at the beginning or during the course of the trial, a sentence range on the condition that the defendant confesses to all or some of the charges (§ 257c secs. 1–3). That proposal becomes binding if both the defense and the prosecution agree. The prosecutor thus effectively has the power to veto a lenient sentence suggested by the court and to insist on a full trial.

If a case goes to trial, the prosecutor makes a formal recommendation on verdict and sentence after all the evidence has been taken. The defense lawyer responds with a closing statement, and the defendant has the right to address the court in person (§ 258). The prosecutor's sentence recommendation is by no means binding on the court; judges

---

[3] If the defendant files an appeal against the penal order, the sentence after trial can be more severe than the one contained in the penal order. There is no double jeopardy protection because the penal order is deemed to be a provisional judgment without full fact-finding; see Meyer-Gossner and Schmitt (2015, § 411, marginal note 11).

[4] See Sec. II below for more on the German version of plea bargaining.

sometimes impose a more severe sentence but often remain a bit below the sentence proposed by the prosecutor.

The main burden of sentencing falls on the trial court. Depending on the seriousness of the case, trial courts consist of one, three, four, or five judges; and in all but the least serious cases (which are tried before a single professional judge), two lay judges sit with one, two, or three professional judges.[5] Germany has no jury system, but laypersons and professional judges hear cases, deliberate, and decide together on both the verdict and the sentence. If the judges are not unanimous, the majority decides; but a two-thirds majority is needed for any finding of guilt or any other decision to the defendant's detriment (§ 263).[6] There is no separation between the trial on the issue of guilt and the sentencing hearing; both issues are dealt with in the same trial proceeding. Evidence relating to the sentence is also presented at the trial, even before the defendant has been found guilty. At the end of the trial, the presiding judge announces the judgment comprising the finding of guilt or acquittal and, if guilt, the sentence.

In determining the sentence, the court is guided by the minimum and maximum that the Penal Code sets for each offense. But as mentioned before, the code often indicates very broad sentence ranges without structuring the court's discretion. In many instances, the court may impose a fine or a prison sentence of several years. Nor does the law offer any meaningful guidance as to how to select the sentence within the broad spectrum offered by the offense definition. This is true even where the law is comparatively specific about aggravating and mitigating circumstances.

Take, for example, the sentence ranges provided for assault offenses: simple assault (bodily maltreatment of another person or impairment of his health) can be punished by a fine (with a minimum of €5) or by imprisonment up to 5 years (§ 223 Penal Code). If the offender has used certain dangerous means, such as a poisonous substance or a weapon, the minimum sentence is 3 months' imprisonment; the maximum is 10 years

---

[5] For details, see §§ 29 and 76 *Gerichtsverfassungsgesetz* (Court Organization Act). Offenses against the security of the state, including cases of terrorism, are tried before a panel of three or five professional judges of the State Court of Appeals (§§ 120, 122 *Gerichtsverfassungsgesetz*).

[6] Given the composition of "mixed" courts, the two-thirds rule means that the two lay judges together can veto any finding of guilt.

(§ 224).[7] In cases of mayhem (e.g., when the assault leads to the victim's loss of an eye or of an important member of his body), the sentence range is from 6 months' to 15 years' imprisonment (§ 226).[8] If the assault results in the death of the victim and the offender has at least been negligent as to that result, the sentence may be set between 1 year's and 15 years' imprisonment (§ 227). This statutory arrangement has at least three remarkable aspects: first, the sentence range depends to a considerable extent on the result of the assault (which may or may not have been intended by the offender); second, there is significant overlap of separate sentence ranges (e.g., a 3-year prison sentence may be imposed for any assault offense); third, even though the legislature intended to narrow sentencing discretion for each type of assault offense, the courts retain extremely broad leeway. For each variant of aggravated assault, the sentencing court has a range of at least 10 years' prison time to choose from.

Given such broad sentencing ranges, one might expect the law to spell out aggravating and exonerating factors and to explain how judges should apply them in any given case. But we look in vain for any equivalent of sentencing guidelines. The Penal Code (§ 46) provides only one very general (and partially contradictory) rule: "The offender's blameworthiness shall be the basis for sentencing. The court shall take into account the effects that the punishment is expected to have on the offender's future life in society."

The first sentence indicates that the harm done and the offender's blameworthiness are the primary considerations (see Streng 2013, § 46, marginal notes 19–21). But at the same time, the court should determine what effects the punishment may have on the offender's chances of rehabilitation and of leading a crime-free life in the future. Unfortunately, the code does not indicate how a court should calculate the sentence when these two considerations point in different directions, for example, when an offender deserves great blame for having intentionally committed a serious crime, but where a long prison sentence would ruin his chances of rehabilitation. German courts have interpreted § 46 of the Penal Code to mean that a concern for rehabilitation can be taken into

---

[7] A fine may be substituted for any sentence of imprisonment of less than 6 months (§ 47 sec. 2).

[8] A sentence of more than 10 years may be imposed only if the offender knew that the serious consequence would occur or intended it to occur.

consideration only within the framework of a sentence proportionate to the offender's blameworthiness.[9] Sentencing courts are thus precluded from imposing sentences that are too severe in relation to the offender's blameworthiness; but they must also avoid imposing sentences that are not sufficiently severe and therefore fail to reflect the seriousness of the offender's culpable wrongdoing.[10] It should be noted that any reference to general or special deterrence is conspicuously absent from the general principles of sentencing under German law; the assumption is that any sentence that is proportionate to the offender's blameworthiness is also sufficient to have a deterrent effect (see Streng 2013, § 46, marginal notes 42–43).

The German Penal Code (§ 46 sec. 2) lists a number of considerations that courts should take into account in determining the sentence, including the offender's motives, the consequences of the offense as foreseen by or foreseeable for the offender,[11] the offender's personal and economic situation, and his or her conduct after the offense, in particular, any effort to repair the harm. But neither is this list of sentencing considerations conclusive nor does the law indicate whether (or under what circumstances) the factors named should mitigate or aggravate the sentence. The law thus provides nothing more than an open-ended checklist for courts without giving any substantive guidance for choosing the sentence within the broad range offered by each offense definition.

Sentences can be appealed by the prosecution as well as the defense. But appellate courts, in particular, the Federal Court of Justice as the highest German court in criminal matters, so far have mostly subscribed to a "hands-off" policy in matters of sentencing, emphasizing the principle that sentencing is the domain of trial court judges, who after all have heard all the witnesses and have seen and interrogated the defendant in person.[12] Appeals courts have not shown any intention of setting general sentencing guidelines for certain types of offenses, neither

---

[9] See 7 Entscheidungen des Bundesgerichtshofes in Strafsachen (hereinafter BGHSt) 28 at 32 (1954); 24 BGHSt 132 at 133 (1971). For a critical analysis of this theory, see Hörnle (1999, pp. 23–76).

[10] See 29 BGHSt 319 (1980); 57 BGHSt 123 at 133–134 (2012). For criticism of this view, see Roxin (2006, p. 93).

[11] The Penal Code (§ 46 sec. 2) speaks of "culpably caused" consequences.

[12] In the German system, only appeals on legal questions reach the highest courts, and there is no evidence taken before the Courts of Appeals; see §§ 337, 350–52 Code of Criminal Procedure.

through "guideline judgments" nor otherwise. Instead, they have emphasized that the concept of "blameworthiness," which according to § 46 section 1 of the Penal Code is to be the basis of sentencing, does not require the trial court to identify one particular sentence that exactly reflects the offender's blameworthiness. The courts instead have declared that in each case there is a range of possible sentences each of which can be regarded as reflecting the offender's blameworthiness. Within that range, the trial court should approach the upper or lower limit depending on considerations of rehabilitation, as indicated by the second sentence of § 46 section 1 of the Penal Code (20 BGHSt 264 at 266). Appellate courts have overturned trial courts' sentencing decisions in a fair number of instances (for an overview, see Maurer [2005, pp. 126–74]). However, in most of these cases, the appellate court did not flat-out rule that the sentence was disproportionate to the offender's guilt but rather reproached the trial court for not sufficiently explaining in the judgment the reasons that prompted it to impose a sentence that the appellate court judges regarded as surprisingly lenient or severe, given the facts of the case as recorded in the written judgment.[13] As a result, one can say that trial courts enjoy very broad discretion in sentencing and that they are fairly safe from being overruled on appeal as long as they give plausible reasons for their decisions.

It is no surprise, then, that empirical studies have found a considerable amount of variation in sentencing among criminal courts, variations that cannot be explained other than by local traditions or individual preferences of judges.[14] Such irrational variations have not been of great concern, and in any event they have not led to any serious effort to reform sentencing law or practice.

II. Sanctioning Practice: Present

Before discussing the results of the interactions among legislatures, prosecutors, and courts in sanctioning (suspected) offenders, I must note the imperfection of statistical materials on the German criminal justice

---

[13] See Miebach (2012, § 46, marginal notes 50–63), with many references to appellate court case law.

[14] The breadth of variation differs, however. See Albrecht (1994, pp. 329–80; little variation by location), Langer (1994), Oswald (1994), and Hupfeld (1999). For a comprehensive analysis based on empirical studies, see Streng (2012, pp. 234–44; 2013, § 46, marginal note 3).

system. Although police, prosecuting agencies, and courts all collect and report data on their activities, these statistics are not integrated. Therefore, the base numbers of offenses reported to and processed by the police, accepted and dealt with by prosecutors' offices, and recorded by courts do not match. That Germany is a federal state consisting of 16 states is a further complicating factor. But the data from the criminal justice agencies of the 16 states are almost perfectly integrated in comprehensive statistics, so that data for all of Germany are available. German unification is a significant problem in looking at patterns over extended periods. Although the justice systems of the former East and West Germany were unified in accordance with Western standards in 1990, it took until 2005 to create comprehensive court statistics covering all the new states. We therefore have no comparable databases before that date.

With these limitations in mind, I first look at the police level. In 2013, police recorded (hereafter, I use the European term "registered") 5.9 million reports of alleged crimes, with the great majority being reported by people other than police, often victims or witnesses (Bundesministerium des Innern 2014, p. 4). Police managed to "clear" (according to their own standards) 54.5 percent of these incidents and thus counted 3.2 million "cleared" offenses. Among the offenses reported to the police, violent crime amounted to not more than 2.5 percent; the largest group was theft offenses, which made up half of reported crime (p. 4).

In 2013, the police counted 2.1 million individuals as suspects, of whom only 26 percent were female. Twenty-six percent of all suspects had a foreign passport—a significantly higher proportion than the 9 percent foreign citizens among the registered population of Germany (Bundesministerium des Innern 2014, p. 5).[15] Roughly one-fifth of all suspects, 450,000, were younger than 21, including children, who are not punishable under German law.

Very similar figures appear in police crime statistics for years in the immediate past. It is therefore safe to connect these data to prosecution statistics. In 2013, German prosecutor's offices received 4.6 million cases.[16] Given that the police identified only 2.1 million individual sus-

[15] One also has to take into account that a significant number of persons with a German passport have a family background in a foreign country. But this group is not counted separately either in official population statistics or in crime statistics.

[16] See Statistisches Bundesamt (2014a, p. 26). The figures cited in the text have been extrapolated from the same source.

pects, that figure seems exceedingly high. The explanation is simple: Under German law, the police cannot drop cases but are bound to file all reported crimes with the prosecutor's office, even those without a known suspect. These cases are immediately dismissed.

Surprisingly, figure 1 shows that only in 10 percent of all cases received does the prosecutor eventually file an indictment and submit it to trial. What happened to the remaining 90 percent of the cases? More than a fifth (21 percent) were diverted to some other agency, including prosecutor's offices in other cities; some cases were continued by administrative agencies and were likely to be sanctioned as noncriminal administrative infractions. Twenty-eight percent of all cases that reached the prosecutor were dismissed for lack of sufficient evidence. This includes the fairly large group of cases in which the police had not identified a suspect and there were no further clues for continuing an investigation. But among the 1.3 million dismissed cases, there is also a large proportion that the police filed as "cleared" but for which the prosecutor did not think that the evidence was sufficient for conviction in court. Another 24 percent were dismissed as insignificant.

According to § 153 of the Code of Criminal Procedure (and a similar provision in the Juvenile Court Law), the prosecutor may choose not to prosecute any crime that is not a felony if the suspect's blameworthiness would be regarded as minor and if there is no public interest in prosecution. Under § 154 of the Code of Criminal Procedure, the prosecutor may dismiss prosecution for one or more offenses if he or she charges the suspect with (at least) one other separate offense that weighs more

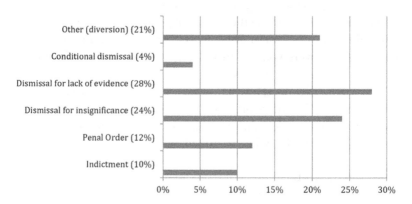

FIG. 1.—Prosecutorial dispositions, 2013. Source: Statistisches Bundesamt (2014a, p. 26).

heavily than those that are dismissed. This provision is designed to sim-plify prosecution of suspects who have committed multiple offenses, such as serial burglaries or frauds. We have little information on how prosecutor's offices apply these provisions of the code in practice, and there appear to be vast regional differences.[17] We do know that German prosecutors in 2013 cleared their dockets of more than 1 million cases by making use of these options of discretionary dismissal. A further 4 per-cent of cases were dismissed under § 153a of the Code of Criminal Pro-cedure, which allows for a deal between the prosecutor and the suspect: the latter is to pay "penance money" in order to have his or her case dismissed.

In sum, in 2013 there was an overall nonprosecution rate of 77 per-cent, which includes, however, cases without a known suspect and cases that were disposed of by being transferred to other agencies. Of the re-maining cases, the majority (i.e., 12 percent of all cases) were brought before the court through the written penal order proceeding, which leaves less than a half million cases (or 10 percent of all cases) in which the prosecutor took the "regular" path by filing a written accusation and requesting a trial.

How did the courts deal with the approximately 1 million cases filed by German prosecutors in 2013? For an answer, we have to switch to court statistics (Statistisches Bundesamt 2014b, pp. 30–68). The figures here are not directly comparable with the prosecutorial statistics. Court statistics of 2013 (which form the statistical basis of fig. 2) mostly relate to cases that prosecutors filed the year before. More importantly, court statistics deal with persons, not cases; one criminal case often covers two or more individuals accused as codefendants. Court statistics therefore refer to a base figure of approximately 1.3 million persons who either re-ceived a penal order or were indicted in a first-instance local court or district court.[18] Given the high selectivity of prosecutors in taking cases

[17] For example, prosecutors in Hamburg used discretionary dismissals in 32 percent of their cases, whereas prosecutors in Nuremberg dismissed only 17 percent (Statistisches Bundesamt 2014a, pp. 26–27).

[18] There were 566,000 applications for penal orders received by criminal court judges (Statistisches Bundesamt 2014b, p. 13). There are no statistics on the number of ap-plications for penal orders rejected by judges, but it is safe to assume that almost all penal orders requested were initially issued. Penal orders that were appealed by defendants are counted among trials in court statistics. Ninety-eight percent of criminal cases are tried in local courts (*Amtsgericht*), which have authority to impose sentences up to 4 years' impris-

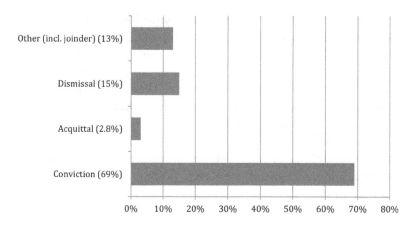

F<small>IG</small>. 2.—Disposition by trial courts, 2013. Source: Statistisches Bundesamt (2014*b*, pp. 13, 30, 68).

to court, it would be reasonable to expect that almost all of these individuals are eventually convicted and sentenced. But that is not the case. Only 69 percent of all defendants were convicted either by penal order or by judgment after trial. The rate of acquittals (including cases that the court refused even to set for trial) was fairly low at 2.8 percent.

Trial courts dismissed 15 percent of their cases for various reasons. In some instances, the defendant was permanently absent or was not fit to stand trial. But in 13 percent of all cases, the trial court dismissed the case for the same "discretionary" reasons that are (and would have been) available to the prosecutor: because the case was of insignificant seriousness, because it was negligible in relation to another ongoing or expected prosecution of the same defendant, or because the defendant agreed to make a penance payment.[19] Finally, there is a fairly large group of "other" dispositions (13 percent of the total), which include joinder of the case with another one.

For the details of sentencing dispositions in 2013 (see fig. 3), we have to switch to yet another set of statistics (Statistisches Bundesamt 2015,

---

onment. Only the most serious cases (including homicide) are tried in district courts (*Landgericht*).

[19] The data of this statistic are collected separately from the court statistics quoted above.

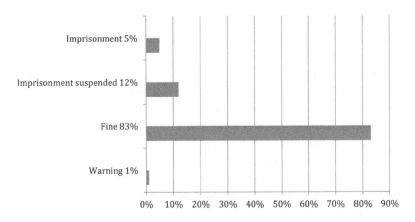

Fig. 3.—Sentences, 2013. Source: Statistisches Bundesamt (2015, pp. 58, 92, 93).

p. 20).[20] Its figures show that defendants who were convicted of a criminal offense ran a very low risk of actually going to prison. This statistic starts from a figure of 936,000 individuals adjudicated in 2013
and 756,000 persons convicted. Because the sanctions for juveniles are
diverse and difficult to compare, I refer only to the 652,000 persons
who were sentenced as adults. Of these persons, 1 percent received only
a warning (p. 58), 83 percent were sentenced to pay a fine, and 17 percent received a prison sentence (pp. 58–92).[21] But 70 percent of all prison
sentences were suspended and the offenders placed on probation
(pp. 92–93). Only a little more than 5 percent of all convicted offenders
actually went to prison. That figure is a bit misleading, however. Some
of those who receive probation later commit new offenses and then have
to serve the original prison sentence.[22] Moreover, an offender who is sentenced to a fine but is unwilling or unable to pay may be taken to prison

[20] The data of this statistic are collected separately from the court statistics quoted
above.

[21] *Verwarnung mit Strafvorbehalt*, § 59 Penal Code. The offender is sentenced to pay a
fine, but the sentence is suspended and will be enforced only if the offender commits another offense within a certain period. Because of rounding errors, the overall figure
exceeds 100 percent.

[22] According to § 56 of the Penal Code, "probation" means that the court fixes a prison
sentence of which the execution is suspended. If the offender commits a serious new crime
or otherwise fails to adhere to the conditions imposed on him, suspension can be revoked
and the offender must then serve the prison sentence (§ 56f).

for serving an amount of time equivalent to the unpaid portion of the fine (§ 43). Even so, it is safe to say that imprisonment is an exceptional sanction in German practice.

Of the 35,000 adults sentenced to imprisonment in 2013, 0.25 percent (92 persons) received a life sentence, which in practice is imposed only for aggravated intentional homicide. Four percent received prison sentences between 5 and 15 years, 24 percent 2–5 years, 14 percent 1–2 years, 30 percent 6 months to 1 year, and 27 percent less than 6 months (Statistisches Bundesamt 2015, pp. 157–58; see fig. 4). The latter figure is surprising, because German law discourages courts from imposing prison sentences of less than 6 months; such sentences may be imposed (and not suspended) only if "special circumstances" of the offense or the offender's personality make it necessary in order to influence the offender or "to defend the legal order" (§ 47 sec. 1).

In sum, German sentencing practice relies heavily on fines and suspended prison sentences. Offenders who serve prison time are the exception rather than the rule. Such statistical findings can be the function of a broad reach of the criminal law: if everyday occurrences such as minor traffic violations are counted as criminal offenses, then the prevalence of fines can easily be explained. It is worth noting, therefore, that in the 1960s, Germany broadly "decriminalized" many areas and trans-

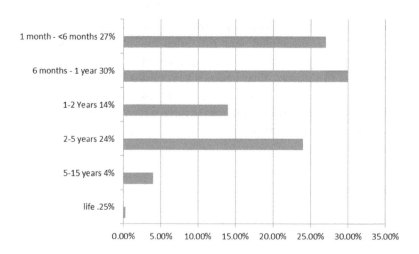

Fig. 4.—Length of prison sentences, 2013. Source: Statistisches Bundesamt (2015, pp. 157, 158).

formed the bulk of traffic offenses and other minor violations into mere administrative infractions; they do not appear in the statistics presented here. It is thus mostly "real" crime that the German criminal justice system tends largely to dispose of by doing nothing (i.e., by prosecutorial or court dismissal) or by imposing fines that equal the offender's income of 3 months or less.[23]

A comparison of today's figures with those of the year 2000 gives an impression of changes in the last 15 years. These changes may indicate changed circumstances or policy choices.

First I look at the development of reported crime. Perhaps surprisingly, more criminal offenses were reported to the police in 2000 than in 2013: the gross number fell from 6.3 million to 6.0 million (BKA 2001, p. 23; Bundesministerium des Innern 2014, p. 16). Even if we account for Germany's slightly shrinking population, reported crime has decreased: the rate per 100,000 inhabitants fell from 7,625 to 7,404 (Bundesministerium des Innern 2014, p. 7). Among identified suspects, the proportions of women (23 percent in 2000, 25 percent in 2013) and foreign citizens (26 percent in 2000, 25 percent in 2013) remained roughly the same. In each year, about 3 million theft offenses were reported to the police, making larceny the most frequent crime that came to the attention of the authorities. One remarkable shift has been the decrease of young suspects: 30 percent of suspects in 2000 were younger than 21 years old, which shrank to 21 percent by 2013 (BKA 2001, p. 72; Bundesministerium des Innern 2014, pp. 12, 13). Within the same time span, the proportion of persons under 20 years of age among the general population decreased from 21.1 percent to 18.1 percent.[24] The dwindling of the most crime-prone population (young men between 16 and 25) may provide at least part of an explanation for the overall reduction of the crime problem.

Looking at prosecutorial dispositions, statistics suggest a fairly stable development (see fig. 5). The 2001 statistics on prosecutor's offices in all of Germany do not present any striking differences from present practice. The gross number of disposed cases, including unidentified suspect

---

[23] Fines are calculated as a product of a number of days and the daily income of the individual offender ("day fine" system; see § 40 Penal Code). Ninety-three percent of fines imposed by the courts amount to 90 day fines or less (Statisches Bundesamt 2015, p. 194).

[24] See https://www.destatis.de/DE/ZahlenFakten/GesellschaftStaat/Bevoelkerung /Bevoelkerungsstand/Tabellen_/lrbev01.html.

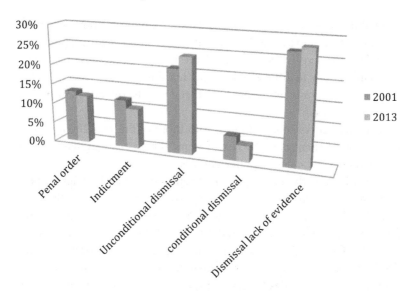

FIG. 5.—Prosecutorial dispositions, 2001 and 2013. Sources: Statistisches Bundesamt (2003, pp. 135–42; 2014a, p. 2).

cases, was 4.5 million in each year. Both the number and the proportion of indictments fell (from 561,000 to 456,000 and from 12 percent to 10 percent), whereas the proportion of unconditional dismissals of "insignificant" cases increased from 21 percent to 24 percent. Somewhat surprisingly, the share of conditional dismissals, that is, dismissals in exchange for a payment (§ 153a Code of Criminal Procedure), decreased significantly from 6 percent to 4 percent. Sustained criticism of this practice may have made some prosecutors wary of using this option.

Court dispositions also have been broadly stable. Regrettably, court statistics for 2000 are much less detailed than those for 2013, especially with regard to penal orders. I therefore present a comparison only for cases that went to trial, including appeals against penal orders (fig. 6). The number of these cases disposed of by criminal courts shrank dramatically, from 846,000 to 713,000. The proportions have nevertheless remained fairly stable. One discernible trend is the reduction of the conviction rate, which dropped from 53 percent to 45 percent, and the concomitant increase of acquittals and other dispositions without conviction. Because the statistics are not completely comparable, the in-

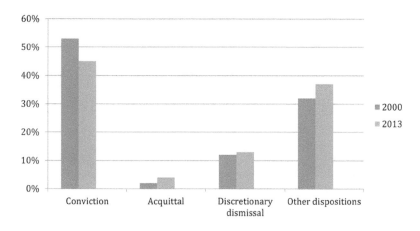

Fig. 6.—Disposition by trial courts, 2000 and 2013. Sources: Statistisches Bundesamt (2012, pp. 20, 21; 2014*b*, pp. 30, 52).

crease of acquittals from 2.4 percent to 4.4 percent in 2013 may not reflect reality; it may also be due to an increase of dispositions by penal order, which preclude acquittal.

Finally, we may compare sentencing structures. German criminal courts in 2013 dismissed a surprisingly high proportion of cases. If defendants were convicted, most had to pay fines or were given suspended prison sentences. How does that picture compare with the situation in the year 2000?

Comparison here faces a significant problem of statistics. Data on sentencing dispositions were not recorded for all of the present German territory before 2005. Before that time, statistics extended only to the former West German states and Berlin, which in 2000 constituted roughly 83 percent of the German population. We therefore cannot directly compare statistical figures but only proportions within the (differing) overall numbers of sentencing cases (fig. 7). As a first impression, it is interesting to note that the raw overall number of statistically recorded convicted persons (including juveniles) rose only from 732,000 in 2000 to 756,000 in 2013, that is, by just 3 percent. This means that the conviction rate in relation to inhabitants actually fell dramatically, because the population on which the 2013 statistic was based was larger by 17 percent than the population for the 2000 statistics, which recorded only convictions in the "old" Federal Republic. The rate of convicted persons

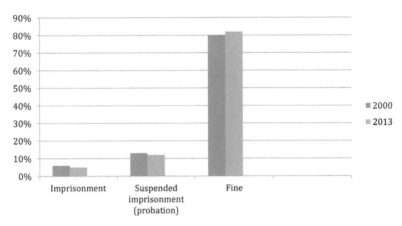

FIG. 7.—Sentencing, 2000 and 2013. Sources: Statistisches Bundesamt (2001, pp. 10, 11, 48; 2015, pp. 12, 16, 158).

among 100,000 members of the population with German citizenship fell from 1,055 in 2000 to 918 in 2013.

Within the given statistical population of each year, the proportion of sanctions within the sentencing spectrum has remained almost unchanged. The number of life sentences fell from 107 in 2000 to 92 in 2013. Sentences of immediate imprisonment were imposed on 6 percent of offenders in 2000 and 5 percent in 2013. Suspended prison sentences fell slightly from 13 percent to 12 percent, and fines increased from 80 percent in 2000 to 82 percent in 2013. If there is any trend discernible, it is toward reduced severity: custodial sentences have been on the retreat, and fines further expanded their vast territory.

Not much has changed in German sentencing since the year 2000. There is a slight tendency toward more dispositions without sanctioning and toward lesser severity, but certainly no dramatic change. As crime rates gradually recede, prosecutors and courts pursue a steady course and administer criminal justice with moderation and prudence.

III. What about Criminal Justice Policy?
Does that mean that criminal justice policy in Germany has been at a standstill? Not if you believe the media and those who are involved in politics. But before taking a closer look, it is time to revert to the trends

I thought I was able to discern 15 years ago when writing about "The Road Ahead—Downhill?" In that article (Weigend 2001), I predicted:

- A further diversification of criminal sanctions.
- A movement toward expanding the role of restitution to the victim.
- An expansion of community service.
- Good prospects for sanctions that restrict offenders' leisure time, including home arrest with electronic monitoring.
- A trend "toward greater punitiveness" and a greater emphasis on the deterrent quality of sentencing.
- A tougher climate of nonindividualist and, in the last consequence, irrational sentencing.
- A significant overall increase in sentencing severity and a greater number of offenders remaining in prison for the full length of their sentence.

I am happy to report that Cassandra, for once, has been wrong. None of the above predictions, whether happy or pessimistic, have come true. The level of sentencing has not changed to any discernible extent, and certainly not toward greater severity. Nor has there been any noticeable expansion of the traditional sentencing options, at least not in statistically relevant practice. I do not go into the futile question of why I was so wrong but briefly report on what became of the ideas that seemed so promising at the beginning of the century.

Restitution and reconciliation between offender and victim have been attractive ideas for long, and they still are. The German legislature in 1994 introduced a new provision, § 46a Penal Code, which permits a reduction of the sentence and in less serious cases even dispenses with punishment altogether if the offender has made restitution or sought personal reconciliation with the victim; the Code of Criminal Procedure exhorts courts and prosecutors to encourage victim/offender mediation (§§ 155a, 155b).

But these efforts have not led to a large-scale replacement or even complementing of traditional criminal sanctions by restitution and reconciliation. As a typical example, the option of requiring the suspect to seek reconciliation with the victim as a precondition for having prosecution dismissed (§ 153a sec. 1 no. 1 Code of Criminal Procedure) in 2013 was used in only 6 percent of all cases of conditional dismissal (Statistisches Bundesamt 2014a, p. 26). The main reason for this neglect of victim-related sentencing is the special effort required of the prosecutorial bureaucracy: whereas a payment by the suspect to the state can easily be made and proven, the initiation, maintenance, and monitoring of personal contact between the suspect and the victim require much time and effort.

The same applies to most types of "community service." Making a suspect or a convicted offender work in a social institution or for the protection of the natural environment can undoubtedly have a major rehabilitative effect, and German state laws foresee this option in lieu of sending to prison a person who has failed to pay a fine. But the positive effect of community service, from an administrative perspective, is offset by the need to hire and train staff to supervise the workers and to support them in fulfilling their duties (cf. Streng 2012, pp. 72–77).[25] "Leisure time sanctions" continue to be discussed, especially the possibility of revoking or suspending an offender's driving license as a sanction for a nondriving offense.[26] But this proposal has not yet been adopted by the German legislature.

The German debate on criminal justice policy matters in recent years has been dominated by other topics. Perhaps the most controversial was the introduction in 2009 of § 257c of the Code of Criminal Procedure, which legalized the long-standing practice of "plea bargaining" German style, that is, agreement between the trial court and the parties about a maximum sentence even before the beginning of the trial.

The practice of sentence negotiation had been discussed for more than 20 years before the legislature finally established ground rules. The judge or either of the parties may take the initiative toward negotiations about a possible sentence, before or during trial. If there appears to be a chance of an agreement, the court proposes a sentence range (say, 3–4 years' imprisonment) that it finds appropriate if the defendant makes certain procedural moves, most frequently a full or partial confession. If both parties agree, the court—barring exceptional circumstances—is bound by its proposal and must impose a sentence within that range. If one party objects or if the defendant does not fulfill his part of the deal,

---

[25] The Code of Criminal Procedure (§ 153a sec. 1 no. 3) provides for the possibility of community service as a precondition of dismissing prosecution. But this option is even less popular than victim/offender reconciliation and in 2013 has been used in only 3 percent of all relevant cases (Statistisches Bundesamt 2014a, p. 26).

[26] Under present law, a 3-month suspension of the driving license is available only as a sanction for offenses committed in connection with driving a vehicle (§ 44 Penal Code).

the proposal becomes moot, and the trial continues. Even in case of a sentence promise, the court remains obliged to "seek the truth," for example, by trying to establish the truthfulness of the defendant's confession (§ 257c sec. 1, second sentence, Code of Criminal Procedure). But this obligation is of little practical relevance (for possible reforms of the practice, see Meyer [2015]).

It is reasonable to suppose that sentence bargaining has had some impact on overall sentencing outcomes. But it is far from clear what that impact might be and, in particular, whether bargained sentences are more lenient than those that would be handed down after a full trial.[27] German law does not provide for any formal reduction of the sentence in exchange for the defendant's confession; and since the presiding judge of the trial court tends to be the main negotiator and the prosecutor can veto any sentence proposal, it is not clear whether a defendant is well advised to agree in advance of trial to a sentence proposed by the court. It therefore remains a matter of speculation whether the lack of an overall increase in sentencing severity in the last few decades is partly a result of the spread of plea bargaining.

Another "hot" topic of recent years has been the reform of security detention (§ 66 Penal Code), a special measure for recidivists who are considered to be dangerous even after they have served their prison sentence. Detention of such persons can be ordered by the trial court and may theoretically last for life (§ 67d sec. 3) but needs to be reviewed every year (§ 67e sec. 2). After some tinkering on the relevant provision by the legislature, the European Court of Human Rights found the German law to be in violation of article 5 section 1 of the European Convention on Human Rights, and the German Constitutional Court then declared the law to be unconstitutional.[28]

The legislature subsequently passed a new version of the law, which emphasizes the difference between imprisonment and security detention and obliges administrators to provide the detainee with opportunities to demonstrate that he is no longer dangerous even when at large (§ 66c Penal Code). This debate has raised important questions of principle,

---

[27] For empirical studies of sentence bargaining in Germany, see Altenhain et al. (2007) and von Frankenberg (2013).

[28] The two cases are *M. v. Germany*, Judgment of 17 December 2009, no. 19359/04, and *Bundesverfassungsgericht*, Judgment of 4 May 2011, 128 Entscheidungen des Bundesverfassungsgerichts 326.

concerning, inter alia, the relationship between culpability, punishment, dangerousness, and prevention. It has also raised concern among the public because some men who had been certified as continually very dangerous had to be released as a consequence of the decisions of the highest courts. But the practical impact of all this on overall sentencing practice has been minimal: in 2013, security detention had been imposed on 32 defendants (Statistisches Bundesamt 2015, p. 368).

Other debates have centered on the introduction of new crimes and on raising maximum sentences for existing ones. Examples of recently enacted new offenses are stalking (§ 238 Penal Code, introduced in 2007), forced marriage (§ 237 Penal Code, introduced in 2011), and female sexual mutilation (§ 226a Penal Code, introduced in 2013). Sanctions have been enhanced for child and juvenile pornography, terrorism, and human trafficking.

Some of these measures were prompted by directives of the European Union. Others have been the result of debates on perceived gaps in the protection of values that are important to some interest groups of society. Most of these new measures have remained symbolic. The raising of maximum sentences tends to have very little impact on sentencing practice (which normally keeps close to the lower end of sentence ranges), and convictions for some of the new crimes are very rare.[29] Symbolic criminal laws nevertheless are inimical to an open, liberal society because they restrict individual freedom and open the door to arbitrary criminal prosecution.

IV. Conclusion

Prosecutorial and judicial practices in Germany so far have withstood the international trend toward greater punitiveness, and the German legislature has shown some restraint against the frequent calls for an expansion of the criminal law. On the whole, the German criminal justice system can be characterized as stable and comparatively liberal. The lack of activism especially in the area of sentencing may result more from bureaucratic inertia than from conscious policy decisions. But whatever the explanation, the development of German sentencing policy shows that no news can be good news.

---

[29] For example, in 2013 there were 230 convictions of stalking (§ 238), and one person was convicted of forced marriage (§ 237; Statistisches Bundesamt 2015, p. 102).

REFERENCES

Albrecht, Hans-Jörg. 1994. *Strafzumessung bei schwerer Kriminalität*. Berlin: Duncker & Humblot.

Altenhain, Karsten, Ina Hagemeier, Michael Heimerl, and Karl-Heinz Stammen. 2007. *Die Praxis der Absprachen in Wirtschaftsstrafverfahren*. Baden-Baden: Duncker & Humblot.

BKA (Bundeskriminalamt). 2001. *Polizeiliche Kriminalstatistik 2000*. Wiesbaden: Bundeskriminalamt.

Bundesministerium des Innern. 2014. *Polizeiliche Kriminalstatistik 2013*. Berlin: Bundesministerium des Innern.

Hörnle, Tatjana. 1999. *Tatproportionale Strafzumessung*. Berlin: Duncker & Humblot.

Hupfeld, Jörg. 1999. "Richter-und gerichtsbezogene Sanktionsdisparitäten in der deutschen Jugendstrafrechtspraxis." *Monatsschrift für Kriminologie und Strafrechtsreform* 82:342–58.

Kudlich, Hans. 2015. "Ecclestone, Verständigungsgesetz und die Folgen: Reformbedarf für § 153a StPO?" *Zeitschrift für Rechtspolitik* 48:10–13.

Langer, Wolfgang. 1994. *Staatsanwälte und Richter*. Stuttgart: Enke.

Maurer, Matthias. 2005. *Komparative Strafzumessung*. Berlin: Duncker & Humblot.

Meinberg, Volker. 1985. *Geringfügigkeitseinstellungen von Wirtschaftsstrafsachen*. Freiburg: Max Planck Institut.

Meyer, Frank. 2015. "Praxis und Reform der Absprache im Strafverfahren." *Strafverteidiger* 35:790–98.

Meyer-Goßner, Lutz, and Bertram Schmitt. 2015. *Strafprozessordnung mit GVG und Nebengesetzen*. 58th ed. Munich: Beck.

Miebach, Klaus. 2012. "Comments on § 46 Strafgesetzbuch." In *Münchener Kommentar zum Strafgesetzbuch*, 2nd ed., vol. 2, edited by Bernd Heintschel-Heinegg. Munich: Beck.

Oswald, Margit E. 1994. *Psychologie des richterlichen Strafens*. Stuttgart: Enke.

Rieß, Peter. 1983. "Entwicklung und Bedeutung der Einstellungen nach § 153a StPO." *Zeitschrift für Rechtspolitik* 17:93–99.

Roxin, Claus. 2006. *Strafrecht Allgemeiner Teil*. 4th ed. Munich: Beck.

Statistisches Bundesamt. 2001. *Rechtspflege: Strafverfolgung 2000 (Fachserie 10, Reihe 3)*. Wiesbaden: Metzler Poeschel.

———. 2003. *Rechtspflege: Gerichte und Staatsanwaltschaften 2001 (Fachserie 10 Reihe 2)*. Wiesbaden: Metzler Poeschel.

———. 2012. *Justizgeschäftsstatistik: Geschäftsentwicklung bei Gerichten und Staatsanwaltschaften seit 1995*. Wiesbaden: Metzler Poeschel.

———. 2014a. *Rechtspflege Staatsanwaltschaften 2013 (Fachserie 10 Reihe 2.6)*. Wiesbaden: Metzler Poeschel.

———. 2014b. *Rechtspflege Strafgerichte 2013 (Fachserie 10 Reihe 2.3)*. Wiesbaden: Metzler Poeschel.

———. 2015. *Rechtspflege Strafverfolgung 2013 (Fachserie 10 Reihe 3)*. Wiesbaden: Metzler Poeschel.

Streng, Franz. 2012. *Strafrechtliche Sanktionen*. 3rd ed. Stuttgart: Kohlhammer.
———. 2013. "Comments on § 46 Strafgesetzbuch." In *Nomos Kommentar Strafgesetzbuch*, 4th ed., vol. 1, edited by Urs Kindhäuser, Neumann Ulfrid, and Paeffgen Hans-Ullrich. Baden-Baden: Nomos.
Turner, Jenia I., and Thomas Weigend. 2014. "The Constitutionality of Negotiated Criminal Judgments in Germany." *German Law Journal* 15:81–105.
von Frankenberg, Kiyomi. 2013. *Grundlagen konsensualer Konfliktlösungsprozesse*. Berlin: wvb Wissenschaftlicher Verlag Berlin.
Weigend, Thomas. 2001. "Sentencing and Punishment in Germany." In *Sentencing and Sanctions in Western Countries*, edited by Michael Tonry and Richard S. Frase. Oxford: Oxford University Press.
———. 2008. "The Decay of the Inquisitorial Ideal: Plea Bargaining Invades German Criminal Procedure." In *Crime, Procedure and Evidence in a Comparative and International Context: Essays in Honour of Professor Mirjan Damaška*, edited by John Jackson, Máximo Langer, and Peter Tillers. Oxford: Hart.

Alessandro Corda

Sentencing and Penal Policies in Italy, 1985–2015: The Tale of a Troubled Country

ABSTRACT

Significant changes in Italian political, socioeconomic, and institutional contexts since 1985 have led to markedly harsher policies and laws. Sentencing law and penal policies have changed substantially. In the late 1980s, the legislature embraced rehabilitation in corrections and enacted a new Code of Criminal Procedure modeled on principles and values typical of adversarial legal systems. The demise in the early 1990s of the so-called First Republic due to the massive bribery scandal known as *Mani Pulite* ("Clean Hands") profoundly affected the structure and functioning of the political system, perceptions of crime, and shaping of penal policies. Despite stable and declining crime rates, over time governments have enacted policies overrelying on criminal sanctions. Particular categories of offenders, undocumented immigrants and drug offenders, have been hit especially hard. Rapidly growing imprisonment rates produced overcrowding that was tackled mostly with alternatives to implementation of custodial sentences and pretrial detention. Persisting signs of punitive moderation for the most part are attributable to the inherent inefficiency of the criminal justice system, the "disintegration" of punishment at different stages of the process, and realpolitik policies adopted to address supranational concerns.

"All happy families resemble one another, each unhappy family is unhappy in its own way." The opening words of Tolstoy's *Anna Karenina*

Electronically published July 7, 2016

Alessandro Corda is postdoctoral research fellow in Comparative and Cross-National Justice System Studies, University of Minnesota Law School. He is grateful to Michael Tonry and Rossella Selmini for comments on an earlier draft of this essay.

vividly capture the current situation of the Italian criminal justice system after nearly three decades of substantial changes. In the second half of the 1980s, Italy embarked on a seemingly never-ending series of changes that oscillated between emphasis on rehabilitation and reintegration of ex-offenders and adoption of increasingly punitive policies.

Between 1985 and 1990 the Italian Parliament passed important pieces of legislation to put an end to domestic political terrorism and fight more effectively against organized crime. In the same period, the legislature endorsed rehabilitation in corrections, redesigning rules to reward inmates' good behavior with an array of early release schemes. In 1989, 1 year after enactment in 1988, a new Code of Criminal Procedure inspired by and modeled on due process principles typical of adversarial legal systems came into force, in stark contrast with a long-standing inquisitorial tradition. Enactment of collective clemency measures in 1986 and 1990 reinforced the image of a period of penal moderation.[1]

During the early 1990s, the collapse of the "First Republic" transformed the structure and functioning of the Italian political system but also perceptions of crime and the shaping of penal policies. The transition to the "Second Republic" witnessed an increasing politicization of penal institutions and criminal justice actors. The most visible result was a transformation of the traditionally moderate Italian penal culture into a more punitive one, especially with regard to some categories of offenders.

Italy's postwar political system was not a paradigmatic instance of consensus-based—or consociational—democracy in which destabilizing effects of cultural segmentation and social cleavage are neutralized by cooperative mechanisms like coalition governments and corporatist political traditions (Lijphart 1969, 1999). Rather, in Italy, "adversarial electoral competition and polarized pluralism went together with patterns of elite collusion that were largely hidden from view" (Bogaards 2005, p. 516). Italy therefore represented a peculiar case of consensus democracy: in a climate of Cold War ideological polarization, the Christian Democratic Party (DC) dominated the government from 1948 through the early 1990s with strong opposition from the largest Communist party

---

[1] Although I focus here on the adult system, it is important to note that in 1988 the Parliament enacted a substantial reform of the Italian juvenile justice system that emphasizes a marked preference for diversion mechanisms, with custodial sentences as a last resort (Gatti and Verde 2002; Scalia 2005; Nelken 2006).

(PCI) in the Western world.[2] However, systemic elite cooperation in all levels of government and society was regarded as necessary to help the system function and the country flourish. This arrangement bore high costs such as pervasive clientelism and excessive power of political parties in all aspects but also throughout all strata and sectors of society and economy. This phenomenon became known as "rule by parties," or "particracy" (*partitocrazia*). The parties that contributed to drafting, and were committed to, the Constitution took control of almost every institution and powerful position; they became the system (Guzzini 1995). The lack of alternation in power, insufficient turnover of the political class, and "crystallization of relationships between members of government and interest groups" led in the long run to systemic corruption (Mershon and Pasquino 1995, p. 48). Beginning in the late 1960s, corruption "lost its elite character" and became commonplace at any level of society. Paoli (2001, p. 165) offers an effective summary:

> First, kickbacks were paid by the *suppliers* of goods and services to the government.... Companies paid off officials at different stages of the bidding process in order to be included in the list of qualified bidders, to be selected as the winning contractor, to get an inflated price for the job, or to be able to cut corners on quality. In some cases, long-term agreements were reached between companies and the representatives of political parties to manipulate bids and keep potential competitors from winning access to the market. At the same time, kickbacks were also paid by the *demanders* of political favors or subsidies. Licenses, authorizations, credits, tax reductions, and state enterprises about to be sold became the object of bribery. Third, kickbacks were routinely paid by those who could be called *avoiders*, i.e., individuals and firms seeking to escape taxes or to get a favorable interpretation of the law. Many examples could be quoted to illustrate these two types of corruption, ranging from petty bribes to obtain a passport, a driver's license, or a cemetery plot to billion-lira kickbacks to avoid taxes or sanctions. In particular, illegal payments to *Guardia di Finanza* officials in charge of revising companies' tax declarations became very frequent and systematic in the 1980s.

[2] The DC and the PCI (together controlling almost 70 percent of the votes) often found themselves in electoral dead heats, but no real alternation in power took place between 1948 and 1994. Italy experienced a period of "blocked democracy," with the Christian Democrats being the cornerstone of every government.

Beginning in 1992, the "Clean Hands" (*Mani Pulite*) investigations (also commonly known as *Tangentopoli*, literally Bribeville) conducted by Milan magistrates attacked the First Republic's systemic bribery and illegal funding of the major political parties (Della Porta 1996; Nelken 1996; Rhodes 1997, 2015). The scandal detonated with unprecedented effect and resulted in the disappearance of all the main parties, in particular the Christian Democrats and the Socialists. Meanwhile the fall of the Berlin Wall resulted in dissolution of the Communist Party in 1991 (Sassoon 1995; Mack 2010, pp. 251–56). Popular referendums in 1991 and 1993 led to reform of the electoral law: a long-lived proportional representation voting system was replaced with a largely majoritarian winner-take-all system (Donovan 1996). These events completely reshaped the political landscape. The general elections of 1994—the first of the Second Republic—led to formation of two new party coalitions, the center-left and the center-right, that dominated Italian politics for almost two decades (Waters 1994; Carter 1998; Fabbrini 2009, pp. 35–36).

The collapse of the First Republic left a profound popular distrust of political parties, including their ability to respond to crime. The Clean Hands investigations did not trigger a moral regeneration of the Italian party system (Della Porta and Vannucci 2007). It had "a short-term impact on corruption" and led to "an escalation of institutional tensions between political powers—especially the coalition headed by Silvio Berlusconi—and the judiciary." Its legacy has been "a deep-rooted pessimism concerning the integrity of political and economic elites" (Vannucci 2009, p. 258).

Such a widespread lack of legitimacy undermined previous perceptions of a strong state able to show penal moderation (Whitman 2003, p. 143). This, and the effects of an economic downturn and increased immigration from non-EU countries in the early 1990s, favored the rise of attitudes that were "more rigid towards deviance, more punitive and favorably disposed towards 'law and order' campaigns" (De Giorgi 2006, p. 37), especially with respect to offenders regarded as social outsiders (Melossi 2000, 2013). The discourse on crime and penal policy reached a level of politicization never before experienced in Italy.

Explicit law-and-order campaigns were not prominent until the early 2000s, but the new and unstable party coalitions soon embraced this new public sentiment. Right-wing political entrepreneurs had an easy target (Tarchi 2002; Fella and Ruzza 2013). The center-left coalitions were unable to offer compelling alternative narratives and often accepted right-wing proposals for fear of losing elections by appearing soft on crime. Despite stable or dropping crime rates in recent years, "tough on crime" slogans have become deeply embedded: the promise of being harsh with street criminals, drug and sex offenders, and undocumented immigrants became familiar at national and local levels.

In earlier times, use of clemency measures was a recurring, deeply rooted feature of the Italian criminal justice system. Repudiation of that tradition and the enactment, especially after the 2001 general elections, of stiffer penalties targeting specific offenders led to rapid growth of imprisonment and overrepresentation in prisons of undocumented immigrants, street criminals, and drug offenders.

The Italian prison population grew steadily after 1990, recently declining only in reaction to critical judgments of the European Court of Human Rights. The population of 39,594 at year-end 1985 fell as a result of an amnesty for nonfinancial offenses punishable by up to 4 years and a collective pardon up to 2 years. As figure 1 shows, after another amnesty and collective pardon in 1990, there were 24,844 prisoners

FIG. 1.—Imprisonment rates at year-end per 100,000 of the general population, 1985–2015. Source: ISTAT and Ministry of Justice (multiple years).

at year-end and an imprisonment rate of 43.8 per 100,000 inhabitants. Things changed quickly: 3 years later there were 50,348 prisoners, the highest figure since the early 1950s. Since the late 1990s, the trend has been upward with one major break represented by a highly contested 2006 collective pardon. In 2005, for the first time Italy had an imprisonment rate above 100 (102.5). The threshold of 60,000 inmates was passed in 2009 (64,791). The all-time high was 114.5 per 100,000 at year-end 2010 (67,961).

Over the past 5 years, the upward trend reversed because of European Court of Human Rights judgments that in 2009 and 2013 declared conditions in Italian prisons to be degrading and inhuman by reason of overcrowding. To preempt additional lawsuits, the government enacted laws to reduce inmate numbers and prevent recurrence of similar future situations.

The new laws boosted existing schemes of early release and administration of custodial sentences outside prison and curbed overreliance on pretrial detention. In addition, the Constitutional Court in early 2014 struck down a 2006 law that eliminated distinctions in sentencing between soft and hard drugs and introduced stiff penalties for possession. As a result, the inmate population of 53,623 in 2014, after 5 consecutive years above 60,000, was at a level comparable to that of the mid-1990s and early 2000s. The imprisonment rate fell below 100 per 100,000 (88.2) compared with a 2013 Council of Europe member state average of 140 (Aebi and Delgrande 2015) and an EU member state average of 128.2. Italy had the lowest rate in southern Europe (Spain, 139; Portugal, 138; Greece, 111; and France, 100; World Prison Brief 2015). The most recent figures confirm the downward trend: at year-end 2015, the rate was 85.3 per 100,000 (52,164 inmates).

Compared with common law jurisdictions, the Italian penal system defies the traditional categorization between civil law and common law countries. Among the most salient features:

Hybrid Criminal Proceedings. Since enactment of the 1989 Code of Criminal Procedure, the Italian criminal process has been characterized by core traits of inquisitorial civil law jurisdictions and selected borrowings from common law adversarial systems. No other civil law country has undertaken so massive a transplant of adversarial system principles and rules. Italy broadened the rights of defendants and in various ways increased the state's burden to obtain a conviction. However, inconsistencies and structural ambiguities persist.

Multiple Appeals. Unlike common law jurisdictions, in which appeals focus on legal errors, both defendants and prosecutors may request a new trial on the facts before a court of appeals. Following the appellate trial, decisions may be reviewed solely on matters of law by the Court of Cassation, the court of last resort. It may confirm or nullify the court of appeals' judgment; it may also nullify the verdict and order either a new trial or resentencing before a different court of appeals, which must apply the Court of Cassation's interpretation of the contested legal issues.

Statutes of Limitations. Statutes of limitations run even after formal charges are filed, with the exception of offenses punishable with life sentences. For all other offenses the statute of limitations expires when the passage of time since the commission of the crime equals the maximum penalty provided for by law, even when a criminal proceeding is ongoing.[3] In 2004–13, a total of 1,552,435 cases were dropped because of statutes of limitations (Ministry of Justice 2015*b*).

Mandatory Prosecution. Article 112 of the Italian Constitution obligates the prosecutor to file charges whenever there is sufficient evidence to prosecute. Known as the principle of mandatory prosecution, or the legality principle, it signifies that prosecuting authorities have no power to choose whether to bring criminal charges or what charges to bring.

Independence of the Judiciary. The 1948 Constitution, enacted after the dark times of the fascist dictatorship, placed both judges and prosecutors within the judiciary, in order to insulate them from political pressures, promote impartiality, and assure the equality of all citizens before the law. For decades members of the judiciary were part of the culture of systemic elite collusion, but both prosecutors and judges have gradually become less sensitive to political expectations and have begun to perceive themselves as charged with a civic responsibility toward society at large. Since the 1970s, the fights against political terrorism, organized crime, and systemic corruption have shaped the new role of the judiciary, whose members have become engaged and vocal concerning criminal justice policy. While in the United States concern is expressed about politicization of the criminal justice system, Italian commentators often criticize the excessive activism of members of the judiciary.

---

[3] In any case, it cannot be less than 6 years for felonies and 4 years for misdemeanors. Some specific events may partly prolong the deadline (see arts. 157–161 of the Penal Code).

This essay recounts the evolution of Italian sentencing policies and practices over the past three decades, describing in particular the path that since the early 1990s led to the abandonment of practices and conventions that characterized the criminal justice system for most of the twentieth century, namely, an inquisitorial system, comparatively low imprisonment rates, recurring use of clemency measures, and relatively low politicization of policies and institutions.

The transition from the First to the Second Republic was characterized by a decisive trend toward increased punitiveness in public discourse and legislation. Both center-right and center-left governments have been unable to promote and enact comprehensive reforms aimed at achieving an enlightened Beccarian system of punishment predicated on promptness and moderation. Instead they have reacted to and sometimes fed emotional demands of the public, often based on notorious crimes and more or less justified alarms, fears, and scandals. The response has usually been more punishment. Most responses were mainly symbolic, aimed at public reassurance, but some hit selected targets harder. The growth of the incarceration rate has been the most visible outcome of this change.

Two major factors contributed to resisting increased punitiveness and functioned as forces of moderation. The first involves the structure of the judiciary: despite the principle of mandatory prosecution, prosecutors routinely filter public fear and emotions in exercising their powers and prerogatives; judges possess significant power to reduce the potential overharshness of penal statutes when determining sentences. Second, the inefficiency of the criminal justice system makes it unable to meet the demands of increasing caseloads. Put differently, inadequate resources significantly undermine implementation of legal changes designed to send more people to prison, and for longer. Recent emergency overcrowding legislation, although it provided substantial relief to the penitentiary system, did not create much-needed bipartisan momentum toward criminal justice and sentencing reform. Italian penal policies and practices can be described as a congeries of contradictions, mixing elements of undue severity, symbolic penal welfarism, and "deflation mechanisms" in order to manage heavy caseloads.

The essay proceeds as follows: Section I provides an overview of the Italian sentencing process, focusing on its hybrid nature between inquisitorial and adversarial systems; I analyze the roles, functions, and organizational cultures of prosecutors, police, and courts. Section II focuses on authorized sanctions and sentencing patterns. In Section III, I describe and discuss major policy changes since the mid-1980s. Finally, in Section IV, I reflect on the main findings and suggest future directions.

I. The Criminal Process

In October 1989, the new Code of Criminal Procedure (CCP) came into force, completely reshaping the machinery of Italian criminal justice. The new code abandoned features of the inquisitorial civil law tradition that had characterized criminal proceedings for more than a century. From a comparative perspective, the new CCP represented "the most serious attempt to transfer adversarial criminal procedures into an inquisitorial jurisdiction since 1791, when the French attempted to import the English system during the heat of the Revolution" (Langer 2004, p. 47). This shift radically transformed the institutional infrastructure and internal dynamics of the criminal justice system.

A. The Prosecutor

The Italian public prosecutor enjoys a distinctive status among Western jurisdictions. Quintessential features of the civil law tradition such as effective hierarchical organization, strong top-down guidelines, and internal controls (Damaška 1986, pp. 19–23) are gone. However, prosecutors retain the status of judicial figures. They are part of the same professional category as pretrial, trial, and appellate judges (the word "magistrate" is commonly used to refer to both judges and prosecutors). Members of the judicial profession are characterized by a strong sense of solidarity; usually they refer to one another as "colleagues." Like judges, prosecutors are neither appointed nor elected; they are career civil servants chosen on the basis of the results of a public examination typically taken a few years after finishing law school. Prosecutors may switch roles and become judges (and vice versa) upon request with only minimal requirements to satisfy. Judges and prosecutors have the same salary structure, receive the same salary increases, and have equivalent career advancement opportunities (Grande 2000, p. 236). Prosecutors and judges see themselves as branches of one professional body and are widely regarded as very effective in promoting and lobbying for the interests of their professional association. This has been criticized as inspired by a "corporatist logic" insofar as it sometimes prioritizes professional interests over achievement of law reform goals (Alberti 1996, p. 285).

1. *The Prosecutor's Independence.*   Italian prosecutors have very strong external independence, that is, independence from external political pressures. In this regard, the prosecutor's role was radically transformed over time. From Italy's unification in 1861 until the end of World War II, the prosecutor represented the executive branch of government within the judiciary, operating under the direction of the Ministry of Justice. With the enactment of the post–fascist period Constitution, the prosecutor was located within the judiciary and vested by the legality principle with the duty to file charges whenever sufficient evidence exists to prosecute a case. The only significant outside control pertains to the disciplinary power of the Ministry of Justice (shared with the chief prosecutor of the Cassation Court) to bring action for possible misconduct. However, the merits of these actions and possible sanctions (ranging from censure to dismissal) are decided by the High Council for the Judiciary (HCJ), the "self-governing body" of the judiciary established in 1958 and two-thirds composed of judges and prosecutors elected by their peers.[4] Thus, even within this body, members of the judiciary exercise significant power. The High Council's constitutional mandate, besides deciding on disciplinary measures, is to ensure the autonomy and independence of the judiciary. It also decides on magistrates' assignments, transfers, and career advancement.

Prosecutors and judges are institutionally insulated from political pressure, but they are not immune from politics. First, members of the judiciary are organized in factions defined by more or less progressive values that play a critical role in determining elections to the High Council (Guarnieri 1994, pp. 251–53; 2015, p. 122). Second, relations between the judiciary and the political system were historically strong at least until the 1970s because of the collusion between elite classes that long characterized the Italian political system (Alberti 1996, pp. 285–86; Della Porta 2001, p. 4). This situation has changed greatly since then.

Evolution in understanding of their role led prosecutors to adopt a more visible judicial activism in the 1970s, particularly in their fights against environmental crimes, political terrorism, and organized crime (Sberna and Vannucci 2013, p. 582). In the early 1990s, the massive brib-

---

[4] The HCJ is currently made up of 27 members: the president of the republic, the first chief judge of the Court of Cassation, the chief prosecutor of the Court of Cassation, eight members appointed by Parliament (so-called lay members), and 16 judges and prosecutors elected by their colleagues.

ery scandal known as *Mani Pulite* (Clean Hands) strengthened the credibility and autonomy of the judiciary, especially prosecutors, who came to be perceived by large strata of the public as the only upright and trustworthy component of government. Critics have argued that the judiciary attempted to fill the void left by politics by "actively seek[ing] the support of the public opinion," prioritizing "civic involvement over institutional neutrality" (Della Porta 2001, p. 18).

In any case, the enduring legacy of that period and the fall of the First Republic has been an ongoing tension between the judiciary—prosecutors in particular—and the political system (Guarnieri and Pederzoli 1997). Starting in the mid-1990s, particularly under center-right coalition governments, the legislature and the executive have repeatedly attacked the legitimacy of judicial action and attempted by statute to curb prosecutors' institutional independence and investigative powers. The recurring refrain is of a threat of the "rule of judges" over the rule of law (Bruti Liberati, Ceretti, and Giasanti 1996; Gallo 2014). For years, Silvio Berlusconi, leader of the center-right coalition and several times prime minister, has claimed to be the victim of a "crusade" by left-wing prosecutors and judges (*New York Times* 2011).

Italian prosecutors also possess remarkable internal independence. In carrying out their duties and functions, they are not obliged to comply with guidelines, orders, or instructions from a supervisor (Alberti 1996, pp. 284–85; Nelken 2013, p. 244). Even within the offices where they work, prosecutors enjoy vast autonomy despite the formal hierarchical structure. Substantive professional evaluations of prosecutorial activity are considered per se to be "a threat to judicial independence." Accordingly, except in cases of patent and serious violations of their duties, the HCJ exercises strong self-restraint in assessing prosecutors' performance. The supervisory powers of the heads of prosecutors' offices are very limited and are closely monitored by the HCJ to prevent the establishment of top-down organizational culture that might limit the operational independence of individual prosecutors; this is a professional feature that is to be "protected and encouraged" (Di Federico 2008, p. 308). Critics have argued that so much independence, coupled with the legality principle, leads de facto to a system of discretionary prosecution in which unaccountable individuals shape penal policies (Di Federico 1998).

   2. *The Prosecutor's Role in the Proceedings.* The constitutional redesign of the prosecutor's role was intended to shield him or her from undue

political pressures and promote independent exercise of his powers. In drafting the new CCP, the legislature sought to structure a system of criminal proceedings grounded in adversarial principles and rules, focusing on the impartiality of the decision maker and parity of arms between the contending sides. Nonetheless, the institutional closeness between judges and prosecutors was left untouched. The fact that the adversarial changes in criminal procedure were not matched by reform of the judiciary created ambiguity as to whether prosecutors should be considered parties to the proceedings or impartial figures "helping the judge" in truth-finding.

The tension is between the prosecutor's "inquisitorial quasi-judicial status" and his or her functions as the accuser in a largely adversarial process (Panzavolta 2005, pp. 606–7; Montana 2012, p. 102). One major ongoing debate concerning the judiciary, not surprisingly, revolves around the need to better delineate the prosecutor's role in a system that has embraced core values of adversarial proceedings. Some advocate a clear separation of career paths of prosecutors and judges that would create two separate tracks in recruitment, career advancement, and disciplinary systems. Others support a separation of functions that would make it much more difficult for a prosecutor to become a judge, and vice versa, by introducing an additional examination and specifying a time window within which final decisions must be made about career paths within the judiciary (Amodio 2004, p. 499).

Legal provisions and their interpretations are not much help in specifying the "inner identity" of the prosecutor. While some provisions imply a truth-seeking function, others suggest a figure no longer responsible for collecting exculpatory evidence and required only to build a strong case and win in court. Scholars have not been reluctant to criticize. Grande (2000), for instance, rhetorically asks whether the prosecutor—independent from the executive, free from substantial hierarchical guidance and control, and in charge of the investigation phase—should be seen as a fourth branch of government alongside the legislative, executive, and judicial branches. She describes a structural identity crisis of a modern Minotaur, at the same time a "lawyer without passion, a judge without impartiality" (pp. 234–35; quoting Calamandrei [1936] 1942, p. 20).

Semistructured qualitative studies have attempted to capture and portray the prosecutors' self-perception and defense attorneys' perceptions of them. Prosecutors see themselves first and foremost as members of the judiciary, functionally different from yet culturally equivalent to judges (Montana and Nelken 2011, p. 290; Montana 2012, p. 111). They perceive themselves as a player within the criminal process "who performs a neutral and impartial investigation to find the truth"; prosecutors acknowledge their cultural distance from common law prosecutors who they believe exclusively work to obtain convictions (Montana 2009*b*, p. 489). Unlike county attorneys in the United States who are often elected on a pledge to fight crime, Italian prosecutors do not have to launch crusades against crime or carry out anyone's agenda. They take a bureaucratic approach to decision making. As members of the judiciary independent from the executive, they need not convey messages but instead can "filter" social emotions and collective fears through an institutional framework insulated from the political level. "Italian prosecutors accept that one of their functions is to provide a response to public fear," but at the same time they translate the public's meaning and understanding of social alarm "using a dictionary that depends on their own legal culture" (p. 487). Accordingly, prosecutors "convert" the amorphous and highly emotional notion of social alarm into more objective and verifiable criteria such as the seriousness of the offense and the risk that a statute of limitation will expire.

From the defense attorneys' perspective, the quasi-judicial role of the prosecutor is a source of major concern. In a recent survey, prosecutors were described as exercising broad discretion while enjoying ready acquiescence from the judges to their requests and motions. That proximity to the decision maker was described as associated not only with shared constitutional standing and common training but also with the final goal—to establish substantive rather than merely evidentiary guilt or innocence. Defense attorneys described, and rued, what in their view are cooperative dynamics in the interplay between prosecutors and judges (Di Federico and Sapignoli 2014).

3. *The Relationship of the Prosecutor with the Police.* Today's Italian criminal justice system substantially differs from common law systems in which police officers handle investigations with almost complete autonomy (Harris 2012, p. 56). Before 1989, things in Italy were not so different. The police had almost unfettered discretion, which was viewed as potentially subject to interference of the executive branch (Goldstein and Marcus 1977, pp. 258–59). Furthermore, the legality principle underlying mandatory prosecution could be undermined by the police (Caianiello 2012, pp. 257–58). One main goal of the new CCP was to

involve the prosecutor as soon as possible after a crime was reported. The new rules were a long-overdue implementation of article 109 of the Constitution providing that "the judicial authority directly disposes of the judicial police."

No special police forces were created; instead the police were made subject to prosecutorial oversight during the investigation stage (Fassler 1991, pp. 252–53). The judicial police remain part of the executive and belong to its hierarchical structure but are subject to direction and supervision by the prosecutor (Illuminati 2004, p. 308). Thus the Italian system draws a clear line between crime prevention and law enforcement, and crime repression by investigative assistance to the prosecutor (Caianiello 2012, p. 258). The police "without delay" must inform the prosecutor that a crime is alleged to have occurred (*notitia criminis*). In the meantime, the police at its own initiative may act to ensure that the offense does not produce further consequences, preserve sources of evidence, and gather information that might prove relevant to the prosecution. After the prosecutor takes control, the police should carry out only activities that have been ordered or delegated.

This framework promotes joint and cooperative efforts. The creation of police units linked to, and located in, the prosecutor's offices has been meant to overcome mutual distrust and potential clashes arising from different professional cultures, backgrounds, and institutional aims.

In practice, prosecutors do not and cannot direct every investigation in detail. When misdemeanors and simple felony cases are not prioritized, prosecutors provide very limited supervision and the investigation is conducted almost entirely by the police. The police set the agenda, and the prosecutor is involved only when authorizations are required or acts must be validated (e.g., searches and seizures). During investigations of this type, interactions are not much different from those in common law jurisdictions (Illuminati and Caianiello 2007, pp. 133–34; Montana 2009*a*, p. 318). When a case is prioritized, the prosecutor prompts, directs, and reviews investigative activities. He or she is in charge formally and practically (p. 325).

4. *Prosecutorial Discretion.* Prosecutorial discretion remains highly debated and has been since at least the late 1980s, when a few chief prosecutors issued informal guidelines to manage backlogs. They represented a shift toward more proactive, managerial, and efficiency-oriented approaches, in contrast with the "fatalistic" attitude about case flow that characterized most offices (Nelken 2013, pp. 250–51). Initially, the guidelines were intended solely for internal purposes.

When a few offices became more open about adoption of criteria that rejected the "first-come, first-served rule" implied by the principle of mandatory prosecution, the HCJ initially reacted skeptically. By the late 1990s, it acknowledged the practical impossibility of timely investigation of every reported crime and the need to elaborate criteria. The HCJ stressed that priorities should not be products of discretionary choices made by single prosecutors for they lack authority to decide whether or not to investigate a given case. The priority criteria should primarily be based on the magnitude of the social harm caused by the crime. A new statute provided guidance in establishing priority criteria including the seriousness of the offense, the harm caused, the potential prejudice of delayed investigations, and the need to vindicate the interest of the victim. The statute required each prosecutor's office to notify the HCJ of any guidelines issued (art. 227 of the Legislative Decree no. 51 of 1998; Torrente 2007, pp. 244–45).

Efficiency-based criteria have also been adopted. One notable example, issued by the Turin chief prosecutor following the 2006 collective pardon, required prosecutors to put on a "dead track" cases for which the likely sentence would have been fully or mostly covered, hence substantially nullified, by application of the pardon (Maddalena 2007). More recently, in 2014, in light of persisting backlogs and understaffed courts, the Rome chief prosecutor capped the charges his deputies can file every year for crimes that are not classified as "serious" (*Corriere della Sera* 2014). The adoption of guidelines has become increasingly popular (Verzelloni 2014) and is widely supported by legal scholars (Caianiello 2012, pp. 260–61).

An influential judge has noted two main risks. The first is localism: priority criteria should be adopted by the office of the public prosecutor at the district court of appeals level rather than by individual offices of the public prosecutor at the trial level to avoid emergence of patchworks of different practices within the same judicial district. Second, drafters of priority criteria should reject the temptation to shape penal policies. Guidelines should be based on objective considerations—principally the seriousness of the offense—and take account of the number of cases that can be properly handled with available human and financial resources (personal communication with Giovanni Canzio [then Milan Court of Appeals president, now first president of the Cassation Court], July 2, 2015).

5. *Diversion Tools.* Two noteworthy new laws aim at substantially reducing the number of cases being tried by means of prosecutorial di-

version. Law no. 67 of 2014 introduced in the adult system a form of deferred adjudication largely based on a similar juvenile justice proceeding. The defendant is placed on probation (community service) for a fixed period; if probation is successfully completed, the case is dismissed. The special proceeding must be requested by the defendant before the trial and is applicable only to offenses carrying a maximum penalty up to 4 years of imprisonment and to a few specified offenses. Deferred adjudication may not be granted more than once.

The second form of prosecutorial diversion was introduced by Law no. 28 of 2015. It provides for a new reason for dismissal: the charge is not simply dropped, but the offender is legally shielded from punishment when the harm caused by an offense punishable by fine only or imprisonment up to 5 years is "particularly low" and the perpetrator is not a "habitual offender." The request is made by the prosecutor to the preliminary investigation judge or the trial judge; the victim may oppose the dismissal. This special order becomes part of the offender's criminal record, thereby preventing further applications of the same measure if a pattern of habitual recidivism is established.

B. Establishment of a Hybrid System

Although adversarial and inquisitorial models are ideal types that are rarely found in pure versions in real-life legal systems (Langer 2014), the Italian system borrows from both in a way that makes the main goal being pursued unclear and leads to practical inefficiencies. The Italian system is thus "caught between two traditions," and significant legal and cultural resistance toward adversarial principles persists to this day (Pizzi and Marafioti 1992, p. 3; Marafioti 2008).

There are at least four persisting factors of hybridization. First, the new CCP has not clearly redesigned the role of the prosecutor. It is not easy to say whether the prosecutor is an adversary party or a quasi-judicial actor. In practice, the prosecutor commonly behaves as a non-partisan actor who helps the judge establish the truth.

Second, the trial judge retains significant powers that are widely used in the evidence formation process: the judge is seldom reluctant to take over a party's examination or cross-examination. He or she may introduce evidence (e.g., a court-appointed expert witness). While US federal judges tend to act as impartial adjudicator-referees, the activism of Italian trial judges reflects a persisting inquisitorial approach (Pizzi and Montagna 2004, p. 465). Rather than act as a neutral umpire, the judge plays a role that expresses the system's implicit primary concern: to ascertain truth and do justice.

Third, in contrast to the adversarial model, the victim reports the crime and serves as a witness but may also bring a civil claim for damages in the criminal trial (the *partie civile* as in the French system). If the victim brings a civil action, he or she participates as an additional party throughout the process. During the investigation the victim can request access to the case file and ask for additional investigation, present evidence and witnesses at trial, and appeal an acquittal and parts of the judgment related to monetary compensation.

Fourth, the reformed Italian system retained broad appellate review on matters of both fact and law: in adversarial criminal law systems a new trial for the same crime violates double jeopardy protection; only rarely are factual decisions reconsidered on their merits. Under Italian law, a ruling is not final until appeal rights are exhausted and double jeopardy protection does not apply to what is viewed as a continuation of the same trial. This represents a further inconsistency: the vertical protection of appellate review of facts has historically characterized inquisitorial systems, which do not afford defendants horizontal protections such as rights to confrontation and cross-examination. The prosecutor may appeal an acquittal; in adversarial systems a not guilty verdict ends the case.[5] This difference was a major source of American consternation concerning Amanda Knox, an American exchange student accused of murdering her British roommate in Italy in 2007, particularly when the Court of Cassation ordered a new trial after she was acquitted by an appeals court following a conviction at trial (Mirabella 2012, p. 253).

C. *The Process*

For four decades after adoption of the 1948 Constitution, the Italian criminal process was dominated by rules set out in 1930 by the fascist regime. Over time the Constitutional Court and the legislature softened provisions that limited the rights of the accused during the investigation and at trial. Overall the system retained a structure based heavily on the

---

[5] Law no. 46 of February 20, 2006, abolished prosecutorial appeals of acquittals delivered by a trial court. The Constitutional Court struck it down because it created undue inequalities between the defense and the prosecutor, disadvantaging the latter.

1808 French Code d'Instruction Criminelle. It provided for a mixed system: a secret investigation followed by a public trial, with the former manifestly dominating the latter (Illuminati 2010, pp. 303–7). Likewise, under the Italian Code of 1930, the criminal process was divided into the pretrial investigation (*istruzione*) and the trial (*dibattimento*). The pretrial phase was dominated by an investigating judge modeled on the French *juge d'instruction*. On paper a public prosecutor worked side by side with the investigating judge but in practice had little power and few substantive functions (Amodio and Selvaggi 1989, p. 1214; Marafioti 2008, pp. 81–82).

The prosecutor began the proceeding, but the investigating judge collected the evidence. The investigating judge was the real "case manager." He or she was the major player, charged to obtain all relevant information for deciding whether to prosecute. The prosecutor was auxiliary (Panzavolta 2005, p. 579). The criminal proceeding was based on a "single dossier": the collected evidence and documentation of investigative activities. The judge who conducted the investigation decided whether the case would be sent to trial. In case of indictment, the dossier migrated into the case file of the trial judge.

A public trial was held but represented "a mere formality" (Illuminati 2005, p. 570): the defense lawyer could call witnesses but could neither examine them nor cross-examine prosecution witnesses. The trial judge instead asked questions suggested by the parties or on his or her own initiative. The public trial often merely reiterated investigative activities by reading minutes documenting them. Witnesses interviewed in the earlier stage merely confirmed what they had then said before the trial judge. The dossier and supporting material thus constituted the basis for the prosecution, the verdict, and the sentence (Pizzi and Marafioti 1992, p. 4). In practice a continuum existed, with the investigation phase and the investigating judge performing the truth-seeking crucial for the final outcome.

The 1989 CCP, rooted in symbolic and practical considerations, departed from the past: the criminal proceeding was divided into three stages and strictly separated the trial from the preliminary investigation. The Parliament wanted the criminal justice system to reflect the modernization and democratization of state institutions, breaking any links with an earlier system shaped under the authoritarian fascist regime. The principles of orality and immediacy were embraced with evidence being presented and tested before the trial judge. The single dossier system was rejected. These are the three stages of criminal proceedings:

- the *preliminary investigation*, in which the prosecutor, helped by the judicial police, and under the supervision of a neutral pretrial investigation judge, collects evidence in order to decide whether to prosecute;
- the *pretrial hearing*, in which a judge not previously involved determines whether charges should be brought on the basis of evidence that probable cause exists to believe a crime was committed and the accused committed it;
- the *trial*, in which the prosecutor and the defendant have equal opportunities to present their cases before a trial judge principally charged to ensure observation of the rules of due process.

The 1989 changes sought greater efficiency, thus attempting in part to address persisting backlogs of cases. The goal was to limit the full adversarial trial to about 20 percent of cases while handling the rest by means of newly created "special proceedings" that gave defendants significant sentence reductions for waiving their rights to trial. The aim was to hold full trials only for the most serious cases while providing "fast-track procedures" for cases in which inculpatory evidence was clear (Pizzi and Marafioti 1992, pp. 6, 16ff.; Grande 2000, pp. 252–53).

1. *The "Penalty upon Request of the Parties."* This is a form of sentence bargaining. If the parties agree on the merits and on the sentence before trial, they may request the judge to review and accept their agreement. This is available for a penalty up to 5 years of imprisonment including a discount of up to one-third (Maffei 2004, pp. 1061ff.). The code does not identify eligible offenses but effectively excludes crimes with sentencing ranges that do not authorize a custodial penalty within the 5-year limit (e.g., the sentencing range for murder is 21 years to life).

2. *The "Summary Trial" Proceeding.* This eliminates the adversarial trial by providing a significant sentence discount (up to one-third of what would be imposed at trial or 30 years in case of a life sentence) in exchange for enabling the pretrial hearing judge or the trial judge to resolve the case on the basis of information collected during the pretrial investigation.

3. *The "Penal Decree."*   In misdemeanor cases punishable with a fine only (in the first place or as a substitute for short custodial sentences up to 6 months), this proceeding allows early imposition of the sentence by the judge supervising the investigation upon request of the prosecutor. The main benefit for the defendant is the reduction of the sentence up to half of the statutory minimum. Such a decree may be opposed by a petition to the trial court, in which case a full adversarial trial is held unless the defendant opts for one of the available special proceedings.

Two additional special proceedings provided for by the new CCP do not reward the defendant but speed the process. The pretrial hearing can be eliminated when the merits of the decision to prosecute are clear (the "immediate trial" procedure) or when the accused was caught in commission of a crime and lawfully arrested or has confessed (the "direct trial" procedure).

Thus, the Italian criminal process resulting from the 1989 changes retained the principle of mandatory prosecution (the abandonment of which would have required an amendment to the Constitution) and created special proceedings to achieve greater efficiency. More than 25 years later, it is fair to say the alternative "simplified" procedures did not achieve the goal for which they were intended. Figure 2 shows the most recent comprehensive data available. At year-end 2013, the full "ordinary proceeding" encompassing investigation, pretrial hearing, and trial was the standard process (63.9 percent of cases). When the new immediate and direct trial procedures that provide for a full trial are added, the percentage of fully adversarial cases argued before a trial judge reaches more than 67 percent (182,850 proceedings out of 271,602).[6] Summary trials requested by the defendant after the pretrial hearing and reviews of proposed sentence bargains do not trigger a full adversarial proceeding.

---

[6] This includes verdicts of guilt or innocence and trials ending with declarations of expiration of statutes of limitations that, as previously noted, run regardless of whether a decision to prosecute has been made. Some courts did not report broken-down figures and thus have not been counted, leading to the 271,602 dispositions considered in the chart, which include cases tried before first-instance tribunals (sitting as a single judge or panel of three judges) and courts of assize, where summary trial is exceptional. Dispositions in appeal proceedings against decisions of the justice of the peace before first-instance trial judges (4,483) are not counted. The National Institute of Statistics (ISTAT 2015) estimates that overall 359,840 cases were decided at the trial stage. The Ministry of Justice, DG-Stat (2015d) estimates 359,865.

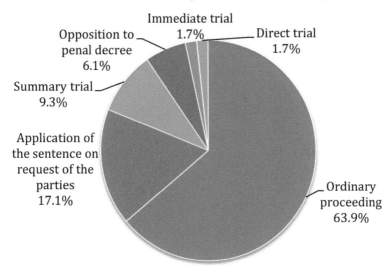

FIG. 2.—Cases adjudicated with a known defendant, by type of proceeding, 2013. Source: Ministry of Justice, DG-Stat (2015*a*, 2015*b*, 2015*d*).

Many dispositions do not involve trials, as figure 3 shows for the pretrial stages (preliminary investigation and pretrial hearing): 70.5 percent of cases involving a known accused in which an investigation was formally initiated were eventually dismissed (563,983 cases); 11.7 percent (93,327 cases) were indicted and sent to trial; and 17.8 percent were handled by summary trial, penalty on request of the parties, or nonopposed penal decree (143,181 cases).[7]

The following description discusses the ordinary three-stage proceeding, which, in theory and practice, is the paradigmatic case-processing method. The 1989 CCP abolished the investigating judge and assigned the investigation to the prosecutor, with police assistance.

A new official, the preliminary investigation judge (*giudice per le indagini preliminari* [GIP]), was created to supervise the prosecutor. Unlike the former investigating judge, the GIP is "a judge without a file."

[7] Some pretrial judges did not report broken-down figures. The figure refers to 800,491 reported cases. ISTAT (2015) reports that 897,791 cases involving a known accused were conclusively handled at the preliminary investigation and pretrial hearing stages.

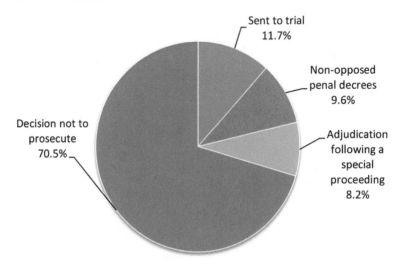

FIG. 3.—Cases processed during pretrial stages, known accused, by type of decision, 2013. Source: Ministry of Justice, DG-Stat (2015*c*).

He or she plays no active role in the investigation and is not a party to the proceeding, but is a neutral supervisor. The main duty is to assure that the prosecutor fully complies with rules provided by the CCP and with the rights of the accused. The GIP also decides prosecutorial requests for pretrial custodial and noncustodial measures to prevent the accused from fleeing, reoffending, or interfering with the investigation. Also at the prosecutor's request, the GIP can authorize wiretapping and validate arrests. Finally, he or she also exceptionally authorizes and presides over the gathering of evidence to be used at trial when it might otherwise be unavailable (e.g., a critical witness diagnosed with a terminal disease or perishable evidence that must be examined promptly; Amodio 2004, p. 491).[8]

The pretrial investigation is now purely instrumental to the decision of whether charges should be pressed (Del Duca 1991, pp. 82–83). When the prosecutor decides to proceed on the basis of the gathered evidence,

---

[8] In this case the defense counsel has the right to participate in the proceeding and may cross-examine the witness or appoint an expert. This is for evidence that will be included in the trial dossier; hence the proceeding (named *incidente probatorio*) must fully comply with all adversarial rules that would be applicable at trial.

the decision on the indictment is made at the pretrial hearing.[9] Before this, the prosecutor must notify the accused, the defense counsel, and the victim that the investigation is complete. Before the pretrial hearing, the investigative file must be disclosed to the accused and defense counsel with opportunity to inspect it. The pretrial hearing is chaired by a single pretrial hearing judge (*giudice dell'udienza preliminare* [GUP]) who was not previously involved in the investigation. This is a "trial before the trial." Its aim is to establish probable cause. The prosecutor and defense counsel present their cases and the GUP decides either to dismiss the case or to indict the accused.

The trial follows. The main goal of CCP drafters was to separate investigation from adjudication by breaking the chain that previously connected them. Accordingly, the trial court cannot have access to or use evidence other than that produced and admitted at trial. The new code fully embraced the Hearsay Evidence Rule: with minor exceptions, and in contrast to the past, out-of-court statements cannot be introduced to prove the truth of the matter asserted. They can be used only for witness impeachment purposes.

Hence, there is now the "double-dossier" principle (Ruggieri and Marcolini 2012, p. 395). When the trial begins, a new dossier is assembled "in order to avoid bias to the trial judge's 'virgin mind'—meaning a totally unbiased approach, guaranteeing that the judge would acknowledge only the evidence produced in court and decide only on that basis" (Illuminati 2005, p. 572). Evidence is presented orally in court; in principle, nothing documenting acts performed during the investigation may become part of the trial dossier. Key principles of the adversarial model, such as orality, confrontation, and direct cross-examination, are honored. The limited material from the investigation dossier that migrates into the trial dossier includes records of activities that cannot be reproduced at trial, documents from foreign authorities, and the defendant's criminal record. Statements or evidence contained in the prosecutor's files (e.g., a police interrogation record) and the defense counsel's files (e.g., an affidavit of testimony) may also be added to the trial dossier if the parties mutually agree.

The current framework is the result of a decade-long struggle between the legislature and the Constitutional Court that started when

---

[9] If the prosecutor believes that no probable cause exists, he asks the GIP to dismiss the case. The GIP has authority to compel the prosecutor to request the indictment.

many judges challenged key provisions of the 1989 code. In 1992, Constitutional Court judgments openly challenged the legislative decision to shift the focus of the criminal process from the investigation to the trial and grant the defendant the full panoply of adversarial guarantees. The Court struck down provisions concerning the hearsay evidence rule by announcing a new principle of the "nondispersion of evidence" under which "no available information should be wasted, regardless of how it has been collected" (Panzavolta 2005, p. 599). The Court linked this to the goal of establishing the "material truth" as a main aim of the criminal process. From that perspective, allowing migration to the trial dossier of statements given to the prosecutor and the police was not only necessary but consistent with the quintessential task of seeking the truth in the most effective way possible (Amodio 2004, pp. 493–94).

These cases gave prosecutors carte blanche to introduce at trial out-of-court statements obtained in nonadversarial proceedings and highlighted judicial resistance to the adversarial values set out in the new CCP. The demarcation between the investigation and trial stages was deemed an unacceptable limitation on their ability to seek the truth (Pizzi and Montagna 2004, pp. 449ff.; Illuminati 2005, p. 574). When the Parliament reenacted the original rules, the Constitutional Court signaled its disapproval by granting certiorari to new challenges to the adversarial provisions of the CCP. Parliament in 1999 permanently secured the adversarial system by amending article 111 of the Constitution: the core principle of a right to adversarial proceedings stated in article 6 of the European Convention of Human Rights was incorporated into the Italian Constitution. This granted criminal defendants the rights to examine witnesses or have them examined and to obtain attendance and examination of witnesses under the same conditions as the prosecution.

The Italian system is still in search of its true identity. As an influential judge, notoriously fond of the inquisitorial tradition of the 1930 CCP, noted, the essential problem is whether the Parliament wants a continental inquisitorial system or a common law adversarial system. There can be no middle ground since the criminal process cannot simultaneously be "a device to ascertain the historical truth of the facts" and "a device to resolve a dispute between two parties," in which the more capable and persuasive party prevails in a fair competition. Opting for a truly adversarial system implies that "the truth does not matter anymore" (Davigo 1999, p. 209).

D. The Court System

The criminal courts for adults (ages 18 and up) are divided into three instances (see fig. 4).[10] The first two, trial and appeal courts, are triers of facts. The highest-level judges of the Court of Cassation review only matters of law. In contrast to common law systems, there is no bifurcation into guilt and sentencing phases: courts of first instance and courts of appeal determine both guilt and the sentence to be imposed following the closing arguments.

1. *Courts of First Instance.* Justices of the peace—introduced in 2000—try minor offenses, typically misdemeanors and felonies for which the victim must file a formal complaint for the prosecutor to press charges. The justice of the peace represents "a mixed model that combines retributive and reparative aspects" with primary aims of "lightening the workload of the system of ordinary justice, minimizing recourse to criminal sanctions, and favoring reparative conduct and reconciliation between the parties to a dispute" (Henham and Mannozzi 2003, p. 300). If mediation fails, fines, home custody, and community service may be imposed.[11]

Tribunals are courts of first instance with jurisdiction over all criminal matters outside the jurisdictions of the justices of the peace and the assize courts. Tribunals usually consist of a single judge but in designated cases operate as a three-judge panel.

The assize courts try the most serious offenses (punishable with life imprisonment or carrying a maximum custodial sentence of 24 or more years, plus intentional crimes resulting in deaths). They are composed of eight members, two professional judges and six randomly selected members of the public: a mixed deliberation takes place. Except for the justices of the peace, the only active involvement of laypersons in adjudicating guilt or innocence is in the assize courts of first and second

---

[10] Article 97 of the Italian Penal Code establishes 14 as the age of criminal responsibility. Article 98(1) provides that a person 14 or older but under 18 who commits an offense and is deemed to have "the capacity to understand and to will" shall be punished, but the sentence must be reduced. These cases are handled in the juvenile justice system. Waiver to the adult system is not possible.

[11] Justices of the peace are honorary judges selected on the basis of their titles and professional experience. Usually they are defense lawyers who cannot thereafter practice law before the courts of the city in which they sit. They are appointed for 4 years but can be confirmed for an additional 4-year term.

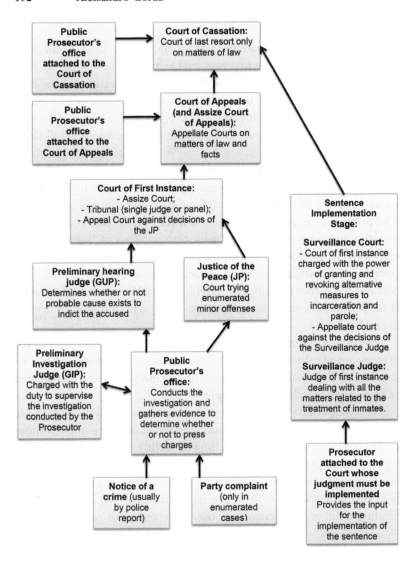

FIG. 4.—The Italian criminal justice process (ordinary proceedings)

instance.[12] The activism of Italian judges, particularly of first-instance courts, is often explained from a behavioral perspective as based on their

[12] According to the Ministry of Justice, DG-Stat (2015d), justices of the peace at year-end 2013 had 147,464 pending cases, courts of first instance had 540,203 (as single- or three-judge panels), and assize courts had 359.

sense of responsibility as fact-finders unlike judges in common law jurisdictions who merely direct lay fact-finders. This makes judges feel particularly responsible for the accuracy of the adjudication, playing "a very active role instead of simply responding to what the parties present and accepting that a weak prosecution case should lead to a 'not guilty' verdict" (Marafioti 2008, p. 94).

2. *Courts of Second Instance.*   Courts of appeals and assize courts of appeals, respectively, hear appeals from tribunals and assize courts. Judgments of the justices of the peace are appealed before tribunals, which then operate as an appellate court. Courts of appeals sit as three-judge panels. Assize courts of appeals consist of two professional judges and six laypersons.[13] Appeals courts do not merely review the merits of appealed cases but are vested with significant powers of fact-finding and are not shy of using them. In particular, the court may decide, inter alia, to reopen the presentation of evidence. With only a few exceptions, both the prosecutor and the defendant may appeal purported errors made at trial. When only the defendant appeals, appellate courts are bound by the prohibition of *reformatio in peius* (literally, "change for the worse"). Even if the initial conviction is affirmed, an altered sentence may not be more severe than the original: defendants have nothing to lose. This is one reason defendants customarily appeal both the conviction and the sentence. Prosecutors rarely file appeals solely to neutralize the prohibition of *reformatio in peius,* but usually only if the sentence was substantially lower than they requested. The reasons for this include lack of incentives (the trial prosecutor will not litigate the appeal) and ethical concerns (prosecutors tend to appeal sentences only if they think a substantial injustice has occurred). Only in a few trial courts do prosecutors systematically appeal sentences in order to prevent operation of the prohibition of *reformatio in peius.*

3. *Court of Third Instance.*   The Court of Cassation is the highest appellate authority for criminal courts. It reviews judgments only on matters of law. In some cases it may remand cases to a new appellate court for retrial (regarding the merits, the sentence, or both) after formulating a binding principle to be followed (e.g., regarding a clear methodologi-

---

[13] At year-end 2013, courts of appeals had 263,932 pending cases, courts of first instance had 5,136 pending cases as appellate courts for judgments of the justice of the peace, and assize courts of appeals had 580 (Ministry of Justice, DG-Stat 2015d).

cal mistake in evaluation of evidence or overlooking a particular aggravating circumstance).[14] The court has seven criminal divisions; allocation of cases is based on the subject matter. When particularly complex and important issues are regularly resolved differently by different divisions, it may resolve the split in a plenary session. Although no *stare decisis* principle formally exists, plenary judgments usually prove highly influential in subsequent decisions by lower courts.

4. *Sentence Implementation Courts.* When a conviction becomes final, a surveillance judge (*magistrato di sorveglianza*) is in charge of supervising implementation of the sentence. For custodial sentences, he or she supervises by means of visits and inmate audits to assure that correctional treatments are carried out consistently with principles set out in the Constitution and that prisoners' rights are observed. A sentence implementation court, the surveillance court (*tribunale di sorveglianza*), decides applications filed by inmates for parole release and applications concerning access to alternatives to incarceration. It also has authority to revoke such measures in case of violations. The surveillance court also serves as an appellate court concerning decisions of the surveillance judge. It sits as a mixed panel of two professional and two lay judges who are experts in fields such as psychology, clinical criminology, social work, and psychiatry. Its decisions may be appealed to the Court of Cassation.

II. Sanctions and Sentencing Patterns

The Italian system provides an interesting comparative case study. Italy is where both the Classical (Beccaria [1764] 1995; Harcourt 2014) and the Positivist schools (Ferri 1968; Sellin 1972) of criminological theory originated in the eighteenth and nineteenth centuries. The influence of both remains visible in almost all penal systems on either sides of the Atlantic. The Classical school emphasis on having the punishment fit the crime was foundational to the development of "just deserts" theories (von Hirsch 1976). The legacy of the Positivist school includes the "dual-track" systems of sanctions and measures in much of Europe. They provide for traditional penal sanctions (mainly imprisonment and fines) for blameworthy offenders and custodial and noncustodial measures (formally "nonpunitive") for incapacitating individuals deemed unacceptably dangerous to society (Simon 2006; de Keijser 2011; von Hirsch 2011).

---

[14] At year-end 2013, the Court of Cassation had 31,871 pending cases.

In this section, I describe the framework and main characteristics of the Italian sentencing system concerning rules and guiding principles for sentencing and currently available penal sanctions. Alternative modes of implementation of custodial sentences are considered and analyzed, and recent sentencing patterns are described.

A. Sentencing: Rules and Principles

The Penal Code and other statutes usually set forth statutory minimums and maximums for each offense. Only rarely is the statutory maximum exclusively indicated. The ranges embody the principles of proportionality and legality (*nulla poena sine lege*). A sentencing range between, say, a month and 20 years would not be constitutionally permissible for it would undermine the foreseeability of the sentence and permit exceedingly harsh or lenient sentences resulting from the judge's subjective evaluation of the case. The same scheme applies to both custodial sentences and fines. Within this range the judge exercises discretion.

1. *The Guiding Criteria.* The Italian Penal Code, adopted in 1930 to take effect in 1931 (Skinner 2011, pp. 425–28), constitutes a middle ground between Montesquieu's position that judges should be "no more than the mouth that pronounces the words of the law, mere passive beings, incapable of moderating either its force or rigour" ([1748] 2000, p. 113) and schemes that allow too much unfettered discretion. The legislature opted for a sentencing scheme based on "limited discretion." Article 132 of the Penal Code provides that "within the limits provided for by law, the judge shall have discretion in applying punishment; he shall be required to specify the grounds which justify the use of such discretionary power. In increasing or reducing punishment the limits prescribed for each type of punishment shall not be exceeded, except in cases expressly defined by the law." Unlike the numerical guidelines in one-third of US states, the Italian system provides statutory sentencing principles that indicate primary and secondary rationale categories plus lists of aggravating and mitigating circumstances and rules for weighing previous convictions (Ashworth 2009, p. 249).

Article 133 sets forth the main factors the court must take into account: (*a*) the seriousness of the current offense, as inferred from the nature, type, means used, and any other aspect of the conduct; the seriousness of the harm caused or the danger threatened; and the scope of intent or degree of negligence; and (*b*) the offender's propensity to commit crime, which may be inferred from the offender's motives, his or her criminal record, and his or her behavior before and after the offense. Ideas of the Classical and Positivist schools are recognizable. The first category of factors focuses on proportionality: the nature of the conduct and the culpability of the defendant. The second is clearly concerned with prediction of future recidivism (Henham 2012, p. 266). A 1981 amendment to the Penal Code introduced article 133-*bis*, which enables the judge to adjust fines (increase up to three times or reduce up to a third) depending on the economic conditions and assets of the convicted offender.

The sentencing judge determines the length of the sentence within the statutory minimum and maximum, following criteria set out in article 133. Upward and downward departures from the indicated range may be made on the basis of statutory aggravating and mitigating circumstances. No mandatory minimums exist. Fixed penalties, extremely rare and limited mostly to fines for some misdemeanors, are generally deemed to contravene the principle of individualization of punishment.

2. *Statutory Harshness and Judicial Moderation.*   The sentencing provisions of the Penal Code were, and are, characterized by a distinctive harshness that reflects the ideology of the authoritarian regime that promulgated them. The code provides comparatively high minimum and maximum penalties for every offense and provides a long list of aggravating circumstances that make it hard not to increase the punishment. In order to ameliorate the code's harshness, judges generally impose sentences close to the statutory minimum (Ruggiero 1995, p. 51; Grande 2000, p. 2; Mannozzi 2002, p. 111).

After the fall of the fascist regime, a "generic mitigating circumstance" was introduced that allows judges to take into account other mitigating circumstances not listed in the code or other statutes to justify a reduction of punishment. The provision was modified in 2005 to provide that the mere absence of previous convictions does not justify a reduction. This was an attempt by the center-right government then in power to end the judicial practice of almost invariably granting sentence reductions to first-time offenders. Leaving aside sentence enhancements for recidivists, the severity of the code is shown by the rule regarding multiple offenses: a single custodial sentence should be ordered with a term equal to the cumulative duration of the punishments for each individual offense. The code thus rejects practices of imposing concurrent sentences or applying a policy that adds modest increments to the base sentence imposed for the most serious crime.

Two postfascist limiting mechanisms mitigate the scheme's severity: in case of multiple current offenses, the aggregate punishment may not exceed the most severe single punishment by more than five times. Furthermore, the overall punishment may not exceed 30 years of imprisonment for felonies and 6 for misdemeanors. Anyone who commits more than one offense as part of a common plan (even at different times) may not receive an aggregate punishment more than three times what would be imposed for the most serious offense (Vassalli 1974, pp. 1040–41).

3. *The Rationale(s) behind Punishment.* Article 27(3) of the Constitution asserts that "punishment must aim at rehabilitating the offender." Such a mandate is absent from common law jurisdictions. The US Supreme Court, for example, defers to legislatures' policy choices: "The Constitution does not mandate adoption of any one penological theory" (*Ewing v. California*, 538 U.S. 11, 25 [2003]). Federal and state laws and guidelines accommodate retributive values alongside other goals including deterrence, incapacitation, and rehabilitation.

The traditionally conservative Italian Constitutional Court has been reluctant to confirm rehabilitation as the primary rationale justifying criminal penalties. At first, the Court adopted a "multifunctional" approach: rehabilitation was portrayed as one among many legitimate objectives (Cavadino and Dignan 2006*b*, p. 140). Rehabilitation should inform sentence implementation but not be central to establishment of sentencing ranges by the legislature or setting of the sentence at trial. The Court observed that deterrence should be the primary aim in drafting sentencing statutes and retribution the main goal in determination of the sentence.

The Constitutional Court thus refused to establish a static and generally valid hierarchy of punishment goals but endorsed an approach differentiating dominant rationales for each major stage within an overall framework primarily shaped by "just deserts" considerations (see, e.g., Judgment of February 12, 1966 no. 12; Judgment of February 17, 1971 no. 22; Judgment of May 25, 1989 no. 282; Judgment of August 7, 1993 no. 1993). More recently, the Court has seemed more open to acknowledging social reintegration as primary throughout, including during legislative decision making, determination of sentences, and implementation of punishments. Although alluding to a framework in which more than one rationale is relevant, the Court noted that "were the aim of rehabilitation limited to the sentence implementation phase, it would run the risk of being greatly compromised any time the type and length of the penalty are not calibrated (neither at the legislative nor at the sentencing stage) on the offender's need for social reintegration" (Judgment of July, 2 1990 no. 313, my translation; see also Judgment of April 30, 2008 no. 129).

B. *Authorized Penalties and Their Implementation*

The 1930 Penal Code attempted to reach a viable compromise between the Classical and Positivist schools. Classicists wanted penalties and sentencing provisions to focus on harm caused by the offense and the culpability of the offender. Positivists were highly skeptical of the concept of culpability and insisted that the primary aim must be to address and neutralize threats posed by dangerous individuals.

1. *The Dual-Track System.*   The code still reflects this compromise especially concerning sanctions, providing a dual track (*doppio binario*) of criminal sanctions for competent offenders and safety (or preventive) measures for individuals deemed dangerous. This proved particularly harsh for dangerous individuals with full or diminished criminal capacity: in such cases both types of sanctions may be jointly applied, usually with the safety measures being served after completion of the criminal sanctions (Pellissero 2013, p. 107). Safety measures are based on a prognosis of dangerousness irrespective of whether an individual has committed a crime. Article 202 of the Penal Code includes commission of an offense or a "quasi offense" (only in enumerated cases) with social dangerousness as preconditions for an "administrative safety measure." The code engages in mislabeling when it refers to "administrative" measures that are clearly punitive in substance and goal. Safety measures may be custodial or noncustodial. The former are counted in official statistics as part of the total number of incarcerated individuals as they involve restrictions on freedom of movement and constant monitoring (e.g., in mental hospitals for offenders, treatment and custody centers, working penal colonies, and labor facilities). On September 1, 2013, the reported number of people confined under security measures was 1,204 (Aebi and Delgrande 2015, p. 101, table 5.2).

2. *Main and Supplementary Criminal Penalties.*   Criminal penalties are divided into main and ancillary penalties (see table 1). Main penalties (*pene principali*) consist of custodial sentences and fines. Ancillary penalties (*pene accessorie*) automatically supplement the main sentence and are explicitly provided for as penal consequences of conviction. They in-

TABLE 1

Authorized Sanctions for Felonies and Misdemeanors

Available Penal Sanctions

Felonies:
- a. Principal sanctions:
  - a.1. Life imprisonment
  - a.2. Imprisonment (*reclusione*) from 15 days to 24 years
  - a.3. Fine (*multa*) from €50 to €50,000
- b. Ancilllary sanctions:
  - b.1. Disqualification from running for and holding public offices
  - b.2. Disqualification from the exercise of a profession or trade
  - b.3. Legal disqualification
  - b.4. Disqualification for managerial and executive positions of private legal persons and corporations
  - b.5. Inability to bargain with governmental entities
  - b.6. Termination of employment
  - b.7. Loss or suspension of the exercise of paternal authority
  - b.8. Publication of the judgment of conviction (for both felonies and misdemeanors)

Misdemeanors:
- a. Principal sanctions:
  - a.1. Detention (*arresto*) from 5 days to 3 years
  - a.2. Monetary penalty (*ammenda*) from €20 to €10,000
- b. Ancillary sanctions:
  - b.1. Suspension from the practice of a profession or trade
  - b.2. Suspension from managerial and executive positions of private legal persons and corporations

clude various forms of disqualification (e.g., from holding public office or practicing a profession). When the law does not specify a duration, it is the length of the main sentence.[15] The death penalty for peacetime offenses was abolished after the fascist regime was overthrown. The 1948 Constitution allowed capital punishment only in cases provided for by the military law of war. The death penalty in military law was abolished in 1994 and replaced with life imprisonment. An amendment to article 27(4) of the Constitution, implementing Protocol 13 of May 3,

---

[15] Whenever the law prescribes that a conviction shall entail a temporary collateral punishment and the duration thereof is not expressly specified, the period of the ancillary sanction shall be equal to that of the principal punishment imposed or that which would have to be served in the case of a conversion due to the inability to pay of the convicted person. In no case, however, may it exceed the minimum and maximum limits prescribed for the particular type of ancillary sanction punishment (art. 37 of the Penal Code).

2002, to the European Convention on Human Rights and Fundamental Freedoms on the Abolition of the Death Penalty in All Circumstances, made Italy fully abolitionist. Section 4 now reads, "The death penalty is not allowed."

Life imprisonment with the possibility of parole is the most severe authorized penalty. Life prisoners become eligible for parole release after serving 26 years. The most commonly applied penalties are imprisonment for a term and fines. For main penalties, the code distinguishes different types of custodial sentences and fines for felonies and misdemeanors. Prison terms for felonies (*reclusione*) can range from 15 days to 24 years; for misdemeanors, detention (*arresto*) can vary from 5 days to 3 years. These are outer limits: a specific range is specified for every offense. Fines can range from €50 to €50,000 for felonies (*multa*) and from €20 to €10,000 for misdemeanors (*ammenda*). Terms of imprisonment and fines may be imposed alone or together depending on provisions for each offense. If an offender cannot afford to pay the fine, this is replaced with supervision or community work with a conversion rate of 1 day of work for every €250 outstanding.

3. *Fully Suspended Custodial Sentences.*   Fully suspended custodial sentences were introduced in 1904 on the basis of reformers' rejection of short terms of incarceration for deterrent purposes followed by community supervision. It was widely believed that sending first offenders to serve short prison terms would cause more crime because of criminal associations made during imprisonment and stigma. Suspended custodial sentences are hard to classify as custodial or noncustodial. They are a legal fiction. The offender, unless he or she commits a new offense, serves time in the community without spending a day in prison. The code provides that the sentencing judge, after imposing a prison term up to 2 years (2 years and 6 months for 18–21-year-olds and people over 70), may suspend it for 5 years (2 for misdemeanors). If the defendant does not reoffend and complies with conditions, the judge will dismiss the sentence and declare the original offense extinguished. No trace will remain on the person's criminal record.

On paper nothing happens automatically. The judge is to make decisions case by case after evaluating the offender's capacity to abstain from further crimes. In practice, the suspended sentence's original character and purpose have been lost. It is routinely used to alleviate strain on overcrowded prisons or as an incentive to defendants to agree to the special sentence bargaining proceeding described earlier and consequently to waive trial. At year-end 2013, 5,123 offenders were serving a fully suspended custodial sentence with conditions (Aebi and Chopin 2015, p. 17, table 1.1).

4. *Alternatives to Incarceration.* Over four decades, a wide range of alternatives to incarceration have been introduced. They are applied by the sentence implementation court immediately after sentencing (in which case the offender will spend no time in prison unless the measure is revoked) or after partial service of the prison sentence. These are not "intermediate punishments" but are substitute ways to implement prison sentences. They were first introduced by Law no. 354 of 1975 as part of a fundamental overhaul of custodial sentences. The goal was to implement the rehabilitative aim of punishment declared in article 27(3) of the Constitution. Later on, Law no. 663 of 1986 put Italy at the forefront internationally by its emphasis on resocialization and treatment (Grande 2002, pp. 3ff.).

The most commonly used alternatives include probation (*affidamento in prova ai servizi sociali*), home custody (*detenzione domiciliare*), and semiliberty (*semilibertà*).

Probation is the most frequently used alternative implementation of a custodial sentence. It may be used when an offender has received a custodial sentence of no more than 3 years or has less than 3 years to serve. The supervision period corresponds to the original length of a sentence or the balance yet to be served. When probation is granted, the probation service supervises compliance with treatment and other conditions and assists in resocialization.

Home custody may be granted to offenders with up to 2 years' custodial sentence to serve, either as an original sentence or as the remainder of one when the requirements for probation are not met. For some categories of individuals (e.g., pregnant women, mothers of children under age 10, people over 60 or under 21, seriously ill offenders) the time to be served must not exceed 4 years. Offenders 70 or older may request home custody at any time.

Semiliberty allows prisoners who have served at least half of their sentence (two-thirds for a few sentences and 20 years for lifers) to spend part of the day in the community to work or participate in training programs or other activities deemed useful for reintegration. Semiliberty usually represents the step before becoming eligible for parole release.

Decisions concerning such measures are made by the sentence implementation court (*tribunale di sorveglianza*) discussed above. These dispositions trigger imposition of tailored conditions and requirements. A violation may result in more burdensome conditions or revocation (Gualazzi and Mancuso 2010, pp. 284–91).

Statutory limitations preclude use of alternatives to implementation of incarceration for offenders who committed particularly serious offenses or for recidivists. Automatic suspensions of penalties up to 3 years allow offenders to apply for an alternative before starting to serve the sentence. Beyond these boundaries, sentence implementation courts enjoy wide discretion in granting, denying, revoking, or rescinding such measures. In the absence of specific rules or guiding criteria, "back-door" judges in practice exercise a resentencing power (Gualazzi, Mancuso, and Mangiaracina 2012, pp. 80–81), focused on the offender's postconviction behavior aimed at rehabilitation and, in case of nonparticipation in programs, incapacitation. The Italian sentencing system thus shifted from a rigid mostly desert-based approach to a more flexible "correctional model" (Pavarini 2001, pp. 416–19).

Legislation permitted the progressive shift from institutional control toward community supervision. Influential scholars stressed that alternatives must be handled with care. Bricola (1977) asserted that alternatives must be implemented in a way conducive to social reintegration and not simply create new modes of formal social control. Pavarini (1994, p. 55) pointed out that the multiplication of "soft" modes of social control would "curb not so much the room for segregation, but the field controlled by informal social control." In other words, this literature was concerned that community supervision would become a strategy of "social discipline," ultimately resulting in net-widening. This hypothesis was validated in the 1990s when the proliferation of alternatives did not lead to lower imprisonment rates in Europe, including Italy. Both imprisonment and community supervision rates increased across the continent (Aebi, Delgrande, and Marguet 2015). However, in responding to two recent European Court of Human Rights' judgments condemning prison overcrowding, the government mostly relied on alternatives.

C. Sentencing Patterns

Tables 2 and 3 show types of sentence imposed in felony and misdemeanor cases, including prison sentences by length for the 2000–2014 time series for which most reliable data are available. Lengths are per

TABLE 2

Sentences for Felonies

Year	Fine (*Multa*) Only	Imprisonment (*Reclusione*)				
		Up to 1 Year	1–2 Years	2–5 Years	5–10 Years	>10 Years
2000	19.40	63.30	11.87	3.96	1.04	.44
2001	20.52	61.97	11.87	4.06	1.10	.48
2002	20.71	61.33	11.65	4.44	1.27	.58
2003	20.34	62.09	11.23	4.67	1.10	.49
2004	19.16	62.66	11.24	5.37	1.03	.47
2005	16.94	65.22	11.14	5.27	.92	.43
2006	16.36	65.29	11.14	5.90	.88	.36
2007	17.40	62.74	11.61	6.84	1.02	.33
2008	18.10	60.15	12.80	7.34	1.10	.37
2009	18.01	58.39	13.55	8.22	1.36	.41
2010	18.82	57.57	13.27	8.31	1.53	.46
2011	18.06	57.80	13.94	8.27	1.47	.40
2012	21.52	57.84	13.00	7.34	1.32	.36
2013	21.26	57.20	12.80	7.10	1.24	.40
2014	21.75	57.33	12.68	6.67	1.13	.44

Source.—ISTAT (2013, p. 15; 2014, p. 200, table 6.14; 2015, pp. 205–6, table 6.14).

case, whether for a single offense or multiple offenses. Table 2 presents sentences for felonies and table 3 for misdemeanors.

Imprisonment (*reclusione*) up to a year is the most frequently imposed felony sentence; over the last 6 years, less than 60 percent were above that threshold, although for 9 consecutive years after 2000 more than 60 percent were above it. Percentages of sentences between 5 and 10 years and above 10 years (which include life sentences) have been stable. Those between 1 and 2 years and especially those between 2 and 5 years have grown. These increases seem not to be attributable to more punitive attitudes of the courts but to numerous upward adjustments of statutory ranges for high-volume felonies, especially property crimes, and introduction of new aggravating circumstances.

Both center-right (2001–6; 2008–11) and center-left (2000–2001; 2006–8) governments embraced enhancement of statutory penalties as a prompt, seemingly cheap, and psychologically reassuring strategy to address increased public concerns about crime. Misdemeanor convictions followed a similar pattern, with a significant reduction of sentences to custody up to a year particularly since 2008 and a noticeable increase in

TABLE 3
Sentences for Misdemeanors

Year	Fine (*Ammenda*) Only	Custody (*Arresto*)				
		Up to 1 Month	1–3 Months	3–6 Months	6–12 Months	>12 Months
2000	50.53	34.08	12.50	2.24	.53	.12
2001	43.87	47.11	6.61	1.75	.58	.08
2002	58.47	32.13	6.23	1.86	.53	.09
2003	67.39	20.24	7.34	2.37	.54	.11
2004	58.87	31.54	5.85	1.93	.44	.09
2005	48.90	42.47	5.78	1.82	.45	.08
2006	47.00	45.12	5.21	1.78	.62	.10
2007	50.15	41.45	5.75	1.95	.51	.12
2008	55.07	35.26	6.96	1.99	.58	.12
2009	55.49	28.99	12.20	2.64	.58	.11
2010	53.26	26.07	15.98	3.86	.70	.13
2011	51.22	22.83	18.46	6.23	1.09	.17
2012	57.47	24.50	15.79	6.81	1.18	.17
2013	49.00	23.82	16.50	5.70	.87	.08
2014	50.16	22.94	15.21	9.39	2.04	.44

SOURCE.—ISTAT (2013, p. 15; 2014, p. 200, table 6.14; 2015, pp. 205–6, table 6.14).

sentences ranging from 1 to 3 months, and even more in those between 3 and 6 months.

III. Major Developments in Italian Penal Policy

The First Republic's political system was largely consensual, peaking in the "Historic Compromise," an accommodation between the Christian Democrats and the Communist Party from 1973 through 1980 (Ginsborg 1990, pp. 354–70). This softened demands for overly punitive policies. Debate about crime and penal policy was concentrated at elite levels. "Collective feelings of insecurity" were expressed "as a political demand for change" (Pavarini 2001, p. 145). Crime and responses to it were treated as political but not politicized matters.

When harsh laws were enacted, they seldom symbolically aimed at "going to war" with vast categories of nonserious offenders. Laws against political terrorism were enacted during the 1970s and 1980s (Della Porta 1992; Cento Bull and Cooke 2013, pp. 30ff.). They, and anti-mafia legislation in the early 1980s and 1990s, provided good examples of "emergency" provisions regarding pretrial detention, sentence enhancements, cooperation agreements, and sentence implementation based on policy rationales separate from those underlying the rest of the criminal justice system (La Spina 2004, 2014; Paoli 2007). The social alarm caused by those phenomena did not extend to "other less serious forms of crime, nor give rise to a widespread feeling of lack of safety" (Selmini 2011, p. 166).

Melossi (2001, p. 413) provides a cultural explanation of the low levels of punitiveness through the 1990s. Low levels of penal repression were linked, he argues, to the "soft authoritarianism" typical of Italian history and tradition, resulting from the vast presence and influence of the Catholic Church. Political parties with different ideological backgrounds shared the same policy of mildness. During the second half of the 1980s, Italy's imprisonment rate never exceeded 70 per 100,000. A crucial role was played by recurring amnesties and general pardons, alone or combined. Clemency measures in 1986 and 1990 were not the only noteworthy efforts. Following the prison law reform of 1975, the Parliament in 1986 further embraced rehabilitation in corrections, redesigning the rules governing sentence implementation. The new law rewarded inmates' good behavior with an array of early release schemes, including greater access to alternatives to incarceration. The focus on treatment was favored by the Christian Democrats, "who saw corrections as a synonym for redemption," and the Communists, "who believed in re-education in a social and moral sense" (Gonnella 2013, p. 228). The demise of the First Republic in the early 1990s and the advent of a new political system gradually led to radical changes.

In this section, I focus on the changes in penal policies since the early 1990s. These include rejection of clemency measures, the development of an increasingly punitive approach to crime and punishment, the Italian version of the "war on drugs," and recent measures of decarceration adopted in response to two European Court of Human Rights judgments.

A. Harsher Policies and the Abandonment of Clemency

The rejection of clemency measures by means of a constitutional amendment was the first visible marker of change. Until 1992, amnesties and pardons were granted by the head of state upon the enactment of legislation delegating authority to do so; only a simple majority was required for such bills.[16] As judicial inquiries related to the Clean Hands investigation spread, concerns emerged that the Parliament could pass an amnesty bill to stop the investigations and prevent trials. To address public anxiety, the Parliament passed a constitutional amendment setting a very high threshold for amnesties and general pardons. Supermajorities were required: two-thirds of the members of Parliament must vote in favor of each section of the bill and then of the entire bill.

Once a recurring feature of Italian penal policy, measures of collective clemency have become hard to pass and are widely perceived as "politically unacceptable" (Nelken 2009, p. 303). This can be seen concerning the 2006 collective pardon proposed by the center-left government. Primarily justified as an emergency measure to reduce prison overcrowding, the bill was harshly criticized in the media as a threat to public safety. It is still commonly cited as a main reason for defeat of the center-left coalition in the 2008 general elections. The 2006 general pardon was an extraordinary event and not a prelude to a general shift toward more lenient policies generally. During the 2008 campaign, the center-right coalition—which in part supported and voted for the general pardon— repeatedly criticized its opponents for being "soft on crime" and returned to power with a "zero tolerance" agenda (Shea 2009, p. 89).

The difference with the past could not be starker. Until 1992, 20 clemency bills had been passed since 1948. With few exceptions, they granted both amnesty and collective pardons, usually containing provisions specifying the maximum statutory penalty of crimes covered by the amnesty, specifying the number of years of the sentence to be pardoned, and designating certain types of ineligible offenses or offenders (usually recidivists; Piraino 2007). Historically, such measures were meant to reduce the overall severity of a penal system inherited from an authoritarian regime and to prevent prison overcrowding. The recurrent use of amnesty and pardon bills has been described as a distinctive feature of Italian penality, whose "governing through tolerance" policies were influenced by the Catholic "tendency to be extremely tolerant in

---

[16] In Italian law, amnesty is a collective measure that extinguishes criminal liability and removes all effects of a conviction, including a criminal record: it erases the offense, not only the penalty imposed. Unlike individual pardons, collective pardons apply to designated categories of offenders rather than being issued on an individual basis. Collective pardons mitigate punishment but neither speak to the criminality of the underlying offense nor expunge the conviction from the offender's rap sheet.

individual and social issues" including crime, in contrast to the Protestant, and mostly North American, "preoccupation with law and order" (Melossi 1994, p. 213). Amnesties and pardons also functioned as short-term solutions that postponed long overdue debates on structural reforms (Gonnella 2013, pp. 226–27; Barbarino and Mastrobuoni 2014).

B. The Second Republic and the "Politics of Fear"

The fall of the Berlin Wall and the demise of the First Republic radically changed the social and political environments in which penal policies were shaped. The advent of a new (mostly) majoritarian political system set the stage for a new understanding of crime and criminal justice as "political" issues. The rise of new populist parties made it easier to appeal directly to discontent, for example, concerning the moral panic surrounding the first massive wave of immigration from non-EU countries and the growing sense of insecurity caused by the early 1990s recession (Pavarini 1997). At the same time, the disappearance of strong ideologies and movements made the general public more receptive to messages and slogans that previously would have been dismissed as oversimplifications or misrepresentations.

Of course, the political lexicon, and penal policies, did not change overnight. Until the latter 1990s, for example, media commonly referred to property and street crimes as forms of "micro-criminality." The prefix was not meant to underestimate the seriousness of such offenses. Rather, it signified that problems should be dealt with by police and prosecutors in a "neutral" way without being exploited by political parties for electoral reasons. Property crimes had low visibility and were not portrayed as fundamental threats that required exceptional responses. There was still room for an approach to safety inspired by liberal values and community participation (Selmini 2005).

In the late 1990s, it became evident that the country no longer considered safety a matter simply of "external security" or "public order" but an "internal" challenge in which criminals and "outsiders," especially street criminals and undocumented immigrants, were viewed as "common enemies" (Melossi and Selmini 2009, p. 160). Italy "was a late-comer to a political realization that had come to many developed Western countries over the preceding decades" (Zedner 2003, p. 153). Until the late 1990s, populist "law and order" campaigns mostly failed (Nelken 2005, p. 225). Yet it is no surprise that the "zero tolerance" mantra was first adopted around 1998 by a center-left government (Caputo 2001, pp. 1063–67).

The 2001 general election campaign was a turning point. The mediatization of crime was systematically used by the center-right coalition led by Silvio Berlusconi to foster moral panics for electoral goals (Altheide 2003; Ceretti and Cornelli 2013, p. 44). The presence in the coalition of the Northern League (*Lega Nord*), a populist anti-immigration party, contributed to making tough-on-crime measures a top campaign priority (Ruzza and Fella 2009, pp. 91–92). One of Italy's leading contemporary historians, Paul Ginsborg (2004, pp. 94–95), recounted that "[Berlusconi's coalition] program was a strong and simple one: decrease taxation, streamline the state administration, provide public works for the southern un- and under-employed; establish greater security in the cities, stamp out illegal immigration and its high co-relation with petty and not-so-petty crimes; reform the judicial system and put an end to the prying and punitive actions of excessively independent magistrates."

The victory of the center-right coalition (in power from 2001 to 2006 and again from 2008 to 2011) inaugurated the shift from a corporatist penal ideology focused on rehabilitation (Cavadino and Dignan 2006*a*, pp. 441, 443–44) to one in which explicitly exclusionary policies became common (Cavadino and Dignan 2006*b*, pp. 139–40). The right-wing parties effectively spoke to and incited what sociologist Zygmunt Bauman calls "derivative fear," "a steady frame of mind that is best described as the sentiment of being susceptible to danger; a feeling of insecurity . . . and vulnerability" that acquires "a self-propelling capacity" (2006, p. 3).

The radical change was not justified by changes in crime rates. Despite the center-right parties' narrative of a "dramatic increase" in crime, data tell a different story. As figure 5 shows, crime per 100,000 inhabitants reported by the police, after climbing until 1991, has since fluctuated, being overall substantially stable.[17]

In the mid-1970s, Italy, like other Western nations, shifted from being a low-crime society toward being a high-crime one (Garland 2001), although with distinctive characteristics (Ceretti and Cornelli 2013, p. 27).

---

[17] Throughout this essay the expression "crimes reported by the police to judicial authorities" refers to crimes known to the police from their own activities and from citizens' reports and complaints. The data provided do not refer to prosecuted cases.

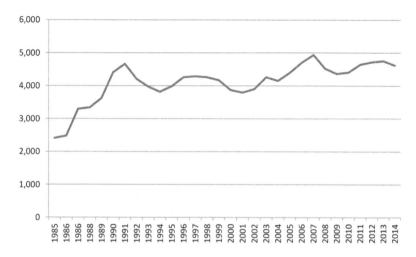

F<small>IG</small>. 5.—Numbers of crimes reported by the police to the prosecutors' offices per 100,000 of the general population. Source: ISTAT (multiple years).

Rapid increases in thefts and robberies that characterized much of Europe in the early 1960s became visible in Italy only a decade later and peaked in the early 1990s. For a long time, homicide rates were high compared with those of most European peers, reaching 3.4 per 100,000 inhabitants in 1991 largely because of "mafia wars" in southern Italy in the 1980s and early 1990s (Barbagli 2004, pp. 144–48). Since then, rates have plummeted, reaching 0.78 per 100,000 in 2014. Recent increases in theft and robbery rates produced levels comparable to those observed during the second half of the 1990s. Before the recent increase, property crimes followed an erratic path (Barbagli and Colombo 2011).

Figure 6 shows historical trends in rates of homicide (multiplied by 10 to match the figure's scale), total violent crimes (murder, attempted murder, and physical assault), and three common property crimes (larceny/snatch thefts, robberies, and household burglaries).[18] The property crime data confirm recent upward trends, especially for household burglaries (250.6 in 2009 to 416.6 in 2013). The upward trend in violence is

---

[18] Unlike the FBI's Uniform Crime Reporting definition of violent crime, in Italy the crime of robbery is usually listed among property offenses following the categorization adopted in the Penal Code.

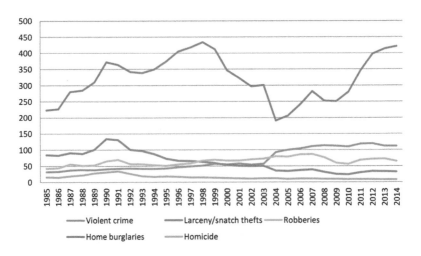

FIG. 6.—Homicides, violent crimes, larceny/snatch thefts, robberies and home burglaries reported by the police to the prosecutors' offices (rate per 100,000). Source: ISTAT (multiple years).

mainly due to physical assaults, which steadily grew from rates below 40 per 100,000 inhabitants in the late 1980s to above 100 as of 2005. This seems largely attributable to a shift over time in the social meaning of assault, leading to "rising thresholds of intolerance to violence" and patterns of increased reporting (Tonry 2013, p. 311; 2014, pp. 38–48). Sexual assault has been excluded from the data on violent crime because of a significant statutory change in 1996 that combined into one two formerly separate offenses (sexual harassment, including unwanted touching and kissing, and rape). With various forms of sexual harassment counted as sexual assault, overall rates inevitably went up (from 1.2 per 100,000 in 1985 to a mean of 7.8 since 2006), portraying a pattern that would be misleading when compared with pre-1996 data trends (Selmini and McElrath 2014, p. 404).

C. "Double Standard" in Penal Policy Making

Penal policies of the center-right governments were enacted in the shadow of conflict between the political branches of government and the judiciary. The government repeatedly attempted to curb the independence of judicial authorities and shield Prime Minister Berlusconi from prosecution in multiple trials and investigations (Nelken 2002; Quigley 2011).

The policies of Berlusconi's second government (previously he served as prime minister for a short period after the 1994 general elections) from 2001 to 2006 were markedly ambivalent: soft on white-collar criminals and first-time offenders and tough on low-level and career criminals and immigrants. The preceding center-left government in 2000 had greatly relaxed penal provisions related to tax frauds, but also in 2001 it introduced the first model of corporate criminal liability in the country's history. The center-right government was characterized by an almost blatant "double standard" (Forti and Visconti 2007, pp. 495–96): lenient toward economic offenders and tough on stereotypical street offenders. A 2002 statute substantially weakened penal provisions against accounting frauds, false claims, and slush funds partly by decriminalizing behavior and by reducing the severity of applicable sentences. This has recently been partly offset by top-down harmonization of white-collar offenses affecting EU financial interests and changes to related sentencing provisions.

In 2002 Berlusconi's government strengthened the 1998 immigration law enacted by the center-left government. The maximum period of administrative detention of undocumented aliens awaiting deportation was extended and penalties for illegally reentering the country were increased. The law increased efficiency in tracking illegal immigration and related criminal activities (especially compared with previous underregulation; Barbagli 2004, p. 153) but racialized immigration discourse by treating undocumented aliens as scapegoats and enemy outsiders (Totah 2002). Since 1998, many non-EU immigrants have had the status of guests on "probation" in terms of papers and permits they need to be considered legal residents; they are constantly at risk of breaking rules. On December 31, 2014, inmates from non-EU countries constituted 13,797 of the 53,623 people held in Italian prisons (25.72 percent).

Following a short-lived center-left government led by Romano Prodi (2006–8), which enacted the 2006 collective pardon, the center-right coalition won the 2008 elections, this time on a clear law-and-order platform primarily targeting transient communities, such as Roma people, and non-EU citizens from developing countries (Shea 2009). "Security packages" of 2008 and 2009, called "urgent measures for public security," criminalized, among other conduct, illegal immigration and "making use of minors to beg for money," the latter an offense punishable with imprisonment up to 3 years and clearly aimed at Roma people (Ambrosini 2013).

Overall, new policies enacted by the center-right government were mostly symbolic, concerned more with showing that the executive branch was "doing something" and "reassuring" the general public than with pursuing or producing tangible results (Massetti 2015, p. 498). The crime of illegally entering the country enacted in 2009 provides a telling example. The government initially planned to make illegal immigration a felony punishable by imprisonment. However, concerns expressed by the international community and the risk of exacerbating prison over-crowding soon led it to change course. Illegal entrance or residence was made a misdemeanor punishable with a fine. The aim was not actually to collect fines from needy undocumented immigrants but to speed up deportations. However, the many appeals provided by the Italian judicial process made deportation harder than before—a clear example of a more punitive policy on paper that proved self-defeating if not counterproductive. Not surprisingly, the law creating the offense soon became unenforced. The center-left government in power since 2014 has repeatedly expressed willingness to repeal it.

The real punitive turn in immigration policy, irrespective of the government in power, has been in "administrative" detention of undocumented aliens for screening or pending deportation. Over time, this "has evolved into a de facto punishment" and "has become an instrument of deterrence used by the police to try to wear down the resistance of those who do not cooperate with their removal" (Campesi 2015, p. 449). The "security packages" enacted in 2008 and 2009 also critically contributed to expansion of a more hidden but not less pervasive facet of "administrative penality" at the local level. Local authorities used new powers to promulgate a vast array of municipal measures and orders to fight such forms of urban disorder as minor drug dealing, begging, prostitution, illegal sale of goods, and illegal occupation of public spaces. As noted by Selmini (2016, p. 6), "the widespread use of these orders, especially in the biggest cities, remarkably reshape[d] urban policing at the local level, with municipal police becoming heavily involved in zero-tolerance type strategies."

D. Sentence Enhancements for Repeat Offenders

A 2005 tough-on-crime law recast the rules governing sentence enhancements for repeat offenders. The government sought to address the media and general public complaint that even habitual offenders "stay in prison for too little and end up being released too soon." The drafters focused on judicial nullification of sentence enhancements (often disregarded or counterbalanced by use of mitigating circumstances) and on rehabilitative elements of the implementation phase of custodial sentences that allowed offenders to leave prison early. The bark of the new law outweighed its bite: under the new rules, sentence enhancements remained discretionary.[19] They were also applicable only to intentional felonies. Judicial discretion was radically curbed mainly with regard to the magnitude of sentence increases if enhancement was deemed appropriate.[20] The recidivist premium was made mandatory only for particularly serious charges, including organized crime offenses, drug trafficking, murder, aggravated sexual assault, and kidnapping for ransom (Pavarini 2006; Torrente 2009, pp. 5–8).

Nonetheless, a 2015 decision of the Constitutional Court (Judgment no. 185 of July 23, 2015) struck down the provision making sentence enhancement mandatory for certain offenses, ruling against any irrebuttable presumptions of increased dangerousness as a result of a new offense, even a particularly serious one. Sentence enhancements based on criminal history must be determined case by case following assessment of the threat to society the offender poses. A presumptive incapacitative sentence would unduly frustrate the rehabilitative aim of punishment set forth in the Constitution.

The 2005 law represents an example, according to Dolcini (2007), of the "selective approach" to penal policy making adopted by the center-right cabinet. While making penalties for repeat offenders potentially much harsher, at the same time the 2005 bill introduced a new regulation of statutes of limitations, now equivalent to the statutory maximum pro-

---

[19] The judge shall examine the criminal record of the offender and assess whether or not—on the basis of, e.g., the temporal distance between the crimes and their nature—increased culpability, dangerousness, or both exist. Guidance shall be provided by criteria set forth in art. 133 of the Penal Code.

[20] The 2005 law distinguishes among three different types of recidivism: (*a*) "simple recidivism" (i.e., committing an intentional felony having another one on record), triggering a fixed enhancement of a third of the sentence to be imposed for the current crime; (*b*) "aggravated recidivism," allowing the court to increase the sentence from a third up to a half when the new offense is of the same character as the one on record, it has been committed within a 5-year window since the previous conviction, or it has been committed during the execution of the prior sentence; and (*c*) "multi-aggravated recidivism," if more than one aggravating factor applies. In such cases, if the court decides to impose the recidivist premium, the enhancement shall be by a half, thus determined in a fixed amount. In case a recidivist reoffends (reiterated recidivism), the penalty may be enhanced by a half or two-thirds in case one or more of the aggravating factors listed at point *b* above applies.

vided for by the law for each offense. The various reforms of white-collar crimes passed over the years and characterized by a generalized lowering of statutory minimums and maximums in practice have restricted the potential applicability of recidivist premiums to certain types of offender only (street criminals, drug dealers, undocumented aliens in particular), who in fact now consistently represent more than a half of the sentenced recidivists (pp. 540–41).

E. War on Drugs Italian Style

Since the early 1990s, supply-side law enforcement has been nearly the only response to drugs. Law no. 162 of 1990 harshened legal system responses to production and distribution of drugs and possession for personal consumption. However, a clear line was drawn between hard and soft drugs: production and distribution of hard drugs were to be punished within a statutory range of 8–20 years' imprisonment; for soft drugs, the range was 2–6 years. In 1993 a successful ballot initiative abolished imprisonment for personal consumption of hard or soft drugs. Italian drug policy was thus characterized by tolerance of personal consumption and a clear distinction in punishment between types of drugs, largely driven by a late-1980s heroin epidemic (Rezza et al. 1992). A major policy concern was that drug smuggling was the largest income source for organized crime (Paoli 2003).

A major change of direction occurred in 2006, a few months before general elections. The center-right coalition changed the 1990 drug law. At the 2003 annual meeting of the UN Commission on Narcotic Drugs held in Vienna, Deputy Prime Minister Gianfranco Fini called for a zero-tolerance drug policy eliminating the distinction between soft and hard drugs and penalizing possession of illegal drugs for personal use. "The attitude of the state must change," Fini said. "It cannot remain indifferent to illegal drugs, even when they are for personal consumption" (*The Independent* 2003).

Law no. 49 of 2006 (the Fini-Giovanardi Law after its two main sponsors) followed suit. It embraced an openly moralistic prohibitionist approach that equated soft and hard drugs for punishment purposes. The new version of article 73 of Law no. 162 provided 6–20 years' imprisonment for production and distribution of any type of drug, regardless of addictive effects. This is draconian in comparison, for example, with the 10–18 range for reckless murder and the 6–12 range for aggravated sexual assault.

The new law reinstated personal drug use as a criminal offense. Above a specified quantity threshold, a presumption of possession for distribution applies. For possession of an amount slightly above the threshold, the range is 1–5 years. The new policy was largely based on the gateway theory that use of less dangerous drugs leads to use of more addictive and destructive ones. The early report on the draft of the bill dismissed the libertarian notion of drug use as harmless wrongdoing: "Taking drugs is not a harmless exercise of freedom that does not tolerate interference, but rather it is an act of rejection of the most fundamental duties of individuals towards the communities in which they live. . . . The state has the duty to respond to such behavior with a complex framework of measures" (quoted in *L'Unità* 2003).

The center-left governments in power from 2006 to 2008 and, more recently, since 2013 have not changed the Fini-Giovanardi Law. The opposition came, surprisingly, from a Constitutional Court ruling in early 2014 (Judgment no. 32 of February 25, 2014) that struck down the provision eliminating the distinction between soft and hard drugs and thus reinstating the previous, less severe penalty regime. The provisions were found to violate the delegation of powers by the Parliament to the government, which promulgated the drug reform under a legislative decree that was originally aimed solely at dealing with matters related to the Turin Winter Olympic Games of 2006.

The 2006 changes quickly and visibly affected admissions to prison and the incarceration rate. Table 4 shows trends in prison admissions. Previously, many newly incarcerated persons each year were not affected by drug-related penal provisions as they were personal consumers or distributors of soft drugs and thus were immediately eligible for probation as a prison alternative, sometimes coupled with mandatory drug treatment. The increases in statutory minimum penalties made it much harder for many drug offenders to avoid prison, at least in part.

In 2006, of 90,714 people admitted to prison, 25,399 were article 73 related; in 2008 they were 28,865 of 92,800 total admissions. Numbers have recently declined, as a result of enactment of various decarceration measures in the aftermath of the European Court of Human Rights prison overcrowding decisions and the Constitutional Court judgment reintroducing the distinction between hard and soft drugs. The percentage of admissions in 2014 under article 73 was the lowest since 2007.

Table 5 shows the effects of drug offenders on the composition of the prison population at year-end. On December 31, 2014, convicted or

TABLE 4

Trends in Prison Admissions

	Total Admissions to Prison for All Types of Offense			Total Admissions to Prison for Violations of Article 73			Prison Admissions for a Violation of Article 73 (%)
Year	Italians	Foreigners	Total	Italians	Foreigners	Total	
2005	49,281	40,606	89,887	15,670	10,107	25,777	28.68
2006	47,426	43,288	90,714	15,074	10,325	25,399	28.00
2007	46,581	43,860	90,441	15,392	11,593	26,985	29.84
2008	49,701	43,099	92,800	16,564	12,301	28,865	31.10
2009	47,993	40,073	88,066	15,909	12,460	28,369	32.21
2010	47,343	37,298	84,641	15,695	10,446	26,141	30.88
2011	43,677	33,305	76,982	14,226	10,226	24,452	31.76
2012	36,014	27,006	63,020	11,376	9,088	20,465	32.47
2013	33,572	25,818	59,390	10,042	8,109	18,151	30.56
2014	27,470	22,747	50,217	7,225	6,747	13,972	28.38

SOURCE.—Anastasia and Cianchella (2015, p. 5, table 1).

remanded drug offenders were 33.56 percent of the total, down from 37.33 percent in 2013. The peak under the zero-tolerance statute occurred in 2009, when 40.21 percent of prisoners were drug offenders. The effects of the Constitutional Court judgment are clear: There were 8,913 fewer people in custody in 2014 compared with 2013; the year-to-year reduction in article 73–related inmates was 5,351.

The effects of the Fini-Giovanardi Law are further evidenced by comparison of police and prison data related to article 73 in 2006–13. Figure 7 shows that the rate of reported drug offenses per 100,000 population has been substantially stable since enactment of the 2006 law but that the imprisonment rate for those crimes greatly increased. Many more people were in pretrial detention or serving a custodial sentence for drug-related offenses.

F. California Calling: Addressing Prison Overcrowding

The Italian prison population rose substantially after the early 1990s for three main reasons. First, new laws increased lengths of sentences for particular crimes (e.g., drugs), and other changes limited eligibility of some offenders for early release. Second, enactment of clemency measures became much more difficult politically. Third, no efforts were made to increase the capacity of the prison system despite clear popula-

TABLE 5

Drug Offenders in Prison

Date	Total Number of Inmates (Sentenced and Pretrial)	Incarcerated Individuals for a Violation of Article 73	Incarcerated Individuals for a Violation of Article 73 (%)
12/31/2006	39,005	14,640	37.53
12/31/2007	48,693	18,222	37.42
12/31/2008	58,127	22,727	39.10
12/31/2009	64,791	26,052	40.21
12/31/2010	67,961	27,294	40.16
12/31/2011	66,897	26,559	39.70
12/31/2012	65,701	25,269	38.46
12/31/2013	62,536	23,346	37.33
12/31/2014	53,623	17,995	33.56

SOURCE.—Anastasia and Cianchella (2015, p. 6, table 2).

tion growth. This led to the European Court of Human Rights (ECHR) decisions I have mentioned several times.

Sulejmanovic v. Italy (application no. 22635/03) put the Italian government on notice in 2009. The applicant complained about overcrowding and insufficient daily exercise outside his cell. He shared a cell with six people, each thus having approximately 29 square feet of personal space. This is much less than the minimum standard of 75.3 square feet per prisoner recommended by the Committee for the Prevention of Torture and Inhuman or Degrading Treatment or Punishment. The Court agreed, finding that the personal space allotted Sulejmanovic constituted inhuman or degrading treatment in violation of article 3 of the Convention.

Following this judgment, the Italian government failed to tackle the problem effectively; the most consequential measure adopted was to allow home custody for execution of prison sentences not exceeding 1 year. The government announced a new master plan to increase prison capacity (which was never acted on). At year-end 2010, Italian prisons held 67,961 prisoners in facilities designed for 45,022. That constituted 151 percent overcrowding.

Following *Sulejmanovic*, numerous applications were submitted by inmates to the ECHR alleging violations of article 3 due to overcrowding. In 2013, in *Torreggiani and Others v. Italy* (application no. 43517/09), the ECHR unanimously found a violation of article 3 and gave Italy 1 year

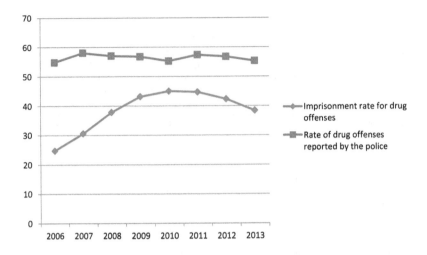

Fig. 7.—Imprisonment rate and rate of drug offenses reported by the police to the prosecutors' offices per 100,000 of the general population, 2006–13. Source: ISTAT (multiple years).

to provide "redress in respect of violations of the Convention resulting from overcrowding in prison." In early June 2012, when the ECHR notified the Italian government of its willingness to issue a "pilot judgment," there were 66,487 inmates against a design capacity of 45,558. The prisons were operating at 145.9 percent of capacity. Italy was required to adopt a combination of remedies aimed at addressing large numbers of individual cases. Overcrowding was acknowledged to be a structural problem.

The *Torreggiani* judgment will probably call to American readers' minds the US Supreme Court decision in *Brown v. Plata*, 131 S. Ct. 1910 (2011). The Court ruled 5–4 that overcrowding in California's prisons violated prisoners' Eighth Amendment rights to adequate health care; the California system was operating at nearly double its design capacity. The Court asserted that dealing with constitutionally inadequate health care required a population limit and ordered California to reduce its inmate population to 137.5 percent of design capacity within 2 years. California adopted a realignment plan that is under way (Simon 2014).

In Europe, where the culture of human rights in relation to criminal penalties is deep-seated, the ECHR may not directly require a national government to free incarcerated offenders for failing to take adequate measures to solve a certain problem within a designated period. The main remedy available is to award compensatory damages to successful applicants after a Convention violation is established (Heyns and Killander 2013, p. 684).

In the first half of 2014, the Italian Parliament enacted several measures aimed at reducing the overcrowding rate. No sentencing provisions in a narrow sense were modified; rather the focus was on sentence implementation. These are the main changes:

- Good time credit (sentence remission) has been increased from 45 to 75 days per half year except for a specific list of offenses.
- Home custody has been authorized for prison sentences up to 18 months.
- Substitution of probation for a prison term has been extended to cover sentences up to 4 years imposed in court or already partly served.
- New provisions make custody before trial the last resort to which the pretrial investigation judge may resort on request of the prosecutor. Pretrial detention is applicable only when less intrusive options are insufficient. Except for offenses such as organized crime, terrorism, domestic violence, and stalking, pretrial detention was banned when the pretrial investigation judge estimates that the sentence imposed at trial will not exceed 3 years.

Figure 8 shows the pattern of decarceration since 2006, when the last collective clemency measure took effect. Changes since 2010 had the primary goal to increase the proportion of custodial sentences served outside a prison by diverting some offenders and accelerating eligibility for release into alternatives for prisoners who have partly served their prison term.

Since the ECHR cases were decided, the number of sentenced individuals serving custodial sentences in an alternative regime outside prison has continuously grown. The decrease in inmate numbers is also partly attributable to earlier eligibility of many prisoners for release on parole due to increased good time credits. The number of detainees in pretrial detention is the lowest since the early 1990s.

At year-end 2015, the decarceration measures had had substantial effect. There were 52,164 inmates in Italian prisons designed to accommo-

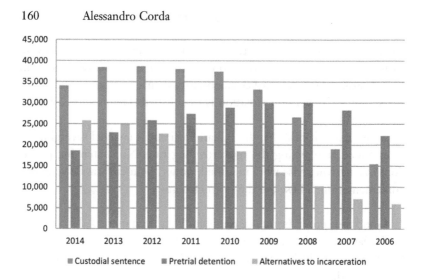

Fɪɢ. 8.—Individuals held in custody, either serving a custodial sentence or in pretrial detention, and serving custodial sentences under an alternative regime outside prison at year-end, 2006–14. Source: Ministry of Justice (2015*a*).

date 49,592 (thus "only" 5.2 percent over capacity). Prison admissions have plummeted. Admissions in 2015 were 45,823, compared with 92,800 in 2008 during the peak of "zero tolerance."

My impression is that the policy changes were enacted merely as emergency measures to avoid unfreezing of nearly 3,000 applications pending before the ECHR that alleged degrading conditions and to stop the filing of new ones. Italy potentially faced massive compensatory damages (each *Torreggiani* applicant case received between €10,000 and €20,000 depending on length of confinement). The ECHR's rulings have not sparked a genuine debate on reform of Italy's criminal justice system generally and sentencing policies and practices in particular. The new initiatives are a reactive response to what Aviram dubbed "humonetarianism," the short-term "tendency to view criminal justice and correctional policies primarily through a prism of cost" (2015, p. 6).

IV. Conclusions

Italian penal culture has experienced a substantial transformation since the mid-1980s. In 1986 Italy embraced penal welfarism at a time when in common law countries and elsewhere it had been dismantled since the 1970s in favor of harsher penalties and enhanced social control. This choice together with expanded procedural protections in the 1989 Code of Criminal Procedure seemed to express a tradition of penal moderation based on the legitimacy of the state and consensual approaches to penal policy.

In retrospect, those changes were the swan song of a political system that was about to succumb because of its structural inability to reform itself (Briquet 2009). The Clean Hands investigation initiated what appears to be still a never-ending political transition that increasingly affected penal policy making.

Since at least the late 1990s, governments of different orientation have enacted policies that overrely on criminal sanctions, by creating new offenses or specifying harsher sentences. The shift from a consensual to an openly conflictive majoritarian political system has led to much higher sensitivity to populist arguments concerning penal policies. The appeal of tough-on-crime policies for short-term electoral gains has not been a monopoly of the center-right parties. The center-left governments also embraced them, although to a lesser extent and according to a different ideological platform.

In the past two decades, massive immigration and large cuts in public spending on welfare and law enforcement heightened public concerns about security of individual property and personal safety. Crime-related anxieties have consistently ranked first among the public's top fears, being only recently surpassed by unemployment and financial instability (Demos et al. 2015). Overall, the slow but constant substitution of highly individualized self-responsibility for collective solidarity has led to a widespread "sentiment of vulnerability" that has triggered demands for harsher penalties (Bauman 2009, p. 110). At the same time, the justice system has been expected to address issues that should have been handled by other institutions and different social policies.

At least three factors, however, reduce the "punitive potential" of the developments discussed in this essay. First, an independent judiciary strongly insulated from political directives and pressures has played, and likely will continue to play, a crucial role. Prosecutors "filter" social fears and excessive penal demands by performing their functions in neutral yet sensitive ways. Judges use their discretionary powers in determining sentences to reduce the effects of severe statutory ranges. The Constitutional Court struck down laws that contributed to the shift toward greater severity.

Second, the pendulum has swung multiple times over the past three decades between increased punitiveness and greater procedural fairness. The outcome has been a criminal justice system sometimes at war with itself. In contrast to the United States, where the adversarial system over time has become an efficient assembly line of guilty pleas (Bibas 2012), the Italian adversarial initiatives of the 1980s and 1990s overlooked foreseeable effects on efficiency. The Italian infrastructure includes long pretrial investigations and gives defendants and their lawyers incentives to abuse guarantees "which are seen by some as measures pretending to protect the accused's rights" but slow down and often prevent the final adjudication of cases (Nelken 2009, p. 306). No real incentives exist to opt for a simplified "fast-track" alternative proceeding: the incentive (a reduced sentence) is not balanced by any kind of disincentive (a realistic "trial penalty"). The opposite is true: not only does the prohibition of *reformatio in peius* prevent the appellate courts from increasing sentences imposed at trial but the statutes of limitations run out for a relatively large number of cases—especially low- and medium-level offenses—during the process because of the multiple appeals that are available.

Third, the growth of the prison population and gigantic backlogs of cases persuaded the Parliament to try to tackle those problems. However, despite their tangible outcomes, deferred and nonprosecution schemes and alternatives to implementation of custodial sentences were not inspired by a revamped culture of tolerance. The increased centrality of alternatives is not a manifestation of a comprehensive strategy to abandon imprisonment or reinvigorate constitutional mandates of rehabilitation as the main goal of punishment. To the contrary, those initiatives have largely been impromptu efforts to come to terms with issues at a time when procrastination was no longer viable. Today's instances of Italian penal welfarism look more declaratory than real, mirroring the progressive structural weakening of social welfare generally.

The current Italian sentencing system is characterized by a high degree of inefficiency. Sentences are largely "disintegrated" at various stages of the process. The excessive length of trials coupled with initiatives widening the range of alternatives further undermines the certainty and predictability of punishment. Selectiveness is another major feature of the Italian sentencing system: for perpetrators of certain offenses (typically members of criminal organizations, drug and sex offenders), extended pretrial detention and disproportionately high statutory maximums make experience with the Italian penal machinery more likely. This is also true of offenders who commit common crimes but lack knowledge and resources to take full advantage of the existing "devices of moderation."

During the period covered by this essay, 1985–2015, Italy experienced increased levels of punitiveness. The effects are evident at national and local levels and include newly established policies and ways in which political and media discourse on crime and punishment have changed. In my view, Italy's recent penal history does not represent, as Gallo (2015) has argued, a distinctive challenge to the narrative on trends of "Western punitiveness."

The persistent mildness of the criminal justice system results from the combination of inadequate resources, inefficient organization, and inconsistent penal values rather than from considered policy choices. Recent initiatives affecting sentence implementation have been driven by realpolitik policies in reaction to the prison overcrowding crisis. Current proposals for decriminalization of minor crimes and substantial reform of criminal sanctions are embryonic and largely contested. It is too early to tell whether faint signs of change will eventually be seen as early steps in a long overdue comprehensive reconstruction of the sentencing system or simply as tiles soon to be undone or contradicted in the Penelope's shroud of never-ending reforms of the troubled Italian penal system.

REFERENCES

Aebi, Marcelo F., and Julien Chopin. 2015. *SPACE II—Council of Europe Annual Penal Statistics: Persons Serving Non-custodial Sanctions and Measures.* Survey 2013. Strasbourg: Council of Europe.

Aebi, Marcelo F., and Natalia Delgrande. 2015. *SPACE I—Council of Europe Annual Penal Statistics: Prison Populations.* Survey 2013. Strasbourg: Council of Europe.

Aebi, Marcelo F., Natalia Delgrande, and Yann Marguet. 2015. "Have Community Sanctions and Measures Widened the Net of the European Criminal Justice Systems?" *Punishment and Society* 17(5):575–97.

Alberti, Adriana. 1996. "Political Corruption and the Role of Public Prosecutors in Italy." *Crime, Law and Social Change* 24:273–92.

Altheide, David L. 2003. "Notes Toward a Politics of Fear." *Journal for Crime, Conflict, and the Media* 1(1):37–54.

Ambrosini, Maurizio M. 2013. "We Are Against a Multi-ethnic Society: Policies of Exclusion at the Urban Level in Italy." *Ethnic and Racial Studies* 36(1):136–55.

Amodio, Ennio. 2004. "The Accusatorial System Lost and Regained: Reforming Criminal Procedure in Italy." *American Journal of Comparative Law* 52(2):489–500.

Amodio, Ennio, and Eugenio Selvaggi. 1989. "An Accusatorial System in a Civil Law Country: The 1988 Italian Code of Criminal Procedure." *Temple Law Review* 62(4):1211–24.

Anastasia, Stefano, and Maurizio Cianchella. 2015. "La punizione della detenzione e del consumo di droghe: Cosa è cambiato ad un anno dalla sentenza della Corte Costituzionale?" In *6° Libro bianco sulla legge sulle droghe*, 2nd ed., edited by Franco Corleone, Stefano Anastasia, and Leonardo Fiorentini. http://formazione.fuoriluogo.it/pubblicazioni/libro-bianco/.

Ashworth, Andrew. 2009. "Techniques for Reducing Sentence Disparity." In *Principled Sentencing*, 3rd ed., edited by Andrew von Hirsch, Andrew Ashworth, and Julian Roberts. Oxford: Hart.

Aviram, Hadar. 2015. *Cheap on Crime: Recession-Era Politics and the Transformation of American Punishment*. Oakland: University of California Press.

Barbagli, Marzio. 2004. "Lost Primacy: Crime in Italy at the End of the Twentieth Century." *Journal of Modern Italian Studies* 9(2):143–60.

Barbagli, Marzio, and Asher Colombo. 2011. *Rapporto sulla criminalità e la sicurezza in Italia*. Milan: Gruppo XXIV ore Ministero dell'Interno.

Barbarino, Alessandro, and Giovanni Mastrobuoni. 2014. "The Incapacitation Effect of Incarceration: Evidence from Several Italian Collective Pardons." *American Economic Journal: Economic Policy* 6(1):1–37.

Bauman, Zygmunt. 2006. *Liquid Fear*. Cambridge: Polity.

———. 2009. "The Demons of an Open Society." In *Globalization and the State: Sociological Perspectives on the State of the State*, edited by Willem Schinkel. Hampshire, UK: Palgrave Macmillan.

Beccaria, Cesare. 1995. *On Crimes and Punishments and Other Writings*. Edited by Richard Bellamy; translated by Richard Davies, with Virginia Cox and Richard Bellamy. Cambridge: Cambridge University Press. (Originally published 1764.)

Bibas, Stephanos. 2012. *The Machinery of Criminal Justice*. New York: Oxford University Press.

Bogaards, Matthijs. 2005. "The Italian First Republic: Degenerated Consociationalism in a Polarised Party System." *West European Politics* 28(3):503–20.

Bricola, Franco. 1977. "Le misure alternative alla pena nel quadro di una 'nuova' politica criminale." *Rivista Italiana di Diritto e Procedura Penale* 20(1):13–76.

Briquet, Jean-Louis. 2009. "A Crisis of Legitimacy in Italy: The Scandals Facing the First Republic 1992–1994." *International Social Science Journal* 60:297–309.

Bruti Liberati, Edmondo, Adolfo Ceretti, and Alberto Giasanti. 1996. *Governo dei gudici: La magistratura tra diritto e politica*. Milan: Feltrinelli.

Caianiello, Michele. 2012. "The Italian Public Prosecutor: An Inquisitorial Figure in Adversarial Proceedings." In *The Prosecutor in Transnational Perspective*, edited by Erik Luna and Marianne Wade. New York: Oxford University Press.

Calamandrei, Piero. 1942. *Eulogy of Judges*. Translated by John Clarke Adams and C. Abbott Phillips Jr. Princeton, NJ: Princeton University Press. (Originally published 1936.)

Campesi, Giuseppe. 2015. "Hindering the Deportation Machine: An Ethnography of Power and Resistance in Immigration Detention." *Punishment and Society* 17(4):427–53.

Caputo, Angelo. 2001. "Politiche e riforme penali nel quinquennio di governo dell ulivo." *Questione Giustizia* 6(6):1045–67.

Carter, Nick. 1998. "Italy: The Demise of Post-war Partyocracy." In *Political Parties and the Collapse of the Old Orders*, edited by John Kenneth White and Philip John Davies. Albany: State University of New York Press.

Cavadino, Michael, and James Dignan. 2006a. "Penal Policy and Political Economy." *Criminology and Criminal Justice* 6(4):435–56.

———. 2006b. *Penal Systems: A Comparative Approach*. London: Sage.

Cento Bull, Anna, and Philip Cooke. 2013. *Ending Terrorism in Italy*. London: Routledge.

Ceretti, Adolfo, and Roberto Cornelli. 2013. *Oltre la paura: Cinque riflessioni su criminalità, società e politica*. Milan: Feltrinelli.

Corriere della Sera. 2014. "Processi a numero chiuso a Roma non più di 12 mila casi all anno." March 7.

Damaška, Mirjan R. 1986. *The Faces of Justice and State Authority: A Comparative Approach to the Legal Process*. New Haven, CT: Yale University Press.

Davigo, Piercamillo. 1999. "Sete di giustizia e sepolcri imbiancati." *Micromega* 14(2):183–216.

De Giorgi, Alessandro. 2006. *Re-thinking the Political Economy of Punishment: Perspectives on Post-Fordism and Penal Politics*. Aldershot, UK: Ashgate.

De Keijser, Jan. 2011. "Never Mind the Pain; It's a Measure! Justifying Measures as Part of the Dutch Bifurcated System of Sanctions." In *Retributivism Has a Past: Has It a Future?* edited by Michael Tonry. Oxford: Oxford University Press.

Del Duca, Louis F. 1991. "An Historic Convergence of Civil and Common Law Systems: Italy's New 'Adversarial' Criminal Procedure System." *Dickinson Journal of International Law* 10:73–92.

Della Porta, Donatella. 1992. "Institutional Responses to Terrorism: The Italian Case." *Terrorism and Political Violence* 4(4):151–70.

———. 1996. "The System of Corrupt Exchange in Local Government." In *The New Italian Republic: From the Fall of the Berlin Wall to Berlusconi*, edited by Stephen Gundle and Simon Parker. London: Routledge.

———. 2001. "A Judges' Revolution? Political Corruption and the Judiciary in Italy." *European Journal of Political Research* 39(1):1–21.

Della Porta, Donatella, and Alberto Vannucci. 2007. "Corruption and Anticorruption: The Political Defeat of 'Clean Hands' in Italy." *West European Politics* 30(4):830–53.

Demos et al. 2015. *Rapporto sulla sicurezza e l'insicurezza sociale in Italia e in Europa*. 8th ed. http://www.demos.it/2015/pdf/3346fondazione_unipolis_rapporto_sulla_sicurezza_febbraio_2015.pdf.

Di Federico, Giuseppe. 1998. "Prosecutorial Independence and the Democratic Requirement of Accountability in Italy: Analysis of a Deviant Case in Comparative Perspective." *British Journal of Criminology* 38(3):371–87.

———. 2008. "Prosecutorial Accountability, Independence, and Effectiveness in Italy." In *Promoting Prosecutorial Accountability, Independence, and Effectiveness*. Sofia, Bulgaria: Open Society Institute Press.

Di Federico, Giuseppe, and Michele Sapignoli. 2014. *I diritti della difesa nel processo penale e la riforma della giustizia*. Padua: CEDAM.

Dolcini, Emilio. 2007. "La recidiva riformata: Ancora più selettivo il carcere in Italia." *Rivista Italiana di Diritto e Procedura Penale* 50(2–3):515–45.

Donovan, Mark. 1996. "Electoral Reform and Political Change in Italy." In *The New Italian Republic: From the Fall of the Berlin Wall to Berlusconi*, edited by Stephen Gundle and Simon Parker. London: Routledge.

Fabbrini, Sergio. 2009. "The Transformation of Italian Democracy." *Bulletin of Italian Politics* 1(1):29–47.

Fassler, Lawrence J. 1991. "The Italian Penal Procedure Code: An Adversarial System of Criminal Procedure in Continental Europe." *Columbia Journal of Transnational Law* 29:245–78.

Fella, Stefano, and Carlo Ruzza. 2013. "Populism and the Fall of the Centre-Right in Italy: The End of the Berlusconi Model or a New Beginning?" *Journal of Contemporary European Studies* 21(1):38–52.

Ferri, Enrico. 1968. *The Positive School of Criminology: Three Lectures*. Pittsburgh: University of Pittsburgh Press.

Forti, Gabrio, and Arianna Visconti. 2007. "Cesare Beccaria and White-Collar Crimes: Public Harm; a Study in Italian Systemic Corruption." In *International Handbook of White-Collar and Corporate Crime*, edited by Henry R. Pontell and Gilbert Geis. New York: Springer.

Gallo, Zelia A. 2014. "Legitimacy and Punitiveness: The Role of Judicial Actors in Italian Penality." In *Punishment and Incarceration: A Global Perspective*, edited by Mathieu Deflem. Bingley, UK: Emerald.

———. 2015. "Punishment, Authority, and Political Economy: Italian Challenges to Western Punitiveness." *Punishment and Society* 17(5):598–623.

Garland, David. 2001. *The Culture of Control: Crime and Social Order in Contemporary Society*. Chicago: University of Chicago Press.

Gatti, Umberto, and Alfredo Verde. 2002. "Comparative Juvenile Justice: An Overview of Italy." In *Juvenile Justice Systems: International Perspectives*, 2nd ed., edited by John A. Winterdyk. Toronto: Canadian Scholars Press.

Ginsborg, Paul. 1990. *A History of Contemporary Italy: Society and Politics, 1943–1988*. London: Penguin.

———. 2004. *Silvio Berlusconi: Television, Power and Patrimony*. London: Verso.

Goldstein, Abraham, and Martin Marcus. 1977. "The Myth of Judicial Supervision in Three 'Inquisitorial' Systems: France, Italy, and Germany." *Yale Law Journal* 87:240–83.

Gonnella, Patrizio. 2013. "Italy: Between Amnesties and Emergencies." In *Punishment in Europe: A Critical Anatomy of Penal Systems*, edited by Vincenzo Ruggiero and Mick Ryan. Basingstoke, UK: Palgrave Macmillan.

Grande, Elisabetta. 2000. "Italian Criminal Justice: Borrowing and Resistance." *American Journal of Comparative Law* 48:227–59.

———. 2002. "The Rise and Fall of the Rehabilitative Ideal in Italian Criminal Justice." *Global Jurist* 2(1):1–15.

Gualazzi, Alessandra, and Chiara Mancuso. 2010. "Italy." In *Release from Prison: European Policy and Practice*, edited by Nicola Padfield, Dirk van Zyl Smit, and Frieder Dünkel. London: Routledge.

Gualazzi, Alessandra, Chiara Mancuso, and Annalisa Mangiaracina. 2012. "Back Door Sentencing in Italy: Common Reasons and Main Consequences for the Recall of Prisoners." *European Journal of Probation* 4(1):73–84.

Guarnieri, Carlo. 1994. "Justice and Politics: The Italian Case in a Comparative Perspective." *Indiana International and Comparative Law Review* 4:241–57.

———. 2015. "The Courts." In *The Oxford Handbook of Italian Politics*, edited by Erik Jones and Gianfranco Pasquino. Oxford: Oxford University Press.

Guarnieri, Carlo, and Patrizia Pederzoli. 1997. "The Judicialization of Politics, Italian Style." *Journal of Modern Italian Studies* 2(3):321–36.

Guzzini, Stefano. 1995. "The Long Night of the First Republic: Years of Clientelistic Implosion in Italy." *Review of International Political Economy* 2(1): 27–61.

Harcourt, Bernard E. 2014. "Beccaria's on Crimes and Punishments: A Mirror on the History of the Foundations of Modern Criminal Law." In *Foundational Texts in Modern Criminal Law*, edited by Markus D. Dubber. Oxford: Oxford University Press.

Harris, David A. 2012. "The Interaction and Relationship between Prosecutors and Police Officers in the US and How This Affects Police Reform Efforts." In *The Prosecutor in Transnational Perspective*, edited by Erik Luna and Marianne Wade. New York: Oxford University Press.

Henham, Ralph. 2012. *Sentencing and the Legitimacy of Trial Justice*. Abingdon, UK: Routledge.

Henham, Ralph, and Grazia Mannozzi. 2003. "Victim Participation and Sentencing in England and Italy: A Legal and Policy Analysis." *European Journal of Crime, Criminal Law and Criminal Justice* 11(3):278–313.

Heyns, Christof, and Magnus Killander. 2013. "Universality and the Growth of Regional Systems." In *The Oxford Handbook of International Human Rights Law*, edited by Dinah Shelton. Oxford: Oxford University Press.

Illuminati, Giulio. 2004. "The Role of the Public Prosecutor in the Italian System." In *Tasks and Powers of the Prosecution Services in the EU Member States*, edited by Peter J. P. Tak. Nijmegen, Neth.: Wolf Legal.

———. 2005. "The Frustrated Turn to Adversarial Procedure in Italy: Italian Criminal Procedure Code of 1988." *Washington University Global Studies Law Review* 4:567–81.

———. 2010. "The Accusatorial Process from the Italian Point of View." *North Carolina Journal of International Law and Commercial Regulation* 35:297–318.

Illuminati, Giulio, and Michele Caianiello. 2007. "The Investigative Stage of the Criminal Process in Italy." In *Suspects in Europe: Procedural Rights at the Investigative Stage of the Criminal Process in the European Union*, edited by Ed Cape, Jacqueline Hodgson, Ties Prakken, and Taru Spronken. Antwerp: Intersentia.

The Independent. 2003. "Italy Signs Up to Zero-Tolerance Drugs Crackdown." April 18. http://www.independent.co.uk/news/world/europe/italy-signs-up -to-zero-tolerance-drugs-crackdown-115664.html.

ISTAT (National Institute of Statistics). 2013. *I condannati con sentenza definitive nel periodo 2000–2011*. http://www.istat.it/it/archivio/103655.

———. 2014. *Annuario statistico italiano 2014*. http://www.istat.it/it/files/2014 /11/Asi-2014.pdf.

———. 2015. *Annuario statistico italiano 2015.* http://www.istat.it/it/archivio/171864.

Langer, Máximo. 2004. "From Legal Transplants to Legal Translations: The Globalization of Plea Bargaining and the Americanization Thesis in Criminal Procedure." *Harvard International Law Journal* 45:1–64.

———. 2014. "The Long Shadow of the Adversarial and Inquisitorial Categories." In *The Oxford Handbook of Criminal Law,* edited by Markus D. Dubber and Tatjana Hörnle. New York: Oxford University Press.

La Spina, Antonio. 2004. "The Paradox of Effectiveness: Growth, Institutionalisation, and Evaluation of Anti-mafia Policies in Italy." In *Organised Crime in Europe: Conceptions, Patterns, and Policies in the European Union and Beyond,* edited by Cyrille Fijnaut and Letizia Paoli. Dordrecht, Neth.: Springer.

———. 2014. "The Fight against the Italian Mafia." In *The Oxford Handbook of Organized Crime,* edited by Letizia Paoli. New York: Oxford University Press.

Lijphart, Arend. 1969. "Consociational Democracy." *World Politics* 21(2):207–25.

———. 1999. *Patterns of Democracy: Government Forms and Performance in Thirty-Six Countries.* New Haven, CT: Yale University Press.

L'Unità. 2003. "La legge di fini: Mezza canna e finisci in cella." November 14.

Mack, Charles S. 2010. *When Political Parties Die: A Cross-National Analysis of Disalignment and Realignment.* Santa Barbara, CA: Praeger.

Maddalena, Marcello. 2007. "L'obbligatorietà dell azione penale." *Critica Penale* 62(1):5–26.

Maffei, Stefano. 2004. "Negotiations on Evidence and Negotiations on Sentence: Adversarial Experiments in Italian Criminal Procedure." *Journal of International Criminal Justice* 2:1050–69.

Mannozzi, Grazia. 2002. "Are Guided Sentencing and Plea Bargaining Incompatible? Perspectives of Reform in the Italian Legal System." In *Sentencing and Society: International Perspectives,* edited by Cyrus Tata and Neil Hutton. Aldershot, UK: Ashgate.

Marafioti, Luca. 2008. "Italian Criminal Procedure: A System Caught between Two Traditions." In *Essays in Honour of Professor Mirjan Damaška,* edited by John Jackson, Máximo Langer, and Peter Tillers. Oxford: Hart.

Massetti, Emanuele. 2015. "Mainstream Parties and the Politics of Immigration in Italy: A Structural Advantage for the Right or a Missed Opportunity for the Left?" *Acta Politica* 50(4):486–505.

Melossi, Dario. 1994. "The 'Economy' of Illegalities: Normal Crimes, Elites, and Social Control in Comparative Analysis." In *The Futures of Criminology,* edited by David Nelken. London: Sage.

———. 2000. "Changing Representations of the Criminal." *British Journal of Criminology* 40(2):296–320.

———. 2001. "The Cultural Embeddedness of Social Control: Reflections on the Comparison of Italian and North-American Cultures Concerning Punishment." *Theoretical Criminology* 5(4):403–24.

———. 2013. "The Processes of Criminalization of Migrants and the Question of Europe as a Land of Immigration." In *European Penology?* edited by Tom Daems, Dirk van Zyl Smit, and Sonja Snacken. Oxford: Hart.

Melossi, Dario, and Rossella Selmini. 2009. "Modernisation of Institutions of Social and Penal Control in Italy/Europe: The 'New' Crime Prevention." In *Crime Prevention Policies in Comparative Perspective*, edited by Adam Crawford. Cullompton, UK: Willan.

Mershon, Carol, and Gianfranco Pasquino. 1995. "Introduction." In *Italian Politics: Ending the First Republic*, edited by Carol Mershon and Gianfranco Pasquino. Boulder, CO: Westview.

Ministry of Justice. 2015*a*. *Condannati sottoposti a misure alternative alla detenzione incarichi in corso al 31 dicembre, 1997–2014*. https://www.giustizia.it/giustizia /it/mg_1_14_1.wp?facetNode_1=0_2&facetNode_2=0_2_2&previsiousPage =mg_1_14&contentId=SST1192560.

———. 2015*b*. *Prescrizioni penali serie storica, 2004–2013*. https://webstat.giustizia .it/Analisi%20e%20ricerche/Prescrizioni%20penali%20Serie%20storica %202004-2013.pdf.

Ministry of Justice, Direzione Generale di Statistica (DG-Stat). 2015*a*. *Procedimenti penali con autore noto definiti con sentenza nei tribunali ordinari, con rito monocratico primo grado, per distretto*. Anno 2013. https://reportistica.dgstat .giustizia.it/VisualizzatoreReport.Aspx?Report=/Pubblica/Statistiche%20della %20DGSTAT/Materia%20Penale/2.%20Modalita%20di%20definizione /1.%20dati%20distrettuali/6.%20tribunale%20ordinario%20monocratico.

———. 2015*b*. *Procedimenti penali con autore noto definiti con sentenza nei tribunali ordinari, con rito collegiale, per distretto*. Anno 2013. https://reportistica.dgstat .giustizia.it/VisualizzatoreReport.Aspx?Report=/Pubblica/Statistiche%20della %20DGSTAT/Materia%20Penale/2.%20Modalita%20di%20definizione/1 .%20dati%20distrettuali/5.%20tribunale%20ordinario%20collegiale.

———. 2015*c*. *Procedimenti penali con autore noto definiti nei tribunali—Sezione GIP/GUP per principali modalità di definizione e distretto*. Anno 2013. https:// reportistica.dgstat.giustizia.it/VisualizzatoreReport.Aspx?Report=/Pubblica /Statistiche%20della%20DGSTAT/Materia%20Penale/2.%20Modalita%20di %20definizione/1.%20dati%20distrettuali/7.%20tribunale%20ordinario%20gip %20gup.

———. 2015*d*. *Movimento dei procedimenti penali con autore noto negli uffici giudiziari per tipologia di ufficio: Dato nazionale*. Anno 2013. https://reportistica.dgstat .giustizia.it/VisualizzatoreReport.Aspx?Report=/Pubblica/Statistiche%20della %20DGSTAT/Materia%20Penale/1.%20Movimento%20dei%20procedimenti /1.%20dati%20nazionali/2.%20tutti%20gli%20uffici.

Mirabella, Julia Grace. 2012. "Scales of Justice: Assessing Italian Criminal Procedure through the Amanda Knox Trial." *Boston University International Law Journal* 30:229–60.

Montana, Riccardo. 2009*a*. "Paradigms of Judicial Supervision and Co-ordination between Police and Prosecutors: The Italian Case in a Comparative Perspective." *European Journal of Crime, Criminal Law and Criminal Justice* 17(4): 309–33.

———. 2009*b*. "Prosecutors and the Definition of the Crime Problem in Italy: Balancing the Impact of Moral Panics." *Criminal Law Forum* 20(4):471– 94.

————. 2012. "Adversarialism in Italy: Using the Concept of Legal Culture to Understand Resistance to Legal Modifications and Its Consequences." *European Journal of Crime, Criminal Law and Criminal Justice* 20(1):99–120.

Montana, Riccardo, and David Nelken. 2011. "Prosecution, Legal Culture, and Resistance to Moral Panics in Italy." In *Routledge Handbook of International Criminology*, edited by Cindy J. Smith, Sheldon X. Zhang, and Rosemary Barberet. New York: Routledge.

Montesquieu, Baron de. 2000. "Extract from: The Spirit of the Laws." In *Modern Political Thought: A Reader*, edited by John Gingell, Adrian Little, and Christopher Winch. London: Routledge. (Originally published 1748.)

Nelken, David. 1996. "The Judges and Political Corruption in Italy." *Journal of Law and Society* 23(1):95–112.

————. 2002. "Legitimate Suspicions? Berlusconi and the Judges." *Italian Politics* 18:112–28.

————. 2005. "When Is a Society Non-punitive? The Italian Case." In *The New Punitiveness: Trends, Theories, Perspectives*, edited by John Pratt, David Brown, Mark Brown, Simon Hallsworth, and Wayne Morrison. Cullompton, UK: Willan.

————. 2006. "Italian Juvenile Justice: Tolerance, Leniency, or Indulgence?" *Youth Justice* 6(2):107–28.

————. 2009. "Comparative Criminal Justice: Beyond Ethnocentrism and Relativism." *European Journal of Criminology* 6(4):291–311.

————. 2013. "Can Prosecutors Be Too Independent? An Italian Case-Study." In *European Penology?* edited by Tom Daems, Dirk van Zyl Smit, and Sonja Snacken. Oxford: Hart.

New York Times. 2011. "Berlusconi, Magnetic and Divisive, Whose Politics Were Personal." November 13. http://www.nytimes.com/2011/11/13/world/europe/berlusconi-both-drew-and-divided-italians.html?_r=0.

Panzavolta, Michele. 2005. "Reforms and Counter-reforms in the Italian Struggle for an Accusatorial Criminal Law System." *North Carolina Journal of International Law and Commercial Regulation* 30:577–622.

Paoli, Letizia. 2001. "Crime, Italian Style." *Daedalus* 130(3):157–85.

————. 2003. *Mafia Brotherhoods: Organized Crime, Italian Style*. Oxford: Oxford University Press.

————. 2007. "Mafia and Organised Crime in Italy: The Unacknowledged Successes of Law Enforcement." *West European Politics* 30(4):840–80.

Pavarini, Massimo. 1994. "The New Penology and Politics in Crisis: The Italian Case." *British Journal of Criminology* 34(S1):49–61.

————. 1997. "Controlling Social Panic: Questions and Answers about Security in Italy at the End of the Millennium." In *Social Control and Political Order: European Perspectives at the End of the Century*, edited by Roberto Bergalli and Colin Sumner. London: Sage.

————. 2001. "The Politics of Punishment: The Death of Prison Reform in Italy." In *Imprisonment Today and Tomorrow*, edited by Dirk van Zyl Smit and Frieder Dünkel. Boston: Kluwer Law International.

————. 2006. "The Spaghetti Incapacitation: La nuova disciplina della recidiva." In *La legislazione penale compulsiva*, edited by Gaetano Insolera. Padua: CEDAM.

Pellissero, Marco. 2013. "The Doppio Binario in Italian Criminal Law." In *Preventing Danger: New Paradigms in Criminal Justice*, edited by Michele Caianiello and Michael L. Corrado. Durham, NC: Carolina Academic Press.

Piraino, Flavio. 2007. "Amnistia, indulto e popolazione detenuta nell Italia repubblicana." *L'Altro Diritto: Centro di Documentazione su Carcere, Devianza e Marginalità Repubblicana.* http://www.altrodiritto.unifi.it/ricerche/law-ways /piraino.htm.

Pizzi, William T., and Luca Marafioti. 1992. "The New Italian Code of Criminal Procedure: The Difficulties of Building an Adversarial Trial System on a Civil Law Foundation." *Yale Journal of International Law* 17(1):1–40.

Pizzi, William T., and Mariangela Montagna. 2004. "The Battle to Establish an Adversarial Trial System in Italy." *Michigan Journal of International Law* 25:429–64.

Quigley, Brendan. 2011. "Immunity, Italian Style: Silvio Berlusconi versus the Italian Legal System." *Hastings International and Comparative Law Review* 34: 435–63.

Rezza, Giovanni, Maria Dorrucci, Umberto Filibeck, and Irinus Serafin. 1992. "Estimating the Trend of the Epidemic of Drug Use in Italy, 1985–89." *British Journal of Addiction* 87(12):1643–48.

Rhodes, Martin. 1997. "Financing Party Politics in Italy: A Case of Systemic Corruption." *West European Politics* 20(1):54–80.

———. 2015. "Tangentopoli—More than Twenty Years on." In *The Oxford Handbook of Italian Politics*, edited by Erik Jones and Gianfranco Pasquino. Oxford: Oxford University Press.

Ruggieri, Francesca, and Stefano Marcolini. 2012. "Italy." In *Toward a Prosecutor for the European Union: A Comparative Analysis*, vol. 1, edited by Katalin Ligeti. Oxford: Hart.

Ruggiero, Vincenzo. 1995. "Flexibility and Intermittent Emergency in the Italian Penal System." In *Western European Penal Systems: A Critical Anatomy*, edited by Vincenzo Ruggiero, Mick Ryan, and Joe Sim. London: Sage.

Ruzza, Carlo, and Stefano Fella. 2009. *Re-inventing the Italian Right: Territorial Politics, Populism, and "Post-Fascism."* London: Routledge.

Sassoon, Donald. 1995. "Tangentopoli or the Democratization of Corruption: Considerations on the End of Italy's First Republic." *Journal of Modern Italian Studies* 1(1):124–43.

Sberna, Salvatore, and Alberto Vannucci. 2013. "It's the Politics, Stupid! The Politicization of Anti-corruption in Italy." *Crime, Law and Social Change* 60 (5):565–93.

Scalia, Vincenzo. 2005. "Italian Juvenile Justice: A Lesson in Tolerance?" *Youth Justice* 5(1):33–45.

Sellin, Thorsten. 1972. "Enrico Ferri." In *Pioneers in Criminology*, edited by Hermann Mannheim. Montclair, NJ: Patterson Smith.

Selmini, Rossella. 2005. "Towards Città Sicure? Political Action and Institutional Conflict in Contemporary Preventive and Safety Policies in Italy." *Theoretical Criminology* 9(3):307–23.

———. 2011. "The Governance of Crime in Italy: Global Tendencies and Local Peculiarities." In *Travels of the Criminal Question: Cultural Embeddedness and*

Diffusion, edited by Dario Melossi, Maximo Sozzo, and Richard Sparks. Oxford: Hart.

———. 2016. "Urban Policing in Italy: Some Reflections in a Comparative Perspective." In *Policing European Metropolises*, edited by Adam Edwards, Elke Devroe, and Paul Ponsaers. London: Routledge, forthcoming.

Selmini, Rossella, and Suzy McElrath. 2014. "Violent Female Victimization Trends across Europe, Canada, and the United States." In *Why Crime Rates Fall and Why They Don't*, edited by Michael Tonry. Vol. 43 of *Crime and Justice: A Review of Research*, edited by Michael Tonry. Chicago: University of Chicago Press.

Shea, Evelyn. 2009. "Elections and the Fear of Crime: The Case of France and Italy." *European Journal on Criminal Policy and Research* 15(1–2):83–102.

Simon, Jonathan. 2006. "Positively Punitive: How the Inventor of Scientific Criminology Who Died at the Beginning of the Twentieth Century Continues to Haunt American Crime Control at the Beginning of the Twenty-First." *Texas Law Review* 84:2135–72.

———. 2014. *Mass Incarceration on Trial: A Remarkable Court Decision and the Future of Prisons in America*. New York: New Press.

Skinner, Stephen. 2011. "Tainted Law? The Italian Penal Code, Fascism, and Democracy." *International Journal of Law in Context* 7(4):423–46.

Tarchi, Marco. 2002. "Populism Italian Style." In *Democracies and the Populistic Challenge*, edited by Yves Meny and Yves Surel. Basingstoke, UK: Palagrave Macmillan.

Tonry, Michael. 2013. "Understanding Crime Trends in Italy and Elsewhere." In *Organized Crime, Corruption, and Crime Prevention: Essays in Honor of Ernesto U. Savona*, edited by Stefano Caneppele and Francesco Calderoni. Heidelberg: Springer.

———. 2014. "Why Crime Rates Are Falling throughout the Western World." In *Why Crime Rates Fall and Why They Don't*, edited by Michael Tonry. Vol. 43 of *Crime and Justice: A Review of Research*, edited by Michael Tonry. Chicago: University of Chicago Press.

Torrente, Giovanni. 2007. "Le storie organizzative di due procure della repubblica: Tra obbligatorietà dell azione penale e selezione del crimine." In *Processi di selezione del crimine: Procure della repubblica e organizzazione giudiziaria*, edited by Claudio Sarzotti. Milan: Giuffrè.

———. 2009. *Punishment and Recidivism: The Italian Case*. Turin: UNICRI.

Totah, Michele. 2002. "Fortress Italy: Racial Politics and the New Immigration Amendment in Italy." *Fordham International Law Journal* 26:1438–1504.

Vannucci, Alberto. 2009. "The Controversial Legacy of '*Mani Pulite*': A Critical Analysis of Italian Corruption and Anti-corruption Policies." *Bulletin of Italian Politics* 1(2):233–64.

Vassalli, Giuliano. 1974. "The Reform of the Italian Penal Code." *Wayne Law Review* 20(4):1032–69.

Verzelloni, Luca. 2014. "Il lungo dibattito sui criteri di priorità negli uffici giudicanti e requirenti." *Archivio Penale* 66(3):815–22.

von Hirsch, Andrew. 1976. *Doing Justice: The Choice of Punishments*. New York: Hill & Wang.

———. 2011. "Reflections on Punishment Futures: The Desert-Model Debate and the Importance of the Criminal Law Context." In *Retributivism Has a Past: Has It a Future?* edited by Michael Tonry. Oxford: Oxford University Press.

Waters, Sarah. 1994. "Tangentopoli and the Emergence of a New Political Order in Italy." *West European Politics* 17(1):169–82.

Whitman, James Q. 2003. *Harsh Justice: Criminal Punishment and the Widening Divide between America and Europe*. New York: Oxford University Press.

World Prison Brief. 2015. *Europe: Country Reports*. http://www.prisonstudies .org/map/europe.

Zedner, Lucia. 2003. "The Concept of Security: An Agenda for Comparative Analysis." *Legal Studies* 23(1):153–76.

Krzysztof Krajewski

Sentencing in Poland: Failed Attempts to Reduce Punitiveness

ABSTRACT

Poland, like all central and eastern European communist countries, had no-toriously harsh sentencing practices and high imprisonment rates, in sharp contrast to western Europe. After 25 years of political, economic, and social reforms, sentencing in Poland remains very different from patterns in western Europe. It is unclear whether that results from particularities of the trans-formation after 1990 or from shadows of the communist past and mentality. After 1989 substantial efforts were made to reduce punitiveness. A major liberalization took place in the early 1990s under the old communist penal code, the product primarily of changes in sentencing practice, and not in the law. Trends reversed after a new 1998 code took effect. Legislation meant to liberalize sentencing practice instead produced increased use of imprison-ment. This resulted mainly from the changing political and social atmosphere. Imprisonment increased while sentencing policies became milder. This seems to result not from especially frequent use of imprisonment or harsh sentences but from abuse of sentencing the main alternative, the suspended sentence. It is imposed often, but is often revoked, with recipients ending up behind bars.

Writing 15 years ago on sentencing in Western countries, Michael Tonry observed great formal similarities concerning crime, criminal jus-tice systems, and sentencing theory and practice. He pointed out that

Electronically published June 21, 2016
Krzysztof Krajewski is professor in the Department of Criminology, Jagiellonian Uni-versity, Krakow.

175

there is widespread commitment to democratic values and Enlightenment ideals, and the institutions of criminal justice are everywhere much the same. These include professional police, public prosecutors' offices, and an independent judiciary, and reliance on imprisonment as the primary sanction for very serious crimes and chronic criminals and on various community penalties for others. There is much more similarity than difference in the content of criminal law doctrine, rules of evidence, and procedural safeguards. Nonetheless, and despite broad similarity in most countries in crime trends over the past 30 years, sentencing and punishment policies and patterns vary enormously. (Tonry 2001, p. 3)

The proposition that similarities in how criminal justice systems operate in western Europe, North America, and Australia result from those societies' underlying core values and their liberal democratic political systems seems right, even if the term "western" is somewhat misleading. The term emerged primarily from the political realities of the Cold War, with the Eastern bloc being the West's ideological and political opposite (Harries 1993). Nevertheless, it was commonly used also in comparative analyses (Tonry and Frase 2001; Tonry and Farrington 2005). For the entire period 1945–90 it was probably quite legitimate to juxtapose liberal democracies of the West to communist autocracies of the East, encompassing the Soviet Union and its satellites in central and eastern Europe and in that contrast to include crime control policies.

However, things have changed. The fall of the communist systems in the Soviet Union and central and eastern Europe in 1989–90 completely altered the meaning of the term "West." During the 1990s and 2000s, former communist countries of central and eastern Europe joined the "Western club" by becoming members of the North Atlantic Treaty Organization and the European Union. There is no doubt that the political systems of Bulgaria, the Czech Republic, Estonia, Hungary, Latvia, Lithuania, Poland, Slovakia, Slovenia, and Romania today correspond to basic values of liberal democracy. The same may be said of their criminal justice systems. The entire process of political transformation in those countries centered on "Westernization." During the 1990s, all of them implemented broad reforms of criminal justice systems to comply with Western standards, primarily as reflected in the European Convention on Human Rights and other conventions, recommendations, standards, and guidelines of the Council of Europe. Those reforms had profound effects on how their criminal justice systems operate, including their sanction systems and sentencing patterns (van Zyl Smit and Snacken 2009). The EU accession process during the 2000s intensified these changes.

However, this integration of the West and the East during the 1990s and 2000s had a significant impact on increased diversity among liberal democracies. Former communist countries were eager to return to Europe and to become more like the established democracies. They also brought, inevitably and understandably, their historical experiences, which before World War II were not always liberal and democratic. Moreover, they were burdened by 50 years of Soviet domination and authoritarian national regimes, which left deep traces on those societies. To recover from the communist past proved to be a much more complicated enterprise than many people foresaw. Criminal justice systems may offer an especially good example.

During the past 25 years of reform, criminal justice systems in those countries were changed almost beyond recognition. Those features mentioned by Tonry without a doubt are present in countries of the region. Yet, substantial differences persist, not primarily in how criminal justice systems function, but precisely in their sentencing outcomes. Certain features, such as exceptionally high imprisonment rates (usually well above the European average), very frequent use of suspended sentences as the alternative to imprisonment, and marginal roles played by fines and community service, characterize almost all countries of the region and make their penal policies different from those in western Europe (Krajewski 2014a). It is legitimate to ask why. Possibly political, economic, and social transformation brought with it substantial negative collateral consequences, including rapid growth in crime (Jasiński 1996; Lévay 2000, 2012; Łoś 2003; Gruszczyńska 2004; Krajewski 2004; Šelih 2012). This must have had at least some impact on crime control policies and made its patterns different from those in western Europe, which were not confronted at that time by similar phenomena. However, it is equally legitimate to wonder whether criminal justice policies in the region remain burdened by extremely punitive crime control policies of the communist past (Krajewski 2013) and cultural transmission of certain professional ideologies that were dominant before 1990 (Krajewski 2012).

Poland is probably one of the best examples of these tendencies. Immediately after the fall of the communist system in 1989, the country initiated broad reforms of the criminal justice system and the criminal law. The main tasks were to introduce Western values and standards and to reduce notorious punitiveness inherited from the communist past

(Frankowski and Wąsek 1993, 1995). The idealized example—to what extent corresponding to reality is another matter—of enlightened, rational, and evidence-based crime control policies implemented in western Europe during the 1960s, 1970s, or 1980s always constituted the main model principle for Polish reforms. Reduction of the imprisonment rate, at least to the western European average, was perceived as the most important task. This was the purpose of a broad reform of the prison system that was implemented successfully in 1990–91. This was also the purpose of amendments to old communist criminal codes made during 1990–95, although they eliminated only the most conspicuous excesses of the communist penal legislation.

The main step toward rationalization of criminal policy and sentencing patterns was meant to be the completely new Criminal Code, Code of Criminal Procedure, and Code for Implementation of Punishments that were adopted in 1997 and became effective in 1998. The underlying philosophy of the new penal code was meant to change the sentencing process completely, not only by providing new sentencing guidelines and establishing detailed provisions giving priority to noncustodial sanctions but also by generally lowering statutory minimums and maximums for many offenses (Krajewski 2004; Rzeplińska and Wiktorska 2015).

It is interesting to note, however, that despite all those efforts, patterns of sentencing and developments regarding the imprisonment rate were to a large extent independent of the legislative changes. During 1990–98, the imprisonment rate declined substantially and sentencing patterns became perceptibly milder, but this happened under the old communist legislative framework, which at that time underwent only cosmetic changes. After the new codes became effective, the situation started to deteriorate and to return to patterns well known from the communist era: use of fines and community service decreased, the imprisonment rate started to grow, and prisons began to become overcrowded again.

There may be multiple reasons for these developments. The growth of crime resulted in a surge in levels of fear of crime (Łoś 2002). This combined with traditionally punitive attitudes of the population (Krajewski 2009). The political atmosphere switched from the "liberal optimism" of the 1990s to populist "tough-on-crime" rhetoric of the 2000s. A previously unknown phenomenon of the "politics of law and order" exerted growing influence. This change of rhetoric by politicians, by the media, and in public discourse probably played a crucial role and significantly affected sentencing patterns (Kossowska et al. 2012). Under the new circumstances, designedly liberal penal policies began to have illiberal outcomes.

However, there is another consideration. The persistence for the last 15 years of high imprisonment rates does not result directly from severity of sentencing patterns. Imprisonment is not used especially often by Polish courts, and most prison sentences are not very harsh. The problem is that the main alternative to imprisonment is the suspended sentence, broad use of which to avoid sending most offenders to prisons may be entirely reasonable. The problem is that there are serious deficiencies in the probation system (Wójcik 2015). That is one reason why suspended sentences are often revoked. A substantial proportion of prison inmates were not initially sentenced to prison but received suspended sentences that were revoked for reoffending or other violations of conditions and obligations. This is a major problem shared by all criminal justice systems in central and eastern Europe: lack of appropriate and effective alternatives to imprisonment, primarily because of the communist past. Countries in the region were not involved when creation of alternatives to imprisonment became important developments in Western countries in the 1950s and 1960s. The Eastern countries of the region remained within the mentality of Soviet penal ideology, which paid little attention to such issues. The consequences persist and are a main cause of failed attempts to reduce punitiveness.

The rest of this essay develops issues just introduced. Section I provides a brief overview of the sentencing process; it is typical of the inquisitorial structure of continental criminal processes. Section II presents and analyzes changes in sentencing philosophy underlying the three modern Polish criminal codes of 1932, 1969, and 1997. Particular attention is paid to their general sentencing principles and guidelines and how changes reflected different penal ideologies in various periods. Special attention is paid to differences between the communist criminal code of 1969 and the current one. The latter was a reaction to communist punitiveness and was intended to change judicial thinking about punishment radically. It was not successful. Section III presents the structure of sanctions available under the 1997 penal code, including differentiation between punishments and security measures.[1] Measures other than pun-

---

[1] Many European systems distinguish between sanctions (or punishments), which traditionally are meant to be proportioned to the seriousness of crimes, and measures, which are preventive and need not be proportionate (de Keijser 2011).

ishment are discussed. Section IV provides the available statistical data on sentencing patterns in Poland since 1990 (and in some cases earlier). It attempts to characterize differences and similarities in sentencing patterns before and after the fall of the communist system through the 2000s. These data are also used to explain reasons for the persistence of punitive outcomes. Legislation is not the only factor that influences sentencing; outcomes always express underlying penal ideologies and are shaped by political, social, and economic factors.

I. The Sentencing Process

Neither under previous codes nor under current law has sentencing in Poland ever been separate from adjudication. Evidence concerning guilt and sentencing is presented during one proceeding and according to the same evidentiary standards. After presentation of the evidence, the parties make their arguments about guilt and punishment. The public prosecutor offers concrete recommendations (orally, never in writing) concerning sentencing. This recommendation in no way binds the court. Defense lawyers usually argue for acquittal or in favor of mitigated punishment. It is common to urge punishment as a lesser included offense carrying a milder statutory minimum or maximum or that extraordinary mitigation of punishment be ordered. After the final speeches, the judge, or judicial panel, retires for deliberations.

On returning, the court pronounces the accused guilty or not guilty and announces the sentence. Judges must always provide oral explanations for both. Discussions of the basis for determining guilt predominate, although some mention of reasons for the punishment is always included. There is no obligation to provide written reasons. This must be done only if at least one party demands it within a designated period following sentencing. Parties usually do this only if they intend to appeal. Either party may appeal the sentence. If the sentence or the verdict is appealed only by the accused, neither the appeals court nor the original court may impose a harsher sentence if the sentence is quashed.

The information on which Polish courts base their sentencing decisions is usually not very comprehensive (except sometimes for the most serious violent offenses). In principle, information relevant to sentencing should be collected during the investigation and prior to the trial. However, no special presentencing reports are prepared. The court usually has information concerning previous convictions. In some cases, the court receives a special report prepared by a probation officer, but this is not mandatory, with the exception of felonies (which under Polish law are the most serious offenses carrying imprisonment for no less than 3 years) and violent offenses committed by young offenders under 21.[2] When a special report is prepared, probation officers interview the accused's family, neighbors, and colleagues and collect other information. In especially serious cases or when issues of legal responsibility arise, courts receive specialist information and assessments from psychiatrists, sexologists, psychologists, or other specialists. Purely psychological assessments are seldom available. In some cases information is offered by the accused or his lawyer in hopes of mitigating judgments about responsibility and sentencing.

Because information on the accused is usually scant, judges make their sentencing decisions intuitively on the basis of the little information they have. This is primarily offense, not offender, related. Information pertinent to individual prevention or rehabilitation needs, including alcohol abuse or other chemical dependence, is very often lacking. Polish law provides for, as noted, treatment measures to be imposed parallel to punishments; this requires formal assessment by specialists in addiction therapy. Courts very often, however, waive such assessments.

Polish law, within the framework of the "treatment instead of punishment" principle, provides for measures comparable to those used in American drug courts, but they are not used. The reason is that courts thereby save time and money on specialist assessments. It is much easier to impose a suspended sentence, without obligations or supervision. This disposes of the case but does not address the problems. After all, as policemen, prosecutors, and judges sometimes say, "we are not social workers."

This is not only because Polish judges lack training in criminological knowledge. It also partly results from introduction of simplified procedures similar to Anglo-American plea bargaining, referred to in Poland as consensual procedures. The most common one, article 335 of the Code of Criminal Procedure (CCP), allows the suspect during the investigation to make an agreement with the public prosecutor about his guilty plea and the prosecutorial sentencing recommendation. The prosecutor

---

[2] The age limit for criminal responsibility is 17. Offenders under 17 are considered to be juveniles (*nieletni*) and are subject to special juvenile responsibility. Young offenders between 17 and 21 (*mlodociani*) are criminally responsible, but the criminal code contains special sentencing rules regarding them (Krajewski 2006, 2014*b*).

asks the court to impose a sentence according to that agreement, which usually happens. This procedure was introduced in 1998 to save time, resources, and money and, after original hesitations, became extremely popular. Article 387 CCP established a special form of plea bargaining during the trial. Forty-five percent of convictions took place under article 335 in 2011 and 11 percent under article 387, for a total of 56 percent of all convictions. Public prosecutors are under strong pressure to settle as many cases as possible in that way.

The consensual sentencing procedures partly explain why, as I show below, Polish courts in recent years have imposed a huge proportion of suspended prison sentences unaccompanied by conditions or supervision by a probation officer and many short prison sentences.

II. Sentencing Principles and Aims

Polish penal law shares common features with the penal codes of Germany, Austria, and other central European countries such as the Czech Republic, Hungary, and Slovakia. Issues regarding penal responsibility are regulated in the penal code. It consists of a so-called general part and a special one. The general part contains basic rules of penal responsibility, general principles, and guidelines regarding sentencing. The special part defines offenses and specifies penalties, including statutory minimums and maximums.

This structure characterized all three twentieth-century Polish penal codes. The first, adopted in 1932 and in force until 1969, was a modern piece of penal legislation influenced strongly by the ideas of Franz von Liszt, Enrico Ferri, and the related "sociological school in penal law." That code remained in force after the communist takeover in 1946–48, supplemented by much additional legislation. In 1969, the communist authorities adopted a new code that reflected principles and ideas of Soviet penal law. Despite this, many provisions extended traditions established in 1932. In many respects Polish penal law was less "Sovietized" than those in neighboring countries of central Europe. The 1969 code remained in force until 1998—8 years after the fall of the communist regime. During that time it was amended to reduce its severity, but the changes were not fundamental.

A new penal code, adopted in 1997, took effect September 1, 1998. Its main aims were to change the philosophy underlying penal responsibility and substantially to reduce the code's severity. It has frequently been amended. It is not an exaggeration to speak of governmental and parliamentary hyperactivity in penal law, independently of which parties have been in power. Commentators complain that the current code bears little similarity to the 1997 original. It is a patchwork of inconsistent provisions. The general part is sometimes almost irreconcilable with changes to the special part. On July 1, 2015, yet another major reform of the general part entered into force. It was prepared in part as a response to certain problems regarding sentencing patterns that are discussed below and resulted in a high imprisonment rate and prison overcrowding. The main purpose of the reform was to limit the use of suspended sentences and to provide broader opportunities to use other alternatives to imprisonment, such as fines, community service, and electronic monitoring. Of course, it will not be possible to observe any effects of the new regulations for at least 2 or 3 years. Therefore, the analysis below refers exclusively to legal regulations in force prior to July 1, 2015, and sentencing outcomes resulting from those regulations.

All three codes established basic principles and guidelines concerning sanctions and other penal measures. Those provisions illustrate the evolution of underlying criminological and penological assumptions. Of course, sentencing rules and practices were and are influenced by the—sometimes inconsistent—provisions of the general parts of each code.

The 1932 code, especially its general part, was the creation of one man, Juliusz Makarewicz, professor of penal law at the university in Lwów (Lemberg). It is commonly referred to as "Makarewicz's code," although its final version was prepared by a committee. Makarewicz represented the ideas and concepts of the sociological school in penal law of the time, especially its German version.[3] As a young man, he attended Franz von Liszt's seminars, which decisively shaped his ideas. The 1932 penal code represented offender-oriented penal law and sentencing rules (as opposed to the offense-oriented approach of the classical school). This is shown in article 54 on principles and guidelines regarding imposition of punishment: "The court shall impose the penalty according to its own discretion,

---

[3] The sociological school had strong influence in Poland between the two world wars. An example is Leon Radzinowicz, at that time identified with the Italian sociological school and his mentor Enrico Ferri. Radzinowicz had no significant influence on drafting of the 1932 code, but his prolific writing before his emigration in 1937 contributed significantly to popularization in Poland of the Italian sociological school.

paying attention first of all to the perpetrator's motives and particular features of his act, his attitude towards the victim, the level of his intellectual development and particular features of his character, his way of life before commission of an offense, and his behavior after it."

No explicit reference is made to purposes of punishment, including either individual or general prevention. This accorded with positivist ideas and von Liszt's tripartite classification of offenders into those who are to be deterred, those who are to be rehabilitated, and those who are to be incapacitated. It was up to the judge to assess which purposes prevailed for given offenders. Such an assessment required consideration of various factors regarding the offender. Nevertheless, it was a common assumption that article 54 stressed individual prevention as the main purpose of punishment, while pushing general prevention, that is, general deterrence, to the background.

This does not mean that the code directly encouraged mild sentencing outcomes. Individual prevention may also justify harsh sentences and long periods of confinement. The code contained many detailed provisions making such outcomes possible. These included indeterminate, postpenal security measures for "incorrigible" and "professional" offenders. They were influenced by the positivist differentiation between punishments and measures. However, the code gave substantial discretionary sentencing powers to the judge. Statutory minimums and maximums were broad. Relatively few provisions provided for increases of such minimums and maximums (in case of recidivism). Those increases in most cases were optional, and broad discretion was left to the judge.

The equivalent provision in the 1969 penal code was more extensive. Article 50 provided the following:

§ 1. The court shall impose the penalty according to its own discretion, within the limits prescribed by the law, assessing the degree of social danger of the act and taking into consideration the aims of a penalty with regard to its social impact as well as the preventive and educational aims which it would have the penalty attain in relation to the person sentenced.

§ 2. Guiding itself by the directions specified in § 1, the court shall take into consideration, in particular, the kind and extent of the damage caused by the offense, the motives and the perpetrator's manner of acting, his traits and personal conditions, as well as his way of life prior to the commission and his behavior after the commission of the offense, and also his participation with a juvenile at the time of committing the offense.

This formulation constituted a significant change from the 1932 code, although in principle § 2 might be considered a continuation, in slightly changed wording, of article 54. Like its predecessor, this provision indicated circumstances and facts to be taken into account in deciding on punishment. In principle, many are identical or similar to those in the earlier provision, even if the formulation "the level of his intellectual development and particular features of his character" was replaced by more general language, "his traits and personal circumstances." The significant change was the formulation that the court take into consideration "the kind and extent of the damage caused by the offense." The 1969 code paid at least equal attention to the characteristics of the offense as to the personal characteristics of the offender.

However, apart from those changes, the 1969 code did not indicate what should be considered during the sentencing process. It added article 50, § 1, which had no earlier equivalent and which referred clearly to the purposes of the punishment. This wording was always broadly interpreted as making a significant change in penal philosophy. Of crucial importance was the stress on the "social danger of the act," which constituted the main criterion.[4] Apart from "the kind and extent of the damage caused by the offense," it provided an "objective" sentencing criterion and meant that the offense, not the offender, was the center of attention.

The 1969 code included additional aims of punishment, meant to supplement social danger, into article 50. The first one referred to the "social impact of a penalty." This was always interpreted as requiring that the penalty should seek to make other people refrain from crime. This is, of course, general deterrence. A penalty based on the degree of social danger of an act should also fulfill "preventive and educational" purposes. Educational purposes equaled rehabilitative effects. Together these provisions were understood to encompass prevention of reoffending and incapacitation.

---

[4] The concept of the "social danger of an act" was a cornerstone of Soviet penal law. It underlined the "substantial definition of an offense" in contrast with the "formal definitions" characteristic of "bourgeois penal law." This meant primarily that an act formally contrary to law but not socially dangerous did not constitute an offense. But this concept was also of crucial importance for the sentencing process. For further details, see Pomorski (1981).

There was some discussion in the literature of the communist period of the relation between the directives and the punishment aims in § 2. Some argued that all the directives were of equal importance, that all should be considered and together result in an integrated outcome. Others were of the opinion that the directives were often impossible to reconcile. It is seldom possible to combine equally requirements of retribution, general deterrence, and rehabilitation. Something had to have priority, and the question was what. For some the judge had to decide this (in principle as under the 1932 code). For others this was too liberal. Therefore, it was often assumed—with some support in the wording of the provision—that the degree of social danger should always have priority but that its impact could be modified by the requirements of general deterrence, incapacitation, and rehabilitation.

Independently of the legal disputes, the 1969 provision clearly represented a switch from offender-oriented to offense-oriented criminal law. However, this did not imply a switch toward purely retributive or just deserts sentencing. In practical terms, priority was given to offense severity combined with general deterrence. These became the crucial desiderata in sentencing until the fall of the communist regime.

Independently of the legal intricacies, the punitive ideology promoted by the communist authorities made the Polish criminal justice system and sentencing patterns extremely severe and contributed decisively to the enormous scale of imprisonment under the communist regime. This was aggravated by provisions restricting judicial discretion, providing for mandatory increases in statutory minimums and maximums, and requiring especially harsh treatment of certain categories of offenders. A typical example was article 60, which contained special rules specifying harsher sentences for recidivists.

Article 50 of the 1969 code was neither the sole nor the most important cause of punitive sentencing practices in communist Poland. That resulted from the general atmosphere in a country governed by an authoritarian communist regime, limitations on judicial independence, and various means by which the Communist Party could directly or indirectly influence general sentencing patterns, and often decisions in individual cases. Direct influence violated official ideas of judicial independence even at that time, but it was not uncommon.

Indirect influences were more subtle. For example, public prosecutors had unlimited discretion to appeal sentencing outcomes and demand harsher penalties. Judges whose sentences were appealed too often could get into trouble. The Supreme Court had authority to issue detailed guidelines regarding sentencing practices in given categories of cases, for example, forbidding suspended sentences under certain conditions or directing that some categories of offenses or offenders be treated more severely (usually in the name of general deterrence). Sentences contrary to such guidelines could be appealed by the public prosecutor (Krajewski 2012, pp. 83–89).

Thus, punitive sentencing outcomes under communism resulted from features of the political system and from the penal philosophy of the communist authorities. But legal provisions in force at the time made such outcomes possible or even encouraged them. This relation between legal provisions on sentencing and the conditions in which the criminal justice system functions is evident in a substantial decline in punitiveness in the years 1990–97 after the fall of the communist system. It happened without major changes to article 50, which survived unaltered until 1997. Given the new circumstances and a completely different political atmosphere, sentencing practice changed substantially without legal provisions being changed.

This relative distance between legal provisions regulating sentencing and sentencing outcomes in practice is also evident in the penal code adopted in 1997. There is no doubt that harshness of sentencing practice under communism and the size of the prison population were main concerns of academic lawyers, criminologists, and many practitioners. This concern shaped drafting of the new penal code. Its general intent was to reduce the severity of the criminal justice system. One expression of this was the new wording of code provisions on sentencing criteria. Article 53 of the 1997 code was formulated similarly to its predecessor, but with significant changes:

§ 1. The court shall impose the penalty according to its own discretion, within the limits prescribed by the law, having in mind that pain inflicted on the offender or its severity does not exceed the degree of culpability, taking into account the degree of social harmfulness of the act, taking into consideration the preventive and educational aims the penalty would have to attain in relation to the person sentenced, as well as the needs in shaping the legal awareness of the society.

§ 2. Imposing the penalty the court takes into account, in particular, motives and the perpetrators' manner of acting, commission of an offense together with a juvenile, type and degree of breach of duties with which the offender was charged, type and magnitude of the negative consequences of the offense, traits and personal conditions of the offender, way of life prior to the commission of the offense, and his behavior after the commission, in particular his attempts at repairing the damage or satisfying in other forms the public sense of justice, as well as the conduct of the victim.

Two changes to § 1 are of crucial importance. First, although the new provision retains "the degree of social harmfulness of the act" as a factor, it tries to limit its impact by direct reference to the degree of culpability.[5] The penalty should be proportionate not to the offense per se but to the offender's culpability. More precisely, the penalty should not exceed the degree of culpability independently of other offense characteristics. Thus, culpability constitutes an impassable limit. A penalty exceeding the degree of culpability (because, e.g., of the "objective" characteristics of an offense) should be considered excessive. The drafters believed that reduction in the severity of sentencing was crucially important. However, this required explicit mention in the code of retributive considerations.

Second, preventive and educational aims were retained, but mention of the punishment's social impact (associated earlier with general deterrence) is missing. Instead "needs in shaping the legal awareness of the society" was introduced. This formulation refers to the concept of "positive general prevention" that is influential in some European countries (see, e.g., Lappi-Seppälä 2011). This concept is usually contrasted with "negative general prevention," which is associated with general deterrence. The premise is that social effects of punishment include positive reinforcement of basic social norms, a process that has nothing to do with a punishment's severity.

It is not easy to characterize general sentencing principles and aims in contemporary Polish penal law. The 1932 code was offender-oriented, giving unequivocal priority to individual prevention, and the 1969 code was offense-oriented, emphasizing punishments proportionate to the gravity of the offense, but with stress also on general deterrence. The 1997 code is less clear. Prevention and education are emphasized, but with links to offenders' culpability. This may be interpreted as a turn toward a retributive and culpability-oriented criminal law.

However, this is not quite true. Culpability is an important concept in Polish penal law, but it does not play as large a role as in Germany and some other European countries. Article 53 does not directly say that pun-

---

[5] In the current code the word danger (*niebezpieczeństwo*) was replaced by harmfulness (*szkodliwość*). The drafters wanted to distance the code from the communist past, although, in principle, most favored retaining a "substantive definition" of the offense.

ishment should be proportionate to the degree of culpability, but that it should not be exceeded. Clear characterization of current provisions is not easy. The new code moved away from a purely offense-oriented penal law emphasizing proportionality to offense seriousness and stressed positive general prevention. This did not involve a return to offender-oriented penal law based primarily on individual prevention.

III. Authorized Sanctions

Poland's system is in principle a "two-track" system of penal law. The code provides for two types of response to commission of an offense: punishments and security measures. The code also recognizes so-called penal measures (earlier called supplementary punishments). Under certain conditions they may be applied in addition to punishments proper and are in fact special types of punishment. Punishments are imposed on the majority of offenders and have—at least in part—a retributive purpose. They are related to culpability, have to be proportionate, and are always of determinate character. Security measures result exclusively from public safety considerations unrelated to culpability.

A. Security Measures

Security measures are used in a small minority of cases, primarily for offenders declared to be criminally insane and not criminally responsible but considered to pose a threat to public safety. Such offenders may be detained indeterminately, for as long as their condition warrants, without being punished. In such cases security measures are imposed instead of punishment. The purpose is to protect the public and to treat the individual's mental condition. If treatment brings about improvement and doctors certify that he or she no longer poses a threat, such a person is to be released.

Treatment-oriented security measures are also possible in addition to punishment, primarily for alcohol- and drug-dependent offenders. In such cases measures are usually implemented prior to punishment, and the court decides afterward whether a penalty should be executed.[6] Such measures are partially indeterminate. They are implemented as long as necessary, but no longer than 2 years. Polish penal law, unlike some other

---

[6] This was the case prior to substantial changes that entered into force on July 1, 2015. Such measures are now to be implemented after the sentence has been served and are indeterminate; i.e., there is no upper limit on their implementation.

European countries' laws, does not provide for purely isolative postpenal security measures for offenders who are criminally responsible but are considered dangerous.[7] Security measures are used in a tiny minority of court decisions and are beyond the scope of this essay.

B. Punishments

Polish penal law differentiates between punishments proper and penal measures. Article 32 of the penal code established five basic punishments: fines, limitation of liberty (equivalent to community service), deprivation of liberty (i.e., imprisonment), 25 years of deprivation of liberty, and life deprivation of liberty.[8] There are thus three main sanctions—fines, community service, and imprisonment, the latter differentiated between regular imprisonment (1 month to 15 years)—and two extraordinary imprisonment categories (25 years and life).

Probation does not feature as a separate punishment. This does not mean, however, that probation is unknown. Chapter 8 of the penal code regulates "probationary measures" that encompass conditional discontinuation of proceedings, suspended sentence, and early conditional release, or parole. Early conditional release is decided during the imprisonment sentence and does not constitute a sanction per se (although it modifies the earlier imposed sanction). Conditional discontinuation of proceedings and suspended sentence are in practice distinct punishments although the penal code does not formally recognize them as such. This practice—present also under the two earlier penal codes—generates legal

---

[7] Before July 1, 2015, art. 95a of the penal code, introduced in 2005, provided for postpenal detention of certain categories of sexual offenders (in principle, those convicted for sexual abuse of children). They could be detained indeterminately after serving their sentences, for as long as they were considered to pose a public safety threat. But in principle, the main purpose of such detention was treatment, and not only isolation. Additional possibilities of detaining certain categories of dangerous offenders after they serve their sentences were introduced in the fall of 2013 (Krajewski 2014c), but they were constructed in a way that put them completely outside the scope of penal law. Since July 1, 2015, possibilities of postpenal isolation were significantly broadened, although such isolation must still always involve some treatment and cannot be exclusively isolative.

[8] The 1997 penal code finalized the gradual abolition of capital punishment, which was authorized under the 1932 and 1969 codes. The last execution occurred in 1988. Courts subsequently imposed death sentences, but no executions took place. An informal moratorium lasted until 1995, when the Parliament enacted a formal moratorium. The 1997 code abolished the death penalty altogether and reintroduced life imprisonment as the most severe penal sanction (under the 1969 code, 25 years was the most severe form of imprisonment).

debates on the character of suspended sentence. Formally, the suspended sentence (arts. 69–75 of the penal code) is not a separate punishment but a mode of implementing imprisonment sentences. However, from a purely penological perspective, this is not true. In practice the suspended sentence is a separate type of punishment and is the most common one. Therefore, for all practical reasons, Polish penal law recognizes four basic types of punishment.

A fifth type of penal reaction is available, although it is not considered to be punishment proper. This is the conditional discontinuation of proceedings (arts. 66–68). It was introduced in 1969 and was to be used for relatively minor offenses committed by first-time offenders. In practice, it is used as a form of probation. Conditional discontinuation may be ordered for offenses subject to prison sentences of 3 years or less (in some exceptional cases 5 years or less).[9] It involves a trial period from 1 to 2 years (3 years since July 1, 2015), may be accompanied by various obligations, and may be supervised by a probation officer. Importantly, though, a conditional discontinuation does not involve a conviction and, if successfully completed, does not result in a criminal record.[10]

The 1997 code attempted in various ways to make sentencing less punitive than under the 1969 penal code. This included changes in the wording of the provision listing available punishments (art. 32). In the current code, the list starts with the least severe penalty, the fine, and ends with the most severe, life imprisonment. In the 1932 code the order was reversed, starting with the death penalty and ending with fines. In the 1969 code the list started with 25 years' imprisonment and ended with fines, with the death penalty mentioned in a separate paragraph as exceptional punishment. Under the 1932 code, the death penalty was simply an available penalty among many. The 1969 code sought to limit its use by stressing its extraordinary character, in effect sending a message to the judges.

Reversal in the 1997 code was intended to change judicial thinking, communicating that punishment consideration should always start from

---

[9] The reform of July 1, 2015, broadened possibilities for conditional discontinuation and made it a general rule that this measure may be used in cases of offenses carrying up to 5 years' imprisonment.

[10] Under the 1969 code, conditional discontinuation could be imposed by judges or public prosecutors. Under the 1997 code, for constitutional reasons, it may be imposed only by the judge following a motion by the prosecutor.

the least severe option. Only then should more severe punishments be considered. This way of thinking is also reflected in the special part. Under the two earlier codes, offense definitions were always followed by authorized punishments listed from most to least severe. Under the current code the listing was reversed. The intent was to stimulate the use of alternatives to imprisonment. Whether this had any practical effect is not clear.[11]

1. *Day Fines.* The 1997 code, like its predecessor, provides general rules regarding statutory minimums and maximums for punishments. Article 33 introduced day fines to make it possible to administer fines evenhandedly and independently of the offender's means. First, the judge must determine the number of day fines. This should be the same for offenders convicted of the same or comparable crimes. In the second step the judge sets the daily rate on the basis of the offender's financial circumstances. Day fine units may range from 10 to 540. The daily rate may range from 10 zlotys (about US$3.00) to 2,000 zlotys (US$625.00).

Paradoxically, this system intended to stimulate the use of fines in lieu of imprisonment had the opposite effect. The imposition of fines dropped substantially in the early years after the law was enacted. It started to recover only about 10 years ago. Among other explanations was that the required calculations proved too complicated for judges accustomed to imposing fines in concrete amounts. They chose other punishments.

2. *Community Service.* Limitation of liberty is the Polish equivalent of community service. It was first introduced by the 1969 code and was retained in the current code. Durations range from 1 to 12 months, and it is to be imposed only in full months. The 1969 code provided for a minimum of 3 months and a maximum of 2 years.[12] Limitation of liberty consists of three types of obligations. First, the offender is not allowed to change his or her place of residence without the court's permission. Second, the work indicated by the court must be performed. Third, he or she must be always available to report to the court about implementation of the penalty.

---

[11] There is clear evidence that under the 1969 code it worked in just the opposite way. As there were then no prospects for abolition of the death penalty, an attempt was made to limit its use by making it exceptional. But paradoxically, under the new code the courts imposed the death penalty more frequently than under the 1932 code.

[12] The reform of July 1, 2015, returned to the 2-year upper limit of this punishment.

The main component of the penalty is the work. This may be fulfilled in two basic forms. The first involves community service in a literal sense: 20–40 hours per month of unpaid, controlled work in an appropriate company, health care institution, social welfare institution, or charity or for a local community, as indicated in the court's order. The second may be applied only to those who are employed. The court may order 10–25 percent of the offender's salary to be deducted for some common or charitable purpose or for the state treasury. During implementation of the penalty, such a person may not terminate employment without court approval.

Both forms were available under the 1969 code. Until 1989, the second form was most frequently used. The reason was that there was practically full employment under the communist regime; an overwhelming majority of employees worked in state-owned enterprises or institutions.[13] It was often pointed out that this form does not constitute real community service, and it was commonly referred to as a "fine in installments." After 1989 the situation changed drastically. With growing unemployment and many people working in the underground economy, salary deductions were often impossible. At the same time community service proper ran into serious implementation problems. Neither private nor state-owned companies may be forced to employ convicts to do work. Hospitals and charities are reluctant to accept such workers. The only possibilities are usually special systems of public works run by local governments that involve contracts with the Ministry of Justice. In recent years effort has been made to improve implementation of community service orders to stimulate their use. But they remain significantly underused. The reform of July 1, 2015, undertakes yet another effort to change this, although the main obstacles are not legal regulations but implementation.

3. *Imprisonment.* Under the 1997 code, imprisonment may in principle normally range from 1 month to 15 years and is to be imposed in full months and years (it is not possible to impose terms expressed in days or weeks). Some serious felonies carry 25 years' imprisonment or 25 years or life. The 1-month minimum is less than in the 1969 code, which set a 3-month minimum.

---

[13] Full employment in former communist countries was completely artificial and resulted only from extremely low productivity and unimaginable waste in the state-controlled and centrally planned economy.

During drafting of the 1969 code, strong arguments were made against short prison sentences. They were said to be ineffective and harmful: ineffective because they did not allow for any reasonable rehabilitative efforts, and rehabilitation then constituted the dominant official rationale for punishment (in practice, deterrence prevailed); harmful because it was generally believed that sending offenders, especially first-timers, to prison for a short time provided only opportunities for contacts with criminals. The lower limit was set at 3 months, with the intent to replace the shortest prison terms with community service and fines.[14] That did not happen. The longer minimum probably contributed to an increase in average lengths of prison sentences in the 1970s and 1980s. The drafters of the 1997 code decreased the minimum in hopes of shortening average sentence lengths. Once again, the results were other than intended. Average lengths did not fall, but there was a huge increase in the imposition of shorter incarceration sentences.

The general statutory maximum of 15 years is of special significance for multiple convictions. Under Polish law, multiple convictions are in principle subject to something called the total or aggregate penalty for convictions during a single trial or—under certain conditions—in several separate trials over a designated period. The aggregate penalty in principle should not be lower than the highest penalty imposed for any of the affected offenses and should not exceed the sum of all penalties for all offenses. However, penalties may not be aggregated beyond the general statutory maximum of 15 years.[15] In a great majority of cases, service of sentences consecutively is not possible, which reduces the amount of time spent behind bars.

4. *Penal Measures.* Penal measures are listed in article 39. They include deprivation of public rights; bans on occupying certain positions, pursuing certain occupations, or being involved in specified business ac-

---

[14] The 1932 code recognized two forms of deprivation of liberty: jail and imprisonment. The minimum for jail was 1 week (maximum 5 years), while for imprisonment it was 6 months (maximum 15 years). Therefore, it was jail sentences that involved the possibility of real short-term imprisonment.

[15] The aggregate punishment of someone sentenced for three offenses for 2, 3, and 5 years in theory may amount to no fewer than 5 and no more than 10 years (in practice usually somewhere in between). Someone sentenced to 5, 8, and 12 years will have an aggregated sentence of no fewer than 12 and no more than 15 years, even though the terms total 25 years. If one sentence is for 15 years, the aggregate will be 15 years. If one is for 25 years or life, the aggregate will be 25 years or life.

tivities; bans on conducting activities related to the upbringing, treatment, and education of minors and on taking care of them; duties to refrain from being in specific milieus or places; bans on contacts with specified persons, restraining orders regarding specified persons, or bans on leaving a specified place of residence without the court's permission; bans on attending mass (including sports) events; bans on entering places of gambling and taking part in gambling; orders to leave premises occupied commonly with the victim; withdrawals of the driving license; forfeitures; duties to repair damage or redress inflicted harm; payments of a specified amount for a public purpose; cash benefits; and public announcements of conviction.[16]

Such measures existed in the two earlier codes, where they were called supplementary penalties (as contrasted with the main punishments of imprisonment and fines). However, there were fewer. The change of label has no substantive significance. They may, and in certain situations must, be imposed in addition to the penalty proper, although it is possible, under certain circumstances, for them to be the sole sanction. Penal measures are intended primarily to individualize punishments and adjust them to specific features of an offense and an offender. They have mixed character, although they are mostly preventive (like all bans, prohibitions, orders, and deprivations), with retribution or other purposes of punishment being secondary. Most may be imposed for a period from 1 to 10 years. In some cases the upper limit is 15 years, and bans on attending mass events may last from 2 to 6 years. In some circumstances they may involve life imposition (e.g., withdrawal of the driving license).

C. Judicial Discretion

Polish sentencing judges have traditionally had broad discretionary powers. Under current article 53, "the court imposes the penalty according to its own discretion." However, the judge (or judicial panel) is bound by general sentencing principles and by any applicable statutory minimums or maximums for particular offenses. In imprisonment sentencing, judges always have a choice within limits. In many instances they can choose between types of sanctions. The code provides for most offenses the full range (fines, community service, or imprisonment) and

---

[16] Originally there were eight such measures, but four new ones were recently added, including for sexual offenders, football hooligans, perpetrators of domestic violence, and compulsive gamblers.

for some only imprisonment.[17] For offenses carrying only imprisonment, the minimum and maximum ranges are 1 month to 3 years, 3 months to 5 years, 6 months to 8 years, 1–10 years, and 2–12 years. All offenses carrying statutory minimums below 3 years are considered misdemeanors. For offenses subject to minimums of 1, 3, or 6 months, fines (10–360 daily units) or community service (1–12 months) is an authorized alternative. However, fines or community service can also be used for misdemeanors carrying minimums above 6 months. For offenses subject to maximum prison terms up to 5 years, the court may use fines or community service even if the offense definition does not mention those sanctions. In such cases community service may last up to 2 years. The drafters considered this provision of fundamental importance for stimulating use of alternatives to imprisonment.

All offenses subject to a statutory minimum of 3 years' imprisonment or more are felonies. Most carry a sentence of no less than 3 and no more than 15 years. Thus for most felonies judges have broad discretion. This category includes aggravated rape, aggravated robbery, hijacking with deadly consequences, aggravated forms of unlawful deprivation of liberty, trafficking in human beings, taking hostages, and active involvement in a terrorist organization. Some felonies carry higher minimums: 5 years (currency counterfeiting), 8 years (homicide), 10 years (use of devices of mass destruction), or 12 years (aggravated homicide or murder).

Most felonies subject to such high minimums are offenses against humanity, war crimes, serious offenses against the state, and high treason. If a felony carries a minimum of 5 years, 25 years of imprisonment may be imposed. If the minimum is 8, 10, or 12 years, 25 years or life imprisonment is authorized. In practical terms the affected crimes are homicide, crimes against humanity, war crimes, and some crimes against the state.

The special part of the new code provides broad ranges, giving the judge substantial discretion. Statutory maximums for prison sentences are not especially severe by European standards, and even less compared with American standards:

- simple assaults (art. 158): 1 month to 3 years;
- simple theft, minor robberies, serious assaults (arts. 279, 283, 158): 3 months to 5 years;

[17] Some criminal offenses defined in laws outside the penal code are punishable by fines or community service, but not imprisonment.

- serious bodily harm (art. 156): 1–10 years;
- burglary (art. 279): 1–10 years;
- robbery (art. 280): 2–12 years;
- aggravated robbery (art. 280, firearms or other weapons): 3–15 years;
- rape (art. 197): 2–12 years;
- aggravated rape (art. 197): 3–15 years, and if especially cruel, 5–15 years;
- homicide (art. 148): 8–12 to 15 or 25 years or life imprisonment.

Statutory minimums are not absolutely binding and never completely limit judicial discretion. Judges may impose sentences below them if they believe circumstances so warrant. For felonies, such extraordinary mitigation should not result in a sentence less than one-third of the minimum. Thus the statutory minimum of 8 years for homicide may be reduced to 2 years and 7 months. For more common felonies with 3-year minimums, the floor is 1 year. This authority is often used.[18]

The code also allows extraordinary aggravation. The classic instance concerns recidivists. Offenders who commit certain repeated offenses (similar offenses, within a certain time at liberty since the previous conviction, and after serving some minimum of imprisonment) may have their penalties increased. This authorizes a sentence up to 150 percent of the normal maximum (e.g., 3 years instead of 2). The judge may use this authority, but need not. The 1969 code, by contrast, was absolutely binding and provided for automatic increases in minimums and maximums. These provisions were widely criticized as unduly impinging on judicial discretion and being unacceptably harsh, resulting in disproportionate sentences for petty offenses by recidivists. The 1997 code significantly increased judicial discretion and reduced excessive severity.

The 1997 code thus provides broad discretionary authority to sentencing judges, even for felonies. Since 1998 there have been many attempts, a few successful, to limit those powers and require more rigid minimums and longer sentences. One example concerns homicide. For many politicians and some in the media, many homicide cases resulted in insufficiently severe punishments. Changes were made, but some judicial discretion was preserved. The minimums for some aggravated killings were increased from 8 to 12 years, but life sentences were not mandated.

---

[18] In 2003, of 415 convictions for homicide without aggravating circumstances, 169 sentences were for less than 8 years; extraordinary mitigation of penalty was involved.

There were other attempts to limit judicial discretion in sentencing some violent offenses. Nonetheless, broad discretionary powers were preserved for most offenses.

As mentioned earlier, Polish law does not recognize suspended sentences as a separate type of sanction, but only a means of implementing a sentence. In practice, they are a distinct sanction. Suspension, technically conditional suspension of the execution of a sentence, is always possible, not only for imprisonment but also for community service and fines. The latter two possibilities were introduced in 1997 to give judges more flexibility. In practice, suspended community service and fines remain rare. Suspended prison sentences are a main tool of Polish penal policy.

General premises for suspending a prison sentence are set out in article 69. Prison sentences up to 2 years may be suspended. The code requires a positive criminological prognosis: "Suspended sentence must be sufficient to achieve purposes of punishment, especially to prevent reoffending." Other reasons for suspending sentences relate to offenders' characteristics and individual prevention: attitudes, traits, personal conditions, lifestyle, and postoffense behavior. The 1969 code added that suspension should not take place "if the reasons related to the social impact of the penalty speak against it." This made clear that suspension may be denied for the sake of general prevention and general deterrence. This limitation is absent from the 1997 code. The current code precludes suspension only for multiple recidivists, unlike the 1969 code, which forbade it for all recidivists. This is another respect in which the new code provides greater flexibility and discretion.

Suspended sentences involve elements of probation, normally for a trial period from 2 to 5 years, often with two additional elements. First, the court may impose various obligations. These include reporting to the court or probation office, apologizing to the victim, supporting another person in his or her care, performing remunerated work or continuing with education or vocational training, abstaining from alcohol abuse or drug use, participating in educational and correctional programs, participating in treatment programs, avoiding particular milieus or places, not contacting or approaching the victim or any other person, leaving premises occupied together with the victim, and satisfying any other conditions aiming to prevent reoffending.

Second, the court may order supervision by a probation officer. The officer is supposed primarily to oversee performance of conditions. However, designation of a probation officer is optional only. So, it is possible to impose a suspended sentence without supervision. Moreover, imposition of obligations is optional. Thus suspended imprisonment without conditions is possible. Two-thirds of suspended sentences involve neither obligations nor supervision.

Suspended sentences may be accompanied by a fine of up to 270 daily units. If there are no obligations and no supervision, the fine may be the only effective punishment.

If the offender commits no further offenses and there are no other behavioral problems, the criminal record is deleted 6 months after the end of the suspension period. The offender will then have no official criminal record. If the period ends negatively, in some designated cases the court must order execution of the suspended prison sentence and in some others it may do so. It is mandatory to order such execution if during the trial period the convicted person committed an offense similar to the previous one and was sentenced for this offense to immediate imprisonment. If during the trial period the convicted person commits a similar offense, but without being sentenced to immediate imprisonment, or commits any other offense or refuses to comply with obligations imposed, does not pay a fine, or in any other way violates conditions related to suspension of the sentence, execution of the sentence is optional.

IV. Punishment Patterns

The 1997 Polish Penal Code as it took effect on September 1, 1998, is rightly considered a substantial attempt to reduce the notorious severity of the Polish criminal justice system. But its effects on sentencing practice, and on the imprisonment rate, were much below expectations. Some excesses were reduced, but overall, Polish criminal justice remains harsh by the standards of most European countries, including many of its neighbors in central Europe, except the Baltic countries, and non-EU countries such as Ukraine or Belarus (although all countries of the region have still harsher sentencing practices than any country in the "old" European Union).

Figure 1 shows that the enormous imprisonment rate under communism fell substantially after 1989. This was partly due to a broad amnesty bill adopted in the fall of 1989, after the first noncommunist government took power. For most of the 1990s the imprisonment rate remained

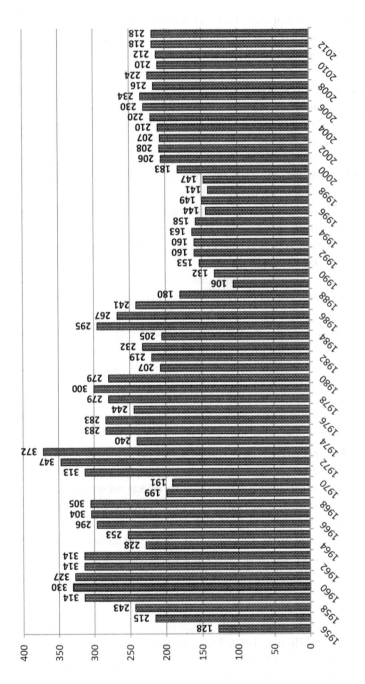

FIG. 1.—Imprisonment rate in Poland, 1956–2013. Source: Data are taken from the criminal justice statistical data collected by the Ministry of Justice and published regularly in Statistical Yearbooks of the Republic of Poland.

much lower than in the 1980s. Sentencing became less harsh and judges sent offenders to prison less often. However, after the new code took effect in 1998, the imprisonment rate grew rapidly, exceeding 200, and today it remains extremely high by European standards (though slightly lower than 10 years ago). It is a paradox that legislation meant to reduce severity increased it. It is not clear whether this is related to provisions of the new code, to the many subsequent amendments, or to external factors.

Figure 2 shows convictions since 1993. Especially at the beginning of the 2000s, the number grew sharply. This is no wonder. The period after 1990 was characterized by growth of crime and a rise in recorded crime rates (Krajewski 2004). But much of the increase is attributable to the criminalization of drunken driving in article 178a in 2000. Before that, drunken driving was an administrative violation and was not included in general crime statistics. Drunken driving poses a serious problem in Poland, and tightening of the law could be justified. However, the consequences for the criminal justice system and for statistical data on sentencing were profound. Since 2000, convictions under article 178a have constituted roughly a third of all convictions! Without that change, criminal convictions would be substantially lower.

There were substantial consequences for sentencing outcomes. Drunken driving is punishable by a fine, community service, or imprisonment from 1 month to 2 years. All sanctions are used and fines play a significant role, but the most common punishment—especially for first offenders—is the suspended prison sentence. Article 178a had major consequences for the frequency of use of suspended sentences and also of prison terms under 2 years (often used for repeat offenders). The effects of article 178a distort aggregate data on sentencing outcomes in Poland. This has to be borne in mind when analyzing these data.

Figure 3 provides the data on immediate prison sentences, suspended prison sentences, limitation of liberty (community service), and fines imposed since 1989. This time series goes back further than other official data, so comparison with the communist period is necessary. Under communism immediate imprisonment played a much larger role than today. In 1989, the last year of the communist regime, immediate imprisonment amounted to 30 percent of all sentences, compared with 9–10 percent during the last 10 years. The major decreases occurred before 1999, the first full year under the new code. The political transformation, not changes in the law, contributed most to the changes.

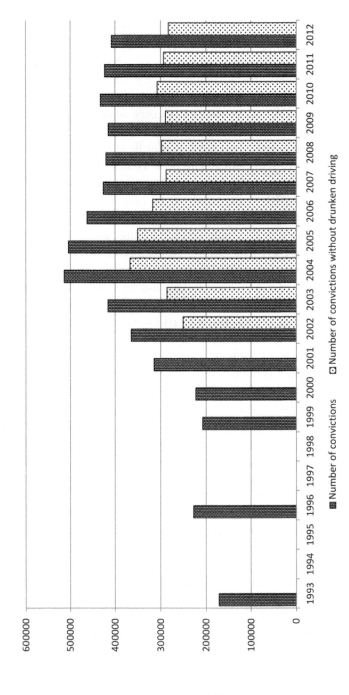

Fig. 2.—Number of convictions in Poland, 1993–2012. Source: Data are taken from the criminal justice statistical data collected by the Ministry of Justice and published regularly in Statistical Yearbooks of the Republic of Poland.

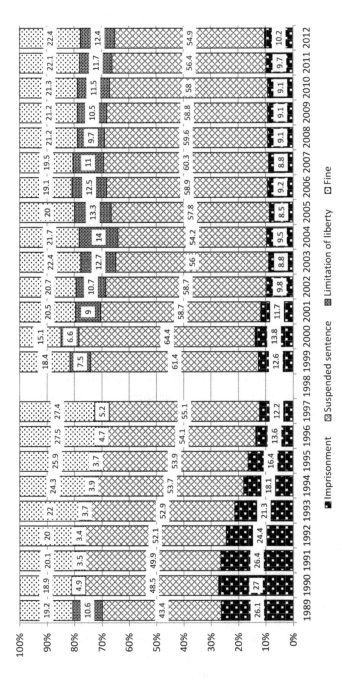

■ Imprisonment ▨ Suspended sentence ▨ Limitation of liberty ☐ Fine

Fig. 3.—Structure of penalties imposed by courts in Poland, 1989–2012. Source: Data are taken from the criminal justice statistical data collected by the Ministry of Justice and published regularly in Statistical Yearbooks of the Republic of Poland.

During the 1990s, the use of fines expanded and the use of community service contracted. The use of fines increased from 19.2 percent in 1989 to 27.4 percent in 1997. The use of community service shrank by almost half. This happened largely because economic changes made it much more difficult to deduct payments from the offender's salary and organization of public works became more difficult. This may be one reason why courts imposed regular fines more often.

The most commonly used punishment continued to be the suspended prison sentence. Frequency of use increased substantially after the communist period, rising from 43.4 percent in 1989 to 55.1 percent in 1997. Judges often substituted suspended sentences for cases in which immediate imprisonment previously was used. At that time, the suspended sentence was the most readily available alternative to imprisonment.

After the effectuation of the new penal code, the proportion of immediate imprisonment sentences decreased further. Use of fines decreased immediately after 1997, despite introduction of the day fine system. The reason is probably that judges considered the new system too complicated and preferred to use suspended sentences. Use of fines later increased but never regained the 1997 level. In 2012, 22.4 percent of all sanctions were fines, compared with 27.4 percent in 1997.

Expansion of fine use may be somewhat misleading and result largely from the introduction of article 178a. Fines constitute a substantial proportion of sanctions for drunken driving. The same may be at least partly true for community service. Frequency of its use has increased substantially since 1998, and it is used more often than at the end of the communist regime. Like fines, though, community service is especially common for drunken drivers.

The most frequently imposed alternative to imprisonment continues to be the suspended sentence: 55–60 percent of all punishments imposed since the new penal code took effect. Polish judges do not appear to be eager to send offenders to prison. Such broad use of suspended sentences can be criticized. Many claim that they are popularly perceived as being no sanction at all and that frequent use fosters a widespread impression that many offenders get away with their crimes. In practice, the suspended sentence carries no special burdens. Figure 4 shows, for example, that supervision by a probation officer is ordered in only a third of cases and therefore bears little resemblance to probation in other Western countries. The attempt to keep people out of prison has been futile. The prisons are full and overcrowded and the imprisonment rate is high.

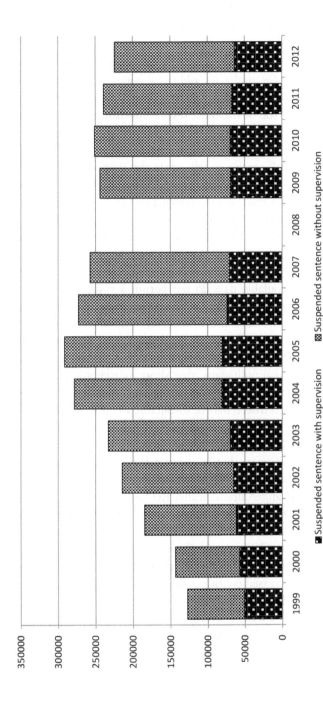

Fig. 4.—Suspended sentence with and without supervision, 1999–2012. Source: Data are taken from the criminal justice statistical data collected by the Ministry of Justice and published regularly in Statistical Yearbooks of the Republic of Poland.

Suspended sentences are one reason for this; court orders to execute suspended sentences are very common.

Figure 5 shows developments concerning immediate imprisonment through 2012. Until 1998, under the old penal code, only 2–3 percent of prison sentences were short (then, 3–6 months), and their use was stable. The same was true of the most severe imprisonment sentences (above 5 years). Changes took place in between, and interestingly enough, they indicate that severity of sentencing at that time was declining. The proportion of midlength sentences fell, while the proportion between 6 months and 1 year rose. Poland experienced a sharp rise in violent offenses (primarily assaults and robberies) during that period, so it appears that sentencing patterns became milder.

Under the new code after 1999, sentences below 6 months substantially increased. In 1999 they were about 5 percent of all prison sentences; in 2007, 12 percent; and in 2012, almost 20 percent. The reasons for this change are unclear. Available data do not permit a confident answer. Sentencing practice became milder, with shorter sentences replacing longer ones. However, the lesser use of fines and community service sentences after 1998 may mean that courts used short-term imprisonment instead. This could have occurred in response to recommendations by some academics, and also politicians, that short incarceration be used more often as "shock therapy" for some categories of offenders (Tyszkiewicz 2006). If that was true, it may be disputable whether the new pattern was really milder than the previous one.

However, this would be true only if courts after 1999 dealt with a comparable pool of offenses, that is, if recorded offense patterns remained stable. However, after 2000, offense patterns with the introduction of article 178a changed dramatically. Relatively short prison sentences are especially common for drunken driving, especially for repeat offenders. Thus it may be that the use of short-term imprisonment did not change substantially. What changed was the pool of offenses and offenders suitable for their use. Nonetheless, the proportion of prison sentences above 1 year decreased continuously during the 2000s, indicating that sentencing overall became milder.

A similar pattern can be seen regarding immediate and suspended prison terms altogether. Between 2000 and 2012, the proportion of 1–6-month prison sentences (fig. 6) increased enormously: from 19 percent to 43 percent. The proportion of sentences of 6 months to 1 year fell from 50 to

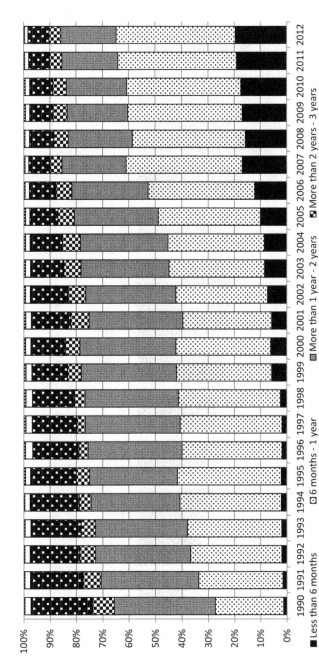

FIG. 5.—Incarceration rates, 1990–2012. Source: The data are the same data published in Siemaszko, Gruszczyńska, and Marczewski (2009, p. 99).

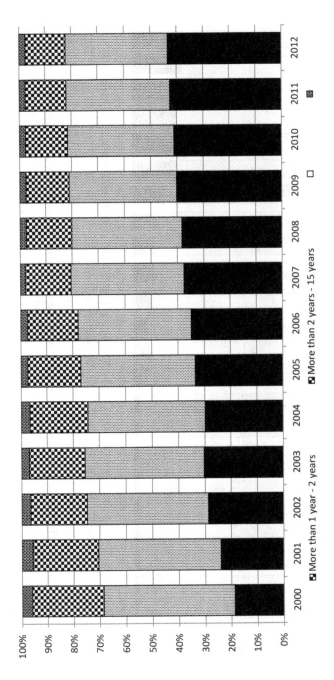

Fig. 6.—Incarceration and suspended imprisonment sentences, 2000–2012. Source: Data are taken from the criminal justice statistical data collected by the Ministry of Justice and published regularly in Statistical Yearbooks of the Republic of Poland.

38 percent and of 1–2 years from 28 percent to 15 percent. This means that shorter imprisonment sentences were imposed increasingly often.

Imprisonment sentences longer than 2 years in principle may not be suspended. It is evident from figure 7 that those patterns were fairly stable. Changes primarily affected the most common low and moderate severity offenses, but not the most serious.

Figure 8 provides data on average lengths of prison sentences. During the years 2003–7, the average for all imprisonment sentences (suspended and not) was stable, but in 2007 it dropped significantly. However, there were marked differences for executed and suspended sentences. During the 4 years for which data are available, the average for executed sentences was decreasing and in 2007 was 29 percent lower than in 2003. Average lengths of suspended sentences remained fairly stable. This may confirm a pattern suggested by some experts that the courts indulge in an unexpected practice—completely contrary to the law—of imposing harsher imprisonment sentences if they are going to suspend them.

In principle, if there are two similar offenses, the court may impose a particular sentence—say 6 months' imprisonment in both cases—and suspend one of them because there is a positive prognosis regarding one offender. This would be appropriate reasoning under the provisions regarding conditional suspension. However, judges may foresee that they will suspend a sentence and only later on decide on its length, making it longer than an executed sentence in a similar case. This may be motivated probably by an aim to reinforce an offender's motivation not to reoffend. This may also be done for the sake of public perceptions: longer imprisonment is supposed to compensate somehow for the suspension. This practice may have serious consequences. Offenders whose suspended sentences are revoked may spend more time in prison than do those originally sentenced to incarceration.

The problem may be of crucial importance in the light of some additional data. The patterns just described do not suggest that Polish criminal justice is especially punitive and do not convincingly explain the high imprisonment rate. Recent analyses indicate that the explanations may lie in the implementation of alternatives to imprisonment. Many offenders sentenced originally to fines, community service, and suspended prison sentences wind up behind bars. First, a high proportion of fine defaulters are imprisoned for default. Second, many of those sentenced to community service breach their work obligations and are sent to prison. Third, most importantly, huge numbers of offenders on

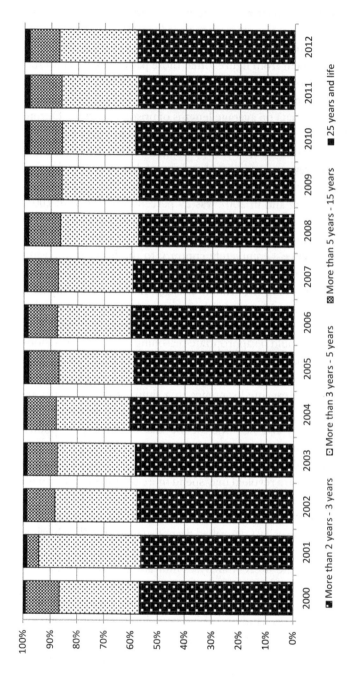

FIG. 7.—Incarceration sentences above 2 years' imprisonment, 2000–2012. Source: Data are taken from the criminal justice statistical data collected by the Ministry of Justice and published regularly in Statistical Yearbooks of the Republic of Poland.

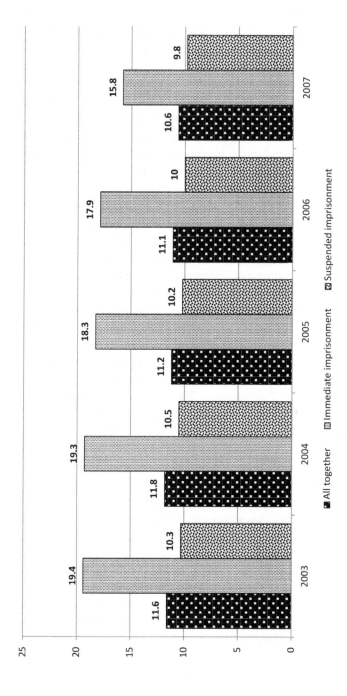

Fig. 8.—Average length of imprisonment sentence, 2003–7 (in months). Source: Skupiński (2009a, p. 16).

suspended sentences have their suspensions revoked (Nawój-Śleszyński 2014); the courts order their sentences implemented because they re-offend or misbehave in some other way. Data for 2008 and 2011 shown in figure 9 confirm this. In both years, the group most often incarcerated was offenders whose suspended sentences were revoked. Together with incarcerated fine defaulters and community service failures, this group constituted 66.5 percent of those incarcerated in 2008 and 63.7 percent in 2011. The Polish criminal justice system on its face may not appear to be especially punitive, but the implementation of alternatives results in imprisonment of substantial proportions of those who receive them (Mycka and Kozłowski 2013).

The explanation can be found in serious legal, financial, organizational, and other obstacles to implementation of alternatives. Judges prefer to use suspended sentences, especially unsupervised ones, because they are the simplest to implement. They require no implementation at all. All other sanctions require investment of organizational, financial, and other re-sources to implement them in a reasonable way.

Consider fines. In many countries the fine is the most common sanc-tion (especially in Scandinavia, where fines can amount to more than 90 percent of all sanctions). In Poland the fine represents only 22 percent of sanctions, although this understates their true prevalence. Polish crim-inal law divides punishable law violations into criminal (*przestępstwa*) and administrative offenses (*wykroczenia*). The latter are commonly called contraventions or violations in English. Their punishment is authorized in the separate contraventions code. Contraventions, mostly petty viola-tions of public order rules, usually are punishable only by fines and are adjudicated by special divisions of criminal courts; a contravention con-viction does not create a criminal record. Polish courts adjudicated 516,200 contraventions in 2012, of which 450,000 may have resulted in convictions, the overwhelming majority resulting in fines. If they were reflected in criminal court data, fines as a proportion of sanctions would increase more than fivefold.

Imposition and enforcement of fines present considerable challenges. Under communism, fines were treated with suspicion for ideological reasons. Introduction of the day fine system was supposed to stimulate their use by allowing courts to adjust them to offenders' finances and ad-minister them more equitably. Unfortunately, it did not work out that way. Judges found the system too complicated, and there were serious im-plementation problems. The courts needed precise, reliable information

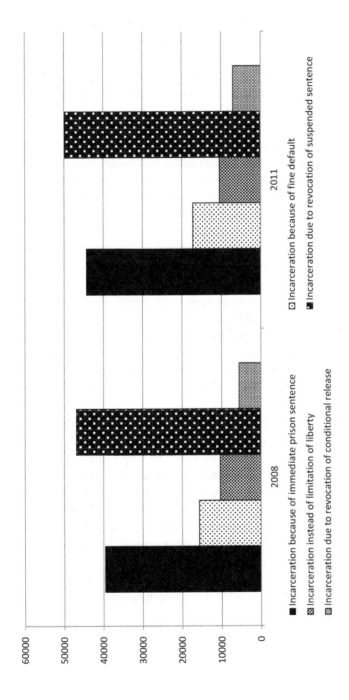

Fig. 9.—Reasons for incarceration (preliminary detention excluded). Source: Mycka and Kozłowski (2013, pp. 26–27).

on the accused's finances, but this was seldom available in an economy in transition, with a huge underground economy, many people employed unofficially, and much of the population hiding their real income from the tax authorities. To establish credible information, courts would have to undertake intensive investigations for which they lack time and resources.

Judges say also that most offenders are lower-class persons, often unemployed, with no or extremely low income, and living on the verge of poverty. Using fines for such offenders makes little sense, they say: fines in such cases will not be paid, are mostly impossible to execute, and will land the convicted person in jail for default.[19] It is probably true that fines are much easier to administer in wealthy societies than in relatively poor ones.

Similar problems arise with community service. Frequency of use has increased, but implementation remains complicated. In Section II, I discussed practical impediments. Many practitioners believe that implementation is too complicated and requires too much effort and that it is simpler to send people to jail or suspend their sentences. It is necessary to underline that this pattern of broad use, or even abuse of suspended sentences as the alternative to imprisonment, seems to be not only Polish particularity. As mentioned already earlier, it seems to be present in all former communist countries of central and eastern Europe (Krajewski 2014*a*).

Suspended sentences are the most commonly imposed sanction and the principal alternative to incarceration (Skupiński 2009*b*). They may result from well-intentioned efforts by judges to keep as many offenders as possible out of prison, but they are often imposed without adequate information on an offender's background and other problems. Most are unsupervised and do not involve meaningful treatment, educational, or preventive obligations. Many offenders during the suspended sentence period are left alone with their alcohol, drug, mental health, and other problems. Even when the court orders supervision by a probation officer, overcommitted officers with huge caseloads have difficulty providing reasonable assistance (Wójcik 2015). Under such circumstances it is not

---

[19] The code prohibits imposition of fines when there are no prospects of payment and chances of execution are low (art. 58, § 2). This was intended to prevent sending defaulters to jail.

surprising if many offenders persist in bad habits, reoffend, or otherwise attract attention that lands them in prison.

V. Back to the Future

The history of sentencing in Poland in the past 25 years features repeated attempts to reduce severity. The 1997 code is the most striking example. The drafters usually spoke of "rationalization" rather than "liberalization," but it is clear that among their main purposes were to reduce severity, lower the imprisonment rate, and move Polish practices closer to western European norms. So far these efforts have largely failed, indicating that statutory changes are often not enough to effect major changes in how the criminal justice system works.

Ironically, significant liberalization and reduction of the imprisonment rate occurred during the 1990s under the communist criminal code, which was notorious for its rigidity and punitiveness, and without major changes in its sentencing provisions. Sentencing practice changed to reflect the changing mood in the country associated with political, economic, and social transformation and liberalization. Changes in penal law proposed by academic lawyers and criminologists during the 1990s were implemented quite successfully within the old legal framework.

After the new penal code took effect in 1998, further "rationalization" of sentencing practices was intended and expected. Unfortunately, the opposite happened. Changes thought to be irreversible began to be reversed. The new code failed to achieve further progress or to consolidate what had been accomplished thus far. Criminal justice policy became the focus of an onslaught by the media and some politicians because of its "unacceptable mildness." This view found public support in a country plagued by a substantial growth in crime rates and high levels of fear of crime.

All this resulted in hyperactivity of the Parliament in amending and "improving" a code that in some parts is scarcely recognizable in the eyes of its drafters. The changes mostly made things harsher. The sentencing provisions, including most statutory minimums and maximums, were little changed, but sentencing practices shifted in ways that led to substantial increases in the size of the prison population and in the imprisonment rate. To what extent this resulted from changes in the political and social atmosphere in a more conservative and punitive direction is unclear. The coincidence is conspicuous.

The increases in severity have not resulted primarily from harsher laws and stricter sentencing practices. Polish judges are not unusually punitive. They attempt to keep substantial proportions of convicted offenders out of prison, probably because they understand the ineffectiveness of incarceration. Unfortunately, the tools most available to them are probably the wrong tools. The overuse of simple suspended prison sentences results in a small proportion of offenders being initially incarcerated. However, the comparative absence of supervision, conditions, and treatment results in many winding up behind bars. The Polish criminal justice system is paralyzed by a catch-22: the more offenders sentenced to alternatives, the higher the imprisonment rate. It is too early to say whether most recent changes introduced on July 1, 2015, will finally bring some substantial change or prove to be yet another failed attempt to reduce the severity of punishment.[20]

REFERENCES

de Keijser, Jan W. 2011. "Never Mind the Pain, It's a Measure! Justifying Measures as Part of the Dutch Bifurcated System of Sanctions." In *Retribution Has a Past: Has It a Future?* edited by Michael Tonry. Oxford: Oxford University Press.
Frankowski, Stanisław, and Andrzej Wąsek. 1993. "Evolution of the Polish Criminal Justice System after World War II—an Overview." *European Journal of Crime, Criminal Law and Criminal Justice* 1:143–66.
———. 1995. "Polish Criminal Law and Procedure." In *Legal Reform in Post-Communist Europe: The View from Within*, edited by Stanisław Frankowski and Paul B. Stephan III. Dordrecht, Neth.: Nijhoff.
Gruszczyńska, Beata. 2004. "Crime in Central and Eastern European Countries in the Enlarged Europe." *European Journal on Criminal Policy and Research* 10:123–36.

---

[20] The general election in October 2015 gave an absolute majority to the radically conservative Law and Justice Party. The new government quickly reversed two important innovations of the previous liberal government. First, changes meant to give the public prosecution service greater political independence were nullified, and it was again placed under the direction of the minister of justice (Krajewski 2012). Second, a major procedural change in 2015 that introduced trials based on the adversarial system was canceled; the previous inquisitorial trial structure was revived. Radical reforms of the penal code may be expected, with one aim only: to make sentencing harsher.

Harries, Owen. 1993. "The Collapse of the West." *Foreign Affairs* 72(4):41–49.
Jasiński, Jerzy. 1996. "Crime in Central and East European Countries." *European Journal on Criminal Policy and Research* 5:40–50.
Kossowska, Anna, Konrad Buczkowski, Witold Klaus, Irena Rzeplińska, and Dagmara Wojciechowska-Fajst. 2012. "Politicians, Media and Society's Perception of Crime." In *Crime and Transition in Central and Eastern Europe*, edited by Alenka Šelih and Aleš Završnik. New York: Springer.
Krajewski, Krzysztof. 2004. "Crime and Criminal Justice in Poland." *European Journal of Criminology* 1:377–407.
———. 2006. "The Juvenile Justice System in Poland." In *Juvenile Law Violators, Human Rights, and the Development of New Juvenile Justice Systems*, edited by Eric L. Jensen and Jørgen Jepsen. Oxford: Hart.
———. 2009. "Punitive Attitudes in Poland: The Development in the Last Years." *European Journal on Criminal Policy and Research* 15:103–20.
———. 2012. "Prosecution and Prosecutors in Poland: In Quest of Independence." In *Prosecutors and Politics: A Comparative Perspective*, edited by Michael Tonry. Vol. 41 of *Crime and Justice: A Review of Research*, edited by Michael Tonry. Chicago: University of Chicago Press.
———. 2013. "Penal Developments in Poland: New or Old Punitiveness?" In *European Penology?* edited by Tom Daems, Dirk van Zyl Smit, and Sonja Snacken. Oxford: Hart.
———. 2014a. "Different Penal Climates in Europe." *Kriminologijos Studijos* [Criminological studies] 1:86–111.
———. 2014b. "Juvenile Justice in Poland." In *Oxford Handbooks Online*. http://www.oxfordhandbooks.com/view/10.1093/oxfordhb/9780199935383.001.0001/oxfordhb-9780199935383-e-012?result=1&rskey=6qkvzM.
———. 2014c. "Rule of Law vs. Public Security: Controversy Regarding Dangerous Offenders in Poland." In *A büntető hatalom korlátainak megtartása:a büntetés mint végső eszköz. Tanulmányok Gönczöl Katalin tiszteletére*, edited by Andrea Borbíró, Éva Inzelet, Klara Kerezsi, Miklós Lévay, and Lena Podolentz. Budapest: ELTE Eötvös Kiado.
Lappi-Seppälä, Tapio. 2011. "Sentencing and Punishment in Finland: The Decline of the Repressive Ideal." In *Why Punish? How Much? A Reader on Punishment*, edited by Michael Tonry. Oxford: Oxford University Press.
Lévay, Miklós. 2000. "Social Changes and Rising Crime Rates: The Case of Central and Eastern Europe." *European Journal of Crime, Criminal Law and Criminal Justice* 8:35–50.
———. 2012. "Penal Policy, Crime, and Political Change." In *Crime and Transition in Central and Eastern Europe*, edited by Alenka Šelih and Aleš Završnik. New York: Springer.
Łoś, Maria. 2002. "Post-Communist Fear of Crime and the Commercialization of Security." *Theoretical Criminology* 6:165–88.
———. 2003 "Crime in Transition: The Post-Communist State, Markets and Crime." *Crime, Law and Social Change* 40:145–69.
Mycka, Krzysztof, and Tomasz Kozłowski. 2013. "Paradoksy polskiej polityki karnej, czyli jak zapełniamy więzienia nadużywając środków probacji" [The

paradoxes of Polish sentencing policies, or how we fill up prisons by abusing probation]. *Probacja* [Probation] (2):5–38.

Nawój-Śleszyński, Aldona. 2014. "Rola środków penalnych związanych z poddaniem sprawcy próbie w kształtowaniu rozmiarów populacji więziennej w Polsce" [The impact of probationary measures on the size of the prison population in Poland]. *Probacja* [Probation] (2):5–30.

Pomorski, Stanisław. 1981. "Communists and Their Criminal Law: Reflections on Igor Andrejew's 'Outline of the Criminal Law of the Socialist States.'" *Review of Socialist Law* 7:7–34.

Rzeplińska, Irena, and Paulina Wiktorska. 2015. "Controlling Criminality." In *Criminality and Criminal Justice in Contemporary Poland*, edited by Konrad Buczkowski, Beata Czarnecka-Dzialuk, Witold Klaus, Anna Kossowska, Irena Rzeplińska, Paulina Wiktorska, Dagmara Woźniakowska-Fajst, and Dobrochna Wójcik. Farnham, UK: Ashgate.

Šelih, Alenka. 2012. "Crime and Crime Control in Transition Countries." In *Crime and Transition in Central and Eastern Europe*, edited by Alenka Šelih and Aleš Završnik. New York: Springer.

Siemaszko, Andrzej, Beata Gruszczyńska, and Marek Marczewski. 2009. *Atlas przestępczości w Polsce 4* [Atlas of crime in Poland 4]. Warsaw: Oficyna Naukowa.

Skupiński, Jan. 2009a. "Kara bezwzględnego pozbawienia wolności i populacja więzienna: Współczynniki prizonizacji w Polsce i w Europie" [Incarceration sentences and prison population: Imprisonment rates in Poland and in Europe]. In *Alternatywy pozbawienia wolności w polskiej polityce karnej* [Alternatives to deprivation of liberty in Polish penal policy]. Warsaw: Wydawnictwo Naukowe Scholar.

———. 2009b. "Warunkowe zawieszenie wykonania kry pozbawienia wolności" [Conditional suspension of execution of imprisonment sentences]. In *Alternatywy pozbawienia wolności w polskiej polityce karnej* [Alternatives to deprivation of liberty in Polish penal policy]. Warsaw: Wydawnictwo Naukowe Scholar.

Tonry, Michael. 2001. "Punishment Policies and Patterns in Western Countries." In *Sentencing and Sanctions in Western Countries*, edited by Michael Tonry and Richard S. Frase. Oxford: Oxford University Press.

Tonry, Michael, and David P. Farrington. 2005. *Crime and Punishment in Western Countries, 1980–1999*, edited by Michael Tonry and David P. Farrington. Vol. 33 of *Crime and Justice: A Review of Research*, edited by Michael Tonry. Chicago: University of Chicago Press.

Tonry, Michael, and Richard S. Frase 2001. *Sentencing and Sanctions in Western Countries*, edited by Michael Tonry and Richard S. Frase. Oxford: Oxford University Press.

Tyszkiewicz, Leon. 2006. "Rzut oka na niektóre aktualne problemy prawa karnego, polityki kryminalnej i kryminologii" [An overview of main current problems of penal law, penal policy, and criminology]. In *Zagadnienia współczesnej polityki kryminalnej* [Problems of contemporary penal policy], edited by Teresa Dukiet-Nagórska. Bielsko-Biała: Wydawnictwo STO.

van Zyl Smit, Dirk, and Sonja Snacken. 2009. *Principles of European Prison Law and Policy*. Oxford: Oxford University Press.

Wójcik, Dobrochna. 2015. "Supervised Freedom." In *Criminality and Criminal Justice in Contemporary Poland*, edited by Konrad Buczkowski, Beata Czarnecka-Dzialuk, Witold Klaus, Anna Kossowska, Irena Rzeplińska, Paulina Wiktorska, Dagmara Woźniakowska-Fajst, and Dobrochna Wójcik. Farnham, UK: Ashgate.

Jacqueline Hodgson and Laurène Soubise

Understanding the Sentencing Process in France

ABSTRACT

French sentencing is characterized by broad judicial discretion and an ethos of individualized justice focused on rehabilitation. The aims are to prevent recidivism, and so protect the interests of society, while reintegrating the offender. By contrast, the political Right, characterized by the recent Sarkozy regime, favors deterrence through harsher penalties, minimum prison sentences, increased incarceration, and preventive detention of offenders considered dangerous. The sentencing process can be understood only within the broader context of inquisitorially rooted criminal procedure. The central part played by the prosecutor (including in case disposition through alternative sanctions) and her role in recommending sentences that the court almost invariably endorses, together with the unitary nature of the judicial profession, means that there is remarkable consistency in penalties imposed. The *contrainte pénale*, based on a reconsideration of the range of available penalties put forward by the Consensus Commission and legislated in 2014, is unlikely to have great impact without investment in the probation service and a change in the judicial culture that still favors simple sentencing options, including imprisonment, compared with alternatives now in place.

As in many other jurisdictions, sentencing law and policy over the last two decades in France have been preoccupied with such issues as addressing the increasingly overcrowded prison population, incorporating the victim's perspective in appropriate ways, preventing and punishing

Electronically published June 21, 2016

Jacqueline Hodgson is professor of law and director of the Criminal Justice Centre, and Laurène Soubise is a doctoral candidate, both in the School of Law, University of Warwick.

recidivism more severely, defining and managing dangerous offenders, and balancing the effectiveness of alternatives to imprisonment with a political rhetoric of being tough on crime. Sentencing is an emotive and political issue—prison overcrowding and recidivism both featured in the French presidential campaign in 2012—and even where there is some consensus as to the nature of the problem, there is little agreement among politicians on how best to tackle it. Sentencing policies have followed the political fortunes of the Left and the Right. Recent legislation, the law of 15 August 2014 (Loi no. 2014-896 of 15 August 2014, Relative à l'individualisation des peines et renforçant l'efficacité des sanctions pénales), is no exception. It began life almost 2 years earlier as an initiative by the incoming socialist President François Hollande to reform the mandatory minimum sentences introduced in 2007 and the *rétention de sûreté*, a measure that allows the continued detention after completion of the sentence of those considered to be dangerous and at high risk of reoffending because of a serious personality disorder. The *peines planchers*, as these mandatory minimum sentences came to be called, were targeted at recidivists but were extended in 2011 to first-time offenders in the case of some aggravated offenses. Both measures were strongly associated with the politics of former right-wing President Nicolas Sarkozy and were criticized as ineffective in preventing reoffending, while at the same time contributing to the increasing prison population. While Sarkozy was in power, first as minister of the interior then as president, the prison population increased from around 48,000 in 2002 to 64,000 in 2012. The rate of imprisonment rose from 79.2 per 100,000 inhabitants to 99.2 in the same period.

In order to inform this most recent sentencing reform, the minister of justice, Christiane Taubira, established a Consensus Commission to find ways of reducing reoffending and to examine the issue of "dangerousness" in the offending population. The commission, which used an unusual methodology for a law reform inquiry,[1] included a panel of 22 experts who selected a "jury" of 20 (presided over by Françoise Tulkens, a former judge in the European Court of Human Rights) made up in

---

[1] This method is more common in the medical field. The idea is to identify the essential issues and the points of disagreement. By bringing a range of perspectives, informed by research from France and elsewhere and having a structured debate, the aim is to build a consensus base on which to build. See the account of the methodology at http://conference -consensus.justice.gouv.fr/note-dinformation-2/methode/.

equal part of expert practitioners and nonspecialists who, in turn, heard from some 30 experts in a series of public hearings. This approach was advanced as scientifically rigorous, independent and with no link to government, and transparent, as hearings were held in public. It considered research evidence from France and elsewhere in order to have a more scientific basis to inform its recommendations. For example, in an attempt to cut across the usual political debates and media portrayals, the commission looked at the nature of recidivism, competing definitions, and frequencies of reoffending across offense types in order to develop a range of effective penal responses.[2]

The commission produced a bold set of recommendations, which the minister of justice was committed to taking forward, but which the interior minister, Manuel Valls, opposed. This is perhaps predictable given the different perspectives and values typically advanced by these two different offices: the interior minister representing the police and law and order and the justice minister representing the judiciary and the balance of constitutional protections (see, e.g., the account of the reforms in Hodgson [2005, chap. 2]). While both ministers agreed that recidivism was a key problem to be addressed, they differed sharply in the choice of solution. The interior minister favored incarceration, building more prison places, and taking a tough stance on sentencing; the justice minister, following the commission's evidence and recommendations, favored greater use of alternative sanctions, sending fewer people to prison in order to decrease levels of reoffending, and continuing to reduce the prison population. This represented a complete clash of values and of policy, typical of the functional differences between these two ministers and their contrasting perspectives. However, in an unprecedented move that demonstrates just how high the political stakes had become, without informing the justice minister, Valls wrote to President Hollande, voicing his strong opposition to the proposals and urging him to arbitrate on the matter. The letter was published in *Le Monde* in July 2013, amid a storm of controversy surrounding a decision by a *procureur* (public prosecutor) to release from prison three offenders sentenced to short sentences because the prison was full (Johannès 2013).

The legislation made it onto the statute book a year later, and the final text of the law retained important reforms such as the creation of a new probation sentence, the *contrainte pénale*, for middle-ranking offenses

---

[2] The commission cited Huré (2012) as the only study on media portrayal of recidivism.

(*délits*); the abolition of the *peines planchers*; and the removal of the automatic revocation of suspended sentences on the commission of a further offense. However, the *rétention de sûreté*, associated so strongly with the Sarkozy regime, was retained and automatic early release on parole was rejected.

   This essay addresses some of the key themes in sentencing in France and examines recent trends in policy. The French approach is to adapt the penalty to the offender, striving for a justice that is individualized without being arbitrary. Key to this is the relatively unfettered discretion of the judiciary in determining sentence and the notion of sentencing as a process rather than a single event that takes place at the conclusion of the trial. The judge responsible for the execution of the sentence (the *juge d'application des peines* or JAP) will review the penalty, taking account of the offender's employment and family situation and efforts she has made to make good the harm caused. The sentence served by the offender may be quite different from that handed down at trial: electronic tagging may be substituted for a portion of custody once the sentence has begun; noncustodial alternatives may be permitted if the offender has made good progress toward her own rehabilitation; or prisoners may be permitted to continue or take up employment through day release schemes.

   The sentencing discretion of the judge has been diluted, through measures such as the *suivi socio-judiciaire*, controversially mixing treatment and punishment, and the introduction of a measure permitting the detention of dangerous offenders beyond the term of their sentence—the *rétention de sûreté*. Both of these were products of the Sarkozy regime, along with a system of minimum sentences for some offenses, curtailing the traditional and constitutionally guaranteed discretion of the sentencing judge. Pulling in the opposite direction has been the need to address prison overcrowding. Right-wing administrations have favored harsher sentences and building more prisons, but the government of Hollande has focused on rehabilitation and prevention of recidivism through socially adapted (rather than simply harsher) penalties as a means to reduce the prison population.

   Here is how this essay is organized. We begin in Section I with an account of the general principles of sentencing in France and their context within the inquisitorially rooted system of French criminal justice. The centrality of the public prosecutor (the *procureur*) during each phase of the criminal process is underlined, including her role in proposing a sentence to the court and in administering a variety of alternative penalties. Also significant are the relatively diminished role of the defense lawyer and the professional unity of the judicial body (the *magistrature*), which includes the prosecutor, the investigating judge (*juge d'instruction*), the trial judge, and the JAP. Sentencing patterns over recent decades are examined, noting that, despite the introduction of a range of alternative sanctions, including direct alternatives to custody, imprisonment continues to be the sentence of choice. Sentencing appears to be consistent across the country. This may be explained by the unity of judicial culture and the judicial hierarchy for both prosecutors and trial judges, which helps to ensure the application of national and local policies—in particular that the prosecutor's sentencing request in most instances is followed by the court.

Section II discusses the process and laws of sentencing. The offender's relationship with the state is also part of the overall sentencing story. The idea of individualized justice is ingrained in the trial structure (where the antecedents and biography of the accused are set out before the evidence has even been heard), reflecting the relationship with the state in which the trial and sentence are part of the individual's rehabilitation as a citizen.

The law of 15 August 2014 was significant in placing punishment and rehabilitation on the same footing rather than in opposition. Rehabilitation is seen by the current government as a key part of the task of reducing reoffending, and the legislation introduced a further noncustodial sentencing option aimed at rehabilitation, the *contrainte pénale*, a form of probation order. Research suggests, however, that judges prefer simple prison sentences to the myriad of alternatives available because it is often unclear what is available for different levels of offense. The *contrainte pénale* appears to be even more complex, making it unlikely to appeal to a busy judiciary. Furthermore, there are existing measures that achieve the same objectives of imposing obligations on the offender, backed by the threat of a fixed prison term, but are simpler to apply. The August 15 reform also repealed minimum sentences, following the Consensus Commission's findings that these tended to increase the prison population with no corresponding reduction in reoffending.

The final sections provide practical examples of the work of the JAP in adapting sentences to the needs of the individual. These illustrate the close working relationship between the two *magistrats*, the public prosecutor and the JAP, and the focus on personal rehabilitation. While accused and convicted persons in adversarial procedures are often almost silent, as it is their lawyers who advance the defense case, in the French process, the judge addresses the accused (or here, the offender) directly. Yet, in admonishing the accused in court or delivering a moralizing lecture to the convicted offender, the *magistrat* is affirming the potential of rehabilitation and the value of the individual as a citizen.

The future of sentencing policy and practice in France will depend on how the traditionally conflicting perspectives of the ministries of justice and of the interior are resolved and on the politics of the government in power. It will also depend on resources: new probation measures will require increases in probation personnel, which have been promised. The prosecutor as sentencer is also an important trend that will continue to define the sentencing landscape: around half of all cases prosecuted are disposed of by the prosecutor through some form of alternative sanction. Many cases are dealt with through abbreviated procedures in which the prosecution case and sentence are effectively rubber-stamped by the court.

I. Sentencing and Sanctions

Overall, crime rates have fallen regularly in France since 1996. However, this hides important disparities between different types of offenses. Offenses against property have been falling from a peak in 2001, but the number of offenses against the person more than doubled between 1996 and 2011 (table 1).

Before examining patterns in sentencing and policy trends, we first outline the roles of key legal actors and the path followed by a typical case.

A. The French Criminal Justice System

Founded on the inquisitorial principle, the French system of criminal procedure is now best described as mixed. At the investigation stage, the police or the *gendarmerie* carry out the investigation under the supervision of a judicial officer. In 98 percent of cases, this will be the public prosecutor (*procureur*); less than 2 percent of cases, the most serious and complex, are handled by the investigating judge (*juge d'instruction*; Ministère de la Justice 2014, p. 14). The evidence collected during the investigation is compiled in the case file, which will then constitute

TABLE 1

Recorded Crime: 1996–2011

	Offenses against Property	Offenses against the Person	Frauds and Economic and Financial Offenses
1996	2,765,191	228,030	310,910
1997	2,685,053	244,880	295,511
1998	2,753,458	257,233	287,415
1999	2,716,865	282,963	295,734
2000	2,820,509	316,404	352,164
2001	3,063,922	362,175	366,208
2002	3,059,062	381,053	355,342
2003	2,881,838	389,172	349,473
2004	2,708,934	391,857	329,955
2005	2,633,571	411,350	318,680
2006	2,534,097	434,183	334,064
2007	2,363,519	433,284	345,416
2008	2,243,498	443,671	381,032
2009	2,227,649	455,911	370,728
2010	2,184,460	467,348	354,656
2011	2,146,479	468,012	350,040

SOURCE.—Observatoire Nationale de la Délinquance et des Réponses Pénales (ONDRP), Bulletin Annuel 2011 (2012), p. 17 (http://www.inhesj.fr/fr/ondrp/les-publications/bulletins-annuels/15).

NOTE.—The ONDRP created three indicators relating to crime recorded by the police and the *gendarmerie*. Offenses against property encompass various offenses of theft and criminal damage. Offenses against the person encompass acts or threats of violence and sexual offenses. Frauds and economic and financial offenses encompass frauds and various other offenses such as counterfeiting, money laundering, etc. Some offenses appear in several indicators (e.g., robberies appear in both offenses against property and offenses against the person) and others appear in none (e.g., drug-related offenses). Aggregated data for police and *gendarmerie* are available only until 2011 as the *gendarmerie* changed its recording software in 2012 and the ONDRP considers that data generated by the new software cannot be compared with data for previous years and cannot be aggregated with police data.

the basis of the trial if the case is prosecuted. Offenses are divided into three categories, from the more minor *contraventions*, through middle-ranking *délits*, to the most serious *crimes*. Many *contraventions*, such as traffic offenses, are dealt with in a quasi-administrative way, but the remainder are tried by a single judge in a *tribunal de police*. *Délits* are tried in a *tribunal correctionnel*, which is traditionally formed of three professional judges, although cases can also be tried by a single judge. Lay jurors are used only for *crimes*, which are tried by a *cour d'assises*, where three professional judges sit alongside six jurors (nine on appeal). Jurors and judges decide together on guilt and sentence.

French public prosecutors have great influence over the punishment handed down by the courts. Not only do they decide whether to prosecute or not and on what charge, but they also recommend a sentence at trial. Furthermore, they have extensive disposal powers. Only a small percentage of cases received by public prosecutors result in fully fledged trials. In 2012, 5 million cases were brought to the attention of the prosecution service (table 2). Of these, prosecution was legally possible in only 1.3 million cases (such as identified suspect, sufficient evidence, statute of limitations). Prosecutors dismissed 141,000 cases (11 percent) for legal policy reasons: withdrawal of complaint, mentally impaired suspect, low-level harm, and so forth. Almost half of the cases (45 percent) were settled by public prosecutors through alternatives to prosecution. The remaining cases were tried by a criminal court, of which 140,561 went through a speedy "on-file" procedure called *ordonnance pénale* (discussed below) and 63,886 went through the French guilty plea procedure (also discussed below).

TABLE 2
Case Disposal by Public Prosecutors: 2004–13

	Recorded Crime	Prosecutable	Dismissed	Settled by Prosecution	Tried by Criminal Court
2004	5,399,181	1,455,657	366,414	414,721	674,522
2005	5,143,257	1,461,904	323,594	461,203	677,107
2006	5,311,024	1,526,396	299,459	519,110	707,827
2007	5,273,909	1,476,535	241,597	550,204	684,734
2008	5,101,119	1,500,411	219,520	611,945	668,946
2009	5,030,578	1,487,675	182,552	631,439	673,684
2010	4,966,994	1,260,428	139,856	529,728	590,814
2011	5,771,017	1,250,966	136,971	556,308	557,687
2012	4,982,173	1,293,189	141,252	583,369	568,568
2013	4,899,894	1,306,758	137,317	566,821	602,620

SOURCE.—Ministère de la Justice, Statistiques: Activité des parquets des TGI (http://www.justice.gouv.fr/statistiques.html, accessed June 4, 2015).

NOTE.—The following terms are translated from the original source. Recorded crime: *plaintes et PV reçus*; prosecutable: *affaires poursuivables*; dismissed: *procédures classées sans suite*; settled by prosecution: *procédures alternatives réussies and compositions pénales réussies*; tried by Criminal Court: *poursuites*.

Recent years have seen the development of prosecutorial powers to divert cases from court (Saas 2004; Hodgson 2012). Born from local initiatives, alternatives to prosecution have become a criminal justice pathway in their own right: they represented only 10 percent of prosecutorial decisions in cases cleared up in 1994 but one-third in 2000 (Aubert 2008) and almost half in 2012. Prosecutors can decide not to prosecute a case but to engage alternatives to prosecution, such as warnings (*rappels à la loi*), mediations, voluntary regularization or reparation, and rehabilitation schemes, but also *compositions pénales*, which allow the prosecutor to impose a financial penalty or community work if the suspect admits the offense (arts. 41-2 and 41-3 of the Code of Criminal Procedure, CPP). The execution of a *composition pénale* does not formally count as a conviction. However, it prevents prosecution for the same facts (*ne bis in idem*), and it forms part of the person's criminal record (art. 768 CPP). Even when prosecutors decide to prosecute the suspect, they have a choice of procedures from which to select. Introduced in 1972 for *contraventions*, the *ordonnance pénale* is a summary procedure in which no public hearing or debate takes place. The judge makes her decision solely on the papers provided by the prosecutor. This procedure was extended to certain *délits* in 2002 and is par ticularly used in road traffic cases. In 2012, it represented over 30 percent of prosecutions for *délits* (table 3). Inspired by common law guilty pleas, the CRPC procedure (*comparution sur reconnaissance préalable de culpabilité*) was introduced in 2004 and progressively extended to almost all *délits* (except for certain exclusions, such as serious and sexual assaults). It allows the prosecutor to offer a sentence of up to 1 year in prison or half of the maximum penalty if the defendant admits the offense. In 2012, it represented over 13 percent of prosecutions for *délits*.

This sentencing power given to the *procureur* in the *composition pénale* and the CRPC procedures have been the objects of debate. In 1995, the Conseil Constitutionnel struck down the *injonction pénale*, a predecessor of the *composition pénale*, considering that a criminal sentence could not be pronounced by a public prosecutor but required the intervention of a judge (decision no. 95-360 DC 2 February 1995). A *composition pénale* or a CRPC must therefore be validated by a judge, but this check by a judge has been described as "quick," "succinct," or even "artificial," underlining that the judge can only accept or reject the sentence proposed by the prosecutor and that a deeper check would go against the ob-

TABLE 3

Alternatives to Prosecution, *Ordonnances Pénales*, and CRPC: 2004–12

	Prosecutions		Alternatives to Prosecution	
	Ordonnances Pénales	CRPC	*Compositions Pénales*	Other Alternatives
2004	58,822	2,187	25,777	388,944
2005	105,765	27,200	40,034	421,169
2006	129,577	50,250	51,065	468,045
2007	129,914	49,712	59,770	490,434
2008	136,124	56,326	67,230	544,715
2009	144,711	77,530	73,392	558,047
2010	126,997	69,232	65,460	464,268
2011	136,103	63,452	65,221	491,087
2012	140,561	63,886	73,241	510,128
2013	145,066	65,100	73,732	493,089

Source.—Ministère de la Justice, Statistiques: Activité des parquets des TGI (http:// www.justice.gouv.fr/statistiques.html, accessed June 4, 2015).

Note.—Other alternatives include *rappels à la loi* (warnings), regularization/reparation, and mediation.

jectives of rapidity for which the measures were first introduced (Saas 2004; Hodgson 2012).

While *procureurs* belong to the same professional body as judges, the defense lawyer has been described as a "professional outsider" and traditionally has a limited role in an inquisitorially based system (Hodgson 2005, p. 112). However, recent decades have seen a growing role of the defense lawyer in France, first at trial and, more recently, during the pretrial phase, influenced by decisions of the European Court of Human Rights (ECtHR 14 October 2010, *Brusco v France*, no. 1466/07). That said, lawyers' role remains marginalized as, although they can now attend, they must not intervene during police interrogation and are permitted to put questions to the suspect only at the end of the interview and to make observations that would then be attached to the case file. Nonetheless, this can allow them to introduce mitigating elements in favor of the suspect, such as pointing out that she has a stable lifestyle with a job and family, which could influence the decision of the public prosecutor. At trial, a fuller mitigation argument will be made by the defense lawyer with regard to remorse, difficult personal history, addiction, and so forth. The court will also be informed by a probation report and the defendant's criminal record. The presence of defense lawyers is mandatory for the CRPC hearing, and their role is crucial in negotiating the sentence with the *procureur* and in advising their client whether to accept the sentence being offered.

If the court finds the accused guilty, the trial judge will hand down the sentence, having heard any mitigation from the defendant or her lawyer. However, in some cases there will be a second stage to the sentencing process, in which the JAP, responsible for the execution of the penalty, will adapt the sentence to the needs of the individual offender in order to make it more effective and to prevent reoffending. The JAP determines the terms and conditions under which the sentence will be served. Article 707 of the CCP provides that the sentence should be kept under review and adapted depending on the evolution of the personality of the convicted person and her financial, familial, and social situation, which must be evaluated regularly. This adaptation may consist of awarding or removing sentence reductions to reflect good or bad behavior and efforts made by the prisoner to reintegrate by, for example, passing exams or improving her literacy skills. The JAP is also empowered to commute short prison sentences to noncustodial alternatives before the sentence has been served or to release the prisoner on probation or under certain conditions toward the end of her sentence in order to prepare for her permanent release.

B. Sentencing Patterns

Imprisonment and fines remain the principal punishment imposed by French courts. Despite legislative creativity in establishing a range of noncustodial sentences, they are used relatively rarely by French courts, representing only about 10 percent of the sentences imposed in 2012 (table 4). They mainly comprise suspension of driving licenses, fine days, and community service (*travail d'intérêt general*, or TIG). They also include citizenship courses and the "reparation-sanction," which forces the offender to repair the damage caused to the victim, either through financial compensation or through reparation in kind or material reparation. In 2012, over 66,000 noncustodial sentences were imposed, including about 17,000 suspensions of driving licenses (25 percent), 24,271 fine days (36 percent), and 16,588 community service sentences (24 percent).

Between 2000 and 2014, the total number of prisoners rose from 51,441 (85 per 100,000 population) to 67,075 (101.6 per 100,000). This

TABLE 4
Main Penalties Imposed by Courts

	2004	2005	2006	2007	2008	2009	2010	2011	2012
Total	596,304	618,010	632,531	642,803	639,853	633,736	609,992	593,143	610,502
Imprisonment:	311,872	319,126	318,171	322,034	323,772	309,558	301,586	292,786	301,833
Partially suspended	28,337	27,293	26,031	28,495	33,498	33,553	33,684	32,468	31,143
Fully suspended	198,582	198,825	197,026	195,665	197,374	188,744	178,337	169,064	173,125
Fine	204,880	204,782	214,051	223,093	218,677	223,882	212,524	206,049	213,139
Noncustodial	49,672	58,281	62,669	61,358	60,832	64,118	61,481	62,159	64,479
Educative measure	22,716	28,033	29,664	28,417	28,550	28,111	27,257	25,510	24,705
Discharge	7,164	7,788	7,976	7,901	8,022	8,067	7,144	6,639	6,347

SOURCE.—Ministère de la Justice, Statistiques: Les condamnations (http://www.justice.gouv.fr/budget-et-statistiques-10054/donnees-statistiques-10302
/les-condamnations-27130.html, accessed June 4, 2015).

NOTE.—Noncustodial sentences mainly comprise suspension of driving license, fine days, and community service. An educative measure can be imposed on juvenile offenders (return to parents or guardian, placement in a medical or educative institution, return to children services, reparation, etc.).

increase is due to the explosion of the number of prisoners serving short sentences (see table 5). Whereas in 2000, inmates sentenced to over 5 years in prison represented 41.8 percent of the total with 13,856 prisoners, this proportion dropped to just 22.7 percent in 2014 with 13,902 prisoners. Meanwhile, the number of inmates sentenced to less than a year in prison has gone up from 8,365 in 2000 (25.3 percent) to 22,213 in 2014 (36.3 percent). Additionally, the number of prisoners sentenced to between 1 and 3 years' imprisonment jumped from 6,766 in 2000 to 18,288 in 2014. This trend could be explained by several factors including a change in the structure of reported crime, the introduction of increased sentences for road traffic offenses, the introduction of mandatory minimum sentences for repeat offenders in 2007, and the abolition of the practice of mass pardons by former President Sarkozy from 2007. Mass pardons traditionally took place every year on Bastille Day, but the

TABLE 5

Prison Sentences Quantum for *Délits*: 2000–2014

	<1 Year		1–3 Years		3–5 Years		>5 Years		
	Number	%	Number	%	Number	%	Number	%	Total
2000	8,365	25.3	6,766	20.4	4,139	12.5	13,856	41.8	33,126
2001	7,739	24.5	6,128	19.4	3,562	11.3	14,202	44.9	31,631
2002	9,301	28.7	6,599	20.3	3,300	10.2	13,244	40.8	32,444
2003	9,875	28.6	7,936	23.0	3,468	10.0	13,250	38.4	34,529
2004	10,954	29.2	8,835	23.6	4,357	11.6	13,333	35.6	37,479
2005	11,504	29.5	8,929	22.9	4,569	11.7	14,039	36.0	39,041
2006	12,146	30.5	8,810	22.1	4,486	11.3	14,342	36.0	39,784
2007	15,141	36.1	8,445	20.1	4,295	10.2	14,035	33.5	41,916
2008	17,371	36.8	11,025	23.4	4,644	9.8	14,161	30.0	47,201
2009	17,422	34.7	13,716	27.3	5,103	10.2	14,002	27.9	50,243
2010	17,445	34.4	14,174	28.0	5,628	11.1	13,442	26.5	50,689
2011	17,535	34.2	14,780	28.8	5,709	11.1	13,248	25.8	51,272
2012	20,641	35.9	17,226	30.0	6,202	10.8	13,428	23.4	57,497
2013	21,961	36.4	18,169	30.1	6,647	11.0	13,563	22.5	60,340
2014	22,213	36.3	18,288	29.9	6,858	11.2	13,902	22.7	61,261

SOURCE.—Ministère de la Justice, *Séries statistiques des personnes placées sous main de justice 1980–2014*, p. 35 (http://www.justice.gouv.fr/prison-et-reinsertion-10036/les-chiffres-clefs -10041/series-statistiques-des-personnes-placees-sous-main-de-justice-26147.html, accessed September 8, 2014).

NOTE.—The total represents the stock of inmates on January 1 of each year who were convicted for a *délit* (middle-ranking offense).

constitutional reform of July 23, 2008, restricted the right of the president to grant a pardon to individual cases only. Kensey and Ouss (2011) found that, on average, prisoners released between May 1996 and April 1997 were relieved of an average of 8 percent of their sentences as a result of mass pardons. Forty-three percent benefited from at least one pardon during their sentence. Since 2007, such reductions in sentence do not occur.

Since the Second World War when the files were kept by the French police recording the names and addresses of Jewish people from 1940 (in the occupied zone) and 1941 (in the nonoccupied zone) (on the discovery of these files in 1991–92, see Combe [1994]), French official statistics contain no references to race, religion, or ethnicity; only nationality is recorded. Whereas nonnationals constitute around 6 percent of the general population in France, they represented 19 percent of prisoners (including people under electronic tagging and external placements) in France on January 1, 2015 (Ministère de la Justice 2015, p. 6). Yet, this proportion has decreased significantly as nonnationals represented over 30 percent of inmates in January 1994. By contrast, non-French people represented 5.6 percent of offenders serving a noncustodial sentence on January 1, 2015 (p. 8). The vast majority of foreigners in French prisons come from Africa (49.1 percent, particularly former French colonies in Algeria, Morocco, and Tunisia) and the European Union (38 percent). There is very little research on the impact of nationality, ethnicity, or immigration status on the treatment of defendants in the French criminal justice system. Body-Gendrot (2014) compiled existing research on the subject and concluded that the overrepresentation of non-French in the criminal justice process may result from wrongful bias; but disparities could also be explained by socioeconomic disadvantages or differences in records of past criminality. Roché, Gordon, and Depuiset (2014) conducted a study on the impact of ethnicity on sentencing in two juvenile courts between 1984 and 2005. Although they found some evidence of sentencing bias, they did not discover massive and systematic discrimination based on ethnicity.

C. Sentencing Policy Trends (1994–2014)

The relevant provisions of the *Code Pénal* (CP, Criminal Code) and the course of their recent development are discussed in detail throughout this essay. It may be useful, however, to provide a brief overview of some of the most significant legislative and statistical trends and the legal and political forces that have shaped them. The CP is the core text governing French sentencing; but as governments change, sentencing reform is characterized by swings between putting in place either more rehabilitative or more repressive measures, depending on the political hue of each administration. The first codification of criminal law since 1810 (a variety of amendments were made, but the same code remained in place), the new CP introduced in 1994 merely brought the finishing touches to the sentencing developments of the nineteenth and twentieth centuries. It ratified the wide discretionary sentencing powers progressively given to judges throughout the years. Judges are virtually unfettered in their choice of the nature and quantum of the sentence, and they do not have to give reasons for their sentencing decisions (art. 132-17 CP). The Cour de Cassation, France's highest criminal court, repeatedly asserted that, with regard to sentencing decisions and as long as they remain within the boundaries of the law, judges have an absolute discretion for which they cannot be made accountable (Cass. Crim., 28 January 1991, no. 89-84987). In order to fight the proliferation of short prison sentences, the CP introduced a limited obligation to give reasons for the imposition of a nonsuspended prison sentence for *délits* (art. 132-19 CP). Chassaing (1993) also criticized the CP for not revising the sentence maximums, leaving them in many instances very high, on the grounds that they were merely symbolic and were never imposed in practice. The new CP also reaffirmed the principle of the individualization of sentences to the circumstances and to the character of the offender, dedicating a whole section of the code to this. It retained the alternatives to imprisonment introduced in 1975 (Loi no. 75-624 of 11 July 1975 introduced sentences involving the forfeiture or restriction of rights, such as suspension of driving license, confiscation of vehicle) and 1983 (Loi no. 83-466 of 10 June 1983 created the TIG [unpaid work in the community] and the fine day) but failed to include them within offense definitions, which continued to refer only to imprisonment and fines. The new CP also neglected to define sentencing rationales. It fell to the Constitutional Court to confirm that prison sentences aim both to reform and to reintegrate the offender (decision no. 93-334 DC of 20 January 1994).

Since the acceptance of the new CP, particularly from 2002, crime control political rhetoric has progressively dominated the French public debate on criminal justice reform with some impact on sentencing policy

(Salas 2005; Garapon and Salas 2007). However, more rehabilitative inspirations have had a role in the separate phase of sentence execution, which has remained more sheltered from the influence of penal populism.

1. *The Dominance of Crime Control Ideas.* The 2002 French presidential campaign focused on insecurity and zero tolerance. The Front National, the extreme Right party, made it to the second round of the election. Nicolas Sarkozy, first as minister of the interior (2002–7) and then as president of the Republic (2007–12), clearly positioned himself as the defender of victims. Defending his vision of crime policy in a 2012 speech to judges and public prosecutors, he declared, "the judicial institution, is first and foremost the institution of victims. And you, as *magistrats*, you work for them first and foremost" (Robert-Diard 2012). As a result, his crime policy has been criticized for too closely reflecting high-profile crime stories (Salas 2005; Garapon and Salas 2007; Mucchielli 2008; Wyvekens 2010). Referring to crime policy reform between 2002 and 2007, Mucchielli (2008) describes a "security frenzy." During this period, 30 legislative acts amended the CP and 40 amended the CPP. Numerous new offenses were created (see Danet [2008, pp. 21–22] for an overview). Maximum sentences were also increased, either directly—the law of 18 March 2003 increased sentences applicable to many road traffic offenses—or through the introduction of new aggravating circumstances. The fight against repeat offending also shaped the adoption of several successive acts. The Act of 12 December 2005 widened the scope of equivalent offenses taken into account for the aggravating circumstance of repeat offending to apply and reduced the sentence discount automatically available—barring bad behavior—for recidivists. The reluctance of the ministry of justice to constrain judicial discretion meant that Sarkozy failed to impose minimum sentences for recidivists as minister of the interior. Once he was elected president, however, the law of 10 August 2007 introducing these mandatory minimums was one of the first legislative acts pushed through by his government. Although controversial, these *peines planchers* were later extended to offenses of serious violence by the law of 14 March 2011.

An important development was a new philosophy mixing repression and treatment within a single measure as a new means of reducing recidivism. The law of 17 June 1998 introduced the *suivi socio-judiciaire*, which allows for judicial—and even medical—control of sexual offenders after their release from prison. It involves several obligations, in particular, bans from certain locations and from carrying out activities in contact with children and an obligation to seek psychiatric treatment. Failure to respect those obligations is sanctioned by imprisonment. The 1998 law met with cross-party approval: it was voted by a left-wing majority in Parliament but found its origins in a bill proposed by the outgoing right-wing government just months before. This particular focus on dangerous offenders, mixing repression and treatment in a single measure, has continued through several subsequent laws. The Act of 12 December 2005 introduced judicial surveillance of dangerous offenders; the person is placed under the control of a judge, who can require the offender to report any change of address to probation, to seek medical treatment, to wear an electronic tag, or to be under house arrest (for people sentenced to over 15 years in prison). In addition, a psychiatric report is necessary to establish dangerousness and to check whether medical treatment is appropriate. The law of 25 February 2008 introduced the *rétention de sûreté*, which allows the continued detention after sentencing of those considered to be dangerous and at a high risk of reoffending because of a serious personality disorder. The Act of 10 March 2010 required sexual offenders to undertake a hormonal treatment called "chemical castration." These laws have been denounced as "confusing mental illness and criminality, dangerousness and recidivism" (Herzog-Evans 2011, p. 100). When these two conflicting notions of responsibility are mixed together—criminal culpability and mental illness—the responses of treatment and of punishment also risk being confused: offenders are treated and the mentally ill are punished (Wyvekens 2010). The effects of these new legal provisions and the number of people affected are not yet known, as they apply to offenders sentenced to long periods of imprisonment (e.g., over 15 years for the *retention de sûreté*) toward the end of their sentence.

2. *Rehabilitative Inspirations.* Until 1958, the role of the judge was limited to the imposition of the sentence at the close of the trial; after that, the administration of sentences was left to prisons. In 1958, the CPP established the JAP to oversee the execution of prison sentences. Since then, their role has grown. This redefinition of sentence execution as a judicial function contrasts with the administrative control of sentence execution in common law countries. For example, in England and Wales, the parole board, the body that carries out risk assessment of prisoners to determine who may safely be released into the community, is an independent administrative authority.

The JAP's role in sentence execution has seen a significant increase since 2000 because of contextual but also structural causes. The incarceration of politicians, businessmen, and various celebrities from the mid-1990s, together with the publication in 2000 of a book written by a doctor working in a famous Paris prison (Vasseur 2000), placed the conditions of detention in French prisons firmly under the spotlight. A new interest was taken in violations of human dignity in prisons, in particular because of the state of overcrowding. Parliamentary commissions were tasked to report on the conditions of detention in French prisons (Commission d'Enquête de l'Assemblée Nationale 2000; Commission d'Enquête du Sénat 2000). The return to a crime control ideology from 2002 mainly affected the substantive criminal law and criminal procedure, and the less visible terrain of sentence execution was largely untouched as the focus was of necessity on dealing with the persistent problem of overcrowding. Furthermore, parole and other sentence adjustments were no longer perceived as privileges for offenders anymore, but as tools to prevent recidivism (Warsmann 2003). Further structural causes linked to the legal context can also be identified. Thus, the inclusion by the European Court of Human Rights of sentence reductions within the scope of article 6, paragraph 1 ECHR in its Campbell and Fell decision (1984) and the decision in 1995 by the Conseil d'État to open disciplinary sanctions in prison to judicial review (CE, 17 February 1995, Marie) seem also to have played an important role in cementing the role of the JAP.

Studying people released between May 1996 and April 1997, Tournier and Kensey (2001) showed that, on average, prisoners served 69 percent of their imposed sentence, with 27 percent of the discount due to discretionary sentence discounts and 4 percent to parole decisions. To the best of our knowledge, this is the only study on sentences actually served. Since 2004, each offender sentenced to imprisonment is given automatic sentence reduction credits. The credits are calculated on the basis of the nonsuspended sentence as 3 months for the first year and 2 months for the remaining years or 7 days per month for shorter sentences. The JAP can withdraw sentence reduction credits for bad behavior up to a maximum of 3 months per year or 7 days per month. Prisoners can receive further sentence reductions for "serious efforts of social readaptation" (art. 721-1 CPP), such as passing an exam or learning to read and write. In addition, the Acts of 15 June 2000 and 9 March 2004 greatly increased the JAP's powers, allowing them to adjust sentences to take into account the evolution of the offender's situation and personality (art. 707 CPP). They are also permitted to commute short prison sentences to noncustodial sentences before they have been served (art. 723-15 CPP). Article 707 CPP specifies that "sentence execution favors, within the respect of society's interests and the rights of the victim, the integration or the reintegration of convicted persons, as well as the prevention of recidivism." By contrast to the more crime control–oriented policies described above, the Act of 24 November 2009 accentuated this rehabilitative objective by allowing sentences up to 2 years long to be adjusted prior to being served.

II. The Law of 15 August 2014

This context of a growing prison population and tensions between repressive and rehabilitative objectives, as well as the access to power of a new governing party in 2012, called for a new reform of French sentencing. The new sentencing law of 15 August 2014 is not revolutionary; it is in line with established historical principles of French sentencing, principles that many have argued were called into question by the reforms of the previous administration. The new law establishes a solid foundation by articulating the sentencing rationales of the criminal justice system. Prior to this, article 132-24 of the Code Pénal attempted to reconcile several sentencing aims and functions by providing that "the nature, quantum and regime of imposed sentences are set so as to reconcile the effective protection of society, the punishment of the offender and the interests of the victim with the necessity to promote the integration or reintegration of the convicted person and to prevent the commission of new offenses."

The article was buried in the depths of the Code Pénal's sentencing provisions. The law of 15 August 2014 creates a new article 130-1 CP, placed at the start of the code's section on sentencing. It stipulates that "in order to ensure the protection of society, to prevent the commission of new offenses and to restore the social balance, while respecting the interests of the victim, the sentence has the following functions: '1. To punish the offender; and 2. To promote his reform, his integration or his reintegration.'"

The new article 130-1 articulates an ideology in which punitive and rehabilitative objectives are not opposed, as the drafting of article 132-24 had suggested, but are complementary. There is no political consensus on sentencing aims in France, and the wording of the new article was criticized during its parliamentary debate as evidence of a permissive ideology underpinning the law, which puts on an equal footing the two objectives of punishment and reintegration of the convicted person. The opposition contended that sentences must first and foremost remind offenders of the consequences of infringing the law. The Consensus Commission, whose recommendations formed the basis of the bill, and the government disagreed. The new law gives expression to the view that the punishment of the offender cannot be the sole aim of sentencing; the objective of rehabilitation is an essential part of the battle against recidivism. In this section, we examine two themes that have shaped the French sentencing debate of recent years and make a further appearance in the new law: the individualization of sentences and place of imprisonment within French sentencing.

A. Individualization, Judicial Discretion, and Minimum Sentencing

The new act reaffirms what has become the central principle in French sentencing: the principle of individualization, which gives wide discretionary powers to the sentencing judge by requiring her to tailor the sentence to the offender. The centrality of this principle is the result of historical developments over two centuries. In reaction to the arbitrariness of the prerevolutionary ancien régime, the 1789 Déclaration des Droits de l'Homme et du Citoyen (DDHC—Declaration of the Rights of Man and of Citizens) expressed the principles of proportionality and of legality in its article 8: "The Law must prescribe only the punishments that are strictly and evidently necessary; and no one may be punished except by virtue of a Law drawn up and promulgated before the offense is committed, and legally applied."

The first criminal code of 1791 promulgated fixed sentences, denying any discretionary power to the judge. This was in line with the revolutionary impetus for curbing the power of judges who were considered as nothing more than "the mouth of the law," as Montesquieu put it in *The Spirit of the Laws* (1748, bk. XI, chap. 6). The 1810 criminal code abandoned fixed sentences, instead providing minimums and maximums: for instance, assaults were punished by imprisonment between 15 days and a year and a fine between 500 and 20,000 francs (art. 320). Promoted by liberal lawyers and reformers, the law of 28 April 1832 introduced the mechanism of extenuating circumstances, which allowed the court to depart from minimum sentences imposed by the Code Pénal, taking into account the personality of the accused or the circumstances of the offense. The principle of individualization was theorized at the end of the nineteenth century by Raymond Saleilles, who argued that it was not possible to set sentences rigidly in advance, since they should be adapted to individual circumstances rather than defined in a purely abstract law, ignoring the diversity of cases and individuals (Ottenhof 2001). The principle was strengthened throughout the twentieth century, in particular, with the consideration of the age of the offender and the creation of a separate regime for juveniles, culminating with the new Code Pénal, which came into force in 1994. Minimum sentences were removed entirely, and a whole new section was dedicated to "the personalization of sentences." The Conseil Constitutionnel (French Constitutional Court) granted constitutional status to the principle of individualization, inferring this from the principles of proportionality and necessity found in article 8 DDHC, which has been part of the French Constitution since 1958 (decision no. 2005-520 DC of 22 July 2005, para. 3).

The introduction of the *peines planchers* (minimum sentences) in 2007 was seen as a challenge to this principle of individualization, as it limited the power of judges to adapt the sentence to the personal circumstances of repeat offenders. Judges were permitted to depart from these minimums only if they could demonstrate special circumstances, such as "exceptional guarantees of reintegration" (former art. 132-18-1 CP). However, when called on to rule on the constitutionality of this reform, the Conseil Constitutionnel considered that the principle of individualization was not an obstacle to the legislator fixing rules ensuring the effective repression of offenses, and it did not imply that the sentence had to be determined entirely according to the individual's characteristics (decision no. 2007-554 DC of 9 August 2007, para. 13).

Some commentators welcomed this constraint on the principle of individualization, which they believed could lead to great inequalities between offenders. Pradel (2007), for example, has argued in favor of the introduction of "Anglo-Saxon sentencing guidelines" to promote harmonization between courts. He claimed that the *peines planchers* moved toward greater certainty of sentences, a powerful deterrent against repeat offending. Others, such as Herzog-Evans (2007), argued that the new mechanism did not make sentencing more certain, but simply more severe. Furthermore, experiments in other jurisdictions suggest that, as a sentencing policy, minimum sentences are destined to fail: the US experience has been an explosion in the prison population, with no effect on reducing criminality or repeat offending.

The Consensus Commission conducted a close examination of the *peines planchers*. They heard evidence from a range of experts—including legal academics, criminologists, and sociologists, and also practitioners such as *magistrats*, probation officers, and psychiatrists—and examined the findings of earlier research studies. They concluded that there was no scientific evidence to suggest that the *peines planchers* were effective in preventing recidivism and furthermore that they had noticeably contributed to prison overcrowding. The commission asserted that it was right to give judges broad discretion in sentencing, emphasizing that "their decision should not be constrained in any way by a minimum sentence which does not take into account the whole background of the individual concerned, the nature of offenses and the necessary individualization of the sentence" (Conférence de Consensus 2013, p. 11). The Act of 15 August 2014 reaffirms this principle in article 132-1 CP, which states that "any sentence imposed by the court must be individualized. Within the limits set by law, the court sets the nature, quantum and regime of pronounced sentences according to the circumstances of the offense and the personality of the offender, as well as her material, familial and social situation." It repeals all minimum sentences. It also abolishes the automatic revocation of suspended sentences in case of a new conviction, giving judges the discretion "to avoid inappropriate blind revocations." The clear policy that emerges is a strict application of the individualization principle, reaffirming the total discretion of the judge. This wide judicial discretion is at odds with the international trend toward greater regulation of sentencing through mandatory standards or guidelines. The desire for consistency and predictability of sentences is felt elsewhere, so why not in France?

One explanation might be the absence of wide variations in sentencing, in contrast with other countries. Several factors could be perceived as favoring sentencing uniformity in France. The most obvious factor is provided by the control of individual discretion through the broad right of both defense and prosecution to appeal against the sentence imposed in first instance (unfortunately, no data are available showing the proportion of appealed decisions or the success rate). Furthermore, the exercise of judicial discretion is less solitary in France, where three judges often sit together, compared with, for example, England and Wales. Although there has been a great increase in the number of offenses that can be tried by a single judge, those judges are accustomed to making sentencing decisions collectively. Another guarantee against variations is that, in contrast to England and Wales, public prosecutors recommend a sentence in court and are part of the *magistrature* (French career judiciary), the same professional body as judges.

In an extensive 2013 study of sentencing decisions in five different court centers, Saas, Lorvellec, and Gautron (2013) demonstrated the symmetry that exists between sentences called for by public prosecutors and the sentences actually imposed by the court; for example, the court imposed a fine when it had been requested by the prosecutor in 91.6 percent of cases (p. 171). Faget (2008, p. 23) has also commented on the common "invisible judicial culture" in which those legal actors work. The common training and membership of the same professional body create strong bonds and a common outlook among *magistrats*, who are already characterized by a strong social resemblance (Hodgson 2005, pp. 69–70). Faget also noted that the appraisal of all judges by a hierarchical superior in order to determine career progression contributes to a "culture of obedience" that encouraged conformity of behaviors and decisions (2008, p. 11).

Saas, Lorvellec, and Gautron do not provide detailed tables for each court center in their 2013 study because of a lack of space but provide some further support for their conclusions in the comments of a public prosecutor who worked in several courts and found a remarkable degree of consistency in sentencing practices. By contrast, a journalist evoked "a national lottery" when referring to variations in judicial decisions (Simonnot 2003). Mucchielli and Raquet (2014) also found some variations in sentencing in their study of *comparutions immédiates* in Nice, by comparison with similar studies in Lyon and Toulouse. Similarly, Roché, Gordon, and Depuiset's (2014) study of serious crime cases in juvenile courts showed important variations between courts and significant differences across sentenced individuals.

A better explanation for the broad acceptance of the principle of individualization is provided by French legal culture. In contrasting the pervasiveness and visibility of character evidence in French trials, with the separation of character from the case facts in England and Wales, Field (2006, pp. 544–45) points to the vision of relations between state and citizen very different from that of Anglo-Saxon liberalism: "Character evidence in England and Wales is marginalized to emphasize that punishment and censure relates to the particular crime charged and not to a more broad-ranging judgment of the standing of the accused in the community. . . . In France, the trial is presented as part of a process of rehabilitating the accused as a citizen of the state. The legitimacy of that notion of criminal trial is related to the legitimacy of a positive concept of the citizen against which it is appropriate to judge the character and life of the accused." Different concepts of the relationship of the individual to society help explain why the individualization of the sentence has become such a fundamental starting point in France in a way that it has not in common law jurisdictions such as England and Wales.

One of the most striking features of the French criminal justice process for common law researchers is the unitary structure of the trial. In common law jurisdictions, the finding of guilt is often separated from sentencing: in England and Wales, for example, in the more serious contested cases, it is a function of different actors in the Crown Court—the jury decides on guilt, while the judge decides on the sentence. This separation does not exist in magistrates' court cases, however, where the magistrates or district judge determines both sentence and verdict. The Crown Prosecutor makes no recommendation as to sentence beyond sentence type; she may argue for a custodial sentence, for example, but not for a specific term.

In France, however, guilt and sentence are discussed at the same time, and the *procureur* makes arguments as to both, with a precise sentence recommendation. This has important consequences for the criminal justice system. For instance, an English or American researcher would struggle to recognize the common law guilty plea procedure in the French version of the CRPC. This is partly due to the negotiation that takes place between the public prosecutor and the defendant, not so much on guilt—an admission at the police station is usually necessary to go down this procedural pathway—but on sentence. Interestingly, the 2014 act introduced the formal separation of finding of guilt and sentencing at the trial stage. In order to encourage judges to tailor sentences to offenders, the new law introduces the possibility for judges to adjourn the sentencing decision after the finding of guilt (art. 132-70-1 CP). The court can ask the probation service for further information about the personality of the offender or her material, familial, or social situation. This innovation could prove the most revolutionary aspect of the 2014 law, depending on the use judges make of this new possibility.

B. Centrality or Subsidiarity of Imprisonment in French Sentencing?

In a bid to convince judges to impose noncustodial sentences, the Act of 15 August 2014 reiterates the idea that imprisonment should be a sentence of last resort. A new paragraph of article 132-19 CP now affirms that "a nonsuspended sentence of imprisonment can only be pronounced in last resort if the seriousness of the offense and the character of the offender make this sentence necessary and if any other sanction is clearly unsuitable." It makes it mandatory for judges to justify their decision to sentence a defendant to imprisonment taking into account "the circumstances of the offense and the character of the offender, as well as his material, familial and social situation." However, the law is far from innovative, as this wording is an exact replica of the third paragraph of article 132-24 CP introduced by Sarkozy's government in 2009 (Loi no. 2009-1436 of 24 November 2009 *pénitentiaire*). The new law merely abolishes the exception created by the December 2005 law that allowed courts not to provide any justifications for imposing prison sentences in cases of repeat offending.

Since the 1970s, keen to promote alternatives to custody to resolve prison overcrowding, successive governments have introduced a plethora of new sentences. Over the years, noncustodial sentences have slowly piled up: fine days, community service (TIG), electronic tagging, and so on, but also a myriad of punishments that involve the forfeiture or restriction of rights (suspension or invalidation of driving license, prohibition to exercise a commercial or industrial profession, exclusion from certain places [e.g., licensed premises], prohibition from contacting certain people [e.g., victim or coaccused], bans from carrying arms, bans from using checks or payment cards, impounding or confiscation of a thing). Suspended sentences also come in various forms: *sursis simple* (a simple suspension, with only the condition that the offender should not reoffend), *sursis mise à l'épreuve* (SME—with numerous possible conditions, such as keeping in touch with a probation officer, medical treatment, etc.), and *sursis-TIG* (with the condition to do community work). More recently, the Act of 9 March 2004 introduced citizenship courses and the Act of 5 March 2007 created the *sanction-réparation* that forces the offender to pay compensation to the victim.

Yet, despite all these legislative efforts, imprisonment remains the sentence of choice, although those sentences are typically not served in full because of the automatic sentence reductions detailed above. When *ordonnances pénales* that do not allow for imprisonment sentences are excluded, imprisonment sentences represent 63 percent of convictions (37 percent—totally suspended sentence; 26 percent—not suspended or partially suspended; "Étude d'impact du projet de loi relatif à la prévention de la récidive et à l'individualisation des peines" [2013, p. 18]). Although this is difficult to measure, some authors have suggested that the multiplication of noncustodial sentences has had a net-widening effect, as the new sentences apply to cases in which another noncustodial sentence would have been imposed without reducing the imprisonment rate (Herzog-Evans 2013). The gradual stacking up of noncustodial sentences has created a tangled undergrowth in which even professionals get lost. Definitions of offenses indicate only the maximum term of imprisonment and the maximum fine that can be imposed for each offense, but the legislator has also authorized judges to impose alternative noncustodial sentences instead. Judges have to refer to separate provisions to make sure that the alternative sentence they are considering is indeed applicable to the specific offense they are dealing with. Some critics argue that, as a result of this, judges and prosecutors tend to stick with the familiarity of imprisonment and fines to avoid venturing into the maze of alternative sentences (Saas 2010).

The new Act of 15 August 2014 creates a new probation sentence: the *contrainte pénale*. The new sentence will apply only to adult offenders, not to juveniles, and is aimed at offenders who need "personalized and sustained socioeducative support" (new art. 131-4-1 CP). Under this sentence, the convicted person is the subject of measures of control and assistance for a period between 6 months and 5 years. The probation service will have to draw up its proposed measures for the offender and submit them to the sentencing judge (the JAP; see below for a detailed account of the process). The new law provides for regular reevaluation of the measures in place, taking into account the evolution of the situation, which could even result in the sentence being ended earlier than originally planned.

The creation of this new sentence gives effect to recommendations of the Council of Europe. The Council of Europe's Recommendation on Probation Rules was adopted on January 20, 2010, and defines probation as "the implementation in the community of sanctions and measures, defined by law and imposed on an offender. It includes a range of activities and interventions, which involve supervision, guidance and assistance aiming at the social inclusion of an offender, as well as at contributing to community safety" (Recommendation CM/Rec [2010] 1). Yet there already exist several sanctions in the French sentencing system that fit within this description, in particular, TIG and SME, but more broadly any sentence that imposes obligations on the offender. It has been argued that the SME was a better solution, as it is more flexible and easier to use, in particular, in cases in which the offender does not respect the obligations imposed on her by the probation service (Herzog-Evans 2013). Under the SME, the failure to respect obligations can lead to the revocation by the JAP of the suspended prison sentence originally imposed by the court. The new law provides for a complicated process in cases of failure to respect the obligations imposed under a *contrainte pénale*: the court that imposes the *contrainte pénale* must provide the maximum prison sentence that can be imposed for failure to respect the obligations (art. 131-4-1 CP); if the offender fails to respect her obligations, the JAP can remind her of these obligations or modify them (art. 713-47 CPP); if that is insufficient, the JAP can apply to another judge to decide the length of the prison sentence that the offender will have to serve, within the maximum provided by the original sentencing court (art. 713-47 CPP).

By creating a new noncustodial sentence on top of those already in existence, the new law can be criticized for adding a layer of complexity and for failing to respond to the criticisms expressed against existing alternative sentences detailed above, in particular, that introducing new sentences has not had much effect on the ground. This has been recognized by the government itself, which states in the impact study of its bill that noncustodial sentences represent about 15 percent of imposed sentences, 66 percent of which are fine days ("Étude d'impact du projet de loi relatif à la prévention de la récidive et à l'individualisation des peines" [2013]). The Consensus Commission recommended the inclusion of all the existing sentences imposing obligations on the offender under a new probation sentence. This would have had the advantage of simplification, but it was considered too onerous in terms of resources. The government decided to reserve the *contrainte pénale* for offenders in need of intense support, keeping other alternative sentences for those for whom a lighter touch is sufficient. It remains to be seen whether this added layer of complexity will deter judges further from imposing noncustodial sentences. The government considered going further and replacing references to imprisonment with the *contrainte pénale* in the definition of specific offenses, thus forcing judges to impose it instead of prison. It decided against this, as it would have meant reducing the scope of the new sentence to a limited number of offenses instead of targeting offenders who need special support. However, the door has not been completely closed to this proposition, as article 20 of the law provides that the government should report to Parliament within 2 years of the law coming into effect, to examine the possibility of replacing imprisonment with the *contrainte pénale* for certain offenses.

III. The Sentence as Process

To the English observer, the French approach to sentencing has a number of striking features that mark it out as very different from that in England and Wales, where responsibility for passing sentence rests squarely with the trial judge. The court in England and Wales sentences the accused after hearing the prosecution case, any mitigation from the defense, the accused's previous criminal convictions, and information on the person's work and social circumstances. Typically, where there has been a "not guilty" plea, the court will adjourn after the decision to convict in order to gather more information to inform its sentencing decision. The sentence is announced in open court along with reasons for the choice and severity of the penalty. Apart from rules allowing for early release from prison, the sentence pronounced in court is the sentence served. The French system also differs strikingly from American practices in which, in theory, sentencing decisions are for the judge to make, but in practice, all but 3–5 percent of convictions result from guilty pleas in which the sentence is effectively negotiated between the prosecutor and the defense counsel, with the prosecutor's voice almost always being determinative (e.g., Lynch 2003).

In France, the position is rather different: the sentence imposed by the trial judge may simply be the starting point in determining the sentence that will be carried out. Sentencing is not a single event but an ongoing process, through which penalties can be adapted weeks or months after conviction, in a closed hearing with a *procureur* and a sentencing judge, the JAP. This might include substituting a noncustodial measure in place of a short prison term or altering the way in which imprisonment is served—allowing the convicted person to continue in employment, for example. The rationale is to ensure that the sentence is appropriate to the individual and so is effective in preventing reoffending and assisting in the individual's reinsertion into society. For less serious sentences, this process will begin immediately after the trial and court sentence. For those serving more than 2 years in prison (art. 723-15 CPP), it will take place toward the end of their sentence. In short, the sentence pronounced in court may be very different from the sentence that will be served in practice.

Before we tease out some of the underlying assumptions and practices revealed through this approach, a few examples from recent research provide a sense of these hearings and the scope of this sentence adaptation and adjustment (see also Padfield [2011*a*, 2011*b*, 2011*c*, 2011*d*] for further brief examples).[3] Present at all of the hearings were the JAP, the *procureur*, and a court clerk. The first three cases took place in the chambers of the JAP.

Case one concerned a man sentenced to 18 months in prison for the sexual assault of his daughter. He applied to serve his sentence by being electronically tagged, and the probation service recommended the route of *semi-liberté*, which requires the person to spend each night in prison but allows her to go to work during the day as part of a strict schedule of her movements. The JAP checked the employment schedule and that the person had been attending his medical treatment appointments as required. The JAP asked the man how the treatment was going and how things were with his children. The *procureur* suggested that he begin executing the sentence when he returned from holiday with his family.

Procureur: There is something else I would like to speak to you about. I know you have problems with alcohol and you would like to benefit from the *semi-liberté* system but I need you to realize that you cannot come back to prison in the evening completely drunk. You need to be very careful.

JAP: Do you understand what the *procureur* is saying? It is important.

[Convicted person explains that he is trying to get a place in a rehabilitation program.]

JAP: I think we could delay the sentence execution to allow you to do this. What do you think?

---

[3] These are the observations of Laurène Soubise in the course of her current PhD fieldwork examining the independence and accountability of prosecutors in France and in England and Wales.

Convicted person: I think it would help me.

Procureur: I'm not opposed to it. Obligation to get medical treatment is essential.

JAP: Is there anything else you would like to add?

Convicted person: I've already paid 50 euros towards compensation. I'm going to leave my flat when I go to prison so I will be able to pay more.

Procureur: You're going to leave your flat? Are you sure it's a good idea? Where will you go when you have permission to be on leave? We need to have a stable address if we let you come out of prison occasionally!

[He explains that he will stay with a family member.]

Case two concerned a man sentenced to 5 months in prison for theft and assaulting a police officer. The probation service reported that the man's behavior had been problematic and he had been complaining that justice is too slow. Both the *procureur* and the JAP lectured the man about his behavior: he was not the victim here; he chose to commit the offenses. The man went on to say that he had no income and so could not pay compensation to the victims.

JAP: I won't adjust your sentence without compensation to victims. I don't take into account just your interests when deciding whether or not to adjust your sentence, but also society's interests and the interests of the victims.

Procureur: You were sentenced to do some community work and you didn't do it. You were sentenced to prison because of that and now we are trying to adjust this prison sentence. You are not showing that you have made any effort; you need to improve your attitude quickly, otherwise you will go to prison.

Case three concerned a man sentenced to 3 months in prison for possession of cannabis, who was asking for this to be commuted to unpaid work. He could not read or write, and he had recently become a father. After asking how he was managing as a father the judge asked:

JAP: What about the drugs consumption?

Convicted person: I only take cannabis now. I stopped heroin and alcohol. I've reduced my consumption a lot, but I haven't been able to stop completely yet.

The man was still under the treatment of health care professionals. The *procureur* did not object to the sentence adjustment to unpaid work and proposed 105 hours together with an obligation to receive health care treatment, to pay prosecution costs, and with an obligation to work or receive training (especially with reading and writing).

Cases four and five were similar hearings but took place in prison and concerned serving prisoners applying for some form of early release from prison—either on a day release scheme or by being electronically tagged. In addition to the JAP, the *procureur*, and a clerk, a representative from probation and a duty lawyer were also present.

Case four concerned a young man who had been released under the *semi-liberté* regime but was unable to continue for health reasons. He was fitted with an electronic tag instead. A week later he was returned to prison. The JAP asked him what happened.

Convicted person: I thought I was going to have the same schedule as with *semi-liberté*. . . . I had three beers, three joints and some tablets as well. [He explains that he had an argument with his stepmother and she called the police because she was scared, and he has been in prison since the electronic tagging was suspended a week ago.]

JAP: The probation report sounds as though you are blaming the JAP for the failure of the electronic tagging.

Convicted person: No, I think it's my fault. Wearing a tag is not at all like I thought it would be.

[Probation are asked for their opinion. They think tagging is the best solution, but as it is now the summer vacation, there will be insufficient support available for the prisoner to ensure it works this time. They suggest looking at it again in September. The *procureur* agrees.]

Convicted person: I would like to take my exam next week.

Lawyer: [speaking for the first time] This is a difficult situation. It is very important that he sits this exam. His father says that he has worked hard for it. He wrote a letter to his stepmother to apologize. He needs to study and the prison have refused to let him have his books in.

[The *procureur* suggests that he can apply for a day release to take his exam.]

JAP: Here is my decision: I suspend the electronic tagging. *Semi-liberté* is not possible. If you ask for day release to take this exam I am prepared to allow it.... You have got an addiction and you are not dealing with it properly. You will spend the summer in prison and we will reexamine the situation in September.

Convicted person: Can I get my books in?

JAP: Yes, it seems perfectly legitimate. Probation will speak to the prison about it.

Case five concerned a man with a long list of convictions. He received 100 fine days at €10 per day for theft and 30 fine days at €20 for drug use, both 4 years ago. He has not paid anything and so owes €1,600. He has been in prison for a year on other offenses and could be released in a few months.

Procureur: Can you pay now?... The judge cannot give you longer than six months to pay. Can someone lend you the money?

[After a long discussion, the prisoner agrees to pay. The *procureur* and the JAP want to be sure that he will be able to pay, and the *procureur* makes clear that the consequences will be serious if he does not.

Convicted person: I promise to pay.

JAP: OK I will summon you to appear before me three months after your release and you will bring the receipts then. If you don't, you will be sent back to prison.

When looking at sentencing policies and practices through a comparative lens, it is important to understand the legal culture and practices within which they function. These cases are typical and illustrate several important features of the French process, which are discussed below: the range of offenses for which sentences are adjusted; the close and cooperative working relationship between the *procureur* and JAP (as part of the same professional grouping, *magistrats*) and with probation; the minor part played by the defense lawyer; the frank and direct communication between the *magistrats* and the convicted person; the importance of the victim's interests; and the need for convicted persons to demonstrate that they are making efforts toward their own rehabilitation into society.

A. Adapting the Sentence to the Offender: The Juge d'Application des Peines (JAP)

Alongside other continental European models of criminal justice, the French legal system is typically portrayed as a top-down hierarchical process, in which discretion is closely circumscribed. This is reflected in the structures of legal authority designed to ensure the promulgation of orders and the *politique pénale* of the executive, through the minister of justice (for a classic account, see Damaška [1986]). In practice, *procureurs* as well as judges enjoy a great deal of discretion (Hodgson 2002, 2005). It is the *procureur* who decides whether to charge the suspect, whether then to pursue a formal prosecution or an alternative such as mediation, what offense to prosecute, whether to involve the *juge d'instruction* in the investigation, how to present the case at trial, and the sentence to recommend to the court. These decisions are governed in part by legal constraints, including targets set centrally (see Vigour 2006; Alt and Le Theule 2011), but they also reflect local priorities and the working practices of individual *procureurs*.

The scope of discretion is most visible in the treatment of individual cases. Running alongside, and arguably in tension with, the rhetoric around uniformity and hierarchical order, the French criminal justice process attaches great weight to the importance of a properly "adapted" criminal response. This approach recognizes that a one-size-fits-all model of justice may appear to promote equality of treatment but in fact produces injustice. As one of Hodgson's *procureur* respondents explained:

"Of course there are problems of standardisation . . . you cannot follow the same *politique pénale* everywhere because the cases are different, the populations are different, the problems are different. . . . In one instance you will prosecute far more offenders than in another, because there is less delinquency. . . . A uniform system of justice, which is delivered in the same way everywhere and so which does not take account of differences, would effectively be a nondemocratic system of justice" (interview respondent [*procureur*] A6, quoted in Hodgson [2005, p. 230]).

The impact particular crimes might have on the local community are important in determining how they should be dealt with:

If you arrest someone with 10g of hashish here [a major city], we will not prosecute. It is of no interest, it is not a threat to public order. But in a town of 15,000 inhabitants, where everybody knows one another, where nothing ever happens, you find 10g of hashish and in fact, you need a different kind of judicial response because everybody is going to panic, because everybody is going to say, "There are drugs, we have never had this before, this is a major event" . . . depending on the scale of the problem, attitudes will be different . . . you can say that one court was less severe and another court was more severe. This is because there is a context, and one can say that actually, justice, from one angle, will not be the same for everyone, but it will be designed to have the same degree of effectiveness. So effectiveness is not necessarily achieved by treating all things in the same way. (Interview respondent [*procureur*] E5, quoted in Hodgson [2005, p. 230])

This notion of adaptation is also strongly present within the sentencing process and was one of the chief sources of opposition to the introduction of *peines planchers*, which were seen by critics to tie the hands of the judiciary and to emphasize punitiveness over effectiveness. In the same way in which prosecution policy is "adapted" to local conditions in order to be effective, so too there is a keen desire to ensure that the sentence fits the offender as well as the crime.

Defendants sentenced to imprisonment for a *délit* at a criminal hearing are not immediately incarcerated, unless the court issues a detention order. They will later be summoned by the JAP if the decision becomes definitive (i.e., no appeal is formed against it within the legal time limit). Sentences up to 2 years' imprisonment can be adjusted after conviction (i.e., a noncustodial sentence can be substituted or the way the prison sentence is served can be altered). The range of offenses that might be dealt with in this way is illustrated by the five cases outlined above—sexual assault, drug possession, theft. The convicted person works with probation as well as the JAP to find a sentence that will work for her and is practicable to carry out. For example, electronic tagging requires the consent of the householder to have equipment installed and the support of probation to agree on a schedule of movements; carrying out a prison sentence in *semi-liberté* requires the offender to have a set schedule that can be approved in advance.

For their part, the JAP and the *procureur* speak to offenders about their life, their family, their work, and their sentence so far, and where applicable, why they have been returned to prison, to ensure that they can find a solution that will promote the rehabilitation of the individual, so that she can lead a useful life in society without reoffending. In case one, prison was delayed in order that the offender could attend a drug and alcohol rehabilitation program; in case three, the *procureur* ensured that literacy and numeracy training were undertaken as well as drug treatment. Without the ability to read and write, the offender was unlikely to gain employment. In case four, the JAP ensured that the prisoner could study for and then sit his exam, and a second try at electronic tagging would be considered in a few months. In case five, both the JAP and the *procureur* were prepared to give the offender another chance to pay at least some of the fines owed from 4 years ago, sympathizing with his poverty. In case two, however, the offender had already benefited from a more individualized sentence, but he had failed to do what was required and made no effort to provide any guarantee of compliance. In essence, he had used up his chances.

Armed with information about individuals, their personality, and their current circumstances, the JAP seeks to assess what will be most effective in reforming them—in particular, imposing a sentence that is realistic and can be executed successfully. For their part, offenders are expected to demonstrate that the proposed sentence is realistic and that they will stick to what is agreed. Case five seemed especially generous in this respect. The offender had not been able to pay the fines for 4 years and had gotten into more trouble. Payment to victims is taken more seriously than payment of fines. The production of work schedules, undertaking treatment programs, and beginning to pay compensation to victims are all crucial parts of this process. It is clear that no sentence adjustment is possible without evidence of some, albeit very small, steps being taken to compensate the victim in accordance with the order of the trial court. As the JAP explained to the offender in case two, "I won't adjust your sentence without compensation to victims."

B. *The Relationship between Offender and Magistrat*

In more adversarial systems of criminal justice as in England and Wales and the United States, we are accustomed to judges and prosecutors remaining at a distance from the accused, all contact being mediated through the defense lawyer. The direct relationship between the *magistrat* and the offender in France is very different. Before trial, the accused may be brought before the *procureur* before appearing directly before the court. During the *instruction* investigative phase, the *juge d'instruction* questions the accused directly. At trial, the judge maintains a constant dialogue with the accused; the defense lawyer plays a diminished role, usually consisting of a brief mitigation speech. This direct contact between judge and offender is also a marked feature of the JAP hearings. It is unusual for a lawyer to be present, and the hearing is relatively informal. There is no raised bench, no formal procedures, and no legalistic terminology. Judge, *procureur*, and offender will discuss the matter together. There may be reports from the probation service, but the JAP will also ask the offender directly about home life, the impact of becoming a parent, employment, how drug treatment programs are going, and so on. They will also ask direct questions about offending and in particular how the offender is managing drug or alcohol problems.

This direct engagement of the *magistrat* with the offender is part of a wider culture in which the criminal justice process (representing the state) seeks to reform the individual citizen. The judge will try to get a sense of the offender as an individual and often knows some personal background about her life in the years preceding her offending. This approach is not unique to the JAP hearings: an emphasis on the person, the accused or offender as citizen, is pervasive. Defendants in England and Wales are essentially "processed" through the courts, objects rather than subjects of their own trial (Hodgson 2006); likewise in the United States (Bogira 2006). Although French defendants might also feel that they are processed through the courts as they struggle to understand the process,[4] they are addressed directly, required to account for themselves and to respond to the accusations against them. In contrast to an

---

[4] See the Ministry of Justice (January 2014) survey at http://www.justice.gouv.fr/art _pix/j21-p-jpj.pdf.

adversarial procedure, their character is before the court from the outset (before any finding of guilt) and is seen as an essential part of evaluating the evidence (Field 2006).

The role of the *procureur* in these hearings is also important. As a *magistrat* (along with the JAP, the *juge d'instruction*, and trial judges), the *procureur*'s function is defined in different terms from that of an adversarial public prosecutor; in particular, her professional ideology requires her to represent the public interest. *Procureurs* work with other agencies in the development of local crime policies and intervene in noncriminal cases in which actions threaten the public interest. For example, the *procureur* may attend hearings at the commercial court to defend the "economic public order," which may include the protection of jobs in a company takeover. She is also seen to represent the interests of the victim—typically by insisting that some attempt is made at paying compensation to the victim—as well as the wider public interest. However, the way in which the public interest is understood within the neutral terms of the professional ideology of the *magistrat* is not always reflected in the practice of the public prosecutor. Hodgson (2005) has argued that the predominant crime control ideology of *procureurs* is often clothed in the legitimacy of public interest. Acting in the public interest, or seeking the truth in an investigation, is, in practice, often synonymous with obtaining an admission.

However, the *procureur*'s role in representing the public interest during the postconviction sentencing process seems to be a little different. In the examples observed, it was not rooted in a crime control ideology as is so often seen in the trial and pretrial role, but seemed to be closer to the more neutral rhetoric of the *magistrat*. Rather than seeking a punitive response, the *procureur* worked in a spirit of cooperation to see what could be agreed to (delaying prison to accommodate a rehabilitation program; substituting prison for electronic tagging or unpaid work; having a day release from prison to sit an exam), while ensuring that the sentence is credible ("you cannot come back to the prison in the evening completely drunk") and the victim's interests in receiving compensation are respected. Interestingly, observations of the CRPC meetings between the *procureur*, the accused, and the defense lawyer were similarly cooperative and nonconflictual.

Offenders appear to be comfortable with this direct relationship, and they are often frank in their conversations with *magistrats* telling them how they feel, what they struggle with and not trying to disguise, for example, continued unlawful behavior. Noticeably absent in the sentencing process is the defense lawyer, other than a duty lawyer in prison hearings, for those who want one. Again, this reflects the relatively diminished role of the defense lawyer throughout the criminal process, compared with her institutionalized function within more adversarial procedures. In the French court, typically, several cases are heard together, and then after a short adjournment, the verdicts and sentences are all announced together. The defense lawyer will normally have left the court and so will not be present for the verdict or the sentence (this does not hold true of cases involving serious crimes tried in the *cour d'assises*). Lawyers tend also not to be present during the JAP hearings, as they do not have a formal role in the procedure. There is a higher degree of trust in *magistrats* as representatives of the public interest (rather than punitive, crime control–oriented prosecutors, e.g.), as well as a culture of direct engagement between judge and accused or offender, as noted above. This contrasts sharply with more adversarial procedures, where the defense lawyer would seek to shield the accused from direct questioning that might risk incriminating admissions.

As well as being direct, judges and *procureurs* speak to accused and convicted persons in often quite moralizing tones. At one level, this may be objectionable because it is patronizing, but there is also a potentially positive strand to this approach. In England and Wales and the United States, by contrast, there is almost no contact between the prosecutor or judge and the accused. Defendants are objects to be processed through the system by the criminal justice repeat players—the prosecutors, defense lawyers, magistrates—who speak for, about, and at the accused. There are few moralizing speeches about the need to break out of a cycle of drug use and criminality or the potential that might be realized in a person. Defendants are seen as undeserving of this and unlikely to benefit. In short, their value as useful members of society is implicitly denied. In France, this process of "othering" is much less pronounced. Only in the Youth Court in England and Wales are defendants addressed as they are in France: asking them why they would commit an offense and risk their liberty or what the welfare of their family is; encouraging them to take up offers of training and make something of their life. The discourse of *magistrats* focuses on the reintegration into society of the offender as citizen. In admonishing the accused or the convicted person, in delivering moralizing lectures, the *magistrat* is affirming the potential of rehabilitation and the value of the individual.

C. Too Much Discretion, Not Enough Public Accountability?

Theoretical accounts of the inquisitorial model of procedure have characterized it by its hierarchical structures of authority and the absence of individual discretion. Contemporary French criminal justice, however, is characterized by both hierarchy and discretion; the two are not mutually exclusive. Rather, it is a question of degree. The discretion of the *procureur* is framed by the wider criminal justice policy promulgated from the minister of justice through the prosecution hierarchy, but in practice, this places little constraint on the actions of the *procureur*. Policies are expressed in broad terms, and there is little or no policing of their implementation at the local level. Centrally determined targets around methods of case disposition, together with local interagency cooperation, provide some framing, but *procureurs* enjoy considerable latitude in their interpretation of the public interest in individual cases. Hodgson's (2005) empirical study of *procureurs*, for example, demonstrated the ease with which the repressive crime control practices of the *procureur* were fitted into a more neutral discourse of public interest.

Critics of the JAP process of individualization in sentencing tend not to question *magistrats'* commitment to their professional ideology and values, but object to the existence of broad discretion per se. It is perhaps unrealistic to separate out these two; a judge who exercises discretion in an excessive or arbitrary way is not acting in accordance with the public interest professional ideology. Pradel is one such critic, arguing that with judicial discretion comes the risk of excessive discretion and so arbitrariness and inequality (Pradel 2007). Policies such as minimum sentences avoid this. In contrast to countries such as England and Wales, where the judiciary might be seen as preventing the excesses of the executive by holding its members accountable under the rule of law, in France, the state-centered nature of French political culture is such that judges are mistrusted by government, and it is the democratically elected executive that claims to hold the unelected judiciary to account. One might compare the JAP to the *juge d'instruction*: operating within a legal framework and with the *procureur* participating in the entire process, the JAP exercises a broad discretion according to what she considers to be appropriate in the individual case. And like the *juge d'instruction*, the process takes place behind closed doors and without reasons. This lack of transparency requires a great deal of trust in the *magistrat*. This is characteristic of the entire French criminal justice process: Mouhanna (2001,

p. 82) describes trust as a pragmatic response to the irreconcilable demands of justice. It also risks the JAP replacing the trial judge as sentencer and so moves the truth of sentencing out of court and into the judge's chambers.

The new ability of the court to adjourn sentencing in order to gather up information on the offender represents a different way of doing sentencing. Rather than considering such information in private after trial and sentence have been concluded in court, it allows for relevant information to be brought before the trial judge and taken into account at the time the sentence is passed in court. It might be argued that this is more efficient, as well as bringing the truth of sentencing back into the courtroom. Saas (2010) questions whether this will have an impact on judicial behavior, given judges' reluctance to take advantage of the more recent diversification of sentences that are available to them. The Consensus Commission also noted the continued preference for fines and imprisonment; the diversification of trial procedures has not been matched by a diversification of sanctions. The role of the *procureur* is key here, as the sentence she recommends is invariably followed by the trial court—in type if not in severity. However, in contrast to the JAP, the *procureur* has little information on the person's background, and this may be a barrier to the proposal of alternative sanctions to the court.

IV. Looking Ahead

It is difficult to predict what the future holds for sentencing reform in France. The ministry of justice has recently turned its attention to yet another reform of the juvenile justice system. The French juvenile justice system is regulated by the Ordonnance of 2 February 1945, which has been amended no fewer than 36 times. During the 2012 election campaign, President Hollande had promised the abolition of the *tribunaux correctionnels pour mineurs* composed of three professional judges and instituted by the Act of 11 August 2011 to try repeat offenders aged between 16 and 18 years old risking a prison sentence of 3 years or over. Prior to the 2011 reform, these defendants were tried along with other juvenile defendants by a *tribunal pour enfants* (youth court) composed of a professional judge and two lay judges with professional experience of juvenile questions. The 2011 act was criticized by professionals as going against the spirit of the 1945 *ordonnance*, which favors an educative over a repressive approach. However, *Le Monde* reported in January 2015 that the new courts had tried only 787 young defendants between January 2012 and November 2013 and had not imposed more severe sentences (Johannès 2015). It is therefore unlikely that their abolition will have much more than a symbolic effect. Nevertheless, it has been reported that the government was hesitant to propose the reform because of the proximity of regional elections in 2016, followed by presidential elections in 2017 (Johannès 2015).

The question of radicalization in French prisons has been at the forefront of public debates following the attacks in Paris in January 2015. A recent parliamentary report pointed out that recent terrorist attacks in Paris and Toulouse were all committed by former prisoners. Yet it also admitted that it was established that their radicalization did not take place in prison and that a minority of people traveling to Iraq or Syria to join extremist groups had spent time in prison beforehand. Khosrokhavar (2013) identified the main cause of radicalization in prison as the existence of deep frustrations, in particular, the near impossibility of performing religious duties for Muslim inmates. This combines with overcrowding, understaffing, and high turnover of both staff and prisoners. Keen to be seen to act against radicalization in French prisons, the ministry of justice announced the recruitment of 60 Muslim ministers in January 2015. Furthermore, a provision of the intelligence bill currently being discussed in Parliament gives greater powers and resources to prison administrators to monitor electronic communications and prisoners' interactions. This has been opposed by the minister of justice, who argues that, as the guarantor of individual freedom, the justice system cannot be seen to be the prescriber of phone tapping and microphones' installation in prison cells. It was further claimed that such a move would undermine the necessary trust between guards and inmates (Suc 2015).

The return of Nicolas Sarkozy to the political stage as president of the main opposition party could spell a remake of the 2012 presidential election if François Hollande also seeks a second mandate in 2017. Whether the Left will remain committed to broadly rehabilitative ideals remains to be seen. Some in the Socialist Party, such as Manuel Valls, who was promoted to the position of prime minister in March 2014, would like to see the adoption of a tougher line, in response to the accusations of naïve leniency traditionally levied against left-wing parties. In view of the rise of the extreme-right party—the Front National—in the polls, a surge in penal populism cannot be ruled out, with both mainstream parties attempting to outbid the other through tough-on-crime manifestos.

REFERENCES

Alt, Eric, and Marie-Astrid Le Theule. 2011. "La justice aux prises avec l'éthique et la performance." *Pyramides* 22:137–59.

Aubert, Laura. 2008. "L'activité des délégués du procureur en France: De l'intention à la réalité des pratiques." *Déviance et Société* 32(4):473–94.

Body-Gendrot, Sophie. 2014. "Ethnicity, Crime, and Immigration in France." In *The Oxford Handbook of Ethnicity, Crime, and Immigration*, edited by Sandra M. Bucerius and Michael H. Tonry. Oxford: Oxford University Press.

Bogira, Steve. 2006. *Courtroom 302: A Year behind the Scenes in an American Criminal Courthouse.* New York: Vintage.

Chassaing, Jean-François. 1993. "Les trois codes français et l'évolution des principes fondateurs du droit pénal contemporain." *Revue de Science Criminelle* 3:445–55.

Combe, Sonia. 1994. *Archives interdites: Les peurs françaises face à l'histoire contemporaine.* Paris: Albin Michel.

Commission d'Enquête de l'Assemblée Nationale. 2000. "La France face à ses prisons." Paris: Assemblée Nationale.

Commission d'Enquête du Sénat. 2000. "Prisons: Une humiliation pour la république." Paris: Sénat.

Conférence de Consensus. 2013. "Pour une nouvelle politique publique de prévention de la récidive." Paris: Ministère de la Justice. http://conference-consensus.justice.gouv.fr/wp-content/uploads/2012/10/CCR_DOC-web-impression.pdf.

Damaška, Mirjan. 1986. *The Faces of Justice and State Authority—a Comparative Approach to the Legal Process.* New Haven, CT: Yale University Press.

Danet, Jean. 2008. "Cinq ans de frénésie pénale." In *La frénésie sécuritaire: Retour à l'ordre et nouveau contrôle social*, edited by Laurent Mucchielli. Sur le vif. Paris: La Découverte.

"Étude d'impact du projet de loi relatif à la prévention de la récidive et à l'individualisation des peines." 2013. http://www.legifrance.gouv.fr/content/download/5254/78897/version/1/file/ei_recidive_individualisation_peines_cm_09.10.2013.pdf.

Faget, Jacques. 2008. "La fabrique de la décision pénale: Une dialectique des asservissements et des émancipations." *Champ Pénal/Penal Field* 5 (May).

Field, Stewart. 2006. "State, Citizen, and Character in French Criminal Process." *Journal of Law and Society* 33(4):522–46.

Garapon, Antoine, and Denis Salas. 2007. "La victime plutôt que le droit." *Esprit* (November):74–82.

Herzog-Evans, Martine. 2007. "Prévenir la récidive: Les limites de la répression pénale." *AJ Pénal*, 357–63.

———. 2011. *Droit de l'exécution des peines.* 4th ed. Paris: Dalloz.

———. 2013. "Récidive et surpopulation: Pas de baguette magique juridique." *AJ Pénal* 3:136–39.

Hodgson, Jacqueline. 2002. "Hierarchy, Bureaucracy, and Ideology in French Criminal Justice: Some Empirical Observations." *Journal of Law and Society* 29(2):227–57.

———. 2005. *French Criminal Justice: A Comparative Account of the Investigation and Prosecution of Crime in France.* Oxford: Hart.

———. 2006. "Conceptions of the Trial in Inquisitorial and Adversarial Procedure." In *The Trial on Trial,* vol. 2, *Judgment and Calling to Account,* edited by Antony Duff, Lindsay Farmer, Sandra Marshall, and Victor Tadros. Oxford: Hart.

———. 2012. "Guilty Pleas and the Changing Role of the Prosecutor in French Criminal Justice." In *The Prosecutor in Transnational Perspective,* edited by Erik Luna and Marianne Wade. Oxford: Oxford University Press.

Huré, Isabelle. 2012. "La médiatisation de la loi sur la rétention de sûreté: De la répression à la précaution." In *Dialectique carcérale—Quand la prison s'ouvre et résiste au changement,* edited by Pierre V Tournier. Paris: L'Harmattan. http://ezproxy.usherbrooke.ca/login?url=http://www.harmatheque.com/ebook /9782296568150.

Johannès, Franck. 2013. "Manuel Valls et Christiane Taubira s'affrontent sur la réforme pénale." *Le Monde,* August 13.

———. 2015. "Justice des mineurs: La réforme attendra." *Le Monde,* January 31.

Kensey, Annie, and Aurélie Ouss. 2011. "Mesure des effets d'une nouvelle politique pénale: La suppression de la grâce collective." *Champ Pénal/Penal Field* 8. http://champpenal.revues.org/8030.

Khosrokhavar, Farhad. 2013. "Radicalization in Prison: The French Case." *Politics, Religion and Ideology* 14(2):284–306.

Lynch, Gerard E. 2003. "Screening versus Plea Bargaining: Exactly What Are We Trading Off?" *Stanford Law Review* 55:1399–1408.

Ministère de la Justice. 2014. "Les chiffres-clés de la Justice 2014." Paris: Ministère de la Justice. http://www.justice.gouv.fr/budget-et-statistiques-10054 /chiffres-cles-de-la-justice-10303/les-chiffres-cles-de-la-justice-edition-2014 -27571.html.

———. 2015. "Les chiffres clés de l'administration pénitentiaire au 1er janvier 2015." Paris: Ministère de la Justice. http://www.justice.gouv.fr/art_pix/chiffres _cles_2015_FINALE_SFP.pdf.

Montesquieu, Charles. 1748. *The Spirit of the Law.* New York: Cosimo Classics.

Mouhanna, Christian. 2001. *Polices judiciaires et magistrats: Une affaire de confiance.* Perspectives sur la justice. Paris: La Documentation Française.

Mucchielli, Laurent, ed. 2008. *La frénésie sécuritaire: Retour à l'ordre et nouveau contrôle social. Sur le vif.* Paris: La Découverte.

Mucchielli, Laurent, and Emilie Raquet. 2014. "Les comparutions immédiates au TGI de Nice, ou la prison comme unique réponse à une délinquance de misère." *Revue de Science Criminelle* (1):207–27.

Ottenhof, Reynald, ed. 2001. *L'individualisation de la peine: De saleilles à aujourd'hui. Suivi de l'individualisation de la peine: Cent Ans après saleilles.* Collection Criminologie et Sciences de l'Homme. Ramonville: Erès.

Padfield, Nicola. 2011*a*. "An Entente Cordiale in Sentencing? Part 1." *Criminal Law and Justice Weekly* 175:239–41.

———. 2011*b*. "An Entente Cordiale in Sentencing? Part 2." *Criminal Law Justice Weekly* 175:256–58.

———. 2011*c*. "An Entente Cordiale in Sentencing? Part 3." *Criminal Law Justice Weekly* 175:271–73.

———. 2011*d*. "An Entente Cordiale in Sentencing? Part 4." *Criminal Law Justice Weekly* 175:290–92.

Pradel, Jean. 2007. "Enfin des lignes directrices pour sanctionner les délinquants récidivistes (commentaire de la Loi du 10 août 2007 sur les «peines plancher»)." *Dalloz* 32:2247–57.

Robert-Diard, Pascale. 2012. "Nicolas Sarkozy défend sa vision de la justice pénale." *Le Monde*, January 27. http://www.lemonde.fr/politique/article/2012 /01/27/nicolas-sarkozy-defend-sa-vision-de-la-justice-penale_1635518_823448 .html?xtmc = sarkozy_justice&xtcr = 2.

Roché, Sebastian, Mirta B. Gordon, and Marie-Aude Depuiset. 2014. "Case Study: Sentencing Violent Juvenile Offenders in Color Blind France: Does Ethnicity Matter?" In *The Oxford Handbook of Ethnicity, Crime, and Immigration*, edited by Sandra M. Bucerius and Michael H. Tonry. Oxford: Oxford University Press.

Saas, Claire. 2004. "De la composition pénale au plaider-coupable: Le pouvoir de sanction du procureur." *Revue de Science Criminelle* 4(December):827–43.

———. 2010. "Le juge 'Artisan de la peine.'" *Les Cahiers de la Justice* 4:71–85.

Saas, Claire, Soizic Lorvellec, and Virginie Gautron. 2013. "Les sanctions pénales, une nouvelle distribution." In *La réponse pénale: Dix ans de traitement des délits*, edited by Jean Danet. Rennes: Presses Universitaires de Rennes.

Salas, Denis. 2005. *La volonté de punir: Essai sur le populisme pénal.* Paris: Hachette Littérature.

Simonnot, Dominique. 2003. *Justice en France: Une loterie nationale.* Paris: La Martinière.

Suc, Matthieu. 2015. "Assimiler l'administration pénitentiaire à un service de renseignement est dangereux." *Le Monde*, April 13.

Tournier, Pierre V., and Annie Kensey. 2001. "L'exécution des peines privatives de liberté: Aménagement ou érosion?" *Questions Pénales* 14(5):1–4.

Vasseur, Véronique. 2000. *Médecin-chef à la prison de la Santé.* Collection Documents. Paris: Le Cherche Midi.

Vigour, Cécile. 2006. "Justice: L'introduction d'une rationalité managériale comme euphémisation des enjeux politiques." *Droit et Société* 63–64:425–55.

Warsmann, Jean-Luc. 2003. "Les peines alternatives à la détention, les modalités d'exécution des courtes peines, la préparation des détenus à la sortie de prison." Paris: Ministère de la Justice.

Wyvekens, Anne. 2010. "La rétention de sûreté en France: Une défense sociale en trompe-l'œil (ou les habits neufs de l'empereur)." *Déviance et Société* 34 (4):503–25.

Veerle Scheirs, Kristel Beyens, and Sonja Snacken

Belgian Sentencing as a Bifurcated Practice?

ABSTRACT

Belgian sentencing is in a period of turmoil. Belgian judges value their independence. Most believe in the desirability of individualized sentencing and resent intrusions on their autonomy. Although many continue to hold classsical views about the purposes of sentencing, new practices and laws, triggered partly by several decades of rising imprisonment rates and recent efforts by policy makers and correctional officials to contain it, have changed the penal landscape. The public prosecutor has increasing authority to divert cases from investigation and from sentencing judges, leading to de facto sentencing powers for prosecutors. Recent and upcoming innovations have created new freestanding sanctions of work penalties (often elsewhere called community service), electronic monitoring, and probation. A more fully bifurcated legal system is emerging with longer prison sentences for some offenses and offenders, including postprison preventive detention, and more community punishments aiming for a reduced use of imprisonment for others. Many judges are unconvinced though about the desirability of reduced imprisonment use for some convicted offenders. It remains to be seen what Belgian sentencing will look like when practices incorporating recent changes have stabilized.

Sentencing in Belgium should be seen as a set of social practices that are best understood from a constructionist perspective, emphasizing the importance of processes of interaction and translation through which sentencing judges produce their decisions in interaction with other criminal

Electronically published June 22, 2016

Veerle Scheirs is a part-time professor and postdoctoral researcher in penology, and Kristel Beyens and Sonja Snacken are professors of penology, all in the Criminology Department, Vrije Universiteit Brussel.

justice actors (Hawkins 2003; Latour 2005; Hutton 2013). Studying sentencing as a social practice reflects the broader and institutional dynamics of contemporary sentencing (Hutton 1995, 2002, 2006; Beyens 2000; Tata 2007; Beyens and Scheirs 2010).

Judges and other officials in a variety of ways attempt to anticipate and sometimes circumvent decisions others have made or might make. A combination of several decades' increase in imprisonment rates, responsive development of administrative devices that avoid implementation of many short prison sentences and shorten others, increased prosecutorial powers to divert cases from the courts, and enactment of laws establishing work penalties, electronic monitoring, and probation as independent sanctions make this a time of flux. Correctional practitioners in various ways convert—judges might say subvert—prison sentences into other dispositions, and judges sometimes adjust the sentences they impose to anticipate decisions other officials may make that would undermine what judges want to accomplish in individual cases.

Tension exists among competing conceptions of the sentencing process and its goals. Many judges remain committed to traditional neoclassical conceptions of sentencing in which the aims are primarily retributive and deterrent, both of which are readily served by the traditionally available Belgian sanctions of fines and imprisonment. Many judges also remain committed to a model of sentencing in which they make individualized sentencing decisions on the basis of their assessments of the crime and its effects and the culpability and character of the defendant. In Belgium's largely inquisitorial criminal justice system, the dossier containing police, prosecutorial, and sometimes investigating judges' reports provides substantial information on which to base such decisions. As a result, judges request and rely on social reports prepared by judicial assistants less than they might, demonstrate little interest in or support for guidelines or other devices to reduce sentencing disparities, and express frustration when prison sentences they impose sometimes are not implemented and other times are shortened.

Other justice system practitioners and some public officials, by contrast, though not rejecting retributive and other traditional aims of sentencing, have other objectives in mind that have led to passage of laws enhancing prosecutorial authority to divert cases and creating new independent sanctions to supplement fines and prison sentences. The steady increases in the Belgian prison population over several decades, and in prison overcrowding, have crystalized sentiments to change direction.

That and recognition of the destructive effects of imprisonment on prisoners have precipitated passage of new laws on mediation and new community sanctions.

Belgium appears to illustrate the development, as in many other countries, of bifurcated systems of sentencing that, compared with earlier periods, attempt to divert large numbers of offenders from imprisonment and develop more socially constructive ways to deal with them, but increase the uses of confinement, surveillance, and controls for particular kinds of offenses and offenders. Development of new independent community sanctions illustrates the former. Extension of postimprisonment preventive detention laws to new categories of putatively dangerous offenders exemplifies the latter.

Belgium has a modified inquisitorial legal system. As in most continental systems, important powers are distributed among the public prosecutor, the investigating judge, and the judges who adjudicate criminal charges and impose sentences. In addition, a number of other institutions are involved. These include the Judicial Council, the Chamber of Indictment, sentence implementation courts, and Houses of Justice. For readers who are not familiar with the Belgian system, we briefly describe each. The Judicial Council is composed of one judge who supervises the investigation judges by deciding on the extension of remand custody and the eventual indictment or nonindictment of the suspect. The investigation of the most serious offenses is supervised by the Chamber of Indictment, which decides on the indictment and referral to the court of assizes. Sentence implementation courts are multidisciplinary courts deciding on the conditional release of offenders sentenced to a prison sentence of more than 3 years. The Houses of Justice are responsible for the implementation and supervision of community penalties in Belgium.

We start this essay in Section I by situating sentencing within the broader Belgian penal context. We pay specific attention to the increased sentencing powers of the public prosecutor, the importance of decisions by investigating judges, and a variety of developments and problems relating to implementation, and sometimes avoidance, of the sentences judges order.

In Section II we describe the main custodial and noncustodial sentencing options available to judges as well as upcoming and ongoing reforms. Belgian sentencing policy and practice have long been bifurcated. Belgium has experienced prison population inflation and resulting overcrowding for nearly three decades. This fostered the expansion of non-custodial sanctions in the 1990s. At the same time, prison sentences and particularly long prison sentences retained their credibility. Sentencing policy was neglected by politicians for nearly two decades, but important new developments occurred in 2014 with the introduction of new, independent noncustodial sentencing options.

In Section III we discuss aspects of Belgian sentencing practice that raise questions of comparative interest: relatively low levels of attention to sentencing disparities as a problem and therefore the absence of law reform pressures to achieve greater consistency through guidelines or other constraints on judicial discretion; the limited role of social reports; the effects on sentencing policy and practice of partial and fragmented implementation of short prison sentences; and the relation of Belgian bifurcation policy and practice to international debates about increased punitiveness.

I. The Belgian Context

Belgium is a relatively small, but institutionally complex, federal country of around 11.2 million people. It has a federal parliament and government, three language communities (Flemish, French, and, much smaller, German), and three geographically based regions (Flemish, French, and Brussels). Each region and language community has its own parliament, government, and decisional powers under a constitutional monarch. Most matters relating to the criminal justice system, including prosecution, sentencing, and implementation of sentences, are federal. However, in some areas authority is divided between federal and community institutions. Prisons, for instance, are a federal responsibility, but all aspects of social welfare and social reintegration of prisoners fall under the authority of the regional governments (e.g., social aid to offenders, victims, and their families; probation and the supervision of offenders; Snacken 2007; Beyens and Scheirs 2010).

A. Case Processing

Belgium has a moderate inquisitorial penal system, in which the public prosecution plays an important and ever increasing role, but with some adversarial elements (Tak 1993). Police officers must report every offense to the prosecutor, who decides the steps to be taken by the police to investigate the offense. Criminal procedures are instigated by the public prosecutor, who bears the burden of proof in any formal proceedings. Public prosecutors are generally seen as having a double constitutional status: they are part of the executive (and thus participate in the formulation of criminal justice policy) when investigating offenses and part of the judiciary (and hence neutral and independent) when participating in the trial (Parmentier, Fijnaut, and Van Daele 2000). They act at different court levels: the police court for petty offenses, the correctional court for misdemeanors and most felonies, and the courts of assizes for the most serious felonies.

The investigation is led by the public prosecutor (*information/opsporingsonderzoek*) or by the investigating judge (*instruction/gerechtelijk onderzoek*), who can order diverse police actions, such as interrogation of suspects, searches, telephone surveillance, arrests, and other actions. Investigation by the public prosecutor can lead to an array of decisions, ranging from waiver of prosecution to formal charges before the police (petty offenses) or correctional court (misdemeanors and felonies). Investigation by an investigating judge precludes waiver of prosecution. It is supervised by the Judicial Council (Chambre du Conseil/Raadkamer) and leads to indictment or nonindictment (*non lieu/buitenvervolgingstelling*) of the suspect. The most serious crimes are tried by courts of assizes, composed of three professional judges and 12 lay jurors. The investigation is then supervised by the Chamber of Indictment (Chambre des Mises en Accusation/Kamer van Inbeschuldigingstelling), which decides on the indictment and referral to the court of assizes.

The investigation results in preparation of a written dossier containing all documents produced by the police, the public prosecutor, and, if one is involved, the investigating judge, as well as reports from experts and social reports. This dossier is made available to the suspect at least 10 days before the trial (often extended to allow sufficient time for preparation of the defense), unless the suspect is put on remand (access to the dossier 24 hours before the first and 48 hours before each subsequent extension; 3 days before referral to court by the Judicial Council).

Adversarial elements include the rights of victims to lodge civil claims before the investigating judge (*partie civile/burgerlijke partij*), thus preventing waiver of prosecution and requiring judicial investigation of the case, and to request certain investigating initiatives from this judge (Act 12 March 1998). Access to the written dossier has been extended to victims of crime. The trial is adversarial, with the public prosecutor and the suspect being guaranteed "equality of arms" by a judge whose main duty is to seek the "truth." Victims can make claims for compensation as civil parties before the sentencing judge. The written dossier is thus of major importance for all parties involved.

There are three categories of offenses: *contraventions* (petty offenses), *délits* (misdemeanors), and *crimes* (felonies), which lead in principle to different levels of severity of sanctions: fines, probation, work penalties, electronic monitoring, and imprisonment in that hierarchical order. In contrast to American and other Anglo-Saxon legal systems, the Belgian sentencing framework is laid down in the penal code, which provides definitions of crimes and sets minimum and maximum penalties for each. Within that range, the judge is free to determine the sentence. The criminal code and other legislation establish conditions for use of non-custodial sanctions in relation to sentence length and the criminal record of the offender and preclude use of some sanctions for certain offenses.

Belgian judges determine sentences, taking into account the gravity of the offense and the culpability of the offender. Aggravating circumstances and their roles in determination of sentences are specified in legislation. The significance of extenuating circumstances is left to the discretion of the investigating judge or the sentencing judge. The original offense may be downgraded into a lower category, and the legal minimum sentence may be mitigated in other ways. In other words, the Belgian penal code provides judges with a decision-making framework and a legal hierarchy of sentencing options. Within this framework, they possess wide discretion (Snacken et al. 2013).

B. Crime Patterns

Trends in crime and criminal justice processes in Belgium are difficult to assess because of poor data quality and a lack of continuity in statistical data series. Data quality has significantly improved during the past decade, but reliable longer-term data are seldom available.

Overall crime rates, according to official police data, have been stable in recent years, fluctuating around 1 million offenses per year (993,796 in 2000 and 956,297 in 2014). Between 2005 and 2014, property crimes were the most common offenses recorded by the police (between 40 and 43 percent). Violent, including sexual, offenses represent less than 8–9 percent of the total (Crime Statistics, http://www.polfed-fedpol.be).

The absence of reliable data over a longer period has often been criticized by Belgian criminologists (see, e.g., Snacken 2007; Maes 2010; Daems, Maes, and Robert 2013) and hampers the depth of our analysis. Even so, the available figures help us to contextualize some of the patterns in penal legislation and sentencing practices over the last decade.

C. Public Prosecution

Decisions whether to prosecute are governed by the "principle of the general interest." The justifications are listed in a circular letter of the College of General-Prosecutors (Coll. 11/2010 of 18 May 2010). Prosecutors may waive prosecutions "for reasons of opportunity," such as the pettiness of offenses committed by first offenders. Prosecution may also be waived for technical reasons, such as failure to identify a suspect, lapse of time, absence of an offense (e.g., suicide), or death of the suspect. The decision to waive is provisional and can be reconsidered if a prosecution has not been barred by lapse of time under applicable statutes of limitations.

Public prosecution has other ways to deal with offenses besides referral to a court. "Transactions" are prosecutorial fines imposed on suspects following admissions of guilt. Payment of the fine ends the prosecution. Its application was extended by the Acts of 28 June 1984 and 10 February 1994 to offenses potentially subject to prison sentences up to 5 years and by the Act of 14 April 2011 to sentences up to 20 years but in which the prosecution would propose only a fine.

"Penal mediation" was introduced in the Act of 10 February 1994. Prosecutions may be dropped if the victim and the offender reach an agreement on compensation. Mediation is conducted by social workers acting as "justice assistants." They are located in facilities called Houses of Justice, which are separate from the courts. The Houses of Justice are also responsible for preparing social reports (not exactly the same as Anglo-Saxon presentence investigation reports), implementing community sentences, coordinating and improving cooperation between judicial and parajudicial services (victim support; mediation services; implementation of community sanctions, probation, and parole), and offering initial legal aid to all. Mediation concludes with a contract that must be approved by the prosecutor. Therapy, training, and community service by the offender can be part of the contract. The public prosecutor retains authority to prosecute if no agreement can be reached.

In recent years, the prosecution service caseload decreased by more than 25 percent (from 925,522 cases in 2003 to 667,039 in 2014). In the vast majority of cases, the public prosecutor does not refer a case to a court or to the Judicial Council. In 2014, as table 1 shows, less then 3 percent of all cases were referred to court (2.9 percent).

In contrast, as table 2 shows, most cases that came to the prosecutor's attention resulted in a prosecutorial waiver. In 2014, prosecution was waived in 72.6 percent of the cases. A majority of prosecutions are waived for technical reasons (62.8 percent), especially relating to an unknown offender (31.9 percent), insufficient proof (15.6 percent), and the low seriousness of the offense (5.8 percent). This high level of technical waivers must be understood within a legal framework in which police officers must report every offense to the prosecutor, even if no suspect is known at the time of reporting. Waivers for reasons of opportunity represent a much smaller group (2.6 percent) and are related to other criminal justice policy priorities and capacity limits (7.8 percent), the victim-offender relationship (1.7 percent), regularization of the situation (5.6 percent), and the limited criminal record of the suspect (1.8 percent; Annual Statistics of Public Prosecutions Services 2015, table 1 [http://www.om-mp.be/page/152/1/statistieken.html]).

D. Mediation in a More Victim-Oriented Climate

Penal mediation serves two policy purposes: to increase the recognition of and participation by crime victims in criminal justice procedures and to enhance the visibility and speed of penal reactions to petty crimes.

TABLE 1
Prosecutorial Decisions, 2014

	Percentage
Waiver	72.6
Further investigation	8.6
Joining cases	12.2
Transaction	1.1
Successful penal mediation	.4
Referral to court	2.9
Referral to the Judicial Council	2.2
Total	100

SOURCE.—Annual Statistics of Public Prosecutions Services, 2015 (http://www.om-mp.be/page/152/1/statistieken.html).

TABLE 2
Prosecutorial Waiver Decisions, 2014

	Number	Percentage
Reasons of opportunity	143,434	29.64
Criminal policy priorities	37,916	7.8
Limited seriousness of the offense	28,109	5.8
Regularization of the situation	26,978	5.6
Coincidental offenses	10,400	2.2
Absence of criminal record	8,687	1.8
Victim-offender relationship	8,278	1.7
Lack of police capacity	6,801	1.4
Limited consequences of the offense	4,915	1.0
No decision within reasonable time	4,784	1.0
Age of the suspect (e.g., juveniles)	146	.03
Attitude of the victim	3,424	.7
Compensation of the victim	2,996	.6
Other opportunity reasons	0	0
Technical reasons	303,698	62.8
Unknown offender	151,181	31.9
Insufficient proof	75,431	15.6
No offense	64,318	13.3
Other technical reasons	0	1.0
Other	36,863	7.6
Total	483,995	100

SOURCE.—Annual Statistics of Public Prosecutions Services, 2015 (http://www.om-mp.be/page/152/1/statistieken.html).

Hence, the public prosecutor can make therapy, training, and community service available to the suspect.

Two forms of mediation exist. "Penal mediation" is performed by justice assistants for the public prosecutor and terminates prosecution if successful. "Restorative mediation" is conducted by independent nongovernmental organizations (NGOs). Its consequences depend on the parties involved, and it does not have a binding effect on the sentencing judge.

In 2002, community service was transformed into an independent, freestanding sanction (called the "work penalty") and was eliminated as a possible condition of mediation and probation. However, as a result of requests from practitioners, the prosecutor's authority to settle mediation with community service was reintroduced in 2005 (Act of 22 June 2005; Beyens 2010). Prosecutors are said to like community service because it can give a retributive flavor to penal mediation (Beyens 2010), which may explain the requests for its reintroduction. However, penal mediation represents only a small proportion (0.4 percent) of prosecutorial case dispositions (Annual Statistics of Public Prosecutions Services 2015, table 1).

Another Act of 22 June 2005 introduced restorative mediation. It is available for nearly all offenses and at every criminal justice system stage from police investigation through prosecution, judicial inquiry, sentencing, and sentence implementation. Restorative mediation can be initiated at the demand of a person with a direct interest in the criminal procedure.

The act of 2005 describes mediation as "a process that allows people involved in a conflict, if they agree voluntarily, to participate actively and in total confidentiality in solving difficulties that arise from a criminal offense, with the help of a neutral third person and based on a certain methodology." The goals are to find a solution for the difficulties resulting from a crime, to facilitate communication between parties, and to help them reach an agreement that can lead to pacification and reparation. The act strongly emphasizes the importance of confidentiality, neutrality, and voluntary participation. The mediators are not directly linked to the criminal justice system but work for independent NGOs specializing in mediation and restorative justice. Sentencing judges have a responsibility to inform parties about the possibility of restorative mediation. If it succeeds, the offender and the victim decide whether the agreement will be communicated to the judge. Judges can, but need not, take the agreement into account in their decision-making process (Van Garsse 2010).

The infamous Dutroux case in 1996, involving the abduction, rape, and murder of several children and young girls while the suspect was under parole (Snacken 2007), led to increased attention for victims of crime and to several legislative changes enhancing their rights in criminal and parole procedures. Almost all "post-Dutroux" legislative changes relating to sentencing or sentence implementation expressly authorize the judge to take the interests of victims into account when imposing a sentence. However, it is unclear whether or how this authority has influenced judicial decision making in practice.

At the same time, several other victim-oriented initiatives occurred at the level of sentence implementation. In the late 1990s, "restorative justice consultants" (*herstelconsulenten*) were introduced in Belgian prisons in order to initiate restorative justice activities and foster a restorative prison culture. Recognized as an official aim of implementation of prison sentences by the 2005 Prison Act (Act 12 January 2005), restorative justice was integrated into the normal tasks of prison governors in 2008. The victim also has a more prominent place in current legislation on conditional release (Act of 17 May 2006). Three of five counterindications for conditional release refer to the victim: risks of harassment, the attitude of the offender toward the victim, and his or her efforts to pay compensation (see Scheirs 2014).

E. Increasing Prosecutorial Powers

The public prosecutor plays an important role in deciding whether or not cases will be prosecuted. When referring a case to court, prosecutors can request or recommend a specific sentence or penalty to the judge. Several studies confirm that these sentence recommendations influence judges' decision making (e.g., de Keijser and van Koppen 2004; Schuyt 2007; Raats 2013).

The public prosecutor's discretionary power to sanction the suspect has increased, for example, by using financial transactions (settlements by the payment of a fine) as prosecutorial penalties without judicial oversight. Until 2011, transactions could be used for all offenses potentially subject to up to 5 years' imprisonment (Acts of 28 June 1984; Act of 10 February 1994). Transactions were then mainly used for petty traffic offenses (Snacken 2007). Since 2011, however, transactions may be used for all offenses potentially subject to a prison sentence up to 20 years.

The prosecutor may resort to a transaction at any stage of the procedure, even after the case has been referred to the court, but before the verdict (Act of 14 April 2011). Payment of the fine ends the prosecution. Transactions in serious cases are mainly used for huge, complex frauds in which the success rate of bringing cases to court is low. This so-called "buy-off law" for white-collar offenders is, however, highly controversial as it is widely seen as a form of "class justice" (*klassenjustitie*). More than 80 percent of respondents in a survey before the national elections in May 2014 indicated that they opposed this "new" legislation because it meant that the rich could avoid prosecution altogether (VRT 2014). However, despite its increased use, prosecutorial transactions remain a marginal phenomenon (1.1 percent of cases dealt with by the public prosecutor; see table 1; Annual Statistics of Public Prosecutions Services 2015).

In sum, Belgian public prosecutors exercise increased sentencing powers. These have been provided by policy makers to counter a perception of impunity that could have been raised by the large number of waivers of prosecution and the backlog of cases before the courts, and thus to reinforce the legitimacy of the criminal justice system. As Kaminski, Snacken, and van de Kerchove (2007) emphasize, implementing criminal policy through a hierarchical organization such as the prosecution service is more feasible than through independent sentencing judges working case by case. This, however, results in increasing sanctioning by prosecutors with decreasing procedural safeguards, such as a fair trial, and the emergence of new penal actors assisting the prosecutor in this process, such as the justice assistants (penal mediation) and administrative agents (transactions) (Raes 2006; Kaminski, Snacken, and van de Kerchove 2007).

F. The Investigating Judge

Investigation is carried out by the police under supervision of the public prosecutor. Restrictions on fundamental freedoms such as searches or pretrial custody may, however, be imposed only by an investigating judge. If the prosecutor believes that such an action is necessary, the case must be transferred to an investigating judge. Investigating judges are part of the judiciary; they must impartially investigate both incriminating and exonerating facts (*à charge et à décharge*). They are independent of the public prosecution and the executive branch of government; their work is supervised by the Judicial Council or the Chamber of Indictment, which are also parts of the judiciary.

However, an exception to this general principle can be found in the so-called "mini-instruction" introduced in 1998 (Act of 12 March 1998). A mini-instruction allows the public prosecutor to complete the investigation without referral to the investigating judge, with the exception of arrests, home searches, and telephone taps (De Hert and Ölçer 2004). Mini-instructions decrease the workload of the investigating judges in less severe cases. However, they augment the increasing powers of the public prosecutor.

In case of an arrest, the investigating judge must decide within 24 hours (in some cases 48 hours) whether to hold the suspect in custody until trial or to release him or her with or without conditions. Pretrial custody can (theoretically) be imposed only in cases of absolute necessity for public security reasons and for offenses that may be punished with at least 1 year of imprisonment (Act of 20 July 1990). The act states that pretrial custody may never be used as a sanction or to exert pressure on a suspect.

If the punishment for the alleged offense does not exceed 15 years' imprisonment, custody may be ordered only for cases in which there are risks of recidivism, absconding, collusion, or meddling with evidence.

Table 3 shows increases in pretrial detention through 2010. Between 2000 and 2010, there was a 29 percent increase from 9,171 in 2000 to 11,778 in 2011 (16 percent between 2000 and 2013, but data are incomplete). In the same period, the number of offenders released with conditions almost doubled from 2,300 in 2000 to 4,439 in 2010 (Rekenhof [Court of Audit] 2011, p. 50). In practice, risks of recidivism dominate decision making (Van Roeyen and Vander Beken 2014). Conditions often relate to the apparent underlying causes of offending, such as drug addiction.

Research by Raes and Snacken (2004) on the use of pretrial custody and its alternatives indicates that prosecutors request a social report by the investigating judge in a large number of cases, predominantly in order to obtain pretrial custody.[1] In the majority of cases, the investigating judge accedes to the request.

The research also showed how organizational and interactional circumstances affect custody decisions. The decision whether to deprive a suspect of his liberty must normally be made within 24 hours of arrest. A large part of this time is taken up by the police and the prosecutor, leaving the investigating judge sometimes no more than 15 or 30 minutes in which to decide. Without sufficient information on the circumstances of the offense and the offender on which to base a release decision, the safest decision is to hold the suspect in custody. Police officers in their reports often express their expectation that the investigating judges will impose custody. Failure to do so is often perceived as showing a lack of respect for the difficulties the police faced in finding and arresting the suspect. Although investigating judges make their decisions autonomously, their operational dependency on the police may create pressures to honor their requests in order to maintain good relationships (Raes and Snacken 2004; Snacken 2007; Snacken, van Zyl Smit, and Beyens 2013).

---

[1] Social reports can be compared with presentence reports. However, their main aim is to provide social background information on the defendant rather than to provide sentencing advice. We therefore prefer to use the term "social report."

TABLE 3

Pretrial Custody and Release with Conditions,
2000–2013, Number of Cases

Year	Remand	Index	Freedom with Conditions	Index
2000	9,171	100	2,300	100
2001	9,230	101	2,224	97
2002	10,434	114	2,855	124
2003	10,745	117	3,156	137
2004	10,090	110	3,460	150
2005	11,810	129	3,713	161
2006	10,842	118	4,107	179
2007	10,309	112	4,563	198
2008	10,842	118	4,917	214
2009	12,123	132	4,949	215
2010	12,161	133	4,439	193
2011*	11,788	129	NA	NA
2012*	10,183	111	NA	NA
2013*	10,611	116	NA	NA

SOURCE.—FOD Justitie (2011, 2012, 2014); Rekenhof (2011).

* Incomplete data.

In law and in practice, pretrial custody is intrinsically linked to sentencing. From a legal point of view, detention is treated as an anticipated part of the sentence. The time served in pretrial detention is subtracted from the sentence of imprisonment. Thus, in practice, custody is used as an immediate punishment and as a security measure to protect society against "dangerous" elements. Sentencing judges often impose sentences of imprisonment that are equal to or only slightly longer than the period of pretrial custody (Snacken et al. 1999; Beyens 2000; Raes and Snacken 2004; Snacken 2007). The reason is that judges tend to consider the time spent in remand detention as adequate to meet the retributive aim of punishment and adjust the sentence accordingly (Snacken et al. 2013).

The Act of 27 December 2012 adjusted the remand procedure to authorize GPS tracking as an option for the investigating judge. This new legislation became operational in January 2014. GPS tracking was introduced to serve as an alternative to pretrial custody and not as an extra condition of freedom with conditions (Beyens and Roosen 2013). With its implementation, the government sought to reduce the number of people in pretrial custody by 5–10 percent. However, research by Maes et al. (2012) on the introduction of electronic monitoring as an additional alternative to pretrial detention gives reason to be skeptical about achieving this ambition, pointing out the dangers of net widening and heightened risks of incarceration for noncompliance. And indeed, this option is being used cautiously by investigating judges because of operational issues and a gap in the legislation that will soon be resolved (personal communication, Flemish Centre of Electronic Monitoring). Only 40 suspects were on GPS monitoring on October 5, 2015.

II. Sentencing Options

The Belgian sentencing judge is a career official working in a professional culture that highly values the independence of the judiciary, its wide discretion, and opportunities for individualization (Beyens 2000). Sentencing options are laid down in the criminal code and criminal legislation. The sentencing judge has a wide variety of options.

The Belgian court system consists of police courts, correctional courts, appeal courts, and courts of assizes. The majority of cases are dealt with by the police courts (79.3 percent of all convictions; see table 4). Police courts have jurisdiction over all petty offenses and designated misdemeanors such as traffic offenses leading to unintended death or injuries. Correctional courts have jurisdiction over other misdemeanors and felonies in which mitigating circumstances have been accepted by the Judicial Council at the time of referral. This is standard practice, aiming at avoiding cumbersome referrals to the courts of assizes, which are reserved for the most severe felonies such as murder.

TABLE 4
Convictions by Type of Court, 2013, Percentages

	Number	Percentage
Supreme Court	0	0
Appeal court	4,103	2.3
Court of assizes	82	.05
Correctional court	32,777	18.4
Police court	141,262	79.3
Judicial Council	2	0
Total	178,224	100

SOURCE.—Dienst Strafrechtelijk Beleid (Criminal Justice Service), Statistics of Convictions, Data Extraction October 21, 2015 (http://www.dsb-spc.be).

In 2013, correctional courts handled 18.4 percent of all convictions (32,777 judgments). The courts of appeal, which hear cases on the basis of appeals by the prosecutor or the sentenced person, entered 2.3 percent of all convictions in 2013 (4.103). The courts of assizes deal with the small number of most serious felonies (0.05 percent of all judgments in 2013).

The total number of convictions has varied over the years, with a minimum of 153,779 in 2000 and a maximum of 206,236 in 2012 (index 124). The number of cases in which the conviction is suspended for 1–5 years without a formal conviction increased from 8,134 in 2000 to 9,843 in 2012 (index 121) but decreased to 7,492 in 2013. These represent a small proportion of all decisions (4.0 percent in 2013). Internments of mentally ill offenders increased from 321 in 2000 to 374 in 2012 (index 117) and 342 in 2013 but remain at a constant proportion of 0.2 percent of all convictions (see table 5).

A. Sentencing Options

The Belgian sentencing judge has a wide variety of sentencing options: a fine (unconditional or conditional, with or without probation), imprisonment (unconditional or conditional, with or without probation), a suspended sentence with or without probation, a work penalty (unconditional or conditional, with or without probation orders), electronic monitoring, probation, internment of mentally ill offenders, and preventive detention of repeat and sexual offenders.[2] This last option allows the sentencing judges to impose an additional prison sentence up to 15 years, which could result in additional confinement after completion of the main sentence (see below).

Until 2002, Belgian sentencing judges had only two main options: fines and imprisonment. Both could be suspended, with or without conditions of probation. Community service was introduced in 1994 as an additional condition to probation. In 2002 it became a freestanding sentencing option called a "work penalty." This change of terminology and legal status entailed a different application and implementation of this sanction. In 2014 electronic monitoring and probation were introduced as freestanding sanctions.

---

[2] We do not discuss internment of mentally ill offenders.

TABLE 5
Numbers of Convictions, Suspended Sentences, and Interments of Mentally Ill Offenders, 2000–2013, Numbers and Percentages

	Convictions			Suspended Convictions			Interments			Total
	Number	Percent	Index	Number	Percent	Index	Number	Percent	Index	
2000	153,779	94.8	100	8,134	5.0	100	321	.2	100	162,234
2001	164,514	94.2	107	9,769	5.6	120	342	.2	107	174,625
2002	165,651	94.0	108	10,135	5.8	125	366	.2	114	176,152
2003	177,983	95.4	116	8,305	4.4	102	345	.2	107	186,633
2004	190,594	95.8	124	7,893	4.0	97	378	.2	118	198,865
2005	219,488	95.6	143	9,699	4.2	119	409	.2	127	229,596
2006	198,755	94.8	129	10,491	5.0	129	459	.2	143	209,705
2007	174,694	94.6	114	9,587	5.2	118	448	.2	140	184,729
2008	176,342	95.6	115	7,631	4.1	94	412	.2	128	184,385
2009	188,689	95.9	123	7,621	3.9	94	405	.2	126	196,715
2010	183,904	95.7	120	7,756	4.0	95	413	.2	129	192,073
2011	186,093	95.8	121	7,796	4.0	96	390	.2	121	194,279
2012	206,236	95.3	134	9,843	4.5	121	374	.2	117	216,453
2013*	178,224	95.8	116	7,492	4.0	92	342	.2	107	186,058

SOURCE.—Dienst Strafrechtelijk Beleid (Criminal Justice Service), Statistics of Convictions, Data Extraction October 21, 2015 (http://www.dsb-spc.be).

* Incomplete data.

Recent figures (see table 6) illustrate, however, that the largest proportion of convictions are dealt with by use of fines (57.8 percent of petty offenses, misdemeanors, and felonies in 2013) and license bans (31.2 percent). Prison sentences are imposed on 8.2 percent of offenders, of which 3.4 percent are conditional imprisonment.

B. Imprisonment

In 2013, 26,505 prison sentences were imposed (8.2 percent of all imposed sentences); 10,882 offenders (3.4 percent of all imposed sentences) were sentenced to conditional imprisonment (see table 6). Use of conditional imprisonment is restricted to offenses punishable by an unconditional prison sentence up to 5 years and to offenders who have not previously been sentenced to a conditional prison sentence of more than 12 months.

Because of the absence of reliable data, we cannot describe and explain trends in sentences to imprisonment. The most recent figures date from 2003 and indicate that sentences to short terms of imprisonment have decreased and sentences to long terms of imprisonment have increased (see Snacken 2007).

Sentence implementation has become a major issue and is often directly linked by critics to the credibility of punishment. To explain what is at stake, we first describe some key aspects of sentence implementation.

As figure 1 illustrates, like several other European countries, Belgium has experienced a rising prison population since the early 1990s. Between

TABLE 6

Sentences, 2013, Percentages

	Number	Percent
License ban	100,521	31.2
Fine*	186,234	57.8
Work penalty	8,971	2.8
Suspended imprisonment	10,882	3.4
Imprisonment	26,505	8.2

SOURCE.—Dienst Strafrechtelijk Beleid (Criminal Justice Service), Statistics of Convictions, Data Extraction October 21, 2015 (http://www.dsb-spc.be).

* The number of convictions resulting in a fine includes suspended fines. Owing to the absence of data, suspended and unsuspended fines cannot be distinguished.

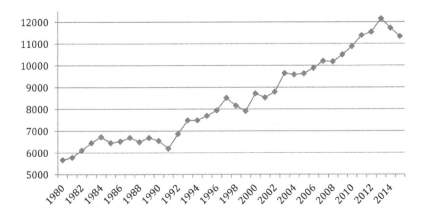

FIG. 1.—Daily prison population, 1980–2015. Source: FOD Justitie (2003–14); De Ridder and Beyens (2014).

1980 and 2013, it more than doubled from 5,677 in 1980 to 12,158 in 2013 (excluding electronic monitoring as a way to execute prison sentences), resulting in an imprisonment rate increase from 65 per 100,000 population in the 1980s to 90 in 2003 and 109 in 2013 (Aebi and Delgrande 2014). Prison capacity also increased, but much more slowly, resulting in prison overcrowding of 24.1 percent (FOD Justitie [Prison Service] 2014). Overcrowding is particularly severe in remand prisons in big cities. However, since 2013 a slight but clear decrease of the prison population has occurred. On October 26, 2015, Belgium had a prison population of 11,099 in facilities with a capacity of 10,012 places, resulting in an overcrowding rate of 10.8 percent and an imprisonment rate of 99 per 100,000 population. Custodial sentences have increased for violent and sex offenses, drugs (dealing/trafficking), and organized crime (Snacken 2007).

The rise of the prison population is particularly due to increasing numbers of remand prisoners (although their numbers have not increased in recent years), internees, and prisoners sentenced to between 3 and 10 years (Maes 2010). In 2014, 31.2 percent of the prison population were being held awaiting trial, 58.5 percent had been convicted, and 9.4 percent were imprisoned after a decision of internment (FOD Justitie [Prison Service] 2014, p. 50). The increasing presence of prisoners serving long sentences can partly be explained by a policy of not or only partly executing prison sentences up to 6 months and partly by conversion of prison sentences up to 3 years into electronic monitoring.

Imprisonment is widely used for nonnationals: between 1980 and 2013 their numbers increased fourfold. The presence of foreign prisoners without a legal residence increased significantly between 2003 and 2013 for all legal categories: pretrial, up 30 percent; convicted, up by a factor of 2.5; and interned, up by a factor of 2.9 (De Ridder and Beyens 2014). These increasing numbers can be explained by more frequent and longer application of pretrial custody, difficulties in implementation of noncustodial sanctions (due to problems of housing, employment, and control possibilities), and practical difficulties in use of early release (De Ridder, Beyens, and Snacken 2012).

Offenders considered not responsible for their offenses as a result of mental illness are subjected to indeterminate measures in order to help them and protect the public. Although the annual number of internment decisions has only slightly increased over the last 10 years (see table 5; index 117 between 2000 and 2012), they are the fastest-growing group in prison. This indicates an increasing average length of stay (De Ridder and Beyens 2014).

Decisions to release prisoners are highly sensitive and often debated. The early release system has undergone fundamental changes in recent decades. One was the transfer of most authority to release prisoners from the executive branch of government to independent, multidisciplinary sentence implementation courts.

Depending on the length of sentence, separate systems of early release exist. First, the minister of justice has authority to release prisoners sentenced to up to 3 years. These prisoners are semiautomatically released after an administrative procedure without procedural safeguards. Since February 2007, sentence implementation courts have had jurisdiction over prisoners sentenced to more than 3 years.

The sentence implementation courts make decisions after a hybrid inquisitorial and adversarial procedure in which the public prosecutor, the prison governor, and the prisoner are heard. These courts are chaired by a judge assisted by two nonjudicial assessors with expertise in social reintegration or prison matters. The decision-making process is highly discretionary.

However, the legislation provides that a conditional release order is to be awarded if the time conditions have been fulfilled and if no counterindications are present that cannot be addressed by imposing license conditions. Persons sentenced to more than 3 years' imprisonment can be released conditionally after serving one-third of the sentence. Recidivists can be released after having served two-thirds. People sentenced to 30 years or to life imprisonment must serve at least 15 years. Legal recidivists must serve at least 19 or 23 years of their sentences depending on earlier convictions (for more details, see Scheirs [2014]; Scheirs, Beyens, and Snacken [2015]).

The legally prescribed one-third minimum may seem lenient, but prisoners often serve more than the minimum before they are released (mean of 14.4 months extra; Maes and Tange 2014). Considerations that gravitate toward denial of release require an individual assessment by the sentence implementation courts. Designated considerations include the absence of prospects for social reintegration, risk of committing new serious offenses, risk that the offender will harass victims, the offender's attitude toward his or her victim, and efforts to pay the civil parties.

According to the Act of 17 May 2006 on the External Legal Position, a single sentence implementation judge should decide about the provisional release of prisoners sentenced up to 3 years. However, transfer of this authority from the prison governor and minister of justice to independent sentence implementation judges has been postponed several times (because of fear of even more prison overcrowding). Most recently, the transfer of authority was postponed to September 2017.

There are indications, however, that this part of the legislation will never be implemented and will be replaced by another release system (Geens 2015). Until now, decisions about release of prisoners sentenced to up to 3 years have been made by the minister of justice and the prison administration, under a quasi-automatic release scheme (see Snacken, Beyens, and Beernaert 2010; Scheirs, Beyens, and Snacken 2015). Over 80 percent of all released sentenced prisoners are released by decision of the minister of justice.

C. Noncustodial Sentences

Several laws enacted in recent decades promoted the use of noncustodial sanctions to reduce the use of prison sentences. This has led to the amplification of noncustodial sanctions and measures. Suspended sentences, applicable to both fines and imprisonment, were introduced in 1888. For a long time, fines and suspended imprisonment were the only noncustodial sentencing options. Individualization was the main objective, but strongly embedded in a neoclassic sentencing framework, guided by deterrence and retribution. Unsupervised conditional prison sentences have long been widely used and are today. Judges see them as a "second chance" for the offender, who is regarded as a rational actor who can be deterred by the threat of imprisonment (Snacken 1986; Beyens 2000).

In 1964, almost a century later, probation was introduced as the Belgian expression of the "era of resocialization," not as an independent sanction but as a "probation measure" to be added to a suspended fine or prison sentence. This fitted with a general tendency during that period toward the humanization of punishment and an inclusionary view of the offender. It also illustrated the Belgian continued neoclassical sentencing framework. Only some 30 years later did significant new developments occur in Belgian community punishment. Since 2000, a "new generation of community penalties" (Bottoms, Rex, and Robinson 2004) has been ushered in, with the introduction of intermediate penalties that can be situated between those commonly perceived as "too soft" (probation, training orders, and community service) and imprisonment (Morris and Tonry 1990). Community penalties obtained independent legal status. For some, the rehabilitative aspect was reframed in a more desert-oriented neorehabilitative framework (Beyens 2016).

1. *Fines.* As table 6 shows, the largest proportion of convictions are dealt with through fines: 57.8 percent of petty offenses and misdemeanors in 2013. Consecutive analyses by the Court of Audit show that one of two fines is not paid (Rekenhof [Court of Audit] 2007, 2014). Because of prison overcrowding, prison sentences are not imposed as sanctions for nonpayment, except when an offender is already in prison for another offense; then prison as a sanction for nonpayment is automatically implemented.

This does not prevent judges from imposing fines. Unfortunately, no research has been carried out into the decision-making practices of Belgian judges concerning imposition of fines.

2. *Suspended Sentences and Suspended Conviction* (Opschorting). Forty-one percent of all prison sentences are suspended (conditional imprisonment). This illustrates the continuing credibility and importance of this sanction, which fits well with the Belgian traditional neoclassical sentencing culture (see van Zyl Smit, Snacken, and Hayes 2015).

Since February 10, 2013, suspended fines can be coupled with an obligation to participate in a specific training program (Act 27 December 2012). This mainly aims at traffic offenses, where fines are the most commonly imposed sanction. Traffic safety training courses aim at reducing recidivism in a variety of traffic offenses (driving under the influence of alcohol or drugs, aggression, speeding; Belgisch Instituut voor de Verkeersveiligheid [Belgian Road Safety Institute] 2013).

3. *Work Penalty.* Community service was introduced in 1994 as a condition of probation at the sentencing level and as a condition of mediation at the prosecution level (without a conviction).[3] The prosecutor can impose between 20 and 120 hours of community service. At sentencing, until 2002, community service could be imposed only in connection with a suspended sentence or suspended conviction (Act of 10 February 1994). The length of community service varied between 20 and 240 hours. Owing to its unclear and subordinate legal status as a condition of probation, community service was used only for a small selection of first-time offenders. Beyens (2000), conducting semistructured interviews with judges using vignettes after some years of application, found that they typically had a dismissive attitude toward community service. They believed that it lacked the necessary "punitive bite." They viewed it as "a favor" that had to be "deserved," and they reserved it for "redeemable," socially integrated, employed, motivated, remorseful, reliable young offenders, with no criminal mind-set. Legal provisions with regard to criminal record were strictly applied; judges used it only for first offenders.

In 2002, community service as a probation add-on was replaced by a stand-alone sentencing option, renamed the "work penalty" (Act of 17 April 2002). Together with imprisonment and the fine, it became the third main sanction in the Belgian Penal Code, which boosted its legal status. The explicit legislative aims were to introduce the work penalty as a substitute for imprisonment and to avoid social stigmatization. It is not mentioned on the certificate of good conduct that offenders need to apply for a job. Nonetheless, the sentence appears on the central sentence register.[4] This possibility of safeguarding social and judicial rehabilitation was and remains a strong incentive for defendants and defense lawyers to agree to a work penalty and is a key factor in its swift acceptance.

To maximize their scope, work penalties can be imposed for most offenses, except only a few very serious ones such as kidnapping, rape,

---

[3] For a more in-depth and extended analysis of the history, implementation, and use of the work penalty in Belgium, see Beyens (2010).

[4] In Belgium all criminal records are registered in this central sentence register.

sexual offenses with minors, murder, and manslaughter, and they can substitute for a prison sentence up to 5 years. In contrast to suspended sentences and probation, a criminal record does not preclude imposition of a work penalty, which has been an important step forward that has increased its use. Work penalties can range between 20 and 300 hours (600 hours for recidivists), and defendants (or their lawyer) must give their consent during the court hearing. To prompt judges to impose work penalties, a refusal to impose a work penalty, when it is requested by the defendant (or his lawyer) or is proposed by the prosecutor, must explicitly be explained in the verdict.

Upgrading the legal status of the work penalty ushered in a significant change in judges' sentencing behavior. The number of offenders receiving a work penalty rose from 4,537 in 2003 to 10,457 in 2014 (FOD Justitie/Departement Welzijn [Houses of Justice] 2015, p. 92), more than a doubling in 11 years. Compared with the moderate use of community service as a condition of probation, this is a striking success. The punitive dimension of work penalties is expressed in the restriction of freedom, having to comply with work schedules, and being subject to external control.

Lefevre (2009) and Verbist (2013) repeated Beyens's (2000) research using the same four vignettes with a small sample of judges, aiming to evaluate their receptivity to the work penalty and trying to compare sentencing decisions with those documented by Beyens. While Beyens found that judges' experience with community service was limited, more than 15 years later judges showed much greater willingness to impose work penalties. They considered it to be a burdensome sentence that can serve different ends, including retribution, deterrence, rehabilitation, and redress to the society. The decision to impose a work penalty can take account of the nature of the offense, the criminal record, remorse, indemnification of the victim, the defendant's presence at the court hearing, and nonexecution of short prison sentences. The freestanding character of the work penalty seems to be of decisive importance. The work penalty's greater credibility is also related to the policy of effectively implementing the substitute prison sentence.[5]

Work penalties are regarded as more credible sentencing options than are short prison sentences that are not executed, thus countering the

---

[5] Ministerial Circular letter no. 1771 of 17 January 2005 concerns provisional release and the nonimplementation of certain sentences.

public's perception of impunity and enhancing the legitimacy of the sentencing system. In practice, however, substitute prison sentences are almost automatically converted into house arrest with electronic monitoring, which means that people sentenced to a work penalty can end up serving a period of electronic monitoring, which is very confusing for outsiders (Beyens 2010, 2016). The work penalty can be regarded as a typical "chameleon" sanction (Van Kalmthout 2006).

Social inquiry reports to inform the sentencing decision are optional. Work penalties are increasingly being imposed without a social report (Beyens and Scheirs 2010). This reinforces the idea that they are retributive punishments in which the offender pays her or his debt to society.

4. *Electronic Monitoring.* Electronic monitoring (EM) was introduced in 2000. Initially, it was promoted as a humane and rehabilitative way to implement a prison sentence and thereby avoid harms associated with detention. A balance was sought between social guidance and technical control, with technology used as a means to support rehabilitative goals (Beyens, Bas, and Kaminski 2007; Beyens and Kaminski 2013).

Over time, EM's rationale has evolved, as has its application in practice.[6] It is increasingly used as a surveillant and retributive way to implement prison sentences, with technology becoming a means in itself. The penological goal of avoiding detention harms and the focus on reintegration and rehabilitation have not been abandoned completely, but budgetary considerations have become more prominent. Today, EM is organized on two tracks. For prisoners with a prison sentence up to 3 years, EM is used as a "front-door" strategy, aiming to reduce the prison population. Most of these sentences are almost automatically converted to EM by the prison governor or for "difficult" cases, such as sexual offenses, by the Detention Management Service (Directie Detentiebeheer).[7] This explains the declining number of prisoners with sentences up to 3 years. For offenders sentenced to more than 3 years, EM can be granted by the sentence implementation courts 6 months before the prisoner is eligible for conditional release. In this context, EM serves as a "back-door" strategy (see also Scheirs, Beyens, and Snacken 2015).

[6] For a more in-depth analysis, see Beyens and Roosen (2013) and Beyens (2016).

[7] Ministerial Circular letter of 28 August 2012 pertains to home detention with voice verification for persons convicted to one or more prison sentences of which the executable part is no longer than 3 years and who are 2 months or less from their early release date. Ministerial circular letter ET/SE-2 of 17 July 2013 on the regulation of EM as a modality for prison punishment where the executable part does not exceed 3 years.

Figure 2 shows the evolution of the number of persons under EM. During the early years, the numbers rose slowly; more recently, almost exponentially. The use of EM did not immediately lead to a decreasing prison population. However, the steep rise of EM cases since 2013 has coincided with a decrease in the prison population, suggesting that massive conversion of prison sentences into EM has caused the drop in the prison population. EM thus seems to be used to support an expansionist penal policy: the search for cheap and quick additional but virtual prison capacity has become the main driver.

EM was initially used exclusively as a way to implement prison sentences. In 2014, pretrial use of EM with GPS tracking was authorized. With the Act of 7 February 2014, EM also became an independent penalty at the sentencing level for offenses punishable by prison sentences up to 1 year. EM can be used for the duration of the prison sentence that otherwise would be imposed. The judge also pronounces a substitute imprisonment, to be applied if the EM sentence is not performed. In these cases, 1 day under EM equals 1 day in prison.

The public prosecutor, investigating judge, or sentencing judge may request a brief information or social inquiry report from the Houses of Justice in connection with consideration of EM at the sentencing level. Cohabitants of the supervisee must be heard when conducting a

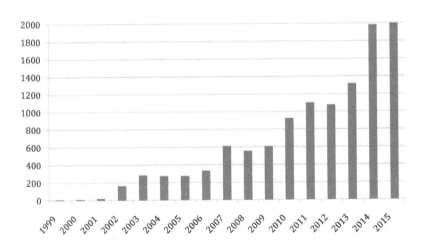

FIG. 2.—Daily EM population, 1999–2015. Source: FOD Justitie (2003–14); Beyens and Kaminski (2013); Vander Beken (2013).

social inquiry report. Research shows the importance of this because EM can have a serious effect on family life (Devresse et al. 2006; Vanhaele-meesch 2013). The defendant or his lawyer must consent to it at the court hearing. The judge fixes the duration of EM. Individualized conditions may be imposed, but only to counter risks of recidivism or to the victim's well-being.

Research prior to the introduction of EM as an independent sentencing option had observed that there was no particular demand for it from the judiciary. Judges stated that introduction of EM as a sentencing option would be impractical and time-consuming because of the need to gather detailed information about the social situation of the offender. However, the main critique by the researchers concerned the risk of net widening if EM was introduced as an independent sanction (Vanneste et al. 2005). Those reservations did not prevent the introduction of EM as a sentencing option, which confirms the eagerness of politicians and policy makers to use this technology (Beyens and Kaminski 2013). In the law, autonomous EM is positioned between the prison sentence and the work penalty, which suggests that it is regarded as a more punitive sentence than the work penalty. However, work penalties can be imposed for offenses punishable with a prison sentence of up to 5 years, while EM can replace only prison sentences up to 1 year.

As the autonomous EM was implemented only on May 1, 2016,[8] its success with the judiciary is still unclear. At first sight, EM could be regarded by judges as an interesting, more credible alternative to prison sentences up to 1 year that now are not implemented by the Prison Service or transformed into EM because of prison overcrowding. From this perspective, EM as a sentencing option restores the judges' autonomy and provides the possibility of punishing offenders who avoid prison today anyway. Minister of Justice Koen Geens has proposed abolition of prison sentences up to 1 year altogether and replacing them with community penalties such as the work penalty, EM, and probation (Geens 2015). This is courageous and bold (Scheirs et al. 2015). Whether his bill will pass the Parliament remains to be seen.

---

[8] Chambre des Représentants de Belgique, *Projet de loi modifiant le droit pénal et la procédure pénale et portant des dispositions diverses en matière de justice*, Chambre 3e Session de la 54e Législature, Doc 54 1418/001, http://www.dekamer.be/FLWB/PDF/54/1418/54K1418001.pdf.

5. *Probation.* The introduction of probation in 1964 fits the growing interest in rehabilitative measures in the 1960s. According to the Act of 29 June 1964, probation conditions can be imposed only in combination with a suspended sentence up to 5 years or with a suspended conviction. Conditions can consist of obligations (e.g., to follow treatment, attend specific training, be available for the justice assistant, look for a job, report any change of domicile) or of prohibitions (e.g., to visit pubs, drink alcohol, or take drugs; geographical bans). A follow-up period of 1 up to 5 years can be imposed. Probation officers, renamed "justice assistants" since 1999, are responsible for social guidance and follow-up; they have to report to the Probation Commission, which is presided over by a magistrate.

Unlike the work penalty, probation had a hesitant start and, 50 years later, is still imposed in a modest way. Purely rehabilitative measures do not fit easily with the neoclassical thinking of Belgian sentencing judges. In 2014, only 6,873 new mandates were issued, compared to 10,457 work penalties (FOD Justitie/Departement Welzijn [Houses of Justice] 2015, p. 69). The introduction of community service as a condition of probation fostered its use up to 2002, when its abolition reduced the use of probation. This shows that judges used community service as a probation condition and valued its added retributive value.

With the Act of 10 April 2014, probation was also introduced as an independent main penalty, for up to 2 years. Probation as a condition of a suspended sentence or suspended conviction, introduced in 1964, was not abolished. Both forms of probation will coexist. This has been an important focus of criticism since they have different philosophies. The recent act articulates the need for "judicial guidance" while the Act of 29 June 1964 refers to "social support." That terminology illustrates that probation as an autonomous penalty has a more punitive connotation (Decaigny 2014). Furthermore, judicial requests for social reports are not provided for.

However, while determination of the duration of the probation order, between 6 months and 2 years, is left to the judge, he or she is allowed to give only indications on the content of the probation penalty. The Probation Commission will eventually decide the content of the penalty, on the basis of a report by the justice assistant and taking into account the judge's indications. A similar logic exists for the independent work penalty; the judge imposes the number of hours, but the content of the work is determined during sentence implementation.

These developments could be interpreted as illustrations of a neore-habilitationist approach, that is, rehabilitation within desert limits (Morris 1992). Decaigny (2014) points out though that the role of the sentencing judge has been eroded and that the obligation to inform the defendant about the implications of the probation penalty and to require consent is paradoxical: how can the judge inform the defendant about a sentence of which the details will be determined by another actor, later, and how and to what can a defendant consent?

As with the work penalty and EM as independent penalties, there are no restrictions concerning criminal record, which communicates the Parliament's desire to encourage the use of these penalties and meets the demands of judges to be able to individualize sentences. The minister of justice proposes enlarging the application of probation measures within a suspended sentence or suspended conviction by expanding the allowed criminal record from 12 months' to 3 years' imprisonment (Geens 2015).

6. *Overall.* The variety and scope of noncustodial sanctions have been extended greatly in recent years. The changes were not products of a comprehensive reform but happened piecemeal. Proposals by the Subcommittee on Sentencing of the Holsters Commission in 2003 to undertake a comprehensive reform of the sentencing framework were not initially followed up (Aertsen et al. 2004). While many ideas eventually were represented in legislation, the absence of a comprehensive approach has led to inconsistencies in the sentencing framework and conflicts with established practices. The Justice Plan of the current minister of justice (Geens 2015) and proposed legislation do aim to harmonize sentencing policies concerning freestanding community penalties.

III. Discussion

Here we discuss some aspects of Belgian sentencing practice, with particular reference to comparative perspectives. We focus on concerns about consistency in Belgian sentencing, the limited role of presentence reports, the effects on sentencing policy and practice of the fragmented implementation of prison sentences, and how Belgian bifurcation policy and practice fit into debates about increased punitiveness.

A. Consistency

Disparities and the need for consistency are major issues in sentencing research. Unlike judges in some Anglo-Saxon and American legal systems, Belgian judges have no guidelines or sentencing starting points to assist them in decision making. However, as described in Section I, the Penal Code sets out a decision-making framework and a legal hierarchy of sentencing options. Within these margins, Belgian judges are relatively free to determine sentences.

A need for greater consistency has only occasionally been a topic in judicial and political debates and has not resulted in reform attempts. Belgian sentencing judges are apprehensive about the idea of sentencing guidelines. In a 2006–7 survey, 75 percent of sentencing judges opposed guidelines, which were seen as corroding judicial independence. Subsequent interviews with judges confirmed those results. Guidelines were felt to interfere with judges' capacity to individualize sentences and to be inconsistent with the nature and philosophy of the Belgian judicial system. Disparity was regarded as an intrinsic aspect of individualized decision making.

However, the judges were much less reluctant to consider informal consultations and guidelines for prosecutors (Beyens and Scheirs 2009, 2010). By contrast, Monsieurs, Vanderhallen, and Rozie (2011) conclude that Belgian magistrates are generally positive about achievement of increased consistency and implementation of nonbinding guidelines. Forty-nine percent of magistrates in their study believed that sentencing and prosecution guidelines should be developed. Raats (2014) also concluded that sentencing judges are open to the possibility of nonbinding guidelines. These more recent results may indicate a shift in judicial views and the traditional aspiration to have maximum autonomy in decision making. The recent introduction of new freestanding community penalties that shuffle the order in the penalty ranking may suggest recognition of a need for additional guidance.

B. Sentencing: Dossiers and Social Reports

In Belgium's moderate inquisitorial system, the dossier containing reports from the police, the public prosecutor, and sometimes the investigating judge, as well as psychiatrists or other expert reports, is of vital importance. As in other countries, judges, public prosecutors, and investigating judges can request a social report to assess the suitability of a noncustodial sanction. In Belgium, social reports are produced by justice assistants. They aim to inform the judge about the social and personal circumstances of the defendants and assess their potential suitability for a community penalty.

Internationally, social reports play a crucial role in penal decision making (e.g., Beyens and Scheirs 2010). In Belgium, however, despite an increase in the total number of reports, community sanctions are increasingly imposed without a social report. In Beyens and Scheirs's interviews with judges about the use and importance of social reports, about 50 percent indicated that they never or almost never requested one. Half of respondents in a sample of justice assistants reported that sentencing judges made insufficient use of social reports.

There are two explanations of the limited role of social reports. First, they play a less central role in decision making than in more adversarial common law systems, in which plea negotiations are common and trials uncommon, where reports are commonly the main way judges learn about defendants' personal and social circumstances. In Belgium, the judicial dossier provides an overview of all the elements of the case, sometimes including a social report. This dossier occupies a central place in the judicial process. Additionally, sentencers can communicate directly with the defendant or her or his attorney at the hearing. Many judges say they have more confidence in their own interpretation and evaluation of the information in the dossier or in interrogation of the defendant than in the social reports written by justice assistants. They often believe that enough information is available and that requesting an additional social report would slow the process and be an additional cost for an overburdened system.

Second, sentencing judges complain about the quality of the social reports, which are often viewed as the product partly of naivete and gullibility by young, inexperienced, and mostly female justice assistants. They are seen as less authoritative and credible than reports written by the police (Beyens and Scheirs 2010).

C. Relations between Sentencing and Implementation of Sentences

Sentencing judges and other penal actors are influenced by the actions and decisions of other criminal justice actors at earlier stages of the process (Hawkins 2003). Sentencing judges, however, also try to anticipate probable decisions at later stages and sometimes to develop compensatory mechanisms (Beyens and Scheirs 2009, 2010; Beyens, Snacken, and van Zyl Smit 2013).

Continuous prison overcrowding has induced ministers of justice and the prison administration to resort to a common practice of nonimplementation of sentences up to 6 months and to nearly systematic early release or conversion into electronic monitoring for offenders reciving sentences up to 3 years. This has led to discontent among the judiciary and nourished the idea that offenders can avoid their punishments. As a result, investigating judges often see pretrial custody as a "short sharp shock" to compensate for the expected nonexecution of very short sentences. They feel less inhibited about holding offenders in custody, or keeping them there, because they regard this as an advance installment of a prison sentence that will probably be imposed but is unlikely to be executed since pretrial custody is almost always taken into account by judges imposing an equal or greater term of imprisonment. This can be regarded as a compensation mechanism in the presentencing stage and leads to a growing prison pretrial population (Raes and Snacken 2004; Snacken 2007; Beyens, Snacken, and van Zyl Smit 2013).

Other compensation mechanisms can be seen when sentencing judges impose much longer sentences than they deem "deserved" in order to ensure a minimum time spent in prison. Beyens and Scheirs (2009, 2010) investigated judges' knowledge of this perceived pattern and their reactions to it. Many said they had poor knowledge of the implementation of their sentences. They criticized a lack of transparency in the implementation system and wanted more feedback and information. Several judges confused the two release systems (those for sentences up to 3 years and more than 3 years). They were not in favor of early release mechanisms in general and opposed the idea that implementation of sentences occurred at the initiative of other relatively autonomous officials. However, judges were less negative about conversion of prison sentences into EM than they were about the early release system.

We observed a great deal of judicial frustration and received many complaints about the erosion of "their" decisions and claims that it led to a loss of proportionality and punitiveness. Judges were frustrated by their loss of authority and questioned the meaningfulness of their work: "Does it make sense that we impose sentences?" was a recurring rhetorical question. Different coping strategies for dealing with their perceived loss of authority could be distinguished. Although many judges were not well acquainted with the different modalities of release, they tend to anticipate possible release decisions in their sentencing. Some admitted that they anticipate the nonexecution of prison sentences and that they lengthen sentences to be sure the convicted person will spend at least a certain period in prison. They tend to impose sentences with the symbolic length of 36 months and 1 day or 37 months, to be sure that the release decision will be made by the sentence implementation court and not by the prison administration (see also Pieters 2010). Other judges reject this form of compensation and say that they do not attempt to take into account potential later changes to their decisions.

In other words, the perceived nonimplementation of short prison sentences has created a bifurcation practice and policy in which sentencing judges impose longer prison sentences to be sure that the convicted person will serve at least what the judge considers the deserved prison sentence. Early release measures to tackle overcrowding thus became mechanisms of penal inflation as a result of adaptive sentencing (Snacken 2007; Beyens, Clémence, and Scheirs 2010; Beyens, Snacken, and van Zyl Smit 2013; Snacken et al. 2013).

These practices illustrate the interdependency and mutual influence of penal actors at different stages. Although the general mechanisms are similar in civil and common law systems, the details vary depending on the competences of the penal actors involved (Snacken et al. 2013).

D. Bifurcation or Increased Punitiveness?

Despite official rhetoric advocating a "reductionist" penal policy (Rutherford 1984), the Belgian experience can be characterized as a policy of bifurcation, with use of imprisonment as a last resort for most offenses and offenders and with wider application of noncustodial sanctions, while at the same time with use of more custodial sentences and restrictions on parole for specific offenses and offenders.

"Placement at the government's disposal," a traditional form of preventive detention for habitual offenders that had become obsolete, was revived and extended to serious physical and sexual assaults, even for first-time sex offenders (Act of 5 March 1998). The "placement" can result in additional imprisonment imposed of at least 5 and up to 20 years. Its application is compulsory or discretionary, depending on the seriousness of the new offense and the level of recidivism. In case of recidivism with a new felony or in case of death of the victim resulting from terrorism, rape, assault, torture, or abduction, preventive detention is compulsory.

Assessment of the need for its implementation after the underlying prison sentence was served used to be performed by the minister of justice: it could be implemented as a public protection measure but could also result in a conditional release. Authority was transferred to the sentence implementation courts by the Act of 26 April 2007, which reduced the maximum term to 15 years. Since the Act of 17 March 2013, the decision to release such a prisoner can be made only by consensus of all five members of the "extended" implementation court. For these cases, the sentence implementation court is composed of five members, as two judges from the correctional court are added to the president and the two assessors. Between 2003 and 2008, the number of convictions containing an additional disposal remained constant (between 21 and 36 offenders). It is unclear whether its use has increased since the transfer of authority to the sentence implementation courts. Similarly, we described above the enlarged use of custodial sentences for foreign prisoners without a legal residence.

While judges welcome the enlarged possibilities for use of noncustodial sanctions and measures, they generally continue to view these as favors or warnings to offenders, which should not fundamentally replace imprisonment as the standard reaction to crime (Snacken 2007; Beyens, Snacken, and van Zyl Smit 2013). Judicial culture in Belgium has remained fairly neoclassical and never experienced the "rise and fall of rehabilitation" described by Garland (2001). Its emphasis on individual responsibility, retribution, and deterrence in relation to "normal adult offenders" results in favoring fines, conditional or unconditional imprisonment, and work penalties (Beyens 2000; Snacken 2007). Protection of the public and incapacitation are seen as important aims when sentencing serious offenses or "dangerous" offenders (Beyens 2000). "Dangerous" offenders are linked to violent and sexual offenses and to violent and unpredictable forms of organized crime. These offenders are seen as antisocial and hyperrational (Snacken et al. 2013; Scheirs 2014).

Noncustodial sanctions are still seen by judges as a favor for offenders who deserve a second chance. Probation measures (as implemented in 1964), for instance, are considered only for offenders with an "intervenable need" (Maurutto and Hannah-Moffat 2006) or for redeemable or "troubled" offenders (Gelsthorpe and Loucks 1997). When the offender is perceived as incorrigible or untreatable (the so-called "troublesome" offenders; Gelsthorpe and Loucks 1997), he or she will most probably be sentenced to imprisonment or a work penalty. The latter is regarded as more credible than short prison sentences that are not executed. Likewise, EM has become a more purely retributive form of sentence implementation focusing on control of the offender, with no or minor emphasis on rehabilitation (Beyens and Roosen 2013). With the introduction of EM as a freestanding sentence, this trend will likely continue. Independent community sentences, however, have a judicial rehabilitative aspect, as they do not appear on the criminal record of the offender, which adds to the reintegrative goal. Nonetheless, the sentencing judge will still be able to take these previous penalties into account while making new decisions.

Despite efforts to reduce reliance on deprivation of liberty, this analysis illustrates that both penal legislation and penal practice remain ambivalent.

IV. Conclusion

Sentencing policies and practices are social practices. Sentencing judges base decisions on case files, which have already been constructed by other criminal justice professionals earlier in the criminal justice process (Hawkins 2003; Hutton 2006). Sentencing decisions reflect broader institutional dynamics of contemporary penality. Situating sentencing practices within the broader Belgian penal context shows that sentencing has been structurally transformed by developments at both ends of its penal field: the increasing diversionary and sentencing powers of the public prosecutor at the forefront and the increasingly fragmented implementation and conversion of prison sentences into community sanctions at the back end. The first development leads to decreasing procedural safeguards for offenders. The loss of the punitive bite of short prison sentences through their non- or part execution has led to perceptions of impunity and a loss of credibility of the criminal justice system. In that sense, the recent introduction of new independent community penalties can be seen as reinforcements of sentencing judges' position and authority but covering a downsized field.

It remains to be seen to what extent these new sentencing options and upcoming reforms will alter the traditionally bifurcated Belgian sentencing policy and practices. The noncustodial measures will not entirely replace short prison sentences at the lower end, while long prison sentences and enlarged "preventive detention" for "dangerous" offenders may lead to increased punitiveness at the upper end. We do not expect them fundamentally to alter the mainly neoclassical sentencing culture, illustrated by the continued success of traditional fines, suspended sentences without probation measures (conditional imprisonment), and the freestanding work penalty. Rehabilitation retains an ambivalent position within the aims of sentencing, reinforced through the introduction of an independent probation sanction and marginalized in the independent work penalty, electronic monitoring, and lack of social reports.

Despite the enlarged scope of noncustodial sentences, we also observe more punitive elements in Belgian sentencing policies and practices. This bifurcation results in an overall increased level of punitiveness, including imprisonment and supervision and control in the community, resulting in a net increase in judicial actions that lead to more people under judicial control.

REFERENCES

Aebi, Marcelo, and Natalia Delgrande. 2014. *SPACE I, Council of Europe Annual Penal Statistics*. Strasbourg: Council of Europe.
Aertsen, Ivo, Kristel Beyens, Sabine Devalck, and Freddy Pieters. 2004. *De Commissie Holsters Buitenspel?* Brussels: Politeia.
Belgisch Instituut voor de Verkeersveiligheid (Belgian Road Safety Institute). 2013. *Jaarverslag Annual Report*. http://jaarverslag.bivv.be/centrum-voor-rijgeschiktheid /driver-improvement/.
Beyens, Kristel. 2000. *Straffen als Sociale Praktijk: Een Penologisch Onderzoek naar Straftoemeting*. Brussels: VUBPRESS.
———. 2010. "From 'Community Service' to 'Autonomous Work Penalty' in Belgium: What's in a Name?" *European Journal of Probation* 2(1):4–21.
———. 2016. "The New Generation of Community Penalties in Belgium: More Is Less ...." In *Community Punishment: European Perspectives*, edited by Gwen Robinson and Fergus McNeill. London: Routledge.
Beyens, Kristel, Ralf Bas, and Dan Kaminski. 2007. "Elektronisch Toezicht in België: Een Schijnbaar Penitentiair Ontstoppingsmiddel." *Panopticon, Tijdschrift voor Strafrecht: Criminologie en Forensisch Welzijnswerk* 28(3):21–40.
Beyens, Kristel, Françoise Clémence, and Veerle Scheirs. 2010. "Les juges belges face à 1 exécution des peines. " *Déviance et Société* 32:401–24.
Beyens, Kristel, and Dan Kaminski. 2013. "Is the Sky the Limit? Eagerness for Electronic Monitoring in Belgium." In *Electronically Monitored Punishment: International and Critical Perspectives*, edited by Mike Nellis, Kristel Beyens, and Dan Kaminski. London: Routledge.
Beyens, Kristel, and Marijke Roosen. 2013. "Electronic Monitoring in Belgium: A Penological Analysis of Current and Future Orientations." *European Journal of Probation* 5(3):56–70.
Beyens, Kristel, and Veerle Scheirs. 2009. "Geruchten, Frustraties en Verdeeldheid: De Belgische Strafrechter Over de Strafuitvoering." *Proces, Tijdschrift voor Berechting, en Reclassering* 88(2):76–93.
———. 2010. "Encounters of a Different Kind: Social Enquiry and Sentencing in Belgium." *Punishment and Society* 12(3):309–28.

Beyens, Kristel, Sonja Snacken, and Dirk van Zyl Smit. 2013. "Truth in the Implementation of Sentencing: Belgium and Elsewhere." In *European Penology?* edited by Tom Daems, Dirk van Zyl Smit, and Sonja Snacken. Oxford: Hart.

Bottoms, Anthony, Sue Rex, and Gwen Robinson. 2004. *Alternatives to Prison: Options for an Insecure Society.* Cullompton, UK: Willan.

Daems, Tom, Eric Maes, and Luc Robert. 2013. "Crime, Criminal Justice, and Criminology in Belgium." *European Journal of Criminology* 10(2):237–54.

Decaigny, Tom. 2014. "Nieuwe Correctional Hoofdstraffen: De Straf Onder Elektronisch Toezicht en de Autonome Probatiestraf." *Tijdschrift voor Strafrecht* 15(4):211–25.

De Hert, Paul, and P. Ölçer. 2004. "De Methodologische Armoede van het Debat over de Onderzoeksrechter of Rechter-commissaris: Pleidooi voor de Onderzoeksrechter." *Orde van de Dag* 28:53–73.

de Keijser, Jan W., and Peter van Koppen. 2004. "Compensatoir Straffen: Over de Relatie Tussen Bewijs, Overtuiging en Straf." In *Het Maatschappelijke Oordeel van de Rechter: De Wisselwerking Tussen Rechter en Samenleving*, edited by Jan W. de Keijser and Henk Elffers. Den Haag: Boom.

De Ridder, Steven, and Kristel Beyens. 2014. "Illegalen in de Gevangenis: Een Eerste Analyse op basis van de Gevangenispopulatie in België op Basis van de Verblijfstatus." In *Criminografische Ontwikkelingen III: Van Survey tot Penitentiaire Statistiek*, edited by Lieven Pauwels et al. Antwerp/Apeldoorn: Maklu.

De Ridder, Steven, Kristel Beyens, and Sonja Snacken. 2012. "Does Reintegration Need Rehab? Early Release Procedures for Prisoners without a Legal Permit of Residence in Belgium." *European Journal of Probation* 3(4):21–36.

Devresse, Marie Sophie, Heidi Luypaert, Dan Kaminski, and Kristel Beyens. 2006. *Onderzoek Betreffende de Evaluatie van de Reglementering, van de Besluitvorming en van het Verloop van het Elektronisch Toezicht.* Brussels: UCL, VUB, FOD Justitie.

FOD Justitie (Prison Service). 2011. *Activiteitenverslag Directoraat-generaal Penitentiaire Inrichtingen DG EPI Annual Report.* Brussels: Federale Overheidsdienst Justitie.

———. 2012. *Activiteitenverslag Directoraat-generaal Penitentiaire Inrichtingen DG EPI Annual Report.* Brussels: Federale Overheidsdienst Justitie.

———. 2014. *Activiteitenverslag Directoraat-generaal Penitentiaire Inrichtingen DG EPI Annual Report.* Brussels: Federale Overheidsdienst Justitie.

FOD Justitie/Departement Welzijn. 2015. *Jaarverslag 2014 Justitiehuizen Activity Report 2014 of the Houses of Justice.* Brussels: FOD Justitie/Departement Welzijn.

Garland, David. 2001. *The Culture of Control: Crime and Social Order in Contemporary Society.* Oxford: Oxford University Press.

Geens, Koen. 2015. *Het Justitieplan, een Efficiëntere Justitie voor meer Rechtvaardigheid.* Brussels: FOD Justitie.

Gelsthorpe, Loraine, and Nancy Loucks. 1997. "Magistrates' Explanations of Sentencing Decisions." In *Understanding the Sentencing of Women*, edited by Carol Hedderman and Loraine Gelsthorpe. London: Home Office.

Hawkins, Keith. 2003. "Order, Rationality, and Silence: Some Reflections on Criminal Justice Decision-Making." In *Exercising Discretion: Decision-Making in the Criminal Justice System and Beyond*, edited by Loraine Gelsthorpe and Nicola Padfield. Cullompton, UK: Willan.

Hutton, Neil. 1995. "Sentencing, Rationality, and Computer Technology." *Journal of Law and Society* 22(4):549–70.

———. 2002. "Reflections." In *Sentencing and Society: International Perspectives*, edited by Cyrus Tata and Neil Hutton. Aldershot, UK: Ashgate.

———. 2006. "Sentencing as a Social Practice." In *Perspectives on Punishment: The Contours of Control*, edited by Sarah Armstrong and Lesley McAra. Oxford: Oxford University Press.

———. 2013. "From Intuition to Database: Translating Justice." *Theoretical Criminology* 17(1):109–28.

Kaminski, Dan, Sonja Snacken, and Michel van de Kerchove. 2007. "Mutation dans les champ des peines et de leur execution." *Déviance et Société* 31(4):487–504.

Latour, Bruno. 2005. *Reassembling the Social: An Introduction to Actor Network Theory*. Oxford: Oxford University Press.

Lefevre, J. 2009. *Rechters en Werkstraf: Een Kwalitatief Onderzoek*. Brussels: Vrije Universiteit.

Maes, Eric. 2010. "Evoluties in Punitiviteit: Lessen uit de Justitiële Statistieken." In *Hoe Punitief is België?* edited by Ivo Aertsen, Kristel Beyens, Tom Daems, and Eric Maes. Ghent: Maklu.

Maes, Eric, Benjamin Mine, Caroline De Man, and Rosamunde Van Brakel. 2012. "Thinking about Electronic Monitoring in the Context of Pre-trial Detention in Belgium: A Solution to Prison Overcrowding?" *European Journal of Probation* 4(2):3–22.

Maes Eric, and Carrol Tange. 2014. "Langgestrafte Veroordeelden in de SURB-wachtkamer voor Voorwaardelijke Invrijheidstelling: En Attendant Godot?" In *Exit Gevangenis? De werking van de Strafuitvoeringsrechtbanken en de wet op de Externe Rechtspositie van Veroordeelden tot een Vrijheidsstraf*, edited by Kristel Beyens, Tom Daems, and Eric Maes. Antwerp: Maklu.

Maurutto, Paula, and Kelly Hannah-Moffat. 2006. "Assembling Risk and the Restructuring of Penal Control." *British Journal of Criminology* 46(3):438–54.

Monsieurs, Annemie, Miet Vanderhallen, and Joëlle Rozie. 2011. "Towards Greater Consistence in Sentencing: Findings from a Survey of Belgian Magistrates." *European Journal of Criminology* 8(1):6–16.

Morris, Norval. 1992. "Desert as a Limiting Principle." In *Principled Sentencing*, edited by Andrew von Hirsch and Andrew Ashworth. Boston: Northeastern University Press.

Morris, Norval, and Michael Tonry. 1990. *Between Prison and Probation: Intermediate Punishments in a Rational Sentencing System*. New York: Oxford University Press.

Parmentier, S., C. Fijnaut, and D. Van Daele. 2000. "From Sisyphus to Octopus: Towards a Modern Public Prosecutor's Office in Belgium." *European Journal of Crime, Criminal Law, and Criminal Justice* 3:159–61.

Pieters, F. 2010. "Maar wat als en Mogelijkerwijze." In *Hoe Punitief is België?* edited by Ivo Aertsen, Kristel Beyens, Tom Daems, and Eric Maes. Ghent: Maklu.

Raats, Sanne. 2013. "De Beïnvloedbare Strafrechter: Een Empirisch Onderzoek naar het Ankereffect van de Strafeis van het Openbaar Ministerie." *Rechtskundig Weekblad* 31:1202–10.

———. 2014. "De Straf Gemeten en Gepast: Op weg naar Consistentie in de Straftoemeting." PhD dissertation, Department of Law, Universiteit Antwerpen.

Raes, An. 2006. "Naar een Communicatieve en Participatieve Justitie?" PhD dissertation, Department of Criminology, Vrije Universiteit Brussel.

Raes, An, and Sonja Snacken. 2004. "The Application of Remand Custody and Its Alternatives in Belgium." *Howard Journal of Criminal Justice* 43(5):506–17.

Rekenhof (Court of Audit). 2007. *Uitvoering van de Penale Boeten.* Brussels: Rekenhof.

———. 2011. *Maatregelen tegen de Overbevolking in de Gevangenissen.* Brussels: Rekenhof.

———. 2014. *Uitvoering van de Penale Boeten Opvolgingsaudit.* Brussels: Rekenhof.

Rutherford, Andrew. 1984. *Prisons and the Process of Justice: The Reductionist Challenge.* London: Heinemann.

Scheirs, Veerle. 2014. *De Strafuitvoeringsrechtbank aan het Werk.* Antwerp: Maklu.

Scheirs, Veerle, Maaike Beckman, Kristel Beyens, Steven De Ridder, Philippe Kennes, Marijke Roosen, and An-Sofie Van Houche. 2015. "De Atleet in Koen Geens: Enkele Penologische Reflecties bij zijn Justitieplan." *Panopticon* 36(4): 361–74.

Scheirs, Veerle, Kristel Beyens, and Sonja Snacken. 2015. "Who Is in Charge? Conditional Release in Belgium as a Complex Bifurcation Practice." In *Offender Release and Supervision: The Role of Courts and the Use of Discretion*, edited by Martine Herzog-Evans. Nijmegen, Neth.: Wolf Legal.

Schuyt, Pauline. 2007. "Bij de Volgende Verdachte Rechtsaf: Een Tom Tom voor de Strafoplegging?" In *Macht en Verantwoordelijkheid: Essays voor Kees Schuyt*, edited by Jan Willem Duyvendak, Godfried Engbersen, Marigo Teeuwen, and Imrat Verhoeven. Amsterdam: Amsterdam University Press.

Snacken, Sonja. 1986. *De Korte Gevangenisstraf: Een Onderzoek naar Toepassing en Effectiviteit.* Vol. 13. Antwerp: Kluwer Rechtswetenschappen.

———. 2007. "Belgium." In *Foreigners in European Prisons*, vol. 1, edited by A. M. van Kalmthout, F. B. A. M. Hofstee-van der Meulen, and F. Dünkel. Nijmegen, Neth.: Wolf Legal.

Snacken, Sonja, Aline Bauwens, Dirk van Zyl Smit, Hanne Tournel, and Rudy Machiels. 2013. "Prisons and Punishment in Europe." In *The Routledge Handbook of European Criminology*, edited by Sophie Body-Gendrot, Mike Hough, Klara Kerezsi, René Lévy, and Sonja Snacken. London: Routledge.

Snacken, Sonja, Kristel Beyens, and M. A. Beernaert. 2010. "Belgium." In *Release from Prison: European Policies and Practice*, edited by Nicola Padfield, Dirk van Zyl Smit, and Frieder Dünkel. Cullumpton, UK: Willan.

Snacken, Sonja, An Raes, Samuel Deltenre, Charlotte Vanneste, and Paul Verhaeghe. 1999. *Kwalitatief Onderzoek naar de Toepassing van de Voorlopige*

Hechtenis en de Vrijheid Onder Voorwaarden. Brussels: Vrije Universiteit Brussel en Nationaal Instituut voor Criminalistiek en Criminologie.

Snacken, Sonja, Dirk van Zyl Smit, and Kristel Beyens. 2013. "Sentencing." In *The Routledge Handbook of European Criminology*, edited by Sophie Body-Gendrot, Mike Hough, Klara Kerezsi, René Lévy, and Sonja Snacken. London: Routledge.

Tak, P. J. P. 1993. *Criminal Justice Systems in Europe: The Netherlands*. Deventer, Neth.: Springer.

Tata, Cyrus. 2007. "Sentencing as Craftwork and the Binary Epistemologies of the Discretionary Decision Process." *Social and Legal Studies* 16(3):425–47.

Vander Beken, Tom. 2013. "Van Vette vis tot Dieetpil: Vijftien jaar Elektronisch Toezicht in België." In *De machines van Justitie*, edited by Tom Daems, Tom Vander Beken, and Delphine Vanhaelemeesch. Ghent: Maklu.

Van Garsse, L. 2010. "Victim-Offender Mediation in a Maximalist Perspective." Paper presented at the Probation Works Conference, Malaga, Spain, May.

Vanhaelemeesch, Delphine. 2013. "Tussen Gestrafte en Bestraffer: De Ervaringen van Huisgenoten van Personen met Elektronisch Toezicht." In *De Machines van Justitie: Vijftien jaar Elektronisch Toezicht in België*, edited by Tom Daems, Tom Vander Beken, and Delphine Vanhaelemeesch. Antwerp: Maklu.

Van Kalmthout, A. M. 2006. "De Werkstraf in Vergelijkend Perspectief." *Panopticon, Tijdschrift voor Strafrecht, Criminologie, en Forensisch Welzijnswerk* 27(4):19–33.

Vanneste, Charlotte, Franky Goossens, Eric Maes, and S. Deltenre. 2005. *Onderzoek met Betrekking tot het Invoeren van Elektronisch Toezicht als Autonome Straf*. Brussels: Nationaal Instituut voor Criminalistiek en Criminologie.

Van Roeyen, Sofie, and Tom Vander Beken. 2014. "Een wet om aan te Houden: Het Beslissingsproces van Onderzoeksrechters in het kader van de Voorlopige Hechtenis." *Panopticon* 35(6):502–19.

van Zyl Smit, Dirk, Sonja Snacken, and David Hayes. 2015. "One Cannot Legislate Kindness: Ambiguities in European Legal Instruments on Non-custodial Sanctions." *Punishment and Society* 17(1):3–26.

Verbist, D. 2013. *De Visies van Rechters op de Autonome Werkstraf: Een Emprisich Onderzoek*. Brussels: Vrije Universiteit.

VRT 2014. *De Foto van Vlaanderen*. Resultaten van een Grootschalig Media-onderzoek. http://deredactie.be/cm/vrtnieuws/binnenland/2.32738?eid=1.1916375.

Julian V. Roberts and Andrew Ashworth

The Evolution of Sentencing Policy and Practice in England and Wales, 2003–2015

ABSTRACT

Sentencing in England and Wales has evolved in a direction apart from other common law countries. Although sentencing problems found in many Western nations are present, legislative and judicial responses have been very different. The use of custody rose steeply in the 1990s and has remained stable around that level in recent years. Crimes of violence and sexual aggression have, however, attracted increasingly longer sentences. The other principal changes are a steep increase in indeterminate sentence offenders, now accounting for some 19 percent of the prison population, and a striking rise in the volume of suspended sentences that has reduced the use of community sentences rather than terms of imprisonment. Net widening has therefore occurred. The principal distinction between England and most other jurisdictions is that statutorily binding guidelines now exist for both magistrates' and higher courts. Unlike most US guidelines that assign offenses to levels of seriousness within a single sentencing grid, the English guidelines are offense specific. The Sentencing Council has also issued "generic" guidelines applying to all categories of offending. The guidelines have been evolving for over a decade now and cover most common offenses. Growing,

Electronically published June 20, 2016

Julian V. Roberts is professor of criminology, University of Oxford. Andrew Ashworth is Vinerian Professor of English Law Emeritus, University of Oxford, and adjunct professor of law, University of Tasmania. The authors thank Keir Irwin Rogers for assistance in collecting statistics and the editor for very helpful comments on an earlier draft. Views expressed are solely those of the authors.

307

but still limited, research suggests modest positive effects on consistency and proportionality in sentencing.

England may reasonably be regarded as the home of sentencing scholarship and research. The first sentencing text was published in the nineteenth century by an English magistrate (Cox 1877). Approximately a century later, the first influential modern sentencing texts appeared (Thomas 1970; Cross 1971). With respect to empirical research on sentencing, over a century ago the statistician Francis Galton published a remarkably prescient article in the journal *Nature*. Galton drew attention, for the first time, to the fact that certain custodial sentence lengths were used by judges very frequently, while others were seldom or never imposed. Galton argued that the natural human preference for particular numbers "interferes with the orderly distribution of punishment in conformity with penal deserts" (1895, p. 175). Galton's insight is remarkable because aside from discussion of the issue in the philosophical literature, no publication had clearly articulated the principle of desert-based, proportional sentencing, the first clear statement of penal desert being the seminal volume *Doing Justice* almost a century later (von Hirsch 1976).

During the nineteenth century, numerous writers decried the lack of consistency and proportionality in sentencing (for a comprehensive discussion, see Radzinowicz and Hood [1979]). Thus one author wrote that "the mode of fixing the duration of penal restraints is from beginning to end little else than guessing. And how ill this system of guessing works we have abundant proofs. . . . Daily do there occur cases of extremely trifling transgressions visited with imprisonment of considerable length; and daily do there occur cases in which the penalty imposed is so inadequate that the offender, time after time commits new offenses" (Spencer 1860, p. 65). Crackenthorpe (1900, p. 194) noted that sentencing "discrepancies were still more startling when we turn from first sentences to those that follow after previous convictions. Some judges ignore such convictions altogether, others treat them as a ground for severely augmenting the subsequent sentence."

This concern over sentencing disparities led to calls for a more systematic approach to determining sentence. In fact, the earliest proposals for a sentencing commission, sentencing principles, and guidelines also emerged in England. A key development was the 1901 "Memorandum on Normal Punishments" prepared by Lord Alverstone on behalf of the judges of the King's Bench Division (see Radzinowicz and Hood 1979). This memorandum contained offense ranges or "normal sentences" for many common offenses.[1] For example, for cases of indecent assault, the scheme proposed imprisonment for a period of between 1 and 12 months. Attempted murder in which life was endangered carried a range of penal servitude for a period of between 7 and 12 years (Report of the Advisory Council on the Penal System 1978, app. E).

Around the same time, a clear prototype guidelines system foreshadowing the current scheme was published in an article entitled "Can Sentences Be Standardised?" (Crackenthorpe 1900). Crackenthorpe proposed a sentencing table and guidelines system that would prescribe sentences for common crimes, based on judicial practice, and containing "starting points from which the judge would make his reckoning" (p. 114). The system would not involve "laying down hard-and-fast rules, for . . . a large discretion would still be left to the judge who has to try the case" (p. 114). These specific proposals ultimately foundered, but approximately a century later, a system along these lines was finally implemented.

More recently, sentencing in England and Wales has evolved in a direction apart from almost all other common law countries. Although the problems of sentencing found in many Western nations—penal populism, a high rate of incarceration, and widespread public perceptions of leniency accompanied by criticism of the courts—are also present in England, the legislative and judicial responses have been different.[2] The principal distinction between England and most other jurisdictions is that statutorily binding guidelines now exist for both magistrates and

---

[1] Ironically, in light of the volume of professional and public commentary on disparity, this memorandum begins with a defensive claim that "there is nothing in the sentences of Judges of the High Court of Justice which are recorded in the criminal statistics . . . to indicate the existence of any established difference of principle or of general practice in the sentences of Judges" (see Advisory Council on the Penal System 1978, p. 191).

[2] For the sake of brevity hereafter we usually use simply "England" to represent these two components of the United Kingdom. With the exception of the definitive sentencing guidelines and the Sentencing Council, most of the other sentencing provisions are also found in Scotland and Northern Ireland. A Scottish Sentencing Council was created in 2015, and it has a duty to prepare sentencing guidelines for the consideration of the High Court of Justiciary, Scotland's supreme criminal court, which may approve them in whole or in part, and with or without modifications (see https://www.scottishsentencingcouncil .org.uk). Sentencing guidelines of an advisory nature exist for Northern Ireland and may be found on the website of the Judicial Studies Board for Northern Ireland (see http:// www.jsbni.com/Publications/sentencing-guides-magistrates-court/Pages/default.aspx).

higher courts.[3] For this reason we pay particular attention to this innovation.

We explore developments in English sentencing over the period 2003–15. Our discussion begins with the passage of the Criminal Justice Act 2003, the most important sentencing statute of recent years.[4] Our point of departure is an earlier review essay by Ashworth (2001). We address the following key questions:

- How has the relative use of different sanctions changed over the period, particularly the use of custody as a sanction?
- To what extent have statutory and nonstatutory influences contributed to these changes in sentencing practice?
- Has sentencing become more consistent, principled, parsimonious, or transparent?
- Is the use of imprisonment likely to increase or decline in the near future?

Section I of this essay provides background information on sentencing in England and Wales, noting the key role played by lay magistrates in the lower courts. We then summarize the principal empirical trends regarding prison admissions and sanctions imposed in the Crown Court and magistrates' courts over the past decade (2003–14). We note the relatively stable use of different punishments (often referred to here as "disposals") but also the dramatic increase in the use of the suspended sentence order since it was amended in 2005. Section II summarizes critical statutory and policy developments since the Criminal Justice Act 2003 and notes several reports that have called for a reduction in the use of custody as a sanction. Section III discusses the statutory authority that issues sentencing guidelines: the Sentencing Council for England

---

[3] South Korea now has a guideline scheme (http://www.scourt.go.kr/sc/engsc/index.jsp; Park 2010), and starting point sentences have been introduced in China (Roberts and Pei 2016). Guidelines have been developed but not adopted in New Zealand (Young and King 2013) and proposed (yet not developed) as part of sentencing reform in Israel (Roberts and Gazal-Ayal 2013). Other jurisdictions such as Uganda have developed advisory, judicially based guidelines (Kamuzze 2014), but England and Wales remains the only Western jurisdiction outside the United States to have instituted a detailed system of guidelines containing specific sentence ranges.

[4] For discussion of the evolution of sentencing policies prior to this legislation, see Ashworth (2001, 2010); for general information on sentencing in England and Wales, see Roberts (2015) and Ashworth and Roberts (2016).

and Wales. We identify the principal differences between the composition, mandate, and duties of this body and analogous sentencing commissions in the United States. One important distinction is that the English council has no explicit mandate to modify its guidelines to respond to changes in the prison population. Instead, the council forecasts the impact of each new guideline on the number of prison places, and it is for another authority—the executive or the legislature—to correct any significant overcrowding in the prison population. This section of the essay also describes the nature and effects of the definitive sentencing guidelines, the first of which were issued in 2004 by a previous statutory body, the Sentencing Guidelines Council. Section IV draws some conclusions about the current state of sentencing in England and Wales.

I. Sentencing Practices in England and Wales

There are two levels of trial court in England and Wales: the Crown Court sits with judge and jury and adjudicates the more serious cases. Approximately two-thirds of Crown Court cases involve a guilty plea, and these are dealt with by judge alone—juries play no part in sentencing.[5] However, most cases are sentenced in the magistrates' courts, where the arrangements are different. While in other common law jurisdictions sentencing is conducted by professional judges sitting alone or with a jury, the magistrates' courts in England and Wales are unique in relying largely on lay adjudicators and sentencers.[6] The lay magistracy has existed for over six centuries, and there are currently approximately 26,000 sitting magistrates. They receive limited training on appointment and usually sit in benches of three, assisted by a legally qualified adviser.[7] Some

---

[5] In a small number of US jurisdictions, juries play a role in felony sentencing, but the common law norm is for sentencing by professional judges.

[6] A number of jurisdictions such as Germany and Italy use hybrid tribunals composed of professional judges and members of the public, and some countries use lay justices for certain decisions such as bail; but England is alone in using lay magistrates to both hear trials and sentence offenders.

[7] Legal advisors play a critical yet rather hidden role in shaping sentencing in the magistrates' courts. For example, they generally provide the little ongoing training offered magistrates. In addition, they may offer advice that affects the sentence imposed. Anecdotal evidence suggests that legal advisors sometimes advise that some cases in which immediate custody seems likely may receive a suspended sentence order (SSO). This may help explain the striking rise in the use of SSOs that we document in this essay. Very little research has explored their influence on sentencing patterns, and documenting their role remains a research priority.

magistrates' courts, particularly in large cities, have a professional district judge who sits alone.[8]

The maximum sentence that may be imposed in a magistrates' court is 6 months' imprisonment or a total of 12 months' imprisonment if there are two or more convictions. The importance of the magistrates' courts is signaled by the fact that in 2014, fully 93 percent of all offenders sentenced were sentenced at that level (Ministry of Justice 2015c). All cases begin in a magistrates' court, which, if it believes that its own sentencing powers are inadequate, may decline jurisdiction and commit the case to the Crown Court for sentencing.[9] Appeals against sentences in the magistrates' courts are heard in the Crown Court; appeals from the Crown Court are heard by the Court of Appeal (Criminal Division).

Another unique characteristic of English sentencing is the more modest role of the prosecutor. Although specific and robust sentencing submissions from both parties are the norm in common law countries, English prosecutors generally limit themselves to highlighting the important aggravating circumstances and providing information that may be useful to the court at sentencing including any relevant guidelines or guideline cases.[10] This more circumscribed prosecutorial role is slowly changing. Prosecutors now address the guidelines category they believe is appropriate to the case at bar, although they stop short of routinely recommending specific sentences, which is common practice in North American jurisdictions.

A. Recent Prison Population and Sentencing Trends

The picture of sentencing trends emerging from the last 10 years changes depending on the specific indicator of severity employed or

---

[8] The magistrates' court statistics do not provide a breakdown indicating the percentage of cases sentenced by the district judges rather than panels of lay magistrates, but given the number of the former, it is likely that lay magistrates are responsible for the vast majority of decisions.

[9] The divided jurisdiction has been the subject of much commentary and research. Over the years, the government has contemplated both increasing the powers of the magistrates and also reducing their jurisdiction through the greater use of district judges. One recurrent observation is that magistrates not infrequently decline jurisdiction and transfer a case to the Crown Court, only for the offender to ultimately receive a sentence well within the magistrates' sentencing powers.

[10] See the Criminal Procedure Rules, Rule 37.10(3) available at http://www.cps.gov.uk /legal/s_to_u/sentencing_-_general_principles/#a01.

the level of court.[11] Our general conclusion is that England has experienced a period of relative stability with respect to sentence severity measured by the immediate custodial rate, although this generalization is subject to several important qualifications, particularly with respect to sentence lengths and the number of indeterminate sentences. The principal trends over the past decade include the following:

- The prison population has been reasonably stable in recent years, around the level achieved after its sharp rise in the previous decade.
- The number of sentenced cases has declined significantly at both levels of court.
- The rate of cases sent to immediate custody or given a fine has been stable.
- The rate of suspended sentence orders (SSOs) has increased significantly, yet most of these orders appear to have replaced community sentences rather than custodial sentences, leading to considerable net widening and no significant reduction in the use of immediate custody.
- The rate of community orders imposed in indictable cases has declined significantly in the Crown Court.
- The average custodial sentence length has increased, particularly for violent and sexual offenses.

B. Prison Population Trends[12]

Between 1993 and 2015, the prison population almost doubled, rising from to 44,200 to 86,000 (Ministry of Justice 2015b). Over the more recent period covered in this essay (2003–15), the increase has been less steep. The principal causes of the increase over the 20-year period were harsher sentencing, including higher custody rates and longer prison sentences; tougher enforcement outcomes for community penalties and prisoners released on license; and a more serious mix of offenses

---

[11] For earlier discussion and data relating to sentencing and the prison population, see Hough, Jacobson, and Millie (2003) and Ministry of Justice (2013).

[12] The focus of this essay is on sentenced admissions to prison rather than the total prison population, including remand prisoners. For information on the remand population, see Player et al. (2010).

appearing for sentencing (Ministry of Justice 2013).[13] As of November 2015, the population count was 85,982, approximately the same as a year earlier (85,902). A further 2,111 prisoners were serving home detention curfews (Ministry of Justice 2015c).

Overall, prisons were functioning as of August 2014 at 112 percent of Certified Normal Accommodation (CNA). This masks considerable variability: a significant number of institutions are substantially over-populated. For example, in August 2014, Wandsworth prison in London housed 1,578 prisoners against a CNA of 843, an overpopulation of 167 percent (Ministry of Justice 2015c, p. 3). In fully two-thirds of prisons, the number of prisoners exceeds the CNA. Some of these prisoners are held in overcrowded conditions, with two prisoners in a cell constructed for one.

C. Sentencing Trends

Across all courts in 2014, a total of 1,215,695 cases were sentenced, a drop of 21 percent from the peak in 2004 (table 1). The decline in case-load reflects the fall in recorded crime rates over this period and to a lesser degree increased use of "out-of-court" disposals. A different pattern emerges for the two levels of court: over the decade there was a 26 per-cent decline in cases sentenced in the magistrates' courts yet a 13 percent increase in cases sentenced in the Crown Court. The volume of cases has continued to decline in the magistrates' courts and for the past 2 years has now been dropping in the Crown Court, where the number sen-tenced fell by 16 percent between 2011 and 2013.

Table 1 reveals that the proportionate use of different disposals has changed little over the last decade—at least when all cases (indictable and summary) sentenced in all courts are considered. Although the vol-ume of all disposals (except the SSO) has declined (to reflect the drop in cases sentenced), the courts are using the principal sanctions in relatively constant proportions over the years. Fines, for example, were imposed in 70 percent of cases in 2014, the same percentage as a decade earlier. The proportionate use of immediate custody was also invariable, accounting for 7 or 8 percent of all cases over the period 2003–14. The rate of com-munity orders declined (from 13 percent in 2003 to 9 percent in 2014)

---

[13] And in this order: the Ministry of Justice (2013) report ascribes fully 85 percent of the increase in the prison population over the 20-year period to changes in the rate and length of immediate custodial sentences.

TABLE 1
Volumes and Rates of Disposals, All Courts, England and Wales, 2003–14

	2003	2004	2005	2006	2007	2008	2009	2010	2011	2012	2013	2014
Immediate custody:												
Cases	107,670	106,322	101,236	96,017	95,206	99,525	100,231	101,513	106,170	98,047	92,799	91,313
Rate	7	7	7	7	7	7	7	7	8	8	8	8
Suspended sentence:												
Cases	2,717	2,855	9,666	33,509	40,688	41,151	45,157	48,118	48,153	44,642	48,628	52,979
Rate	.2	.2	1	2	3	3	3	4	4	4	4	4
Community sentence:												
Cases	191,422	201,503	204,247	190,837	196,424	190,171	195,903	189,321	175,525	149,327	123,087	112,638
Rate	13	13	14	13	14	14	14	14	13	12	11	9
Fine:												
Cases	1,033,617	1,082,690	1,025,064	961,535	941,534	890,296	946,146	893,931	856,808	823,298	792,942	853,335
Rate	69	70	69	68	67	65	67	66	65	67	68	70
Other disposals:[a]												
Cases	154,401	153,982	142,240	138,673	140,890	140,921	119,468	132,464	126,083	114,513	112,271	105,430
Rate	10	10	10	10	10	10	9	10	10	9	10	9
Total offenders sentenced	1,489,827	1,547,352	1,482,453	1,420,571	1,414,742	1,362,064	1,406,905	1,365,347	1,312,739	1,229,827	1,169,727	1,215,695

SOURCE.—Adapted from Ministry of Justice (2015a, table Q5.1); Roberts and Irwin-Rogers (2015).

[a] Includes absolute discharge, conditional discharge, and otherwise dealt with.

but much more markedly when we consider indictable cases (see below). Figure 1 graphs the use of the principal disposals for indictable cases in all courts over the period 1999–2014.[14] Figure 2 presents the use of immediate custody over the same period for both levels of court.

Variation emerges when trends in the two levels of court are compared. In the Crown Court, the proportion of sentences involving immediate custody declined from 63 percent of all indictable cases in 1999 to 56 percent in 2014 and remained stable in the magistrates' court at 4 or 5 percent over the entire decade. This pattern of penal stability must now be qualified by noting some important shifts in practice.

D. Decline of Community Orders and Increase in Suspended Sentence Orders

One theme noted in the previous review was the revival of community disposals (Ashworth 2001, pp. 67–72). Ashworth reported that community sentences accounted for 24 percent of sentences for indictable offenses in 1996, up from 14 percent a decade earlier. This trend has now reversed itself. As can be seen in table 2, the rate of community sentences for indictable offenses in all courts has declined from a peak of 37 percent in 2005 to 21 percent in 2014. The fall has been particularly striking in the Crown Court: in 2004, 30 percent of disposals in indictable cases involved a community penalty; by 2014 this had fallen to 12 percent (table 3). Where have these cases gone? The answer lies in the increased use of the suspended sentence of imprisonment.

The decade witnessed a dramatic rise in the use of the SSO, principally in the Crown Court. Although the SSO has been available to courts since 1967 (Criminal Justice Act 1967, sec. 39; see Ashworth [2015] for discussion), the disposal was reinvigorated when the Criminal Justice Act 2003 removed the restriction that this form of custody be imposed only in exceptional circumstances.[15] The anticipated consequence was an increase in the volume of SSOs, and so it has proved. Suspended sentence orders accounted for only 2 percent of Crown Court cases in 2004 but fully 27 percent in 2014 (table 3). The English experience is at odds

[14] The category of "indictable cases" includes all serious cases and excludes summary offenses. Many indictable cases for offenses such as theft and aggravated assaults are dealt with by the magistrates' courts.

[15] The SSO has since been further amended by the Legal Aid, Sentencing and Punishment of Offenders Act 2012. As a result of these amendments, sentences of imprisonment of up to 2 years may now be suspended, a reform that may increase still further the number of suspended sentences imposed.

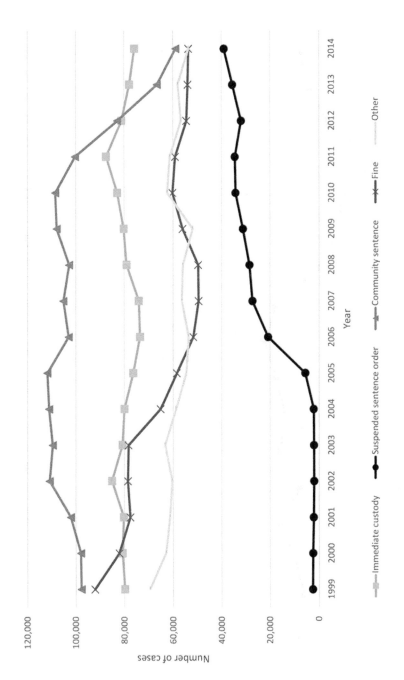

FIG. 1.—Trends in all disposals, indictable offenses, all courts, 1999–2014

Number of cases

120,000
100,000
80,000
60,000
40,000
20,000
0

1999 2000 2001 2002 2003 2004 2005 2006 2007 2008 2009 2010 2011 2012 2013 2014

Year

Immediate custody —●— Suspended sentence order —▲— Community sentence —✕— Fine — Other

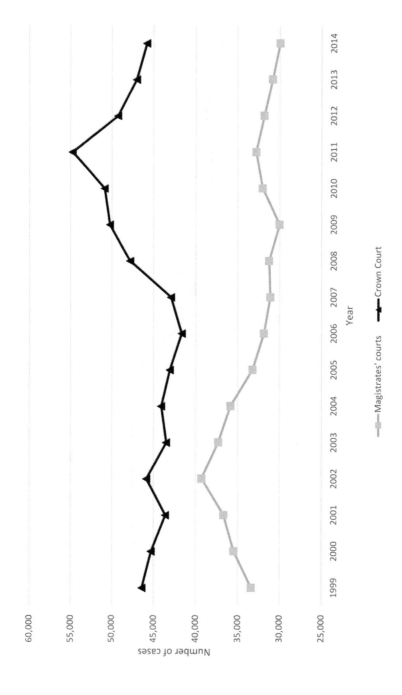

FIG. 2.—Trends in immediate custody, indictable offenses, by magistrates' courts and Crown Court, 1999–2014

TABLE 2
Volumes and Rates of All Disposals, Indictable Offenses, All Courts, 2003–14

	2003	2004	2005	2006	2007	2008	2009	2010	2011	2012	2013	2014
Immediate custody:												
Volume	80,794	79,938	76,291	73,532	74,037	79,058	80,265	82,939	87,558	81,082	77,843	75,770
Rate	24	25	25	24	24	25	25	24	26	26	27	27
Suspended sentence:												
Volume	2,055	2,143	5,610	20,799	27,254	28,455	31,131	34,176	34,422	31,883	35,429	38,928
Rate	1	1	2	7	9	9	10	10	10	10	12	14
Community sentence:												
Volume	109,549	111,013	111,724	102,971	105,142	102,782	107,924	108,495	100,286	82,815	66,487	58,879
Rate	33	35	37	34	34	33	33	31	29	27	23	21
Fine:												
Volume	77,097	63,999	57,382	50,665	48,452	48,736	55,351	59,437	58,288	53,667	53,159	53,571
Rate	23	20	19	17	16	15	17	17	17	18	18	19
Other disposals:[a]												
Volume	62,971	58,713	54,495	53,521	56,306	55,910	51,921	62,375	61,304	56,669	57,981	53,661
Rate	19	19	18	18	18	18	16	18	18	19	20	19
Total offenders	332,466	315,806	305,502	301,488	311,191	314,941	326,592	347,422	341,858	306,116	290,899	280,809

Source.—Adapted from Ministry of Justice (2015a, Crown Court Data Tool; Magistrates' Court Data Tool); Roberts and Irwin-Rogers (2015).
[a] Includes absolute discharge, conditional discharge, and otherwise dealt with.

TABLE 3
Volumes and Rates of All Disposals, Indictable Offenses, Crown Court, 1999–2014

	1999	2000	2001	2002	2003	2004	2005	2006	2007	2008	2009	2010	2011	2012	2013	2014
Immediate custody:																
Volume	46,400	45,304	43,599	45,865	43,490	44,090	43,070	41,653	42,919	47,795	50,242	50,889	54,749	49,252	47,012	45,817
Rate	63	64	63	63	60	61	60	57	56	57	57	54	57	58	58	56
Suspended sentence:																
Volume	1,971	1,877	1,605	1,488	1,542	1,539	2,536	9,922	14,777	16,883	18,835	20,782	20,572	19,039	20,335	22,095
Rate	3	3	2	2	2	2	4	14	19	20	21	22	21	22	25	27
Community sentences:																
Volume	19,658	18,519	18,378	20,496	21,914	21,575	21,140	16,085	13,532	13,949	14,645	17,267	15,322	12,996	9,972	9,408
Rate	27	26	27	28	30	30	29	22	18	17	16	18	16	15	12	12
Fine:																
Volume	2,119	1,876	1,966	1,832	2,079	1,849	1,815	1,562	1,735	1,570	1,594	1,735	1,379	1,162	1,387	1,293
Rate	3	3	3	3	3	3	3	2	2	2	2	2	1	1	2	2
Other disposals:																
Volume	3,835	3,483	3,300	3,315	3,717	3,733	3,627	3,519	3,853	3,448	3,575	4,419	3,773	2,870	2,610	2,713
Rate	5	5	5	5	5	5	5	5	5	4	4	5	4	3	3	3
Total offenders sentenced	73,983	71,059	68,848	72,996	72,742	72,786	72,188	72,741	76,816	83,645	88,891	95,092	95,795	85,319	81,316	81,345

Source.—Adapted from Ministry of Justice (2015a, Crown Court Data Tool); Roberts and Irwin-Rogers (2015).

with developments in other jurisdictions, most notably the Australian state of Victoria, where the suspended sentence has been abolished (Freiberg and Moore 2009).

In terms of numbers of cases, 2,055 offenders convicted in 2003 of an indictable offense received a suspended sentence; by 2014 this figure had risen to almost 40,000 (table 2). In terms of all sentenced cases the number rose from 2,717 in 2003 to 52,979 in 2014 (table 1).[16] Table 4 focuses on the Crown Court and demonstrates that the increased use of the SSO occurred for all categories of offending.[17]

In other jurisdictions, the creation (or expansion) of sentences comparable to the suspended sentence has usually reduced the use of immediate sentences of imprisonment.[18] This goal has not been achieved in England. Table 3 confirms this. As noted, the percentage of indictable cases in the Crown Court receiving an SSO rose from 4 percent in 2005 to 27 percent in 2014 (table 3); yet the proportionate use of immediate custody was relatively unchanged, dropping slightly from 60 percent of cases in 2005 to 56 percent in 2014. The Crown Court has experienced a steady and significant decline in the number of community orders. As seen in table 3, this disposal accounted for 29 percent of all Crown Court indictable cases in 2005; by 2014 this had declined to 12 percent.

Table 5 highlights the shift from community sentences to the SSO for violent offenses in the Crown Court. As can be seen, the proportion of custodial sentences for this category of offending was stable over the decade. The volume of community sentences imposed for crimes of violence dropped significantly, from one-third of all disposals in 2003 to less than one-tenth in 2014, while suspended sentences rose from 3 percent to 31 percent over the same period. Table 6 presents the same data for the magistrates' courts. Once again we see a dramatic increase in the use of suspended sentences—increasing from less than 1 percent of cases in 2003 to 17 percent in 2014. This was accompanied by an equally dramatic

---

[16] Although the very significant increase in the volume of SSOs has attracted little scholarly commentary or research, it has not escaped the attention of the news media or critical advocacy groups ("Almost 12,000 offenders walked free from court with suspended sentences" [Cuthbertson 2014]). Critics of the expanded use of the SSO have failed to appreciate that most of these cases would formerly have attracted a community order.

[17] Category-specific data are not yet available for 2013.

[18] For example, Lappi-Seppälä (2001) for Finland, Cid (2005) for Spain, and Roberts (2004) for Canada.

TABLE 4
Percentage of Indictable Offenses Resulting in Suspended Sentence Orders by Offense Group, Crown Court, 2003–14

	2003	2004	2005	2006	2007	2008	2009	2010	2011	2012	2013	2014	Change, 2003–14
Violence	3	2	4	18	24	26	26	27	26	26	28	31	+933%
Sexual offenses	2	2	3	6	9	8	8	8	8	8	10	11	+450%
Theft offenses	1	1	2	12	17	17	17	17	16	17	19	20	+1,900%
Robbery	1	1	1	5	8	8	8	9	9	10	10	10	+900%
Criminal damage and arson	2	2	3	12	16	16	15	15	16	15	18	18	+800%
Drug offenses	2	2	3	13	17	18	19	21	22	24	29	31	+1,450%
Possession of weapons	3	3	5	17	19	21	26	24	25	26	33	33	+1,000%
Public order offenses	2	2	3	17	27	30	27	28	27	27	29	33	+1,550%
Miscellaneous crimes against society	2	2	4	13	18	20	23	24	24	25	27	29	+1,350%
Fraud offenses	7	8	8	20	33	36	35	34	36	39	40	43	+514%
All indictable offenses	2	2	4	14	19	20	21	22	21	22	25	27	+1,250%

SOURCE.—Ministry of Justice (2014, table A5.1; 2015a, Crown Court Data Tool).

TABLE 5
Trends in Relative Use of Disposals, Violent Offenses, Crown Court, 2003–14

	2003	2004	2005	2006	2007	2008	2009	2010	2011	2012	2013	2014	Change, 2003–14
Immediate custody	56	58	58	53	52	54	54	51	55	58	58	57	+2%
Suspended sentence order	3	2	4	18	24	25	27	27	26	27	28	31	+933%
Community sentence	33	31	30	22	16	15	15	17	16	13	10	9	−73%
Fine	2	2	2	1	1	1	1	1	1	1	1	<1	−50%
Other disposal	6	7	6	6	7	5	3	4	2	1	3	2	−67%

SOURCE.—Ministry of Justice (2014, table A5.1; 2015a, Crown Court Data Tool).

TABLE 6
Trends in Relative Use of Disposals, Violent Offenses, Magistrates' Courts, 2003–14

	2003	2004	2005	2006	2007	2008	2009	2010	2011	2012	2013	2014	Change, 2003–14
Immediate custody	17	18	18	16	15	16	15	15	18	22	22	23	+35%
Suspended sentence order	<1	1	3	10	12	12	14	13	13	14	15	17	+3,300%
Community sentence	60	61	61	54	54	55	57	54	48	41	37	34	−43%
Fine	9	8	6	6	6	5	6	6	8	12	13	13	+44%
Other disposal	14	12	12	14	13	12	12	11	12	12	13	13	−7%

SOURCE.—Ministry of Justice (2014, table A5.1; 2015a, Magistrates' Court Data Tool).

fall in the use of community sentences, from 61 percent in 2003 to 34 percent in 2014, while the use of immediate custody increased (table 6).

E. Evidence of "Net Widening"

In light of the fact that an SSO has the legal status of a term of custody, it is surprising that the courts appear to be imposing it in cases that formerly attracted a community order. Numerous scholars (e.g., Ashworth and Player 2005; Wasik 2014; Ashworth 2015, pp. 318–22; Hedderman and Barnes 2015) have drawn attention to this example of "up-tariffing," which occurs when a sentence designed to replace immediate custody (because it is a form of custody) is ultimately applied to less serious cases (see Morris and Tonry 1990, pp. 156–57). Sparks (1971) and Bottoms (1981) found the same "malfunction" in the application of the suspended sentence to cases bound for a community sanction, following the introduction of the suspended sentence in the Criminal Justice Act 1967.

It is cause for concern that the SSO is being applied to cases that formerly would have attracted a noncustodial sentence.[19] In other jurisdictions when a noninstitutional sentence of custody has been introduced that does not involve immediate imprisonment, the statutory framework requires courts to first impose a sentence of immediate imprisonment and only then to decide whether the sentence may be suspended.[20] The guidance from the Sentencing Guidelines Council (2004) advocated this approach. The SGC specified a three-step methodology that courts should follow before imposing an SSO. First, a court has to find that the custodial threshold has been passed; second, it has to determine that custody is "unavoidable," and only then should it proceed to consider if the sentence may be suspended. Following this logic should ensure that all SSOs were cases for which immediate custody would otherwise have been imposed.

The statutory provision in England and Wales strongly suggests that suspending a sentence of imprisonment should take place only once a

---

[19] In one of the few empirical studies Mair, Cross, and Taylor (2008) report "persistent accounts of the misuse of the SSO on the part of magistrates" (p. 40).

[20] The suspended sentence in Spain carries this structure. The Canadian conditional sentence of imprisonment is in certain respects analogous to the SSO in that a term of institutional custody is imposed on the offender, who is then permitted to discharge the sentence in the community, usually at his residence. Failure to respect the conditions of the order normally results in a breach hearing and may ultimately lead to committal to custody (see Roberts 2004).

court has established that the custodial threshold has been passed. The empirical trends noted here suggest that courts are imposing the SSO in a way that differs markedly from what was originally envisaged. They appear to be applying the suspended sentence to the more serious offenders within the community sentence caseload. Finally, the precise impact of the net widening on admissions to custody and the size of the prison population remains unquantified because data on the rate of breach and rate of admission to custody for breach are not currently published.

F. Longer Sentences of Imprisonment

A second important shift in sentencing practices relates to custodial sentence lengths. Table 7 summarizes the average custodial sentence length (ACSL) in months for both levels of court combined, 2003–14. As can be seen, across all offenses there has been an increase in ACSL from 12.6 months at the beginning of the decade to 15.6 in the most recent year (2014), an increase of approximately one-quarter. This reflects an increase in ACSL for indictable offenses from 15.7 to 18 months and, in particular, offenses involving violence and sexual offenses. Table 8 provides ACSL data for the two levels of court and demonstrates that the increase in ACSL arises from longer sentence lengths for indictable offenses in the Crown Court; sentence lengths declined somewhat for all cases sentenced in the magistrates' courts from 3.0 in 2003 to 2.4 months in 2014 (table 8). It is worth noting that the ACSL trends underestimate the true increase in time served in custody since they do not include the

TABLE 7

Average Custodial Sentence Length (in Months), All Courts, 2003–14

	2003	2004	2005	2006	2007	2008	2009	2010	2011	2012	2013	2014
Indictable offenses	15.7	16.1	15.8	15.3	15.2	16.0	16.5	16.2	16.8	17.0	18.0	18.3
Summary offenses	3.2	3.2	3.1	3.0	3.0	2.8	2.8	2.7	2.6	2.7	2.7	2.6
All offenses	12.6	12.9	12.6	12.4	12.4	13.3	13.7	13.7	14.3	14.5	15.5	15.6

Source.—Adapted from Ministry of Justice (2015a, table Q5.2); Roberts and Irwin-Rogers (2015).

TABLE 8
Average Custodial Sentence Length (in Months), Crown Court and Magistrates' Courts, 2003–14

	2003	2004	2005	2006	2007	2008	2009	2010	2011	2012	2013	2014
						Crown Court						
Indictable	26.8	27.0	25.9	25.2	24.6	25.1	25.0	25.0	25.5	26.5	28.3	28.9
Summary	3.6	3.6	3.7	3.9	3.5	3.3	3.2	3.3	3.0	3.1	3.3	3.1
All offenses	26.3	26.5	25.5	24.7	24.0	24.5	24.3	24.3	24.7	25.9	27.6	28.1
						Magistrates' Courts						
Indictable	3.0	3.0	2.9	2.9	2.8	2.7	2.6	2.5	2.6	2.5	2.4	2.3
Summary	3.2	3.2	3.1	3.0	2.9	2.8	2.7	2.6	2.6	2.6	2.7	2.6
All offenses	3.1	3.0	3.0	3.0	2.9	2.7	2.7	2.5	2.6	2.5	2.5	2.4

SOURCE.—Adapted from Ministry of Justice (2015a, Crown Court Data Tool; Magistrates' Court Data Tool); Roberts and Irwin-Rogers (2015).

significant number of indeterminate (i.e., Indeterminate Sentences for Public Protection, discussed below) cases.

Increases in sentence lengths were particularly striking for violent and sexual offenses. Table 9 reveals a 12 percent increase in ACSL for violent offenses and an even more striking 49 percent increase for sexual offenses over the period. Further research is needed to determine why these offense categories have attracted greater than average increases. It seems, however, that courts have focused the increased punitiveness on the more serious crimes of violence. Other serious violent crimes have seen similar increases. For example, the ACSL for manslaughter rose from 64 months in 2009 to 94.4 in 2014, an increase of 45 percent, and the average minimum term imposed on offenders convicted of murder rose from 14.5 years in 2004 to 21.2 years in 2014.

These latter changes may have been triggered by the introduction of Schedule 21 of the Criminal Justice Act 2003. This schedule introduced higher starting points for minimum terms for murder and has been criticized by scholars and the judiciary alike (e.g., Jeremy 2010; Wasik 2014). However, both the Sentencing Council and the Court of Appeal have taken the view that Parliament's approach to the minimum sentences for murder indicates that "crimes which result in death should be treated more seriously and dealt with more severely than before."[21] Thus sentence levels for manslaughter, and also for attempted murder and causing grievous bodily harm with intent, have been raised to reflect this (Lord Phillips 2007).

II. Sentencing Policy Developments, 2003–15

The Criminal Justice Act 2003 reaffirmed a number of existing sentencing provisions and introduced a raft of changes. The objectives of sentencing were placed on a statutory footing for the first time, and guidance was provided regarding the use of prior convictions (see von Hirsch and Roberts 2004; Ashworth and Player 2005; Ashworth 2015). The 2003 act also established seriousness thresholds for the use of custodial sentences. Specifically, a sentencing court should impose custody only when no other sanction adequately reflects the seriousness of the crime (sec. 152 [2]). In addition, when imposing a term of custody, the court should employ the shortest period that is commensurate with

---

[21] The words of Lord Judge C. J. in *Wood* ([2010] 1 Cr App R (s) 6, at [23]).

TABLE 9

Average Custodial Sentence Length (in Months), All Violent and Sexual Offenses, Crown Court, 2003–14

	2003	2004	2005	2006	2007	2008	2009	2010	2011	2012	2013	2014	Change, 2003–14
Violent offenses	26.8	26.7	25.9	24.2	24.1	24.9	24.8	24.7	26.3	28.7	30.9	29.9	+12%
Sexual offenses	43.8	43.6	44.5	44.2	46.2	47.4	52.0	51.5	56.4	58.2	62.8	65.1	+49%
All indictable offenses	26.8	27.0	25.9	25.2	24.6	25.1	25.0	25.0	25.5	26.5	28.3	28.9	+8%

SOURCE.—Adapted from Ministry of Justice (2015*a*, Crown Court Data Tool); Roberts and Irwin-Rogers (2015).

the gravity of the offense (sec. 153 [2]). The extent to which these various statutory provisions are applied in practice remains an open question. Since 2003, a number of academics have argued that the custodial threshold is too easily crossed, too subjective, and in need of tightening (e.g., Padfield 2011).

The pace of change in sentencing legislation in England and Wales has been relentless over the last 12 years, as in the previous decade. Many of the changes have been designed to "toughen up" sentencing, and largely for political reasons, but that is by no means the whole story. Brief mention can be made here of four major policy developments or themes:

- the introduction of a new form of indeterminate sentence ("imprisonment for public protection," or IPP) that was applied overextensively and swelled the prison population unexpectedly between 2005 and 2008, before a legislative retreat in 2008 and, ultimately, the abolition of IPP in 2012;
- the reshaping of community sentences and changing attitudes to breach of those sentences;
- the reform of the legal structure for the sentencing of youths in 2008, leading to a substantial reduction in the use of formal interventions and of custody for young offenders;
- a continuing refusal of governments to engage with—or even acknowledge—the recommendations made by independent inquiries into criminal justice, particularly in relation to the use of imprisonment.

A. New Indeterminate Sentence: The IPP

In 2002 the government set out to ensure "that the public are adequately protected from those offenders whose offense do not currently attract a maximum penalty of life imprisonment but who are nevertheless assessed as dangerous" (Home Office Sentencing Review 2001, para. 5.41). The 2003 act introduced the IPP, mandatory for offenders convicted of one of 153 offenses (some with maximum sentences as low as 5 or 3 years) who were presumed dangerous if they had a previous conviction for another such offense. Several thousand offenders were placed on IPP sentences, even in cases in which the minimum term (commensurate with the seriousness of their offense) was as low as 2 years or even 1 year.

By 2008 the government recognized that indeterminate sentences were being significantly overused—creating injustice to offenders and unexpected strain on the prisons—and IPP was amended so as to make it discretionary rather than mandatory (see Jacobson and Hough 2010). The coalition government accepted that IPP was a mistaken policy, and it was abolished in 2012 and replaced by a much narrower provision.[22] However, some 4,600 offenders remain in prison on indeterminate sentences, unable to persuade the Parole Board that they are suitable for release,[23] and the European Court of Human Rights has held that their continued detention is not lawful.[24]

B. Reshaping Community Sentences

The government stated in 2002 that it wished to promote the wider use of community sentences while also making them tougher so as to increase the confidence of courts and the public. The Criminal Justice Act 2003 abolished distinct orders such as the probation order and the community service order in favor of a generic community sentence, with a range of 12 possible requirements (now increased to 15; Ashworth 2015, pp. 359–70) including unpaid work, curfew, drug treatment, and so on. Courts were empowered to impose the requirements appropriate in each case. The 2003 act also toughened the provisions regulating judicial response to breach of a community order, with courts required to impose imprisonment if the breach is "willful and persistent."

Whether these changes would have led to greater use of community sentences was never tested as such, because, as explained in Section I, the 2003 act also reintroduced the suspended sentence and courts have preferred to make extensive use of it. In 2012, it was accepted that courts need greater flexibility when dealing with breach of a community sentence, and courts now have a wider range of options in response to breach. While there are good local initiatives in community sentences, courts seem to prefer the "bite" of a suspended sentence combined with one or more requirements, and it remains difficult to persuade courts to

[22] Under the Legal Aid, Sentencing and Punishment of Offenders Act 2012, a life sentence is "automatic" for offenders convicted of a second violent or sexual offense for which the (minimum) sentence for both offenses was 10 years or more.

[23] See www.parliament.uk/briefing-papers/Sn06086.pdf, p. 7.

[24] The British government has still not met the terms of the court's critical judgment in *James, Wells and Lee v. United Kingdom* ([2013]) 56 E.H.R.R. 399).

make significantly greater use of community sentences—as can be seen from the sentencing statistics summarized earlier.

C. Reform of Youth Sentencing

Youth court sentencing may be seen as one of the success stories of English sentencing and carries lessons for sentencing at the adult level. Largely owing to the work of the Youth Justice Board and its local agencies, the youth justice system in England and Wales has been substantially reoriented in the last decade. The principal legislative changes were made by the Criminal Justice and Immigration Act 2008: the referral order (referring the offender to a community-based Youth Offender Panel to consider the young offender's needs and how best to respond to them) was reinforced; for more serious offenders a youth rehabilitation order was introduced, with the requirements dependent on risks and needs, and for the most serious offenders, a youth rehabilitation order with intensive supervision and surveillance was introduced. Custodial sentences of detention and training remain for very serious offenders, but the court may not impose custody unless it is satisfied that the offender cannot properly be dealt with by a youth rehabilitation order. These legislative changes, reinforced by sentencing guidelines (Sentencing Guidelines Council 2009), succeeded in enhancing trends that had started a few years earlier. Thus the number of youths receiving their first caution or conviction exceeded 100,000 in the years 2005, 2006, and 2007 but had fallen spectacularly to 23,000 by 2013–14 (Youth Justice Board 2014).[25] The number of youths in custody stood at 3,200 in 2002 but had declined to 1,056 by 2015.

The Youth Justice Board had targeted localities with high custody rates and appears to have been successful in promoting alternative approaches (through restorative justice initiatives and new schemes for unpaid community work). The guidelines on the sentencing of youths (Sentencing Guidelines Council 2009) were used in training magistrates, and this may have assisted changes in practice. Although there remain concerns, such as the high reconviction rate of young offenders released from custody, this aspect of the English sentencing system has demonstrated that community sentences can be deployed successfully in place of many custodial sentences.

[25] In this context a "caution" (reprimand or warning) is an out-of-court response to an offense, which is administered by the police and recorded.

D. *Independent Reports Critiquing the Use of Imprisonment*

We noted that the prison population in England and Wales doubled between 1993 and 2003. The resultant imprisonment rate is much higher than those in Germany, the Nordic countries, France, and Italy (see Sec. IV.B below). A review commissioned by the then government from Lord Carter (2007) recommended measures to reduce the use of custody (discussed below), but this part of his report was not adopted. The report of an independent inquiry into "English Prisons Today," sponsored by the Howard League, advocated greater "justice reinvestment" and more sparing use of custody (Howard League for Penal Reform 2010). A subsequent independent inquiry by the British Academy sets out a strong moral and political case against the current high use of imprisonment and argues for changes in the sentencing structure to reduce the reliance on prison sentences (British Academy 2014).

These well-reasoned reports, which rely considerably on comparisons with other European sentencing systems, have elicited no formal response from any government. Even where governments have taken notice of independent reports, such as Baroness Corston's (2007) report on women in the criminal justice system, progress has been desperately slow: the number of women in English prisons trebled between 1992 (1,500) and 2002 (4,500) before falling back only slightly to 4,200 in 2012 (on Scotland, see Angiolini [2012]). A review by the House of Commons Justice Committee (2013) found that most of the Corston recommendations had not been implemented.

One significant argument has been that penal policy should be removed from the political arena and placed in the hands of an independent body, following the transfer of major elements of British fiscal policy to an independent Monetary Policy Committee (Lacey 2008; British Academy 2014). No government has shown any enthusiasm for losing its power over sentencing policy, perhaps believing that greater penal severity is a vote-winning policy (cf. the surveys of public opinion by Hough and Roberts [2012] showing a more nuanced set of attitudes).

III. Origin and Impact of the Sentencing Guidelines

The most striking development in English sentencing since Ashworth (2001) was published is the inception and evolution of guidelines. The only guidelines at the time of the earlier review were voluntary guidelines published by the Magistrates' Association and occasional guideline judgments handed down by the Court of Appeal (Ashworth and Roberts 2013a, pp. 3–5). Since then, guidelines for most common offenses have been developed and now apply to both levels of court. In addition there is now a significant and growing body of empirical literature on the effects of the guidelines. For these reasons, the experience in this country carries important lessons for other countries contemplating introducing some form of guidelines.

Parliament created the Sentencing Advisory Panel in 1998, its principal role being to give advice to the Court of Appeal, having conducted a public and professional consultation on proposed guidelines. The Court of Appeal would then decide whether to adopt these guidelines in whole or in part and would incorporate them into a judgment of the court. Guideline judgments were issued for offenses such as burglary, handling stolen goods, and child pornography (Ashworth and Wasik 2010). However, following a major report on sentencing (Home Office for Penal Reform 2001), the Criminal Justice Act 2003 established the Sentencing Guidelines Council, with a judicial majority, to receive advice from the Sentencing Advisory Panel and to issue definitive guidelines. The SGC was itself required to consult the minister of justice and the relevant House of Commons committee on its draft proposals—a democratic input into the process, although the SGC retained power over the final contents of the guidelines.

A substantial number of definitive guidelines on topics such as sexual offenses, general principles, and youth sentencing were created during this period (see Ashworth 2006; Ashworth and Wasik 2010; Roberts 2012, 2015; Ashworth and Roberts 2013b; Wasik 2014).

In 2010, sentencing entered a new era. The Coroners and Justice Act 2009 had introduced important changes. These may be traced to two significant developments. The first was the review of the use of imprisonment in response to the high and rising prison population (Carter 2007). In 2007, Lord Carter recommended that the government "immediately implement a package of measures that could moderate the demand for custody" (p. 3).[26] The second development was the creation

---

[26] Lord Carter set 2014 as the date by which the government should reduce the population by 4,500 places. So much for that deadline. The economic crisis that followed shortly after might have accelerated efforts to moderate the use of custody, although no such steps were undertaken. Prior to assuming power as the leading partner in the coalition government, the Conservative Party announced its opposition to a sentencing commission that was "simply a device to manage down the prison population" (p. 30).

of the Sentencing Commission Working Group (SCWG). The SCWG reviewed sentencing guidelines in other jurisdictions and issued a public consultation document that attracted considerable response from the judiciary and other stakeholders (Jacobson, Roberts, and Hough 2008; Sentencing Commission Working Group 2008).

A consensus emerged from respondents that a grid-based guidelines system such as that found in several US jurisdictions was not appropriate for England and Wales. Instead of such a scheme, the SCWG recommended a revamp of the current arrangements. Both the Carter report and the report of the SCWG stressed the need for more accurate predictions of the prison population. Greater accuracy, it was argued, could be achieved if the government were better able to predict the use of sentences of imprisonment by the courts. This could be achieved by ensuring a tighter fit between the guidelines and judicial practice. These two reports spawned the Coroners and Justice Act 2009. This legislation introduced a number of changes to the sentencing guidelines.

A. The Sentencing Council and Its Guidelines

The act created a new statutory body—the Sentencing Council for England and Wales—to replace the previous two organizations.[27] The new council retains a judicial majority among its 14 members. Before being replaced by the Sentencing Council in 2010, the Sentencing Guidelines Council had issued definitive guidelines for a range of offenses. These guidelines remain in force until such time as the Sentencing Council revises and reissues them—a task that will take several years to complete. In the meantime, the new council has issued a number of guidelines. The first such guideline relating to assault offenses was issued in March 2011. Since then the council has issued other offense-specific guidelines— following a slightly different model—as well as "generic" guidelines relating to sentencing in multiple conviction cases and allocation decisions.[28] In 2016, the council issued for consultation a guideline to replace the existing guideline relating to sentence reductions for a guilty plea.

---

[27] The Sentencing Advisory Panel (created in 1998) and the Sentencing Guidelines Council (in 2003).

[28] The guidelines pertain to burglary; environmental offenses; drug offenses; theft offenses; totality and offenses taken into consideration; sexual offenses; offenses involving dangerous dogs; fraud, bribery, and money laundering; health and safety offenses, corporate manslaughter, and food safety and hygiene offenses. All guidelines are available at http://sentencingcouncil.judiciary.gov.uk/.

The English guidelines require a sentencing court to follow a clear methodology in determining sentence. For example, when sentencing an offender convicted of one of the assault offenses, a court should work through nine steps to arrive at a final sentence (Sentencing Council of England and Wales 2011). Thus, under the definitive guideline for causing grievous bodily harm, the first task (at step one) is to determine which of the three levels of seriousness is appropriate for the case appearing for sentence. The court must take into account an exhaustive list of the principal elements of the case appearing for sentencing—for example, the degree of premeditation and whether a vulnerable victim was deliberately targeted—to determine which of the three ranges is most appropriate.[29] Thus the most serious cases that involve greater harm and higher culpability will fall into the category with the longest sentence length range (9–16 years).[30]

Once a court has determined the appropriate category range, it employs the starting point sentence within the range as a point of departure. For the most serious category, the starting point—from which a court will calculate a provisional sentence—is 12 years' custody. The second step involves adjusting the sentence within the chosen range by considering other factors deemed less important, such as previous convictions and personal mitigation. Having completed this step, the court then follows seven other steps to determine the final sentence. For example, step four requires a court to take into account whether and when the offender entered a guilty plea (Roberts and Rafferty 2011).[31]

B. The Statutory Compliance Requirement

Across many US guidelines, courts have to find "substantial and compelling" reasons to depart from the guidelines range. In England, the statutory compliance requirement is rather different and was amended as part of the most recent reforms. The Coroners and Justice Act 2009 amended the duty of a court to comply with the guidelines. Under the previous regime the statute stated that courts "must have regard" to

---

[29] These factors are all contained in an exhaustive list provided by the guideline.

[30] The ranges for the lesser categories are 5–9 years' custody for cases of intermediate seriousness and 3–5 years' custody for the least serious forms of causing grievous bodily harm with intent.

[31] The council has departed from this format for some of its more recent guidelines; see, e.g., the guideline for fraud, bribery, and money laundering offenses (Sentencing Council 2014a).

any relevant guidelines. Section 125 of the new act states that "(1) Every court: (a) must, in sentencing an offender, follow any sentencing guidelines which are relevant to the offender's case, and (b) must, in exercising any other function relating to the sentencing of offenders, follow any sentencing guidelines which are relevant to the exercise of that function, unless the court is satisfied that it would be contrary to the interests of justice to do so." This amended language thus tightened the compliance requirement on courts. However, in the process of legislative review, the requirement was softened by Parliament inserting clarification about the nature of a departure (Roberts 2011).

Courts may exercise their discretion in three important ways under the guidelines. First, although step one requires a court to identify an offense category and then apply that category's range, the guideline notes that courts may "move outside the category range" if they believe it is justified by the presence of a significant number of aggravating or mitigating factors. The guidelines proposed in New Zealand, in contrast, require the court that has chosen a range to remain within that range (Young and Browning 2008).

Second, having settled on a final sentence, a court is not bound to remain within the category range of the offense but only the much wider total guideline range. For example, consider the offense of assault occasioning actual bodily harm. If a court decides at step one that the case falls into the intermediate category of seriousness, it begins to work within a range running from a community order to 51 weeks' custody. However, for the purposes of complying with the statute, the court may impose any sentence within the total offense range that is much wider (from a fine to 3 years' imprisonment; see Ashworth 2010; Roberts 2012). Finally, a court may elect to depart from the guideline entirely if it decides that it would be contrary to the interests of justice to follow the guideline. The consequence is that courts have considerable discretion within the guideline ranges, as well as the ability to impose a sentence outside the range, if following the guideline would be contrary to the interests of justice.

The critical issue for present purposes is the relationship between the English guidelines and sentencing patterns, in particular the use of custody.

C. Relationship between Use of Custody and Sentencing Guidelines

Although the English council may be distinguished from its US counterparts on a number of dimensions, the principal distinguishing characteristic concerns its mandate. Many US states direct their sentencing commissions to monitor sentencing practices and to adjust the guidelines in response to key changes, for example, in the size of the prison population. Frase (2005) observes that the Minnesota guidelines "were not expected simply to model and perpetuate past judicial decisions. . . . The new guidelines were thus intended to be norm changing, not simply norm-reinforcing" (p. 146). Minnesota's was the first commission to take prison capacity and existing correctional resources into account when determining and revising guidelines (see Frase 2005). The Minnesota Commission was enabled to make policy decisions as well as to promote more consistent sentencing outcomes within the existing policy framework.

No such authority was conferred on the Sentencing Council of England and Wales. The SCWG created to explore the relationship between the guidelines and prison capacity ultimately rejected any link between the two. The SCWG concluded that "it is not practicable to impose a duty [on the Sentencing Guidelines] authority to . . . fit within current and reasonably foreseeable capacity" (2008, p. 28). This feature of the English guidelines has important consequences for the use of custody as a sanction. As seen in the empirical trends summarized in Section I, the guidelines have not constrained the use of custody as a sanction, nor has their onset been associated with any generalized escalation in severity.[32] While sentence lengths have increased for indictable offenses in the Crown Court (particularly for violent and sexual offenses), this appears unrelated to the guidelines per se.

This outcome is unsurprising. In issuing guidance to courts, the Sentencing Council attempts to reproduce current judicial practice; the point of departure when devising or revising a guideline is existing practice as revealed by sentencing statistics, reported judgments, and transcript analyses.[33] This point is confirmed by the council's resource impact assessments that are conducted prior to the development of each guideline. These assessments generally predict that the impact of the proposed guideline is neutral with respect to the number of prison places, exactly what one would expect if the guideline is based on existing prac-

---

[32] As noted later in the essay, the assault guideline appears to have triggered an escalation in severity for one offense.

[33] Current practice always has the point of departure for the development of guideline ranges. This is true of Minnesota in the late 1970s, Canada in the mid-1980s, and Uganda in 2013. Commissions differ in the degree to which their guidelines attempt to change existing sentencing patterns.

tice (see, e.g., Sentencing Council 2014*b*). The guidelines are designed to have no impact on the prison population, and this is generally borne out in practice. The one exception to this is the assault guideline. A recent evaluation published by the Sentencing Council (2015*b*) revealed that for one assault offense (actual bodily harm) the introduction of the guideline had triggered a significant increase in sentence severity.[34]

The council has departed from established practice in only two examples, when current trends were regarded as being disproportionate. For example, in its drug offenses guideline the council recommends shorter sentence lengths for drug mules than would have been the case had it followed existing judicial practice. In general, however, the council's guidelines would appear to have been neutral with respect to the use of custody as a sanction, neither promoting nor discouraging courts from imposing custodial sentences.

Two explanations may be offered for the council's conservative policy regarding the use of custody. First, as a primarily judicial body, there is an understandable reluctance to engage with issues of sentencing policy;[35] reducing the use of custody is seen by the judiciary as a matter left to the elected legislature to resolve. Indeed, other constituencies may also feel it is inappropriate for an unelected body to reduce (or inflate) custody rates or sentence lengths unless these changes are grounded in a principled or empirically derived justification. The English guidelines are designed to promote a "consistent approach to sentencing." Second, as noted, the mandate of the council contains no specific directive to consider the size of the prison estate when devising its guidelines nor to address racial or other disparities. Although we shall later note one statutory duty that could justify consideration of the cost-effectiveness of different disposals—with consequences for the size of the prison population—the council has developed its guidelines thus far without regard to the size of the prison population, although it has produced impact projections each time it has produced a guideline.[36]

---

[34] Presumably the council will address this inflationary effect when it revises the guideline and issues a revision for public consultation in 2016.

[35] Tonry (2004, p. 107) suggested that a primarily judicial majority is unwise because judges may constitute a force for conservatism.

[36] This exercise suggests that the council is not indifferent to the consequences of its guidelines on the size and costs of the prison estate.

One response to the question "Why have the English guidelines not constrained the use of custody as a sanction, or promoted the use of alternatives to imprisonment?" might therefore be "Because the guidelines were not created with such objectives in mind." Yet there is a clear danger to the council's noninterventionist approach. By adopting judicial practice as the basis for its guidelines, the council not only fails to implement a more parsimonious approach to imprisonment; it also institutionalizes current judicial practice, for better or worse.[37] If we assume, for the purposes of argument, that the recent increase in custody for sexual and violent offenses (e.g., table 7) was not caused by any changes in the seriousness of cases coming before the courts or prevented by the guidelines, then the shift will eventually be institutionalized by the council in its guidelines.

The statutory duties of the council do not preclude a more interventionist approach to sentencing practices, including shaping the use of custody as a sanction. For example, section 120 (11) of the Coroners and Justice Act 2009 directs that when exercising its functions relating to reviewing guidelines, the council "must have regard to" a series of considerations, one of which (e) is "the cost of different sentences and their relative effectiveness in preventing reoffending." The council might draw on this statutory duty to justify promoting the use of alternative sanctions, particularly as a substitute for short prison sentences.

For example, the council could replace short prison sentences with community orders in some of its offense-specific guidelines.[38] If the council were to accept that community orders represent a clearly more cost-effective punishment than, say, a 2-month prison term, it might adjust its guidelines accordingly. Substituting the community penalty for prison would be undertaken not in pursuit of a policy goal to reduce the size of the prison population but in recognition that short prison terms represent a more expensive way of achieving the statutory objectives of sentencing. To date, the council has declined to pursue such a policy change. Another approach would involve reacting to any upward or downward drift in sentencing practices. If a change was detected—for ex-

---

[37] It is significant that the guidelines do not include the statutory thresholds for different sanctions. It is assumed that the court will consider the thresholds, but highlighting them in the guideline would surely be a prudent step.

[38] Reducing the number of short prison terms would have only a modest impact on the prison population. Since these offenders serve such short prison terms, they represent less than 10 percent of the total population (see Mills 2011).

ample, the striking increase in sentence length for sexual offenses—the council might determine if the shift was attributable to case characteristics or some legislative intervention such as a change in the maximum penalty. In the absence of a legitimate cause such as these, the council could issue guidance for the offenses affected by the change. Without such monitoring, the overall proportionality of the sentencing process may be undermined.

In the event, the council has declined to adopt these strategies, although academic commentators and a recent report funded by the British Academy have urged the council to "take a fresh look at its statutory duties and powers in relation to the costs and effectiveness of different forms of sentence" (British Academy 2014, p. 106). Without a more directive statute—one responsive to the size of the prison population or to the relative costs of imprisonment—the council is unlikely to change course.

D. Responding to the Riots

Barely a year after the creation of the council in 2010, England experienced a rare but not unprecedented wave of social disorder. Riots erupted in a number of cities over the course of three nights in August 2011. In addition to a small number of extremely serious crimes, each affected city witnessed large numbers of offenders, primarily young adults, taking advantage of the disorder (Lewis 2011). The consequence was a sudden wave of expeditious prosecutions, most of which were for minor commercial burglary, as the offenders had stolen from looted or abandoned shops. The resulting sentencing was exemplary in severity; in some court locations the custody rate for commercial burglary doubled, and sentence lengths were significantly longer than those imposed prior to the riots.[39]

The sudden wave of prosecutions caused a short-term spike in the prison population. The riot prosecutions demonstrated both the limitations on the ability of the council to react expeditiously to a sentencing problem and the need for comprehensive guidelines. Since the council is required to conduct a protracted consultation on any proposed guideline, issuing timely guidance for courts on the question of how to sen-

---

[39] Ministry of Justice statistics reveal that the immediate custody rate in the Crown Court for offenses related to the public disorder was 81 percent compared to 33 percent for similar offenses committed a year earlier (Ministry of Justice 2012; for commentary, see Lightowlers and Quirk [2015]).

tence offenses committed during such a period was impossible. Instead the Court of Appeal issued judgments that upheld strikingly harsher sentences in order to deter future cases.[40] These judgments meant that offenders sentenced for riot-related offenses paid a much higher and quite unexpected premium for their offending. The council subsequently added the factor "offense committed during a period of social disorder" to all its subsequent guidelines, beginning with the burglary offenses guideline issued in 2012. The English riots illustrate the need for a sentencing guidelines authority to be able to respond immediately to such events, in order to preserve the principles that undermine sentencing and the sentencing guidelines.

E. Effects of Guidelines on Consistency of Outcome and Application

It is too soon to draw definitive conclusions about the effects of the guidelines on consistency and proportionality because the guidelines have been in place for a relatively short period and the evaluation research is limited. It takes a considerable amount of time to develop a guideline, issue it for public and professional consultation, and then revise it in response to feedback. The whole process takes approximately a year before a definitive guideline is issued. Nevertheless, some conclusions about the effects of the guidelines may be drawn. First, however, it is worth noting an important addition to the knowledge base of sentencing in this jurisdiction.

Between 2010 and 2015, sentencers in the Crown Court were required to complete a data form for every sentenced case. The council initiated this database to fulfill its statutory duty to monitor compliance with the guidelines. The survey was designed to produce a census rather than a sample of sentencing decisions in the Crown Court. The Crown Court Sentencing Survey (CCSS) form contained important elements of the offense and required the sentencer to indicate which guidelines factors were taken into account at sentencing. The data have been used by the Sentencing Council to develop and revise its guidelines and also to discharge its various statutory duties (Sentencing Council 2015b). Since the release of data to the public domain, the survey has been exploited by academic researchers (e.g., Raine and Dunstan 2009; Pina-

---

[40] The leading decision, handed down from the Court of Appeal by Lord Judge C. J., was *Blackshaw* ([2011] EWCA Crim 2312); for commentary, see Ashworth (2012) and Roberts (2012).

Sanchez and Linacre 2013; Roberts 2013; Roberts and Pina-Sanchez 2014; Irwin-Rogers and Perry 2015; Maslen 2015).[41]

The Sentencing Council's survey provided unique insight into sentencing practices and goes far beyond merely documenting the extent to which courts comply with the council's guidelines.[42] Information derived directly from the sentencer permits a much more accurate calibration of the influence of various factors on sentence outcomes.[43] Unfortunately for researchers, in 2015 the council made the decision to terminate the Crown Court survey. The council took the view that the guidelines monitoring (which is a statutory requirement of the Coroners and Justice Act 2009) could be more efficiently achieved by time-limited and offense-specific data collection. This may be so, but the consequence is that the fine-grained, annual data that provided a unique insight into sentencing in the Crown Court will now be lost.

Although the council has a statutory duty to "monitor the operation and effect of its sentencing guidelines" and to "consider what conclusions can be drawn" from this monitoring (sec. 128 [1][a], [b]), this statutory obligation has been rather narrowly interpreted. The council publishes annual "departure" rates for offenses covered by its guidelines (e.g., Sentencing Council 2015*b*), but this report simply notes the percentage of cases falling outside the total offense ranges. Moreover, since the statutory definition of a departure sentence rests on the total offense range—rather than on the more limited guideline category range—for this reason alone, the departure rates are very low. For example, data from 2014 show that fully 97 percent of assault and burglary offenses fell within the overall guidelines range (Sentencing Council 2015*a*, tables 6.1, 6.3).

---

[41] In 2013, the council made the first full year of data available to external researchers through its website.

[42] As far as we are aware, no other jurisdiction derives data directly from the sentencing authority, although some US guidelines require courts to complete a form in the event that a "departure" sentence is imposed (see Minnesota Sentencing Guidelines Commission 2015). As with all surveys, the CCSS had limitations, one of which is its coverage. In 2014, the response rate was approximately 65 percent (see Roberts and Hough [2015] and Sentencing Council [2015*a*] for further information and discussion).

[43] For example, research drawing on the CCSS has shown that sentence reductions for a guilty plea and sentence enhancements for previous convictions are both much more modest than would be thought from examination of the aggregate sentencing statistics. In the latter example, the ministry statistics include all relevant prior convictions, whereas the CCSS records only those that were considered relevant by the court at the time of sentencing (see Roberts and Pina-Sanchez 2014). This issue is discussed later in the essay.

The creation of the Sentencing Council and the introduction of the guidelines have stimulated more academic scholarship and commentary. Padfield (2013) describes the increased debate on sentencing in the academic literature as "one of the greatest successes of the introduction of guidelines" (p. 50). Academic analyses to date suggest a positive impact on consistency across courts and also the application of the offense-specific guidelines. Pina-Sanchez and Linacre (2013) drew on the CCSS to explore the degree of variability in sentencing assault, robbery, and burglary. They demonstrated that for these offenses, the guideline factors were being applied in a consistent way across courts. Using a more sophisticated multivariate methodology than previous researchers, Pina-Sanchez (2015) explored the impact of the new assault guideline on variability in sentencing outcomes across courts.[44] He conducted a pre-post analysis using the council's data set and reports that "consistency improved in all the offenses studied after the new guideline came into force" (p. 87). Irwin-Rogers and Perry (2015) drew on the same data set to explore the impact of sentencing factors in cases of domestic burglary. Their multivariate analyses "provided a strong indication that the courts were sentencing in a manner that was consistent with the domestic burglary guideline and in particular the principle that the factors in step one of the guideline should have more of an influence on sentence severity than the factors in step two" (p. 210). Finally, we noted earlier that the council's drug offenses guideline had attempted to change sentencing practices for so-called drug mules. Subsequent evaluation research by Fleetwood, Radcliffe, and Stevens (2015), again drawing on the CCSS, detected a significant downward shift in sentences imposed on these offenders to reflect their lower level of culpability. These researchers concluded that "the sentencing guideline appears to have achieved greater proportionality" (p. 435).

These findings with respect to sentencing trends, while restricted in time and scale, are encouraging. Additional research into public views of sentencing has suggested another benefit of the guidelines. One of the statutory duties of the Sentencing Council is to "have regard to . . . the need to promote public confidence in the criminal justice system" (Coroners and Justice Act 2009, art. 120[11][d]). One empirical explora-

---

[44] For example, Mason et al. (2007) were unable to control for a range of contaminating variables in their survey of sentencing variation across different court areas.

tion of public opinion suggested that greater public awareness of the guideline may promote public confidence in sentencing and possibly mitigate criticism of sentencers. Members of the UK public were strongly supportive of the concept of guidelines.[45] In addition, respondents who had been informed of the guidelines were less likely to rate specific sentences as being too lenient than people who reacted to the same cases without having been made aware of the guidelines (Roberts et al. 2012).

F. "Glasnost" in English Sentencing

Beyond more consistent and principled sentencing, guidelines confer benefits in ways that are not easily measured. A systematic and public-facing set of guidelines also promotes greater understanding of sentencing and enhances the predictability of the sentencing process. The guideline regulating sentence reductions for a guilty plea is a good illustration of the greater transparency and predictability of sentencing practices since the onset of the guidelines. In almost all other common law jurisdictions, although the practice of awarding plea-based discounts is universal, the magnitude of these discounts remains hard to predict.

Canada is a good example of this lack of clarity. There is no guideline regulating sentence reductions and no appellate guidance regarding the appropriate levels of reductions (Renaud 2004, chap. 4). Moreover, since Statistics Canada does not record plea as a factor in its annual Adult Criminal Court Survey (personal communication, Canadian Centre for Justice Statistics, April 2013), researchers are unable to determine with any precision the magnitude of sentence reductions awarded by the courts. Accused persons contemplating entering a plea and who consult their legal advisors are unlikely to receive anything other than imprecise predictions regarding the benefit if they plead guilty. This undermines the purpose of sentence discounts, yet this constitutes the norm around much of the common law world. Litigants, advocates, and researchers—indeed, all interested parties—are better placed in England and Wales.[46]

---

[45] Ninety-three percent of respondents endorsed the view that guidelines were definitely or probably a good idea.

[46] Even in neighboring Scotland there is little clarity with respect to the magnitude of discounts, a sliding scale on the English model being rejected in *Murray* ([2013] HCJAC 129). This lack of clarity is self-defeating. As Leverick notes, "If defendants cannot predict with confidence that a discount will be awarded or suspect that it will be minimal, they may elect to take their chances at trial" (2014, p. 343).

Greater clarity exists in England and Wales as a result of three significant developments. First, as noted, the individual guidelines themselves provide a relatively clear indication of the sentence ranges that may be imposed for specific offenses. Second, a generic guideline applicable across all offenses identifies specific levels of reduction that should be awarded to reflect a guilty plea. Third, the CCSS makes it possible to determine the extent to which the guidelines are actually followed in practice.[47]

The greater transparency and predictability introduced by the guidelines can be illustrated by reference to the guideline for plea-based sentence reductions. According to the current guideline (see Sentencing Guidelines Council 2007), if a guilty plea is entered at the earliest reasonable opportunity, the recommended reduction is one-third.[48] The magnitude of the reduction should diminish the later the guilty plea is entered. For cases in which the plea was entered after the first reasonable opportunity but before the day of trial, the recommended reduction is one-quarter. Defendants who change their plea to guilty on the day the trial commences should receive a reduction of only 10 percent. The guideline thus creates a sliding scale of discounts depending on the timing of the plea, a pattern consistent with arrangements in other common law jurisdictions.[49] Empirical research documents a relatively close fit between the guideline recommendations for guilty plea discounts and the reductions actually awarded in the Crown Court. Thus, while the guideline recommends a reduction of one-third for early plea cases, in 2012, four-fifths of offenders pleading at this stage of the process re-

---

[47] Although US commissions routinely monitor compliance with their guidelines, this has not been the case in England and Wales, until the creation of the Sentencing Council and the CCSS. The previous statutory body—the Sentencing Guidelines Council—did not have the resources to monitor judicial compliance with its guidelines.

[48] This guideline was issued by a former statutory body responsible for issuing guidelines and remains in effect until the current council issues a revised guideline. The council has a statutory duty to prepare a guilty plea reduction guideline (Coroners and Justice Act 2009, sec. 120[3][a]), and a draft for consultation was issued in 2016.

[49] Courts retain some discretion in determining the level of reduction awarded. The statutory foundation for the practice makes it clear that timing of the plea is not the only determinant of the reduction accorded. Section 144 (1) of the Criminal Justice Act 2003 notes two elements, and not simply the timing: "In determining what sentence to pass on an offender who has pleaded guilty to an offence in proceedings before that or another court, a court must take into account: (a) the stage in the proceedings for the offence at which the offender indicated his intention to plead guilty, and (b) *the circumstances in which this indication was given*" (emphasis added).

ceived exactly this level of reduction. The remaining cases can be explained by the presence of factors other than the timing of the plea that also affect the magnitude of the reduction (see Roberts 2013).[50]

One of the four key objectives of sentencing reform identified by the SCWG in 2008 was to achieve "transparency," which it defined as the "ability of Parliament, the public, and sentencers to have an understanding, through the existence of clear and comprehensive sentencing guidelines . . . of how offenders may expect to be sentenced, together with an understanding of the aggravating and mitigating factors that may be taken into account" (2008, p. 8).[51] If the guidelines have failed to achieve some other important goals, they have at least made significant progress toward this objective.

IV. Conclusions

This essay has discussed the major changes taking place in sentencing in England and Wales between 2003 and 2015. Much more could have been said about the sentencing policies pursued by the Court of Appeal (on which see Ashworth [2015], especially chap. 9), which continue to have a significant effect despite the proliferation of sentencing guidelines. There has also been an expansion in the use of civil preventive orders, imposed by civil or criminal courts so as to prohibit certain forms of conduct, with a maximum sentence of 5 years' imprisonment for breach of the order (Ramsay 2013; Ashworth and Zedner 2014, chap. 4), and an increase in the use of out-of-court punishments (Padfield, Morgan, and Maguire 2012). Without elaborating on these and other tendencies, however, we conclude here by identifying three major themes in recent English policy:

• the continued attraction of penal populism to policy makers, despite empirical findings showing that members of the public are accepting of alternatives to custody, particularly when the alternatives carry cost savings;

---

[50] The correspondence between empirical reductions and guideline recommendations becomes weaker for the late plea cases simply because a number of other factors come into play (see Roberts and Bradford 2015, table 2).

[51] The other three objectives were predictability, consistency, and compatibility between the supply of and demand for correctional capacity (see pp. 8–9).

- the relatively high use of imprisonment compared with countries such as Germany (and several other European countries) and, in particular, the high use of indeterminate sentences;
- the continued resistance of the British government to judgments of the European Court of Human Rights relating to imprisonment, manifested in a refusal to implement certain judgments.

A. Penal Populism and Public Opinion

Sentencing policy continues to be driven by political initiatives, despite evidence that a uniformly punitive approach to punishing offenders is inconsistent with community views. A number of empirical investigations in recent years have documented public tolerance of alternatives to custody. For example, Roberts and Hough (2011) document widespread public support for a range of mitigating factors at sentencing. Research has demonstrated that the public is sensitive to the issue of cost-effectiveness, even if the political parties remain committed to custody whatever the cost. With respect to alternatives to custody, although the government may not see community sentences and custody as fungible, the public appears to think differently. In addition, there is acceptance of alternatives to custody for a range of offenses (Roberts and Hough 2011).

The most compelling example of political indifference regarding current levels of punishment comes from the period of austerity triggered by the worldwide recession of 2008. The UK government has implemented spending cuts throughout all public services, including criminal justice. Yet the cuts to the criminal justice system have deliberately avoided reducing the use of custody as a sanction. Instead, the government has targeted the legal aid budget and introduced a raft of reductions to policing and central departments such as the Ministry of Justice. This reluctance to promote alternatives is even more surprising in light of the ministry's own research having demonstrated that short-term custody (less than 12 months in prison) was consistently associated with higher rates of proven reoffending than community orders and SSOs (Mews et al. 2015).

With respect to prisons, the current Conservative government has required institutions to reduce the average amount spent per prisoner.[52]

---

[52] In 2014, the coalition government detailed plans to cut the average annual cost of incarceration by £2,200 per inmate.

This strategy is tantamount to attempting to reduce the costs of Accident and Emergency Departments by lowering the average costs, per patient treated, rather than restricting admissions to only those patients who cannot be treated elsewhere. The National Health Service has introduced a number of strategies to reduce the caseload of Accident and Emergency through creation of out-of-hours clinics and on-site general practitioner screening to determine whether a patient presenting at a hospital needs to be admitted or can be safely treated elsewhere. No analogous filtering strategy has been considered to reduce the caseload of the prison estate, which continues to silt up with the penal equivalent of "bed blockers," namely, individuals who could have been equally or more effectively punished in the community or who are serving longer terms than can reasonably be justified on the grounds of desert or dangerousness.

The attitude of successive governments, coupled with the restricted mandate and conservative approach of the Sentencing Council to modifying sentencing practices, leads us to conclude that the custody rate is unlikely to change in the near future. Indeed, according to the latest government estimates, the prison population is projected to increase still further, by 9 percent over the period 2016–20 (Ministry of Justice 2015*d*, p. 2). Aside from a few limited initiatives, the government appears to be content to let the use of custody remain at the current level and to focus on increasing the accuracy of prison projections. The eventual release of the IPP population will help constrain the numbers of prisoners, but the overall picture will likely remain unchanged.

B. High Use of Imprisonment

World prison statistics show that the imprisonment rate per 100,000 of population currently stands at around 148 for England and Wales, compared with 79 for Germany and around 70 for the Nordic countries, and 98 for France (Walmsley 2013). Can this relatively high rate be credited with the decline in recorded crimes in England and Wales? Has the high use of custody served to prevent crime? This seems highly unlikely, since the institution of punishment does not exist in a social vacuum, but rather in "broad socioeconomic, cultural, and political conditions" (Lacey 2008, p. 19). Thus the corporatist approach in Germany means that there is little political or legal discussion of sentencing reform, and moderate sentencing levels are sustained by institutional features such as the form of German legal education (inculcating certain values) and the selection of career judges from the top law school graduates (Hoernle 2013). While it is true that crime rates in England and Wales have declined as levels of imprisonment have increased, the causal inference has to be examined with care: in common with almost all other European countries, France and Germany, which have not had a significant increase in the use of imprisonment, have also experienced declines in their crime rates in recent years.

The high use of imprisonment in England and Wales (relative to many other EU member states) has occurred largely for other reasons, perhaps connected to the nature of the political system, perhaps reflecting changes in the labor market and other economic factors, perhaps as a consequence of changes in the welfare system (Lacey 2008; Wacquant 2009). Thus Lappi-Seppälä (2013) concludes from his European study that "overall victimization rates . . . are unrelated to incarceration rates" (p. 312), although he also warns that the available data are more satisfactory for homicide than for many other types of crime. Our argument here is that serious questions should be asked about the justifications for the current level of imprisonment in England and Wales, relative to other western European countries, not least in respect of the length of English sentences and the extraordinary fact that 19 percent of prisoners are serving indeterminate sentences.

C. Resistance to Judgments of the European Court of Human Rights

The British government is a signatory to the European Convention on Human Rights and has agreed to abide by the judgments of the European Court of Human Rights in Strasbourg. However, in recent years some of those judgments have met with resistance from the UK Supreme Court or from the British government. The first of four examples is the judgment in *Stafford v. United Kingdom* ([2002] 35 E.H.R.R. 1121), in which the Strasbourg Court held that the determination of release from a sentence of life imprisonment was a sentencing matter and that it should therefore be decided by an "impartial and independent tribunal" and not by a government minister. This judgment was accepted, but the system of sentencing for murder was hastily changed by Schedule 21 to the Criminal Justice Act 2003—discussed at the end of Section I above—in which Parliament created significantly higher starting points for minimum terms for murder sentences.

The second example is *Hirst v. United Kingdom* ([2006] 42 E.H.R.R. 41), in which the Strasbourg Court held that the "general, automatic, and indiscriminate" ban on prisoners voting was a disproportionate restriction on an important human right. The British government disagrees with this judgment and has not implemented it, even though the judgment would not prevent a more nuanced ban on voting. A third case is *James, Wells and Lee v. United Kingdom* (2013), already mentioned (see fn. 24), where the Court held that it is unlawful to detain prisoners sentenced to the indeterminate IPP sentence without providing courses that enable them to present a case for release from custody. Over 4,600 IPP prisoners remain in prison after the expiration of the minimum term of their sentences (see fn. 22).

Finally, the British government has signaled its intention not to comply with the judgment in *Vinter v. United Kingdom* ([2014] Crim.L.R. 81) on life imprisonment with a whole life order (the equivalent of life without parole in the United States). The Court's view is that human dignity requires that there must always be the possibility of review of the need for continuing detention. There is disagreement about whether English law provides for this, but the Strasbourg Court has now accepted that English law does ensure compliance because the minister for justice is bound to act compatibly with article 3.[53] While there are other important judgments with which the United Kingdom has complied, the growing resistance to Strasbourg in matters surrounding imprisonment represents a major challenge to the European system for the protection of human rights.

D. Coda

Notwithstanding their limitations and critics, the guidelines remain the most positive story emerging from England and Wales.[54] As noted, they have not constrained the use of custody, nor has the council elected to promote a more cost-effective approach to sentencing. However, the existence of guidelines containing sentence ranges means that a mecha-

---

[53] In *Hutchinson v. United Kingdom*, judgment of February 3, 2015; this case has now been referred to the Grand Chamber, which means that another judgment on this issue is imminent.

[54] As is the case in other jurisdictions, the guidelines have also attracted critics. One critique expressed by some scholars and practitioners is that the guidelines have diminished the role of personal mitigation at sentencing (e.g., Lovegrove 2010; Cooper 2013; cf. Roberts, Hough, and Ashworth 2011). Academics have also criticized the guidelines for providing insufficient guidance regarding the weighting that should be assigned different factors (Dhami 2013). Padfield (2013) has questioned whether the guidelines have successfully ensured fairer and more consistent outcomes, and a recurrent critique is that not-

nism is in place that could comprehensively reduce the use of custody and in a principled fashion, if the political will were to emerge. In light of the government's austerity drive in almost all areas of public expenditure, it may well eventually seek to reduce the current use of imprisonment as a sanction, if only to ensure cost cutting across all sectors. Finally, the guidelines have increased transparency and predictability of sentencing to a greater level than most other common law jurisdictions. If not justifying celebration, this last development is at least cause for some satisfaction.

REFERENCES

Advisory Council on the Penal System. 1978. *Sentences of Imprisonment: Report of the Advisory Council on the Penal System.* London: HMSO.

Angiolini, Elish. 2012. *Report of the Commission on Women Offenders.* Scottish Executive, Edinburgh. http://www.gov.scot/resource/0039/00391828.pdf.

Ashworth, Andrew. 2001. "The Decline of English Sentencing." In *Sentencing and Sanctions in Western Countries,* edited by Michael Tonry and Richard S. Frase. New York: Oxford University Press.

———. 2006. "The Sentencing Guideline System in England and Wales." *South African Journal of Criminal Justice* 19:1–23.

———. 2010. "Coroners and Justice Act 2009: Sentencing Guidelines and the Sentencing Council." *Criminal Law Review* (5):389–401.

———. 2012. "Departures from the Sentencing Guidelines." *Criminal Law Review* (2):81–96.

———. 2015. *Sentencing and Criminal Justice.* 6th ed. Cambridge: Cambridge University Press.

Ashworth, Andrew, and Elaine Player. 2005. "Criminal Justice Act 2003: The Sentencing Provisions." *Modern Law Review* 68(5):822–38.

Ashworth, Andrew, and Julian Roberts. 2013a. "The Origins and Evolution of Sentencing Guidelines in England and Wales." In *Sentencing Guidelines: Exploring the English Model,* edited by Andrew Ashworth and Julian Roberts. Oxford: Oxford University Press.

———. 2013b. *Sentencing Guidelines: Exploring the English Model.* Oxford: Oxford University Press.

———. 2016. "Sentencing: Theory, Policy, and Practice." In *Oxford Handbook of Criminology,* 5th ed., edited by Shadd Maruna, Lesley McAra, and Alison Liebling. Oxford: Oxford University Press.

Ashworth, Andrew, and Martin Wasik. 2010. "Ten Years of the Sentencing Advisory Panel." Annual report. http://www.sentencing.council.org.

---

withstanding the 2009 amendments to the compliance requirement, the guidelines still permit too much judicial discretion at sentencing (e.g., Ashworth 2010; Young and King 2013).

Ashworth, Andrew, and Lucia Zedner. 2014. *Preventive Justice*. Oxford: Oxford University Press.

Bottoms, Anthony. 1981. "The Suspended Sentence in England, 1967–1978." *British Journal of Criminology* 21:1–26.

British Academy. 2014. *A Presumption against Imprisonment*. London: British Academy.

Carter, Lord. 2007. *Securing the Future: Proposals for the Efficient and Sustainable Use of Custody in England and Wales*. London: Ministry of Justice.

Cid, Josép. 2005. "Suspended Sentences in Spain: Decarceration and Recidivism." *Journal of Community and Criminal Justice* 52(2):169–79.

Cooper, John. 2013. "Nothing Personal." In *Sentencing Guidelines: Exploring the English Model*, edited by Andrew Ashworth and Julian Roberts. Oxford: Oxford University Press.

Corston, Baroness. 2007. *Review of Women with Particular Vulnerabilities in the Criminal Justice System*. London: Home Office.

Cox, Edward. 1877. *The Principles of Punishment, as Applied in the Administration of Criminal Law by Judges and Magistrates*. London: Law Times Office.

Crackenthorpe, M. 1900. "Can Sentences Be Standardised?" *Nineteenth Century* (January):103–15.

Cross, Rupert. 1971. *The English Sentencing System*. London: Butterworths.

Cuthbertson, Peter. 2014. *Suspended Sentences: The Case for Abolition*. London: Centre for Crime Prevention. https://drive.google.com/file/d/0B25IaOtJKl vwam5mREhqU3JQUVE/edit?pli=1.

Dhami, Mandeep. 2013. "A 'Decision Science' Perspective on the Old and New Sentencing Guidelines in England and Wales." In *Sentencing Guidelines: Exploring the English Model*, edited by Andrew Ashworth and Julian Roberts. Oxford: Oxford University Press.

Fleetwood, Jennifer, Polly Radcliffe, and Alex Stevens. 2015. "Shorter Sentences for Drug Mules: The Early Impact of the Sentencing Guidelines in England and Wales." *Drugs: Education, Prevention and Policy* 22(5):428–36.

Frase, Richard S. 2005. "Sentencing Guidelines in Minnesota, 1978–2003." In *Crime and Justice: A Review of Research*, vol. 32, edited by Michael Tonry. Chicago: University of Chicago Press.

Freiberg, Arie, and Victoria Moore. 2009. "Disbelieving Suspense: Suspended Sentences of Imprisonment and Public Confidence in the Criminal Justice System." *Australia and New Zealand Journal of Criminology* 42(1):101–22.

Galton, Francis. 1895. "Terms of Imprisonment." *Nature* 52(1338):174–76.

Hedderman, Carol, and Rebecca Barnes. 2015. "Sentencing Women: An Analysis of Recent Trends." In *Exploring Sentencing Practice in England and Wales*, edited by Julian Roberts. London: Palgrave Macmillan.

Hoernle, Tatjana. 2013. "Moderate and Non-arbitrary Sentencing without Guidelines: The German Experience." *Law and Contemporary Problems* 76 (1):189–210.

Home Office Sentencing Review 2001. *Making Punishments Work*. London: Home Office.

Hough, Mike, Jessica Jacobson, and Andrew Millie. 2003. *The Decision to Imprison: Sentencing and the Prison Population*. London: Prison Reform Trust.

Hough, Mike, and Julian Roberts. 2012. "Public Opinion, Crime, and Criminal Justice." In *Oxford Handbook of Criminology*, 5th ed., edited by Mike Maguire, Rod Morgan, and Robert Reiner. Oxford: Oxford University Press.

House of Commons Justice Committee. 2013. *Women Offenders: After the Corston Report*. HC 92. London: HMSO.

Howard League for Penal Reform. 2010. *Do Better, Do Less: Report of the Commission on English Prisons Today*. London: Howard League for Penal Reform.

Irwin-Rogers, Keir, and Thomas Perry. 2015. "Exploring the Impact of Sentencing Factors on Sentencing Domestic Burglary." In *Exploring Sentencing Practice in England and Wales*, edited by Julian Roberts. London: Palgrave Macmillan.

Jacobson, Jessica, and Mike Hough. 2010. *Unjust Deserts: Imprisonment for Public Protection*. London: Prison Reform Trust.

Jacobson, Jessica, Julian Roberts, and Mike Hough. 2008. "Towards More Consistent and Predictable Sentencing in England and Wales." In *Tackling Prison Overcrowding: Build More Prisons? Sentence Fewer Offenders?* edited by Mike Hough, Rob Allen, and Enver Solomon. Bristol: Policy Press.

Jeremy, David. 2010. "Sentencing Policy or Short-Term Expediency?" *Criminal Law Review* (8):593–607.

Kamuzze, Juliet. 2014. "An Insight into Uganda's New Sentencing Guidelines: A Replica of Individualization?" *Federal Sentencing Reporter* 27(1):47–55.

Lacey, Nicola. 2008. *The Prisoners' Dilemma*. Cambridge: Cambridge University Press.

Lappi-Seppälä, Tapio. 2001. "Sentencing and Punishment in Finland: The Decline of the Repressive Ideal." In *Sentencing and Sanctions in Western Countries*, edited by Michael Tonry and Richard S. Frase. New York: Oxford University Press.

———. 2013. "Imprisonment and Penal Demands: Exploring the Dimensions and Drivers of Systemic and Attitudinal Punitivity." In *European Handbook of Criminology*, edited by Sophie Body-Gendrot, Mike Hough, Klara Kerezsi, Rene Levy, and Sonja Snacken. New York: Routledge.

Leverick, Fiona. 2014. "Sentence Discounting for Guilty Pleas: An Argument for Certainty over Discretion." *Criminal Law Review* (6):338–49.

Lewis, Paul. 2011. *Reading the Riots: Investigating England's Summers of Disorder*. London: London School of Economics. http://eprints.lse.ac.uk/46297/1.

Lightowlers, Carly, and Hannah Quirk. 2015. "The 2011 English 'Riots': Prosecutorial Zeal and Judicial Abandon." *British Journal of Criminology* 55(1):65–85.

Lovegrove, Austin. 2010. "The Sentencing Council, the Public's Sense of Justice, and Personal Mitigation." *Criminal Law Review* (12):906–23.

Mair, George, Noel Cross, and Stuart Taylor. 2008. *The Community Order and the Suspended Sentence Order: The Views and Attitudes of Sentencers*. London: Centre for Crime and Justice Studies.

Maslen, Hannah. 2015. "Penitence and Persistence: How Should Sentencing Factors Interact?" In *Exploring Sentencing Practice in England and Wales*, edited by Julian Roberts. London: Palgrave Macmillan.

Mason, Thomas, Nisha de Silva, Nalini Sharma, David Brown, and Gemma Harper. 2007. *Local Variation in Sentencing in England and Wales*. London: Ministry of Justice.

Mews, Aidan, Joseph Hillier, Michael McHugh, and Cris Coxon. 2015. *The Impact of Short Custodial Sentences, Community Orders and Suspended Sentence Orders on Re-offending*. London: Ministry of Justice.

Mills, Helen. 2011. "The 'Alternative to Custody' Myth." *Criminal Justice Matters* (March):34–36.

Ministry of Justice. 2012. *Statistical Bulletin on the Public Disorder of 6th to 9th August 2011–September 2012 Update*. London: Ministry of Justice.

———. 2013. *Story of the Prison Population: 1993–2012*. London: Ministry of Justice.

———. 2014. *Criminal Justice Statistics Quarterly: December 2013*. Sentencing Data Tool. https://www.gov.uk/government/statistics/criminal-justice-system -statistics-quarterly-december-2014.

———. 2015a. *Criminal Justice System Statistics Quarterly December 2014*. Sentencing Data Tool. https://www.gov.uk/government/statistics/criminal-justice -system-statistics-quarterly-december-2014.

———. 2015b. *Offender Management Statistics Quarterly: Prison Population: 30 September 2015*. London: Ministry of Justice.

———. 2015c. *Prison Population Figures 2015: Population Bulletin: Weekly 27 November 2015*. London: Ministry of Justice.

———. 2015d. *Prison Population Projections, 2015–2021: England and Wales*. Statistical Bulletin. London: Ministry of Justice.

Minnesota Sentencing Guidelines Commission. 2015. *Minnesota Sentencing Guidelines and Commentary*. Minneapolis: MSGC.

Morris, Norval, and Michael Tonry. 1990. *Between Prison and Probation*. New York: Oxford University Press.

Padfield, Nicola. 2011. "Time to Bury the Custody Threshold?" *Criminal Law Review* (8):593–612.

———. 2013. "Exploring the Success of Sentencing Guidelines." In *Sentencing Guidelines: Exploring the English Model*, edited by Andrew Ashworth and Julian Roberts. Oxford: Oxford University Press.

Padfield, Nicola, Rod Morgan, and Mike Maguire. 2012. "Out of Court, Out of Sight? Criminal Sanctions and Non-judicial Decision Making." In *Oxford Handbook of Criminology*, 5th ed., edited by Mike Maguire, Rod Morgan, and Robert Reiner. Oxford: Oxford University Press.

Park, Hyungkwan. 2010. "The Basic Features of the First Korean Sentencing Guidelines." *Federal Sentencing Reporter* 22:262–71.

Phillips of Worth Matravers, Lord. 2007. "How Important Is Punishment?" Speech to the Howard League for Penal Reform, London, November 15.

Pina-Sanchez, Jose. 2015. "Defining and Measuring Consistency in Sentencing." In *Exploring Sentencing Practice in England and Wales*, edited by Julian Roberts. London: Palgrave Macmillan.

Pina-Sanchez, Jose, and Robin Linacre. 2013. "Sentence Consistency in England and Wales." *British Journal of Criminology* 53(6):1118–35.

Player, Elaine, Julian Roberts, Jessica Jacobson, Mike Hough, and James Robottom. 2010. "Remanded in Custody: An Analysis of Recent Trends in England and Wales." *Howard Journal of Criminal Justice* 49:231–61.

Radzinowicz, Leon, and Roger Hood. 1979. "Judicial Discretion and Sentencing Standards: Victorian Attempts to Solve a Perennial Problem." *University of Pennsylvania Law Review* 17(5):1288–1349.

Raine, John, and Eileen Dunstan. 2009. "How Well Do Sentencing Guidelines Work? Equity, Proportionality and Consistency in the Determination of Fine Levels in the Magistrates' Courts of England and Wales." *Howard Journal* 48 (1):13–36.

Ramsay, Peter. 2013. *The Insecurity State*. Oxford: Oxford University Press.

Renaud, Gilles. 2004. *Speaking to Sentence*. Toronto: Carswell.

Roberts, Julian. 2004. *The Virtual Prison*. Cambridge: Cambridge University Press.

———. 2011. "Sentencing Guidelines and Judicial Discretion: Evolution of the Duty of Courts to Comply in England and Wales." *British Journal of Criminology* 51:997–1013.

———. 2012. "Points of Departure: Reflections on Sentencing outside the Definitive Guidelines Ranges." *Criminal Law Review* (6):439–48.

———. 2013. "Sentencing Patterns in England and Wales: Findings from the Crown Court Sentencing Survey." In *Sentencing Guidelines: Exploring the English Model*, edited by Andrew Ashworth and Julian Roberts. Oxford: Oxford University Press.

———. 2015. *Exploring Sentencing Practice in England and Wales*. London: Palgrave Macmillan.

Roberts, Julian, and Ben Bradford. 2015. "Sentence Reductions for a Guilty Plea: New Empirical Evidence from England and Wales." *Journal of Empirical Legal Studies* 12(2):187–210.

Roberts, Julian, and Oren Gazal-Ayal. 2013. "Sentencing Reform in Israel: An Analysis of the Statutory Reforms of 2012." *Israel Law Review* 46:455–79.

Roberts, Julian, and Mike Hough. 2011. "Custody or Community? Exploring the Boundaries of Public Punitiveness in England and Wales." *Criminology and Criminal Justice* 11:185–202.

———. 2015. "Empirical Sentencing Research: Options and Opportunities." In *Exploring Sentencing Practice in England and Wales*, edited by Julian Roberts. London: Palgrave Macmillan.

Roberts, Julian, Mike Hough, and Andrew Ashworth. 2011. "Personal Mitigation, Public Opinion and Sentencing Guidelines in England and Wales." *Criminal Law Review* (7):524–30.

Roberts, Julian, Mike Hough, Jonathan Jackson, and Monica M. Gerber. 2012. "Public Attitudes toward the Lay Magistracy and the Sentencing Council Guidelines: The Effects of Information on Opinion." *British Journal of Criminology* 52(6):1072–91.

Roberts, Julian, and Keir Irwin-Rogers. 2015. "Sentencing Practices and Trends in England and Wales, 1999–2013." In *Exploring Sentencing Practice in England and Wales*, edited by Julian Roberts. London: Palgrave Macmillan.

Roberts, Julian, and Wei Pei. 2016. "Structuring Judicial Discretion in China: Exploring the 2014 Sentencing Guidelines." *Criminal Law Forum* 27(1):3–33.

Roberts, Julian, and Jose Pina-Sanchez. 2014. "Previous Convictions at Sentencing: Exploring Empirical Trends in the Crown Court." *Criminal Law Review* (8):575–88.

Roberts, Julian, and Anne Rafferty. 2011. "Sentencing Guidelines in England and Wales: Exploring the New Format." *Criminal Law Review* (9):680–89.

Sentencing Commission Working Group. 2008. *Sentencing Guidelines in England and Wales: An Evolutionary Approach*. London: SCWG.

Sentencing Council of England and Wales. 2011. *Assault: Definitive Guideline*. http://sentencingcouncil.judiciary.gov.uk/.

———. 2014a. *Fraud, Bribery and Money Laundering Offenses: Definitive Guideline*. http://sentencingcouncil.judiciary.gov.uk/.

———. 2014b. *Robbery Guideline Resource Assessment*. London: Sentencing Council of England and Wales.

———. 2015a. *Assessing the Impact and Implementation of the Sentencing Council's Assault: Definitive Guideline*. http://www.sentencingcouncil.org.uk/wp-content /uploads/Assault-assessment-synthesis-report.pdf.

———. 2015b. *Crown Court Sentencing Survey: 2014*. London: Sentencing Council. https://www.sentencingcouncil.org.uk/publications/item/crown-court -sentencing-survey-annual-publication-2014-full-report-2/.

Sentencing Guidelines Council. 2004. *New Sentences: Criminal Justice Act 2003*. London: Sentencing Guidelines Council.

———. 2007. *Sentence Reductions for a Guilty Plea: Definitive Guideline*. London: Sentencing Guidelines Council.

———. 2009. *Overarching Principles: Sentencing Youths*. London: Sentencing Guidelines Council.

Sparks, R. F. 1971. "The Use of Suspended Sentences." *Criminal Law Review*, 384–96.

Spencer, H. 1860. "What Is to Be Done with Our Criminals?" *British Quarterly Review* (July):42–70.

Thomas, David. 1970. *Principles of Sentencing*. London: Heinemann.

Tonry, Michael. 2004. *Punishment and Politics: Evidence and Emulation in the Making of English Crime Control Policy*. Cullompton, UK: Willan.

von Hirsch, Andrew. 1976. *Doing Justice*. New York: Hill & Wang.

von Hirsch, Andrew, and Julian Roberts. 2004. "Legislating Sentencing Principles: The Provisions of the Criminal Justice Act 2003 Relating to Sentencing Purposes and the Role of Previous Convictions." *Criminal Law Review* (August):639–52.

Wacquant, Loic. 2009. *Punishing the Poor*. Durham, NC: Duke University Press.

Walmsley, Roy. 2013. *World Prison Population List*. 10th ed. London: International Centre for Prison Studies.

Wasik, Martin. 2014. "Sentencing: The Last Ten Years." *Criminal Law Review* (7):477–91.

Young, Warren, and Claire Browning. 2008. "New Zealand's Sentencing Council." *Criminal Law Review* (4):287–98.

Young, Warren, and Andrea King. 2013. "The Origins and Evolution of Sentencing Guidelines: A Comparison of England and Wales and New Zealand." In *Sentencing Guidelines: Exploring the English Model*, edited by Andrew Ashworth and Julian Roberts. Oxford: Oxford University Press.

Youth Justice Board. 2014. *Annual Report, 2013–2014*. London: Youth Justice Board.

Anthony N. Doob and Cheryl Marie Webster

Weathering the Storm? Testing Long-Standing Canadian Sentencing Policy in the Twenty-First Century

ABSTRACT

In contrast with many Western nations, the structure of Canadian sentencing and its overall effects on imprisonment did not change dramatically over the past century. To a large extent, Parliament left sentencing to judges. Broadly speaking, imprisonment was seen as a necessary evil to be used sparingly. Sentencing principles legislated in 1996 largely reflected the status quo. However, the period 2006–15 reflected a dramatic break. The Conservative government in power repeatedly attempted to restrict judicial discretion. Prison was touted as the solution to crime. Scores of politically motivated modifications were introduced to sentencing legislation. Perhaps surprisingly, few of these changes had large effects on large numbers of people. There were no appreciable changes to imprisonment rates by the time of the Conservatives' electoral defeat in October 2015.

> The Wind began to blow as hard as it could upon the traveller. But the harder he blew the more closely did the traveller wrap his cloak round him, till at last the Wind had to give up in despair. (Aesop's "Fable of the Wind and the Sun")

Electronically published June 24, 2016

Anthony N. Doob is professor emeritus of criminology, University of Toronto. Cheryl Webster is associate professor in the Department of Criminology, University of Ottawa. We thank Michael Tonry and Allan Manson for suggestions on earlier drafts. Cheryl Webster's work on this article was supported by a grant from the Social Sciences and Humanities Research Council of Canada.

If we were writing this essay in the mid-1990s, the task of describing Canadian sentencing policy would have been considerably different. The theme would have been one of consistency, if not blandness or even monotony. For the better part of the twentieth century, there existed little controversy about what Canada should be doing. Absent were any of the dramatic swings in principles and practices witnessed in the United States and, to a lesser extent, England, as Canada's closest comparators. Canadians remained strongly committed to underlying values that had guided sentencing policy for decades.

We might have begun this essay by pointing out that there was little substantial activity in Canadian sentencing legislation for most of the past century. However, this would not be to say that there was no discussion. Canada had been actively discussing sentencing reform for over 20 years. After the introduction of three very similar sentencing bills in 1984, 1992, and 1994, the final one was enacted in 1996. Notably though, this new law would have been described as being largely an attempt to legislate the status quo. Not surprisingly, little of substance about the proposed sentencing legislation had been debated in the federal Parliament.

We might have pointed out that this new law essentially left the control of sentencing and the development of sentencing policy to trial and court of appeal judges. Similarly, it simply codified Canada's long-standing culture of restraint in the use of imprisonment. We would have emphasized that Canada had experienced a relatively stable imprisonment rate since at least 1950 (see fig. 1) and reminded the reader that governments, committees, and royal commissions established by the Canadian government had a long history of being pessimistic about the use of prison as an effective strategy to reduce crime. In numerous formal statements, government officials were critical of Canada's imprisonment rate, which was high compared to those of most civilized countries other than the United States and needed to be reduced.

To further exemplify this nation's commitment to moderation in recourse to imprisonment, we would have noted that despite its overall relative stability in levels of incarceration, in 1994 Canada had hit its highest rate since 1950—116 adults in prison per 100,000 people in the general population. More importantly, this high level was a matter of concern for both political parties that had shared power since the country was founded in 1867. But we would likely have pointed out that more troubling for Canadians than the absolute level of imprisonment was that the incarceration rate had been increasing more or less steadily, albeit

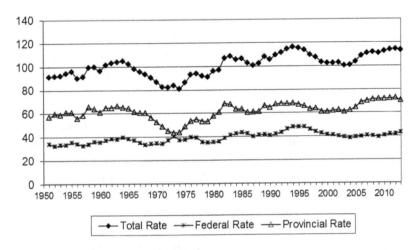

Fig. 1.—Total, federal, and provincial adult imprisonment rates per 100,000 residents (1951–2013).

slowly, since 1974, when at 81 per 100,000 it had hit its lowest point since 1950.

The 43 percent increase in two decades prompted provincial, territorial, and federal governments individually and collectively to search for ways to reverse the trend.[1] Though it was not well known at the time, we might have mentioned that even Alberta, Canada's most conservative province and the political home of Stephen Harper, Canada's prime minister from 2006 to 2015, reduced its imprisonment rate by 32 percent in the early 1990s (Webster and Doob 2014). Nevertheless, we would not have been optimistic that the promise in the 1996 sentencing law that "an offender should not be deprived of liberty if less restrictive sanctions may be appropriate in the circumstances" (sec. 718.2[d]) would be followed in Canada as a whole.

[1] As fig. 1 shows, the increase was more evident in the provincial rate (remand prisoners and those serving sentences under 2 years) than in the federal rate (those serving sentences of 2 years or more). Concern with persistent, albeit slow, rises at both levels of government encouraged the establishment of the Working Group of Federal/Provincial/Territorial Deputy Ministers to explore ways to contain prison populations.

In sum, our description of Canadian sentencing policy would have been a story of one nation that managed to defy the adoption of the, sometimes spectacularly, harsher sentencing policies and practices that emerged in other Western nations and translated into escalating imprisonment rates.

But we are writing this essay in late 2015. Our description of Canadian sentencing policy is considerably—if not dramatically—different than it would have been 20 years earlier. The early years of the twenty-first century brought the election of the newly branded Conservative Party of Canada under the leadership of Stephen Harper. From his three consecutive terms in power from 2006 to 2015 emerges a completely different sentencing landscape that stands—in almost all aspects—in striking contrast with Canada's long-standing past traditions.

Most notably, this government created an unrelenting stream of legislative proposals on criminal justice matters, many involving changes in sentencing laws. Almost all fit neatly into the "tough-on-crime" mantra that had been part of the Conservatives' appeal to Canadian voters. Not surprisingly, Canada witnessed a significant increase in maximum penalties for many criminal offenses and the introduction of a multitude of mandatory minimum sanctions—a relatively rare provision until recently. Even an inattentive observer could not help but notice the virtually complete absence of any moderating forces to this type of "law and order" legislation. The crime legislation produced between 2006 and 2015 was all in one direction: an unprecedented hardening of responses to criminal behavior. Notably though, imprisonment rates did not go up appreciably.

To describe this new Canadian sentencing policy of the twenty-first century, we begin in Section I with a brief outline of the structure of Canada's criminal justice system within which sentencing principles and practices take their form and substance. In Section II, we review the historically entrenched sentencing "culture" that we believe is responsible for Canada's relatively stable level of imprisonment since 1950. This long-standing approach forms the backdrop for understanding the changes that occurred in 2006–15. By juxtaposing these two periods, Section III illustrates the magnitude of the twenty-first-century transformations. Given that this essay was completed shortly after the Conservative Party lost power in the October 2015 general election, we recognize that the full effects of its legislative agenda will not be known for some time and its potential effects may never be known if key parts are modified.

With this obvious caveat in mind, Section IV discusses the broader significance of these changes. In particular, we suggest—analogous to the notion of *Governing through Crime* (Simon 2007) and consistent with recent writing on Canadian Prime Minister Harper's political motives (e.g., Wells 2013)—that the Conservative Party was interested in crime policy to change Canadians' underlying normative beliefs. Criminal justice policies not only reflect social values but may well, at least in Canada, be used by some politicians to attempt to shift social values. If our optimistic prediction is correct that Canada's imprisonment rate will not increase substantially as a result of the Conservative 2006–15 policies, this will show that criminal justice culture weathered the Conservative storm. Section V concludes with speculations on what the Liberal government elected in October 2015 might do in the area of sentencing and imprisonment.

I. A Brief Overview of Sentencing in Canada

Although Canada is a federation of 10 provinces and three territories, criminal law is a federal responsibility. With few exceptions, almost everyone in Canadian prisons is there because of conflict with a federal law. However, the administration of justice is largely under the control of the provinces.[2] Judges are appointed until a fixed retirement age by the provincial governments (for the judges responsible for approximately 95 percent of criminal work) and by the federal government (for the judges who hear a small number of serious criminal cases). The appeals court judges for each province and the national Supreme Court justices are appointed by the federal government. Appointments are made by the government in power and do not require approval by any legislative body.

Prosecutors are largely appointed by the provincial governments and are, in effect, civil servants with all of the stability of employment this term implies. They are assigned to specific locations but can be moved from one location to another. For certain offenses—most notably drugs—federally appointed prosecutors are responsible.

The federal criminal code sets down, for each of over 350 offenses, a maximum sentence and, in some cases, a mandatory minimum sentence.

---

[2] The three territories are under more direct federal control. For simplicity, we refer only to provinces.

Offenses in Canada are classified as either "summary conviction" or more serious "indictable" offenses. A significant number of offenses, including some relatively serious ones such as assault with a weapon or causing bodily harm, are called "hybrid" offenses. They may be tried either as a summary conviction offense (with a maximum sentence of less than 2 years) or as an indictable offense. The decision is in the sole discretion of the prosecutor, giving the prosecutor an additional tool to use in the plea negotiating process.

Mandatory minimum sentences were quite rare in Canada until 1996. There were a few obscure ones (e.g., for certain offenses related to prostitution), but the most frequently used mandatory minimums were and still are for impaired driving offenses (a fine for the first offense and a prison sentence for subsequent offenses). Murder has a mandatory sentence of life in prison with parole eligibility, normally, after 10–25 years. Since 2006, numerous mandatory minimum sentence laws have been enacted; some existing mandatory minimums were increased.

Maximum sentences give little guidance to the sentencing judge or to the public on what to expect as they are typically dramatically higher than sentences that are imposed in practice. For instance, breaking and entering has a maximum sentence of life in prison if a dwelling is broken into, and 10 years otherwise (and normally no minimums). However, only 4.7 percent of sentences handed down for this offense received prison sentences of 2 years or more in 2013. It seems likely that most maximum sentences have never been imposed.

As in many other common law countries, most cases are settled without a trial. In Ontario, Canada's largest province, for example, only 5.1 percent of all adult cases were resolved with a trial in 2014–15. Jury trials for offenses other than murder are very rare even though they are constitutionally available for all offenses punishable by 5 years or more. Most sentences are the result of "joint submissions" by the Crown prosecutor and defense counsel. Judges almost always accept joint submissions and impose the suggested sentence. For routine cases, prosecutors, not judges, are in effect the key players in determining sentences.

All sentences in Canada can be appealed by the prosecutor or the defense; the provincial courts of appeal are charged with hearing them. This level of court is responsible for ensuring that there is some semblance of predictability in sentences. That said, few would disagree with the following description of sentencing, other than the final sentence, contained in a passage from a recent Alberta Court of Appeal opinion.

We must face up to five sentencing truths. First, it is notorious amongst judges, of whom there are now approximately 2,100 in this country at three court levels, that one of the most controversial subjects, both in theory and practical application, is sentencing. That takes us to the second truth. The proposition that if judges knew the facts of a given case, they would all agree, or substantially agree on the result, is simply not so. The third truth. Judges are not the only ones who know truths one and two, and thus judge shopping is alive and well in Canada—and fighting hard to stay that way. All lead inescapably to the fourth truth. Without reasonable uniformity of approach to sentencing amongst trial and appellate judges in Canada, many of the sentencing objectives and principles prescribed in the *Code* are not attainable. This makes the search for just sanctions at best a lottery, and at worst a myth. Pretending otherwise obscures the need for Canadian courts to do what Parliament has asked: minimize unjustified disparity in sentencing while maintaining flexibility. The final truth. If the courts do not act to vindicate the promises of the law, and public confidence diminishes, then Parliament will. (*R. v. Arcand*, 2010 ABCA 363 [CanLII])

The final sentence might be interpreted as expressing the concern among many judges that Parliament might fetter the enormous discretion given to sentencing judges in Canada.

It is difficult to know how sentence lengths (or even the proportions of sentences that result in a prison sentence) have changed in the past 25 years. The reason is partly that judges are required to give credit for time spent in pretrial custody. In 1993, the overall Canadian imprisonment rate was 113 adults in prison per 100,000 total residents. Of this rate, 18 per 100,000 residents were on remand. In 2013, the most recent year for which we have data, the overall imprisonment rate was almost exactly the same (114), but remand constituted 38 per 100,000 of the total. Given that increased proportions of those being sentenced had presumably received some credit for time in presentence custody, it is difficult to estimate how sentence lengths have changed over time.

Those serving sentences of 2 years or more traditionally constitute about 40 percent of Canada's prison population. Hence their numbers can serve as a proxy for the number of people serving relatively long sentences. About 20 people per 100,000 Canadian residents were admitted to prison with sentences of 2 years or more in 1993—a rate that had increased gradually since the late 1970s. Three years later, in 1996 the prison admission rate for those with long sentences had dropped to 15, where it stayed through 2013 (the range during that period was 13–16). Even on this dimension, then, Canadian imprisonment rates look remarkably stable.

Prisoners in both the provincial and the federal systems typically are released at the two-thirds point in their sentences. Although parole is available for most prisoners after they have served one-third of their sentences, a recent study suggests that complete elimination of discretionary parole for those serving fixed-length sentences would increase imprisonment rates only by 2.7 percent (Doob, Webster, and Manson 2014).[3] Therefore, parole has little impact on most sentenced prisoners.

II. The Calm before the Storm: Canada's Approach to Sentencing in the Twentieth Century

Canadian sentencing policy in the late twentieth century can be divided into pre- and post-1996 eras. This temporal demarcation is somewhat arbitrary as changes were more fluid in nature. However, it highlights several relatively contained, yet worrisome, harbingers of things to come.

A. The Pre-1996 Era

In the 1980s and the early to mid-1990s, Canada was aware of the trends in imprisonment rates in the United States, its closest neighbor. Canadian politicians and Canadian parliamentary committees made disparaging remarks about the high levels of US incarceration. Over a 20-year span, overall American imprisonment rates had increased from about 155 in 1974 to 564 in 1994—an increase of 409 adult prisoners per 100,000 residents.[4] Canadian overall rates over the same period grew from 81 to 116 per 100,000—an increase of 35.[5]

---

[3] This excludes those serving life or indeterminate sentences. Of an average of 5,202 sentenced prisoners who entered Canada's federal prisons in the past 5 years, an average of 178 had a life or indeterminate sentence.

[4] Jail figures for US states are not reliably available until roughly 1980. Between 1980 and 2010, the state and federal prison population constituted, on average, 66 percent of the total (prison plus jail; range: 63–70 percent). It is plausible to estimate that the total for the pre-1980 period was approximately 1.52 times the prison rate.

[5] A more appropriate comparison would arguably look to states with imprisonment rates comparable to Canada's 81 per 100,000 residents in 1974. Five states then had imprisonment rates (not including local jails or federal prisons) "comparable" to those in Canada. The increase from 1974 to 1994 in each of these states was dramatically higher

While Canadian developments were far from demonstrating anything remotely similar to American developments, this era was nonetheless characterized in Canada by a continuing concern about its own growth in incarceration. Despite relatively stable rates since at least the 1950s, Canadians had been experiencing a disturbingly persistent, albeit gradual, increase since the mid-1970s. This growth was not the result of government policy changes. As we have described elsewhere (Doob and Webster 2006; Webster and Doob 2007, 2011, 2012), both Liberal and Conservative Canadian governments since the nineteenth century have seen prison as a necessary evil and have not favored heavy use of incarceration.

The irony of what was happening to Canadian imprisonment rates in the mid-1990s is that significant effort had been expended in the previous 10 years studying and making recommendations to address the rising levels. In 1984, the then-Liberal government released a policy statement on sentencing that clearly endorsed restraint in the use of imprisonment. Entitled simply *Sentencing*, it characterized Canada's recent policy statements as supporting "restraint in the use of criminal sanctions, especially that of imprisonment [and] increased availability and use of noncarceral sentencing alternatives" (Canada 1984, p. 4). It noted with obvious disapproval that "statistics are often cited showing that Canada incarcerates, on a *per capita* basis, more people than almost any other western democracy except the United States" (p. 8). The statement also offered strong arguments in favor of conditional release from imprisonment (parole).

Similarly, a policy-recommending royal commission, the Canadian Sentencing Commission (1987), repeated the refrain 3 years later that there should be restraint in the use of imprisonment. However, this commission went further and recommended a mechanism to accomplish this task. It proposed the creation of a system of presumptive sentencing guidelines along with abolition of discretionary parole (for all offenses other than murder, which has a mandatory life sentence, with parole eligibility coming after 10–25 years). However, the guidelines recommended would be different from the standard American grid. Instead, each offense (or group of similar offenses) would have an explicit guide-

---

than in Canada: Colorado, 1974 rate = 79, 1994 rate = 289; Delaware, 76 and 400; New Mexico, 81 and 211; New York, 79 and 367; Washington, 86 and 201.

line, the range of which would vary depending on the offense. There was no hint of a two-dimensional (offense by criminal record) grid, which was seen by the commission as too mechanical and too "American."

As the Sentencing Commission (1987, p. 324) noted, "There is a tradition in this country of not vesting all authority in one body and of providing checks and safeguards in order to achieve a balance of power." For this reason, courts of appeal would maintain enormous power, not only over individual sentences (a power that they have traditionally had) but also to amend the guidelines "for substantial and compelling reasons" (p. 328). Guidelines would be tabled in the House of Commons and would take effect unless a resolution rejecting them passed.

Sentencing guidelines, especially presumptive ones, were predictably not popular with judges. An apparently confidential report of the Supreme Court of Ontario Committee on Sentencing written by five judges rejected the "presumptive" guidelines but did not seem much bothered by "advisory" guidelines.[6] Their argument was simple:

> It is our view that it is generally undesirable and unnecessary to interfere with judicial discretion in the imposition of sentences in criminal cases, save and except to the minimal extent necessary to achieve clarity, consistency, and equity in sentencing policy. Put differently, restraint ought to characterize executive and legislative intervention in the sentencing process. We have no doubt that the proposed presumptive guidelines would inject into the sentencing process an element of coercion which would unnecessarily confine judicial discretion in an area where individualization is crucial.
> In practical terms, the proposed presumptive guidelines would be mandatory. . . . Presumptive guidelines are not necessary and go some

---

[6] The view that sentencing is a judicial, not a public, responsibility was made clear. The report pointed out, implicitly insulting the six judges (of nine members) on the Canadian Sentencing Commission, that "Unlike other reports, this one puts forward a new philosophy and a new scheme for Canadian sentencing. In effect, it changes the role of the courts. Our impression on reading the document, is that while some members of the Commission were judges, the document is entirely the work of professorial and research people. It is their language. No judge wrote this Report. Indeed, from the statistics quoted in the minority report, very few judges or lawyers engaged in the system would approve of it" (unpublished report by the Supreme Court of Ontario Committee on Sentencing [chairman J. A. Brooke], 1987, p. 7). The statistics, in a minority report (p. 340) written by a defense counsel, not a judge, showed that most Canadian judges, defense counsel, and Crown attorneys opposed presumptive guidelines in the mid-1980s. Interestingly, fewer judges than other professionals surveyed opposed them.

distance towards removing or dulling important areas of judicial discretion which assure a just result in a human process. (Supreme Court of Ontario 1987, p. 35)

Our understanding is that the Canadian Judicial Council (consisting largely of the federally appointed chief and associate chief justices across Canada and chaired by the chief justice of Canada) took a similar position in its confidential advice to the government. Canadian judges did not like any guidelines that might be created outside of the normal appellate process, which, of course, is controlled completely by judges.

Thus with strong opposition from federally appointed judges and a lack of support from a parliamentary committee in 1988 (or almost anyone else, for that matter), sentencing guidelines died shortly after being proposed and have never since been seriously considered. However, that same (Conservative Party–dominated) parliamentary committee in 1988 (Daubney 1988) reaffirmed the commitment to attempt to use imprisonment as little as possible, and in 1990, the Conservative government released another policy document proposing, among other things, that "a term of imprisonment should be imposed only

  i)   to protect the public from crimes of violence;
 ii)   where any other sanction would not sufficiently reflect the gravity of the offense or the repetitive nature of the criminal conduct of an offender, or adequately protect the public or integrity of the administration of justice;
iii)   to penalize an offender for wilful noncompliance with the terms of any other sentence that has been imposed on the offender where no other sanction appears adequate to compel compliance" (Canada 1990*b*, p. 8).

Simultaneously, a companion piece was released, reaffirming the importance of conditional release (Canada 1990*a*). While clearly reflecting continuing concern with reducing imprisonment, this document signaled the death of a second key proposal of the Canadian Sentencing Commission—the abolition of parole. When the Conservative government introduced a comprehensive sentencing bill in 1992 (C-90, 34th Parliament, 3rd sess.), it contained the by-then-traditional statement urging restraint in use of imprisonment (particularly in the case of vastly overrepresented Aboriginal offenders), but neither guidelines nor any

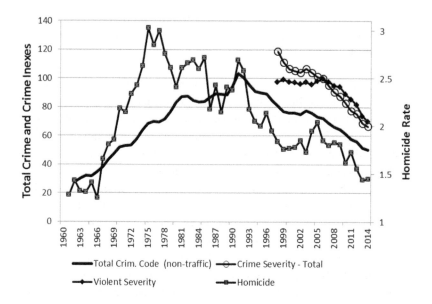

Fig. 2.—Canada: Crime (1962–2014). Total criminal code nontraffic incidents per 1,000 residents. Crime severity and violent severity indexes are set at 2006 = 100 and weight crimes by apparent severity (based on sentences imposed). Homicide rate = homicide victims per 100,000 residents.

movement toward removal of parole was anywhere to be seen. Notably though, this bill—which died when an election was called in late 1993— also contained a familiar statement that sentence severity should be proportionate to the gravity of the offense and the responsibility of the offender for that offense. Though proportionality had been the law in Canada for decades as a result of court of appeal decisions, it had not yet been placed into legislation.

Crime in Canada peaked in 1991 and began to decline. This fall occurred not only in total crime but also in violent crime and homicide (fig. 2). However, this reality was not particular to Canada. It was occurring in many countries, most notably, for Canadians, in the United States. In *The Great American Crime Decline*, Franklin E. Zimring (2007) noted that "there are extraordinary parallels in timing, breadth, and magnitude between the crime declines of the 1990s in the United States and in Canada" (p. 132). However, in the early to mid-1990s, it is unlikely that anyone was confident that Canada was experiencing what would ultimately turn out to be a long-term trend rather than a short blip.

Thus, from a policy perspective, Canadians continued to perceive their rates of imprisonment as a problem. The increasing rate of incarceration between 1974 and 1994 was occurring both for long sentences (a federal government responsibility) and for short ones (a provincial or territorial responsibility). In response, the federal, provincial, and territorial ministers responsible for justice (elected officials) met in January 1995 and instructed their deputies and heads of corrections to come up with a plan "to deal effectively with the growing prison populations" (FPT Ministers 1996, p. 1). It was clear from the initial and progress reports that the ministers were not looking for ways to build additional prisons.

However, it is important to remember that data for only 2 years of "decline" in crime were available when materials were being assembled for the January 1995 meeting; even then, the total crime rate for 1993 was down only to 1990 levels and the violent crime rate had hardly declined at all. The decision to "do something" about imprisonment was made at this January 1995 meeting. It was not a question of which laws to change. It was a question of what to change that would reduce imprisonment. But there were other factors to consider. Canada was in economic difficulties at this time, and spending additional money in the provinces or in the federal government was not seen as attractive.

The province of Alberta was already well on its way toward reducing imprisonment, though the original motivating goal was only to deal with a budget cut. It accomplished its goal—a balanced budget—through administrative measures that reduced provincial imprisonment rates considerably (Webster and Doob 2014). On a national basis, however, we expect that senior officials across Canada knew that, with creative policies and not necessarily legislation, they could address the problems they were facing.

In response, the deputy ministers produced a report. In cautious language so as to annoy no one, it noted that at a time when "government resources have been declining," imprisonment was increasing. Further, it mentioned that "many believe the incarceration rate [in Canada] is excessive in view of domestic factors and international comparisons" (FPT Ministers 1996, p. 2). It observed that "in Finland, prison populations have been reduced through policy changes that de-emphasize imprisonment, reduce penalties, ... set parole eligibility earlier, and increase the use of suspended sentences" (p. 3).

More importantly, they offered 11 recommendations—only two of which involved changes in legislation. Those two were to enact a "shared statement of principles for the Criminal Justice System," which included such values as limiting the use of imprisonment, and to amend the laws governing the release of provincial and territorial prisoners in order to give the provinces and territories more flexibility. Each of these recommendations might be seen as "enabling," but not determining, a reduction in the use of incarceration.

Implicitly, it seems, they knew where the action was. That is, it was in the administration of justice rather than in sentencing law per se. The deputy minister of justice of Alberta was not on the working group that produced the 1996 report. Had he been, he could have shared his experience in dramatically reducing imprisonment in his province without legislative change.

B. The Post-1996 Era

In 1994, the then-Liberal government of Canada introduced two bills that are crucial in understanding sentencing legislation in the following 20 years. The first, probably the more important, was a comprehensive sentencing code (part XXIII of the Criminal Code of Canada) incorporating into legislation what was generally seen as normal practice in sentencing. Though the bill was long and detailed, only three parts received public attention. First, some concerns were raised about the introduction of the "conditional sentence of imprisonment"—a form of suspended sentence—but politically it was not a large issue before the bill became law. The conditional sentence applied only to people who would otherwise be sentenced to prison for less than 2 years and thus was explicitly designed to reduce provincial imprisonment rates.

Second, there was a small controversy surrounding the last phrase in a statement in section 718.2(e) of "other principles" of sentencing, which stated that "all available sanctions other than imprisonment that are reasonable in the circumstances should be considered for all offenders, with particular attention to the circumstances of aboriginal offenders." Though obviously designed to address the contribution of sentencing to the overrepresentation of Canada's Aboriginal peoples in prisons, it was often described, in public discussions, as if it were an invitation to give more lenient sentences to Aboriginal offenders than would be the norm for other offenders.

The third, and by far the most publicized and controversial, section 718.2(a), now reads as follows:[7] "A sentence should be increased or reduced to account for any relevant aggravating or mitigating circumstances relating to the offense or the offender, and, without limiting the generality of the foregoing, (i) evidence that the offense was motivated by bias, prejudice or hate based on race, national or ethnic origin, language, color, religion, sex, age, mental or physical disability, sexual orientation, or any other similar factor . . . shall be deemed to be aggravating circumstances." For inexplicable reasons, this was seen as somehow giving special status to the gay community. The then minister of justice recalled when we interviewed him a few years ago,

> It's an irony that when we tabled [the sentencing bill]—75 pages of proposed legislation . . . the one thing that preoccupied the House of Commons and the public for 6 months before it got passed was the appearance of two words . . . "sexual orientation" in the hate crimes provision. Those boneheads didn't spend a moment talking about the policy of conditional sentences, didn't talk even about the [Aboriginal] provisions for recognizing the particular circumstances of aboriginal punishment, which I thought was daring at the time. I expected to have the roof fall in on me over that. They focused on those two words. . . . It was wild. Anyway, that just shows you the shallowness of the Reform [the far right opposition party that had almost completely eliminated the old Conservative party from the House of Commons in the previous, 1993, election] approach, and it also shows you how, in the public process of politics, the substance can be overlooked and not debated. The actual things that make a difference can slip past if you distract them with something gaudy that catches their eye, right. So, anyway, conditional sentencing, that was a very major change.

When asked whether he had put the words "sexual orientation" into the list of possible "hate crimes" criteria as a ploy to distract people from

---

[7] The original section was written as if the list was exhaustive by not containing the words "or any other similar factor." However, the subsequent addition in committee of those words seemed to have had no effect on the controversy surrounding the section.

the substantive parts of the bill, he laughed and simply said, "I'm not that clever."

So Canada acquired a sentencing code in 1996. Based, in part, on the usual list of traditional objectives (denunciation, individual and general deterrence, rehabilitation, incapacitation, etc.) and, more importantly, incorporating, for the first time, a strong statement of proportionality,[8] it maintained the Canadian tradition of leaving sentencing largely to the judges. It is highly unlikely that judges felt that their discretion was being limited in any important way by these new provisions. The principles—and the original list of aggravating factors (three in number)—largely left judges with legislated maximum sentences that were dramatically higher than sentences normally handed down and very few mandatory minimum sentences. Mandatory sentences were not part of this sentencing bill, which was introduced on June 13, 1994, and became law in 1996.

The second "sentencing bill" of that period did not focus on sentencing. On February 14, 1995, ironically while the first sentencing bill was still in the parliamentary process, the government introduced a firearms control bill that contained a set of mandatory minimum sentences of 4 years in prison for certain violent offenses (e.g., robbery, manslaughter, sexual assault) carried out with a firearm. These provisions were put in the firearms bill as a political "balance" for other provisions requiring the registration of all firearms, notably rifles and shotguns. For some time, there had been restrictions on the possession of handguns (and a broad category referred to as "prohibited weapons" such as automatic weapons and sawed-off shotguns), but rifles and shotguns, once legally acquired, did not need to be registered. This new bill would require registration.

Our own estimate is that the provision had little effect on overall imprisonment rates, in large part because offenders convicted of these serious violent offenses with firearms were already usually receiving sentences in that range (Webster and Doob 2007). In his remarks to a parliamentary committee examining the bill, the minister of justice indicated that his department's expectation was that there would be an increase in the federal penitentiary population as a result of this bill. One senior department official told us that they had set aside funds to

---

[8] "A sentence must be proportionate to the gravity of the offense and the degree of responsibility of the offender" (sec. 718.1).

pay for the expected effect on imprisonment rates. However, the sentencing provisions received only brief mention in the minister's initial speech in the House of Commons. The focus was on the requirement that firearms be registered—a requirement that remained controversial until it was repealed by the Conservative government in 2012.

The two bills—one endorsing proportionality, restraint in the use of imprisonment, and judicial discretion; the other imposing mandatory minimum sentences—were considered in the House of Commons at almost the same time. On the day the firearms bill, which included mandatory minimum sentences, passed the House, the next piece of business was the sentencing bill. As far as we could see in the House of Commons debates, no one mentioned any apparent contradiction between the two pieces of legislation. The contradiction between broad principles that would appear to be designed to reduce imprisonment and specific amendments to the Criminal Code that were designed to look tough was not, it seems, a public policy concern. When the Conservative Party took power in 2006, it focused on specific harsh sentencing provisions but did little to modify the liberal general statutory principles of restrictions on the use of imprisonment.

The 1996 legislation can be assessed in a variety of different ways. It produced, for the first time, a statutory statement of purposes and principles of sentencing. However, this section was not dramatically different from that contained in the earlier Liberal Party sentencing bill in 1984 or the Conservative Party bill in 1992. Three aggravating factors to be considered at sentencing were added: that the offense was motivated by hate, that the victim was the offender's spouse or child, and that the offender abused a position of trust or authority in relation to the victim. Various noncontroversial principles were also included: proportionality, a vague "totality" principle suggesting that consecutive sentences for different offenses being sentenced at the same time should not be overly long, and what might be interpreted as a mild presumption in favor of noncustodial sentences.

One other high-profile change in sentencing in the 1990s serves as a second (after the firearms mandatory minimums) harbinger of things to come. When the Liberal government proposed the abolition of capital punishment in the late 1970s, a challenge was to determine what the sentence for murderers would be. There was apparently no debate on one issue: the sentence would be life in prison. The controversy was rooted in the determination of a period of parole ineligibility. Prior to 1977, if a death sentence was commuted to life in prison, the offender was eligible for release on parole after 10 years. Parliament in 1977 enacted a 25-year parole ineligibility period for first-degree murder and a 10–25-year period (set by the judge) for second-degree murder.

However, in order to provide a "faint hope" of release to those serving life sentences with parole ineligibility periods longer than 15 years, prisoners who had served 15 years were allowed to go before a jury to argue that their parole ineligibility period should be reduced. On a vote of at least 8–4, the jury could reduce the ineligibility period.[9] Even though, for various technical reasons, the first hearings took place in 1987, the number of people becoming eligible for this procedure would not be expected to be very high until the early 1990s.

In 1997, there was public as well as opposition party concern related to two notorious murderers who were eligible for consideration under the "faint hope clause" for a reduction in parole ineligibility. The minister of justice introduced and Parliament passed legislation restricting access to this provision. Applicants thereafter first had to convince a superior court judge that a reduction could plausibly occur before their case could go to a jury, multiple murderers could not apply, and juries had to be unanimous—but only if they voted to reduce the number of years of parole ineligibility. Other than politics, there was no reason for this change.[10] As Roberts (2002) points out, most of those who have had hearings since the change have been successful. Between 1987 and January 1997, there were 105 hearings. In 84 of them (80 percent), the parole ineligibility period was reduced. This success rate did not change significantly after the jury was required to be unanimous. Between January 1997 and April 2013, 76 percent were successful.

For slightly more than a year in 2004–5, Canada had a Liberal minority government. The newly reborn Conservative Party was the official opposition.[11] One bill that related to sentencing involved reworking

[9] But even then, the prisoner would have to convince a parole board that release was appropriate.

[10] The most notorious case involved Clifford Olson, who had killed at least a dozen young boys. The jury that heard his case took less than 15 minutes to reject his request for a reduced ineligibility period.

[11] In the 1993 federal election, the Progressive Conservative Party was reduced to two seats from having a comfortable majority. The hard right "Reform" Party (mainly, initially, a western Canadian party) won 52 seats in the new Parliament. Between 1993 and 2004, the right-of-center parties regrouped and united under Stephen Harper, who served as prime minister from 2006 to 2015.

the law on child pornography and sexual exploitation, allowing for electronic presentation of evidence from children and a few other related matters. The only interesting aspect of this bill from a sentencing perspective was not the mandatory minimum sentences (e.g., 14 or 45 days for sexual touching of children in a dependency relationship with the offender) but that the then minister of justice, Irwin Cotler, indicated in Parliament that he personally did not support the mandatory minimum penalties provisions that had been included as a result of amendments from opposition members of Parliament at the committee stage. Cotler, a former law professor, indicated that he did not believe that mandatory minimums would act as a deterrent to anything but indicated he was willing to go along with the amendments in order to turn the bill into law. Simply put, he saw his choice as a stark one. When appearing before the Senate committee, he was blunt: "Our experience and scientific research show that mandatory minimum penalties are not a deterrent nor are they effective. All research, not only in Canada, but in other countries, shows that mandatory minimum penalties yield results that are the opposite of what people supporting the option wanted to achieve.... I believe that mandatory minimums serve neither as a deterrent nor are they effective. That has been my appreciation of the evidence thus far" (Proceedings of the Senate Standing Committee on Legal and Constitutional Affairs, June 22, 2005).[12]

However, other bills were introduced during this Liberal minority period that had certain commonalities with legislation introduced by the Conservatives who would take power in early 2006. The most hotly debated was arguably a bill designed to restrict the use of conditional sentences of imprisonment. This sanction had been introduced into the Criminal Code as part of the comprehensive sentencing reform bill in 1994–96. For reasons already described, it did not get much attention in the parliamentary process. However, it did receive significant public criticism after it became law, almost certainly because it was not well understood. Details on Canadians' lack of understanding of this sanction are available, but predictably the problem was simple: the sanction was not seen to be as punitive as it almost certainly was in most cases (Roberts, Antonowicz, and Sanders 2000).

---

[12] See http://www.parl.gc.ca/Content/SEN/Committee/381/lega/17eva-e.htm?Language=E&Parl=38&Ses=1&comm_id=11.

The Liberal government's response was to introduce a bill—not enacted—to reduce the availability of conditional sentences—but only presumptively, requiring judges imposing conditional sentences in cases involving more serious charges to justify why it was "in the interests of justice to do so because of exceptional circumstances" to keep the offender out of prison. There was no compelling evidence we are aware of that judges were, in a systematic manner, imposing conditional sentences inappropriately. However, it would be hard to find much fault in a requirement that judges justify their decisions, even though it might be unnecessary.

Another bill (which also did not become law) had similar features. Canada has the usual serious driving offense of dangerous operation of a motor vehicle with maximum sentences of 5–14 years, depending on whether the offense resulted in bodily harm or death, and also more serious general offenses of criminal negligence causing death or bodily harm. In September 2005, in part because of public concern and in part the result of a private member's bill on the subject introduced by a recently deceased Conservative member of Parliament, the Liberals introduced a bill on "street racing." The bill was almost certainly purely symbolic. Had it passed, it would have made participation in street racing at the time of the offense an aggravating factor at sentencing. It seems unlikely that very many judges would not have considered it as such on their own initiative since, among other things, the "aggravating factors" listed in section 718.2 of the Criminal Code are not exhaustive.

In Toronto, Canada's largest city, 2005 was and is still referred to by the media as "the year of the gun." A Google search on "year of the gun" brings up stories emphasizing that the 80 murders that year were more than in any of the previous 10 years (49 to 67).[13] Equally important, a high proportion were carried out with firearms. Since the English-language mass media are concentrated in Toronto, these details received a lot of attention. Unsurprisingly, the Liberals introduced a bill that appears to have been an attempt to restrict the lawful availability of

---

[13] The mass media are not inclined to discuss rates. Nevertheless, the 2005 rate of 3.2 homicides per 100,000 residents in Toronto, as opposed to the larger census metropolitan area, was higher than in any of the previous 10 years (range: 1.93–2.53). Toronto's mass media seemed completely uninterested that there had been 89 murders (rate = 3.90) in 1991. After each of these spikes, overall rates returned to previous levels. Equally notable, in 2005 a higher than average number of murders involved firearms (52 of 80) compared with 27 of 64 the previous year.

firearms. Notably, they proposed a mandatory minimum sentence of a year in prison for being in possession of a loaded handgun (without appropriate authority) or a prohibited weapon (e.g., a sawed-off shotgun, machine gun).[14] They also created new offenses: robbery of a firearm, and breaking and entering for the purpose of stealing a firearm, each subject to 2-year mandatory minimum sentences. We suspect that these two mandatory minimums would be well within the normal range of sentences that could be expected to be handed down for such offenses without the "special" new offense. As far as we can tell, the bill's introduction was not covered by Canada's major newspapers. Four days after the bill was introduced, the minority government fell and an election was called.

Though neither of these bills passed before the election was called, it appears to demonstrate that the Liberals were not averse to using sentencing policy in an attempt to respond to the public's emotional concerns. This politicization of crime would quickly extend to the third national political party as well. Early in the election campaign, a young white woman shopping during the day on Toronto's main shopping street was killed when hit "in the crossfire" by a bullet fired apparently as part of a dispute between black youth gangs. Referred to as the "Boxing Day Shooting," it seemingly helped convince the New Democratic Party, Canada's slightly left-of-center national party, to advocate tough-on-crime measures in an attempt to attract public support. The national parties were thus united on one thing: Canada "needed" tough sentencing laws.

III. The Perfect Storm: Canada's Approach to Sentencing in the Twenty-First Century

One might expect that sentencing policy in the early decades of the twenty-first century would be divided into two somewhat distinct periods, which could be called the minority and the majority Conservative eras. The 2006 federal election and the following one in 2008 resulted in minority Conservative governments, while the 2011 federal election gave the Conservatives a majority government. However, while this

---

[14] The mandatory minimum would be 2 years if the person was in possession of the loaded firearm in a public place.

temporal demarcation would distinguish the distribution of seats in Parliament across the three national parties, it has little bearing on sentencing policy. Perhaps because of the salience of "crime" issues in the 2006 and 2008 elections, but largely because the two national opposition parties were concerned about losing votes in the next election to the Conservatives, there was no organized parliamentary opposition to Conservative criminal justice legislation during either minority period. As such, the Conservative government reigned for 10 years with no consistent opposition to its criminal justice policies generally and sentencing policy in particular. More importantly, the entire period from 2006 to 2015 can generally be characterized as a dramatic break with Canada's long-standing traditions in sentencing. Both the "talk" and the "actions" of the Conservatives, as well as the general lack of serious opposition from the opposition parties, reflected a tough-on-crime approach. As a result, the Conservative government introduced nothing less than a punishment tsunami of new sentencing legislation.

A. Winds Picking Up: An Overview of Early Policy and Promises

The minority periods set the stage and the tone for things to come. The Conservative government's election promises, contained in its formal platform documents, coupled with its actions when it took power, make it clear that in discussing "sentencing," one needs to consider both what the government said and what it actually did. As part of its overall plan, the Conservatives promised, in the 2006 election platform, to do the following:

- introduce mandatory minimum sentences for certain offenses or circumstances (crimes committed while on parole) and legislate that certain sentences must be served consecutively rather than concurrently;
- restrict the use of conditional sentences (a form of suspended sentence that was seen as being used in lieu of normal imprisonment);
- eliminate the "faint hope" clause under which certain people serving life sentences could have their periods of parole ineligibility reduced;
- tighten up on parole release and eliminate "automatic" release at the two-thirds point of fixed-length sentences;
- reduce the credit given to time in presentence custody and make it harder to be released on bail awaiting trial.

In case it was not already clear that the Conservatives did not consider offenders to be full citizens, they also promised to "work for a constitutional amendment to forbid prisoners in federal institutions from voting in elections" (2006, p. 22).[15]

Most of the other recommendations in the "Stand Up for Security" section of their 2006 election platform were similar. They included more police, fewer restrictions on rifles and shotguns, harsher punishments for and more controls on sex offenders, and requirements of adult sentences for all youths convicted of "serious violent or repeat offenses." The only provisions that might be seen as recognizing the "social" causes of crime related to youths (e.g., supporting other levels of government in their efforts to address youth crime and directing $50 million—over a 4–5-year period—toward community programs for "young people at risk" [p. 24]). Further, the causes of crime were clearly linked to punishment. The 2006 platform noted that "the Liberal record on safety and security has been weak. The homicide rate is up, gun violence is a growing menace, drug cultivation offenses have doubled in the last decade, and the government has demonstrated an inability to deport criminals out of Canada—and keep them out" (p. 22).[16]

This type of language and, indeed, the specific policy proposals were different from those used before the turn of the century by the Liberals and by the previous Progressive Conservative Party, which governed with a majority from 1984 to 1993.[17] Not surprisingly, the new Conservatives in 2006 gave crime and justice issues more prominence in

[15] In 2002, federal prisoners were given the right to vote while in prison by the Supreme Court of Canada in *Sauvé v. Canada* (Chief Electoral Officer), [2002] 3 S.C.R. 519, 2002 SCC 68.

[16] Because of the scale we used in fig. 2, it is difficult to see exactly what was happening to homicide rates at this time. The most recent national data available in late 2005 and early 2006 would have been for 2004. The rate was indeed "up" that year. The 2004 rate was 1.95 homicides per 100,000 residents, compared to 1.73 in 2003. A more accurate description of homicide rates in Canada is that they had been dropping fairly steadily between 1991 and 2004. The correlation between "year" (1990–2004) and the homicide rate is −.83, quite a "distance" from a positive ("homicide going up over time") correlation implied by the politicians.

[17] Hatt, Caputo, and Perry (1992) demonstrate that the Progressive Conservative Party during this earlier period used somewhat different language to describe their criminal justice policies than did the Liberals. Nevertheless, this former political party certainly would not have been described as being in favor of imprisonment.

their campaign platforms than did the other national parties. Notably though, they and the Liberals both mentioned a 12 percent increase in the homicide rate in 2004. Everyone seemed to agree that mandatory minimum sentences were advisable for at least some firearms offenses. Even with a minority government, mandatory minimums seemed inevitable.

When the Speech from the Throne was read by the governor general on April 4, 2006, it repeated the kind of general statements that were contained in the Conservative platform.[18] Interestingly though, only about 7 percent of the words written for the governor general by the government were about crime, while roughly a third related to helping communities prevent crime. However, the landscape changed dramatically on May 4, 2006, when the Conservatives introduced two bills into the House of Commons. The first (C-9, 39th Parliament, 1st sess.) was designed to restrict the use of conditional sentences of imprisonment (a matter debated in the previous parliamentary session by the Liberals). The second (C-10, 39th Parliament, 1st sess.) would increase mandatory minimum sentences for a number of offenses involving firearms. In many ways, these two bills were typical of what Canadians could expect over the next decade.

The first was designed in a heavy-handed manner to restrict the use of a nonprison sanction by making it unavailable for any offense punishable by 10 or more years in prison. The problem with this restriction is that legislated maximum sentences in Canada mean little. Neither are they a good measure of the seriousness of the offense, nor are they highly correlated with sentences actually handed down.

The second bill raised mandatory minimum sentences for certain firearms offenses and offenses carried out with firearms. For example, robbery with a firearm at that time had a 4-year minimum. This bill would raise it to 5 years for the first offense, 7 years for the second, and 10 years for the third and subsequent offenses. But the changes were applicable only if the firearm was a handgun or a prohibited weapon (e.g., a sawed-off shotgun or machine gun). There was no increase if a rifle or shotgun was used. Notably though, it was not clear in the government's press release that the proposal was to increase mandatory minimums for these crimes by only 1 year (for the first offense). By describing the bill

---

[18] See http://www.lop.parl.gc.ca/ParlInfo/Documents/ThroneSpeech/39-1-e.html.

as imposing 5-year minimums, it was easy to assume, incorrectly, that there had been no mandatory minimum prior to the coming into force of this act.

Because there was a minority government, the opposition parties were able to modify these bills. But both, eventually, became law.[19] Importantly, changes made by the other political parties did little to mute their punitive bite. However, even this relatively minor moderating role would be lost in 2011 when an election was called and the Conservatives won the majority of seats in the House of Commons. While their crime policy did not change dramatically, the opposition parties did, sometimes, vote against government bills.

B. Unrelenting Rain: Characterizing Changes in "Sentencing" Laws (2006–15)

Government crime bills were introduced in both houses of Parliament, though largely in the House of Commons. The majority never became law—at least the first time that they were introduced. As it turns out, many were introduced two or three times (in different sessions of Parliament) before they became law. But the overall effect was that the media were inundated with tough-on-crime legislation. A nontrivial portion of these bills involved sentencing or other forms of punishment (e.g., changes to the laws governing release, creation of new offenses with harsher penalties than offenses from which they were derived).

The distinction for the public between a bill introduced into Parliament by the government and not enacted and a bill that was made law was not always clear. The government typically created a great deal of publicity around the introduction of a bill. It would issue a press release, often giving a combination of explanations for the "need" for the bill including denunciation, deterrence, and incapacitation. In addition, the Department of Justice would produce a background document explaining the changes in more detail. Often, the relevant ministers would also have a formal press briefing during which they would speak about the importance of the bill. Occasionally, the prime minister would make the announcement.

---

[19] Bill C-10 was not enacted in that session of Parliament but was bundled with four other bills into a single bill in the next session of the same Parliament (Bill C-2, 39th Parliament, 2nd sess.). The mandatory minimum penalty section was modified to become 7 years in prison for the second or subsequent offense.

No crime bill was ever defeated in Parliament—even during the period when the government had a minority of seats in the House of Commons. Having said this, some bills simply languished and died at the end of the parliamentary session. The passing of a bill was often not covered by the press and typically, if mentioned, received very little attention. The parliamentary process was, apparently, not of interest to the Canadian press. Hence from a political perspective, it was the introduction of legislation that was of interest.

In total, the Conservative government enacted 42 crime bills that became law while it was in power. None deviated far from the overall tough-on-crime mantra. Nonetheless, it was not obvious to us how to classify them for purposes of description. We ultimately adopted a two-dimensional grid. Changes in the law could be categorized as having an impact on either a small or a large number of people. Alternatively, the size of the impact on a given individual could be categorized as either large or small. Table 1 applies this four-part classification scheme to bills that became law between 2006 and 2015.[20] It is important to note that this categorization constitutes a rough and subjective classification of bills and does not attempt to classify all parts of all bills. We have a moderate amount of confidence that most of the bills we have identified do not fall into the "large impact" on "many people" cell of this table. But sentencing provisions are scattered throughout many of the 42 bills, rendering it very difficult to know exactly what the impact is of any one of them, let alone their cumulative impact. Some changes (e.g., changes to maximum penalties) we have ignored completely.

As an illustration, section 718 of the Criminal Code (the purpose of sentencing) stated until July 22, 2015, that "the fundamental purpose of sentencing is to contribute, along with crime prevention initiatives, to respect for the law and the maintenance of a just, peaceful, and safe society by imposing just sanctions that have one or more of the following objectives: (*a*) to denounce unlawful conduct." (This is followed by all the usual sentencing purposes.) From July 23, 2015, onward, this section was changed to the following (the italicized words are new): "The fundamental purpose of sentencing is *to protect society and* to contribute,

---

[20] In cases in which essentially the same bill had been introduced but not passed in an earlier session, we have referred only to the bill that was passed. Some bills (e.g., C-10, 41st Parliament, 1st sess.) combined a number of previously introduced bills into one "omnibus" bill.

TABLE 1

Categorization of Changes to Sentencing Laws, 2006–15

	Size of Impact on an Individual Offender	
	Small	Large
Number of people affected:		
Few	• Mandatory minimum for gun crimes (C-10, 39-1)[a] • Sentencing frauds (C-21, 40-3) • Reporting Internet child pornography (C-22, 40-3) • Auto theft mandatory minimums (S-9, 40-3) • Sexual offenses against children (C-54, 40-3) • Restrictions on parole (C-39, 40-3) • Tougher Penalties for Child Predators Act (C-26, 41-2) • Killing or harming police dogs or horses (C-35, 41-2)	• Restrictions on conditional sentences (C-9, 39-1) • Possible sequential parole ineligibility, certain multiple murderers (C-48, 40-3) • Repeal faint hope clause (S-6, 40-3) • Restrictions on pardons (C23A, 40-3) • Further restrictions on conditional sentences (C-10, 41-1) • Restrictions on transfer of international offenders back to Canada (C-10, 41-1) • Penalties for contraband tobacco (C-10, 41-2) • Trafficking in people and prostitution (C-36, 41-2) • Zero Tolerance for Barbaric Cultural Practices Act (S-7, 41-2)
Many	• Increased penalties, impaired driving (C-2, 39-2) • Increase to victim surcharge, no waiving of it (C-37, 41-1) • Changes to principles of sentencing (C-32, 41-2)	• Restricted credit for presentence custody (C-25, 40-2) • Eliminate accelerated parole review (C-59, 40-3) • Broad restrictions on pardons (C-10, 41-1)
No impact	• New offense: drive-by shootings, terrorist/organized crime murder sentence (C-14, 40-2) • Reverse onus, bail, gun crimes (C-35, 39-1, C-2, 39-2) • New crime: street racing (C-19, 39-1) • New aggravating factor: vulnerable victim (C-36, 41-1) • Drug-Free Prisons Act (C-12, 41-2) • Protecting Canadians from Online Crime Act (C-13, 41-2)	
Other punishing impacts	• Sex offender registry (S-2 40-3)	

[a] Bill number, Parliament, and session. Some were so-called omnibus bills in which large numbers of bills that had not passed in previous parliamentary sessions were bundled as a single bill.

along with crime prevention initiatives, to respect for the law and the maintenance of a just, peaceful and safe society by imposing just sanctions that have one or more of the following objectives: (*a*) to denounce unlawful conduct *and the harm done to victims or to the community* that is caused by unlawful conduct." The presumptions in favor of noncarceral sentences also changed. Section 718.2(e) quoted earlier had the italicized words added: "All available sanctions, other than imprisonment, that are reasonable in the circumstances *and consistent with the harm done to victims or to the community* should be considered for all offenders, with particular attention to the circumstances of Aboriginal offenders." We would not expect these changes to have much impact given that judges have become accustomed to the previous wording and no attempt was made to educate them on what these changes might mean. However, we also recognize that we may be wrong. In the 1980s, the Canadian Sentencing Commission (1987) struggled to move away from the notion that society should look to judges to protect it from crime. As the commission mentioned with what one assumes was an attempt at wry humor, "Intuitively, at least, one would rather resort to a security guard than to a sentencing judge to protect one's home" (p. 148). The Conservative government, it would seem, would rather see judges take on this responsibility. In any case, it is not obvious how important this change might be. We expect it to be small. But by definition, it affects all cases.

Another example is more concrete, but just as difficult to assess. We have listed the Tougher Penalties for Child Predators Act as having a small impact for a relatively small number of people. Our rationale is that we assume these offenses do not occur very often. However, there were, by our count, 11 separate increases in mandatory minimum penalties for these crimes (from those that had been in place before) and 31 increases in maximum sentences.

1. *Small Impact on Few People.* With these important caveats in mind, we identified eight sentencing bills that became law that in our assessment had at most a small impact on a relatively small number of people. For example, as mentioned earlier, the second "crime" bill introduced into Parliament by the Conservatives (C-10, 39th Parliament, 1st sess.; passed as part of C-2, 39th Parliament, 2nd sess.) raised the mandatory minimum penalty for those committing certain violent offenses with a handgun or prohibited weapon (from 4 to 5 years for the first offense and from 4 to 7 years for the second and subsequent offenses). Clearly, the change would have an impact on those who, otherwise, would al-

ready have qualified for the minimum sentences. But our calculations suggest that relatively few would be caught by this change. Further, it would add only 8 months in prison to the sentence of at least some of those being sentenced.[21]

Within the same logic, the government passed into law, in 2011, a bill (C-21, 40th Parliament, 3rd sess.) that imposed a mandatory minimum penalty of 2 years in prison for anyone convicted of a fraud (or set of frauds) involving a total value of $1 million or more. Again, it is unlikely that this legislation would affect many, if any, people.[22] Similarly, as part of S-9 (40th Parliament, 3rd sess.; originally C-53, 39th Parliament, 2nd sess., which later morphed into Bill C-26, 40th Parliament, 2nd sess.), the Tackling Auto Theft and Property Crime bill created a new offense of stealing a motor vehicle. Previously, suspects would simply be charged with theft (over or under $5,000). The new offense carried with it a mandatory minimum of 6 months in prison for the third offense. It seems unlikely that this mandatory minimum would make much of a difference.

As mentioned earlier, the Liberals had gone along with amendments from the Conservatives in 2005 to impose some mandatory minimum sentences on certain sex offenses against children. In one case, a mandatory minimum of 15 or 45 days (depending on prosecutorial decisions) was created. In 2011–12, Parliament—with a Conservative majority—increased this mandatory minimum to 90 days or 1 year. We do not know how many people were found guilty of this offense. However, a total of 762 adults were charged with this offense in 2013. To put this in context, 533,360 adults were charged with criminal offenses that year (140,946 for violent or sex offenses).

2. *Small Impact on Many People.* We identified three bills that we thought could have a small impact on many people. The first—the modifications made to the principles of sentencing—was discussed above. We are fairly confident in the classification of the second: the bill changing the penalties for impaired driving (part of C-2, 39th Parliament, 2nd sess.). Prior to passage of this bill, the mandatory minimum penalties for the family of impaired driving offenses were a fine of $600 for the first

---

[21] Prisoners are normally released after serving two-thirds of their sentences.

[22] Experienced defense counsel whom we consulted suggested that it would be a very rare offender who would be affected by this new mandatory minimum. Most already were receiving penitentiary sentences. The exceptions would be someone close to death, or perhaps someone who had completely repaid the victim for the losses.

offense, 14 days in prison for the second, and 90 days in prison for the third and subsequent offenses.[23] These sanctions were raised to $1,000, 30 days, and 120 days. Little explanation was given in Parliament of the need for these changes. The bill was first introduced by the parliamentary secretary to the minister of justice, who, on the issue of penalties, appeared to justify the change in terms of denunciation and deterrence:

> As for the penalties for impaired driving where there is no death or injury, the government believes they do not adequately reflect the seriousness of this offence. We are proposing to raise the minimum fine for a first offence to $1,000. When combined with the prohibitions on driving, provincial licence suspensions, and higher insurance costs, this should be enough to convince the person not to commit the offence again.
>
> However, for those who do commit another offence, we propose that they be subject to imprisonment for a minimum 30 days on a second offence instead of the current 14 days. For a third offense, we propose 120 days rather than the current 90 days' imprisonment. (Rob Moore, January 7, 2007, at 1635)

Notably, no evidence was given on the distribution of penalties actually imposed by courts.

One of the Conservative government's frequent themes was to pit the interests of victims against the interests of "criminals." This point was forcibly made in the Increasing Offenders' Accountability for Victims Act (C-37, 41st Parliament, 1st sess.). Since 1989, Canada has had a provision requiring those convicted of offenses to pay an amount of money into a provincially administered fund for services for victims of crime. The amount was originally established as 15 percent of any fine imposed or up to a set amount of money if there was no fine. Judges set the amount, or if the offender was indigent, they could decide not to impose the surcharge. In 1999, a standard amount—$50 for minor (summary conviction) offenses and $100 for more serious cases—was established when there was no fine. What was important, however, was that these surcharges could be waived if the judge determined that they would cause hardship to the offender or those dependent on the offender.

---

[23] The driving offenses are driving while impaired, driving with a blood alcohol level in excess of 80 milligrams of alcohol in 100 milliliters of blood, and refusing to give a breath sample.

This bill increased the victim surcharge on fines from 15 percent to 30 percent and the amounts for which no fine was imposed to $100 or $200 per charge (depending on the charge). More importantly, the provision allowing judges to waive the requirement was eliminated. Hence all offenders had to pay, even if they had no money and were being sent to prison. Effectively, it created a mandatory minimum fine for all criminal offenses. When the minister of justice was asked how indigent people could pay the victim surcharge, he proposed a solution somewhat more modern than "Let them eat cake." His advice to the poor was simple: "Sometimes they might even have to, God forbid, sell a bit of property to pay and make compensation to their victim" (Seymour 2013).

3. *No Impact.* There were six bills we thought would have almost no impact. Here are two illustrations. One change in the law created a new offense of dangerous operation of a motor vehicle while street racing (Bill C-19, 39th Parliament, 1st sess.), which had a maximum penalty of 5 years in prison or 14 years or life in prison if bodily harm or death resulted. For ordinary dangerous operation of a motor vehicle, the maximum penalties for these offenses are 5, 10, and 14 years. The government's explanation was simple: a new offense was necessary to send a message to Canadians about the seriousness of street racing by creating the new offense with increased penalties. On the day it became law, the minister of justice stated in a press release that it will "help protect Canada's streets and communities from the threat of street racing. People who disregard the safety of our streets must be met with serious consequences. . . . This activity is causing too many tragic and senseless fatalities on Canada's roadways" (Department of Justice, Canada 2006).

Between 2009 and 2013, an average of 4.8 people were charged each year with causing death while street racing across Canada. More than 10 times that number (66.8 per year) were charged with ordinary dangerous driving causing death. It is unlikely that this additional offense had any impact on sentencing. Further, an average of 58.2 adults (across Canada) per year from 2009 to 2013 were charged with any form of street racing, with most (82 percent) being charged with the simple offense of street racing (without injuries or death). Said differently, almost nobody (10.6 people a year) was even at risk of the higher penalties. In contrast, the Liberals in the previous session had proposed to make "street racing" an aggravating factor at sentencing—a proposal that almost certainly reflected traditional judicial decision making without help from Parliament.

A second change appeared to be an attempt to exacerbate a problem that Canada has been experiencing increasingly for roughly 20 years— detention in pretrial custody. Though not technically a "sentencing" issue, it relates to sentencing indirectly because remand custody—no matter what credit is given for time in custody before sentencing—is likely to be more punitive than "sentenced" time in Canada. Currently, 35 percent of Canada's prison population are unsentenced.

When Canada's bail laws came into effect in 1972, the onus was on the Crown in all cases to demonstrate the need to detain any suspect. The grounds for pretrial detention related to the likelihood that the accused would not appear in court as required or would commit a serious offense. Over the next 35 years, various exceptions to this legislation were created in which the onus was reversed, with accused people having to demonstrate why they should be released. By 2006, there were seven such "reverse onus" circumstances. Some reverse onus situations would affect large numbers of accused persons (e.g., an offense committed while the accused was on bail; certain drug offenders). Some were rare but could be understood in terms of the specific nature of the offense (e.g., murder, treason, alarming Her Majesty) or offender (a person not ordinarily resident in Canada). And some were clearly related to other concerns (offenses involving organized crime, terrorism, or threats; for the benefit of foreign entities or a terrorist group).

In its first minority session of Parliament, the government introduced a bill to place a "reverse onus" at the bail hearing of those charged with various firearms offenses (Bill C35, 39th Parliament, 1st sess.; passed in the 2nd sess. of that Parliament as part of C-2). By that time, such cases were almost certainly already, in reality, "reverse onus" since suspects in any case in which a bail hearing is held have to present a strong case in order to be released (Webster, Doob, and Myers 2009).

As one last illustration, the government introduced a bill (C-36, 41st Parliament, 1st sess.) in 2012 with the short title Protecting Canada's Seniors Act. Since one of us is a senior, we had a special interest in it. Fortunately, it is easy to reproduce it in full since it consists of only 24 words: "evidence that the offence had a significant impact on the victim, considering their age and other personal circumstances, including their health and financial situation" is an aggravating factor in sentencing.

Government ministers told Canadians that "our Government has a responsibility to protect elderly Canadians and to ensure that crimes against them are punished appropriately. . . . This legislation would further support our Government's common front to combat elder abuse in all forms. ... The interests of law-abiding citizens should always be placed ahead of those of criminals" (Department of Justice, Canada 2012). No judge we spoke to about this law thought it would have any effect since the relevant factors were almost certainly already being taken into account.

4. *Large Impact on Few People.* The mandatory sentence for murder in Canada is life in prison. However, those convicted of first-degree murder are automatically eligible for parole after 25 years, and those convicted of second-degree murder are eligible for parole on a date set by the judge that must be between 10 and 25 years. One bill (C-48, 40th Parliament, 3rd sess.) allowed but did not require judges to give consecutive parole ineligibility periods for certain people convicted of multiple murders.

Another bill addressed an issue that had bothered Conservative voters for years: the so-called faint hope clause (sec. 745.6 of the Criminal Code). This statutory possibility had been restricted by the Liberals in the 1990s and it was on the Conservative "hit list" in its 2006 party platform (Conservative Party of Canada 2006). It was not addressed until the second session of the Conservatives' second minority government. In 2009, they introduced a bill (C-36, 40th Parliament, 2nd sess.) that proposed the abolition of any possibility of reducing the parole ineligibility period for those found guilty of murder. Although the government allowed the bill to die, it was reintroduced in the Senate in the next session of Parliament (S-6, 40th Parliament, 3rd sess.). It became law shortly before the 2011 election. For a very small number of people who committed murder after the change came into force, the absence of even a faint hope of being eligible for early parole could make a considerable difference. However, the numbers are known to be small. Only 155 people have been granted earlier eligibility for parole since 1987, and as of April 14, 2013, only 139 of these had been released from penitentiary.

Another example that almost certainly involves very few offenders is the set of changes that were made in the "dangerous offender" provisions of part XXIV of the Criminal Code of Canada. An application to have an offender designated a "dangerous offender" and, by extension, be eligible for an indeterminate time in penitentiary must come from the prosecutor. One statutory change created a presumption that certain offenders would be designated as dangerous offenders if they had been convicted of one or more of several serious offenses on two separate occasions. Given the maximum sentences that exist in Canadian law, it seems likely that many of those designated as dangerous offenders would, in fact, have received very long definite sentences. This change was originally proposed in 2006 (C-27, 39th Parliament, 1st sess.) but did not become law until the following session in 2008 (as part of C-2, 39th Parliament, 2nd sess.). In the subsequent 4 years, an average of 36.75 people were designated as dangerous offenders, which is more than the average number in the previous 10 years (23.9). But, of course, one does not know whether the extra 13 people per year received this designation because of the change in the law or whether they will serve more time in prison as a result of being given an indeterminate sentence rather than a long "determinate" one.

Another provision that received almost no discussion was the proposal to make it harder for Canadians convicted of crimes abroad to serve their sentences in Canada. At a UN conference in 1975, Canada proposed that there be agreements between countries to allow people who had been convicted of offenses in other countries to serve their sentences in their home country. The first such treaty was negotiated with the United States in 1978. By the beginning of this century, about 75 Canadians a year were transferred from foreign countries, most often the United States, to serve their sentences (typically for drug offenses) in Canada. Before a transfer could take place, agreement had to be obtained from the prisoner and the two countries involved. The 2011 change in the law made it easier for the minister of public safety to refuse transfers. Ironically, of course, cutting down on international transfers (most with Canada involve moving Canadians into Canada rather than moving offenders from Canada elsewhere) slightly reduces Canada's imprisonment rate.

5. *Large Impact on Many People.* There were only three changes we could identify as having a large impact on large numbers of people. Notably, none was directly related to sentencing, but all three could affect the degree of punishment experienced by offenders.

The clearest example was the decision to eliminate a provision of the Corrections and Conditional Release Act, which created a "class" of penitentiary prisoners who presumptively would be released without an in-person parole hearing at the one-third point in their sentences. Canadian prisoners with fixed-length sentences are normally eligible for parole at the one-third point and are almost automatically released after serving two-thirds on what is referred to as "statutory release."[24] The prisoners who were treated differently under the prior legislation were, essentially, those in penitentiary for the first time (though they could have been previously imprisoned for periods of less than 2 years in a provincial institution) and serving sentences for a nonviolent, non-drug offense. They were virtually automatically released on full parole at the one-third point and were eligible for what is termed "day parole" after serving one-sixth.[25] One identifiable group of prisoners who typically qualified for APR were so-called "white-collar" offenders, typically given long sentences for fraud.

The government first introduced a bill to restrict this provision in 2009 (Bill C-53, 40th Parliament, 2nd sess.), but it did not go through the legislative process and died. After another false start in the next session of Parliament (Bill C-39, 40th Parliament, 3rd sess., which also died on the order paper), APR was completely eliminated with Bill C-59 (40th Parliament, 3rd sess.)—a bill that completed the legislative process just days before the 2011 election was called.[26]

Parole in Canada is more alive in statutory words than in fact (Doob, Webster, and Manson 2014). Largely on the basis of statistics about corrections and parole from federal and provincial/territorial institu-

---

[24] There are provisions for detaining people until the end of their sentences. Of 7,711 people released from federal penitentiaries in 2013, only 200 had been detained past the two-thirds point. It is not known how many of them are detained for the full last third of their sentences.

[25] Offenders on day parole typically are free to work or do some other "productive" activity in the community during the day but must return to a community corrections facility or to penitentiary at night. The original justification of accelerated parole review (APR) was largely cost. The Parliamentary Library's 2011 summary of this first bill was blunt: "APR was designed to allow non-violent offenders at low risk of reoffending to be released as early as possible to serve the rest of their sentences under supervision in the community. By accelerating release of those offenders, APR was intended to enable Correctional Service of Canada (CSC) and the National Parole Board (NPB) to focus their efforts and correctional resources on offenders sentenced for offenses involving violence or serious drug-related offenses and considered to be at high risk of reoffending. Application of this measure was supposed to produce significant savings for the correctional system, since the cost of incarceration is much higher than the cost of supervising offenders in the community.... The economic aspect was not insignificant when APR was introduced, since other legislative amendments had had the effect of lengthening incarceration periods for violent and dangerous offenders and thus significantly increasing the funds allocated each year to incarceration of offenders in the federal correctional system" (Casavant and Valiquet 2011, p. 2).

[26] The bill was supported in the House of Commons by the Conservatives and the (separatist) Bloc Quebecois Party, but not the Liberals or the New Democratic Party.

tions from 2012–13 (Public Safety Canada 2013), we estimated the impact on imprisonment if full parole (i.e., not counting day parole) was completely abolished for those serving determinate sentences (i.e., not looking at dangerous offenders or those sentenced to life in prison, who are largely those serving sentences for murder). If no compensatory changes were made (e.g., in sentencing or the granting of temporary absences from prison), the overall imprisonment rate should increase from the current rate of about 113.1 to 116.1 adult prisoners per 100,000. These estimates relate to a period when the number of people on release as a result of APR had decreased dramatically. Essentially, then, parole for ordinary offenders has already almost disappeared.

The elimination of APR occurred at the end of the 2010–11 fiscal year.[27] That year, an average of 3,331 people were being supervised on full parole. By 2012–13, this number had fallen to 2,853—the lowest in 10 years. Perhaps a more telling statistic in terms of the "accelerated" aspect of APR was that in the 8 years prior to the elimination of APR, those who were released on full parole served an average of between 37.9 percent (in 2010–11) and 39.4 percent (2003–4 and 2004–5) of their sentences. In the first year after the elimination of this provision (2011–12), those released on parole served an average of 41.5 percent of their sentences. In the second year (2012–13), this number had increased to 46.7 percent.

Day parole was available to this class of offenders after serving a sixth of the sentence. The new law made it available 6 months prior to full parole eligibility. Thus, the change would affect only those with sentences of more than 3 years. In the 8 years prior to the change in law, when a person was released on day parole, the release occurred, on average, after 32–33 percent of the sentence had been served. In the 2 years after the elimination of APR, prisoners released on day parole had served, on average, approximately 38 percent of their sentences before being re-

---

[27] The law made the elimination of APR effective immediately, even for those already sentenced. Since the elimination of "early" day parole (at one-sixth of the sentence rather than 6 months prior to full parole eligibility) had the effect of creating retroactive punishment for those with sentences of more than 3 years who were serving penitentiary sentences at the time, it is not surprising that the Supreme Court of Canada (*Canada (Attorney General) v. Whaling*, 2014 SCC 20, [2014] 1 S.C.R. 392) found this provision to be unconstitutional. By the time of their finding, however, most of those caught by it were already eligible for release under the new legislation.

leased. The overall imprisonment rate in federal penitentiaries moved up only marginally (from 39.3 and 40.5 prisoners per 100,000 population in the 2 years prior to the change to 41.5 and 41.6 in the 2 years after). Most of the effect of this change has likely already worked its way through the system.

Corroborating evidence that this change affected prisoners comes from an audit of federal corrections by the federal auditor general. He found that when the parole board had to look carefully at these files—files that presumptively, in the past, it essentially rubber-stamped for approval—it balked at releasing prisoners because they did not appear to have had the standard "programs" offered by Correctional Service Canada (Auditor General of Canada 2014). The decision not to offer this group "programs" is not surprising. The federal penitentiaries have a policy of not using scarce program resources on "low-risk" offenders with no ordinary criminogenic needs. In any case, there is a relatively short time between admission and release for some of these prisoners. The auditor attributed the parole board's decisions not to release this group of offenders to a lack of communication between Corrections and the parole board.

The second example of legislation affecting large numbers of people in nontrivial ways was Bill C-25 (40th Parliament, 2nd sess.), with the ironic (or, more accurately, dishonest) short title of the Truth in Sentencing Act. To understand this act—and the deceit in its title—one has to consider sentencing and correctional law simultaneously. Almost all federal and provincial prisoners (we estimate over 99 percent) serving fixed-length sentences are released at the two-thirds point or earlier. Before 2009, sentencing law in Canada indicated simply that credit could be given for time spent in presentence custody. Judges traditionally awarded 1.5–2 days of time-served credit for each day spent in presentence custody. This ratio reflected a combination of two factors: days in presentence custody do not count toward early release and time spent in remand is almost certainly "harder" time than sentenced time in Canada. In a tiny number of cases in which accused people suffered unusual forms of deprivation, 3 days' credit was given for each day in custody.

Since most prisoners are released before the end of their sentence (typically at the two-thirds point), a day in sentenced custody "counts" more than 1 day toward the sentence. If a prisoner were released at the two-thirds point, each day in prison effectively counts as 1.5 days toward completion of the sentence. Parole complicates matters even more. For instance, for a person released at the one-third point in the sentence, each day in custody would count for 3 days toward the sentence.

A simple example may suffice not only to justify the traditional attribution of 1.5–2 days' credit for every day spent in presentence custody but also to highlight the dishonesty in Bill C-25. Imagine an offender sentenced to 90 days. Not having spent any time in presentence custody, he will likely serve 60 days before being released. Consider a second offender who might also "deserve" a 90-day sentence but who spent 60 days in presentence custody. If this latter offender receives only 1 day's credit for each day in presentence custody, the offender would still have to serve another 30 days in prison postsentence (and would presumably be released after 20 additional days). This offender would serve a total of 80 days for a 90-day sentence. The inequity of treatment is clear. However, if the second offender was given credit at 1.5 days for each day served, the second offender—just as the first—would serve 60 days in prison. The only difference would be whether the prison time was served before or after sentencing.

The misnamed Truth in Sentencing Act ignored these niceties of the law, changing it to read as follows:

719 (3) In determining the sentence to be imposed on a person convicted of an offence, a court may take into account any time spent in custody by the person as a result of the offence but the court shall limit any credit for that time to a maximum of one day for each day spent in custody.

(3.1) Despite subsection (3), if the circumstances justify it, the maximum is one and one-half days for each day spent in custody unless the reason for detaining the person in custody was stated in the record [as being related to a previous conviction] or the person was detained in custody [because the offense was alleged to have occurred while the offender was on bail for another alleged offense].

When the government first introduced these changes, it was absolutely clear that it fully understood that a day in prison postsentence does not, in fact, count simply as 1 calendar day when calculating the date of release. However, the government and the non-Conservative supporters of the bill (which included most members of all opposition parties) were content to justify the bill as creating a law in which "a day is a day" whether spent in prison pre- or postsentence (for a full legislative history, see Doob and Webster [2013]). Some members of both legislative committees understood that the bill was fundamentally flawed. The Senate committee voted to amend it, but the full Senate did not accept the amendment. Hence, the misnamed Truth in Sentencing Act became law.

Notably though, the law was not bulletproof. The words "if the circumstances justify it" in section 719 (3.1) became an issue that was hotly debated. Notwithstanding the "correct" interpretation of this expression, the law appeared to have created the possibility of affecting a large number of people in a nontrivial fashion. In fact, Canada has a serious "remand problem" in that thousands of prisoners spend at least some time in presentence custody. In terms of numbers, 90,188 prisoners were admitted to sentenced custody in 2011, but 148,135 were admitted to prison on remand during the same year. Clearly, the effect of the new legislation could be considerable.

To this list, we would also suggest adding Bill C-10 (41st Parliament, 1st sess.). This law, among a large number of other provisions, introduced broad restrictions on pardons. The government made it impossible, in some cases, and more difficult, in all others, to have a criminal record suppressed. Although not a sentencing bill per se, one collateral effect of conviction is having a criminal record. Criminologists have recently begun to highlight the nontrivial consequences of this label for the lives of ex-offenders (e.g., Pager 2003).

IV. Surveying the Damage: Making Sense of the Changes in Sentencing Laws in This Century

The Conservative Party of Canada was voted out of power in the general election of October 2015 and became the official opposition. The Liberal Party became a majority government, officially ending the Harper decade. Although it is still very early fully to assess the last decade of Canadian politics as it affected sentencing policy, some initial, albeit tentative, impressions seem justified.

A. Taking Stock of the Storm's Vestiges: Describing Changes to Sentencing Policy in the Twenty-First Century

At first glance, this 10-year period looks remarkably "un-Canadian." Arguably the most important—and potentially the most lasting—change was that almost no one in government (or the opposition parties) was talking about restraint in the use of imprisonment or the need to focus on the reintegration of offenders into society. In their place was pre-dominantly a tough-on-crime message whose tangible form was a con-tinuous streak of harsh-sounding provisions made into laws to reflect the seriousness of the crime or deter "bad" people from committing (more) crime.

In many ways, the Conservative government saw the response to any problem related to crime as necessarily having to be punitive in nature. The new legislation that significantly restricted the use of pardons is a case in point. This change arose, in large part, from two cases. The first involved a notorious murder case in which one accused, a woman, had negotiated a plea to manslaughter rather than murder. She was soon to be eligible for a pardon. The second case involved a former hockey coach who had been found guilty, decades after the offenses took place, of sexual offenses against some of the boys whom he had been coaching. He served his sentence and, after the appropriate time had passed (5 years), applied for and was granted a pardon. Some years later, additional men came forward with evidence that he had sexually assaulted them as boys at the same, much earlier, period in his life. He was tried for the additional offenses and was again found guilty. Notwithstanding that this was not only an unusual case but the "new" offenses had taken place decades be-fore the pardon had been granted, and there was no evidence that he had committed offenses after receiving the pardon, these circumstances were seen as demonstrating that "something needed to be done" about par-dons. Indeed, former Public Safety Minister Vic Toews said that this case "confirmed the existence of this tendency [by the Parole Board of Canada] to the automatic granting of pardons" (Standing Senate Com-mittee on Legal and Constitutional Affairs 2010).[28]

Notably, this statement was made at the same session of the commit-tee in which the chair of the National Parole Board spoke. He pointed out that in 2009–10, roughly 7,000 of 32,000 offenders requesting a par-don were rejected as being ineligible and another 425 were rejected be-cause the board felt that they had not demonstrated good conduct in prison. More importantly, he noted,

[28] http://www.parl.gc.ca/Content/SEN/Committee/403/lega/11eva-e.htm?Language=E&Parl=40&Ses=3&comm_id=11.

The aim is to reduce the barriers and stigmas faced by an individual with a criminal record if he can demonstrate a commitment to live as a law-abiding citizen. The program has a dual benefit: to assist the individual to move forward in his rehabilitation and to enhance the safety of communities by motivating the individual to remain crime free and to maintain good conduct. ... Since the pardon program was introduced, interest in securing a pardon has grown. This is in part because the number of Canadians with criminal records has increased. Also, more scrutiny is placed on an individual's past when applying for a job, securing a loan, volunteering in the community, getting certain licences or furthering an education. (Standing Senate Committee 2010)

The government's ultimate response to its manufactured concern about pardons was exclusively punitive. First, it changed the name from "pardon" to "record suspension" because the Conservatives found it inappropriate that a former offender was being "pardoned." Second, it raised the cost for an application (in two steps, from $50 to $150 to $631), arguing that "ordinary Canadians" should not be paying for pardon applications for "criminals." Third, certain offenses were excluded, including most sexual offenses or sexual offenses in relation to children. Fourth, the government extended the waiting time after the expiry of all parts of the sentence from 3 or 5 years (depending on the nature of the prosecution) to 5 or 10 years. Finally, it attempted to make it easier for the parole board to reject an application. At no point was any empirical evidence referred to as a justification for any of these changes. Most notably, the evidence on the length of time that must pass before someone who had been found guilty has no higher a likelihood of reoffending than do others in the community was not raised (e.g., Kurlychek, Brame, and Bushway 2006, 2007; Blumstein and Nakamura 2009; Bushway, Nieubeerta, and Blockland 2011). In sum, the "problem" to be solved by legislative change seemingly did not need to be "real."

In a similar vein, the procedure involving the transfer of "international offenders" back to Canada to serve their sentences was almost certainly unknown to most Canadians. More importantly, it was not, as far as we can tell, seen to be a problem by anyone. No records of offenders being refused reentry by Canada could be found until 2006, when the Harper government started to reject transfers. It became an issue only when the public safety minister began turning down significant numbers of applicants and was himself overturned by the courts, which suggested that he needed to have a justification for rejecting otherwise eligible applicants. Equally notable, the legislative solution to this apparently imaginary problem was at best short-sighted and at worst disingenuous. The government justified the new law to restrict international transfers on the grounds of public safety. However, as Greenspan and Doob (2011) pointed out, this act will not protect Canadians as it "ignores the reality that, eventually, these offenders will return because they're Canadian.... Being deported to Canada at the end of the foreign sentence will mean offenders won't have had the benefit of rehabilitative programs; they probably will have lost contact with family and friends who assist in their reintegration, and Canada will have no special controls over them."

The second clear effect of the sentencing policies of the Harper era is that there was no attempt to value coherence in the law and, by extension, target areas in need of real reform. Rather, it sometimes appeared as if sections of the Criminal Code were randomly selected and penalties were increased for no obvious reasons. We offer a pointed example. During a period when the news was dominated by noncriminal matters such as financial crises, falling oil prices, concern with the health of returning Canadian veterans, controversies surrounding missing and murdered Aboriginal women, scandals involving Conservative senators, increasing unemployment, worldwide concern with global warming, terrorist attacks, and third-world working conditions, the Harper Conservatives in three separate bills amended the single Criminal Code section relating to having sex with animals in front of children.

Until April 30, 2008, section 160 provided that anyone having sex with an animal in front of a child under age 14 was guilty of an indictable offense punishable by up to 10 years in prison (or a maximum of 6 months if the Crown prosecutor chose to proceed by summary conviction). This law was changed on May 1, 2008, to make it an offense if the bestiality took place in front of a youth aged 16 or under. Penalties did not change at this point, but the government implemented higher penalties on August 9, 2012. A mandatory minimum of 1 year by indictment and a minimum of 6 months (to a maximum of 2 years less a day) by way of summary conviction were legislated for having sex with animals in front of children 16 and under. Seventeen days before the 2015 election was called, the maximum sentence for the cases by indictment was raised to 14 years. Throughout this period, the penalties for bestiality in private or in the presence of an adult did not change. No argument or evidence was ever provided for the need for these changes.

Presumably, the purpose of these changes was to try to focus public attention on the punishment sections of the Criminal Code rather than on social and economic problems that were much more difficult for the government to change. Arguably more problematic is that this seemingly arbitrary and piecemeal approach to sentencing reform would appear to have only added to the incoherence of the criminal law. Specifically, bestiality in the presence of a 15-year-old currently is more serious than assault of a 15-year-old with a weapon or causing bodily harm. Depending on prosecutorial choices, assault with a weapon or causing bodily harm is punishable with a maximum term of imprisonment of up to 10 years or 18 months. There is no minimum penalty. In a similar vein, the Conservatives were also concerned with marijuana cultivation and imposed new penalties in 2012. As they are currently written, growing six marijuana plants for sharing with friends makes one liable to a mandatory minimum of 6 months (if one owns the premises) and 9 months (if the premises are rented). The maximum penalty is 14 years in prison.

More generally, it is not surprising that the original list of "aggravating factors" in sentencing has grown considerably since the current overall sentencing structure became law in 1996. At that point, three items were listed as aggravating factors. By the 2015 election, there were eight (Criminal Code of Canada, sec. 718.2[a]).

The third effect is less obvious. An exclusively punitive approach to crime rooted predominantly in deterrence and incapacitation would theoretically be reflected in an increased recourse to prison. Though few bills in our estimate were likely on their own to have a dramatic effect on imprisonment rates, the cumulative effect of a significant number of changes could be nontrivial. Moreover, several of the bills (e.g., the changes in the credit given to people for time in presentence custody) could have considerable impact. Similarly, the creation of a mandatory fine as a "victim surcharge" on all indigent offenders (with imprisonment for nonpayment) is not to be trivialized.

Notwithstanding this logic, the imprisonment data presented in figure 1 suggest that the effect of the legislative changes under the Harper government on Canadian imprisonment rates, as of 2013–14, was not large. While the overall rate of incarceration is almost as high as it has ever been, the rate of increase in the last 10 years has not been huge. Clearly though, one needs to be cautious because the effects of some of the new laws would be unlikely to show up immediately.

Having said this, examining the three changes to legislation that are likely to have a large effect may tell us something about the future. Most obviously, restrictions on pardons will not affect sentencing. Further, while the effect of restrictions on the credit for presentence custody could have been huge, it has likely been significantly muted by a Supreme Court decision "interpreting" the legislation to permit a substantially greater use of a 1.5 : 1 ratio for time served (*R. v. Summers*, 2014 SCC 26 [2014] 1 S.C.R. 575). And finally, although the elimination of APR clearly has a wide punitive bite, it is likely that most of its effect on imprisonment rates has already occurred. We would propose that the explanation for the apparently small impact of these punitive changes on imprisonment might lie elsewhere.

B. Uncovering the Forces behind the Storm: Understanding Changes to Sentencing Policy in the Twenty-First Century

The obvious caveat to our attempt to understand why a government that advertised itself as tough on crime and prided itself on showing no compassion for offenders did not end up being, in practice, especially punitive (at least as measured by levels of imprisonment) is that we may never really know. Our explanations are speculative at best, particularly given the short period since the Harper government was defeated. Moreover, there may be no real way of proving or disproving our speculations. This is especially true if the Harper government's changes would have had a significant future impact on Canadian imprisonment rates but for modifications made to sentencing legislation after 2015. The separation of effects may be impossible to untangle.

1. *Canadian Courts as a Moderating Factor.* As discussed earlier, Canadian judges have traditionally had substantial leeway in assigning sentences. Generally speaking, until the mid-1990s there were very few mandatory minimum sentences and very high, but meaningless, maximum sentences. As noted by the Canadian Sentencing Commission (1987), maximum sentences give Canadian judges almost no direction on how to sentence offenders. To know how a person will be sentenced in Canada, one needs to know current practice in the trial courts and what the provincial court of appeal has said on the subject for the particular offense. We lack good data on it, but it seems likely that there is province-

to-province variation in sentencing (at least for some offenses) because provincial court of appeal decisions are binding only within the province.

The courts have traditionally resisted practices they see as blatantly unfair. There are three ways that courts in Canada can avoid what they see as unjustifiably harsh or unfair laws. Under the Canadian Charter of Rights and Freedoms, judges can find laws to be unconstitutional (most obviously by declaring them cruel and unusual). Second, they can give a benevolent interpretation to the written law. Or the courts can disregard Parliament's intention and compensate in other ways (e.g., by giving a shorter sentence to counterbalance mandatory harshness somewhere else).

These practices of circumvention are arguably well illustrated by the judicial (and likely prosecutorial) response to the previously discussed Bill C-25 (40th Parliament, 2nd sess.), which restricted credit for time served in pretrial detention (the Truth in Sentencing bill). The strict reading of this change in the law was blatantly unfair. If a person were granted 1 day's credit toward the sentence for each day in pretrial detention, those held in pretrial detention would automatically spend more time in prison than an equivalent offender given the same sentence but who spent no time in remand.

Shortly after the provision became law, a Toronto judge held a protracted sentencing hearing, involving witnesses and experts. Its purpose was to hear evidence on credit for pretrial detention in a routine cocaine trafficking case (the offender sold $20 in cocaine to an undercover police officer). For various reasons, he had spent months awaiting trial and sentencing. In a 32,000-word judgment (*R. v. Johnson*, 2011 ONCJ 77 [CanLII]), the judge gave a creative interpretation to the law that allowed him to give the credit for presentence custody that he would have given before the change in the law. The critical section of the new legislation indicated that judges could give more than 1:1 credit "if the circumstances justify it" but that the maximum would be 1.5 days' credit. Justice Melvyn Green decided that the circumstances justified 1.5 days' credit (because sentenced prisoners can earn remission and remand prisoners cannot) and essentially concluded that it did not matter if those same circumstances would hold for almost all offenders being sentenced. He pointed out that this interpretation dealt with the arithmetic issue of credit but did not deal adequately with the fact that the conditions in which the offender had been housed—an overcrowded and outdated jail—were harsher than sentenced custody facilities typically are. By extension, Justice Green decided that "conditions" were to be taken into account directly in determining the actual sentence (prior to the calculation of the credit for time already served). For our purposes, the details are unimportant. What is important is that Justice Green accomplished what he set out to do: hand down what he considered to be a just and fair sentence that attempted to equate total punishment for an offender who had spent time in presentence custody with offenders who had not.

Not surprisingly, this issue eventually made its way to the Supreme Court. The justices seemingly had little difficulty with it. In a unanimous decision (*R. v. Summers* [2014] 1 S.C.R. 575, 2014 SCC 26 [CanLII]), they indicated that judges could routinely give credit of up to 1.5 days in custody. Circumstances, in effect, almost always justified it. However, this "arithmetic" issue deals only with compensating offenders who have served time in pretrial detention for the effect of virtually automatic remission of sentences. However, sentencing in Canada is inexact enough that it would be quite possible for judges to compensate—silently—for the blatant unfairness of the law as written. In other words, it would be almost impossible to know if judges were reducing sentences somewhat (before calculating credit for presentence custody).

Perhaps the most interesting example of judicial creativity in avoiding what are seen as disproportionate sentences comes from the judicial response to the increased—and mandatory—victim surcharges. From the perspective of the accused, it almost certainly matters little whether the money being paid goes to victims or to the provinces' general revenue. Victim surcharges are, essentially, a mandatory financial penalty.

The difficulty arose fairly quickly when judges were faced with indigent clients who had close to zero likelihood of ever being able to pay the surcharge. The government had indicated, in Parliament, that the purpose of making the surcharge mandatory was that judges were routinely waiving it in certain cases (e.g., if the offender was imprisoned) without sufficient reason (in the government's view). There were diverse ways to address that problem. The first was for the judge to ignore the problem and impose the mandatory surcharge, letting the province deal with offenders who could not pay. The second approach was initially used fairly often, apparently. A judge who had not planned to impose a fine, in many but not all instances, could impose a token fine in addition to whatever the appropriate sentence might be. If the offender would normally be given a simple term of probation, the victim surcharge would normally be either $100 or $200 for each charge on which a finding of guilt was made. However, the way the law was written, if a fine were imposed, the legislation indicated that the surcharge was calculated as 30 percent of the fine.[29] As one judge noted in a case in which he chose not to impose a surcharge:

> In [a previous] case I imposed a nominal fine of $1 and the equivalent of 45 days in jail on an offender for two alcohol thefts from [the provincial liquor store]. I explained that I imposed the nominal fine because I concluded that in all the circumstances of the case, the time in jail coupled with $200 in surcharges would be disproportionate given his personal circumstances. By imposing two $1 fines, the surcharge would apply but at a modest rate of 60 cents, 30 percent of each fine, which would not add to the punitive impact of the overall sentence. I have done this in a handful of cases. (*Her Majesty the Queen v. Shaun Michael*, 2014 ONCJ 360 CanLII, para. 102)

The difficulty, as the judge noted, is that in some circumstances fines are not permitted. Hence this method of "circumventing" the law would be unavailable. In this case, Justice David Paciocco took the issue head-on. The accused, an indigent Inuit man from the territory of Nunavut, was found guilty of nine separate charges arising from his addiction to alcohol (three separate incidents involving thefts, resisting arrest, and assaults). He was living on welfare income of approximately $250 per month and had no reasonable prospects of being able to pay a victim surcharge of $900. The judge found the section to be unconstitutional because it violated the Charter of Rights and Freedom's prohibition of cruel and unusual punishment.

2. *Structural Obstacles as a Moderating Factor.* A second possible explanation of why myriad Conservative government sentencing law changes had little discernible effect on imprisonment levels is a variant on the same theme. Although the government may have been fully committed to introducing harsher punishment as its ultimate goal, there may simply

---

[29] A careful reader might wonder about the drafting. The intent may have been to have the surcharge be the larger of 30 percent of the fine or the mandatory minimum. Recent reports suggest that the Department of Justice had contemporaneously cut the number of qualified policy analysts. Assuming this was an error, it could have been the result of a risk-averse policy analyst strictly following orders from a political staff person.

not exist any obvious or easy mechanisms to accomplish this goal. While criminal law is the responsibility of the federal government in Canada, the structure of the criminal justice system and the ways it is administered make it very difficult to make changes. The divisions of responsibility among the federal government, the provincial governments, and municipalities (which are responsible for policing) have meant that the government of Canada has traditionally been reluctant to legislate on criminal justice policy without a consensus, at least among the largest provinces. Spending money on prisons has never been very popular. Particularly given that the provinces pay for the housing of about 60 percent of all prisoners, the provinces would be unlikely to support dramatic increases in their prison populations.

In addition, judges and prosecutors are appointed until retirement age, giving them a significant level of independence from Parliament and the whims of the general public. Further, the structure of sentencing in the Criminal Code leaves all key decisions to the judge. Within this broader context, it is hard to know what the Harper government could actually have done, other than what it did by adding some mandatory minimum sentences, to increase the severity of punishment.

Indeed, with few exceptions, the Harper government found no easy levers to push to render the criminal law broadly more punitive. Canada's flirtation with sentencing guidelines in the 1980s was halted in its tracks by judges, jealous of their power to determine sentences. The closest equivalents to guidelines are the Alberta Court of Appeal's "starting points" (see, e.g., *R. v. Arcand* [2010] ABCA 363 [CanLII]). Furthermore, the government is constrained somewhat by the law. Proportionality has almost been considered as constitutionally required before and after it was first formally put into legislation (see *R. v. Smith* [1987] 1 S.C.R. 1045; *R. v. Ipeelee* [2012] 1 SCR 422 at the Supreme Court of Canada and *R. v. Safarzadeh-Markhali* [2014] ONCA 627 [CanLII] at the Ontario Court of Appeal).

In contrast with California's laws, in which determinate sentencing allowed for easy changes in sentencing severity by the legislature and directly by the public through referenda (Campbell 2014), the public has no direct levers of influence in Canada, and the government appears to be constrained by the courts and by the structure of the law. As Tonry (2013, p. 470) points out, the changes that took place in the United States may have enabled the development of an "out-of-control sentencing system and an imprisonment rate that no one foresaw or would have wanted." In effect, the tough-on-crime approach that started, largely, in the 1980s in the United States may have built on sentencing structures that were designed to achieve something quite different.

The Canadian Sentencing Commissioners were aware of the risk of creating a structure that would enable sentencing to spin out of control. Their recommendations were designed with concern that an opportunistic future legislature might increase sentencing severity for purely political purposes. However, looking back almost 30 years, it is clear that in some areas—areas of which the Ontario judges' committee (Supreme Court of Ontario Committee on Sentencing, 1987) apparently approved—their recommendations might have made sentencing more vulnerable to being turned into a vote-gathering tool. For instance, the Ontario judges approved of a recommendation that maximum sentences for each offense be set according to what is realistic. The commission had proposed that each criminal offense have a maximum sentence legislated (6 months or 1, 3, 6, 9, or 12 years). The idea was that the maximum sentences would set a "standard" for the judges and the public in that serious cases would get the maximum sentence or something near to it. It is easy to see why this approach would be attractive to judges as it would make their sentences more understandable but would not constrain them in any important way.

The guidelines recommended by the Canadian commission and rejected absolutely by the Ontario judges were, by American standards, quite wide. This characteristic reflected, the commission thought, the need to represent a wide breadth of behavior in many offenses. Using the example of breaking and entering of a dwelling, the presumptive range was 3–18 months, with a maximum of 6 years (the current maximum is life). In keeping with its emphasis on proportionality, no explicit weight was given to criminal record.

This is not the place to summarize Canadian Sentencing Commission proposals. However, unlike the current Canadian sentencing structure, they would have been easy to manipulate by a Parliament interested in doing so. Among other things, membership on the proposed permanent commission (which was never established in any form) was to be for 3 years. This would have meant that by 2009 all commission members—each appointed by Order in Council (i.e., by the government) without any discussion—would have been Conservative appointments who could easily have been informally vetted (or formally interviewed) in advance. Judges, by contrast, are appointed until retirement age.

In sum, making sentencing harsher in the structured system recommended by the Canadian Sentencing Commission in the 1980s would have been easy. Changing maximum sentences could have had an effect on sentencing since the worst cases in this scheme could receive the legislated maximums. Modifications of the guidelines would have been simple. They could have been done selectively or they could have all been multiplied by a constant.

Tonry notes that "sentencing reform worked in the United States and, in the 1970s through the mid-1980s, mostly pursued liberal, humane goals of consistency, transparency, procedural fairness, and racial equality. After that, sentencing reform's evil twin—'tough on crime'—took over and produced a system of unprecedented severity, rigidity, and racial inequality" (Tonry 2013, p. 470). Canada, however, left sentencing in the hands of judges. Notably, however, by the end of the period of Conservative rule, most of the judges on the Supreme Court of Canada were appointments of the Harper government. Nevertheless, the Supreme Court handed the government five major defeats in 2013 and 2014. The cumulative "score" of the votes on these cases was 37–1 against the Harper government. Three of the losses involved punishment: the amount of credit for presentence custody, the retroactive removal of early release on day parole for those formally eligible for APR, and access to the courts to review certain decisions by the Correctional Service of Canada to hold people in maximum security. The Supreme Court unanimously rejected the government's positions on all three.

The other two cases in which the government was roundly defeated involved changes to the Canadian Senate and a case addressing the issue of whether a judge nominated by the prime minister to sit on the Supreme Court of Canada had the formal qualifications for that position. With reference to this latter case, the law states that Supreme Court justices from Quebec have to be practicing lawyers or members of either the Superior Court or the Court of Appeal. Months before the nomination was made, the chief justice of Canada, in a private meeting that included the minister of justice, suggested that members of another court, the Federal Court of Canada, might not meet the legislative criteria for membership on the Supreme Court. When Prime Minister Harper nominated someone from the Federal Court and the nomination was challenged (by a private lawyer and subsequently by the Province of Quebec), the Supreme Court decided that the government's nominee was not qualified. All but one Supreme Court justice (one of Harper's most recent appointments) voted that the nominee did not have the requisite qualifications. Shortly after the Supreme Court decision, the prime minister attacked the chief justice of Canada personally, suggesting that she had violated her judicial independence by expressing her views privately to the minister of justice (Fine 2014).

However, Harper's problems with the Supreme Court did not stop there. In a 6–3 decision in 2015, it declared unconstitutional a law mandating a mandatory minimum sentence of 3 years for being in possession of a loaded handgun (*R. v. Nur*, 2015 SCC 15, [2015] 1 S.C.R. 773). The case was complicated because, possibly as a result of thoughtless criminal code amendments, the mandated sentence was up to 1 year in prison (if the prosecutor proceeded by summary conviction) or, for a first offender, from 3 to 10 years (if the prosecutor proceeded by indictment). Such choices are made before the trial begins and the evidence is fully known, and the prosecutor's decision is not subject to appeal. The Court found that there were plausible cases in which a thoughtful prosecutor could proceed by way of indictment (requiring a sentence of at least 3 years) and a court could find that the sentence was disproportionately harsh (and deserving a sentence of a year in prison or less).

Arguably, Canada's incoherent, sloppy, and inexact sentencing structure has served Canada well in recent years. The Harper government apparently decided not to make important changes in the broad principles of sentencing that govern the decisions of judges.[30] Such changes might have raised too many questions but, in any case, would not have been as politically salable as simple increases in specific sentence ranges. Now that Canada has, effectively, abolished discretionary parole, judges are almost completely in charge of sentencing. Other than mandatory

---

[30] They would include the following: "718.1 A sentence must be proportionate to the gravity of the offence and the degree of responsibility of the offender. 718.2 A court that imposes a sentence shall also take into consideration the following principles . . . (b) a sentence should be similar to sentences imposed on similar offenders for similar offences committed in similar circumstances; (c) where consecutive sentences are imposed, the combined sentence should not be unduly long or harsh; (d) an offender should not be deprived of liberty, if less restrictive sanctions may be appropriate in the circumstances; and (e) all available sanctions other than imprisonment that are reasonable in the circumstances [and consistent with the harm done to victims or to the community] should be considered for all offenders, with particular attention to the circumstances of aboriginal offenders" (bracketed words added by the Conservatives in 2015).

minimum sentences and mandatory victim surcharges, then, there appear to be severe limits on what can be done without first changing the overall sentencing structure.

3. *Symbolic Punitiveness as a Moderating Factor.* The explanations thus far for the lack of significant impact of the Harper government's new sentencing laws assume that the government's ultimate goal was to increase the severity of punishment, likely for utilitarian purposes. However, it could be that the goal was more symbolic than instrumental. That is, harsher sanctions may not have been the real goal. Crime and punishment is an easy "wedge" issue. It appeals to the emotions of the Conservative Party's electoral base. The publicity associated with a bill systematically occurred when it was introduced and derived from the government's press releases and associated documents. Most of the proposed changes in sentencing policies could be described or "justified" in the modern equivalent of a bumper sticker: a 140-character Twitter message. It is much more difficult to explain in 140 characters why increased imprisonment might not be a good policy than to assert that it is.

The Harper government may simply have wanted to look tough, without really caring how coherent, principled, or harsh the criminal justice system actually was. Activity may have been what was required, not real change. The repeated changes in the penalty structure for bestiality in front of a child are an example. The titles of many of the bills give an even broader hint as to what may have been going on. For instance, a private member's bill (C-479, 41st Parliament, 2nd sess.), introduced by an "ordinary" Conservative member of Parliament and supported by the Conservative Party, became law in 2015. Its most important provision extended the time period during which a prisoner had to wait for a second or subsequent parole hearing after being refused parole. One might have expected its title to relate to parole. Instead, it was entitled An Act to Bring Fairness for the Victims of Violent Offenders. This apparent disconnect was not unusual.

Equally notable, the names of bills often related to creating public safety, punishing offenders, or helping victims, even in cases in which they did little of anything. The bill that created mandatory minimum sentences for auto thefts was titled Tackling Auto Theft and Property Crime Act. The bill allowing consecutive parole ineligibility periods for multiple murders was called the Protecting Canadians by Ending Sentence Discounts for Multiple Murders Act. The original bill proposing the repeal of the faint hope clause was called the Serious Time for the Most Serious Crime Act. The bill that legislated mandatory minimums for large-scale frauds was christened the Standing Up for Victims of White Collar Crime Act. The bill to create new crimes as well as mandatory consecutive sentences for charges within an incident involving harm to a police dog or horse was given the short title of the Justice for Animals in Service Act (Quanto's Law).[31] And the bill apparently designed to emphasize the Conservative government's view that certain groups of immigrants to Canada were not fully welcome was called the Zero Tolerance for Barbaric Cultural Practices Act.

The symbolic nature of much of the Conservative government's crime legislation may go a long way in explaining not only the fanfare around the introduction of bills, the punitive rhetoric, the slogans, and the emotionally charged titles but also the lack of punitive bite of many of the new laws.

4. *Broader Neoliberal Political Agenda as a Moderating Factor.* A more sinister suggestion derives from an analysis of the Harper government that hardly mentions its crime policies. Wells (2013) suggests that the real agenda of the Harper Conservatives was to change Canadians' values. Hence, it is the talk, and not the action, that was important. The government may have been attempting to change the fundamental social welfare orientation of many Canadians. The possibility that harsher Canadian criminal justice policies were not the Conservative Party's ultimate goal cannot be excluded. Changes in these policies may have been part of a larger political agenda. Analogous to Simon's (2007) suggestion that Western governments often "govern through crime," Canadian Conservatives may have been using crime policy as a mechanism to reinforce conservative values related to individual responsibility in all aspects of life. As Prime Minister Harper stated, "Serious conservative parties simply cannot shy away from values questions.... On a wide range of public policy questions—including foreign affairs and defense, criminal justice and corrections, family and child care, and health care and social ser-

[31] Quanto was the name of a police dog stabbed to death by a suspect running from the police and being chased by Quanto. Quanto's killer received a sentence of 26 months for cruelty to animals, flight from police, and four other charges. Quanto's handler, an Edmonton police officer, presented a victim impact statement to the court (http://www .huffingtonpost.ca/2014/02/25/quanto-police-dog-edmonton_n_4854727.html).

vices—social values are increasingly the really big issues" (quoted in Wells 2013, pp. 58–59).

Punitive punishment policies, therefore, may have been used as a way to shift Canadian values about those who are less than fully self-reliant, "good," members of society. If those who "fail" (educationally, economically, etc.) are seen as "bad people," then "good" Canadian citizens need not be concerned with them precisely because those "unsuccessful in life" are understood to have chosen their particular "lifestyle." Responsibility for social, economic, or criminal justice failure is thereby shifted from the state to the individual. Wells notes, "Every day [Prime Minister Harper] stayed in office, he would make the decisions only a prime minister can make, knowing few would be noticed, almost none would be contested, and that together they would add up. . . . In the Conservative prime minister's own words to his staff, 'the longer I'm prime minister . . . the longer I'm prime minister'" (2013, p. 11).

If crime policy was a means toward a much larger goal, it makes sense that few changes in the law would have been likely to have a large impact on many people. Said differently, a changed criminal law may not have been the ultimate goal of changes in the criminal law.

Former Prime Minister Harper's ideology is well illustrated by the analysis provided by a Canadian political scientist. In response to the discovery of the body of a murdered young Aboriginal woman in Winnipeg, Manitoba, in August 2014, there was renewed pressure on the federal government to establish an inquiry into the apparently large number of missing or murdered Aboriginal women. The government was not supportive, probably in part because no Canadian government has ever been politically or substantively successful in matters related to Aboriginal Canadians. Prime Minister Harper's response to the request for an inquiry was simple: "We should not view this as a sociological phenomenon. We should view it as crime" (CBC News 2014). Political scientist Jakeet Singh pointed out that "Harper is clearly trumpeting a standard component of neo-liberal ideology: that there are no social phenomena, only individual incidents. . . . Neo-liberalism paints all social problems as individual problems. The benefit of this for those who share Harper's agenda, of course, is that if there are no social problems or solutions, then there is little need for government. Individuals are solely responsible for the problems they face" (Singh 2014). If Singh and Wells are both correct, the Harper sentencing agenda, and his approach to crime, make considerable sense.

V. "Sunny Ways"?[32] The 2015 Election and Beyond

Even though 94 separate government "crime" bills were introduced and 42 became law, and crime policy had been a centerpiece of the Harper decade, crime policy did not feature in the 2015 federal election campaign. Perhaps the only exception was a proposal by the Liberal Party to decriminalize, regulate, and tax the sale of marijuana. Although the Liberals in their platform suggested that they would "design a new system of strict marijuana sales and distribution... with the help of experts in public health, substance abuse, and law enforcement" (Liberal Party of Canada 2015, p. 55), they were criticized by the Conservatives in their platform for having as their "only criminal justice priority... to change the law to allow the sale of marijuana in corner stores, making it more accessible to our children" (Conservative Party of Canada 2015, p. 103). The Conservative platform had a variety of statements about crime, but they were seldom if ever discussed publicly by them or others. Crime had spent its course.

On October 19, 2015, the Harper government was replaced by the Liberal government of Justin Trudeau, son of a former Liberal prime minister. As the American realist philosopher Yogi Berra once pointed out, "It is difficult to make predictions, especially about the future." Notwithstanding this truism, criminal justice reform does not appear to be high on the list of priorities of the new government. At the time of the final revision of this essay in December 2015, it is broadly acknowledged that the overriding difference between the Harper government and past and current Canadian governments is one of values.

Little attention was spent on criminal justice matters in the Throne speech—the statement of the government, read by the Queen's representative at the opening of the new Parliament. Only 73 of the 1,638-word speech directly related to criminal justice policy. "Recognizing that Canada is, fundamentally, a safe and peaceful country, the Government will continue to work to keep all Canadians safe, while at the same time protecting our cherished rights and freedoms. To that end, the Government will introduce legislation that will provide greater support for survivors of domestic violence and sexual assault; that will get handguns and

---

[32] In his victory speech the night of the October 2015 election, Prime Minister Justin Trudeau referred to the phrase "sunny ways" used by Sir Wilfrid Laurier (Canadian prime minister, 1896–1911). Trudeau employed the term in an attempt to move away from the acrimonious disputes that characterized much of the election campaign and the Harper decade.

assault weapons off our streets; and that will legalize, regulate, and restrict access to marijuana."[33] None of the crime issues in the speech related to any of the changes made to the law during the previous 10 years.

The new prime minister issued what are termed "mandate letters" to each member of his new cabinet. The two most relevant letters gave few hints on what the government might do about crime. Both appeared to acknowledge that quick fixes to 10 years of chaotic changes in sentencing laws would not be their approach. In particular, the minister of justice's letter suggested that she should

> conduct a review of the changes in our criminal justice system and sentencing reforms over the past decade with a mandate to assess the changes, ensure that we are increasing the safety of our communities, getting value for money, addressing gaps, and ensuring that current provisions are aligned with the objectives of the criminal justice system. Outcomes of this process should include increased use of restorative justice processes and other initiatives to reduce the rate of incarceration amongst Indigenous Canadians, and implementation of recommendations from [a highly publicized inquest into] solitary confinement and the treatment of those with mental illness. (Mandate letter from Justin Trudeau, Prime Minister, Canada, to Jody Wilson-Reybould, Minister of Justice and Attorney General, Canada, November 2015)

Among a set of noncriminal justice matters, the public safety minister was asked to look into controversial legislation related to the relaxation of controls on firearms.

It is impossible to know what will happen with respect to sentencing policy in Canada under the new Liberal government. However, the Liberals' statement, quoted above, concerning marijuana may offer a hint. It appears they do not plan to move quickly on most crime matters. We have written elsewhere that an appropriate way to think about the incoherence created by the scores of recent amendments to the criminal law and sentencing in particular would be to examine broad categories of problems (Doob and Webster 2015). This suggestion is consistent with the only Liberal government statement we could find that

[33] http://www.speech.gc.ca/sites/sft/files/speech_from_the_throne.pdf.

made the news concerning sentencing policy. Referring to the "overuse and quite frankly the abuse of mandatory minimums," Trudeau, in response to a question, said about a month before the election that because he trusted judges, his government would consider eliminating some mandatory minimums. The implication was that it was an issue to be examined in the future. At the time of writing, it appears that some pending constitutional challenges are being delayed because of the expectation of legislative changes that would render the challenges moot (Cheadle 2015).

Given that crime did not feature in the election campaign and that other concerns are high on the new government's agenda, it seems unlikely that "fixing" the criminal law will be a high priority. With crime decreasing for close to a quarter of a century and imprisonment rates not having, at least yet, increased significantly, moving slowly on sentencing policy seems quite reasonable.

More broadly, Prime Minister Trudeau has suggested numerous times since the election that Canada has returned to its roots on criminal justice reform and will work slowly to review what is needed and attempt more thoughtful broad-based reforms. This affirmation could well signal that the Harper era in sentencing policy in the end may have been a short-term blip in an otherwise historically entrenched commitment to restraint in the use of imprisonment. If this optimistic prediction proves correct, it will be a testament to deep-seated social values underlying a Canadian criminal justice culture that will have weathered the Conservative storm.

REFERENCES

Auditor General of Canada. 2014. "Expanding the Capacity of Penitentiaries—Correctional Service Canada." In *Report of the Auditor General of Canada*, chap. 4. http://www.oag-bvg.gc.ca/internet/docs/parl_oag_201405_04_e.pdf.
Blumstein, Alfred, and Kiminori Nakamura. 2009. "Redemption in the Presence of Widespread Criminal Background Checks." *Criminology* 47(2):327–59.
Bushway, Shawn D., Paul Nieubeerta, and Arjan Blokland. 2011. "The Predictive Value of Criminal Background Checks: Do Age and Criminal History Affect Time to Redemption?" *Criminology* 49(1):27–60.
Campbell, Michael C. 2014. "The Emergence of Penal Extremism in California: A Dynamic View of Institutional Structures and Political Processes." *Law and Society Review* 48(2):377–409.
Canada. 1984. *Sentencing*. Ottawa: Government of Canada.

————. 1990*a*. "Directions for Reform: Corrections and Conditional Release." Ottawa: Supply and Services Canada.

————. 1990*b*. "Directions for Reform: Sentencing." Ottawa: Supply and Services Canada.

Canadian Sentencing Commission. 1987. "Sentencing Reform: A Canadian Approach." Ottawa: Minister of Supply and Services.

Casavant, Lyne, and Dominique Valiquet. 2011. "Bill C-59: An Act to Amend the Corrections and Conditional Release Act. Accelerated Parole Review." Ottawa: Library of Parliament.

CBC News. 2014. "Harper Rebuffs Renewed Calls for Murdered, Missing Women Inquiry." August 21. http://www.cbc.ca/news/canada/manitoba/harper-rebuffs -renewed-calls-for-murdered-missing-women-inquiry-1.2742845.

Cheadle, Bruce. 2015. "Liberals Must Decide Which Tory Laws to Fix, Which Ones to Flush: Several Charter Challenges to Conservative Legislation Now Making Way through Courts." CBC News, October 28. http://www.cbc.ca /news/politics/canada-election-2015-liberal-constitutional-laws-1.3292120.

Conservative Party of Canada. 2006. "Stand Up for Canada: Conservative Party of Canada Federal Election Platform." Ottawa: Conservative Party of Canada.

————. 2015. "Protect Our Economy: Our Conservative Plan to Protect Our Economy." Ottawa: Conservative Party of Canada.

Daubney, David. 1988. "Taking Responsibility: Report of the Standing Committee on Justice and Solicitor General on Its Review of Sentencing, Conditional Release and Related Aspects of Corrections." Canada: House of Commons.

Department of Justice, Canada. 2006. "Street Racing Bill Becomes Law." Press release, December 15. http://news.gc.ca/web/article-en.do?crtr.sj1D = &mthd = advSrch&crtr.mnthndVl = &nid = 263089&crtr.dpt1D = &crtr.tp1D = &crtr .lc1D = &crtr.yrStrtVl = &crtr.kw = royal%2Bassent&crtr.dyStrtVl = &crtr.aud 1D = &crtr.mnthStrtVl = &crtr.yrndVl = &crtr.dyndVl = .

————. 2012. "Government Introduces Legislation to Better Protect Canada's Seniors." Press release, March 15. http://news.gc.ca/web/article-en.do?nid = 662759.

Doob, Anthony N., and Cheryl Marie Webster. 2006. "Countering Punitiveness: Understanding Stability in Canada's Imprisonment Rate." *Law and Society Review* 40(2):325–67.

————. 2013. "The 'Truth in Sentencing' Act: The Triumph of Form over Substance." *Canadian Criminal Law Review* 17(3):365–92.

————. 2015. "The Harper Revolution in Criminal Justice Policy ... and What Comes Next." *Policy Options* 36(3):24–31.

Doob, Anthony N., Cheryl Marie Webster, and Allan Manson. 2014. "Zombie Parole: The Withering of Conditional Release in Canada." *Criminal Law Quarterly* 61(3):301–28.

Fine, Sean. 2014. "Harper Alleges Supreme Court Chief Justice Broke Key Rule with Phone Call." *Globe and Mail*, May 1. http://www.theglobeandmail.com /news/politics/harper-alleges-supreme-court-chief-justice-broke-key-rule-with -phone-call/article18382971/.

FPT Ministers (Federal/Provincial/Territorial Ministers Responsible for Justice). 1996. "Corrections Population Growth." Ottawa: Solicitor General of Canada.

Greenspan, Edward L., and Anthony N. Doob. 2011. "Putting Politics before Public Safety." *Globe and Mail*, August 29.

Hatt, Ken, Tullio Caputo, and Barbara Perry. 1992. "Criminal Justice Policy under Mulroney, 1984–1990: Neo-conservatism, Eh?" *Canadian Public Policy* 18(3): 245–60.

Kurlychek, Megan C., Robert Brame, and Shawn D. Bushway. 2006. "Scarlet Letters and Recidivism: Does an Old Criminal Record Predict Future Offending?" *Criminology and Public Policy* 5(3):483–503.

———. 2007. "Enduring Risk? Old Criminal Records and Predictions of Future Criminal Involvement." *Crime and Delinquency* 53(1):64–83.

Liberal Party of Canada. 2015. "Real Change: A New Plan for a Strong Middle Class." Ottawa: Liberal Party of Canada.

Pager, Devah. 2003. "The Mark of a Criminal Record." *American Journal of Sociology* 108:937–75.

Public Safety Canada. 2013. *Corrections and Conditional Release Statistical Overview*. Ottawa: Public Safety Canada.

Roberts, Julian V. 2002. "Determining Parole Eligibility Dates for Life Prisoners: Lessons from Jury Hearings in Canada." *Punishment and Society* 4:103–13.

Roberts, Julian V., Dan Antonowicz, and Trevor Sanders. 2000. "Conditional Sentences of Imprisonment: An Empirical Analysis of Optional Conditions." *Criminal Reports* 30:113–25.

Seymour, Andrew. 2013. "Offenders Should Sell Belongings to Pay Victims, Mackay Says." *Ottawa Citizen*, December 17. http://www.pressreader.com/canada/ottawa-citizen/20131217/281496454100913/TextView.

Simon, Jonathan. 2007. *Governing through Crime*. New York: Oxford University Press.

Singh, Jakeet. 2014. "The Ideological Roots of Stephen Harper's Vendetta against Sociology." *Toronto Star*, August 26. http://www.thestar.com/opinion/commentary/2014/08/26/the_ideological_roots_of_stephen_harpers_vendetta_against_sociology.html.

Tonry, Michael. 2013. "'Nothing' Works: Sentencing 'Reform' in Canada and the United States." *Canadian Journal of Criminology and Criminal Justice* 55(4): 465–80.

Webster, Cheryl Marie, and Anthony N. Doob. 2007. "Punitive Trends and Stable Imprisonment Rates in Canada." In *Crime, Punishment, and Politics in Comparative Perspective*, edited by Michael Tonry. Vol. 36 of *Crime and Justice: A Review of Research*, edited by Michael Tonry. Chicago: University of Chicago Press.

———. 2011. "Explaining Canada's Imprisonment Rate: The Inadequacy of Simple Explanations." In *International and Comparative Criminal Justice and Urban Governance: Convergence and Divergence in Global, National and Local Settings*, edited by Adam Crawford. Cambridge: Cambridge University Press.

———. 2012. "Maintaining Our Balance: Trends in Imprisonment Policies in Canada." In *Canadian Criminal Justice Policy*, edited by Karim Ismaili, Jane Sprott, and Kimberly Varma. New York: Oxford University Press.

———. 2014. "Penal Reform 'Canadian Style': Fiscal Responsibility and Decarceration in Alberta, Canada." *Punishment and Society* 16(1):3–31.

Webster, Cheryl Marie, Anthony N. Doob, and Nicole Myers. 2009. "The Parable of Ms. Baker: Understanding Pre-trial Detention in Canada." *Current Issues in Criminal Justice* 21(1):79–102.

Wells, Paul. 2013. *The Longer I'm Prime Minister: Stephen Harper and Canada, 2006–*. Toronto: Random House Canada

Zimring, Franklin E. 2007. *The Great American Crime Decline*. New York: Oxford University Press.

Arie Freiberg

The Road Well Traveled in Australia: Ignoring the Past, Condemning the Future

ABSTRACT

Identifying the nature and causes of penal change over decades can be a fraught exercise, particularly where those changes are gradual and the reasons for changes are diffuse. Like climate change and weather patterns, Australia's rising prison population is the product of forces that are also evident in Western Anglophonic societies but that vary in scale and speed depending on local conditions. These forces include penal populism, media influences, risk aversion, and distrust of the judiciary. Changes in the balance of power between the legislature, the judiciary, and the executive, increasing the power of the former and restricting the discretionary powers of the latter, all contribute to increasing prison numbers and more persons under correctional supervision. But where some jurisdictions have seen the cost and futility of continuous expansion of penal populations and appear inclined to draw back, Australia seems determined to follow this senseless path.

If American exceptionalism has been the leitmotif of comparative sentencing discourse over the past few decades, then Australian conformism may be the theme of the present and the way of the future. America's past is too often Australia's future, either by direct example, for good or ill, or indirectly through America's pervasive cultural influence.

America's recent penal history has been marked by the phenomenon of "mass imprisonment." Its imprisonment rate exceeds those of all other

Electronically published June 20, 2016
Arie Freiberg is emeritus professor of law, Monash University, Australia.

419

countries. Yet in more recent years, glimmers of moderation are apparent (Tonry 2013; Subramanian, Moreno, and Broomhead 2014). Nationally imprisonment rates have stabilized or fallen, and in some states the addiction to penal severity seems to have abated.

Predictably, and disappointingly, Australian penal policy is following the well-trodden path of more severe sentencing with few signs of divergence. In the June quarter of 2015, Australia's prison population stood at 35,949, a record number (Australian Bureau of Statistics 2015).[1] In 1984, the lowest point in the recent penal cycle, there were around 11,000 prisoners in custody, amounting to an increase of some 326 percent over the 30 years. During the same period, the imprisonment rate more than doubled from 85.6 per 100,000 of the adult population to 196, or by some 229 percent.[2]

Although the criminal justice systems of the nine states and territories are very different, the trend is similar, as figure 1 reveals. If the increase over the past 40 years has been the product of a form of path dependency reflecting deeper forces in advanced Western societies such as the United Kingdom and Canada, then this is a reason for despondency. Our penal trajectories may be predetermined by economic and social forces: neoliberalism, privatization, actuarialism, and managerialism have all been identified as underlying factors (Cunneen et al. 2013, chap. 1); but none is compelling as a single cause, nor is the nexus clear as to how each translates into sentencing policy. Smith (2013) has argued that while the grand theories of culture and punishment including those of Emile Durkheim, Michel Foucault, Norbert Elias, and David Garland may be useful in explaining the long-term penal climate, they have difficulty in explaining local and short-term variation. Short-term in this context refers to decades and long-term to centuries. Smith (2013, p. 119), for example, looks to cultural theory to help explain "the local and embedded process through which such local meanings (weather) can intersect with more general templates (climate) and often produce unexpected results."

The metaphor of climate, weather, and climate change may be apt to describe, and possibly partially explain, the changes in sentencing in

---

[1] There were at the same time 58,067 persons serving community-based corrections orders.

[2] Australian imprisonment rates are generally quoted as a proportion of the population at risk of imprisonment rather than the population as a whole.

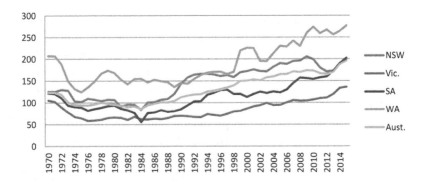

Fig. 1.—Imprisonment rates, selected jurisdictions and Australia, 1970–2015. The one outlier jurisdiction not depicted in the figure is the Northern Territory, which had an imprisonment rate of 903.6 per 100,000. Adapted (with permission) from tables prepared by Hilde Tubex, David Brown, and Alex Steele; Cunneen et al. (2013). A color version of this figure is available online.

some Western countries, including Australia, over the past four decades. The term penal climate has been invoked by various authors (Steenhuis, Tigges, and Essers 1983; Downes and van Swaaningen 2007) and has been described as the general political and cultural atmosphere in which sentencing and correctional policies and actions occur. Green (2008, p. 78) has defined penal climate as being "the degree of public, media, and political pressure exerted upon politicians and sentencers to act toughly or punitively on penal policy issues," which will be influenced by cultural factors and their structural manifestations. Although this definition equates penal with punitive, it can be interpreted more neutrally to describe a political atmosphere that can be either hot or cold, which then produces local sentencing conditions/policies/weather. Green describes a hot penal climate as one that is "marked by a high degree of press, public and political interest in penal issues—often characterized by strongly moralistic and denunciatory sentiments—and this interest tends to produce inhospitable conditions for the deliberative consideration of the range of available knowledge. 'Cool' penal climates are characterized by comparatively minimal interest in penal issues, lower levels of punitive sentiment, and more opportunities to foster policy deliberation" (p. 78).

Travis and Western (2014, p. 4) ascribe the changes in penal policy in the United States resulting in mass incarceration as being due "to an increasingly punitive penal climate surrounding criminal justice policy formed in a period of rising crime and rapid social change," and Simon (2012) also refers to a "penal climate change beginning in the 1970s that [has] produced mass incarceration." Very similar patterns and causes have been documented in the Netherlands (Downes and van Swaaningen 2007). If there has been a general warming of Western penal climates over the past four decades producing similar weather patterns, as seems to be the case, can it be changed? Tonry (2013) has argued that penal climates are both controllable and changeable: "Countries have different criminal justice policies and practices for reasons of political culture and history, not because of crime levels, crime trends, or larger social and economic forces. Anglo-Saxon countries have higher imprisonment rates than Scandinavian ones. Countries and, within the United States, states have the policies and prison populations they choose to have. The next question is why politicians in one country or state chose one thing and those in another country or state chose another" (p. 185).

This essay describes the current penal climate in Australia and its similarity to those in the United States, the United Kingdom, and its local manifestations. It relates to sentencing policy specifically, not penal policy in general, and is not intended to be solely an analysis of imprisonment rates and correctional trends. Imprisonment rates are one product of sentencing policy, but sentencing is about more than sanctions.

Section I examines the changing relationship between the three arms of government, in particular between the legislature and the courts. While courts zealously guard their sentencing discretion, legislatures attempt to restrict it through such measures as mandatory and presumptive sentences, guideline judgments, and standard nonparole periods. The High Court of Australia itself even resists attempts by the courts themselves to guide discretion by prohibiting prosecuting counsel from providing them with information about sentencing ranges, a practice common in most common law jurisdictions. This section also surveys the gradual extension of coercive, quasi-sentencing powers prior to the imposition of, and after the completion of, a sentence. The fraught relationship between legislature and executive agencies such as parole boards is examined in the light of the increasing influence of risk management practices. The abolition of suspended sentences in a number of jurisdictions partly in response to populist pressures and the ambivalent relationship between governments, legislatures, and sentencing advisory bodies are then described.

Section II identifies a number of nonadversarial, restorative, and therapeutic initiatives that run counter to the penal measures that dominate the penal landscape, and Section III attempts to explain the steady
rise in imprisonment rates in Australia. Section IV attempts to draw
these disparate threads together by observing that while some jurisdictions are attempting to reduce their prison populations and temper
their penal climate, Australia continues to emulate the failed policies of
the past.

I. Continuity, Severity, and Conflict

Australia, like the United States and Canada, is a federal country. The
majority of sentencing decisions are made at the state level as the criminal law is primarily a state responsibility. Each state has its own police
force, courts, correctional system, and sentencing laws and procedures,
and like other federations, it displays highly disparate imprisonment
rates, ranging from 904 per 100,000 of the adult population in the
Northern Territory (June 2015) to 118 per 100,000 in the Australian
Capital Territory. It is therefore misleading and dangerous to general-
ize. However, some trends are similar.

In its fundamental sentencing structure, Australian sentencing has not
changed significantly over the past four decades (Freiberg 2006, 2014).
Generally, sentences are set by the courts within the boundaries of maximum penalties set by the legislature and generally, for longer sentences,
incorporate a period served on parole after the expiration of a term usually set by the court, but with release generally at the discretion of an executive agency such as a parole board. Indeterminate sentences, such
as those common in the United States until the 1970s, until recent decades were rare as were mandatory or presumptive sentences. Sentencing power was, in the main, vested in the courts, which were given wide
discretion, little trammeled by externally imposed or internally generated guidelines. It was, however, subject to a well-developed system of
appellate review based on a jurisprudence going back to the UK Criminal Appeal Act 1907 (Freiberg and Sallmann 2008). The concept of proportionality is the fundamental sentencing principle setting both the
upper and lower limits of permissible retribution,[3] but the principle

---

[3] *Veen v The Queen* (No 1) [1979] HCA 7; *Veen v The Queen* (No 2) [1988] HCA 14.

may be overridden by competent legislation, an event that is becoming increasingly common.

Over the past few decades this overarching and relatively stable framework has changed as the balance of powers between the legislature, the courts, and the executive has shifted. The enlarged role of victims and the public in the development of sentencing policy has added to the complexity of the legislative process (Freiberg 2003). Changes in sentencing policy have not been dramatic or at least as large and discontinuous as those in the United States (Tonry 2013), but the "tough-on-crime" period that Tonry identifies as characterizing the time between 1984 and 1996 (Tonry 2014) remains the dominant paradigm in Australia with regrettably few signs of the "equilibrium" said to mark the period 1996–2015 in the United States.[4] The steady, one hesitates to say, inexorable, increase in prison populations appears to be the cumulative effect of a multitude of comparatively limited legislative interventions that seek to limit or guide judicial discretion and constrain executive authority and the increasingly punitive penal climate.

A. Legislatures and the Courts

The legislature is the preeminent body within the Australian sentencing framework, but it is subject to the doctrine of the separation of powers. It sets the maximum penalties for offenses, sets the range of sanctions available to the courts, and determines the degree of discretion invested in subordinate sentencing authorities. Since the 1980s all Australian jurisdictions have enacted specific sentencing statutes that attempt to provide a coherent framework for sentencing and sentence administration.[5] Legislatures are democratically responsible to the public, and governments, or governments-in-waiting, are responsive, sometimes too much so, to what purports to be public opinion.

Responsiveness to what is perceived to be punitive public sentiment is expressed in a variety of measures that appear to reflect a lack of confi-

---

[4] The essence of the tough-on-crime period was laws relating to truth in sentencing, mandatory minimum sentences, and three-strikes laws, increasing prison time and custody rates; see also Travis and Western (2014, pp. 3–4).

[5] The statutes are Sentencing Act 1991 (Vic), Crimes (Sentencing Procedure) Act 1999 (NSW) and Crimes (Administration of Sentences) Act 1999 (NSW), Sentencing Act 1995 (NT), Penalties and Sentences Act 1992 (Qld), Criminal Law (Sentencing) Act 1988 (SA), Sentencing Act 1997 (Tas), Sentencing Act 1995 (WA), and Sentence Administration Act 1995 (WA).

dence in the courts. Most common are the creation of new offenses and increases in statutory maximum penalties, the magnitude of which is often not reflected in concomitant increases in sentencing levels. Unhappy with judicial unresponsiveness to legislative direction, undue leniency, or disparities in sentencing, legislatures have been prone to enact mandatory or presumptive sentences. These take a variety of forms, and there are few of the simple three-strikes-type laws that clearly mandate one form of sentence if the preconditions are met. Instead, they manipulate the structure and relationship between the upper and lower limits of a prison sentence. As the sentencing structure of most Australian sentences over a certain length takes the form of a "head sentence," that is, the maximum term of imprisonment imposed by the court and a nonparole period, there is considerable scope for legislative creativity and variety in the forms of judicial constraint.

A review of the forms of mandatory and presumptive sentences across Australia shows that there are many. Most involve "head sentences." They include mandatory head sentences; mandatory head sentences and mandatory minimum nonparole periods; mandatory sentences that are cumulative on other sentences; mandatory minimum head sentences and mandatory minimum nonparole periods; mandatory head sentences and presumptive or discretionary nonparole periods; discretionary head sentences and mandatory nonparole periods; mandatory minimum sentences fixed in relation to the prison term imposed, mandatory minimum sentences of imprisonment, presumptive nonparole periods, baseline sentences, mandatory imprisonment, and mandatory noncustodial sentences (Freiberg 2014, pp. 733–37).

Although most Australian mandatory or presumptive laws are not of the length and severity of US-style three-strikes legislation and are far less extensive in their scope, their cumulative effect, both practically and symbolically, has been to increase sentence severity.

The most recent manifestation of such laws is what has come to be known as "one-punch" or "coward's-punch" homicide laws. These have resulted from deaths, usually a product of drunken brawls involving young males, in which the sentences imposed have been regarded as inadequate by the families of victims and the media. Laws such as the Crimes and Other Legislation Amendment (Assault and Intoxication) Act 2014 (NSW), the Sentencing Amendment (Coward's Punch Manslaughter and Other Matters Act 2014 (Vic), and the Safe Night Out Legislation Amendment Act 2014 (Qld) prescribe mandatory minimum nonparole periods for homicides committed in circumstances that might not otherwise have amounted to manslaughter and where the sentence was not prescribed (Odgers 2014). The very titles of the acts speak to the symbolic purposes of these statutes (Quilter 2014; Warner 2014; cf. Hemming 2015).

Mandatory or presumptive sentences remove or limit a court's sentencing discretion, a power deeply cherished and vigorously defended by the courts. They have been held to be constitutional by the Australian High Court, even if some courts consider them to be oppressive or unfair.[6] Distasteful as these laws may be, the doctrine of the sovereignty of Parliament places severe limitations on the ability of courts to mitigate or obviate the effects of harsh laws.

Although the Commonwealth of Australia has a written constitution (Constitution Act 1900 [Cth]) as does each state, they are not documents that enshrine human rights in a manner similar to the US Constitution or the European Convention on Human Rights. Despite these limitations, a feature of recent Australian sentencing jurisprudence has been attempts to invalidate laws on constitutional grounds, laws that some consider to be "bad, unjust, ill-advised or offensive to notions of human rights" (Freiberg and Murray 2012, p. 340).[7] These include *ad hominem* laws; mandatory sentencing laws; laws permitting the supervision or detention in custody of offenders beyond the expiration of their sentence; laws permitting an offender to be held indefinitely at "the Governor's pleasure" if the person is deemed to be "incapable of exercising proper control over their sexual instincts"; and laws that attempted to empower the attorney general of a state personally to declare that a person subject to a continuing detention or supervision order be detained if the attorney general was satisfied that the detention of the person is "in the public interest."[8] Two jurisdictions, Victoria and the Australian Capital Territory, have enacted human rights laws that have formed the

---

[6] *Palling v Corfield* [1970] HCA 53; [1970] 123 CLR 52; *Karim v The Queen* [2013] NSWCCA 23; *Magaming v The Queen* [2013] HCA 40.

[7] *Baker v The Queen* [2004] HCA 45 at 87 per Kirby J.

[8] The cases discussed in this paragraph are *Kable v DPP (NSW)* [1996] HCA 29; *Palling v Corfield* [1970] HCA 53; [1970] 123 CLR 52; *Karim v The Queen* [2013] NSWCCA 23; *Magaming v The Queen* [2013] HCA 40; *Fardon v Attorney-General* (Qld) [2004] HCA 46/; *Pollentine v Bleijie* [2014] HCA 30; *Attorney-General (Qld) v Lawrence* [2013] QCA 364.

basis for challenges to laws said to be incompatible with human rights;[9] but because the rights under these statutes are not absolute and are subject to a number of limitations, their effect on sentencing law and practice has been minimal (Freiberg 2014, pp. 75–81). Most of these constitutional and human rights challenges were unsuccessful, but the number and range of measures impugned provide some insight into the nature of the measures designed to deal with lenient sentences or dangerous offenders and of the attempts to "constitutionalize" Australian sentencing.

1. *Judicial Discretion and Hyperindividualism.* A feature of Australian sentencing law that differs significantly from that of other jurisdictions is the fierce judicial defense of sentencing judges' discretion in the face of attempts by legislatures and some appellate courts to limit or guide it. In that respect its path diverges sharply from that taken in the United Kingdom and the United States.

Australian judges are invested with a very wide discretion in order to enable them to impose just and appropriate sentences in all the circumstances of the particular case. They are not bound by recommendations made to the prosecution or by plea agreements made between prosecution and defense counsel. This is discussed further below. Because the circumstances of each case and each offender may be infinitely variable—and because there is a variety of sentencing purposes as well as a large number of aggravating and mitigating circumstances and sentencing options, and because these may appear in an infinite number of combinations—the courts have taken the view that although there may be a range of appropriate sentences, there is no single correct sentence. Sentencing is therefore primarily individualistic and highly discretionary. The proper methodology for arriving at a just and appropriate sentence is through an "instinctive" or "intuitive" synthesis—an exercise in which all considerations relevant to the instant case are simultaneously unified, balanced, and weighed by the sentencing judge (Freiberg 2014, pp. 228–33).

The High Court of Australia has described the process as follows: "By instinctive synthesis, I mean the method of sentencing by which the judge identifies all the factors that are relevant to the sentence, discusses their significance and then makes a value judgment as to what is the

---

[9] The laws enacted are the Charter of Human Rights and Responsibilities Act 2006 (Vic) and the Human Rights Act 2004 (ACT).

appropriate sentence given all the factors of the case. Only at the end of the process does the judge determine the sentence" (*Markarian* [2005] HCA 25 at [51] per McHugh J). The Court has observed that "sentencing is not a purely logical exercise, and the troublesome nature of the sentencing discretion arises in large measure from unavoidable difficulty in giving weight to each of the purposes of punishment. . . . The purposes overlap and none of them can be considered in isolation from the others when determining what is an appropriate sentence in a particular case. They are guideposts to the appropriate sentence but sometimes they point in different directions" (*Veen (No 2)* [1988] HCA 14 at [13]).

Sentencing in Australia is therefore not regarded as a process by which the courts mechanically apply a set of sentencing rules to the facts of particular cases to arrive at invariably correct decisions, but as "an art not a science" and therefore inimical to any form of mathematical precision. The desired outcome is consistency in the application of sentencing principles, not consistency of outcome as expressed in terms of numerical equivalence (*Hili and Jones* [2010] HCA 45 at [48]–[49]). Even the concept of an accepted or acceptable "range of sentences" for the purposes of gauging whether a sentence can be considered to be manifestly excessive or inadequate on appeal is considered questionable as a sentence imposed within a range may be incorrect and one imposed outside the range may not be in error. Ranges, according to the High Court, do not fix the upper or lower limits of sentencing discretion. They are no more than yardsticks against which proposed sentences can be measured (*Hili and Jones* at [54]).

Attempts to limit, guide, or inform judges' sentencing discretion on the grounds that their sentencing practices are too lenient or produce unwarranted disparity have met with firm resistance by the High Court of Australia. Disparity is not as large an issue in Australia in academic writings and in the courts as it is in the United States (cf. Tonry 2013, p. 143); even though there is evidence of unwarranted disparities due to race, gender, regional, and interjudge factors (Australian Law Reform Commission 2006), the cure is generally regarded as being worse than the disease.

Legislative attempts to curb judicial discretion through the variety of mandatory or presumptive sentences are generally difficult to avoid or mitigate, depending on the specificity of their drafting and the scope of exemption or exception clauses. These tend to produce unwarranted parity, an outcome as undesirable as unwarranted disparity.

The past decade or so has seen an ongoing interchange between state courts, the High Court, and legislatures as to the scope of judicial discretion,[10] and although the courts have attempted to read down provisions that limit their discretion, they ultimately defer to clear legislative direction. Three areas of contention are discussed in more detail below: guideline judgments, standard nonparole periods, and prosecution submissions on sentence.

Guideline Judgments. One means of guiding judicial discretion is through guideline judgments. There are no guideline judgments in Australia of the kind that are common in the United Kingdom (Ashworth and Roberts 2013) nor sentencing guidelines similar to those used in a number of states in the United States or in the federal system. There is no formal definition of a guideline judgment. In *R v Wong* ([2001] HCA 64 at [5]), the chief justice of the High Court of Australia observed, "They cover a variety of methods adopted by appellate courts for the purpose of giving guidance to primary judges charged with the exercise of judicial discretion.... Those methods range from statements of general principle, to more specific indications of particular factors to be taken into account or given particular weight, and sometimes to indications of the kind of outcome that might be expected in a certain kind of case, other than in exceptional circumstances."

Informal guidelines judgments of a general kind have been issued in various jurisdictions over the past decades. Some relate to sentencing standards or tariffs with some numerical indicators for some offenses, but most of the informal guideline judgments tend to be principle-based, for example, on the factors that are relevant in deciding how impaired mental functioning should be taken into account in sentencing, on sentencing indigenous offenders, and on family hardship, among others.[11]

For just under a decade from the late 1990s, the New South Wales Court of Criminal Appeal issued guideline judgments for a range of offenses with the aim of providing better guidance to judges and improving consistency in sentencing. Between 1998 and 2004 the court

[10] Although Australia is a federation and each state or territory has its own superior appellate court, the High Court of Australia sits at the apex of the judicial system and has jurisdiction over both state and federal laws.

[11] Examples of the cases discussed in this paragraph include *Police v Cadd* [1997] SASC 6187; *R v Place* [2002] SASC 101; *R v Verdins* [2007] VSCA 102; *DPP v Terrick* [2009] VSCA 220; and *Markovic v R* [2010] VSCA 105.

delivered eight such judgments.[12] The then chief justice, James Spigelman, argued that guidelines were necessary to deal with two major problems that had been identified, but not properly addressed, by the courts: inconsistency and systemic excessive leniency.

However, in 2001 the High Court of Australia, held by a majority in *Wong* that in relation to a federal offense the guideline judgment handed down by the New South Wales Court of Criminal Appeal exceeded the court's jurisdiction by creating sentencing categories that were too prescriptive. In particular, the court held that certain forms of guideline judgment might be unconstitutional because of their prospective nature. Because such a judgment produces no order or declaration, it is not strictly a justiciable matter that is subject to appellate review. Courts cannot generally deal with points of law that may not be the subject of a dispute. Some members of the court were also concerned that a guideline, which identifies a range of results rather than a process of reasoning, passes from being a decision settling a matter before the court to a "decision creating a new charter by reference to which further questions are to be decided" (*Wong* at [80]) and thus passes from the judicial to the legislative.

Three states have laws that empower a court to hand down a guideline judgment,[13] but owing to the High Court's attitude to such sentences and the prevailing sentencing theory of instinctive synthesis, no such formal guidelines have been given by the courts in those jurisdictions in recent years.

However, in December 2014 the guideline judgment drought broke when the Victorian Court of Appeal handed down its first such judgment since it was given the power to do so in 2004. Under Victorian law the Sentencing Act 1991 (Vic) allows the Court of Appeal, on its

---

[12] *R v Jurisic* [1998] NSWSC 423; (1998) 45 NSWLR 209; *R v Whyte* [2002] NSWCCA 343; 55 NSWLR 252 (dangerous driving causing death/grievous bodily harm); *R v Henry* [1999] NSWCCA 111; (1999) 46 NSWLR 346 (armed robbery); *Attorney General's Application No 1* [2002] NSWCCA 518; (2002) 56 NSWLR 146 (impact of further charged offenses); *R v Ponfield* [1999] NSWCCA 435; (1999) 48 NSWLR 327 (break enter and steal); *R v Thomson* [2000] NSWCCA 309; (2000) 49 NSWLR 383 (guilty plea); *R v Wong* [1999] NSWCCA 420; (1999) 48 NSWLR 340 (heroin and cocaine importation); *Attorney General's Application No 3* [2004] NSWCCA 303; (2004) 61 NSWLR 305 (high range prescribed concentration of alcohol).

[13] Western Australia (Sentencing Act 1995 [WA], sec.143), South Australia (Criminal Law [Sentencing Act] 1988 [SA], sec. 29A), and Victoria (Sentencing Act 1991 [Vic], part 2AA).

own initiative or on an application made by a party to the appeal, to give or review a guideline judgment, even if it is not necessary for the determination of the appeal. A guideline judgment in Victoria may set out the criteria to be applied in selecting among various sentencing alternatives, the weight to be given to the various purposes of sentencing, the criteria by which a court may determine the gravity of the offense, the criteria that may be used to reduce the sentence for an offense, and the weighting that is to be given to relevant criteria. However, a guideline judgment in Victoria may not be made in relation to the appropriate level or range of sentences for a particular offense or class of offense.

If the Court of Appeal decides to give or review a guideline judgment, it must notify the Sentencing Advisory Council (see further below) and consider any views stated in writing by the council. It must also give the Director of Public Prosecutions (or its representative) and Victoria Legal Aid (or its representative) an opportunity to appear and make a submission on the matter. The court is then required to have regard to these views. A decision to give or review a guideline judgment must be a unanimous decision of the judges constituting the court.

In *Boulton, Clements, and Fitzgerald* ([2014] VSCA 342), the Victorian Director of Public Prosecutions applied for a guideline judgment in a case relating to the use of a new intermediate order called the Community Correction Order (CCO). This order, which was intended to consolidate a number of intermediate orders as well as to replace suspended sentences, to some extent, contains a number of punitive and rehabilitative conditions. These can be combined with a term of imprisonment, and in the higher courts their maximum duration can be equivalent to the statutory maximum penalty of imprisonment. In the case before the Court of Appeal, CCOs of 10, 8, and 5 years were imposed, which were well outside the historical ranges for such orders. The Director of Public Prosecutions applied for a guideline judgment on the basis that it would help promote consistency of approach in deciding whether a CCO is an appropriate sentencing disposition and considering the exercise of the jurisdiction to impose CCOs for a period up to the maximum term of imprisonment.

In the event, the Court of Appeal upheld all of the appeals, reduced the sentences, and delivered a guideline judgment (Bartels 2015; Krasnostein 2015). The first, and major, part of the judgment discussed the desirability of a guideline judgment in these circumstances and the various principles involved and contained a determination of the appeals before it. The second, and independent, part contained the guidelines themselves, which can be read independently of the substantive judgment. The court was of the view that this new order was new and radical and that a guideline judgment was required to avoid sentencing disparity and to ensure that the new CCO system would be used as intended.

The lengthy judgment traversed a number of significant issues that were in contention such as the application of the principles of proportionality and suitability and their relationship to the sentencing purposes of rehabilitation and punishment, the relationship of CCOs to sentences of imprisonment, the appropriate length of such orders, the combination of imprisonment and CCOs, and the range of offenses for which a CCO may or may not be suitable.

If a guideline judgment is intended to provide some form of guidance, the judgment in *Boulton, Clements, and Fitzgerald* has been successful, being cited nearly 130 times in Victorian cases in the 12 months after its publication. Together with some statutory amendments to the legislation, it has profoundly changed sentencing patterns and contributed to stabilization, if not reduction, in prison populations in Victoria (Sentencing Advisory Council, Victoria 2014, 2015). Whether the success of this process encourages the Victorian or other courts to resurrect this form of guidance remains to be seen.

Standard Nonparole Periods. The High Court's antipathy to legislative attempts to limit judicial discretion by means of what are termed "standard nonparole periods" [SNPP] in New South Wales was expressed again in the case of *Muldrock* ([2011] HCA 39). An SNPP is a form of presumptive nonparole period and was introduced into New South Wales in 2003 with the intention of increasing the severity and consistency of sentences.[14] It required a court to impose a statutorily determined nonparole period for a number of serious offenses unless there were reasons for departing from the SNPP, which were required to be recorded in writing. Some SNPPs overlapped with offenses in relation to which a guideline judgment had been given (54B[2]–[4]).

In *Muldrock*, the High Court ruled that the legislative SNPP should be regarded as only one factor to be considered in determining an

---

[14] The SNPP was intended to represent the nonparole period "for an offense in the middle of the range of objective seriousness" for the prescribed offenses (Crimes [Sentencing Procedure] Act 1999 [NSW], sec. 54A[2]).

appropriate sentence and one that should not be given a "primary, let alone a determinative significance" (at [26]). Factors such as the maximum statutory penalty, the purposes of sentencing, proportionality, parity, and totality, among others, were equally relevant factors, and in that sense the SNPP was not even presumptive. A key goal was to ensure that sentencing courts did not depart from the instinctive synthesis approach and fall into error by adopting what is termed a two-staged approach to sentencing. Under this proscribed approach, also referred to as structured or two-tiered sentencing, the first stage is to identify facts that relate to the objective offense seriousness to determine what an appropriate sentence might be, and the second stage is to take into account any aggravating or mitigating circumstances that might decrease or increase the sentence. This approach carries with it dangers of assigning mathematical weights to sentencing factors, which the court has concluded is both impossible and undesirable (*Markarian* [2005] HCA 25).

Thus in Australia the correct approach to sentencing is to start with the premise that there is no single, correct, objective sentence. It will amount to a legal error for a court to start the reasoning process from some objective starting point such as the maximum penalty, the amount of a drug, the number and seriousness of prior offenses, a numerical guideline, a sentencing tariff or range, a set of comparable sentences, a statutory nonparole period, or even a presumption that a particular sanction must be imposed unless there are exceptional circumstances (Freiberg 2014, pp. 250–51).

Prosecution Submissions on Sentence. Even attempts to assist courts with information provided by prosecuting counsel have proved contentious in the High Court as infringing a sentencing judge's discretion. In Australia, the sentence is the sole responsibility of the judicial officer. Prosecutors may limit the sentencing options available to the court by determining the number and gravity of the charges filed or decide not to proceed with some matters in exchange for guilty pleas on others. An accused person must decide whether to plead guilty to some or all of the charges preferred. However, ultimately it is for the judge alone to decide the sentence to be imposed.

The prosecution has an early influence on sentencing by the role it plays in the choice of charge, the severity and number of charges, whether to treat the charges summarily or on indictment, and whether or not to engage in plea or charge negotiations. Generally, decisions involved in the prosecution process are not capable of judicial review.

The duty of the prosecution is to assist the court at both trial and sentencing. In relation to the latter, the prosecution's task is to see that a proper sentence is imposed in the public interest. Traditionally, the prosecution played little or no part in sentencing. Its primary task was to assist the court in avoiding appealable error. In recent years Australian courts have placed a greater obligation on the prosecution to assist the court by providing information about sentencing practices. In Victoria, the Sentencing Act 1991 (sec. 5[2][b]) requires a sentencing court to have regard to "current sentencing practices," that is, to what sentences other courts were imposing.

In 2008, the Victorian Court of Appeal, in a 3–2 decision in *MacNeil-Brown* ([2008] VSCA 190), held that the duty to avoid appealable error obliged the prosecution to assist the court by submissions as to the range of sentences that could be said to be appropriately open, either at first instance or on appeal. This process not only served the purpose of assisting the courts but was also intended to promote consistency in sentencing, which is regarded as fundamental to maintaining public confidence in the criminal justice system and in the rule of law. However, although there was a duty on the prosecution to assist the court, a sentencing judge was under no obligation or compulsion to receive such assistance even if it were proffered. It was not a breach of procedural justice for a judge to refuse to listen to such a submission, and there were a number of judicial officers who did not wish to be assisted in this way.

The majority of the Victorian Court of Appeal supported its decision on the basis that a submission by the prosecution was not an expression of the personal view of counsel but a submission of law identifying the ambit within which the sentencing discretion may lawfully be exercised in the circumstances of the particular case. They did not believe that the making of a submission usurped or interfered with the exercise of the judge's sentencing discretion: the final decision as to sentence always rests with the court. A judge was not bound in any way to sentence within the range nominated by the prosecution, and indeed it is the duty of defense counsel to respond to any submission. Finally, the submission of sentencing ranges and the use of statistics were not considered to be fundamentally inimical to the intuitive sentencing methodology.

However, in February 2014, the High Court overturned this decision in the case of *Barbaro and Zirilli* ([2014] HCA 2), ruling that the practice of counsel for the prosecution providing a submission regarding the bounds of the available range of sentences was legally wrong. A submission as to range, it said, was a statement of opinion and not law, a remarkable view given the wide-ranging nature of submissions made in courts in an adversarial system. It held that although consistency is important in sentencing, it is consistency in the application of legal principle that is required, not numerical consistency (Warner 2014).

Thus, it is now the law in Australia that a sentencing judge not only is under no obligation or compulsion to receive such assistance but is prohibited from doing so. However, a sentencing judge may look at sentencing statistics and information about sentences imposed in comparable cases, but this is the judge's task, not that of counsel. In fact, the High Court is antipathetic to the use of either form of information (Freiberg and Krasnostein 2011; Krasnostein and Freiberg 2012). Only one judge of the court in *Barbaro and Zirilli* (Gageler J) was of the view that the prosecution may make a submission as to range if the court so requests and in fact has a duty to assist a sentencing court if it perceives that there is a "significant risk that the sentencing court would make an appealable error in the absence of assistance" (at [62]).

The reasoning in *Barbaro and Zirilli* was extended to apply to civil penalties as well as criminal sanctions by the Federal Court of Australia in *Director, Fair Work Building Industry Inspectorate v Construction, Forestry, Mining and Energy Union* (*Union* [2015] FCAFC 59). In this case, a regulator of the building industry had taken action against a union, the result of which was an agreed statement of facts and an agreement as to the pecuniary penalty that was considered appropriate for the court to impose. This was common practice in actions relating to corporate, tax, and consumer protection civil proceedings and provided the basis for extensive plea negotiations between the parties. It was regarded by regulators as an important enforcement and compliance tool but one that recognized that the ultimate decision as to sentencing lay with the courts. Following the High Court's decision in *Barbaro and Zirilli*, the appellate division of the Federal Court held that submissions as to penalty ranges or agreed penalties were contrary to law, although submissions by both parties could be made in respect to the identification of comparable cases, relevant principles, or the facts of the case.

On appeal from the Federal Court, and in a surprising decision, the High Court of Australia held that the reasoning in *Barbaro and Zirillia* should be confined to criminal cases as different public policy considerations applied in civil penalty cases, namely, that these are civil proceedings in which the sanctions are more limited and the standard of

proof is lower.[15] As compromising proceedings is a feature of civil proceedings, it was not inappropriate for regulators to make submissions as
to penalty.

Barbaro and Zirillia has been described as representing "the low-water
mark as far as High Court jurisprudence on sentencing is concerned,"
and there have been calls for legislative intervention to overcome the
effect of the decision, in particular, its chilling effect on plea negotiation
and the rate of guilty pleas (Bagaric 2014, p. 135).

2. *Blurring the Boundaries of Sentencing.*   Understanding where sentencing begins and ends is a key aspect of understanding penal dynamics
and the ebbs and flows of sentencing and sanctioning policy. The answer to the question of what is a sentence is not obvious and will vary
between jurisdictions, over time, and on context.[16] At the front end of
the process there is conflation between bail, bail programs, and presentence or intervention programs that have rehabilitative aims and resemble sentencing orders, and sentencing orders themselves (Freiberg and
Morgan 2004; Law Reform Commission of Western Australia 2009;
Freiberg 2014, p. 97, fn. 687; King et al. 2014, chap. 10). At the back
end are preventive orders that commence at the expiration of a sentence
and can extend supervision or detention, possibly indefinitely. Generally
these can be made only by a court, but their increasing use in relation to
sex or dangerous offenders has the effect of negating the limiting effect
of statutory maximum penalties, one of whose purposes is to place a
known and legally defined limit on judicial power (Sentencing Advisory
Council, Victoria 2010). It also reflects the growing influence of risk-
based justifications for sanctions, a lack of confidence in the ability of
traditional sanctions to protect society, and public fear of sexual and dangerous offenders generally.

The recent growth in the development and use of indefinite sentences, nonproportionate sentences, and ancillary orders to deal with
these classes of offenders has been significant. Since the 1990s, Australian legislatures have introduced such measures as indefinite sentences,

---

[15] *Commonwealth of Australia v Director, Fair Work Building Industry Inspectorate; Construction, Forestry, Mining and Energy Union* [2015] HCA 46. The composition of the court
changed in the period between 2014 and December 2015 when this decision was handed
down, which may partly explain the change in approach to prosecution submissions on
sentence.

[16] For example, for the purposes of an appeal, for the powers of the sentencing court, for
procedural purposes, for constitutional purposes, and for human rights purposes, among
others.

supervision and detention orders, sex offender registration schemes, working with children checks, and a range of civil preventive orders that provide a mechanism to prevent offenders from engaging in certain forms of conduct that pose a risk to the lives or sexual safety of children (Freiberg, Donnelly, and Gelb 2015).[17] Although such provisions have not added significantly to the number of people in custody, like many other measures introduced over recent decades, they reflect communal unease with the criminal justice system and legislatures' attempts to address those concerns in an electorally favorable manner.

Some of the legislative measures designed to deal with sexual and dangerous offenders seek specifically to overcome some of the common law limitations on sentencing. The sentencing statutes of almost all jurisdictions provide that one of the purposes of sentencing is to impose a sentence or order that imposes just, appropriate, or adequate punishment in all of the circumstances of the offense. Imposing a just or proportionate sentence requires a court to consider such matters as the maximum statutory penalty for the offense, the degree of harm caused, and the offender's culpability, among other factors. In relation to some serious sex or dangerous offenders, some jurisdictions permit a court to impose a sentence longer than what is proportionate to the gravity of the offense considered in the light of its objective circumstances for the purpose of protecting the community.[18] As Tonry (2013, p. 175) notes, "Those policies and practices have little or nothing to do with justice toward offenders. They center instead on denunciation of wrongdoing, reassurance of citizens, acknowledgment of popular outrage and insecurity, and demonstration of government resolve."

---

[17] An indefinite sentence is a sentence that can be imposed by a court at the time that the sentence is imposed on an offender that allows a court to order that the person be imprisoned for a certain period of time, after which that sentence may be reviewed and further imprisonment ordered. Supervision and detention orders are intended to provide enhanced protection of the community by requiring offenders to have served custodial sentences for certain offenses, including sexual offenses, who present an unacceptable risk of harm to the community, to be detained in custody or be under strict supervision in the community until they no longer present a risk. The purpose of sex offender registration schemes is to require certain offenders who commit sexual offenses to keep police informed of their whereabouts and other personal details for a period of time in order to reduce the likelihood that they will reoffend and to facilitate the investigation and prosecution of any future offenses that they may commit. Working with children checks aim to protect children from sexual or physical harm by ensuring that those entrusted with their care have their suitability to do so checked by a government body.

[18] Victoria Sentencing Act 1991 (Vic), sec. 6D; South Australia, Criminal Law (Sentencing) Act 1988 (SA), sec. 20BA(1)(a).

Australian courts are generally reluctant to disregard the principle of proportionality. Statutory departures from the principle are regarded as being unusual or exceptional and are generally read down by interpreting them to mean that it must be shown that a proportionate sentence would be inadequate to protect the community. As most sentences for very serious crimes are generally lengthy, there is little scope for imposing even longer sentences in the name of community protection.[19] The dialogue between legislatures, keen on popularity, and the courts, committed to basic common law principles, is continuous and tense.

B. Legislatures and the Executive

Willie Horton is a legendary figure in American political history (Anderson 1995). Having been convicted of murder in 1974 in Massachusetts and sentenced to life without parole, he was released under a weekend furlough program in 1986, during which he raped a woman, assaulted her male partner, and committed a number of other offenses. He was subsequently convicted of these offenses and sentenced to further terms of life imprisonment. The furlough program became a key issue in the 1988 presidential election campaign and inflicted considerable damage on potential candidate Michael Dukakis, then governor of Massachusetts, who was depicted as being soft on crime and allowing a revolving door system to operate in his state.

Parole, temporary leave, early release, remission or good time, and a host of other measures that permit executive agencies such as parole boards or correctional authorities to vary or mitigate a sentence imposed by the court have long been highly sensitive issues. "Truth in sentencing" was a phrase that had wide currency in the early 1980s in Australia, focusing primarily on the operation of remissions, which had the effect of reducing a sentence by between 25 and 35 percent depending on the jurisdiction.[20] Together with the operation of the parole system, which was perceived by some to allow offenders to "get out early" and to alter the announced sentence, the combined effect of these measures was to portray the sentencing as being untruthful or misleading. By the mid-1980s, most jurisdictions had abolished remissions, which had some effect on increasing prison numbers, though the extent of that increase

---

[19] *Tutchell* [2006] VSCA 294 at [33]; *Prowse* [2005] VSCA 287; Freiberg (2014, p. 249).

[20] Remissions differed from parole in that they were formally granted by the prison administration rather than by a formally constituted parole board.

was difficult to determine as courts may have altered their sentences to some extent to take the abolition of remissions into account (Freiberg and Ross 1999, p. 194; Cunneen et al. 2013, p. 59).

The next battleground in relation to truth in sentencing was parole. Parole in Australia is a combination of judicial and executive discretion. In most jurisdictions the sentencing judge sets a nonparole period, and the decision if and when thereafter to release the offender is in the hands of a parole board. In other jurisdictions, release is automatic for most offenders after the expiration of the nonparole period, though this mechanism tends to be confined to shorter sentences.

Parole has been regarded as an important means of integrating offenders back into the community under supervision (Sentencing Advisory Council, Victoria 2012). It had a strong rehabilitative philosophy. However, parole breaches or violations, by either further offending or breach of conditions, particularly those that attract media attention, have undermined confidence in the parole system, which has been described as a system in crisis (Bartels 2013). Although no jurisdiction has abolished parole, it has become far more restrictive, in terms of the decision to release, to terminate or revoke parole, and to rerelease the offender.

Parole policies can be changed merely through a change in policy, as occurred in Western Australia. In 2006, four members of the board resigned in protest against political interference. In 2008, a new chair of the Prisoner Review Board, a Supreme Court judge, declared, with the support of the government, that parole should be severely restricted. Within 2 years, the success rate dropped from 90 percent to 21 percent, with a concomitant increase in the prison population (Cunneen et al. 2013, p. 55; Tubex et al. 2015). In some jurisdictions governments can override parole board decisions to release prisoners without explanation, which has the effect of undermining both judicial and executive decision making.[21]

Victoria's Willie Horton moment came in 2012 when an offender, on parole, raped and murdered a young woman walking home alone in the early hours of the morning. This event triggered a media frenzy and a

---

[21] In South Australia the Executive Council, comprising the governor of the state (the representative of the Queen, not the elected head of government) and senior ministers, can refuse to release offenders convicted of murder despite parole board recommendations, and it has done so on a number of occasions.

wave of emotion and eventually an inquiry into the parole system that resulted in a raft of measures that severely restricted the operation of the parole system. Recent estimates are that 600 additional people are in prison as a result of these parole reforms and highlight the fact that prison populations are influenced not only by the number of offenders entering the system but also by the number not leaving it (Hansard 2014, p. 3).

Victoria's parole reforms are emblematic of the increasingly punitive climate and the power of populism. The report that followed the rape and murder was written by a conservative retired High Court judge who questioned the value of parole. He did not believe that the community was better off by releasing people on parole and suggested that it was worth taking the risk of releasing offenders at the end of their head sentence without supervision rather than releasing them with supervision. He argued that prisoners were not entitled to procedural fairness in parole proceedings (Callinan 2013). The report recommended a significant turnover of membership. It was the third report on parole, following a number of murders by offenders who were on parole, one by a distinguished forensic psychologist (Ogloff 2011) and one by the Victorian Sentencing Advisory Council (2012), both of which were more moderate in their recommendations but were critical of the operation of the parole system. Where the council's report emphasized the value of reintegrative and rehabilitative programs, the Callinan report was primarily focused on incapacitation. Subsequently, the chair and 14 members of the board retired and were replaced by 24 new members. In the year 2013–14, the number of parole orders made fell by 36 percent, the number of cancellations increased from 45 per 100 orders to 58 parole orders made, and there was a 96 percent increase in the number of parole orders denied (Adult Parole Board, Victoria 2014, pp. 2–7).

The bleak and restrictive view of parole articulated in the Callinan report was not reflected in a comprehensive review of parole published in late 2015 by the New South Wales Law Reform Commission (2015), which regarded parole as an integral component of the sentencing system that can serve to protect the community and one that should be retained. Acknowledging communal concerns for safety and the avoidance of risk and reflecting the ascendancy of risk discourse in criminal justice, Victoria's parole legislation was amended to state that in making parole decisions, "the [Parole] Board must give paramount consideration to the safety and protection of the community in determining whether to make or vary a parole order, cancel a prisoner's parole or revoke the cancellation of parole" (Corrections Act 1986 [Vic], sec. 73A). Similarly, the New South Wales Law Reform Commission recommended that the parole legislation be amended to state that "the primary purpose of parole is to promote community safety by supervising and supporting the conditional release and re-entry of prisoners into the community, thereby reducing their risk of offending" (p. 27).

C. Suspended Sentences

Issues of truthfulness and confidence in the criminal justice system also manifest themselves in the debate about the role of suspended sentences in the sentencing hierarchy. Suspended sentences have had a checkered history. They have existed in various forms in most jurisdictions, some being partial suspensions,[22] some being attended by a large number and wide range of conditions, and some with minimal requirements (Sentencing Advisory Council, Victoria 2008; Bartels and Rice 2012; New South Wales Law Reform Commission 2013, chap. 10). In 2013–14, suspended sentences accounted for 35 percent of all custodial sentences imposed in Australia and 4 percent of all sentences (Bartels 2015).

The suspended sentence has been introduced, abolished, and reintroduced in a number of jurisdictions: it is probably one of the most volatile of sanctions. It has been regarded as paradoxical in that it requires a court to form a view that imprisonment is required for the offense but then to consider the same factors it has taken into account, to decide whether the term of imprisonment should be suspended in whole or in part. It is also paradoxical in that although in theory a sentence of imprisonment is regarded as the most severe sentence that can be imposed in Australia, the limited restrictions that are placed on an offender create a perception that it is far less punitive than immediate imprisonment and even less than sanctions such as fines, community-based orders, or forms of conditional dismissals. And although legislatures intend, and courts have held, that the suspended sentence is a very significant punishment, in the public mind the sentence is regarded as a soft option—the offender walking free without punishment (Freiberg and Moore 2009). The sanction of imprisonment that should follow a breach of the order, intended

---

[22] That is, part of the sentence of imprisonment is served in custody and some in the community.

in theory to be regarded as a sword of Damocles, is considered in practice to be a butter knife (Freiberg 2002).[23]

The effect of suspended sentences on imprisonment numbers has been contentious. While in theory they are intended to take the place of sentences of imprisonment, in reality they have diverted only a proportion of prison sentences while escalating sentences that would otherwise have received a fine or community order (McInnis and Jones 2010; Menendez and Weatherburn 2014). There is evidence that they have also resulted in sentence inflation, that is, the imposition of a longer term on the basis that it was not being served in custody (Sentencing Advisory Council, Victoria 2006, p. 34) and in possibly more people being incarcerated, when breaches of sentences that would otherwise not have received a prison sentence result in a prison term being imposed because the top of the sentencing hierarchy has already been reached.

Public concern over suspended sentences, media pressure, and penal populism combined with considered advice (Sentencing Advisory Council, Victoria 2008) has seen suspended sentences being abolished in one jurisdiction, severely restricted in another, and in the process of abolition in another, pending a final report by the state's sentencing advisory body on the process of abolition and transition (Sentencing Advisory Council, Tasmania 2015a, 2015b).[24] In Queensland, a deeply conservative government ordered a review of both court-ordered parole and suspended sentences on the ground that it was responding to community concern about crime (Norton, Ryan, and Howells 2013), but that government lost office in January 2015 and its successor has left the issue in abeyance.

D. Legislatures and Advisory Bodies

Governments do not lack for advice about sentencing, should they need or seek it. Most jurisdictions have long-standing law reform bodies that have examined sentencing laws over recent decades. At the federal level, the Australian Law Reform Commission published a major report

---

[23] Citing R. v. Brady [1998] AJ No. 39 (Alberta Court of Appeal).

[24] Suspended sentences have been abolished in Victoria, completely since September 2014, but were gradually restricted from 2006. In South Australia, suspended sentences are not available for repeat violent offenders and offenders involved in serious and organized crime unless exceptional circumstances exist: Criminal Law (Sentencing) (Suspended Sentences) Amendment Act 2013 (SA).

on federal sentencing (2006) that contained 147 recommendations for reform, including a comprehensive new stand-alone sentencing act. Its primary aim was to ensure broad equality across Australia in sentencing practice;[25] but nearly a decade on from its publication, its recommendations remain largely unimplemented.

At state and territory levels, reviews have been conducted on matters such as sentencing generally (Tasmania Law Reform Institute 2008; New South Wales Law Reform Commission 2013); standard minimum nonparole periods (New South Wales Law Reform Commission 2012b); penalty notices (New South Wales Law Reform Commission 2012a); and court intervention programs (Law Reform Commission of Western Australia 2009). Specialist bodies such as the New South Wales Bureau of Crime Statistics and Research and the Judicial Commission of New South Wales have published numerous reports on specific aspects of sentencing in their jurisdiction.

A more recent change in the Australian sentencing landscape has been the establishment of a number of sentencing advisory councils. In contrast to their American or British counterparts, the primary role of Australian councils is not to promulgate, or assist the courts in preparing, sentencing guidelines or guideline judgments but to provide a mechanism to incorporate community views into the sentencing process: in the words of the Victorian Sentencing Advisory Council, to "bridge the gap between the community, the courts and government by informing, educating and advising on sentencing issues" (Freiberg and Gelb 2008, p. 11).[26]

The first council to be established was in New South Wales in 2002 and is constituted by an act of Parliament (Crimes [Sentencing Procedure Act] 1999 [NSW], part 8B; Abadee 2008). Its statutory functions are to advise and consult with the relevant minister in relation to offenses suitable for SNPPs and their proposed length; to advise and consult in relation to matters suitable for guideline judgments; to monitor and report annually on sentencing trends and practices; and, at the request of the minister, to prepare research papers and reports on sentencing matters and to educate the public about sentencing matters.

---

[25] Although there is a federal system of criminal law and separate sentencing provisions in the Crimes Act 1914 (Cth), federal sentencing is a mixture of federal and state law. There is no separate federal correctional system.

[26] http://www.sentencingcouncil.vic.gov.au/about-us/establishment-functions.

There are 13 members of the council from a variety of professional backgrounds representing the judiciary, prosecution, defense, victims, corrections, academia, and law enforcement bodies. Since 2003, the council has published over 30 reports on topics such as high-risk offenders, suspended sentences, SNPPs, good behavior bonds and nonconviction orders, Aboriginal offenders, alcohol-related violence, and others.[27]

The Victorian Sentencing Advisory Council was established in 2004 under statute (Sentencing Act 1991 [Vic], sec. 108C)[28] with functions including advising the Court of Appeal in relation to guideline judgments, to provide statistical information on sentencing, to conduct research on sentencing (whether at the request of a minister or not), to gauge public opinion on sentencing matters, to consult on sentencing matters with a wide range of people or bodies, and to advise the attorney general on sentencing matters (Freiberg 2008).

The council comprises 14 members of varying professional backgrounds and has been chaired by the author since its establishment. It has been involved in only one guideline judgment application (see above), published over 30 reports and a series of statistical sentencing snapshots relating to sentencing practices in the higher courts, established an online statistical database for the court of summary jurisdiction, and been involved in public information and education programs, both in person and online through an exercise entitled "You Be the Judge."[29]

A sentencing council was established in Queensland in 2010 along lines similar to those of New South Wales and Victoria but was abolished in 2012 by a newly elected conservative government and will be reinstated by the more progressive government that defeated it the following election (D'Ath 2015). A Tasmanian council was created in mid-2010 on a nonstatutory basis. It currently has seven members and very limited resources.[30] A similar, nonstatutory council exists in South Australia, established in 2012, with 18 members and works within the At-

---

[27] http://www.sentencingcouncil.justice.nsw.gov.au/nsw-sentencing-council/publications.

[28] The author is chair of the Victorian Council.

[29] www.sentencingcouncil.vic.gov.au.

[30] http://www.sentencingcouncil.tas.gov.au. The author is chair of the Tasmanian Sentencing Council.

torney General's Department.[31] Its only project to date has been a review of the mental incompetence defense, an issue that is unconnected
with sentencing.

E. Diversity of Voices

The historical paradigm of the criminal justice system as a contest between the state and the offender began to decay in the 1960s with the
growth of the victims' movement, the establishment of victim compensation schemes, and the introduction of victim impact statements in the
sentencing process. Not all victims are punitive or vengeful, but as the
interests and voices of victims in the criminal justice system have become
increasingly recognized and heard, it is likely that they have contributed
to a more punitive penal climate (Freiberg 2003; Kerr 2012). Some
jurisdictions have enacted victims' Charters of Rights, sentencing legislation now regularly requires that the harm done to victims be specifically recognized as a sentencing consideration, victims are formally or
informally recognized through representation on parole boards or similar bodies as well as sentencing councils, and victims' commissioners
have been established by statute. Victims may be legally entitled to information about prisoners and to make representations to releasing authorities regarding whether a prisoner should be released and, if so, the
conditions that may attach to any release order.

The "public" is often invoked in sentencing debates: public attitudes,
public opinion, public or community expectations, or the public interest
generally is not infrequently summoned in support of a political measure
or a judicial decision to justify a measure or decision that might not otherwise find support. The difficulties of determining what the public or
the community might be thinking at any time are obvious, and the examples of misrepresenting what the public might actually believe or expect are legion (Gelb 2006). Views of some members of the public are
now heard not just in the media but also on a number of sentencing advisory and prisoner release bodies.

In Australia, juries are not involved in sentencing, and a review by
the New South Wales Law Reform Commission (2006) recommended
against a greater role for juries in advising judges. In the lead-up to the
2014 Victorian election, the Labor Opposition policy platform stated

[31] http://www.agd.sa.gov.au/about-agd/what-we-do/services-government/sentencing
-advisory-council-south-australia.

that if elected, it would "introduce jury involvement in sentencing to ensure that penalties given for convicted offenders reflect community standard and expectations."[32] In the year or so following its election to office, there is no indication that that promise is being met. There is no evidence that jurors are necessarily more punitive than the courts when fully informed about the circumstances of the case (Warner and Davis 2013).

II. Countercurrents

The penal landscape is not completely gloomy. Although climbing, Australia's imprisonment rate (151/100,000 total population) still ranks well below those of the United States (698/100,000), Singapore (220/100,000), and New Zealand (190/100,000) though above those of England and Wales (148/100,000), Canada (106/100,000), Denmark (61/100,000), and other Nordic countries.[33] Imprisonment remains a sanction of last resort. It is used in around 9 percent of all cases in the courts of summary jurisdiction, which hear about 95 percent of all criminal cases (Australian Institute of Criminology 2014, p. 95). Monetary orders constitute some 68 percent of all orders imposed on male defendants in any court (p. 97), and community work orders and other orders that restrict liberty in the community amount to around 19 percent of all orders (p. 97).

Nonadversarial, restorative, and therapeutic approaches to justice have developed strongly since the early 2000s and continue to grow in number and scope despite being overshadowed by the plethora of non- or antirehabilitative measures described above. Although generally therapeutic and restorative in intent, they generally operate within a legal framework of proportionality and parsimony, and there are strict limits to their dispositive powers (cf. Tonry 2013, p. 174).

The first drug court was established in New South Wales in 1999, and there are now two in that jurisdiction, one in Victoria, and various courts or court "lists" in South Australia, Western Australia, Tasmania, and the

---

[32] See http://www.viclabor.com.au/wp-content/uploads/2014/05/Victorian-Labor-Platform -2014.pdf, p. 63.

[33] World Prison Brief, http://www.prisonstudies.org/highest-to-lowest/prison_population _rate?field_region_taxonomy_tid=All.

Australian Capital Territory.[34] A Family Drug Treatment Court was established in 2014 in Victoria to deal with child protection matters (King et al. 2014, chap. 9). Mental health courts or lists operate in South Australia, New South Wales, Tasmania, Victoria, and Western Australia; family violence courts operate in six jurisdictions; a Neighborhood Justice Centre, or community court, has operated in Victoria since 2007 as well as a "special circumstances" list in the Magistrates Court to deal with people who have received an infringement notice (citation) but who have medical, psychological, or other problems that might mitigate the sanction (chap. 9). A wide range of diversion or intervention programs, which may or may not be court-based, legislative or not, and which are generally presentence, operate around Australia that are intended to be therapeutic, rehabilitative, or supportive. These take the form of pre- or postsentence programs, conditional cautioning programs, bail-related programs, conditional adjournments, or forms of deferred sentencing (chap. 10).

Indigenous sentencing courts have been established in South Australia, New South Wales, Victoria, the Australian Capital Territory, and Western Australia whose aim is to apply problem-solving, restorative, and therapeutic techniques to a group of offenders whose overrepresentation rate in the criminal justice system is unacceptably high (Australia 2013, p. 31; King et al. 2014, chap. 11). Some are similar to circle sentencing schemes developed in Canada, while others are variants of traditional court sentencing processes adapted to involve a wider range of parties than may usually be the case in "normal" sentencing hearings. Unfortunately, the number of cases they deal with is minuscule, around 1–2 percent in comparison with the total number of indigenous offenders sentencing in mainstream courts around the country, and overall, the number of cases dealt with in nonadversarial forums remains too small to slow the growth in prison numbers.

III. How and Why Imprisonment Rates Increased

Tubex et al. (2015) have examined the drivers of penal policies in four Australian jurisdictions that account for the majority of Australian

---

[34] For present purposes, a "court" is a division of an existing court that is established under legislation. A "list" is an administrative arrangement whereby a court hears certain types of cases at certain times or places.

prisoners (New South Wales, Victoria, South Australia, and Western Australia). The different jurisdictions vary in their imprisonment rates for a number of reasons: the rate and composition of crime, the proportion of the population that is indigenous, the remand in custody rate (Australia 2013, p. 10), the rate of use of intermediate sanctions, and the use of parole.[35] They do not vary, however, because of the levels of punitiveness as measured in public opinion surveys (Roberts, Spiranovic, and Indermaur 2011).

Statistically, the modern nadir of imprisonment rates occurred in the mid-1970s when the secular increase commenced with minor fluctuations (see fig. 1). The recent increases were not due to major changes in sentencing philosophy from rehabilitation to retribution: Australian sentencing was always founded on the principle of proportionality. In fact, in the 1980s, reform was focused primarily on increasing the range of intermediate sanctions, though the political debates were concerned with such matters as truth in sentencing. However, the 1990s were dominated by concern about dangerous, violent, and sexual offenders; by the need to protect the community; and by challenges to the centrality of proportionality as a sentencing principle. The 1990s were also a period of the contracting out or privatization of prisons, though there is little conclusive evidence that the pressures of a penal-industrial complex lobbying for an increase in prison capacity for the purpose of profit contributed to the increase in the prison population.

There is no single factor that can be identified as the proximal cause of the increase in Australian imprisonment rates. Mandatory and presumptive sentences play some role, but the number of offenders sentenced under these laws is not great, and most of the provisions affect short terms of imprisonment or marginal increases on existing sentencing lengths (Australia 2013, p. 9). There are few laws with the same effect as the United Kingdom's indeterminate sentencing statutes, the three-

---

[35] In contrast to the United States, there was no significant upsurge in convictions and imprisonment for drug-related crimes and no equivalent of long mandatory sentences for crack cocaine and related offenses. Most prisoners held in custody at any one time are incarcerated for offenses against the person (17 percent) and sexual assault (15 percent; Australia 2013, p. 3; Australian Institute of Criminology 2014, p. 115). The percentage of prisoners imprisoned for violent offenses increased from around 38 percent to around 51 percent between 1986 and 2012, while the percentage of prisoners whose most serious offense type was a property offense declined from around 35 percent to around 15 percent (Australian Institute of Criminology 2014, p. 115).

strikes or similar laws in the United States, or the life sentence provisions in South Africa.

Theories relating to the emergence of a "risk society" provide a valuable context for an understanding of the changing discourse of criminal justice. A greater number of laws now require some form of risk assessment or prediction of future behavior by medical professionals and ultimately by the courts, primarily in relation to the granting of bail or parole, but the effect of such laws on incarceration rates has been small to date. Life sentences in Australia are generally imposed for retributive rather than preventive purposes, and few are imposed without the possibility of parole. Indefinite sentences are rare. Cunneen et al. (2013, p. 116) estimate that about 5 percent of all prisoners are subject to life or indefinite sentences. That proportion varies from 1.5 percent in Victoria to 12.8 percent in South Australia. Persons held in custody under extended detention provisions are included in prison numbers, but the absolute numbers are small (400–500) in comparison with a total prison population of nearly 36,000 inmates.

Rather, it appears, it is the cumulation of a number of measures and influences that has produced the increases. These include the increasing number and proportion of prisoners held in custody after being refused bail; the gradual abolition of remissions (good time), which could amount to around one-third of the length of the sentence;[36] the fixing of presumptive nonparole periods or prescribing a proportionate period between the head sentence and the nonparole period; small increases in the custody rate; increases in sentence lengths (Sentencing Advisory Council, Victoria, 2013); increases in the number of indigenous offenders sentenced to imprisonment; the restriction or abolition of suspended sentences and restrictions on granting parole; and a greater readiness to revoke parole coupled with a reluctance to rerelease the offender (Australia 2013, p. 11).[37] There has also been a steep increase in

[36] Courts generally made adjustments to the length of the sentence imposed to take account of the abolition.

[37] Although those refused bail are not sentenced prisoners, they are included in the total imprisonment rates published by the various bodies responsible for publishing the official statistics. In June 2014, 26 percent of the Australian prison population was unsentenced prisoners. In South Australia, unsentenced prisoners made up 35 percent of the population, while in Victoria they were 18 percent (Australian Bureau of Statistics). Between 1984 and 2012 the rate of unsentenced prisoners in custody increased from around 15 per 100,000 of the population to around 40 per 100,000 (Australian Institute of Criminology

the number of women incarcerated, though because women constitute only around 9 percent of the prison population, even sharp increases in their numbers do not have a significant effect on overall numbers (Australia 2013, p. 16).

No single factor can be identified as the distal cause. Tubex et al. (2015) argue that although Australia is a liberal market economy with neoliberal characteristics that conduce to more punitive policies, this does not necessarily determine penal outcomes. Tonry (2014) has similarly argued against social determinism and suggested that local factors are of more importance in understanding sentencing policy. To the extent that they are similar in direction to jurisdictions that are politically, economically, and culturally alike, such as the United States and the United Kingdom, these trends either may reflect similar underlying forces or are the products of direct or indirect legal hegemony. However, the Canadian experience indicates that political and cultural influences can be resisted, even from a powerful neighbor (Doob 2012), and the Scandinavian experience shows that social democracies do not have to be punitive (Pratt and Eriksson 2013).

In a classic Australian comedy film released in 1997 called *The Castle*, an inept lawyer attempts to fight the compulsory acquisition of a house on constitutional grounds. In his futile attempt to ground his argument in the Australian Constitution and when pressed to find a specific provision, he submits to the court that the answer lies in the vibe of the Constitution. This appeal to the spirit rather than the letter of law echoes the criminological references to the elusive concepts of "penal culture" or "penal climate," ineffable but demonstrable. Cunneen et al. (2013, pp. 1–2) refer to penal culture in relation to imprisonment as referring to "the broad complex of law, policy, and practice which frames the use of imprisonment and to the broad system of meanings, beliefs, ideas and symbols through which people understand and make sense of imprisonment." They note sardonically that culture is a term that is often used to account for the unaccountable (p. 5).

Reference has already been made to the warming of the penal climate, in Green's (2008) terms, which has manifested itself in the measures de-

---

2014, p. 114). The national imprisonment rate for indigenous offenders is 15 times higher than for nonindigenous offenders (Australian Bureau of Statistics 2015; Tubex et al. 2015).

scribed above. The period described can be characterized by a climate of fear and anxiety about crime, even in an era in which crime rates decreased. The fear that was engendered may be evidence of the lingering effects of the increased crimes rates of the 1960s–80s.[38] The appeals to notions of community protection during this period were more salient than abstract notions of proportionality, parsimony, or fairness (Tonry 2013, p. 173). Consequently, proposals for mandatory or presumptive sentencing and preventive orders fell on fertile ground, not for their instrumental value in reducing crime but for their emotional appeal in assuaging real or inchoate fears (Freiberg and Carson 2010; Tonry 2013, p. 170). Managing fear has become more important than managing crime (McSherry 2014).

At the local (state) level, Cunneen et al. (2013) and Tubex et al. (2015) identify the most powerful forces influencing Australian penal policies as being the politicization of criminal justice and sentencing and increasing influence of a populist media dominated by the Murdoch press, which has near monopolies of daily newspapers in a number of jurisdictions. Penal populism is alive and well in the antipodes (Australia 2013, pp. 7–9). Law and order tends to dominate election campaigns, public opinion is preferred over expert evidence, evidence-based policy is secondary to policy-based evidence, and the rhetoric is that prison works. That imprisonment is an effective means of controlling crime strikes a strong electoral chord. The phrase "prison works" has been transformed to "prisons create work," especially in regional areas where unemployment is high. Writing of the changes in Victoria, Tubex et al. (2015, p. 356) observe,

> Victoria's penal policies have been driven by, and are embedded in, a discourse that is directed less at the instrumental level than at the symbolic and emotional levels, mostly triggered by high-profile media events. They are based in differences in the local political environments which are reflective of larger cyclical fluctuations between the conservative and liberal ends of the political spectrum which follow the historical pattern of hope/promise, harsh reality, followed by

---

[38] In Victoria it is estimated that overall crime rates declined by an average of 18.4 percent from 2003; in New South Wales between 1990 and 2010, the murder rate decreased by 50 percent and robbery with a firearm by 66 percent (Australia 2015, p. 6).

disillusionment. Analogous to our understanding of climate change, while weather is changeable, reflecting short-term influences, climate is a long-term phenomenon. Victoria's "penal weather" is becoming more volatile, more reactive to the commission of, and attendant publicity given to horrific crimes and their emotive consequences. Its penal climate, like Australia's, has gradually become harsher.

IV. Conclusion

Australia is often a late adopter of ideas formulated elsewhere. Policies such as truth in sentencing, sex offender registration and notification, boot camps, extended supervision orders, and others that have not been shown to be effective in reducing crime but effective in gaining political office tend to find their way to this country. As Cunneen et al. (2013, p. 142) observe in the context of Western Australia's adoption of anti-social behavior orders, "Embracing criminal justice policies and approaches from elsewhere that appear initially like a good idea or to be popular but that later, at the point at which Australian authorities bring them into law or implementation, are seen to have failed or been abandoned, is a common phenomenon."

The prevailing political mantra is that governments make no apologies for being tough on crime and for adopting any measures that "protect the community" (Australia 2013, p. 7). Decreasing crime rates have not yet reduced fear of crime. The financial burdens of growing correctional populations have not yet been so great as to alter the direction of government policies, though the growing direct and indirect costs of imprisonment have been repeatedly noted (chap. 3). No fiscal cliff appears on the horizon sufficient to halt the march up the world imprisonment rate rankings.

There is no widespread support for changes in direction, although a recent report by a Senate committee recommended that the federal government play a leading role in obtaining and sharing data held by commonwealth agencies in relation to justice reinvestment initiatives particularly through the establishment of a clearinghouse. It also recommended increased funding for justice reinvestment initiatives and the establishment of an independent central coordinating body for justice reinvestment policy, advice, programs, and evaluation (Australia 2013). None of its recommendations has been acted on. Similarly, the Victorian Ombudsman, in her report into the rehabilitation and reintegration of prisoners in Victoria, noted the limited effectiveness of imprisonment in reducing crime rates and the "valuable lessons to be learned from the experience of other jurisdictions" in adopting a justice reinvestment approach (2015, p. 3).

The recent changes in direction in penal policy in the United States focusing on "reducing prison populations and costs, expanding or strengthening community-based corrections, implementing risk and needs assessments, supporting offender reentry into the community; and making better informed criminal justice policy through data-driven research and analysis" (Subramanian, Moreno, and Broomhead 2014, p. 4; Tonry 2014, p. 5) may be evidence that the rate of penal climate warming is moderating, but there are still many penal skeptics in Australia.

Yet there are signs of change. In November 2014, a "law and order" government unexpectedly lost office in Victoria. In January 2015, an even more stridently conservative government was ejected from office in a massive swing against it in Queensland, partly as a reaction to its harsh and unconscionable criminal law and sentencing policies.

Green (2008, chap. 11) has argued that it is possible to effect penal climate change by such means as reinsulating the penal policy-making processes from public influence and by introducing different means of involving the public in penal decision making, through reengaging experts in the public discourse, especially in the mainstream media, through higher standards of public journalism, and through other means. These are highly idealistic and probably impractical measures in the context of powerful, populist media empires. There is no lack of bodies in Australia to provide research and policy advice on sentencing and to incorporate the public in the policy-making process. Its existing sentencing advisory councils have a wider membership and remit than their overseas counterparts, but evidence is not what drives policy in Australia.

In the short term, it would not be difficult to stem the rising tide of incarceration. Repealing many of the legislative measures introduced over the past two decades that restrict sentencing discretion would be one place to start, and reempowering parole boards is another means of reducing prison populations. However, it appears that Australians are destined, or predestined, to follow the path that others have blazed. Too many lawmakers have seen the past and are determined to repeat it, whatever the cost. They are still warming to the task.

REFERENCES

Abadee, Alan. 2008. "The New South Wales Sentencing Council." In *Penal Populism, Sentencing Councils and Sentencing Policy*, edited by Arie Freiberg and Karen Gelb. Sydney: Hawkins Press.

Adult Parole Board, Victoria. 2014. *2013–2014 Annual Report*. Melbourne: Department of Justice.

Anderson, David C. 1995. *Crime and the Politics of Hysteria: How the Willie Horton Story Changed American Justice*. New York: Crown.

Ashworth, Andrew, and Julian Roberts. 2013. *Sentencing Guidelines: Exploring the English Model*. Oxford: Oxford University Press.

Australia Senate. Legal and Constitutional Affairs References Committee. 2013. *Value of a Justice Reinvestment Approach to Criminal Justice in Australia*. Canberra: Commonwealth of Australia.

Australian Bureau of Statistics. 2015. *4512.0—Corrective Services, Australia, June Quarter 2015*. http://www.abs.gov.au/ausstats/abs@.nsf/mf/4512.0.

Australian Institute of Criminology. 2014. *Australian Crime: Facts and Figures*. Canberra: Australian Institute of Criminology.

Australian Law Reform Commission. 2006. *Same Crime, Same Time. Report: Sentencing of Federal Offenders*. Report no. 103. Sydney: Australian Law Reform Commission.

Bagaric, Mirko. 2014. "Editorial: The Need for Legislative Action to Negate the Impact of *Barbaro v The Queen*." *Criminal Law Journal* 38:133–35.

Bartels, Lorana. 2013. "Parole and Parole Authorities in Australia: A System in Crisis?" *Criminal Law Journal* 37:357–76.

———. 2015. "Sentencing Review 2014–2015." *Criminal Law Journal* 39:326–50.

Bartels, Lorana, and Simon Rice. 2012. "Reviewing Reforms to the Law of Suspended Sentences in the Australian Capital Territory." *Flinders Law Journal* 14:253–92.

Callinan, Ian. 2013. *Review of the Parole System in Victoria*. Melbourne: Department of Justice.

Cunneen, Chris, Eileen Baldry, David Brown, Mark Brown, Melanie Schwartz, and Alex Steel. 2013. *Penal Culture and Hyperincarceration: The Revival of the Prison*. Surrey, UK: Ashgate.

D'Ath, Y. 2015. *Media Statements: Court Programs to Address Crime Reinstated*. http://statements.qld.gove.au/Statement/2015/7/1/14court-programs-to-address-crime-reinstated.

Doob, Anthony. 2012. "Principled Sentencing, Politics, and Restraint in the Use of Imprisonment: Canada's Break with Its History." *Penal Field* 9. http://champpenal.revues.org/8335.

Downes, David, and Renee van Swaaningen. 2007. "The Road to Dystopia? Changes in the Penal Climate of the Netherlands." In *Crime and Justice in the Netherlands*, edited by Michael Tonry and Catrien Bijleveld. Vol. 35 of *Crime and Justice: A Review of Research*, edited by Michael Tonry. Chicago: University of Chicago Press.

Freiberg, Arie. 2002. *Sentencing Review: Pathways to Justice*. Melbourne: Department of Justice.

———. 2003. "The Four Pillars of Justice." *Australian and New Zealand Journal of Criminology* 36(2):223–30.

———. 2006. "Twenty Years of Changes in the Sentencing Environment and Courts' Responses." http://njca.anu.edu.au/Professional%t20Development/programs%20by%20year/2006/Sentencing%20Conference/Sen%20conf%20papers%202006/Freiberg.pdf.

———. 2008. "The Victorian Sentencing Advisory Council: Incorporating Community Views into the Sentencing Process." In *Penal Populism, Sentencing Councils and Sentencing Policy*, edited by Arie Freiberg and Karen Gelb. Sydney: Hawkins Press.

———. 2014. *Fox and Freiberg's Sentencing: State and Federal Law in Victoria*. Sydney: Thomson Reuters.

Freiberg, Arie, and William George Carson. 2010. "Evidence, Emotion and Criminal Justice: The Limits of Evidence-Based Policy." *Australian Journal of Public Administration* 69(2):152–64.

Freiberg, Arie, Hugh Donnelly, and Karen Gelb. 2015. *Sentencing Child Sexual Abuse in Institutional Contexts*. Sydney: Royal Commission into Child Sexual Abuse in Institutional Contexts.

Freiberg, Arie, and Karen Gelb, eds. 2008. *Penal Populism, Sentencing Councils and Sentencing Policy*. Sydney: Hawkins Press.

Freiberg, Arie, and Sarah Krasnostein. 2011. "Statistics, Damn Statistics and Sentencing." *Journal of Judicial Administration* 21:72–92.

Freiberg, Arie, and Victoria Moore. 2009. "Disbelieving Suspense: Suspended Sentences of Imprisonment and Public Confidence in the Justice System." *Australian and New Zealand Journal of Criminology* 42(1):101–22.

Freiberg, Arie, and Neil Morgan. 2004. "Between Bail and Sentence: The Conflation of Dispositional Options." *Current Issues in Criminal Justice* 15(3):220–36.

Freiberg, Arie, and Sarah Murray. 2012. "Constitutional Perspectives on Sentencing: Some Challenging Issues." *Criminal Law Journal* 36:335–55.

Freiberg, Arie, and Stuart Ross. 1999. *Sentencing Reform and Penal Change: The Victorian Experience*. Sydney: Federation Press.

Freiberg, Arie, and Peter Sallmann. 2008. "Courts of Appeal and Sentencing: Principles, Policy and Politics." *Law in Context* 26(1):43–74.

Gelb, Karen. 2006. *Myths and Misconceptions: Public Opinion versus Public Judgment about Sentencing*. Melbourne: Sentencing Advisory Council.

Green, David. 2008. *When Children Kill Children: Penal Populism and Political Culture*. Oxford: Oxford University Press.

Hansard. 2014. Victoria: Parliamentary Accounts and Estimates Committee, May 14.

Hemming, Andrew. 2015. "Please Mind the Gap: An Assessment of Fatal 'One Punch' Provisions in Australia." *Criminal Law Journal* 39:130–47.

Kerr, Emily. 2012. "Raising the Fourth Pillar: Public Participation in Australian Sentencing: A Comparative Perspective." *Criminal Law Journal* 36:173–91.

King, Michael, Arie Freiberg, Becky Batagol, and Ross Hyams. 2014. *Non-adversarial Justice*. Sydney: Federation Press.

Krasnostein, Sarah. 2015. *"Boulton v The Queen:* The Resurrection of Guideline Judgments in Australia?" *Current Issues in Criminal Justice* 2:41–58.

Krasnostein, Sarah, and Arie Freiberg. 2012. "Manifest Error: Grounds for Review?" *Australian Bar Review* 36:54–73.

Law Reform Commission of Western Australia. 2009. *Court Intervention Programs*. Project no. 96. Perth: Law Reform Commission of Western Australia.

McInnis, Lea, and Craig Jones. 2010. *Trends in the Use of Suspended Sentences in New South Wales*. Sydney: New South Wales Bureau of Crime Statistics and Research.

McSherry, Bernadette. 2014. *Managing Fear: The Law and Ethics of Preventive Detention and Risk Assessment*. New York: Routledge.

Menendez, Patricia, and Don Weatherburn. 2014. *The Effect of Suspended Sentences on Imprisonment*. Sydney: New South Wales Bureau of Crime Statistics and Research.

New South Wales Law Reform Commission. 2006. *Sentencing and Juries*. Sydney: New South Wales Law Reform Commission.

———. 2012a. *Penalty Notices*. Report no. 132. Sydney: New South Wales Law Reform Commission.

———. 2012b. *Standard Minimum Nonparole Periods*. Report no. 134. Sydney: New South Wales Law Reform Commission.

———. 2013. *Sentencing*. Report no. 139. Sydney: New South Wales Law Reform Commission.

———. 2015. *Parole*. Report no. 142. Sydney: New South Wales Law Reform Commission.

Norton, Francine, Brad Ryan, and Melinda Howells. 2013. "Attorney-General Jarrod Bleijie Orders Review into Queensland Sentencing Laws." ABC News, July 31. http://www.abc.net.au/news/2013-07-31/attorney-general-orders-review -into-qlds-sentencing-laws/4855074.

Odgers, Stephen. 2014. "Editorial: Sentencing Law Reform." *Criminal Law Journal* 38:73–76.

Ogloff, James. 2011. *Review of Parolee Reoffending by Way of Murder*. Melbourne: Department of Justice.

Pratt, John, and Anna Eriksson. 2013. *Contrasts in Punishment: An Explanation of Anglophone Excess and Nordic Exceptionalism*. London: Routledge.

Quilter, Julia. 2014. "One-Punch Laws, Mandatory Minimums and 'Alcohol-Fuelled' as an Aggravating Factor: Implications for NSW Criminal Law." *International Journal for Crime, Justice and Social Democracy* 3(1):81–106.

Roberts, Lynne, Caroline Spiranovic, and David Indermaur. 2011. "A Country Not Divided: A Comparison of Public Punitiveness and Confidence in Sentencing across Australia." *Australian and New Zealand Journal of Criminology* 44(3):370–86.

Sentencing Advisory Council, Tasmania. 2015a. *Phasing Out of Suspended Sentences: Background Paper*. Hobart: Sentencing Advisory Council.

———. 2015b. *Phasing Out of Suspended Sentences: Consultation Paper*. Hobart: Sentencing Advisory Council.

Sentencing Advisory Council, Victoria. 2006. *Suspended Sentences and Intermediate Sentencing Orders: Final Report Part 1.* Melbourne: Sentencing Advisory Council.

———. 2008. *Suspended Sentences and Intermediate Sentencing Orders: Final Report Part 2.* Melbourne: Sentencing Advisory Council.

———. 2010. *Maximum Penalties: Principles and Purposes: Preliminary Issues Paper.* Melbourne: Sentencing Advisory Council.

———. 2012. *Review of the Adult Parole System: Report.* Melbourne: Sentencing Advisory Council.

———. 2013. *Victoria's Prison Population, 2002 to 2012.* Melbourne: Sentencing Advisory Council.

———. 2014. *Community Correction Orders: Second Monitoring Report (Pre-guideline Judgment).* Melbourne: Sentencing Advisory Council.

———. 2015. *Community Correction Orders: Monitoring Report.* Melbourne: Sentencing Advisory Council.

Simon, Jonathan. 2012. "Weather Report: Strange Weather or Climate Change." Governing through Crime blog. http://governingthroughcrime.blogspot.com .au/2012/11/weather-report-strange-weather-or.html.

Smith, Philip. 2013. "Punishment and Meaning: The Cultural Sociological Approach." In *The Sage Handbook of Punishment and Society*, edited by Jonathan Simon and Richard Sparks. Thousand Oaks, CA: Sage.

Steenhuis, D. W., L. C. M. Tigges, and J. J. A. Essers. 1983. "The Penal Climate in the Netherlands: Sunny or Cloudy?" *British Journal of Criminology* 23(1):1–16.

Subramanian, Ram, Rebecka Moreno, and Sharyn Broomhead. 2014. *Recalibrating Justice: A Review of State Sentencing and Corrections Trends.* New York: Vera Institute of Justice.

Tasmania Law Reform Institute. 2008. *Sentencing.* Final Report no. 11. Hobart: Tasmanian Law Reform Institute.

Tonry, Michael. 2013. "Sentencing in America, 1975–2025." In *Crime and Justice: A Review of Research*, vol. 42, edited by Michael Tonry. Chicago: University of Chicago Press.

———. 2014. "Remodeling American Sentencing: A Ten-Step Blueprint for Moving Past Mass Incarceration." *Criminology and Public Policy* 13(4):503–33.

Travis, Jeremy, and Bruce Western, eds. 2014. *The Growth of Incarceration in the United States: Exploring Causes and Consequences*, Washington, DC: National Academies Press.

Tubex, Hilde, David Brown, Arie Freiberg, Karen Gelb, and Rick Sarre. 2015. "Penal Diversity within Australia." *Punishment and Society* 17(3):345–73.

Victorian Ombudsman. 2015. *Investigation into the Rehabilitation and Reintegration of Prisoners in Victoria.* Melbourne: Victorian Government Printer.

Warner, Kate. 2014. "Sentencing Review 2013–2014." *Criminal Law Journal* 38 (6):364–79.

Warner, Kate, and Julia Davis. 2013. "Involving Juries in Sentencing: Insights from the Tasmanian Jury Study." *Criminal Law Journal* 37:246–56.

Michael Tonry

Equality and Human Dignity: The Missing Ingredients in American Sentencing

ABSTRACT

Concern for equality and human dignity is largely absent from American sentencing. Prison sentences are imposed much more often than in any other Western country. Prison terms are incomparably longer. The greater frequency of imprisonment is a product of punitive attitudes and politicization of crime control policies. The longer terms result partly from abolition of parole release in every jurisdiction for all or some inmates, but mostly from the proliferation since the mid-1980s of mandatory minimum, three-strikes, life without parole, and truth-in-sentencing laws. The ideas that offenders should be treated as equals and with concern and respect for their interests largely disappeared, though they had been animating values of earlier indeterminate and determinate sentencing systems. Their disregard is evident in the nature of contemporary laws but also in low-visibility policies and practices including the near absence of meaningful systems of appellate sentence review, low standards of proof at sentencing, and the absence of standards for sentencing of people convicted of multiple offenses at one time or over time.

Sentencing and punishment in the United States are more severe and arbitrary than in other Western countries because two fundamental animating values, ubiquitous elsewhere, are largely absent. The first, encap-

Electronically published June 22, 2016

Michael Tonry, professor of law and public policy, University of Minnesota, and Scientific Member, Max Planck Institute for Foreign and International Criminal Law, is grateful to Alessandro Corda, Richard Frase, Michael O'Hear, and Julian Roberts for comments on an early draft.

459

sulated in the German concept of the *Rechtsstaat*, the state governed by the rule of law, is a strong principle of equality: all citizens in their dealings with the state under particular circumstances should be treated in the same way. Citizens convicted of comparable crimes should be comparably punished. Anything else is a failure to apply the law evenhandedly, to treat citizens as equals (Pifferi 2012).

The second is recognition of human dignity as a fundamental value, along with its corollary that punishments should never be more severe or intrusive than is just or necessary. James Whitman (2003, 2016) refers to this as a "presumption of mercy" that permeates western European criminal law systems. That is why prisoners in western Europe are entitled to vote, wear their own clothing, live in single-occupancy cells, and be accorded privacy. Prison cells often have solid doors, without windows or bars. No one wants to be watched in his or her bedroom or during private moments. Prisoners are no different. They are viewed as citizens behind bars who retain all rights of other citizens except those inextricably associated with confinement (van Zyl Smit and Snacken 2009).

Americans, of course, understand the words equality and human dignity. Most would say they believe in the principles the words embody. However, in the criminal justice system, they are the merest rhetoric. They lack teeth. Neither the words nor the principles that underlie them provide significant constraints on the state's criminal law powers.

Some might say that the constitutional Fourteenth Amendment provision on "equal protection of the law" expresses the equality principle and that the Tenth Amendment provision on "reserved powers," which provides that citizens retain all powers not given to the state by the Constitution, expresses respect for liberty and with that human dignity. Neither claim is credible.

The jurisprudence of equal protection permits unequal treatment for which a "rational basis" can be shown. Courts defer to elected officials and bend over backward to find rational bases even when nothing very plausible is offered. Unequal treatment based on potentially invidious criteria such as race, ethnicity, and religion triggers closer scrutiny; a "compelling state interest" must be shown. Even that seemingly strict standard is a paper tiger. Public safety is considered to be a compelling state interest, which can justify actions based on racial or similar criteria. The courts, for example, allow police to take race and ethnicity explicitly into account in making police street stops and in profiling generally (Johnson 2010).

Even strong statistical evidence of unwarranted racial disparities is not enough to challenge differential treatment. In *McCleskey v. Kemp*, 481 U.S. 279 (1987), the US Supreme Court held that officials must be shown to have intended to discriminate. That is nearly impossible. Few admit to biased motivations. If constitutionally unequal treatment in the justice system cannot be inferred from strong statistical evidence, as it can in employment law, racial disparities as a practical matter are irremediable. American law thus provides no protection against unequal treatment in most criminal justice settings, and little even when potentially invidious criteria are used.

Human dignity is given even less weight. There is no general American legal or constitutional doctrine of human dignity or human rights. The United States in three ways refuses to recognize human rights that other developed countries accept. First, it has signed but failed to ratify some important international agreements, including the Convention on the Rights of the Child and the Convention on the Elimination of All Forms of Discrimination against Women.

Second, other documents, such as the Convention against Torture and Other Cruel, Inhuman, or Degrading Treatment or Punishment (the Torture Convention) and the International Covenant on Civil and Political Rights (the ICCPR), have been signed and ratified but with critical qualifications. For example, a reservation to the Torture Convention provides that "cruel, inhuman, and degrading" shall be interpreted in the United States as being identical in meaning to American courts' narrow interpretation of the Eighth Amendment prohibition of "cruel and unusual" punishment. American agreement to the ICCPR was qualified to provide that its prohibition of capital punishment for juveniles did not apply to the United States.

Third, even international documents to which the United States is a party are not self-executing. The Congress must ratify them. It seldom does so except with limiting qualifications. This means that individuals may not appeal to American or international courts seeking recognition, implementation, or enforcement of human rights provisions of international compacts. International human rights documents do not offer legally enforceable protections. This is in stark contrast to Europe, where the European Convention on Human Rights is enforceable in national courts from which appeals can be taken to the European Court of Human Rights.

The implications of these differences are stark. Below I discuss a German Constitutional Court decision that turns on the view that hope for the prospect of a better future life is a basic human right inferable from the German constitution. It is unimaginable that an American court would draw such an inference from the Declaration of Independence's elaboration of "unalienable rights," including "life, liberty, and the pursuit of happiness." The differences can be seen in sentence severity, imprisonment rates, sentencing laws, disproportionate punishments, and prison conditions:

- The United States is the only Western country that retains capital punishment or frequently imposes sentences of life without parole (LWOPs), other life sentences, and sentences measured in decades (van Zyl Smit and Snacken 2009).
- The American imprisonment rate has been above 700 per 100,000 US residents since 2000. Rates in other developed Western countries in recent years ranged between 70 or less in the Scandinavian countries and the Netherlands and 150 in England and Spain (Aebi et al. 2014).
- Three-strikes and other mandatory minimum sentence laws requiring life or decades-long sentences exist only in the United States. Laws requiring LWOPs exist in no other country. A few countries have laws permitting them, but they are almost never imposed. In most countries, the longest sentence for any offense, except sometimes first-degree murder, is 12–21 years. Almost always those periods are shortened, usually by one-third, for remission, the equivalent of American time off for good behavior (van Zyl Smit and Snacken 2009).
- Proportionality in punishment is everywhere else seen as an elementary requirement of justice: the equality principle requires comparable punishments for comparable crimes. This necessarily implies that less serious crimes will be punished less severely than more serious ones, and vice versa. The US Supreme Court over the past 40 years, however, has effectively eliminated proportionality in punishment as a constitutional principle except in relation to capital punishment: death has been held to be disproportionately severe for any offense other than murder.

• The quality of life in American prisons is incomparably worse than in most continental European countries. At year-end 2014, federal prisons were operating at 128 percent of capacity. Twenty-eight states were operating in excess of capacity including Alabama at 198 percent, Illinois at 171 percent, and Delaware, Hawaii, and Nebraska at 159–162 percent (Carson 2015). The European Court of Human Rights by contrast recently ordered Italy to eliminate overcrowding under threat otherwise of substantial damage awards to prisoners (*Torreggiani and Others v. Italy* [application no. 43517/09], 2013). Northern European countries typically provide single-occupancy cells and often maintain waiting lists for admission in order to avoid overcrowding; American prisoners often live in dormitories, may not vote, almost never have single cells except in segregation units, and in many states receive grossly inadequate medical and mental health care.[1] That last observation was the foundation for the Supreme Court decision in *Brown v. Plata*, 131 S. Ct. 1910 (2011), which ordered California to reduce overcrowding to 137.5 percent of capacity.

The importance of these fundamentally different commitments to equality, proportionality, and human dignity can be seen by looking at how appellate courts handled LWOPs and other laws requiring starkly disproportionate sentences. The US Supreme Court in *Harmelin v. Michigan*, 501 U.S. 957 (1991), upheld the constitutionality of LWOPs. They may even be imposed—as long as they are not mandatory—on juveniles.[2] In *Harmelin*, in which the defendant was a first offender convicted of cocaine possession, Justice Kennedy observed, "The Eighth Amendment does not require strict proportionality between crime and sentence. Rather, it forbids only extreme sentences that are 'grossly disproportionate' to the crime" (p. 1001).

The court laid foundations earlier. In *Rummel v. Estelle*, 445 U.S. 263, 274 (1980), upholding a 25-year-to-life sentence imposed for theft of $120.75, the court observed that the proportionality principle "would . . .

---

[1] Conditions in US prisons are described in chilling detail in the National Academy of Sciences panel report on causes and consequences of mass incarceration (Travis, Western, and Redburn 2014, chap. 6).

[2] The court declared unconstitutional mandatory sentences of life without the possibility of parole for juveniles in *Graham v. Florida*, 560 U.S. 48 (2010), and *Miller v. Alabama*, 132 S. Ct. 2455 (2012).

come into play in the extreme example . . . if a legislature made overtime parking a felony punishable by life imprisonment." Two years later, in *Hutto v. Davis*, 454 U.S. 370, 374 (1982), involving a defendant sentenced to two consecutive 20-year prison terms for possession of 9 ounces of marijuana, the court elaborated: "*Rummel* stands for the proposition that federal courts should be reluctant to review legislatively mandated terms of imprisonment, and that successful challenges to the proportionality of particular sentences should be exceedingly rare."

Two celebrated decisions upholding mandatory minimum 25- and 50-year sentences under California's three-strikes law show that the court meant what it said in *Rummel* and *Hutto*. The defendant in *Lockyer v. Andrade*, 538 U.S. 63 (2003), had been convicted of stealing nine videotapes worth $150 from Kmart. He was sentenced to 50 years to life. The defendant in *Ewing v. California*, 538 U.S. 11 (2003), had been convicted of theft of three golf clubs. He received 25 years to life. Justice O'Connor observed that granting Ewing's appeal "would fail to accord proper deference to the policy judgments that find expression in the legislature's choice of sanctions" (p. 29). Taken together, these cases mean that American courts will almost never strike down sentencing laws or decisions because they are disproportionately severe.

By contrast, the German Constitutional Court in 1977 struck down an LWOP law at a time when the Baader-Meinhof gang and other radical groups were committing political assassinations. The court declared full life sentences to violate the German Constitution and required that every prisoner be allowed to petition for release after at most 14 years, and regularly thereafter, under procedures that afforded a meaningful review of the need for continued confinement and a meaningful possibility of release (*lebenslange Freiheitsstrafe*, 21 June 1977, 45 *BVerfGE* 187).[3] Part of the rationale was that hope for the possibility of a better life in the future is a basic human right that LWOPs completely deny. In 2013, in *Vintner and Others v. The United Kingdom* (nos. 66069/09, 130/10, and 3896/10), the European Court of Human Rights declared LWOPs to violate the European Convention of Human Rights.

---

[3] Kommers (1997, pp. 306–13) provides an English translation of extracts from the opinion. Limits on maximum prison sentences and rationales by which courts in a number of other European countries forbade LWOPs before *Vintner and Others v. The United Kingdom* was decided are discussed in detail in van Zyl Smit and Snacken (2009).

In this essay, I show how the absence of equality and human dignity norms has shaped contemporary American sentencing policies and practices. Section I tells what happened. Respect for equality and human dignity was part of the fabric of American sentencing during most of the twentieth century but largely disappeared in the 1980s. The broad outline of the story is well known. A system of individualized indeterminate sentencing, based largely on rehabilitative ideals, existed from the 1930s to the mid-1970s when it collapsed. It was followed by a short period of determinate sentencing; many states abolished parole release and most either enacted statutory sentencing standards or established sentencing guidelines systems at state or local levels. After that, from the mid-1980s through the mid-1990s, every state and the federal government enacted proportionality-defying sentencing laws of historically unprecedented severity that consistently failed to show concern and respect for offenders. Few such laws were enacted after 1996, but almost none of the severest were repealed and few have been significantly altered. No other developed country in recent decades experienced comparable changes. England and Wales and Canada came closest but enacted no laws remotely as severe as those in the United States. None adopted mandatory minimum sentence laws requiring 10 or more years in prison, three-strikes laws, LWOPs, or truth-in-sentencing laws.

Section II discusses the influence of equality and human dignity norms more generally. The laws of the tough-on-crime period implicitly renounced them. They are also conspicuously absent from other features of twenty-first-century American sentencing. These include the recent shift of primary control over sentencing from judges to prosecutors, the near absence of meaningful appellate sentence review, and a series of low-visibility structural features that defy equality, proportionality, and human dignity norms. These are the absences of meaningful evidentiary standards for sentencing and of principles for sentencing offenders convicted of multiple offenses either at one time or over time.[4] By contrast, no other developed country has given prosecutors dispositive powers over sentencing for serious crimes. All operate systems of meaningful appellate review. Most require that sentencing decisions,

---

[4] There is no American literature on sentencing for multiple current offenses; consequently I do not discuss that subject in any detail. Other English-speaking countries observe a "totality" principle under which the most serious offense receives primary weight and serves as a cap for the total sentence (e.g., Manson et al. 2008; Freiberg 2014; Ashworth 2015).

like convictions, be based on proof beyond a reasonable doubt, tightly regulate the weight given to prior convictions, and have clear rules limiting aggregate punishments for people convicted of more than one offense.

Section III considers, not very optimistically, the prospects for meaningful changes. Repeal or radical alteration of the severe laws enacted in the 1980s and 1990s is a necessary—but enormous—first step (Tonry 2016), but that will not be enough if prosecutors remain the dominant figures in sentencing. Even, however, and improbably, if prosecutorial power were restrained and regulated, the low-visibility problems would remain. They will be solved only if equality and human dignity values somehow become part of American legal and political culture. The path to achievement of that goal is unclear. The only source for optimism is that they were once mainstream American values and may still exist below the surface of American legal culture. Indeterminate sentencing, best exemplified by the *Model Penal Code* (American Law Institute 1962), embodied them. The short-lived determinate sentencing era took them more seriously.

I. American Sentencing, 1965–2015

The story of recent American sentencing policy developments is well known and has recently been told several times (e.g., Travis, Western, and Redburn 2014, chap. 3; Tonry 2016). Here I offer only a recitative.

A. Indeterminate Sentencing

From the 1930s through 1975, indeterminate sentencing systems were ubiquitous. They were of course imperfectly implemented but were not especially controversial until the late 1960s. Their roots lay in distinctive nineteenth-century American developments including the invention and establishment during the Progressive Era of the penitentiary system, juvenile training schools, reformatories, probation, parole, and the juvenile court. The overriding symbol was the indeterminate sentence, which was prominently endorsed at the founding meeting of the American Prison Association in Cincinnati in 1870.[5]

---

[5] Within a few years the organization became, and remains, the American Correctional Association.

The meeting, attended by correctional officials from throughout the United States, other English-speaking countries, and Europe, adopted a Declaration of Principles that emphasized rehabilitation as sentencing's primary goal. Principles II and XXII provided the following: "[II] The treatment of criminals by society is for the protection of society. But since such treatment is directed to the criminal rather than the crime, its great object should be his moral regeneration. . . . [XXII] The state has not discharged its whole duty to the criminal when it has punished him, nor even when it has reformed him. Having raised him up, it has further duty to aid in holding him up" (Wines 1871, pp. 541, 544). Offending was understood to be primarily the result of inadequate socialization and various human deficits that could often be remediated by literacy, vocational training, and moral education. Both juvenile and adult sentences of confinement were to be indeterminate in length so that offenders could be released when they were ready.

By the 1930s, every state and the federal government had adopted full-scale indeterminate sentencing (Rothman 1971). Statutes defined crimes and established maximum probation and prison terms. Judges adjudicated cases and imposed sentences. Parole boards set release dates. Details varied. The distinctive American practices of sentencing offenders to local jails for terms less than a year and to state prisons for a year or more existed then as now. Parole boards decided when state prisoners were released. Sometimes, they were given authority to order release at any time after 1 year had been served; otherwise, after service of the minimum sentence. Prison authorities could award time off for good behavior. This usually reduced both maximum and minimum sentences by a third, and sometimes by more. Judges in most states could set a maximum sentence, but in California and Washington they could not. Every prisoner's maximum term was the period specified in the relevant statute; the minimum was 1 year. Juvenile sentences were much shorter; juvenile correctional authorities made the release decisions. In this short survey, I do not discuss probation and parole supervision, but they, too, were to be individualized and aimed at the rehabilitation and resocialization of offenders. In the federal system and the better-managed state systems, probation and parole officers often were trained social workers. Wardens and other senior officials often had clerical backgrounds.

The drafters of the *Model Penal Code* believed in the principles and values that underlay indeterminate sentencing (e.g., Wechsler 1961). Herbert Wechsler, in explaining the code's approach a year before it was approved, observed, "The rehabilitation of an individual who has incurred the moral condemnation of the law is in itself a social value of importance, a value, it is well to note, that is and ought to be the prime goal of correctional administration" (p. 468). Every judicial sentencing and parole release decision should be individualized. That is why all prisoners, however serious their crimes, including rape and murder, should be eligible for probation and for parole release when the board decided that was appropriate. The code provided for only three classes of felonies, and definitions of crimes were broadly worded. The focus was on the offender and his or her rehabilitative prospects or dangerousness. The offense of conviction was not thought to be especially important. The code created a presumption that every offender should be sentenced to probation and provided criteria judges should consider before deciding that imprisonment should be imposed instead. A similar presumption instructed the parole board to release prisoners when they first became eligible unless another set of specified criteria justified holding them longer.[6]

The code nowhere mentions retribution, deserved punishment, or just deserts as primary considerations. Three provisions nod to retributive ideas, but barely. Section 1.02(c)(2) includes among the purposes of sentencing "to safeguard offenders against excessive, disproportionate or arbitrary punishment." Section 7.01 indicates that one reason to disregard the presumption in favor of probation is that not doing so would "unduly depreciate the seriousness of the offense." Section 305.9(1)(b) contains a comparable provision concerning the parole release presumption.[7]

Indeterminate sentencing never worked as well as its proponents hoped. Correctional systems in the federal system and some states, notably New York, California, Minnesota, Wisconsin, and Washington, were at most times adequately funded, professionally led, and serious about their rehabilitative missions, but in many states they were not. In many states, prisons and jails were awful places; parole boards were composed of unqualified political appointees; prisons, jails, and probation and parole offices were filled with patronage employees; and treat-

---

[6] The American Law Institute's deliberations and the *Model Penal Code* provisions described in this paragraph are described in considerable detail in Tonry (2004, chap. 7).

[7] Section 305.9(1)(b), the parallel section on the parole-release-at-first-eligibility presumption, uses slightly different words to justify delaying release: "his release at that time would depreciate the seriousness of his crime or promote disrespect for law."

ment programs ranged from inadequate to nonexistent (Rothman 1980). Critical accounts by the National Commission on Law Observance and Enforcement (1931) and the President's Commission on Law Enforcement and Administration of Justice (1967) are remarkably consistent and equally damning. Even so, the President's Commission, the National Commission on Reform of Federal Criminal Laws (1971), and the National Advisory Commission on Criminal Justice Standards and Goals (1973) accepted indeterminate sentencing's goals and values and sought to perfect it. So did both editions of the *Model Sentencing Act* (Advisory Council of Judges 1963, 1972).

They were too late. By the early 1970s, influenced by the civil rights, prisoners' rights, and due process movements, a formidable series of damning criticisms had accumulated. Liberals focused on sentencing disparities, unfairness, and racial bias. Conservatives emphasized lenient sentences and inattention to deterrent and incapacitative crime prevention strategies (Fleming 1974; van den Haag 1975; Wilson 1975). Lawyers criticized the lack of rules, opportunities for appeals, and official accountability (e.g., Davis 1969; Frankel 1973). Civil rights advocates made accusations of racial bias and argued that individualization made inconsistent, idiosyncratic, and racially unjust decisions inevitable (American Friends Service Committee 1971). Social scientists concluded that there was no convincing evidence that rehabilitative programs were effective (Martinson 1974; Lipton, Martinson, and Wilks 1975). Reformers proposed that indeterminate sentencing be jettisoned and replaced with statutes and guidelines that set out clear rules governing sentencing and providing bases for appeals (Frankel 1973; Morris 1974; Dershowitz 1976; von Hirsch 1976; Fogel 1979).

The critiques won the day. Not all states abandoned indeterminate sentencing, but almost no one defended it. In 1975, Maine abolished parole release and became the first determinate sentencing state. In 1976, California enacted the Uniform Determinate Sentencing Act, which also abolished parole and set out standards for sentences in the criminal code. Researchers in Vermont and Colorado started work on the first voluntary sentencing guidelines systems. In 1978, Pennsylvania and Minnesota enacted laws creating the first sentencing commissions charged to develop presumptive guidelines systems (Blumstein et al. 1983).

The indeterminate sentencing era was over. In important respects it had honored equality and human dignity values. Equal treatment was not conceived in relation to blameworthiness but to addressing offenders' circumstances and needs. The emphasis on individualization meant that every offender should, in Ronald Dworkin's phrases, be accorded "equal respect and concern" and "treated as an equal" (1978).

Today most people think of equality in punishment as inextricably linked with proportionality, which in turn is linked with offense serious-ness. The *Model Penal Code*'s drafters did not think that way or believe that retribution was an essential or even appropriate consideration. Her-bert Wechsler, later the code's chief architect, and Jerome Michael ob-served that retribution may represent "the unstudied belief of most men" but averred that "no legal provision can be justified merely because it calls for the punishment of the morally guilty by penalties propor-tioned to their guilt, or criticized merely because it fails to do so" (Mi-chael and Wechsler 1940, pp. 7, 11).[8] Instead, the code provided, the focus should always be on the offender. The section that sets out pur-poses of sentencing included these: "(b) to promote correction and re-habilitation of offenders; (c) to safeguard offenders against excessive, dis-proportionate or arbitrary punishment; (d) to give fair warning of the nature of the sentences that may be imposed on conviction of an offense; (e) to differentiate among offenders with a view to a just individualiza-tion in their treatment." Put positively, officials were expected to promote just individualization and the offender's rehabilitation. Put negatively, they were to protect offenders from unfair treatment and safeguard them from excessive and unjust punishments.

Human dignity was addressed in diverse ways. The emphasis on in-dividualization and treatment as an equal was one. Another, consistent with ideas about parsimony and use of the least restrictive alternative,

---

[8] Michael and Wechsler observed, "Since punishment consists in the infliction of pain it is, apart from its consequences, an evil. Consequently, it is good and, therefore, just only if and to the degree it serves the common good" (1940, p. 9). They were not alone. Harvard law professor Sheldon Glueck earlier observed, "The old argument was that punishment was necessary as a 'just retribution' or requital of wickedness. No thoughtful person today seriously holds this theory of sublimated social vengeance" (1928, p. 456). Columbia Uni-versity law professor Jerome Michael, writing with University of Chicago philosophy pro-fessor Mortimer Adler, explained that "the infliction of pain is never justified merely on the ground that it visits retributive punishment upon the offender. Punitive retribution is never justifiable in itself" (Michael and Adler 1933, pp. 341, 344). Harvard law professors Livingston Hall and Sheldon Glueck insisted that "official social institutions should not be predicated upon the destructive emotion of vengeance, which is not only the expression of an infantile way of solving a problem, but unjust and destructive of the purpose of protecting society" (1940, p. 20).

was to minimize intrusion in offenders' lives by means of the presumptions against imprisonment and in favor of parole release.

B. Determinate Sentencing

If Maine's 1975 abolition of parole and federal passage of the Sentencing Reform Act of 1984 are used as beginning and ending dates, which is reasonable, the determinate sentencing period lasted less than 10 years. Normative goals of consistency, predictability, transparency, and accountability emerged directly from the critiques of indeterminate sentencing. The new laws and guidelines, though in substantially different ways from indeterminate sentencing, expressed equality and human dignity values. The new frame of reference was not individualization and rehabilitation, but blameworthiness as manifested in offenders' wrongful behavior. That required that rules be established that tied sentencing decisions to the seriousness of crimes. Equality was sought by means of consistent application of sentencing standards, backed up by rights to challenge their application by filing appeals with appellate courts. Human dignity was acknowledged by concern for fair treatment, by making standards sufficiently flexible that judges could tailor sentences to particular circumstances, and by basing standards on behaviors for which offenders were morally accountable. All of this was encapsulated in the overriding goal of reducing or eliminating unwarranted sentencing disparities.

An outburst of experimentation and innovation occurred. Courts in every state, sometimes at state levels, sometimes in local judicial districts, experimented with or established voluntary sentencing guidelines (Gottfredson, Wilkins, and Hoffman 1978; Blumstein et al. 1983). Parole boards established release guidelines meant to increase consistency (Arthur D. Little 1981). Arizona, Colorado, North Carolina, Illinois, Indiana, and other states followed California's lead in establishing statutory standards for sentencing (Blumstein et al. 1983). Pennsylvania, Minnesota, Washington, and Oregon established systems of presumptive sentencing guidelines backed up by appellate sentence review (Frase 2013). Almost all states enacted laws that mandated minimum sentences, usually of 1 or 2 years for crimes involving guns (Shane-DuBow, Brown, and Olsen 1985).

The federal government and foundations funded many evaluations. The results were clear and relatively uncontroversial, as reports of two

National Academy of Sciences panels separated by three decades attest (Blumstein et al. 1983; Travis, Western, and Redburn 2014):[9]

- Presumptive sentencing guidelines promulgated by a specialized sentencing commission can reduce sentencing disparities generally and in relation to race and gender, facilitate development of systems of appellate sentence review, and improve corrections departments' budgetary and facilities planning.
- Guidelines for parole release, when well designed and implemented, can make more consistent and predictable decisions, even out unwarranted judicial sentencing disparities, and facilitate administrative review of decisions. They can be modified to offset and prevent prison overcrowding.
- Statutory determinate sentencing systems that incorporate sentencing standards into criminal codes have no discernible effects on sentencing patterns or disparities.
- Voluntary sentencing guidelines have no discernible effects on sentencing patterns or disparities.
- Mandatory minimum sentence laws result in unjustly severe and disproportionate sentences in many cases but have few or no deterrent effects, shift power from judges to prosecutors, precipitate widespread circumvention by lawyers and judges, and exacerbate sentencing disparities.

All major national analyses of the effects of sentencing law changes conclude that sentencing guidelines, especially those that tailor guidelines to available prison capacity, suppress population increases. This is usually referred to as adopting a "capacity constraint" policy. Marvell (1995) compared population growth in states that had voluntary or presumptive guidelines with the national average and concluded that guidelines systems incorporating capacity constraints had lower rates of increase. In a 50-state analysis covering a later period, Nicholson-Crotty (2004) concluded that guidelines based on capacity constraints moderate population growth and that guidelines not incorporating them exacerbate it. Stemen, Rengifo, and Wilson (2006) analyzed state sentencing

---

[9] The two National Academy of Sciences reports summarize the major literatures. I have surveyed the major research and evaluations several times in much more detail than this summary provides (Tonry 1987, 1996, 2016).

patterns in 1975–2002 and concluded that states that adopted presumptive guidelines and abolished parole release had lower incarceration and prison population growth rates than other states. Spelman (2009) concluded that, among all sentencing policy approaches of the preceding 30 years, states with presumptive sentencing systems experienced the lowest prison population increases.

The implications of the research findings are clear: establish presumptive sentencing guideline and parole guideline systems, replace statutory determinate sentencing laws and voluntary guidelines systems with presumptive guidelines, and repeal mandatory minimum sentence laws and enact no new ones. That is not what happened. Few systems of presumptive sentencing guidelines were established after the mid-1980s. North Carolina replaced its statutory determinate sentencing system with presumptive sentencing guidelines, but most of those enacted between 1976 and 1985 remain in effect. Mandatory minimum sentence and similar laws proliferated (Tonry 2016).

C. Tough on Crime

The developments of the tough-on-crime period from the early 1980s through 1996, after which few new ornately severe sentencing laws were enacted, can also be briefly summarized.[10] Despite the absence of evidence that deterrent and incapacitative effects of punishment significantly influence crime rates and patterns, a plethora of unprecedentedly severe sentencing laws were enacted. Every state and the federal government enacted mandatory minimum sentencing laws, many requiring prison terms of 5, 10, and more years for drug, violent, and sexual crimes. Half of the states and the federal government enacted three-strikes laws. A partly overlapping half and the federal government enacted truth-in-sentencing laws requiring prisoners to serve 85 percent of their nominal sentences. Many states that did not have LWOP laws enacted them. Many states enacted laws requiring extended sentences for "career criminals." Many enacted preventive detention laws for sexual offenders (often referred to as "sexual psychopaths"). All 50 states, under threats of federal financial penalties if they did not, enacted Megan's Laws establishing sex offender registration and notification systems.

---

[10] Edsall and Edsall (1991), Anderson (1995), Windlesham (1998), and Gest (2001) provide blow-by-blow accounts of the unfolding of the tough-on-crime period.

Those laws are the principal cause of mass incarceration in America. No one as yet has offered a convincing explanation for why so many, of such severity, were enacted.[11] Partisan politics, the responsiveness of voters to law and order appeals, and politicians' fears of being labeled soft on crime are part of the explanation. So too are the politics of race relations, the increased political influence of fundamentalist Protestants, and existential fears of economic and social change and insecurity.

In retrospect, the severe new laws cannot be justified as good-faith efforts to control and prevent crime. The state of the art of knowledge then available on deterrence and incapacitation cautioned that severe sentences were unlikely to have substantial preventative effects. The evidence has changed little since then. The National Academy of Sciences Committee on the Causes and Consequences of High Rates of Incarceration (the "NAS Panel") noted that the "the primary findings have not changed significantly since they were disseminated in a series of National Research Council reports between 1978 and 1986" (Travis, Western, and Redburn 2014, p. 102).[12]

Since both the NAS Panel and I (Tonry 2016) provide detailed reviews of the literature on the effects of truth-in-sentencing, mandatory minimum sentence, and three-strikes laws, here I mostly quote the panel's main conclusions:

- "The incremental deterrent effect of increases in lengthy prison sentences is modest at best. Because recidivism rates decline markedly with age, lengthy prison sentences, unless they specifically target very high-rate or extremely dangerous offenders, are an inefficient approach to preventing crime by incapacitation" (Travis, Western, and Redburn 2014, p. 5).

---

[11] Many people, of course, have tried. They include Garland (2001), Simon (2007), Murakawa (2014), and Gottschalk (2015), and I have tried several times (Tonry 2004, 2009, 2011*b*).

[12] Credible arguments could not be made in 1984–96 that the severe new laws were likely to be effective crime control measures. That such policies are neither instrumentally effective nor cost-effective was repeatedly shown by a series of contemporaneous NAS panels (e.g., on deterrence and incapacitation, Blumstein, Cohen, and Nagin [1978]; on sentencing reform initiatives including mandatory penalties, Blumstein et al. [1983]; on criminal careers, Blumstein et al. [1986]; and on control and prevention of violence, Reiss and Roth [1993]).

- "Mandatory minimum sentence and three-strikes laws have little or no effect on crime rates . . . [and] often result in the imposition of sentences that practitioners believe to be unjustly severe" (p. 83).
- There is substantial evidence that "mandatory minimum sentencing, truth-in-sentencing, [and] life-without-possibility-of-parole laws . . . shifted sentencing power from judges to prosecutors; provoked widespread circumvention; exacerbated racial disparities in imprisonment; and made sentences much longer, prison populations much larger, and incarceration rates much higher" (p. 102).

Little that is positive was learned from the policies adopted during the tough-on-crime period. The NAS Panel observed, "consideration of social science evidence has had little influence on legislative policymaking processes concerning sentencing and punishment in recent decades" (Travis, Western, and Redburn 2014, p. 90). Consideration of values of equality, proportionality, and human dignity almost disappeared. The most severe laws were ham-fisted and forbade judges and parole boards to individualize sentences to take account of distinctive features of particular crimes or of offenders' personal circumstances and characteristics. Judges and prosecutors often manipulated charges or circumvented sentencing laws to avoid injustice, but that exacerbated unwarranted disparities.

Many laws required grossly disproportionate sentences. Mandatory minimum laws for drug crimes often required prison terms for low-level drug dealers that were longer than those received by people convicted of serious violent or major white-collar crimes. Three-strikes laws required minimum 25-year and sometimes life sentences for people convicted of minor crimes including, as the California three-strikes cases show, trivial ones that could have been prosecuted as misdemeanors. Truth-in-sentencing laws cast in stone lengthy prison sentences that were often attributable more to judicial idiosyncrasy than to offenders' behavior. LWOP laws resulted in lifetime sentences for tens of thousands of people, some convicted of offenses committed as juveniles and many for offenses other than homicide.

The lessons are straightforward (Tonry 2014, 2016). Most of the severe laws enacted in the 1980s should be repealed or radically pruned. As experience in the determinate sentencing decade showed, presumptive sentencing guidelines and parole guidelines are the only recent policy initiatives that reduce unwarranted disparities, prevent prison overcrowding, treat offenders with concern and respect, and acknowledge values of equality and human dignity.

II. The Absence of Equality and Human Dignity Values

The lack of respect and concern for offenders and their interests manifested in the laws of the tough-on-crime period are evident to anyone who looks. Predominant influence over sentencing shifted from judges, who are expected to be nonpolitical and impartial, as committed to exonerating the innocent as to convicting the guilty, to elected prosecutors who are primarily interested in achieving convictions and punishment. Less well known are similar failures in three lower-visibility features of contemporary sentencing.

First, although appellate sentence review was a major element of the proposals of the leading proponents of determinate sentencing (Frankel 1973; Morris 1974), it is almost nonexistent except in a handful of states with sentencing guidelines (Reitz 1997). Most offenders who receive idiosyncratic, arbitrary, capricious, or disproportionately severe sentences have no recourse.

Second, although convictions require proof "beyond reasonable doubt," sentencing judges may base sentencing decisions on any evidence that moves them and are generally subject to no established evidentiary standard.

Third, American sentencing systems, unlike those in other developed countries, typically provide no standards at all for sentencing people with previous convictions or—in guidelines systems and under three-strikes, "career criminal," and similar laws—call for dramatically severer punishments. There are likewise no laws or standards for sentencing people convicted of multiple offenses; it is almost always entirely up to the individual judge. This affects a majority of defendants. In 2009, the most recent year for which national data are available, 75 percent of felony defendants had previously been arrested, 60 percent had previously been convicted, and 55 percent faced multiple charges (Reaves 2013, tables 2, 7, 9).

Judge Marvin Frankel (1973) famously disparaged American sentencing under indeterminate sentencing as "lawless." In those three respects, that remains true. Even assuming the honesty and good faith of most judges, their beliefs, attitudes, experience, and personalities inevitably affect how they react to particular offenses and offenders. Consider, for example, the likely differences in sentencing practices of former Supreme Court Associate Justice Thurgood Marshall and of his successor Clarence Thomas or of former Supreme Court Associate Justices William Brennan and Antonin Scalia.

Those three absences could be rationalized under indeterminate sentencing: lengths of prison sentences were meant to be nominal, so the effects of judicial idiosyncrasy were not necessarily important. Parole boards made almost all release decisions and thus served as a mechanism for reviewing judicial sentencing decisions. In any case, all sentences were meant to be individualized. The details of the calculus underlying a particular sentence, like offenses of conviction or criminal history, were relatively unimportant. What mattered was parole release eligibility.

That is all different in contemporary systems. At a time when all jurisdictions have enacted mandatory penalties, many have abolished parole release, and many have adopted "truth in sentencing," the sentencing judge's word is often the last. Without appellate sentence review, there is no way to identify and correct aberrant decisions. Without evidentiary standards of proof, decisions are often based on unreliable and mistaken information. Without rules governing cases involving prior or multiple current convictions, defendants are highly vulnerable to arbitrary, idiosyncratic, and inconsistent sentences.

A. Prosecutorial Sentencing

These problems are exacerbated by the displacement of judges by prosecutors in sentencing in the past 30 years. From the earliest days of determinate sentencing, observers warned that more predictable sentencing would increase prosecutors' power (Coffee and Tonry 1983). A few years after the "mandatory" federal guidelines took effect, the Federal Courts Study Committee observed, "The rigidity of the guidelines is causing a massive, though unintended, transfer of discretion and authority from the court to the prosecutor" (1990, p. 138). When guidelines specify a narrow range of presumptive sentences for each offense, the charge to which the defendant pleads guilty largely determines the sentence. That problem became much worse under mandatory minimum, three-strikes, and LWOP laws that precisely prescribed lengthy prison sentences. As David Boerner (1995), a former Seattle deputy chief prosecutor explained, however, legislators intended this to happen. During the tough-on-crime period they were not troubled. They trusted prosecutors to insist on severe sentences but were much less trustful of judges.

Ninety-five percent or more of convictions in American courts result from guilty pleas. There is no judicial fact-finding, defendants are routinely required to waive any right to appeal, and judges often have nothing to decide about the weight to be given to prior convictions or multiple charges. The prosecutor has sole authority to decide whether to charge an offense subject to a mandatory minimum sentence or LWOP law, or some other offense, or to trigger a three-strikes law. To too many defendants, it is difficult to reject a proposed plea bargain calling for a 5- or 10-year sentence when the alternative if convicted at trial is an LWOP or a 25-year minimum sentence under a three-strikes law. The late William Stuntz observed that "outside the plea bargaining process, such threats would be deemed extortionate" (2011, p. 260). Federal Court of Appeals Judge Gerald Lynch more than a decade ago observed:

> The prosecutor, rather than a judge or jury, is the central adjudicator of facts (as well as replacing the judge as arbiter of most legal issues and of the appropriate sentence to be imposed). Potential defenses are presented by the defendant and his counsel not in a court but to a prosecutor, who assesses their factual accuracy and likely persuasiveness to a hypothetical judge or jury, and then decides the charge of which the defendant should be adjudged guilty. Mitigating information, similarly, is argued not to the judge but to the prosecutor, who decides what sentence the defendant should be given in exchange for his plea. (Lynch 2003, pp. 1403–4)

The prosecutor is in charge. However, 5 percent of cases are decided at trials. Judges determine sentences in those cases and also when plea bargains involve charge dismissals and do not include agreements about a specific sentence. The issues discussed in this section thus remain important in practice. In principle they are highly important.

B. Appellate Sentence Review

Appellate review of sentencing decisions was seldom available in the indeterminate sentencing era. Statutes and judicial decisions defined the elements of crimes but specified only maximum sentences. No statutes, guidelines, court rules, or other standards provided criteria to guide judges' decisions. There were no bodies of appellate case law on sentencing standards. When indeterminate sentencing imploded, Norval Morris (1974) and many others proposed the development of a "Common Law" of sentencing. This was difficult to impossible under individualized indeterminate sentencing. Because sentencing judges were subject to no rules or standards, appellate judges had no criteria to apply in deciding whether particular decisions were reasonable or justifiable. Sentences occasionally were appealed and sometimes were overturned, but on the basis of non-generalizable rationales such as that it offends the conscience or that under all the circumstances it is too severe (Zeisel and Diamond 1977). Those words were no doubt golden to the people they affected, but they provided no general criteria that sentencing judges could be expected to observe.

For those reasons, determinate sentencing proposals envisioned appellate review as a core component (e.g., Frankel 1973). To greater and lesser degree, it took hold in the handful of jurisdictions including the federal system that promulgated presumptive sentencing guidelines (Reitz 1997). Thus Minnesota, Oregon, Washington, Oregon, North Carolina, and Kansas provide appellate sentence review.[13] Elsewhere, it remains nonexistent or minimal.

All other developed countries' legal systems have well-developed bodies of appellate case law on sentencing. English courts, quickly emulated in Canada and Australia, began early in the twentieth century to issue "guideline judgments" that set out standards for ordinary cases (Thomas 1979; Ashworth 2015). Except for the United States, all English-speaking countries have extensive bodies of sentencing case law. All western European systems do also (van Zyl Smit and Snacken 2009). In many countries, for example, Italy, appeals trigger a full retrial in a higher court on all issues including sentences. So as not to discourage appeals, Italian law specifies that when defendants successfully appeal they may be resentenced but subject to a double jeopardy–like restraint that the new sentence cannot be more severe than the sentence initially received (Corda 2016).

C. Standards of Proof

There are few or no limits on the quality or nature of the information on which American judges base their sentencing decisions. In other de-

---

[13] It was especially rigorous under the "mandatory" federal guidelines until the US Supreme Court in *U.S. v. Booker*, 543 U.S. 220 (2005), made them voluntary. Since then, the appellate standard has been that there must be an "abuse of discretion" by the sentencing judge. This has effectively eliminated substantive appellate review in the federal courts (Tonry 2016).

veloped countries, only aggravating circumstances found to be true "beyond reasonable doubt" can justify an increased sentence. A landmark Supreme Court decision, *Williams v. New York*, 337 U.S. 241 (1949), held to the contrary that there are no effective limits on what an American judge may consider. The court reasoned that individualized consideration of offenders' circumstances for fashioning a rehabilitative sentence justified admission of any evidence that might possibly be relevant.

That logic and that case were invoked to uphold the constitutionality of the US Sentencing Commission's "relevant conduct" policy, which required sentencing judges to look beyond the offense of conviction (Tonry 2016, chap. 3). Judges are directed to take into account not only the conviction offense but also any other offenses the judge believes occurred, whether or not a charge was filed or dismissed, and even if the defendant was acquitted. The US Supreme Court in *United States v. Watts*, 519 U.S. 148 (1997), and other decisions upheld the constitutionality of the relevant conduct policy.

So potentially any information is admissible. In the United States, depending on the jurisdiction, the standard of proof at sentencing ranges from low to nonexistent. A few require that facts be found by the civil law "more probable than not" standard; most establish no probative standard (Reitz 2011).

That contrast is especially striking since the adjudicative standard of proof is much higher in criminal than in civil cases—"beyond reasonable doubt" compared with "more probable than not." The reason for this centuries-old difference, which exists in the jurisprudence of all Western countries, is straightforward. Any incorrect legal decision is regrettable, but especially when the stakes are high. In contract law and tort proceedings, the cost of a mistake is that a loss goes uncompensated or someone is wrongly ordered to pay damages.

The stakes are much higher in criminal cases. Life, liberty, reputation, and property are in issue. That is why three centuries ago William Blackstone opined that it is far better that 10 guilty men go free than that one innocent be convicted. In some noncriminal contexts involving especially important or sensitive subjects, findings of fact are subject to "intermediate scrutiny," higher than the ordinary civil law standard but less exacting than the criminal law one.

No American jurisdiction requires that proof of "sentencing facts" be assessed by the criminal law or the intermediate standard. The US Supreme Court in *U.S. v. Blakely*, 542 U.S. 296 (2004), observed, "Sentencing courts have traditionally heard evidence and found facts without any prescribed burden of proof at all" (pp. 332–33). Judges may take into account any information they consider pertinent. Most defendants have no legal basis to challenge the reliability of the evidence or the inferences the judge draws from it.

I find this shocking and do not understand why most people do not. It means that decisions to send people to prison, or for longer or shorter terms, are often made on the basis of information that is incorrect, misunderstood, or misinterpreted. Given the procedural informality and enormous caseloads of American criminal courts, many sentences are no doubt based on inaccurate or mistaken information. That is exacerbated by the ubiquity of plea bargaining. In the cases in which the sentence is set by guilty pleas, no one, including the prosecutor, is held to any established standard.

The absence of a meaningful standard and the resulting injustices pass almost unnoted. Kevin Reitz, one of very few Americans to write about this, probably represents the view of many American lawyers and judges when he assumes such an approach to be inevitable: "Practical reasons exist for the procedural differential between trial and sentencing. Sentencing proceedings occur in a much larger number of cases than full-blown trials—approaching 100 percent of all convictions. [A trial-like process at sentencing] . . . would be unsustainable. . . . Cumbersome rules of process are more expensive, and less workable, in an adjudicative milieu of complexities and shades of grey" (2011, p. 232).

The American approach, however, is not inevitable. Other Western countries tightly limit the evidence that may be taken into account. European judges typically have comparatively little discretion to increase punishments for aggravating reasons, though often they can reduce punishments for mitigating reasons (Hinkkanen and Lappi-Seppälä 2011). There is little latitude for aggravation of punishments. In England and Wales and other common law countries, aggravating facts that might justify increasing a sentence must be proven beyond a reasonable doubt. The requirement in Canada is statutory. Case law in Australia and England establishes a reasonable doubt standard for aggravating factors and a "balance of probabilities" civil law standard for mitigating factors (Ashworth 2011; Doob and Webster 2016; Freiberg 2016).

Other countries' approach to proof of aggravating circumstances is based on the view that findings of fact at the trial and sentencing stages are equally important and should be governed by the same restrictive standard. Ashworth (2015, p. 428) explained concerning English law, "Bearing in mind the great effect on sentence which such issues may have, they ought properly to be resolved according to rules of evidence no less fair than those applicable at trial."

D. Criminal History

In contemporary American sentencing, an offender's prior record often matters more than the offense of which he or she is convicted. Under American guidelines systems, for example, sentences for recidivist offenders are often two, three, or more times longer than those for first offenders convicted of the same offense (Reitz 2010; Frase and Hester 2015). Under "career criminal," "repeat offender," "habitual offender," and three-strikes laws, prior felony convictions can lead to decades-long and life sentences. In both these ways, previous convictions influence sentencing decisions much more heavily in the United States than in other Western countries.

This dubious distinction is another unfortunate legacy. In indeterminate sentencing systems, an offender's criminal history was simply one thing a judge might take into account. Even a judge's decision to increase a sentence because of an offender's criminal record had no necessary significant effect on how long he or she remained in prison. The parole board decided that. The judge's sentence mostly affected the maximum term, and few prisoners served anywhere near that long. Details varied between states. In some the judge could set a minimum sentence, but usually not more than a third of the maximum, and both were usually discounted by time off for good behavior. In other states, the minimum term before release eligibility was 1 year, irrespective of the maximum set by the judge. The judge may have announced a harsher-sounding sentence because of prior convictions, and the parole board may have delayed release somewhat for the same reason, but the overall effects were usually modest. This is why in the 1970s critics often referred to "bark and bite sentencing": the judge's bark was harsher than the parole board's bite. This is also the origin of proposals for truth in sentencing that would make the bark and the bite pretty much the same (Alschuler 1993).

The role of prior convictions in sentencing has received remarkably little attention, most of it precipitated by the English psychologist Julian Roberts (1997; Roberts and von Hirsch 2010). Most people in English-speaking countries, including judges, offenders, and the general public, in our time appear to believe that sentences should be harsher when an offender has previous convictions (Roberts 2008).

When indeterminate sentencing fell apart, the practical consequences of that widely shared intuition were vastly greater than anyone imagined. Members of sentencing commissions simply assumed that criminal records should be part of the sentencing calculus. The process for developing guidelines always included empirical analyses of past sentencing patterns (Gottfredson, Wilkins, and Hoffman 1978; Parent 1988). They invariably showed that criminal histories affected the sentences judges imposed, so it probably seemed natural to incorporate criminal history into guidelines.

That decision, however, was based on a fundamental analytical mistake. The empirical analyses were of sentencing in indeterminate sentencing systems in which judges' reasons for imposing nominal prison terms did not much matter. Criminal records had at most a diffuse and contingent effect on how long offenders stayed in prison; likewise for the earliest sentencing guidelines. The prototypes were "voluntary" and were designed for use in indeterminate systems with parole release (Kress 1980). Business could continue as usual. Evaluations found that the early voluntary guidelines had no effect on judges' decisions, so building criminal history into them made little difference. The parole board made the release decisions.

The next generation of sentencing guidelines, however, was presumptive and was designed for jurisdictions without parole release. The criminal history dimensions became crucial. If, in voluntary guidelines systems, a criminal record might double the nominal lengths of sentences, it did not much matter. The judge could ignore the guidelines, and the parole board could largely ignore the judge's sentence.

When, however, Minnesota's and other early commissions developed presumptive guidelines for use in jurisdictions without parole release, the weight given to criminal history mattered hugely. The new guidelines were presumed to apply in every case, and judges' decisions to do something else could be appealed. The prison sentence the judge announced was no longer nominal, at most an upper limit, but minus easily predicted reductions for good behavior, the length of time to be spent in prison.

Once state and federal commissions began to establish presumptive guidelines prescribing terms of 5, 10, and 20 years, it was a small step for legislators to do the same thing in mandatory minimum sentence, three-strikes, and truth-in-sentencing laws. As a result, the United States has the longest prison sentences in the developed world as tables 1 and 2 show. Table 1 shows for eight European countries the percentages of convicted offenders—3.1–23 percent—receiving executed incarcerative sentences, and of those the percentages receiving sentences of particular lengths. Thus, in Germany, 5.4 percent went to prison and one-fourth of those—1 percent of the total—had terms of 2–5 years. By contrast, as table 2 shows, 73 percent of people charged with felonies convicted in American courts were sentenced to confinement with an average sentence of 52 months.

The 73 percent figure for the United States is not perfectly comparable to the European data shown in table 1. It includes only cases prosecuted as felonies (including many that resulted in misdemeanor convictions). However, the aggregate imprisonment percentage including misdemeanors in the United States is unlikely to be significantly lower. Federal data are available for all offenses including misdemeanors. In 2014, 87 percent of all sentenced offenders received prison sentences, 6 percent received sentences combining community penalties with confinement, and only 7 percent received community penalties alone (US Sentencing Commission 2015, p. 4). There are no national American data on state court sentencing for both felonies and misdemeanors combined.[14] The conventional wisdom in Minnesota is that 75 percent of all convictions result in a prison or jail sentence. Ninety-four percent of felony convictions in Washington State in 2015 resulted in sentences of confinement in a county jail or state prison (Washington Caseload Forecast Council 2016, table 1A). It is highly unlikely that jail sentences for misdemeanants are dramatically less common.

Prior convictions make a huge difference in the United States. Other than by referring to the intuition that prior convictions ought to make some difference (Roberts 2010), however, no one has convincingly explained why in principle they should make much of a difference, especially a drastic one.

The intuition by itself is not an explanation. As Wechsler and others believed about the "the unstudied belief of most men" concerning retribution, intuitions however widely shared may be morally wrong. Some

---

[14] Pennsylvania Commission on Sentencing data for 2014 show that, for felonies and misdemeanors combined, 45 percent of convictions for criminal incidents resulted in prison or jail sentences. For individual felonies, the rates were much higher than in Europe: homicide (100 percent), rape (93 percent), robbery (83 percent), aggravated assault (79 percent), burglary (78 percent), theft (50 percent) (personal communication with Mark H. Bergstrom, executive director of the commission, 2016).

TABLE 1
Length of Prison Sentences in Months, Selected Countries, 2010

Country	% Sentenced to Prison	Of These, % under 6 Months	Of These, % 6–11 Months	Of These, % 12–23 Months	Of These, % 24–59 Months	Of These, % 60–119 Months	Of These, % over 120 Months
Austria	NA	56.1	16.7	11.9	2.0	1.2	…
Finland	3.1	61.2	15.5	11.4	9.3	1.8	.3
France	17.8	57.2	20.3	17.3	2.8	1.4	1.0
Germany	5.4	24.1	28.6	18.8	24.4	3.5	.3
Netherlands	23	74.1	10.8	6.3	4.9	1.2	.4
Sweden	9.6	60.6	14.2	14.3	5.4	3.1	…
Switzerland (2007)	…	87.1	3.4	2.6	4.5	.4	.1
England	7.5	52.7	17.4	12.6	11.4	3.8	.7
United States (2009)	73.0						

SOURCE.—Europe 2007: Aebi et al. (2010); Europe 2010: Aebi et al. (2014, tables 3.2.3.1, 3.2.7.1); United States: Reaves (2013).

TABLE 2

Felony Sentences, US State Courts, by Type and Length of Confinement, 2009

Conviction Offense	Percentage Imprisonment	Incarceration		Percentage Nonimprisonment
		Prison	Jail	
All offenses	73	52 mos.	5 mos.	27
Violent offenses	83	91 mos.	6 mos.	17
Murder/nonnegligent manslaughter	100	373	NA	0
Rape	89	142	NA	11
Robbery	89	90	9	11
Assault	81	62	6	19
Property offenses	75	40 mos.	6 mos.	25
Burglary	79	52	7	21
Larceny	72	31	6	28
Motor vehicle theft	77	34	7	23
Fraud	71	47	5	29
Drug offenses	71	40 mos.	5 mos.	29
Trafficking	80	49	6	20
Other drug offenses	64	29	4	36

SOURCE.—Reaves (2013, tables 24–26).

should be resisted. Many people in earlier times thought it intuitively right that women, blacks, and gay people be treated differently from men, whites, and heterosexuals. Few today believe that those intuitions should be respected or that it was ever right to take them into account.

Some people believe that prior criminality is irrelevant to punishment for new crimes: did the crime, did the time; the slate has been wiped clean (Fletcher 1978; Singer 1979). Others believe, for opaque reasons, that prior crimes justify additional increments of deserved punishments for subsequent crimes. Ambitious, but tortured and unsuccessful, efforts have been made to offer retributive explanations. One is that a prior conviction places a special burden of law-abidingness on the individual (Lee 2010). Another is that the new crime constitutes a sign of disrespect of the state, a breach of citizenship, and a failure to act responsibly (Bennett 2010). All citizens, however, have a civic obligation to be law-abiding, so that cannot be why recidivists deserve greater punishment. And in democratic countries, disrespect and irresponsibility may be rude or unbecoming, but those qualities are not crimes. In a free society, citizens are entitled to be rude, eccentric, irresponsible, or "difficult." Offenders are not differently situated from other citizens in that respect, so disrespect and irresponsibility cannot justify harsher punishment for recidivists (Tonry 2010).

One final argument is that increased punishment of recidivists is not a recidivist premium but the wasting away of a discount for first offenders. Their punishments might be thought of as being mitigated because their crimes may have been out of character or the result of special, unlikely to be recreated, circumstances (von Hirsch 1981, 1985, 2010). For the second offense or perhaps the third, assuming that offenders deserve some continuing benefit of the doubt, they might receive a smaller discount. After that, it should be the deserved punishment, but no more, every time. However accurately that logic describes what judges think they are doing, it cannot explain why sentences become steadily harsher in the United States in direct relationship to the number of prior convictions. Nor can it explain why recidivists receive punishments two, three, or more times harsher than a first offender's.

As with the absences of appellate sentence review and high standards of proof, the United States is alone among Western countries in how prior convictions are handled. Other legal systems give criminal history much smaller weight. In Scandinavian countries, the role is very small. Judges and lawyers typically take the view that what is past is past. The earlier crime has already been punished; that is the end of the matter. Sentencing principles expressed in criminal codes authorize increments of additional punishment because of some prior crimes, but the increments are small and may be imposed only in narrowly defined circumstances (Asp 2010; Hinkkanen and Lappi-Seppälä 2011).

In England, prior convictions are regarded as germane only when—in statutory language—they are "recent" and "relevant" to the new offense, as when all the offenses are burglaries or all are sex offenses; if not relevant, the sentence for the current offense should not be increased (Roberts and Pina-Sanchez 2014). Case law limits how large the increment can be (Baker and Ashworth 2010). In other common law countries, case law doctrines narrowly limit the influence of prior convictions. One standard formulation is that the maximum sentence cannot exceed what would normally be imposed for a serious instance of the offense of conviction by itself (e.g., in Australia: Freiberg 2014).

The uncontrolled power of the prosecutor and the three other low-visibility characteristics of American sentencing are irreconcilable with legality and human dignity values. Anyone, in pondering the possibility that he or she or loved ones were to be convicted of a nontrivial crime, would want to believe that any resulting punishments would be governed by clear rules, be based on strong reliable evidence, be severely limited in scope, and be subject to impartial review of claims of injustice by a higher authority. American sentencing satisfies none of those rudimentary requirements of justice.

At least arguably, proponents of indeterminate sentencing could justify the absence of rules, especially since the influence of ideas about parsimony and least restrictive alternatives—illustrated by the *Model Penal Code* presumptions against imprisonment and for parole release— operated to humanize the system. They might say that criminal history is just one of many circumstances to be taken into account, not necessarily important, and seldom or never dispositive. They would have a difficult time justifying the absence of strong probative standards for assessing the reliability of information. Parole release provided a mechanism for review and for limiting excess and unfairness, but it was an unpredictable and unreliable one.

Proponents of contemporary sentencing systems reflecting more retributive punishment concerns about culpability and blameworthiness cannot with a straight face make any of those claims about parole boards as a fail-safe, probative standards, and criminal history. If support for equality values, and with them concern about treatment of offenders as equals and avoidance of unwarranted disparities, were stronger in the United States, none of these sources of unfairness and injustice would be tolerated. If support for human dignity values were stronger, we would want every case to be evaluated on its merits under fair procedures and on the basis of reliable information.

III. Equality and Human Dignity

'Twas not always so. In earlier times, equality and human dignity values were acknowledged and taken seriously. Nigel Walker's *Sentencing in a Rational Society* (1969), the first major twentieth-century book in English on sentencing policy, and Norval Morris's and my *Between Prison and Probation: Intermediate Punishments in a Rational Sentencing System* (1990) shared the then-uncontroversial premise that sentencing policy should be, and policy makers should want it to be, rational, humane, just, and based on the best available evidence. Crime is a troubling phenomenon and elicits feelings of disappointment, anger, outrage, and sometimes vindictiveness.

During the indeterminate sentencing era, rehabilitation, resocialization, and sometimes incapacitation were considered to be the most effective preventive strategies. During the short-lived determinate sentencing period, the most effective strategies were widely thought to be greater procedural fairness, enforceable but flexible standards, transparency, and accountability, all in the interest of reducing unwarranted disparities and treating offenders fairly and justly. In the tough-on-crime period, both those sets of strategies were eclipsed by policies based on political and ideological considerations that paid little heed to equality, proportionality, or human dignity.

Since 1996, there has been a multitude of new sentencing and punishment initiatives. Some such as drug and other problem-solving courts, restorative and community justice initiatives, and many rehabilitative and reentry programs try to take offenders seriously and treat them humanely. However, those programs coexist with all the severe sentencing laws of the 1980s and 1990s. No three-strikes, truth-in-sentencing, LWOP, or, except in Michigan in 2002, major mandatory minimum sentence laws have been repealed, though minor changes have been made that mostly target minor offenses and first-time offenders (Austin et al. 2013; Tonry 2016, chap. 1).

The paths to take to make American sentencing systems more just, respectful, and humane are clear enough. The *Model Penal Code—Sentencing* (American Law Institute 2007, 2011) lays out one that includes presumptive sentencing guidelines, repeal of mandatory minimum sentence laws, appellate sentence review, and development of more effective community penalties and treatment programs. I have laid out another that includes the same elements in somewhat differing detail as well as revival of parole release systems and creation of new "second-look" systems meant to unwind current mass incarceration and assure that continuing justifications exist over time to continue to confine people sentenced to lengthy prison terms (Tonry 2014, 2016). Both build on the best features of indeterminate (e.g., individualization, least restrictive alternative, effective treatment programs) and determinate systems (published standards, proportionality limits, appeals) and reject the inhumane and unjust laws of the tough-on-crime period.

A large-scale overhaul, however, is unlikely without a widespread change in consciousness or sensibilities. Such changes happen. The collapse in the 1970s in support for indeterminate sentencing was one. The near disappearance in the 1970s and 1980s of white Americans' belief in the racial inferiority of blacks is another (Mendelberg 2001). The extraordinary recent shift in attitudes toward homosexuality, evolving in 40 years from criminal prosecutions to gay marriages, is a third (Carpenter 2013). There are others including changed social norms about female equality, alcohol and driving, and marijuana use.

The overriding difficulty is that there is no easy way to change public consciousness and attitudes. Changes in attitudes, and with them laws and policies, happen slowly, over decades, and are aggressively and systematically promoted by social movements and by individuals and organizations with deep commitments. All of the changes mentioned in the preceding paragraph except the collapse of indeterminate sentencing within a decade after the first serious critiques fit that pattern. There are, however, no comparably broad-based, enduring social movements dedicated to improving the lives and treatment of criminal offenders. Many individuals and some law reform organizations have worked over decades to make the criminal justice system fairer and more just and to promote equality and human dignity values, but compared with the civil rights, gay rights, women's rights, marijuana legalization, and drunk-driving movements, those efforts have been small-scale, peripatetic, and ad hoc.

No individual writing a scholarly article can hope to offer a credible set of proposals for mobilizing a new social movement or changing public consciousness, so I do not try. It is clear that fundamental changes will occur only when a critical mass of opinion converges in the view that American sentencing laws, sentencing severity, and mass incarceration are morally unjustifiable (Tonry 2011*a*). When that happens, even the seemingly intractable problems of prosecutorial sentencing may abate. During the indeterminate sentencing era, many judges, other public officials, and citizens subscribed to its tenets as much as correctional officials did. Contemporary sentencing policies and practices cause enormous damage and accomplish little that is good. Those were the claims that undermined indeterminate sentencing. Those are the claims that should be made today.

REFERENCES

Advisory Council of Judges, National Council on Crime and Delinquency. 1963. *Model Sentencing Act*. Hackensack, NJ: National Council on Crime and Delinquency.
———. 1972. *Model Sentencing Act*. 2nd ed. Hackensack, NJ: National Council on Crime and Delinquency.

Aebi, Marcelo F., Bruno Aubusson de Vacarlay, Gordon Barclay, Beata Gur-szczyńska, Stefan Harrendorf, Markku Heiskanen, Vasilika Hysi, Veronique Jaquier, Jorg-Martin Jehle, Martin Killias, Olena Shostko, Paul Smit, and Rannveig Borisdottir. 2010. *European Sourcebook of Crime and Criminal Justice Statistics: 2010.* 4th ed. The Hague: Research and Documentation Centre, Netherlands Ministry of Justice.

Aebi, Marcelo F., Galma Akdeniz, Gordon Barclay, Claudia Campistol, Stefano Caneppele, Beata Gruszczyńska, Stefan Harrendorf, Markku Heiskanen, Vasilika Hysi, Jörg-Martin Jehle, Anniina Jokinen, Annie Kensey, Martin Killias, Chris G. Lewis, Ernesto Savona, Paul Smit, and Rannveig Þórisdóttir, eds. 2014. *European Sourcebook of Crime and Criminal Justice Statistics.* Helsinki: European Institute for Crime Prevention and Control.

Alschuler, Albert. 1993. "Monarch, Lackey, or Judge." *Colorado Law Review* 64:723–35.

American Friends Service Committee. 1971. *Struggle for Justice: A Report on Crime and Punishment in America.* New York: Hill & Wang.

American Law Institute. 1962. *Model Penal Code—Proposed Official Draft.* Philadelphia: American Law Institute.

———. 2007. *Model Penal Code—Sentencing.* Tentative Draft no. 1. Philadelphia: American Law Institute.

———. 2011. *Model Penal Code—Sentencing.* Tentative Draft no. 2. Philadelphia: American Law Institute.

Anderson, David C. 1995. *Crime and the Politics of Hysteria: How the Willie Horton Story Changed American Justice.* New York: Crown.

Arthur D. Little, Inc. and Goldfarb and Singer, Esqs. 1981. *An Evaluation of Parole Guidelines in Four Jurisdictions.* Washington, DC: National Institute of Corrections.

Ashworth, Andrew. 2011. "Re-evaluating the Standards for Aggravation and Mitigation at Sentencing." In *Mitigation and Aggravation at Sentencing*, edited by Julian V. Roberts. Cambridge: Cambridge University Press.

———. 2015. *Sentencing and Criminal Justice.* 5th ed. Cambridge: Cambridge University Press.

Asp, Petter. 2010. "Previous Convictions and Proportionate Punishment under Swedish Law." In *Previous Convictions at Sentencing: Theoretical and Applied Perspectives*, edited by Julian V. Roberts and Andrew von Hirsch. Oxford: Hart.

Austin, James, Eric Cadora, Todd R. Clear, Kara Dansky, Judith Greene, Vanita Gupta, Marc Mauer, Nicole Porter, Susan Tucker, and Malcolm C. Young. 2013. *Ending Mass Incarceration: Charting a New Justice Reinvestment.* Washington, DC: Sentencing Project.

Baker, Estella, and Andrew Ashworth. 2010. "The Role of Previous Convictions in England and Wales." In *Previous Convictions at Sentencing: Theoretical and Applied Perspectives*, edited by Julian V. Roberts and Andrew von Hirsch. Oxford: Hart.

Bennett, Christopher. 2010. "'More to Apologise For': Can We Find a Basis for the Recidivist Premium in a Communicative Theory of Punishment?" In *Previous Convictions at Sentencing: Theoretical and Applied Perspectives*, edited by Julian V. Roberts and Andrew von Hirsch. Oxford: Hart.

Blumstein, Alfred, Jacqueline Cohen, Susan E. Martin, and Michael Tonry, eds. 1983. *Research on Sentencing: The Search for Reform.* 2 vols. Washington, DC: National Academy Press.

Blumstein, Alfred, Jacqueline Cohen, and Daniel Nagin, eds. 1978. *Deterrence and Incapacitation: Estimating the Effects of Criminal Sanctions on Crime Rates.* Washington, DC: National Academy of Sciences.

Blumstein, Alfred, Jacqueline Cohen, Jeffrey A. Roth, and Christy A. Visher, eds. 1986. *Criminal Careers and "Career Criminals."* Washington, DC: National Academies Press.

Boerner, David. 1995. "Sentencing Guidelines and Prosecutorial Discretion." *Judicature* 78:196–200.

Carpenter, Dale. 2013. *Flagrant Conduct: The Story of Lawrence v. Texas.* New York: Norton.

Carson, E. Ann. 2015. *Prisoners in 2014.* Washington, DC: US Department of Justice, Bureau of Justice Statistics.

Coffee, John C., Jr., and Michael Tonry. 1983. "Hard Choices: Enforcing Sentencing Guideline and Plea Bargaining." In *Reform and Punishment,* edited by Michael Tonry and Franklin E. Zimring. Chicago: University of Chicago Press.

Corda, Alessandro. 2016. "Sentencing and Penal Policies in Italy, 1985–2015: The Tale of a Troubled Country." In *Sentencing Policies and Practices Cross-Nationally and Comparatively,* edited by Michael Tonry. Vol. 45 of *Crime and Justice: A Review of Research,* edited by Michael Tonry. Chicago: University of Chicago Press.

Davis, Kenneth Culp. 1969. *Discretionary Justice: A Preliminary Inquiry.* Baton Rouge: Louisiana State University Press.

Dershowitz, Alan. 1976. *Fair and Certain Punishment.* New York: Twentieth Century Fund.

Doob, Anthony N., and Cheryl Marie Webster. 2016. "Weathering the Storm? Testing Long-Standing Canadian Sentencing Policy in the Twenty-First Century." In *Sentencing Policies and Practices Cross-Nationally and Comparatively,* edited by Michael Tonry. Vol. 45 of *Crime and Justice: A Review of Research,* edited by Michael Tonry. Chicago: University of Chicago Press.

Dworkin, Ronald. 1978. *Taking Rights Seriously.* Cambridge, MA: Harvard University Press.

Edsall, Thomas, and Mary Edsall. 1991. *Chain Reaction: The Impact of Race, Rights, and Taxes on American Politics.* New York: Norton.

Federal Courts Study Committee. 1990. *Report.* Washington, DC: Administrative Office of the US Courts.

Fleming, MacKlin. 1974. *The Price of Perfect Justice: The Adverse Consequences of Current Legal Doctrine on the American Courtroom.* New York: Basic Books.

Fletcher, George. 1978. *Rethinking Criminal Law.* Boston: Little, Brown.

Fogel, David. 1979. *We Are the Living Proof: The Justice Model for Corrections.* Cincinnati: Anderson.

Frankel, Marvin. 1973. *Criminal Sentences: Law without Order.* New York: Hill & Wang.

Frase, Richard S. 2013. *Just Sentencing: Principles and Procedures for a Workable System*. New York: Oxford University Press.

Frase, Richard S., and Rhys Hester. 2015. "Magnitude of Criminal History Enhancements." In *Criminal History Enhancements Sourcebook*, edited by Richard S. Frase, Julian Roberts, Rhys Hester, and Kelly Mitchell. Minneapolis: Robina Institute of Criminal Law and Criminal Justice, University of Minnesota Law School.

Freiberg, Arie. 2014. *Fox and Freiberg's Sentencing: State and Federal Law in Victoria*. 3rd ed. Melbourne: Thomson Reuters.

———. 2016. "The Road Well Traveled in Australia: Ignoring the Past, Condemning the Future." In *Sentencing Policies and Practices Cross-Nationally and Comparatively*, edited by Michael Tonry. Vol. 45 of *Crime and Justice: A Review of Research*, edited by Michael Tonry. Chicago: University of Chicago Press.

Garland, David. 2001. *The Culture of Control*. Chicago: University of Chicago Press.

Gest, Ted. 2001. *Crime and Politics: Big Government's Erratic Campaign for Law and Order*. New York: Oxford University Press.

Glueck, Sheldon. 1928. "Principles of a Rational Penal Code." *Harvard Law Review* 41(4):453–82.

Gottfredson, Don M., Leslie T. Wilkins, and Peter B. Hoffman. 1978. *Guidelines for Parole and Sentencing*. Lanham, MD: Lexington.

Gottschalk, Marie. 2015. *Caught: The Prison State and the Lockdown of American Politics*. Princeton, NJ: Princeton University Press.

Hall, Livingston, and Sheldon Glueck. 1940. *Cases and Materials on Criminal Law*. St. Paul, MN: West.

Hinkkanen, Ville, and Tapio Lappi-Seppälä. 2011. "Sentencing Theory, Policy, and Research in the Nordic Countries." In *Crime and Justice in Scandinavia*, edited by Michael Tonry and Tapio Lappi-Seppälä. Vol. 40 of *Crime and Justice: A Review of Research*, edited by Michael Tonry. Chicago: University of Chicago Press.

Johnson, Kevin R. 2010. "How Racial Profiling in America Became the Law of the Land." *Georgetown Law Review* 98(4):1005–77.

Kommers, Donald P. 1997. *The Constitutional Jurisprudence of the Federal Republic of Germany*. 2nd ed. Durham, NC: Duke University Press.

Kress, Jack M. 1980. *Prescription for Justice: The Theory and Practice of Sentencing Guidelines*. Cambridge, MA: Ballinger.

Lee, Youngjae. 2010. "Repeat Offenders and the Question of Desert." In *Previous Convictions at Sentencing: Theoretical and Applied Perspectives*, edited by Julian V. Roberts and Andrew von Hirsch. Oxford: Hart.

Lipton, Douglas, Robert Martinson, and Judith Wilks. 1975. *Effectiveness of Correctional Treatment: A Survey of Treatment and Evaluation Studies*. New York: Praeger.

Lynch, Gerard E. 2003. "Screening versus Plea Bargaining: Exactly What Are We Trading Off?" *Stanford Law Review* 55:1399–1408.

Manson, Allan, P. Healy, G. Trotter, J. V. Roberts, and D. Ives, eds. 2008. *The Law of Sentencing and Penal Policy in Canada*. 2nd ed. Toronto: Emond.

Martinson, Robert. 1974. "What Works? Questions and Answers about Prison Reform." *Public Interest* 35(2):22–54.

Marvell, Thomas B. 1995. "Sentencing Guidelines and Prison Population Growth." *Journal of Criminal Law and Criminology* 85:696–706.

Mendelberg, Tali. 2001. *The Race Card: Campaign Strategy, Implicit Messages, and the Norm of Equality*. Princeton, NJ: Princeton University Press.

Michael, Jerome, and Mortimer Adler. 1933. *Crime, Law, and Social Science*. New York: Harcourt Brace.

Michael, Jerome, and Herbert Wechsler. 1940. *Criminal Law and Its Administration*. Chicago: Foundation.

Morris, Norval. 1974. *The Future of Imprisonment*. Chicago: University of Chicago Press.

Morris, Norval, and Michael Tonry. 1990. *Between Prison and Probation: Intermediate Punishments in a Rational Sentencing System*. New York: Oxford University Press.

Murakawa, Naomi. 2014. *The First Civil Right: How Liberals Built Prison America*. New York: Oxford University Press.

National Advisory Commission on Criminal Justice Standards and Goals. 1973. *A National Strategy to Reduce Crime*. Washington, DC: US Government Printing Office.

National Commission on Law Observance and Enforcement. 1931. *Report on Penal Institutions, Probation, and Parole*. Washington, DC: US Government Printing Office.

National Commission on Reform of Federal Criminal Laws. 1971. *Report*. Washington, DC: US Government Printing Office.

Nicholson-Crotty, Sean. 2004. "The Impact of Sentencing Guidelines on State-Level Sanctions: An Analysis over Time." *Crime and Delinquency* 50(3):395–411.

Parent, Dale G. 1988. *Structuring Criminal Sentences: The Evolution of Minnesota's Sentencing Guidelines*. New York: LEXIS Law Publications.

Pifferi, Michele. 2012. "Individualization of Punishment and the Rule of Law: Reshaping Legality in the United States and Europe between the 19th and the 20th Century." *American Journal of Legal History* 52(3):325–76.

President's Commission on Law Enforcement and Administration of Justice. 1967. *The Challenge of Crime in a Free Society*. Washington, DC: US Government Printing Office.

Reaves, Brian A. 2013. *Felony Defendants in Large Urban Counties, 2009—Statistical Tables*. Washington, DC: US Department of Justice, Bureau of Justice Statistics.

Reiss, Albert J., Jr., and Jeffrey Roth, eds. 1993. *Understanding and Controlling Violence*. Washington, DC: National Academy Press.

Reitz, Kevin. 1997. "Sentencing Guideline Systems and Sentence Appeals: A Comparison of Federal and State Experiences." *Northwestern University Law Review* 91:1441–1505.

———. 2010. "The Illusion of Proportionality: Desert and Repeat Offenders." In *Previous Convictions at Sentencing: Theoretical and Applied Perspectives*, edited by Julian V. Roberts and Andrew von Hirsch. Oxford: Hart.

———. 2011. "Proof of Aggravating and Mitigating Facts at Sentencing." In *Mitigation and Aggravation at Sentencing*, edited by Julian V. Roberts. Cambridge: Cambridge University Press.

Roberts, Julian V. 1997. "The Role of Criminal Record in the Sentencing Process." In *Crime and Justice: A Review of Research*, vol. 22, edited by Michael Tonry. Chicago: University of Chicago Press.

———. 2008. *Punishing Persistent Offenders: Exploring Community and Offender Perspectives*. Oxford: Oxford University Press.

———. 2010. "First-Offender Sentencing Discounts: Exploring the Justifications." In *Previous Convictions at Sentencing: Theoretical and Applied Perspectives*, edited by Julian V. Roberts and Andrew von Hirsch. Oxford: Hart.

Roberts, Julian V., and J. Pina-Sanchez. 2014. "Previous Convictions at Sentencing: Exploring Empirical Trends in the Crown Court." *Criminal Law Review* 8:575–88.

Roberts, Julian V., and Andrew von Hirsch. 2010. *Previous Convictions at Sentencing: Theoretical and Applied Perspectives*. Oxford: Hart.

Rothman, David. 1971. *The Discovery of the Asylum: Social Order and Disorder in the New Republic*. Boston: Little, Brown.

———. 1980. *Conscience and Convenience: The Asylum and Its Alternatives in Progressive America*. Boston: Little, Brown.

Shane-DuBow, Sandra, Alice P. Brown, and Erik Olsen. 1985. *Sentencing Reform in the United States: History, Content, and Effect*. Washington, DC: US Government Printing Office.

Simon, Jonathan. 2007. *Governing through Crime: How the War on Crime Transformed American Democracy and Created a Culture of Fear*. New York: Oxford University Press.

Singer, Richard G. 1979. *Just Deserts: Sentencing Based on Equality and Desert*. Lexington, MA: Ballinger.

Spelman, William. 2009. "Crime, Cash, and Limited Options: Explaining the Prison Boom." *Criminology and Public Policy* 8(1):29–77.

Stemen, Don, Andres Rengifo, and James Wilson. 2006. *Of Fragmentation and Ferment: The Impact of State Sentencing Policies on Incarceration Rates, 1975–2002*. Final Report to the National Institute of Justice. Washington, DC: National Institute of Justice.

Stuntz, William J. 2011. *The Collapse of American Criminal Justice*. Cambridge, MA: Harvard University Press.

Thomas, David A. 1979. *Principles of Sentencing*. 2nd ed. London: Heinemann.

Tonry, Michael. 1987. *Sentencing Reform Impacts*. Washington, DC: US Government Printing Office.

———. 1996. *Sentencing Matters*. New York: Oxford University Press.

———. 2004. *Thinking about Crime: Sense and Sensibility in American Penal Culture*. New York: Oxford University Press.

———. 2009. "Emerging Explanations of American Punishment Policies: A Natural History." *Punishment and Society* 11:377–94.

———. 2010. "The Questionable Relevance of Previous Convictions to Punishments for Later Crimes." In *Previous Convictions at Sentencing: Theoretical and*

Applied Perspectives, edited by Julian V. Roberts and Andrew von Hirsch. Oxford: Hart.

———. 2011*a*. "Making Peace, Not a Desert: Penal Reform Should Be about Values Not Justice Reinvestment." *Criminology and Public Policy* 10 (3):637–48.

———. 2011*b*. *Punishing Race: An American Dilemma Continues*. New York: Oxford University Press.

———. 2014. "Remodeling American Sentencing: A Ten-Step Blueprint for Moving Past Mass Incarceration." *Criminology and Public Policy* 13(4):503–33.

———. 2016. *Sentencing Fragments: Penal Reform in America, 1975–2025*. New York: Oxford University Press.

Travis, Jeremy, Bruce Western, and Steve Redburn, eds. 2014. *The Growth of Incarceration in the United States: Exploring Causes and Consequences*. Washington, DC: National Academies Press.

US Sentencing Commission. 2015. *Overview of Federal Criminal Cases, 2014*. Washington, DC: US Sentencing Commission.

van den Haag, Ernst. 1975. *Punishing Criminals*. New York: Basic Books.

van Zyl Smit, Dirk, and Sonja Snacken. 2009. *Principles of European Prison Law and Policy: Penology and Human Rights*. Oxford: Oxford University Press.

von Hirsch, Andrew. 1976. *Doing Justice*. New York: Hill & Wang.

———. 1981. "Desert and Previous Convictions in Sentencing." *Minnesota Law Review* 65:591–634.

———. 1985. *Past and Future Crimes: Deservedness and Dangerousness in Sentencing Criminals*. New Brunswick, NJ: Rutgers University Press.

———. 2010. "Proportionality and the Progressive Loss of Mitigation: Some Future Reflections." In *Previous Convictions at Sentencing: Theoretical and Applied Perspectives*, edited by Julian V. Roberts and Andrew von Hirsch. Oxford: Hart.

Walker, Nigel. 1969. *Sentencing in a Rational Society*. London: Allen Lane.

Washington Caseload Forecast Council. 2016. *Statistical Summary of Adult Felony Sentencing—Fiscal Year 2015*. Olympia: Washington Caseload Forecast Council.

Wechsler, Herbert. 1961. "Sentencing, Correction, and the Model Penal Code." *University of Pennsyvania Law Review* 109(4):465–93.

Whitman, James. 2003. *Harsh Justice*. New York: Oxford University Press.

———. 2016. "Presumption of Innocence or Presumption of Mercy? Weighing Two Western Modes of Justice." *Texas Law Review* 94:933–93.

Wilson, James Q. 1975. *Thinking about Crime*. New York: Basic Books.

Windlesham, Lord David. 1998. *Politics, Punishment, and Populism*. New York: Oxford University Press.

Wines, Enoch C., ed. 1871. *Transactions of the National Conference on Penitentiary and Reformatory Discipline*. Albany, NY: Weed, Parsons.

Zeisel, Hans, and Shari Seidman Diamond. 1977. "Search for Sentencing Equity: Sentence Review in Massachusetts and Connecticut." *American Bar Foundation Research Journal* 2(4):881–940.

Index

Aboriginals, 372–373, 405, 412
Adler, Mortimer, 470n8
adversarial systems: civil/common law
and, 10, 112; double jeopardy in, 123;
due process and, 108; inquisitorial
systems, 10, 35, 114, 115, 118, 122,
270; lawyers and, 258; nonadversarial
models, 423, 446, 447; principles of,
129; prosecutor and, 35, 257 (*see also*
prosecutor); social reports and, 297.
See also specific countries
age, of offenders, 33, 36n8, 58f, 59f,
474. *See also* youth justice; *specific
countries*
aggravating factors, 52, 53, 135, 337,
401, 433; assault and, 87–88;
evidence for, 481; overlooked, 85n1,
134; proportionality and, 374, 375,
427; prosecutor and, 374, 375, 427;
recidivism as, 54, 153n20, 236;
street-racing and, 378, 389;
transparency and, 347. *See also
specific topics, countries*
American Prison Association, 466–467
appellate systems, 469; Booker
decision and, 479n13; double
jeopardy, 86n3; history of, 423;
norms and, 465, 471, 476;
proportionality and, 7, 423;
sentencing and, 89, 360, 423,
472, 476–479; trial courts and, 90,

113, 434–435; variations in, 41, 46.
See also specific countries
Ashworth, Andrew, 307–358
assault: aggravating factors, 87–88
(*see also* aggravating factors);
domestic violence, 27, 28, 74t, 77t,
159, 344, 413, 447; firearms and,
197, 374, 378, 381, 382, 386, 390,
413, 414, 471; frequency of, 91;
gangs and, 28, 29, 32, 76t, 379;
homicide (*see* homicide); mental
health and, 49; penal value, 28, 30,
62, 70, 91, 326, 328, 329t, 374;
politicization and, 17, 369, 410, 473;
proportionality and, 448, 475 (*see
also* proportionality); range system,
51; rates of, 91, 149, 150f, 227t, 272,
322t, 323t, 324t, 370, 370f, 371,
486t; repeat offenders, 46, 48, 54,
331n22, 442n24; responsibility
and, 49; robbery and, 85; sexual
offenses and, 48, 70, 71, 150, 159,
272, 300, 307, 340; types of, 28, 63,
65t; women and, 27, 28. *See
also specific topics, countries*
austerity, fiscal, 348, 352
Australia, 4, 419–458; advisory
councils, 442–445, 453; appeals,
479; Barbaro decision, 434, 435,
436; Callinan report, 440; Canada
and, 447; Charters of Rights, 445;

497